With *Friends or Foes?* Norman Saul
continues his multivolume magnum opus
on U.S.-Russian relations over the course
of 200 years. This fourth volume captures
the major changes in relations between two
nations on the verge of becoming dominant
global powers.

Among other things, Saul examines
the rationale for America's f...
recognize the Soviet gov...
the early 1930s, analyzi...
the Red Scare and the r...
Department, Russian ém...
groups, and key individuals—such as
Charles Evans Hughes, Robert Kelley,
Herbert Hoover, Boris Skvirsky, Olga
Kameneva, and Maxim Litvinov—on the
policy process. In addition, he recalls the
American Relief Administration's gigantic
effort to help Russian peasants and garners
new material from American business
records on concession arrangements and
commerce and on Soviet responses during
the first Five Year Plan. He also records
travelers' impressions, cultural exchange,
and the role of academia in each country—
particularly the contribution of Russian
émigré scholars to American education
and the contributions of American
journalists in Russia.

Saul also reveals the tendency on
both sides to preserve an atmosphere of
secrecy, conducting business behind closed
doors and rarely on paper. His prodigious
research in the Hoover Presidential
Library, the Franklin Roosevelt Library,

Friends or Foes?

Also by Norman E. Saul

Russia and the Mediterranean, 1797–1807

Sailors in Revolt: The Russian Baltic Fleet in 1917

Russian-American Dialogue on Cultural Relations, 1776–1914 (editor)

Distant Friends: The United States and Russia, 1763–1867

Concord and Conflict: The United States and Russia, 1867–1914

War and Revolution: The United States and Russia, 1914–1921

Friends or Foes?
The United States and Soviet Russia, 1921–1941

Norman E. Saul

 University Press of Kansas

© 2006 by the University Press of Kansas
All rights reserved

Published by the University Press of Kansas (Lawrence,
Kansas 66045), which was organized by the Kansas Board
of Regents and is operated and funded by Emporia State
University, Fort Hays State University, Kansas State
University, Pittsburg State University, the University of
Kansas, and Wichita State University

Library of Congress Cataloging-in-Publication Data

Saul, Norman E.
  Friends or foes? : the United States and Soviet Russia,
1921–1941 /
Norman E. Saul.
     p. cm.
  Includes bibliographical references and index.
  ISBN 0-7006-1448-6 (cloth : alk. paper)
  1. United States—Relations—Soviet Union. 2. Soviet
Union--Relations--United States. 3. United States—Foreign
relations—20th century. 4. Soviet Union—Foreign
relations—1917-1945.
I. Title.
  E183.8.S65S2744 2005
  327.7304709'042—dc22
                                                          2006000282

British Library Cataloguing-in-Publication Data is available.

Printed in the United States of America

10 9 8 7 6 5 4 3 2 1

The paper used in this publication meets the minimum requirements of the American National Standard for Permanence of Paper for Printed Library Materials Z39.48-1984.

To my grandchildren, who have contributed
more than they will ever know in love and
inspiration: Alex and Ceanne Lyon, Elaina
and Andrew Saul, and Grace Mechler, who are
venturing forth into a new century.

And to the memory of the Honorable George
F. Kennan and his legacy:

The very concept of history implies the scholar
and the reader. Without a generation of
civilized people to study history, to preserve
its records, to absorb its lessons and relate
them to its own problems, history, too, would
lose its meaning.

—George F. Kennan, upon receiving the
Gold Medal for History from the American
Academy of Arts and Letters in 1984

Contents

Illustrations

Preface and Acknowledgments

Sailing through the troubled waters of Soviet-American relations in the interwar years of 1921–1941 is like riding out a series of storms. Unlike earlier periods of Russian-American relations, much of the relationship was up in the air, confused, and contradictory. Fortunately, for this voyage, the seas have been surveyed by some of the best American and Russian historians, from George F. Kennan to Grigory Sevostianov, several of them contemporary to the events. Yet, obstacles certainly remain. For much of the period, official relations did not exist, so the voluminous diplomatic and consular records available on both sides for earlier and later periods are lacking or distorted as seen from afar. Even when they are available after 1933, each country is often viewed by the other through a distant prism or a thick curtain.

Another problem is that many of the principal individuals involved have not left much in the way of records, either by choice, lack of time and motivation, or simply because they had no opportunity. In the case of many on the Soviet side, records that may have existed have been destroyed along with the individuals themselves. Or else they had good reason to remain quiet. Even on the American side, diaries and memoirs—or more or less complete collections of correspondence—are either missing or woefully disappointing. This is certainly true of the records of Presidents Harding and Coolidge, and in certain respects of Herbert Hoover's attempts at deliberate nonrevelation. There was a tendency on both the American and Soviet sides to preserve an atmosphere of secrecy, of nondisclosure, conducting business behind closed doors. Much was done by personal contact, by telephone (without recordings), over lunch or dinner, in the wee hours of the night, or on the spur of the moment. Answering an inquiry of Secretary of Commerce Herbert Hoover about the United States' Russian policy, Secretary of State Charles Evans Hughes replied rather cryptically, berating Hoover, in fact, for putting his query on paper.

In truth there are many matters in the conduct of our foreign relations which in my own Department are necessarily withheld from the general files of the Department as a whole, and from the knowledge even of bureaus or divisions. We have a number of matters where no one but myself and possibly one of my assistants may have the information because of their highly confidential character, and the necessity of avoiding the slightest risk of publicity.[1]

He added in words to the effect that if Hoover had an important matter to discuss, he should not put it on paper but rather discuss it in person. So much for an important part of the historical record. The delight in the discovery of a letter labeled "destroy after reading" only leads to the dismaying afterthought, how many others were destroyed?

In many cases, however, the opposite is true. The real story may be obscured by overwhelming documentation: reality submerged in a sea of paper. An example is the gigantic American famine relief effort, mostly under the auspices of the American Relief Administration in 1921–1923. One can easily get lost in the forest—or a lost forest, literally, in terms of paper production. Everyone was expected to report on everything, often even manufacturing records. Yet, the mission of the historian is still to sift through the debris, fill in as many of the blank pages as possible, read between the lines, and, above all, ferret out in every nook and cranny possible what made that world that was. The result, one hopes, is additional insights into what really happened in Soviet-American relations during a vital, interesting, yet still mysterious and controversial period in the history of the two countries.

Extremely valuable, thankfully, are the rich correspondence files of such guardians of the public and academic trust as Samuel Harper, Boris Bakhmeteff, and William Allen White, who clearly had posterity and the historical record in mind in keeping meticulous files of correspondence, as well as the remarkably complete surviving records of diverse organizations such as the All-Russian Society for Cultural Relations with Foreign Countries, the Communist Party of the United States, the American Relief Administration, and the Council on Foreign Relations. But even all these unrelenting eyes on unfolding history must be treated with caution. Though the opening of Russian archives has revealed much that is new, it has also added to the contradictions and highlighted the questions of distortion and omission. Thus, despite some natural problems in reconstructing

---

1. Hughes to Hoover, 16 December 1921, f. Hughes, box 286, Commerce, Herbert Hoover Presidential Library (hereafter HHPL).

Russian-American relations in this period, on balance the picture is fuller and sharper than in earlier and later periods, because of the proclivity to leave and maintain orderly records by the subjects and institutions involved.

As in the preceding volumes on Russian-American relations, the author depended heavily on the work, experience, and encouragement of colleagues in the field. Not all, certainly, can be recognized here. On the American side, I owe my gratitude and respect to George F. Kennan, Walter LaFeber, John Lewis Gaddis, Ambassador Jack and Rebecca Matlock, the late Alexander Dallin, Basil Dmytryshyn, Ralph Fisher, the late W. Bruce Lincoln, Robert C. Tucker, and Bruce Menning. I am especially indebted to David Foglesong who read the entire manuscript with great care, providing helpful corrections and a real consideration. The friendship and vital support of Russian scholars were also essential in my research: among them are Academicians Grigory Sevostianov and Nikolai Bolkhovitinov, Gennady Kuropiatnik, and the late Robert Ivanov; and especially younger scholars Vladimir Pozniakov, Ilya Gaiduk, Alexander Petrov, Iulia Khemelevskaia, and Elena Kudinova. Kolya and Luda Bolkhovitinov and Volodya and Tanya Pozniakov went well beyond the call of duty in making Moscow hospitable and pleasant for productive research on several occasions and for arranging comfortable living for Mary Ann and me, a most important contribution to productive research. Above all, they imparted a love and appreciation for the Soviet and Russian past, warts and all, in walking tours of Moscow and long, freewheeling conversations into the evenings and nights (before the Metro closed).

Financial assistance for this project, crucial for the opportunity to perform research in important collections but also because of inspirations for the "cause," came from the Herbert Hoover Presidential Library Foundation, the Franklin and Eleanor Roosevelt Institute, and the Institute for Advanced Study in Princeton. The University of Kansas supported the project with a sabbatical leave, a research fellowship from the Hall Center for the Humanities, an international travel grant, and a General Research Fund award (summer stipend). The Center for North American Studies of the Institute of General History of the Russian Academy of Sciences provided essential services in gaining access to materials in Russia and providing genuine and sincere Russian collegial hospitality.

On the American side, I am deeply indebted to those guardians of the public records and promoters of research, the archivists and librarians, who are too numerous to acknowledge individually. I will mention only three as symbolic of the many: Fred Bauman, recently retired, of the Manuscript Division of the Library of Congress; the venerable John Taylor of the military section of the National Archives, who began his tenure there in 1945 and in 2005 was still at his post; and Tatiana Chebotareva, curator of the Bakhmeteff Archive at Columbia University, who has made those dead papers come alive. They are only the tip of the iceberg of the many devoted to the preservation and accessibility of primary resources. More power—and resources—to them!

Russian-American studies are at a crossroads because of many retirements on both sides, difficulties with funding, especially in Russia, and the unfortunate fading of historical interest in things Russian and American on both sides (excepting the sensational news items, now and then). A generation of trained Soviet/Russian scholars that includes Bolkhovitinov, Sevostianov, Kuropiatnik, and others is passing. In this regard one pays tribute to the late Robert (Bob) Ivanov, a true "Russian-American" with a special story. His father sought refuge off a Russian merchant ship in New York in 1912, worked for Ford Motor Company in Dearborn, Michigan, was arrested for radical activity (IWW), and deported to his native Russia in 1920. My friend Bob was named after an American buddy of his father's who was brutally killed in a Detroit jail. Unfortunately, violence on both sides is part of his family's story.

More important than ever, I am indebted to my recent students who patiently tolerated and responded to my various digressions into the lacunae of the subject: among them are Michael Cassella-Blackburn, Ray Leonard, John Steinberg, Laurie Stoff, Luba Ginzberg, Ellen Paul, Wayne Chinander, Father John Mack, Stefan Bergstrom, Kevin Corbett, and Michael Stefany. Likewise, my colleagues in the Department of History and in the Center for Russian and East European Studies gave their time to listen to my seemingly inexhaustible Russian/Soviet-American stories: John (Jay) Alexander, John Dardess, Suresh Bhana, Theodore Wilson, Anna Cienciala, Eve Levin, Rose Greaves, Ray Finch, and the late Joseph Conrad and Donald R. McCoy, all of whose encouragement and criticism were especially valued. They were all forever prompting me to dig out yet one more elusive source—or reexamine another crazy idea. They know how much appreciation is due.

Last but certainly not least is to acknowledge my debt to the professional staff of the Department of History—Sandee Kennedy, Ellen Garber, and Nancie Lockwood—and of the College of Liberal Arts Wood Processing Center—Paula Courtney and Pam LeRow. They were all masters of efficiency in making limited funds go a long way. To the chairs of the department during this research, Tom Lewin and Jeff Moran, thanks for continual encouragement and support. Fred Woodward, director of the University Press of Kansas, has managed to survive four of these volumes, proving himself a master of patience and endurance.

Abbreviations Used in Text and Notes

ACA:	Austin Company Archives
ARA:	American Relief Administration
ARC:	American Red Cross
ARI:	American Russian Institute (New York)
AVPR:	Archive of the Foreign Policy of Russia
CPUSA:	Communist Party of the United States of America
CU-BA:	Bakhmeteff Archive, Columbia University, Manuscripts and Special Collections
d.:	delo (packet)
DEEA:	Division of East European Affairs, Department of State
DPR:	Diplomatic Post Records (RG 84, National Archives)
f.:	folder (American) or fond (Russian)
FDR:	Franklin Delano Roosevelt
FRPL:	Franklin Roosevelt Presidential Library
GARF:	State Archive of the Russian Federation
GUA:	Georgetown University Archives
HHPL:	Herbert Hoover Presidential Library
HIA:	Hoover Institution Archives
HU-HP:	Harvard University, Houghton Library
IHP:	International Harvester Papers
JJDC:	Jewish Joint Distribution Committee (for relief)
LC:	Library of Congress
MD:	Manuscript Division
MUDD-P:	Mudd Library, Princeton University
NA:	National Archives and Records Service
NYT:	*New York Times*
op.:	opis (collection or inventory within fond—Russian)

POF: President's Office File, FRPL
PPF: President's Personal File, FRPL
PSF: President's Secretary's File, FRPL
RFSP: Records of the Foreign Service Posts, Department of State
           (RG 84, NA)
RG: Record Group
RGASPI: Russian State Archive of Social and Political History
           (the party archive)
RU: Russia Unit (ARA)
RWM: R. Walton Moore Papers, FRPL
SHSW: State Historical Society of Wisconsin, Madison
UC-R: University of Chicago, Regenstein Library, Special Collections
UILA: University of Illinois Library Archives

A Note on People and Places

In general, the modified Library of Congress transliteration system, adopted by most academic libraries and presses, has been employed, especially in note citations. The spelling of many Russian names in English, however, remains a mysterious art. Those Russians better known in the West were scripted by European design, and Russians themselves sometimes preferred this rendition. Thus, some names will appear with the "ff" ending that is phonetically correct rather than "v"—Bakhmeteff for Bakhmetev (the pure transliteration), for example. The text thus follows the standard English versions for many, such as Chaliapin rather than Shaliapin, Chagall rather than Shagal, Rachmaninoff instead of Rakhmaninov. A number of other names have also been "anglicized" somewhat arbitrarily for simplicity—or by the writer's whim. The standard Russian ending of "ii" in transliteration has thus often been converted to "y," that is, Stanislavsky for Stanislavskii. The same is true of first names: Maxim rather than Maksim, Leon Trotsky rather than Lev Trotskii—but Kamenev remains Lev. There are some arbitrary exceptions; rather than the usual English spelling for Ambassador Oumansky in the 1930s, the reader will find the more transliterated form of Umansky, more appropriate for indexing. In short, there is an absence of consistency dictated by common sense.

The problem of individuals and places acquiring new names is especially pronounced in the Soviet period, whether to carry on underground revolutionary activity, to adopt simpler, catchier names (Stalin instead of Jugashvilli), or to disguise non-Russian ethnic origins—or, in the case of cities, to honor Soviet "heroes." Nearly all of the names of Soviet personalities highlighted in the text are not their real ones, while place names vary somewhat more whimsically. For example, when does Nizhny Novgorod become Gorky? Or Tver become Kalinin? Or Ekaterinburg finding itself Sverdlovsk? Adding to the confusion is that many of these names have gone back in recent years to the original: St. Petersburg-

Petrograd-Leningrad-St. Petersburg. Moscow and Kiev, fortunately, have a claim to a "unique" preservation of original names, to having escaped sovietization. There are also new names on the map, such as Magnitogorsk, but that is understandable to the American mind, considering the many changes in the American landscape.

Friends or Foes?

1

Nonrecognition

Considering the obvious differences in political and social orientation and development, relations between the United States and Russia from the mid-eighteenth century into the twentieth were remarkably compatible, owing to distance, a mutual sense of Anglophobia, and commercial interests. They had in common features lacking in most other countries: rapid and volatile changes, rich and growing cultural advances, and the conquest of continents through manifest destiny and simple extension of the power of the state. By the late nineteenth century, frictions indeed arose over Russian anti-Semitism, American sympathies with the democratic radical movements against the authoritarian Romanov regime, and imperial interest conflicts in the Far East especially. Yet, due to the happenstance of European alignments, the two countries became allies in the Great War.[1] They were more interlocked than ever before. As the West European Allies counted on American financial and military aid to carry them to victory, they also expected the United States to bail out Russia from impending disaster created by the war. The United States tried to carry out this mission of saving Russia after the February–March revolution that ushered in a new era of democratic promise for Russia, but it provided too little material and moral support too late.[2] The Bolshevik Revolution came first and trumped the American mission.

The period of war and revolution that descended on Europe in 1914 thus largely shaped most of the rest of the century for both countries. Somewhat peripheral to the initial conflict, the non-European world, nonetheless, entered a

1. For more information, see Saul, *Distant Friends: The United States and Russia, 1763–1867* (Lawrence: University Press of Kansas, 1991); *Concord and Conflict: The United States and Russia, 1867–1914* (Lawrence: University Press of Kansas, 1996); and *War and Revolution: The United States and Russia, 1914–1921* (Lawrence: University Press of Kansas, 2001).

2. Several official and unofficial advisers on the scene, ranging from Ambassador David Francis to the director of the Red Cross mission, William Boyce Thompson, had urged the funding of a major propaganda campaign to keep Russia in the war and safe for democracy. Thompson even devoted one million dollars of his own money for that purpose.

new, unpredictable future. The war and peace brought the United States great power status and recognition and (grudging) respect as never before, while, through revolution, Russia became the (red) flag bearer for the idea of an idealized socialist-communist future for the world. The result was two surprising (at least to the old European order) miracles: an opportunity on one hand for the United States to recast the world in its own image along the lines of political self-determination of national identities (Wilson's Fourteen Points), perpetually safe for democracy and immune from future world conflict, and the contrary vision—in Russian guise—of an egalitarian, classless, Panglossian world where everyone would be safe from exploitation and injustice. The failure of both countries—and visions—caused enormous frustration and disillusionment. Perhaps neither ever fully recovered from it. The United States, though victorious in war, failed in its chief world mission to win the peace and retreated into isolationism. Soviet Russia, also achieving victory over opponents, was left in a state of collapse and in a quandary over the failure of the expected world revolution. The world was not made safe for democracy—certainly not the American version of it—and the world socialist revolution remained somewhere over the rainbow.

The era of nonrecognition between Soviet Russia[3] and the United States was predicated upon two developments, not often fully recognized: the first was a great American disappointment in regard to the failure to secure an American path for the Russian future. Instead, it found Russia moving in an opposite direction seemingly in direct conflict with the American conception of society and the world and its imperialist interests and objectives.[4] Not only that, this new Russian mission threatened the rest of the world, especially war-torn Europe and the Middle East, where empires and long-established monarchies were collapsing. As Robert Lansing, secretary of state through the peace conference of 1919, explained later,

> In 1919 the political chaos in Central Europe caused general alarm. Everything seemed to indicate that Bolshevism would sweep through the van-

---

3. The term *Soviet Russia* reflects the basic shift that occurred in the November 1917 Bolshevik Revolution from *Imperial Russia* and the *provisional government*, which is often misnamed *democratic*. This term was preferred, at least in the early years, to the *Soviet Union*. The latter did not formally exist until the USSR constitution went into effect on 1 January 1924. Officially "Russia" is the Russian Socialist Federated Soviet Republic (RSFSR). That entity remained after 1924 as it became the overwhelmingly dominant constituency of the union of Soviet republics that included Ukraine, Georgia, Uzbekistan, and so forth. It reemerged—or "retrograded" back into—the Russian Federation in late 1991, directed first by President Boris Yeltsin and then by Vladimir Putin after 1999.

4. The whole debate on the extent that American imperial ambitions shaped and affected the outcomes of peace is dealt with by several American scholars, most notably by Walter LaFeber.

quished Empires and that if it did France and Italy were in danger of a "Red" revolution. To meet this increasing peril an immediate restoration of peace and a renewal of economic life seemed to be the only available means.[5]

On the other hand, a paranoia consumed the new Soviet leadership, having miraculously come to power, in achieving the goal of creating a new Marxist world from an underdeveloped country that was in a state of economic collapse. Managing simple survival for their own fragile instruments of governance (both state and party) through what they could control by military force came first. None were more surprised by revolutionary victory and the weakness of the resulting regime than Lenin and Trotsky—as well as Stalin and other Bolshevik leaders. If one small, hastily organized conspiratorial group could achieve power in Russia so easily (the Bolsheviks), so might another at any time. Hence the institution of overly centralized control (the Leninist dictatorship of the proletariat) headed by the Bolshevik/Communist Party, technically the Russian Social Democratic Labor Party (Bolshevik), with the Cheka, created in December 1917, as its proletarian/praetorian guard, whose main mission was to ensure the former's survival, regardless of human cost.

From the beginning the new Soviet government in Russia faced many serious problems. The first was what to do about the war that was still in progress and with no end in sight; it had been the main factor in bringing about the situation that allowed the Bolsheviks to take power. The leaders of the October Revolution were committed to an end to the war, though some believed this would be taken care of by world revolution, by converting the imperialist war into civil wars and proletarian revolutions. That, of course, was easier dreamed about than accomplished. The Bolsheviks were going through a difficult transition from theory to reality that would continue for several years. One expedient result would be the Treaty of Brest Litovsk, which formally ended the war between Russia and the Central Powers in March 1918. In the meantime, other options seemed to remain open, with Americans especially establishing regular contacts with Bolshevik leaders in Petrograd and Moscow during the winter and spring months of 1917–1918.[6]

Most active in these communications were military attaché Colonel William Judson and the new chief of the Red Cross mission, Raymond Robins. Even the American ambassador, David Francis, led a diplomatic delegation to see Lenin about solving some delicate diplomatic problems in January 1918. Yet relations were certainly strained, and some Americans, such as Frederick Corse, a trusted

---

5. Lansing to C. F. Hildreth, 5 May 1921, box 70, Lansing Papers, Manuscript Division, Library of Congress (hereafter, MC, LC).

6. For details, see Saul, *War and Revolution*, 251–57 et passim.

adviser of the ambassador, and Consul General Madden Summers advised as little contact as possible with Soviet officials. At the end of February, with German armies approaching Petrograd and the Bolsheviks preparing to move the capital to Moscow, Francis took the compromise action of moving the embassy to Vologda instead. Although most of the British and French diplomats left the country, the Americans remained in Russia along with several smaller missions.

Yet none of the Allied governments was prepared to recognize the new Soviet government, the main reason being the avowed intention of that authority to leave the war with an armistice and negotiations with Germany, construed as a betrayal of the Allies. The deliberations leading up to this peace were prolonged, however, and Robins for one believed that the situation might yet be saved and Russia kept officially in the war with the promise of American assistance then and in the future—the aim being the forced continuation of substantial German forces in the East. A message was sent to Washington with that in mind, but it was bungled in transmission. In fact, Trotsky's initial formula, neither peace nor war, might have worked and, in a sense, still was a possibility. The United States, in any event, was in no position to promise major aid to Soviet Russia, not only because of Bolshevik ideological intentions, but because of the immediacy of facing a major German offensive on the Western Front at the time. Another step toward an American policy of nonrecognition thus occurred in March 1918 in allowing (or making no attempt to prevent) the ratification, with Lenin's insistence, at the Fourth All-Russian Congress of Soviets, of accepting the onerous terms dictated by Germany at Brest Litovsk. The Soviet government thus removed itself from the Allied orbit for the duration of the war.

The next big commitment toward nonrecognition, one that was probably the most decisive, was the decision later in the summer for intervention, that is, to send troops into Russian territory at the two accessible points, in the north at Murmansk and Archangel and in the east at Vladivostok. This action resulted, in part, from the Brest Litovsk peace and its aftermath—the acute possibility of German forces seizing important military supplies in Russian ports, especially Murmansk during the spring of 1918—and led to the Allied encouragement and financial assistance to Russian white military units that were believed to support the Allied war effort wherever feasible. Consul General Summers, married into a family of old Russian nobility, was an ardent supporter of a more stringent anti-Bolshevik policy from the beginning and influenced Francis in that direction. In the midst of the stormy Soviet reestablishment in Moscow and under considerable strain, Summers died suddenly in May. With Robins departed and Francis in limbo in Vologda, the Wilson administration decided in July 1918 to commit a small military force, in conjunction with the British, to the Russian northern ports to protect those supplies and strengthen friendly local authorities.

The shaky and threatened Bolshevik government deeply resented the appearance of military intervention on Russian territory, especially by the United States, in 1918–1919, but, more important, it was a physical move by American forces that—in Wilsonian terms—had to have a moral justification. Russia was not behaving as expected and needed to be taught a lesson—but worse, it had violated the code of civilized nations, as perceived in the Presbyterian mind (Wilson) or through New England puritanism (Henry Cabot Lodge).[7]

Thus the Wilsonian theo-political dogma also needs to be taken into account, since some authors give his worldview prominence;[8] this dogma also reemphasizes the idealistic American crusade to rearrange the world permanently in its own image. In a few words, Russia had opted out of this vision, and Wilson would never forget it, since it left half the European world and a large part of Asia beyond his control. Though military intervention in Russia had little positive effect and may have done more to strengthen bolshevism than weaken it, its legacy remained in the public minds on both sides. Was direct intervention into another major country really in the American character or interest? Mexico or the Caribbean, maybe; Russia, why? The failure of the United States—or Russia—to participate in the League of Nations followed.[9] Wilson's internationalism divided and collapsed in the forests and steppes of Russia.

The Red Scare

A further move cementing nonrecognition was the American witch-hunt of dangerous radicals conducted during 1919. For reasons not clear, the Department of Justice and its new agency of implementation, the Bureau of Investigation (later to become the FBI), felt that the United States and its way of life, its basic freedoms, were threatened by a few thousand people committed to what they thought the Russian Revolution meant in terms of a world free from war, inequality, and destitution. Many of these were expatriates or exiles from the Russian empire, since the United States had been the promised land for immigrants and political dissidents and had more or less welcomed them. Quite a few of them were Jewish, adding another dimension to the ethnic, religious, and class orientations of American policies and labor unrest. The United States also represented a cardi-

7. For a fuller discussion, see ibid. and David W. McFadden, *Alternative Paths: Soviets and Americans, 1917–1920* (New York: Oxford University Press, 1993), 124–51.

8. For example, see Sigmund Freud and William C. Bullitt, *Thomas Woodrow Wilson: A Psychological Study* (Boston: Houghton Mifflin, 1966).

9. For a full discussion, see David Foglesong, *America's Secret War against Bolshevism: U.S. Intervention in the Russian Civil War, 1917–1920* (Chapel Hill: University of North Carolina Press, 1995).

nal refuge of democracy, where anyone, it was believed, could express his or her real—and perhaps exaggerated—sense of injustice. But it was also the citadel of the most extreme capitalistic oppression—low wages, poor working conditions, abrupt worker dismissals—and, most important, home to an established organization dedicated to their grievances, the International Workers of the World (IWW), known popularly as the Wobblies. Many of these idealists were clearly disenchanted with the postwar American scene. They inspired and were backed by the so-called parlor socialists from native Anglo-Saxon backgrounds, such as John Reed, but the twain never quite melded.

Naturally, the established, conservative business and political interests opposed the recognition of the Bolshevik regime and feared further disruptions of the American social and economic scenes. Already in January 1918 Secretary of State Robert Lansing, a leading warrior against bolshevism, warned that a Soviet message to worldwide workers represented "a very real danger in view of the present social unrest throughout the world."[10] Attorney General A. Mitchell Palmer and his dedicated assistant, J. Edgar Hoover, did the dirty work, arresting, incarcerating under brutal conditions, and deporting suspected revolutionaries without trial, most of them guilty only of belonging to activist union groups. In their defense, it must be admitted that these summary actions took place mainly in cities like Chicago, Detroit, and Seattle, all having a history of violence dating back many years. The Seattle general strike that began in the shipyards on 21 January 1919 was especially influential in instigating the Red Scare, since it quickly spread to other, wider labor grievances and to the general population.[11]

Reaction followed. One aim was to silence or at least reduce the voice of the radical press, *The Masses*, *Messenger*, *Defender*, and others that had substantial circulations and had already played a visible role in organizing dissident labor causes. Another result was that the major daily newspapers were clearly aligned in support of the threatened middle class and their representative authorities.[12] Worst of all, the wholesale purge of radicals was indiscriminate, including many who were only on the periphery of dissidence. The suppression cause was undoubtedly assisted by the effects of the Seattle general strike and other militant labor actions, led by the United Mine Workers. That summer on the campaign trail, the president visited Seattle.

---

10. Lansing memorandum, *Lansing Papers, 1914–1920*, vol. 2, PRFR (Washington: GPO, 1940), 353.

11. For an excellent account, see Robert F. Friedheim, *The Seattle General Strike* (Seattle: University of Washington Press, 1964).

12. The best analysis is Regin Schmidt, *Red Scare: FBI and the Origins of Anticommunism in the United States* (Copenhagen: Museum Tusculanum Press, University of Copenhagen, 2000).

He was standing up in the car waving a high silk hat—it was the first time on the trip he had worn one—when with terrifying suddenness all the noise and cheering ended. Standing by the curb in long lines were men in blue denim working clothes. Their arms were folded and they stared straight ahead, not at the President, but at nothing at all. They did not hiss or boo but motionless, noiseless, simply stood there. In their hats they wore signs saying RELEASE POLITICAL PRISONERS.[13]

The wholesale raids of 7 November 1919, mainly targeting members of the Russian Workers Union, netted more than a thousand arrests, of whom 439 were deported—with the assistance of court filings, often manufactured, by the Immigration Bureau. No one seems to have considered that it might have been more in American interest to keep them restrained and under observation in the United States than to inject them into the mainstream cause of world revolution. They included the high-profile radicals Emma Goldman and Alexander Berkman, already in legal process because of their well-known revolutionary activities and prison sentences, as well as many rather ordinary dissidents. The timing of their inclusion in a mass deportation lent a phony legitimacy to the Red Scare and exaggerated the sense of vulnerability in the United States. The roundup of several thousand others soon followed in January and February of 1920, several of whom would also be deported.[14] It is ironic that the United States should feel so threatened by a small number of mostly recent immigrants, while the Bolshevik regime, in genuine fear of survival, was on the verge of collapse.

The November 1919 arrests, with little or manufactured legal justification, were followed by subsequent incarcerations that included barbaric treatment and murders in jail. The deportations remain one of the deepest scars on the American historical record, preceded, accompanied, and followed by many other abuses of racial, political, and military prisoners that would continue well into the twenty-first century. All of this contention was far from being in accord with that Ivy League mentality that generally prevailed in Washington corridors and in the smoke-filled editorial offices of the major newspapers. Most important, the Red Scare shaped public opinion into a mode of hatred and fear of bolshevism, molded into concrete that would take more than ten years to fracture. If not the foundation stone of nonrecognition, the Red Scare provided the mortar for the wall.

13. Gene Smith, *When the Cheering Stopped: The Last Years of Woodrow Wilson* (New York: William Morrow, 1964), 72.

14. Deportation meant forced exportation on crowded ships to the Soviet Union, despite protests by many, since no other country would dare in 1919 receive what the United States declared as dangerous revolutionaries, the preferred term being *Bolshevik anarchists*.

Prisoners of War

Although the United States avoided extended detentions of Soviet prisoners by deporting them instead, several Americans remained in Russian jails for various reasons.[15] They had, however, become a postwar issue. Their repatriation in August 1921 would later become a definite condition for American famine relief, but the Soviet authorities may have been holding them more as hostages to secure recognition than for the various criminal charges. One, Private Russell Hazelwood, a deserter from the American expeditionary forces in North Russia, was epileptic and violent, and his release could easily be obtained, but the United States was not certain it wanted him. Weston Estes, John Flick, Emmett Killpatrick, Marguerite Harrison, Royal Keeley, and Henry La Mare were held on various charges. Estes, who had gone to Russia to organize a film company, claimed that he had been sentenced to be shot seven times.[16] Killpatrick, a Red Cross worker captured along with some White Army soldiers in the south, was very ill, an obvious bother to his Soviet jailers. Harrison was ostensibly a correspondent for the *Baltimore Sun* and Associated Press, who had sneaked over the border from Poland in 1919, while Royal Keeley obtained entry officially on behalf of a risky business venture. Keeley was well received initially but, upon his return from a visit to Europe, was arrested at the border and imprisoned in Moscow.

Marguerite Harrison was a special case. Entering Russia as a reporter, she was, in fact, an agent for American military intelligence, first to scout the German scene at the time of the peace conference, and then extended by her own initiative into Russia. By her own account, she had a somewhat pleasant and adventurous foray for several months in Soviet land that included a fairly free reign in sending dispatches to her news bureau as well as to the U.S. Army Military Intelligence Division. Her contacts included Bertrand Russell and other early prominent visitors to Soviet Russia, who were attracted to what seemed to be a viable socialist experiment.

She was first arrested on 22 October 1919 on charges of spying, subsequently suffering extended internment in primitive Soviet prisons, usually in a small cell along with eight to twelve other women of various Soviet nationalities. Much of their time was spent in fighting various vermin, but otherwise they were reasonably cared for.[17] She goes down in history as the first American woman held

15. Ibid., 131–33.
16. Estes (Moscow) to Sister, 21 April 1921, in vol. 14, DPR, Tallinn, RG 84, NA; and John Flick to ARC, 1 May 1921, box 187, ARC Papers, HIA.
17. For Harrison's detailed description of her life in Lubianka, see *Marooned in Moscow: The Story of an American Woman Imprisoned in Russia* (New York: George H. Doran, 1921), especially, 240–48.

for more that a few days in a Russian/Soviet jail. Senator Joseph France sought Litvinov's assistance on her behalf during the summer of 1921, but she was not freed until her release was specified in the Riga relief agreement in August.[18] Harrison also ranks high in the lucky-unlucky or risky adventure category, since, once released, she returned home, and then set off again via the Pacific Ocean for the Far Eastern Republic in early 1922, which was soon submerged into Soviet Russia. Arrested in Chita for violating her agreement never to return to Russia, she was again confined to a cell in the Lubianka prison in Moscow for several months under worse conditions than previously. Refusing an offer of release in return for serving as a Soviet informer in Russia, she was finally freed when the chief of the American Relief Administration, William Haskell, appealed to Litvinov in early 1923.[19]

Probably the only other truly politically sensitive American prisoner of the Soviets in 1921 was Xenophon Kalamatiano of Odessa Russian-Greek background. He had emigrated with his parents to the Chicago area (Cicero) as a youth in the late 1890s, receiving an excellent education at the Culver Military Academy in Indiana, which excelled in Cossack-style horsemanship (the Black Horse Troop). Enrolling at the University of Chicago, he became the first teacher of Russian there as an undergraduate assistant while also performing as a record-breaking long-distance runner for renowned coach Alonzo Stagg. After graduation, he worked intermittently for American agricultural implement companies in Russia, returning for an extended stay during World War I. After the Bolshevik seizure of power, he assisted anti-Soviet organizations in transferring funds and arms on behalf of local American representatives to the White armies in the south. Arrested by the Cheka in mid 1918 and charged legitimately as an anti-Soviet foreign agent, he endured the worst possible conditions in Bolshevik prisons and was lucky to have survived, thanks mainly to an athletic regimen.[20]

Perhaps just as important, he maintained a sense of humor, as he wrote to Samuel Harper in a smuggled letter:

> I consider that I have been given a box-seat to watch the revolution . . . and am not complaining of such an unusual opportunity. . . . I trust sometime

---

She makes clearer her intelligence operation in a later memoir, *There's Always Tomorrow: The Story of a Checkered Life* (New York: Farrar and Rinehart, 1935).

18. Litvinov note, June 1921, *SAO: gody nepriznaniia, 1918–1926* (Moscow: "demokratiia," 2002), 181–82.

19. Harrison, *There's Always Tomorrow*, 543–64. Soviet police authorities even planned to bring her son to Russia for education at the University of Moscow to induce her cooperation.

20. He credited his long-distance running for his endurance. Kalamatiano to Samuel Harper, 15 September 1921, f. 19, box 9, Harper Papers, R-UC.

to tell you more about them all. At present names on paper are odious things. . . . In May it will be 5 years since I left New York—sometimes I feel very homesick—on the whole, however, as I have suggested above, there is too much of constant interest and excitement here to make the time seem dull. If I pull out alive, and I have every hope of doing so now—although at one time chances seemed to be rather on the undertaker's side—I hope we will have a chance of talking this thing over.[21]

Held in the notorious Butyrki Prison, by 1921 he was, fortunately, out of immediate mortal danger, that is, execution, and receiving ample food supplies through the American Red Cross. Some of this aid was no doubt used to bribe guards to get messages out about his case and that of other American prisoners.[22] Such small-scale shipments to the American prisoners, beginning in December 1920, had, nevertheless, opened a small window into Bolshevik Russia. As information spread and opportunities increased, the Red Cross expanded its limited relief to include other stranded Americans, such as those still overseeing the operations of the International Harvester plant near Moscow.[23]

Besides the few official and semiofficial Americans in Soviet custody, several others were stranded by war and revolution. Among them was Karin Sante, a native Finn, who, as a long-term clerk of the American consulate in Finland, later transferred to Russia, manned the last remnant of the embassy in Petrograd into 1919. Incarcerated in Moscow, she was rescued by friends in the Foreign Service to eventually resume her government work in Washington.[24]

21. To Harper, 19 March 1921, f. 12, ibid. Kalamatiano was fortunate to have influential American friends. To one he confided, "It seems that if I were willing to go to work for this government I might have a chance of getting out. Can't see my way to do it." Quoted in Nankivel to Harper, 9 August 1921, f. 18, ibid. Later, he even expressed regret about his rescue from Soviet incarceration, since it involved a pledge never to return. "I certainly wish this Hoover bunch had left me alone, in which case I would be also at liberty and in Moscow. The old story: may the Lord deliver me from my friends!" To Harper, 8 May 1922, f. 10, box 11, ibid.

22. "Americans in Moscow," ARC report of Edward Ryan (Riga), 31 May 1921, box 187, ARC Papers, HIA, including a detailed list. Ironically and tragically, while teaching history at the Culver Military Academy in 1923, he died of gangrene resulting from frostbite suffered in a winter day of hunting, leaving his full story untold.

23. S. G. McAllister (Brussels IH office) to Colonel Bicknell (ARC, Paris), 15 August 1921, ibid. The State Department followed by authorizing $3,000 to help Americans leave Russia. Young to Albrecht, 29 September 1921, vol. 14 (130–380), DPR Tallinn, RG 84, NA.

24. Especially from J. Butler Wright, former first counselor of the Petrograd embassy, Norman Armour, Zenaida Ragosin, and Methodist minister George Simons. Wright to Simons, 18 January 1921, and Armour to Sante, 12 February 1921, vol. 16, DPR, Tallinn, RG 84, NA. Back in Finland, she married Lars Korsstrom in 1924, regained her consulate position, and was finally allowed entrance to the United States in 1940, concluding her long American government service in the Copyright Office in Washington. For her full story, see Benjamin D. Rhodes, "The Perils of a Foreign Service

The best known "American" resident in Russia at the time of the revolution was Julia Grant Cantacuzene (Kantakuzen) Speransky, a granddaughter of President Ulysses Grant who married a prominent Russian-Greek aristocrat in 1899. She and her family were able to leave rather easily over the Finnish border in early 1918, at least partly because of her connection with Ambassador David Francis and Bolshevik care at the time not to alienate the United States. Cantacuzene would then become quite active in relief for Russian refugee professionals in the 1920s, a strong anti-Soviet and antirecognition advocate, and, after a divorce in the 1930s, a close friend of Canadian statesman MacKenzie King until his death in 1950.

Emma Cochran Ponafidine, daughter of an American missionary in the Middle East, suffered a different fate. She had married in 1885 a Russian diplomat in Persia who volunteered as an officer in the anti-Bolshevik forces and died a natural death in 1919. Though left unmolested on their estate near Tula through those tumultuous years, she encountered considerable difficulty in leaving the country. She seemed, however, to have little trouble in communicating with American consul Charles Albrecht in Reval (Tallinn) about her situation, informing him in January 1921 that she felt like a hostage in Moscow. In refusing her repeated requests to leave, Soviet authorities complained about American policy and hoped for a change with the inauguration of a new president in March, noting that "our government does not ship Russians like cattle home."[25] Albrecht advised her that it would be easier to leave from Petrograd, to which Ponafidine replied that the problem was obtaining permission to get to that city. Another was securing exits for her two sons. This caused further delays, even after the presence of the American Relief Administration personnel on the scene. With the assistance of Archibald Cary Coolidge, however, Ponafidine was finally able to obtain an American passport and transfer with her sons to Petrograd. She chose, however, to make a harrowing escape with them illegally, holding onto ropes on a sledge, across the frozen Gulf of Finland in December 1921.[26] Back in her homeland, Ponafidine would publish a very touching memoir and lecture occasionally.[27]

Clerk: The Career of Karin Sante Korsstrom," *Prologue: Quarterly of the National Archives* 20, no. 1 (spring 1988): 25–41.

25. Ponafidine to Albrecht, 24 January 1921, vol. 16, DPR, Tallinn, RG 84, NA.

26. Albrecht to Ponafidine, 16 April 1921; Ponafidine to Albrecht, 7 and 14 August 1921; and, reporting their arrival in Finland, 30 December 1921, ibid.

27. Ponafidine, *Russia—My Home: An Intimate Record of Personal Experiences before, during, and after the Bolshevist Revolution* (Indianapolis, Ind.: Bobbs-Merrill, 1931), 289–306. The copy at the University of Kansas is inscribed by the author (1931): "The night is not over but dawn approaches." Many of the Russian refugees from Bolshevism would concur.

Veteran lecturer on Russia George Kennan was impressed by Ponafidine's performance in Buffalo. She gave a "simple, sincere and interesting talk about Russian conditions under the Bolsheviks and her escape." Diary, 10 April 1923, box 24, Kennan Papers, MD, LC.

Also managing to get out of Russia through the porous Soviet-Finnish curtain of 1919–1921 were Arthur Prince and Ernest Ropes, descendants of long-established New England merchant families in Russia—and more than thirty more Americans who had waited beyond the last minute to leave in 1918.[28] Another veteran Russian-American businessman, John Lehrs, left Russia in late 1919 and, because of his extensive knowledge of Russia, his fluency in the language, and his many business connections, quickly became a valuable consultant to the relief administration and a key member of the initial staff of the Riga listening post, working mainly at first on the many repatriation cases that included almost any Russian who could claim a relationship to an American.[29] The American Vyborg (Finland) and Tallinn (Estonia) consulates, actually full-fledged intelligence agencies, were the main conduits of information, headed by Harold Quarton and Charles Albrecht, respectively. These posts were the vanguards of American penetration and exit from Soviet Russia in 1920–1921. They were also beset by many other wayward American ventures, such as that launched by Senator Joseph France of Maryland in the spring of 1921, an obvious piece of political grandstanding. His first-hand and much publicized critical account added to the list of reasons for nonrecognition.

The Crane Agenda

Perhaps more important but receiving less notice in the public arena, long-time Russophile Charles R. Crane, accompanied by his son John, returned to Europe from his post as minister to China in June and July 1921 by way of Siberia, among the first foreigners to cross the country after the civil war.[30] They entered with visas from the Far Eastern Republic, oiling their path by dispensing a carload of goods ranging from tea and condensed milk to bottled spirits, and they spent several days in Tomsk, Omsk, and Ekaterinburg visiting churches and a creating a minor sensation as the first visiting Americans since before the

28. Other references are in Quarton to State, 7 July and 3 August 1920, vol. 18, DPR Vyborg, RG 84, NA, and Ropes to Albrecht, 25 July 1921, vol. 14, DPR, Tallinn, RG 84, NA.

29. For some of his work, see Inspection and Control Division Papers, vol. 4: 155 et passim, ARA, HHPL.

30. Albrecht's report on the Crane transit, to State, 9 August 1921, vol. 14, DPR Tallinn, RG 84, NA. Crane was a wealthy businessman and philanthropist (Crane Plumbing of Chicago), who first came to Russia in the 1890s via a joint venture with Westinghouse to manufacture air brakes for the Trans-Siberian Railroad locomotives. He became enamored of Russian music, art, and literature, sponsored trips of several prominent Russians to the United States, and endowed professorships, such as that of Samuel Harper at the University of Chicago.

revolution.[31] As John Crane recorded in his diary of the trip, the Crane entourage had relatively little difficulty with travel accommodations or restrictions. Though they bypassed the most acute famine areas, they heard much about conditions there. After a tour of Vologda that included the last American ambassadorial residence in Russia, Crane visited the Westinghouse factory in Yaroslavl, still under American management, and was surprised to find it in surprisingly good order, railroad equipment maintenance being a high priority of the new government.[32] The main importance of the Crane trip was to show that Soviet Russia was open to a conservative American businessman. He was not alone in braving an encounter with the new Soviet state, but he was probably the most credible.

Crane was relieved to find the Orthodox Church alive though obviously suffering restrictions, closures, and arrests of priests. In conversations with Patriarch Tikhon in Moscow, Crane learned that Tikhon had been appointed head of a nonpartisan famine relief organization but could not leave his compound without approval of a Cheka office that he claimed was staffed entirely by hostile Jews.[33] Crane would support but not actively the serious American concern about religious oppression in Soviet Russia and spoke out supporting nonrecognition in a speech at the University of Wisconsin in early 1922.[34] He also clearly agreed with his son-in-law's later judgment, "I am afraid that they are in Russia to stay for a very long time,"[35] and wanted to make the best of a bad situation by maintaining contacts.

The Colby Note

All that was needed was to follow up the existing situation with a formal framework, explaining the reason and purpose of nonrecognition. Secretary of State Robert Lansing bore some of the blame for Woodrow Wilson's failure to win the peace in Paris in 1919 and was replaced in January 1920 by Bainbridge Colby, a respected Ivy League lawyer with little diplomatic experience. Feeling the pressure to explain exactly what the American policy toward Soviet Russia was, Colby, with the assistance of Norman Davis and John Spargo, concocted in August 1920 an arranged answer to a planted query from the Italian ambassador, so

31. David Hapgood, *Charles R. Crane: The Man Who Bet on People* (New York: Institute of Current World Affairs, 2000), 70–73.

32. John Crane diary, 24–26 July 1921, appendix 1, ibid., 135–38.

33. Ibid., 26 July 1921, 144–46.

34. Josephine (daughter), Madison, to Crane, 24 February 1922, f. 1922, box 14, Crane Papers, BA, CU.

35. Jan Masaryk to Crane, 2 November 1925, f. Jan Masaryk, 1923–1925, box 9, ibid.

that it would be in the form of an official diplomatic note, leaked to the press, and not a public pronouncement by the State Department.[36] The long, wordy reply clearly reflected the Wilsonian principle of self-determination, assuring the rights of Poland, Armenia, and Lithuania to full independence, but the crucial paragraph came near the end, claiming that the Bolshevist government was fully committed to world revolution through the Communist International. But it also assured the self-determination of the Russian state.

> In the view of this Government, there cannot be any common ground upon which it can stand with a Power whose conception[s] of international relations are so entirely alien to its own, so utterly repugnant to its moral sense. There can be no mutual confidence of trust, no respect even, if pledges are to be given and agreements made with a cynical repudiation of their obligation already in the mind of one of the parties. We cannot recognize, hold official relations with, or give friendly reception to the agents of a government which is determined and bound to conspire against our institutions; whose diplomats will be the agitators of dangerous revolt; whose spokesmen say that they sign agreements with no intention of keeping them.[37]

This awkwardly arranged and hastily pronounced dictum in the waning months of the Wilson administration would shape American policy toward Russia for the next thirteen years.[38]

Although a clear statement of nonrecognition, the document also supported the integrity of Russia against complete disintegration, which was a real possibility at the time. Concerned about French, British, Japanese, and even German attempts to carve out dependent entities or spheres of dominance from the former Russian Empire, such as Ukraine, the Baltic states, the Caucasus, and Siberia. The United States in the Colby note supported the maintenance of most of the former Russian-ruled Eurasian territory, during its current weakness and vulnerability, thus helping to restore an empire that would be governed by the Bolsheviks as, eventually, the Union of Soviet Socialist Republics. While avoiding recognition of an immoral power, the United States defended the reassembly

---

36. Drafts, 9 and 10 August 1920, box 3A, Colby Papers, MD, LC. For Spargo's role and his pressing for a clear statement of American policy, see Ronald Radosh, "John Spargo and Wilson's Russian Policy, 1920," *Journal of American History* 52, no. 3 (December 1965), 554–61.

37. Text quoted from Stanley S. Jados, *Documents on Russian-American Relations: Washington to Eisenhower* (Washington, D.C.: Catholic University of America Press, 1965), 48.

38. Embedded in this was some confusion on what "Russia" was at this time: the old Imperial Russia that still existed in "Russia abroad," the illusion of the democratic provisional government, or the new Bolshevik regime, however defined.

or integrity of the Russian (Soviet) empire, including its various non-Russian appendages while recognizing the separation of Poland and Finland. Such contradictions would not be unusual in the course of Soviet-American relations.

The Colby note reversed and canceled the overtures made to the Soviet authorities by the appointment of Norman Hapgood as minister to Denmark in 1919, sponsored by Edward House, and the sending of House's young diplomatic protégé, William C. Bullitt, at about the same time to negotiate directly with the Soviet leaders in Moscow.[39] The rift between the president and House over the peace negotiations undermined the Bullitt mission and was another blow to efforts to repair the damage from intervention, since House was clearly more moderate and open than many close to the administration.

Meanwhile, the mission of Ludwig Martens, one of the grand gentlemen of bolshevism, to reestablish trade connections with the United States ran headlong into the Red Scare atmosphere of 1919. The results were exaggerated suspicions of his ulterior motives, charges that he carelessly mishandled, leading to his expulsion from the country. Martens strived for accommodation but was stabbed in the back by confused and disorganized Bolshevik policies, despite Lenin's reported high regard for him. The appointment of the eccentric Georgi Chicherin as commissar of foreign affairs in 1918 was one problem, since he concentrated on mending relations in continental Europe, while his assistant, Maxim Litvinov, focused on Britain and the United States.[40] Under these circumstances, if Martens could not do it, no one could. Walter Duranty, already becoming established as the foremost American journalist in residence in the shadow of the Kremlin, had a long talk with Martens on 27 September 1922:

> He [Martens] is a reasonable person (and very close to Lenin). We finally came to the conclusion that, broadly speaking, both sides wished for something in the nature of a reestablishment of relations, but unfortunately we neither of us saw just how the present sort of deadlock is to be broken (unless of course the U.S. will make a further move, which is hardly to be expected).[41]

39. On the Bullitt mission, see recent appraisals by Margaret MacMillan, *Paris 1919: Six Months That Changed the World* (New York: Random House, 2002), 78–81, and Michael Cassella-Blackburn, *The Donkey, the Carrot, and the Club: William C. Bullitt and Soviet-American Relations, 1917–1948* (Westport, Conn.: Praeger, 2004), 49–53.

40. For a full account of Chicherin as head of Soviet foreign relations, see Timothy O'Connor, *Diplomacy and Revolution: G. V. Chicherin and Soviet Foreign Affairs, 1918–1930* (Ames: Iowa State University Press, 1988).

41. Duranty to Goodrich, 28 September 1922, f. Recognition, box 23, Goodrich Papers, HHPL.

Though the reasons for nonrecognition were only vaguely defined in Colby's note, subsequent statements, both official and unofficial, reiterated the following points: (1) Soviet failure to acknowledge the large debt of loans incurred by the provisional government in 1917; (2) seizure of the properties of American companies as part of a wholesale nationalization campaign during war Communism; (3) interference by the Moscow-based Communist International in the U.S. internal affairs by supporting antigovernment revolutionary agitation, especially by the communist Workers' Party; and (4) failure of the Soviet government to behave as a normal, legitimate government in these and other respects. For their part, the Soviet authorities insisted that the first two items were open to negotiation and denied the legitimacy of the other two. They did not think it was correct to assume the debt of a government that had used at least some of the funds, through Ambassador Boris Bakhmeteff, to support anti-Bolshevik causes and noted that it had not nationalized (until 1924) the factories and shops of the two major American companies, Singer and International Harvester, each having employed more than 30,000 before the revolution.

Still, Bainbridge Colby was secretary of state for only a short time, and the Wilson administration and its Russian program was clearly trapped in a lame duck session.[42] Veteran Wilsonian Frank Polk, one of the few early proponents of doing business with Bolshevik Russia but who had left the department for a law firm in New York, fired off a poorly aimed salvo to yet one more interim secretary of state, Norman Davis: "How much business are you letting the Russian embassy do? Now that there is no government in Siberia or the Crimea it seems to be dangerous to let those fellows to receive any money or for you to give a certificate that they represent Russia."[43]

Many of those who supported recognition expected a change of policy toward Soviet Russia after the inauguration of William G. Harding as president in March 1921, which happened to coincide with a major shift by the Russian Soviet government. War Communism that accompanied the civil war had done much to foment international opposition by its wholesale nationalization of foreign enterprises, renunciation of debts, and sharply hostile reaction to an internal civil war that was aided and abetted by foreign powers. The new economic policy of Lenin

42. Though providing little insight in terms of diaries or memoirs, Colby was clearly dismayed that *his* policy was later claimed by Hughes, Harding, and Coolidge, emphasizing that it was formed in the last year of the Wilson administration and was *Wilsonian*, "receiving every day fresh vindication and support in the lengthening record of Russian machination and intrigue throughout the world." Colby, *The Close of Woodrow Wilson's Administration and the Final Years* (New York: Mitchell, Kennerley, 1930), 25.

43. Polk to Davis, 27 December 1920, f. Polk, 1920–1921, box 47 Davis Papers, MD, LC.

and the return to a more relaxed, confident normalcy under Harding brought hopes of resolving differences.[44] This was especially the case because some prominent Republican Party leaders were the main banner carriers in favor of recognition, chiefly Raymond Robins and William Borah, an influential progressive Republican senator from Idaho and chair of the powerful Senate Committee on Foreign Relations. Both, however, were tainted by political handicaps: Robins had left the party briefly for the Bull Moose campaign, blamed for losing the presidency for the Republican Party in 1912, and Borah was also an ardent isolationist who had led the party's campaign against the League of Nations.[45]

The American-Russian Chamber of Commerce, organized in 1916, was in the early years a semipublic advocate of the Colby position, financed in part by the Russian embassy from an American loan account. It featured on its board of directors former Russian ambassador Roman Rosen and prominent businessmen such as Alexander Legge (International Harvester) and H. H. Westinghouse. Jerome Landfield, having just left the State Department, served as vice president and actual executive officer, which virtually made it an agency of the State Department.[46] That would soon change.

Private individuals such as Legge and Landfield would play a large role in early Soviet-American relations. Louise Bryant on 2 April 1921 wrote directly to Lenin, who, of course, knew and respected her as the widow of his great American friend of revolution, John Reed, in support of those promoting new trade initiatives with Soviet Russia: "I believe that what they want is the assurance from you that Soviet Russia will not fail to carry out her obligations in regard to contracts and concessions."[47] Her handwritten letter continued by warning Lenin that it was Hughes who turned the Harding cabinet against Russia. "His mindedness takes the attitude of excluding the 'enemy' Soviet Republic of Russia

44. The still recognized pre-Bolshevik ambassador adroitly noted, "Communism has cracked and Lenin is trying to save the day by making concessions. It is just like the autocrats who tried to stop revolution by reform." Bakhmeteff to Landfield, 21 March 1921, f. Landfield, box 19, Bakhmeteff Papers, BA, CU. Landfield, employed by the State Department, was actually paid by the Russian embassy, a strange arrangement, but this money was drying up (or considered too questionable), and he was released, the department still counting on Bakhmeteff to cover from his own account (the 1917 loan) the remaining travel and other expenses owed to Landfield. Bakhmeteff to Redfield, 8 March 1921 and Redfield to Bakhmeteff, 16 March 1921, f. American Russian Chamber of Commerce, box 15, ibid.

45. For the full stories on these American mavericks, see Neil V. Salzman, *Reform and Revolution: The Life and Times of Raymond Robins* (Kent, Ohio: Kent State University Press, 1991).

46. Minutes of meeting of 26 January 1921, f. American Russian Chamber of Commerce, box 15, Bakhmeteff Papers, BA, CU.

47. Bryant to Lenin, 2 April 1921, f. 5 (Lenin Papers), op. 1, d. 1509, RGASPI.

from ever entering the family of nations."[48] She added, "Hoover is also opposed to Russia. He is ambitious and he knows that it means the death of an American politician to oppose relief for Russia at this time. That is the great popular appeal in America. I don't believe Hoover will ever take an open stand against Russia but it is not well to have faith in him." She concluded, however, optimistically, that "prospects for recognition have never looked better."

The CPUSA and the Comintern

Bryant, married to one of the founders of the American Communist Party, John Reed, should have known better. Many Americans, already scared by the perceived radical threat in the labor unrest of 1919, witnessed with alarm the ascendancy of this new political organization, stemming from the left wing of the broader but strong socialist movement, which was more than a generation in the making. The fire was lit by American populism, the women's rights movement, and social welfare advocates, Jane Addams heading the list. Addams and many other respected proponents of economic and social justice were "untouchables" and provided a magnet for new recruits to social causes—and there were many in a rapidly industrializing society that had difficulty absorbing large numbers of poor Southern and black, or immigrant laborers. Anyone would have to accept that exploitation was rampant.

A distinguishing feature of the developing American political left wing, not unlike the Russian, was the presence of many immigrants or children of immigrants. This had the effect of boosting its numbers but at the same time arousing suspicions of those Americans who wanted a purified American patriotic country, invigorated by the creation of new organizations such as the Civic Federation and the American Legion. The atmosphere of postwar disillusionment added to the fear. The connection of the new Communist Party of the United States of America (CPUSA) with the Communist or Third International (Comintern) that was formed in 1919 to replace the defunct Second "Socialist" International earned the American unit special distrust, since the Comintern was generally—and accurately—believed to be an agent of the new regime in Russia in the pursuit of world revolution.[49]

48. Ibid.
49. See especially Theodore Draper, *American Communism and Soviet Russia: The Formative Period* (New York: Viking, 1960).

The American Communist Party, initially dubbed the American Workers' Party, to many rank-and-file Americans seemed to be un-American, because of its large number of foreigners, control from outside, and its own quandary about injecting social values and reform into rampant capitalism. The party's creation corresponded to the much-publicized meeting of the Second Congress of the Comintern in Moscow in 1920, attended by an American delegation. The Comintern, a Soviet creation, was not in a position to provide much monetary aid, but it could make the most of the successful Bolshevik Revolution. At that congress a still relatively active Lenin emphasized a concentration on exploited colonial peoples and on economically deprived minorities in developed countries. The application of this concept to the United States presented a dilemma. Above all, Lenin wanted American recognition—for propagandistic and political reasons. But he also saw a golden opportunity to develop Communist strength in that country through the large number of those with ethnic and economic grievances.

The United States, more than any other country, had attracted many immigrants of various backgrounds seeking new opportunities. Some of them, disappointed with the results and enamored of another promise in the Bolshevik Revolution, quickly joined the new American party. This lent a diversity to its membership that left the party vulnerable to charges of being anti-American, while also alarming agencies as to the wide realm of its potential membership and activity. An example of such an activist is Sen Katayama, a bright Japanese student at Fisk University, disillusioned with the imperialistic direction of his home country, who came to the United States to seek an education. After several years' residence in the United States, he joined the party, attended the Second Congress of the Comintern in 1920 in Moscow, representing both the United States and Japan.[50] Because of his unusual background and Lenin's stress on the colonial world, Katayama was assigned a prominent role in the Comintern organization.

This diminutive Japanese reentered the United States through Mexico in early 1921, under the code name Yavki, funded by $3,500 from the Comintern, as Alexander Borodin reported, "because he has certain particular qualification for this particular job."[51] He apparently had difficulty in receiving the funds, and "Yavki" soon returned, noting that "things are much simpler here [in Russia] than in US—so much squabbling and splitting there."[52] His mission, on direct assignment from Lenin and based on his Fisk background, was to recruit American blacks, and he would remain for many years the main Comintern agent for this

50. Ibid., 165, 170.
51. Report to Comintern council, 1 March 1921, f. 495, op. 18, d. 65, RGASPI.
52. "Yavki" to Comintern, 25 April 1921, ibid.

mission. Katayama remained a key official of the Comintern on American affairs, cultivating black visitors to Russia in general and as delegates to the Comintern congresses.[53]

Other American Communists, such as Charles Scott, received funds from the Comintern during this period, mainly for travel to Russia and back, while others complained of the lack of support from Moscow.[54] Scott reported, "The American working men lack a militant spirit, and their mood is very low. The Communist party does not know how and is unable to make use of the unemployment situation; it cannot co-ordinate the isolated flare-ups of the revolutionary proletariat."[55] He noted that unemployment had risen to 6 million but Communist activity was virtually nonexistent, partly because "American workmen are versatile and find other jobs."[56] Although American Communists complained constantly about the lack of support from the center, mainly due to the fact that the Comintern had few resources to expend in that direction, the Moscow headquarters had plenty to bemoan in the lost opportunities of its American agency. Whatever funds appropriated for the Comintern in the United States were clearly wasted.[57] The real danger to the traditional American way of life, if it existed, was from local concerns about social injustice and efforts to protest it. That would continue, on and off, for many years.

The Comintern foreign committee concluded with little enthusiasm: "American Communists must endeavor to take the lead in this movement for the amalgamation of all the revolutionary elements, and must put forward most emphatically the watch word of the united front."[58] The Comintern and its less-than-credible and wholly incompetent agents sabotaged a genuine American Communist movement, while giving those in political favor a straw dog to attack. The Soviet disillusionment with the American party would continue through the 1920s and through that organization's forced bolshevization. The Comintern was clearly disappointed in the American party's lack of zeal for revolution. This dismay and reluctance to fund activities in that direction continued through the 1920s: "American comrades suffer very much from an absence of *konspirizatsii*."[59] In other words, American Communists had little desire to launch a revolution.

53. Harry Haywood, *Black Bolshevik: Autobiography of an Afro-American Communist* (Chicago: Liberator Press, 1978), 185, 219; Draper, *American Communism and Soviet Russia,* 339.

54. Scott to Zinoviev, 15 October 1921, f. 495, op. 18, d. 38, RGASPI.

55. Ibid.

56. Ibid.

57. See Harvey Klehr, John Earl Haynes, and Fridrickh Igorevich Firsov, *The Secret World of American Communism* (New Haven, Conn.: Yale University Press, 1995). The failure of Soviet-inspired world revolution may be due mainly to the little money they had to pour down the drain into lost causes.

58. Comintern report, 18 December 1921, f. 495, op. 18, d. 38, RGASPI.

59. Scott to Zinoviev, 22 June 1923, ibid.

The New Economic Policy

The whole Comintern agenda and the Western views of a Soviet menace were substantially altered by the initiation of a new policy of retreat from the harsh, unbending policies of war Communism (1918–1921) in March 1921. The country was literally in ruins from war, revolution, civil war, and the ultra-socialist enactments that followed the revolution. War Communism was an odd combination of military necessities—to survive civil war battles—and altruistic ideas of a utopian society. The effort to create the latter was relatively easy in the postrevolutionary world, but how to positively promote the new society remained the problem.

The immense destruction of the civil war caused a consequent collapse of the economy, one of the worst in recorded history before 1921. Basic production levels dropped to about 15 percent of prewar production (reflecting mainly the Red Army producing for the Red Army), and the beginning of the worst famine in Russian history ushered in a new stage of Soviet relations with the West. The vulnerability of the Soviet regime was never more obvious. Lenin faced this reality up front and with a bloodily repressed military revolt at Kronstadt clearly in mind submitted his proposal to the Tenth Party Congress in March 1921. He laid out a new agenda that amounted to a substantial retreat from the idealistic war Communism back to a mixed capitalist economy, along with more open and less antagonistic relations with other countries. The world revolution was not abandoned but placed on hold, at a lower priority—temporarily. Lenin knew that progress in Russia depended on Western administrative and technical knowledge, especially American.

The big question to party activists was, how long was "temporary." Lenin's main followers split on this issue, with the right wing, led by Nikolai Bukharin and Aleksei Rykov, advocating an indefinite continuation of New Economic Policy (NEP) for the sake of humanity and the gradual stabilization of the economy. Others, especially Trotsky, favored a larger role for a centrally planned program of industrial advancement linked to a gradual collectivization of agriculture. The latter would involve more efficient consolidated peasant resources and through mechanization, as it became available, and the freeing up of labor for a massive industrialization drive. This combination of goals would come to fruition in the First Five Year Plan, beginning in 1928. But for now the party was sharply divided over this and several other objectives. Technological borrowing, especially from the United States, would be a major element in both the NEP and the First Five Year Plan.

The New Economic Policy, charted by a realistic Lenin, called for a restoration of a free internal market, an easing of restrictions on individual entrepreneurship, a freer approach to cultural development, and more intercourse in all aspects with other parts of the world. It rekindled all kinds of possibilities for the economy, culture, and even the future charting of the socialist world; the Soviet Pandora's box had sprung open. More than ever before or since, Russia was inviting the world to help rebuild the country but also to test and challenge old values with the new socialistic ones. The clash would significantly change a society already shaken by revolution and civil war, while posing dilemmas for the West. Was this newly reborn Cossack, holding out an olive branch and acting like a Wall Street denizen, to be trusted?

The Washington Conference

One of the few U.S. initiatives in international relations after the Paris peace conference was to call a meeting of major powers (that is, the victors) to Washington in late 1921 to discuss limitations on naval armaments, and, as an important second item on the agenda, the general situation in the Far East. The particular American concern was the persistent Japanese presence on the mainland of Asia, as the result of the war (exclusion of Germany) and Russian intervention (substantial Japanese forces in Russian Siberia). So the issue of the limitation—or setting limits—was accompanied by a goal of removing or, at least, curbing Japanese ascendancy in Asia. Though a naval formula (5-5-3) was agreed upon respecting active battleships of the United States, Britain, and Japan, the larger picture was obscured by the confusing fallout from the Russian revolutions and civil war. Secretary of State Hughes opened the conference in November 1921 with one of his most eloquent addresses, and he adjourned its business perfunctorily with only a few delegates remaining and much left unresolved in February 1922.

The new Bolshevik rulers of Russia, led by Lenin, had openly proclaimed a particular interest in the Far East, especially during the riotous meeting of the "Congress of Peoples of the East" in Baku in 1920. The lack of an invitation to the Washington Conference was considered an insult. Commissar of Foreign Affairs Chicherin issued two strong protests about this exclusion to no avail, since an American invitation to Russia could be construed as recognition.[60] With the motive of putting pressure on Japan to evacuate their overlord position in the area around Vladivostok, the partially ephemeral and transitory "Far Eastern Republic" was invited. This was a left-leaning government, centered in Chita, that filled a vacuum left by the defeat of most of the anti-Bolshevik forces. It

---

60. Paul Dukes, *The USA in the Making of the USSR: The Washington Conference, 1921–1922, and "Uninvited Russia"* (London: Routledge/Curzon, 2004), 20–22, 61–64.

nominally governed Siberia east of Lake Baikal, a territory larger than the United States though thinly populated.

The forces based in Omsk, led by Kolchak, collapsed in July 1919, and their supporting units had surrendered or gradually melded into the local population, or had withdrawn to sanctuaries in Manchuria and China, mainly to Harbin or Shanghai.[61] The American Expeditionary Force of around 13,000, responded to the end of the war and rising anti-intervention sentiment by gradually pulling out between November 1919 and June 1920, leaving Manchuria and strategic areas of Eastern Siberia virtually under Japanese control; relations between the Far Eastern Republic and the Japanese were naturally poor. As Paul Dukes has clearly demonstrated, the Soviets gained much at the Washington Conference simply by the collective pressure on Japan that resulted in its withdrawal from Siberia and then demonstrating an ability to consolidate the Far Eastern Republic into the Soviet realm, thus reconstituting the old Russian empire in Asia.[62]

The Washington Conference is also significant in bringing Boris Skvirsky to the United States as a representative of the Far Eastern Republic. He would stay behind briefly as the representative of that state, which would soon cease to exist, and he then served as the unofficial agent of the Soviet Union, in effect the unrecognized Soviet ambassador. He directed the Russian Information Bureau in Washington from 1922 until the formal establishment of diplomatic relations in 1933. Its primary missions were to furnish information about that country and to facilitate the processing of American visas for Soviet Russia, that is, basically operating as a consulate with offices and staff provided by the Soviet government. Although the Skvirsky agency in Washington and Amtorg, the new trade organization in Washington, were clearly directed by the Soviet government, they pretended to be independent, avoided contact with the State Department, and maintained the facade of official nonrecognition.

At the same time that the Washington Conference was getting under way, another Soviet overture occurred in London, where Leonid Krasin had established a permanent trade mission, known as Arcos. In December 1921 through the American embassy, Krasin asked that in the interests of international peace he be allowed to visit Washington with the object of reestablishing normal business relations through an extension office of Arcos. The State Department response was that the proposal could not be considered without more details and suggested that Krasin consult with the commercial attaché in London, another clear in-

61. For a good account of this tumultuous period in the Russian Far East, see Canfield F. Smith, *Vladivostok under Red and White Rule: Revolution and Counterrevolution in the Russian Far East, 1920–1922* (Seattle: University of Washington, 1974).

62. Dukes, *The USA in the Making of the USSR*, 73–81.

dication that the department was stonewalling all Soviet overtures at the same time that Congress was voting to commit $20 million for Soviet famine relief.[63]

The Genoa Conference and Rapallo Treaty

While American relief was covering much of its territory, Soviet Russia scored another success in the wider diplomatic arena, by being invited, along with Germany, to the Genoa Conference in Italy to discuss the postwar economic reconstruction of Europe in April 1922. The two "outs," who had been forced to accept the dictate of Versailles peace without participating in it, took advantage of the opportunity to meet separately in advance at the nearby resort of Rapallo. Their delegations, led by Chicherin and Walter Rathenau, quickly achieved a surprise agreement to forgive claims of damages from the war and the Soviet seizures of German property and to proceed to a mutually beneficial trade pact with considerable political and economic implications. The fledgling Soviet government had joined forces with the Weimar Republic, the liberal successor to the German Empire.[64]

The result was an upheaval in international relations that left Britain and France scrambling for position, especially since there were rumors (proved correct) of military agreements between the two countries that provided Germany with loopholes to escape some of the most stringent sanctions of the Versailles Treaty. They would quickly soften their policies toward both Germany and Soviet Russia; for the latter it meant diplomatic recognitions and trade overtures, essentially welcoming both back into the European community. The subsequent conference at Genoa with some forty nations participating was left divided and unable to come to any agreement. For the United States, as only an observer, it seemed to confirm the wisdom of staying out of European affairs, but in regard to Russia it strengthened the idea of at least some accommodation in lieu of recognition. Most likely if Martens was still in the country, he would be allowed to stay, as was the case for Skvirsky. Herbert Hoover especially fostered the policy of nonrecognition but business as usual.

63. Harvey (London) to Hughes, 15 December 1921, DEEA, f. 1, box 6, RG 59, NA.

64. For more detailed analyses of this diplomatic event, see George F. Kennan, *Russia and the West under Lenin and Stalin* (Boston: Little Brown, 1961), 208–23; Timothy Edward O'Connor, *Diplomacy and Revolution*, 78–96; and Theodore von Laue, "Soviet Diplomacy: G. V. Chicherin, Peoples Commissar for Foreign Affairs, 1918–1930," in *The Diplomats, 1919–1939*, edited by Gordon A. Craig and Felix Gilbert, vol. 1 (New York: Atheneum, 1974), 269–80.

As background, Soviet representatives had approached Germany about recognition and settlement of claims in early 1921 but had been rebuffed. Subsequently, Germany was presented with an

Soviet delegation at Genoa Conference, 19 April 1922: From left to right, Georgy Chicherin (in top hat), Karl Radek (typically with cigar), Maxim Litvinov (as usual, in the middle), Leonid Krasin (always distinguished), and unidentified. (Prints and Photographs Division, Library of Congress)

Charles Evans Hughes

Harding's designation of the highly respected but conservative Charles Evans Hughes as secretary of state had the effect of setting the Colby note in cement, where it would essentially remain for another ten years, despite many attacks on it, until cracks finally began to appear by the early 1930s.[65] Hughes had strong support for the policy of nonrecognition in the continuity of personnel in the State Department, especially from J. Butler Wright, who had been the first counselor of the embassy under Francis in 1917–1918. Other department personnel—DeWitt Clinton Poole, Basil Miles, Evans Young, Alfred Kliefoth, Felix Cole, Alfred Kumler, and Landfield—all had considerable experience in pre-Bolshevik Russia; they constituted a formidable array of conservative and ardently anti-

enlarged reparations bill by the "Versailles victors," and the League of Nations severed the industrial region of Silesia from the new Germany. Germany was now ready to look to the east.

65. At least some thought that the problem with Hughes was not so much his conservatism as his ignorance, knowing nothing whatsoever about Russia, past and present—and unwilling to learn. Scott Nearing to Borah, 18 January 1924, f. Russia, Dec. 1923–Jan. 1924, box 167, Borah Papers, MD, LC.

*Robert F. Kelley, director of East European Division,
Department of State, 1922–1937. (Prints and
Photographs, Library of Congress)*

Bolshevik opinion. Some opponents made much of the fact that both Poole and
Landfield were married to Russians of the old nobility and that the widow of the
late Consul General Summers in Moscow was a Russian princess, now working as
a translator in the State Department.[66]

They were soon augmented by a new contingent headed by Robert Kelley,
director of the newly (1922) revamped Division of East European Affairs (formerly known as the Russian Bureau).[67] Originally from Massachusetts, Kelley
graduated from Harvard, was a commissioned army officer in World War I, and

66. See, for example, Paxton Hibben to James Goodrich, 26 January 1922, f. Russia, Hibben, box
19, Goodrich Papers, HHPL.
67. For its earlier history, see Linda Killen, *The Russian Bureau: A Case Study in Wilsonian Diplomacy* (Lexington: University Press of Kentucky, 1983).

served as military attaché in Latvia in 1919–1920 as his first appointment to a diplomatic post. In the State Department he impressed many as a serious scholar who would gradually accumulate a distinguished library in the State Department on Russian affairs, but he also represented a conservative, Roman Catholic orientation and was a bulwark of nonrecognition.[68] He would remain as director of the division for fifteen years, a long tenure in a department office, until 1937. This was certainly not the only reason the State Department was strongly opposed to recognition.[69] DeWitt Poole was probably the most vocal and influential voice on nonrecognition, since he had considerable experience in Russia.[70] Kliefoth was a close second, more adamantly anti-Soviet: "Only an evil political combination of professional politicians would change America's attitude," he observed.[71] But he was reassigned to Berlin in 1923 to join Felix Cole, relegated out of Russian affairs—temporarily. Miles left the department in 1921 to serve as the American representative of the International Chamber of Commerce in Paris, Poole was transferred to a diplomatic post in Germany, and Samuel Harper resigned—or was retired by mutual agreement—from his translation and advisory role.[72]

Nonrecognition did not mean, however, that contact between Soviet and American diplomats was not allowed. For the Lausanne Conference that began in November 1922 to settle the complicated arrangements for the future of the new Turkey and a large part of the Middle East, both the United States and Soviet Russia sent delegations, the American one headed by Mark Bristol, the Paris conference high commissioner for the Ottoman Empire, and the Soviets were represented by their commissar for foreign affairs, Georgi Chicherin. Also attending for the United States was career diplomat Joseph Grew, then the U.S. minister to Switzerland. However, the Soviet delegation arrived late and essentially lost their case for the demilitarization of the Black Sea to the lordly Lord Curzon, who

68. For an excellent analysis of how Kelley shaped a whole generation of State Department recruits to a commitment to nonrecognition and anti-Soviet perspectives, see Frederic L. Propas, "Creating a Hard Line toward Russia: The Training of State Department Soviet Experts, 1927–1937," *Diplomatic History* 8, no. 3 (summer 1984), 209–17.

69. F. 1 letters of appointment, box 2, Kelley Papers, Georgetown.

70. James Somerville of the YMCA quoted Poole that "relationships with the Soviet Government was a contradiction in terms, because there can be no such thing as relationships with people whose word cannot be trusted." To Paul Anderson, 26 June 1922, f. ARA, 1921–1924, box 12, Anderson Papers, UILA. After visiting the State Department earlier that year, Paxton Hibben noted, "I found Mr. Poole wholly hostile to any information as to present conditions in Russia and convinced that his own knowledge of conditions, many of which had materially changed of late, was accurate when it was, according to my observation, far from accurate." To Goodrich, 26 January 1922, f. Russia, Hibben, box 19, Goodrich Papers, HHPL.

71. Kliefoth to Bakhmeteff, 19 November 1923, f. Kliefoth, box 18, Bakhmeteff Papers, BA, CU.

72. The anti-Soviet direction of the State Department, ironically, was curtailed to some extent by budget cuts in the Harding/Coolidge administrations.

presided over the proceedings. Behind the scenes interesting contacts occurred. Upon the request of Chicherin, the Norwegian minister to Switzerland arranged a meeting between Grew and the commissar in the latter's rooms at the Savoy on 14 December 1922. The company of five (including a couple of other minor Scandinavian diplomats) sat around a table well supplied with vodka and caviar for mostly small talk. The American minister was impressed with Chicherin's repartee, humor, and knowledge of affairs, such as a comment that "Mussolini was a passion, not a program." In a short conversation alone, Grew asked Chicherin if things were moderating. The answer was yes but not to tell anyone or it might change. Grew expected the Soviet representative to raise the question of a Soviet commercial mission to the United States, but he did not. The meeting was strictly unofficial and social.[73]

As far as Russian affairs were concerned, the State Department was basically in shambles by 1923, a circumstance that may account for the surprisingly mild comment on Russian problems by President Coolidge in his December 1923 message to Congress. Chicherin (or more likely Litvinov) quickly responded by indicating readiness to discuss outstanding issues in a letter directly to the president, released publicly by the Russian Telegraph Agency in New York. It read in part, "As to the question of claims mentioned in your message, the Soviet government is fully prepared to negotiate with a view toward its satisfactory settlement on the assumption that the principle of reciprocity will be recognized all around."[74] Hughes rebuffed this idea with a reiteration of his July pronouncement, which Soviet officials considered an insult.

The secretary of state was bombarded by all and sundry who had any kind of grudge or opposition, religious or ideological, to Soviet Russia and its leaders.[75] He relayed these to Harding and especially later to Coolidge but not the notes from the other, pro-Soviet side, thus filtering the president from objective consideration of the question of recognition to some extent. By contrast, Hoover tried

---

73. Grew diary, 14 December 1922, vol. 20, Grew Papers, HU-HL. The meeting was supported by Richard Washburn Child, U.S. ambassador to Italy, but opposed by Bristol. Interestingly, Grew does not mention this special highlight of his attendance at the Lausanne Conference in his published memoir/diary. Joseph Grew, *Turbulent Years: A Diplomatic Record of Forty Years, 1904–1945*, edited by Walter Johnson, vol. I (London: Hammond, 1953), 512–15. Nor is the meeting mentioned in the major Western study of Chicherin: O'Connor, *Diplomacy and Revolution*.

74. "Soviet Overture Sent to Coolidge," *NYT*, 17 December 1923: 6.

75. See, for example, the correspondence with C. C. Young who had a long history of contacts in Russia in regard to the import of Karakul sheep. He was an avid adherent of nonrecognition, blasting Borah, "who supports recognition of those degenerates." Young to Hughes, 30 January 1924, reel 54, box 66, Hughes Papers, MD, LC. Earlier Hughes responded clearly and succinctly to an inquiry of a friend and judge, Lindley Garrison: "The regime now functioning in Russia and known as the Soviet Regime has not been recognized by the United States." Hughes to Garrison, 19 February 1923, f. Soviet President's file, box 25, DEEA, RG 59, NA.

*Secretary of Commerce Herbert Hoover and Secretary
of State Charles Evans Hughes, 1924. (Prints and
Photographs, Library of Congress)*

to expose the president to various opinions on Russia, paving the way especially
for his friend James P. Goodrich, former Indiana governor and a proponent of
recognition, to see Coolidge. Goodrich wrote him afterward, "My conviction is
that there is a quiet growing sentiment in this country among thinking men for
the recognition of Russia. That sentiment will increase rather than decrease for
it is founded on knowledge gained by contact and not on false and foolish propaganda."[76] After Hughes resigned as secretary of state in 1925, the path to the
president opened up considerably, something Coolidge apparently appreciated.

76. Goodrich to Coolidge, 23 November 1925, f. Coolidge, box 3, Goodrich Papers, HHLP; see
also, Hoover to Everett Sanders (Coolidge's secretary), 12 October 1925, f. 156a, Coolidge Papers,
MD, LC.

The Public Debate

The department's nonrecognition views were seconded by the most respected American and British authorities on Russia, such as the elder George Kennan, Sir Bernard Pares of the London School of Slavonic Studies, and many veterans of Russian service who felt betrayed by events—David Francis (former ambassador), J. Butler Wright (former embassy counselor), businessman and American intelligence agent Xenophon Kalamatiano, Frederick Corse (New York Life), and Walter Dixon (Singer Company). They all had allegiances to the old prerevolutionary Russia and to some degree its more liberal successor (the provisional government)—and to the State Department. They were bolstered by powerful voices of the old Russian nobility by marriage—Julia Cantacuzene-Speransky (granddaughter of President Grant) and Emma Ponafidine, as leading examples—and by prominent refugees in exile such as General Ladyzhinsky, who opened a restaurant on East 57th Street in New York, later known as the Russian Tea Room, that was a notorious monarchist center.[77] Kennan recorded in his diary after hearing Ponafidine speak in Buffalo that she gave a "simple, sincere and interesting talk about Russian conditions under the Bolshevik."[78] Corse believed that the cause of nonrecognition had been won: "I think the less attention we give to Robbins [sic] either by way of showing him up or discrediting him the quicker we will put him into the background, and make him merely an unpleasant memory."[79]

Few thought it necessary to point out that the United States actually did recognize Russia diplomatically and that Boris Bakhmeteff still occupied the grand Russian embassy in Washington and had regular official contact with the State Department. That situation had become something of a public embarrassment, referred to frequently by opponents of the administration. The legitimate excuse for this charade related to unfinished business of the imperial and provisional governments with American enterprises, mainly for orders for munitions and equipment contracted during the war that were later canceled with ensuing losses for the companies involved. For example, an agreement was reached in early 1922 to settle a claim of Curtiss Aeroplane for supplying "flying boats" to Russia for just over a million dollars, paid by the Russian embassy out of the earlier loan held in escrow by the Treasury Department.[80] Some of these cases, especially the claims

---

77. Harper to Kalamatiano, 17 January 1923, f. 12, box 10, Harper Papers, UC-R.

78. Kennan diary, 10 April 1923, f. 1923, box 24 (diaries), Kennan Papers, MD, LC.

79. Corse to Harper, 4 February 1921, box 10, Harper Papers, UC-R.

80. Agreement between Curtiss Aeroplane Co. and Russia, 5 March 1922, f. Coudert Brothers, 1921–1924, box 17, Bakhmeteff Papers, BA, CU. The legal firm of Coudert Brothers in New York handled most of this Russian business to its considerable profit.

to material contracted and paid for by the imperial government, were destroyed in the Big Tom explosion in New Jersey in 1916.

Hughes ratified the Colby note most emphatically in an interview with the press in March 1923.[81] In July Grigory Zinoviev, head of the Comintern, sent a letter to the American Workers' Party advocating an offensive to gain more ground in the labor union sector. Samuel Gompers was quick to appeal to the government, charging foreign interference in labor matters. This forced Hughes to make a formal statement, in which he condemned Soviet interference in American affairs. Gumberg commented, "Mr. Hughes' reply, as well as his former statements on Russia, remind one of a student who has learned his piece so well that he can repeat it any number of times without change. He learned his lesson from Mr. Colby and sticks to it."[82] It was also clear to some that with criticism mounting from the press and privately, Hughes was increasingly unhappy with his role. It is hard to find anyone who had any respect for his conduct of foreign affairs. Hamilton Fish Armstrong politely noted, "I understand his position in Washington . . . is more and more uncomfortable."[83] He saw the possibility of both Hughes and Hoover resigning at an early date in the Coolidge administration—and Hughes did exit.

The eminence that many looked to was Charles Crane, whose philanthropy directly or indirectly endowed much of American scholarship on Russia and whose political clout was indeed great. The heir to a Chicago plumbing company fortune, Crane loved travel, making as many as twenty-three trips to Russia, some for several months at a time. Business—a railroad air brake partnership with Westinghouse—first brought him to the country in the 1890s in connection with a contract to furnish equipment for the Trans-Siberian Railroad. Committed to Russian culture, especially that associated with the Orthodox Church, and to the exposure of Americans to it, Crane was still a Wilsonian liberal. Paul Miliukov was his best Russian friend, and he never recovered from Miliukov's ouster as foreign minister and de facto head of government in May 1917. He despised Kerensky as a failure and the success of the Bolsheviks and their antireligion campaigns.[84] Crane had been a major financial backer of Woodrow Wilson, served briefly as his minister to China, and bravely returned through Russia in 1921 to

81. "Hughes Rejects Plan to Recognize Russia," *Washington Post*, 22 March 1923.

82. To Borah, 23 July 1923, f. 1 (1 July–30 Sept.), box 2, Gumberg Papers, SHSW.

83. Armstrong to Archibald Coolidge, 20 October 1923, f. Coolidge 4 Oct.–14 Nov. 1923, box 18, Armstrong Papers, Mudd-P. For many unsolicited comments, see George Wilson (London) to Hughes, 26 July 1923, reel 54 (box 66), Hughes Papers, MD, LC. It is probably too early to judge Hughes as the worst secretary of state in American history, but he certainly comes close to it, especially if giving due weight to Soviet Russian affairs.

84. For more details on Crane, see *War and Revolution*, 53–66 et passim.

see bolshevism in action. He remained an influential adviser to all presidents through Franklin Roosevelt.[85]

Crane's opposition to recognition was clear and constant, but muted. Some of his closest associates and protégés, such as the Hapgoods, were strong advocates of recognition. Samuel Harper, whose position at the University of Chicago was endowed by Crane, switched from opposition to support of recognition in the 1920s without fear of losing Crane's support. More than a few people, in fact, were outspoken on the left and right wings of recognition: notably Senator William Borah, Raymond Robins, Alexander Gumberg, and Christian socialists Sherwood Eddy and Jerome Davis in favor; Landfield, who left the State Department to edit a journal, Poole, Spargo, Ralph Easley of the National Civic Federation (the equivalent of the John Birch Society of the 1920s), labor leader Samuel Gompers, and Father Edmund Walsh of Georgetown University in opposition. Though Walsh was mainly concerned about persecutions of Roman Catholic clergy in Ukraine, Gompers feared a challenge from socialist leaning and pro-Soviet labor movements, such as the National Labor Alliance for Good Relations with and Recognition of Russia, headed by William Johnstone.

Gompers held a position of considerable power in labor organizations and in the general political scene, more perhaps than at any other time in American history—and everyone, including Soviet leaders, knew it. He constantly stressed the efforts of Communist propaganda to infiltrate the United States and especially to undermine his powerful position as the voice of American labor. In an open letter to Republican senators, he wrote, "It is impossible for me to avoid feeling that in the Communist inquiry there is not being shown that aggressiveness which is essential to the protection of American interests, and, if I may say so, of the interests of all civilization."[86] His would be one of the most powerful voices in opposing recognition.

The left wing was hampered by accusations of being Communists or closely allied and sympathetic to them. It included such Soviet supporters as Anna Louise Strong and Paxton Hibben.[87] The right wing was tainted by the violent antibol-

85. The Crane Papers in the Bakhmeteff Archive at Columbia University have recently (2004) been inventoried by curator Tanya Cheboratova, including new additions. A good biography of Crane is much needed but would be difficult to write, since Crane left an incomplete record, preferring to conduct much of his business through a secretary, by phone, and in person. Moreover, he was involved in so many activities, equally devoted to China and the Middle East, as well as to Russia. But, to adapt a phrase, "When Crane called, you listened," whether you were Wilson, Hoover, Coolidge, or Roosevelt.

86. Gompers to Borah et al., 29 January 1924, f. Russia 1923–1924, box 167, Borah Papers, MD, LC.

87. Both were effective speakers and political manipulators. Strong cultivated Borah as well as Hoover, while Hibben wowed audiences, Harper acknowledging that he was a big hit in Chicago, "especially with the ladies." Harper to Poole, 12 February 1923, f. 14, box 10, Harper Papers, UC-R.

shevism of remnants of the old regime, mostly holed up in European enclaves, who would occasionally surface at political meetings in the United States to the embarrassment of many on both sides. Strong naively offered her services to President Coolidge, noting that she was "personally quite well acquainted with Trotsky, having given him English lessons for three months."[88] Many of the stalwarts of recognition—Hibben, Albert Rhys Williams, Eddy, Gumberg, Davis, and Hapgood—visited Russia in 1923 and came back with generally glowing but biased reports.[89] After the fact, Davis inquired with the State Department about travel to Soviet Russia and was assured that there was no restriction on travel, nor was there any restriction on the import of gold from Soviet Russia.[90]

A congressional delegation, labeled "the unofficial commission"—Representative James A. Frear of Wisconsin, Senator Edwin Ladd of North Dakota, Senator William H. King of Utah, and Representative Albert Johnson of Washington—sponsored by William Randolph Hearst, also surveyed the Bolshevik scene for three months that year with generally positive impressions.[91] Davis, meanwhile, was one of the most effective lobbyists for recognition, holding a prestigious chair at the Yale University Divinity School. His address on the subject before the American Academy of Political and Social Science in Philadelphia in 1924 received wide publicity.[92] In 1926, he proposed the creation of an activist Russian-American Society to include a who's who list of prorecognitionists.[93] With so many constituencies involved, the issue of recognition tended to become lost in the media.

Borah, Robins, James Goodrich, and others, mostly prominent Republicans, continued to lobby the administration for recognition to little avail. Even the more radical partisans, such as Anna Louise Strong, reported forcefully to Coolidge through his secretary in May 1925: "Life in Russia has been improving, steadily for the past four years; there is good order, good transport, a standard of living below that of prewar days, but gradually climbing towards it; an organization of life in some respects consciously hostile to the form of society we know, greatly admiring American technique, but opposed to our whole system of industrial control."[94]

88. Strong to Coolidge, 9 May 1925, f. 156A, reel 85, Coolidge Papers, MD, LC.

89. W. H. Chamberlin (Moscow) to Gumberg, 9 September 1923, f. 1, box 2, Gumberg Papers, SHSW.

90. Leland Harrison to Davis, 13 May 1924, box 22, DEEA, RG 59, NA.

91. Notably, they represented Western and Midwestern states. The best account of their trip is James A. Frear, *Forty Years of Progressive Public Service: Reasonably Filled with Thorns and Flowers* (Washington, D.C.: Associated Writers, 1937), 194–210.

92. Davis to Goodrich, 24 February 1925, f. Russia, Davis, 1925–1926, box 17 Goodrich Papers, HHPL.

93. Davis to Goodrich, 14 April 1926, ibid.

94. Strong to Coolidge, 11 May 1925, f. 156A, reel 85, Coolidge Papers, MD, LC.

The Soviet Disestablishment

One major excuse for the confused and divided American responses to the existence of a Communist-oriented government covering one-sixth of the world was the nature of the personnel that represented it and the diverse policies that they pursued. Lenin—and especially Trotsky—summoned up a variety of reactions, but they were fading away on account of illness or political maneuvering. Few Americans—or Russians—understood the dichotomy between state concerns and those of the Comintern, founded in 1919 to lead (or better supervise) the world revolution, in which many of the new leadership sincerely believed. While the Soviet state with the advent of the New Economic Policy in 1921 pursued commercial connections and diplomatic accommodations with the Western powers, including those that had been directly involved in military intervention to overthrow it, the Comintern agitated, mostly verbally, for the undermining of those governments.

With priorities such as basic survival on their minds, the Bolshevik leaders cast the moderate Georgi Chicherin as commissar of foreign affairs. Following the lead of many old Bolsheviks and faced with the legacy of Brest Litovsk, he concentrated on securing a German alliance and cemented this with the surprise agreement with the Weimar Republic in April 1922 at Rapallo in Italy, just before the convening of the Genoa Conference. Soviet attendance at this important European economic conference, boycotted but observed by the United States, was a breakthrough in establishing more normal relations with the West. Even more important was the arrangement with Germany that removed the mutual claims of war damage and property seizures from the table. This was a definite diplomatic coup for Chicherin.

His assistant commissar, Maxim Litvinov, represented a variation, an understanding with the victors rather than the losers of World War I. Shaped by considerable exposure to Britain before and during that war and married to a British woman, Litvinov would have preferred a Western orientation for Soviet policy and had enough leeway to pursue it.[95] Basically, Lenin and Trotsky, and especially Kamenev, wanted to keep options open. Litvinov's door was usually open to visiting Americans, whether senators or businessmen. Typical was an exchange on a train with former governor of Indiana James Goodrich in 1925. "He expressed himself as very anxious about American recognition and agrees with me that when a Commission of fair-minded men sit down at a table to discuss Russian

---

95. For further analysis, see Hugh Phillips, *Between the Revolution and the West: A Political Biography of Maxim M. Litvinov* (Boulder, Colo.: Westview, 1992), 52–53.

and American affairs, they will agree."[96] Litvinov added that he knew that there were still obstacles.

American avenues of approach followed, such as a correspondence between Goodrich and Litvinov's wife, Fay. The assistant commissar was also patient, relying on such sources as Goodrich for the tenor of American politics regarding recognition. Goodrich wrote Fay Litvinov after Coolidge's 1925 address to Congress,

> The President . . . was entirely silent on the Russian question. We had hoped he would again open the way for Russia as he did in 1923. . . . Mr. Kellogg, . . . while not as dogmatic as Secretary Hughes, still is opposed to recognition, still believes that the Third Internationale is supported by the Russian Government and is carrying on propaganda in this country. The President does not attach so much importance to propaganda as does his Secretary of State.[97]

He then added, with Litvinov's reading in mind, "It must be admitted that there is no wide-spread sentiment in America in favor of recognition. Propaganda carried on in this country during the past eight years has well done its work. The ignorance of the American people concerning the real Russian situation is most discouraging."[98] One who would disagree was the current secretary of state, Frank Kellogg, who succeeded Hughes and was more open and accessible. He achieved fame as the coauthor of the Kellogg-Briand Pact, a golden opportunity to commit the world community of nations to outlawing war, and, especially on insisting that it be open to all, including the Soviet Union.

William Borah

Borah, an American working man's symbolic progressive, was by nature in favor of the underdogs and saw bolshevism as a big step forward over the old regime in Russia; his argument for recognition was simple and direct: the best way to deal with differences—debts, seizures of property, Communist threats—was to have regular relations, adding that Russia was too large and important to be ignored, regardless of the nature of its government. Diplomacy could not achieve much without recognition. Poole added, "He sees in Russia a great and strong friend

96. Goodrich diary, 1925, p. 40, f. Diary, box 17, Goodrich Papers, HHPL.
97. Goodrich to Fay Litvinov, 2 January 1926. f. Russia, Fay Litvinoff, box 20, Goodrich Papers, HHPL.
98. Ibid.

for the United States in the future. . . . He believes that this can be done, and can only be done, through immediate cooperation with the de facto authorities, a condition precedent to which is recognition."[99] In a typical response to one of many such letters, Borah advised,

> Your entire opposition to Russia, as I take it, is based upon Russia's unwillingness to pay her debts. You say you bought $5,000 of the Russian loan, and so forth. Well, Mr. Dietrich, when do you expect to collect that $5,000 under a policy of non-recognition. The most short-sighted, asinine policy that was ever put out by any people, or any individual, is the theory that you can collect a debt from a nation prior to establishing relations with that nation. I haven't the slightest doubt upon facts which I have in my possession that the Russian debts can be adjusted and will be adjusted as soon as recognition is an established fact.[100]

More philosophically, Raymond Robins, one of the most vocal advocates of recognition in 1918, remained convinced of Bolshevik sincerity and desire for friendship with the United States; he too saw the Russian changes as progressive in a loose American sense that should be accommodated. But he spent much of his time in the 1920s enjoying the Maine coast in summer (Southwest Harbor) and in winter developing his Chinsegut forest estate in Florida, now preserved as a state park.[101] Inspired by Robins and Gumberg and by receptive audiences in the Midwest, Borah maintained a steadfast prorecognition line.[102]

A broad spectrum of the Midwest included both inclinations and those undecided, open to discussion, which indeed was lively at the Williamstown (Massachusetts) forums of the Institute of Politics and even in the hallowed halls of

99. Poole to Harper, 7 December 1922, f. 9, box 10, Harper Papers, UC-R.

100. Borah to George Dietrich (Rochester, New York), 3 November 1924, f. Russia 1923–1924, box 167, Borah Papers, MD, LC. In an earlier and more succinct rejoinder, Borah wrote, "I think by recognizing Russia, or recognizing the present government, we have an infinitely better opportunity to exert our influence in the modification of the government of Russia, and certainly in the amelioration of the affairs of Russia, than to treat the Bolsheviks and the people alike as outlaws." To Samuel Dale (Boston), 7 December 1922, f. Russian Matters, 1922–1923, box 144, ibid.

101. Salzman, *Reform and Revolution*, 149–50; he was later plagued by amnesia, a strange disappearance, and a freak accident that left him paralyzed from the waist down and bound to a wheelchair. Robins' wealth began while striking it rich during the Klondike gold rush and was sustained by wise investments.

102. "I have spoken a number of times out here upon the Russian question. I feel that progress is being made all along the line . . . I believe it the first great step toward world peace and toward the restoration of things in Europe which will result in opening up the European Markets to our farmers." Borah to Gumberg, f. 1, (1 July–30 Sept. 1923), box 2, Gumberg Papers, SHSW.

Senator William Borah and Secretary of State Frank Kellogg, 1926. (Prints and Photographs, Library of Congress)

the annual meetings of the American Historical Association. Those in favor of recognition included left-leaning writers such as Theodore Dreiser and Upton Sinclair, film director Cecil B. DeMille, New York attorney Thomas Thacher, Norman Hapgood, Clarence Darrow, Allen Wardwell, Paxton Hibben, James Goodrich, Alice Stone Blackwell, orchestra conductor Leopold Stokowski, and the "voice of the people" in Kansas, William Allen White. Wardwell was especially effective behind the scenes in calming the hot-headed Hibben and encouraging others, especially those supporting trade with Russia.[103]

In the right center were most of the American scholarly establishment from Nicholas Murray Butler (Columbia) and Archibald Coolidge (Harvard) to Samuel Harper (Chicago), Robert Kerner (U.C., Berkeley), and Isabel Hapgood. The academic personage with the greatest political clout was no doubt Butler, who was summoned to confer with president-elect Harding at his Ohio home on "matters relating to our foreign situation and the problem we have to solve

103. Correspondence in box 7, Wardwell Papers, BA, CU.

in dealing with our new world relationship."[104] The meeting duly took place on 18 December with Russia definitely a topic of conversation. However, few details are available except that Butler recommended the appointment of conservative, anti-Bolshevik Elihu Root as secretary of state.[105] The Columbia University president was also a friend of Bakhmeteff and the Miliukov faction.[106]

Borah took heart from this middle ground and support from old, now somewhat lost, Wilsonians such as Norman Hapgood, to whom he wrote, "I wish, Hapgood, we could organize in this country a thorough campaign on Russia. To my mind, it stands right at the threshold of doing anything sane to help not only Europe but our own country in its present economic conditions, particularly, the agriculturists."[107] The latter concern would win him another vocal Senate supporter, Smith Brookhart of Iowa. His main Senate opponent throughout the period was rival Republican Henry Cabot Lodge, united in opposition to the League of Nations but clearly divided on Russian recognition; they had a notable debate on the floor of the Senate about recognition on 20 December 1923. One of the major items was the degree of Soviet-sponsored propaganda in the United States, never clearly resolved, since the definition of propaganda was not clear.[108] No one in or out of the press could complain about not being informed about all aspects of the issue.

A remaining mystery about Harding's views and intentions toward Russia at the beginning of the administration concerns the mission to Russia of businessman Meyer Bloomfield that was personally approved by the president and financed by the State Department, privately by William Phillips, making it about as official as it could be. He spent several months in Russia in 1922 and cultivated a close association with Maxim Litvinov, the Soviet assistant commissar for foreign relations.[109] Apparently, any reports he delivered were oral and private.

The balance, regardless of the administration's ambiguities, was clearly on the side of nonrecognition. Indeed, it would have been quite surprising for any American government in the 1920s to have recognized the Soviet Union. But the current was shifting, especially when so many of those associated with the relief program supported recognition: Frank Golder, Hoover's specially designated American Relief Administration (ARA) historian; William Haskell, the director

104. Harding to Butler, 13 November 1920, vol. 1, Butler Papers, CU.

105. Memorandum of visit, 18 December 1920, ibid.

106. Butler to Bakhmeteff, 27 October 1921, box 1, Bakhmeteff Papers, BA, CU.

107. Borah to Hapgood, 2 July 1923, f. Russian Matters, 1922–1923, box 144, Borah Papers, MD, LC.

108. Borah to Robins, 20 December 1923, f. Russia December 1923–January 1924, box 167, ibid.

109. Bloomfield to Roosevelt, 21 October 1933, recounting his mission, lending support for recognition, and offering his advice, POF 220a, box 2, FRPL. FDR noted in hand on the letter: "If I am up on Thursday I will see him for *one second*."

of operations in Moscow; and James Goodrich, the former governor of Indiana, who served as Hoover's special inspector in the field. Haskell and Goodrich gave opponents of recognition a scare, since their credentials as ordinary Americans, untainted by any previous socialist leanings, were secure. They were also well known from press coverage of their trips to Russia. Though Haskell was taken to task as a renegade for a series of articles in William Randolph Hearst's *New York American* in 1925 in favor of recognition,[110] Goodrich remained a Republican establishment figure of importance with ready access to his old friend Herbert Hoover. Also significant was a revolution in the American-Russian Chamber of Commerce from strong opposition to clear support of recognition in 1922.[111]

That same year another moderate voice emerged with the Council on Foreign Relations and its *Foreign Affairs Quarterly*. It organized three discussion groups: (A) postwar economic and financial problems; (B) the situation in dangerous areas in Europe today; and (C) internal and external concerns of U.S. diplomacy.[112] The subject of the first meeting of Group B at the Century Club on 23 January 1923 was, naturally, Russia, with Arthur Bullard and General Tasker Bliss presiding. Bullard led off by stressing that the Bolsheviks' hope for a world revolution was genuine but that they did not understand the psychology of other peoples. Bliss argued that "while Russia had produced high individual types, the nation as a whole was uncivilized. The higher types having been destroyed by the revolution, we now face practically a primitive uncivilized nation."[113] Coolidge bravely wanted to resurrect a calm discussion: "We must not leave Russia out too long as we are in danger of doing."[114]

Boris Bakhmeteff

All generally agreed that Bakhmeteff's announcement of his resignation as Russian ambassador in April 1922, effective 30 June, was a wise move.[115] "I have no

110. Ralph Easley to Dwight Davis (secretary of war), 16 November 1925, objecting to his status as a regular army officer, in box 2, Bakhmeteff Papers, CU-R.

111. Landfield to Bakhmeteff, 22 April 1922, f. Landfield, box 19, Bakhmeteff Papers, BA, CU.

112. "Announcement of formation of groups," Council on Foreign Relations Papers, box 238, MUDD.

113. Notes of Group B, 24 January 1923, ibid. A second meeting at Harvard on 7 February 1923 was led by Allen Wardwell and Archibald Coolidge and concentrated on the nature of the Soviet government.

114. To Armstrong, 22 November 1923, f. 15 Nov.–31 Dec. Coolidge, box 18, Armstrong Papers, MUDD.

115. Hughes to Bakhmeteff, 29 April 1922, f. State Department, box 21, Bakhmeteff Papers, BA, CU. The financial attaché, Sergei Ughet, remained recognized, as "Russian Financial Attaché," by

government to which I can recognize. [But] only a recognized government in Russia can relieve me of my trust," he said, leaving ambiguity.[116] Under public scrutiny for drawing considerable expenses from the U.S. Treasury, Bakhmeteff had no other recourse. He wrote Harper that "public discussion of our status precipitated the end at a moment when the matter could be wound up with dignity and without having the effect of weakening the policy of the United States. . . . I am going down with flying colors and I appreciate that fact, not on account of personal feeling but of consideration of Russia's interests."[117]

At the same time, few objected to Boris Skvirsky, formerly the representative of the Far Eastern Republic that joined the Soviet Union in 1922, quietly assuming a position as quasi-ambassador of Soviet Russia in Washington, another ambiguity. After Bakhmeteff returned from Europe, he avoided Washington, to the relief of the State Department, and established an office in New York to provide advice on Russian business.[118] The former ambassador was optimistic about what he had heard about conditions in Russia: "It is a great contest of life against the prevailing system of authority. . . . In so far as Soviet power is concerned, the germ has lost its virulency. The people are not held in terror of it any more. . . . The country at last is practically self-dependent."[119] Bakhmeteff was insistent that the United States not recognize that regime. "That would be especially pitiful as America holds a splendid record in Russia. She is the only country against whom Russia does not hold acute hatred."[120] He even reluctantly agreed to lead a roundtable on Russia at the Williamstown (summer) Institute,

---

an exchange of letters of 28 and 29 April 1922, and a formal signed agreement of 26 May 1922. He remained in control of, and responsible for, the embassy building and other continuing business. Kelley memorandum, 10 March 1928, box 22, DEEA, RG 59, NA.

Since Ughet's salary was paid out of the old provisional government loan fund in escrow with the Treasury Department, it might still be argued that the United States recognized the provisional government until October 1933, when Ughet resigned his post and transferred the embassy building to the United States government. Meanwhile, he retained diplomatic status, rank, and immunity. Kelley testimony, Senate hearing, 11 December 1928, ibid.

116. Bakhmeteff to Hughes, 27 April 1922, f. resignation, box 46, Bakhmeteff Papers, BA, CU. A factor in the timing of Bakhmeteff's decision was the recent death of his wife and a desire to visit friends and relatives in Europe.

117. Bakhmeteff to Harper, 9 June 1922, f. Harper, box 3, ibid. He added, "Only now after being relieved of the burden of carrying on official facilities under circumstances extremely trying do I feel how tired I am and how stiff everything has become on account of constant vigilance and circumspection." Ibid.

118. Bakhmeteff to Ira Bennett (*Washington Post*), 10 October 1922, Bakhmeteff Papers, box 1, BA, CU; Harper to Bakhmeteff, 12 February 1923, and Bakhmeteff to Harper, 1 and 28 March 1923, f. Harper, box 3, ibid.

119. Bakhmeteff to Harper, 30 October 1922, ibid.

120. Ibid.

commenting that "Russia is not a subject which lends itself easily to round table discussion the usual way."[121] Practical considerations as usual won out over political and ideological differences as matters of convenience.

One of the main practical considerations, as Bakhmeteff noted, was, naturally, business. Herbert Hoover as secretary of commerce from 1921 made it clear that conducting business with Russia was not officially opposed but was to be done only with the risks in mind His first public statement on the subject, in fact, was quite negative.

> The question of trade with Russia is far more a political question than an economic one so long as Russia is in control of the Bolshevik. Under their economic system no matter how much they moderate it in name, there can be no real return to production in Russia, and therefore, Russia will have no considerable commodities to export, and consequently, no great ability to obtain imports.[122]

This was modified more than a year later to take into account the New Economic Policy and the rise of cooperative institutions that were involved in foreign trade.[123] One of Bakhmeteff's major problems was his repeated statements, especially after conferring with his counterparts in Europe, that bolshevism was doomed, was in "the death grip of communism," all that was needed was to be patient and wait.[124] On the other hand, by 1924 he began to mellow, demonstrating a more realistic perception of the situation: "It would seem that the world is emerging from the post-war period of confusion and entering into an epoch where peoples, sick and tired of politics and politicians, are turning to the raising of children, to the growing of sweet peas and other useful constructive occupations."[125]

Hoover acknowledged that Russia had gold and platinum to export and later saw other opportunities for business. This meant that nonrecognition need not exclude Americans from the Russian market and opportunities that Germans and British were poised to monopolize. Felix Cole, one of the sharpest of the Russia hands in the State Department, drafted an article, "Is America Prepared for Russian Trade," that he sent to Harper for review, who advised that it not be published.[126]

121. To Harper, 6 June 1923, ibid.

122. "Trade with Russia Press Statement," 21 March 1921, f. Russian Trade, 1921, box 536, Commerce, HHPL.

123. "Trade with Russia," Department of Commerce press release, 12 June 1922, f. Russian Trade, 1922, ibid.

124. To Harper, 30 October 1923, f. 7, box 10, Harper Papers, UC-R.

125. Bakhmeteff to Harper, 4 December 1924, box 3, Bakhmeteff Papers, CU-BA.

126. Cole to Harper, 8 February 1923, f. 14, ibid.

Bakhmeteff remembered that those in favor of trade were generally in favor of recognition, and that Norman Hapgood, working for Hearst, was a leader, quoting him on himself: "He's [Bakhmeteff] the man who dictated our Russian policy."[127] Hapgood also recalled the problem of connotation in an age of conservatism, "To be anything novel was to be a Bolshevik."[128] This was entertaining if you were Theodore Dreiser or Cole Porter, but not for Washington administration circles.

Regardless of arguments and issues, and basic rationality, nonrecognition remained assured. One glimmer of hope was Borah's planned hearing before the Senate Foreign Relations Committee in late 1923 and early 1924. The Teapot Dome scandal, however, occupied the center stage in the Senate and the country, and forced suspension and then cancellation of the hearing on Russian propaganda in the United States. Harper comforted Bakhmeteff with his conviction that now, "One need have no worry as to change of policy unless there is a change of administration."[129] He added that the Commerce Department was now as stubborn as the State Department in that regard. Borah's position was also weakened by a few of his senate colleagues, who had been there and seen it, chiefly Senator William King of Utah, who came back from his 1923 trip opposed to recognition. Another constituency that registered in Washington was the earlier Russian émigrés with scholarly credentials in economics and politics, such as economist Leo Pasvolsky and Vera Dean.[130] Borah's ally, Alex Gumberg, was not optimistic about the possibility of gaining headway on recognition.

> Past experience had shown that whenever there was any hint in the press or if there were just rumors that did not appear in print that there was to be some action in regard to the settlement of the Russian problem, all the Czarist propagandists from Bakhmeteff and Brazol down would get very busy. It usually culminated in a protest by Mr. Gompers or the National Civic Federation. All the Washington Russian princesses would use their social influence, and in general all the dark forces praying for a czar would work overtime.[131]

They would eventually tire of the job and succumb to the reality of a major Soviet presence in the world.

127. Bakhmeteff oral history, 487, CU.

128. Hapgood, *The Changing Years: Reminiscences of Normal Hapgood* (New York: Farrar and Rinehart, 1930), 248.

129. October 1924, f. Harper, box 3, Bakhmeteff Papers, BA, CU.

130. For an analysis of their role, see David C. Engerman, *Modernization from the Other Shore: American Intellectuals and the Romance of Russian Development* (Cambridge, Mass.: Harvard University Press, 2003), 148–50; Pasvolsky to Harper, 19 December 1922, f. 27, box 9, Harper Papers, UC-R.

131. Gumberg to Borah, f. Russian Matters, 1922–1923, box 144, Borah Papers, MD, LC.

Facing that reality was not easy for Americans, considering the confusion about identifying what the Soviet regime really was. Commenting on Emma Goldman's *My Disillusionment in Russia*, published in 1923, the veteran interpreter of Russia, George Kennan, in one of his last letters, wrote:

> It does not seem to me to contain much that was not known long ago, or that she could not herself have found out before she was deported, if she had studied with an open mind the evidence that was then in existence. But that is the trouble with most of the socialists, anarchists and other cranks of the kind that I have known. They haven't an open mind, and they can't see straight or think straight until their brains have been shaken up by the stunning shock of a personal experience. In other words they can't believe that there is a club until they have been knocked down by it.[132]

A fitting prologue to Soviet-American relations—but clearly there was already a mystery inside the enigma.

132. To Lyman Beecher Stowe, 5 November 1923, box 9, Kennan Papers, MD, LC. Kennan died in early 1924, along with Woodrow Wilson, ending an era.

2

Relief

That the former Russian Empire was experiencing massive shortages of food, medicine, and other critical supplies in 1921 was no surprise to most of the Western world. The disruptions of central and local administrations and basic services caused by the Great War, sharp declines in both industrial and agricultural production due to isolation and blockade, and a consequent breakdown of the internal transportation system by the winter of 1916–1917 were all well known among the Entente and Central powers from both diplomatic, informal, and journalistic sources. The revolutionary upheavals of 1917 only made matters worse by adding a confusion of bureaucratic changes and ideological programs. The tragic result was the premature deaths of more than 5 million inhabitants of the new Soviet state by starvation and by disease aggravated by malnutrition. American relief that saved at least that many more was for many years one of the neglected chapters of the history of the twentieth century, now substantially repaired by the work of Bertrand Patenaude.[1] Still, it is barely, if at all, mentioned in textbooks on either Russian or American history.

Already in June 1918 Edward House, principal adviser to President Wilson, recommended that a Russian relief program, modeled on the one for Belgium a few years earlier, was required to save many lives and Russia itself, suggesting that Herbert Hoover head this Russian Relief Commission, "and let him take charge of the Russian situation for the time being." He confided to a friend and fellow Wilsonian internationalist, Norman Hapgood, that "I am saying this to you in the deepest confidence for no one knows of the suggest [sic] except the President, Lansing, and Hoover. I wonder how this appeals to you."[2] House apparently conferred with Hoover in the French countryside that summer. Hoover observed that a major American relief effort would probably not keep Russia in the war

---

1. See Bertrand M. Patenaude's definitive *The Big Show in Bololand: The American Relief Expedition to Soviet Russia in the Famine of 1921* (Stanford, Calif.: Stanford University Press, 2002).
2. House to Hapgood, 15 June 1918, f. House, box 9, Hapgood-Reynolds Papers, LC.

but might stave off active support of Russia to Germany after Brest-Litovsk, and that a small bodyguard of five regiments could safeguard shipments to Russia from falling into enemy hands.[3] Only the United States could spare food for Russia in 1918.

But within two weeks House feared his plan was doomed.

> The Russian situation is so confused that it is hard to come to a satisfying conclusion. The advice that one gets from those directly from Russia is absolutely contradictory.
>
> I am quite clear, however, if Hoover is sent in the right way, there are more chances for a successful outcome than in any other plan that has been suggested. There is some danger of the situation slipping out of the President's hands and this I would regard as most unfortunate.[4]

Unfortunately, or inevitably, the question of relief did slip out of the president's grasp, and within weeks, succumbing to Allied pressure, the American die was cast in favor of armed intervention in Russia. Troops were sent to the Russian north and far east to guard the stockpiled supplies and establish a beachhead to support anti-Bolshevik forces. Though temporarily suspended, the idea of a large-scale Russian relief effort remained alive, promoted especially by Walter Lippmann, Norman Hapgood, Hoover, and other humanitarians.[5]

Another effort to provide relief to the interior of Russia was launched during the Paris peace conference in the spring of 1919 by Herbert Hoover. It was, however, overshadowed by the poorly engineered plan to bring all the disparate Russian parties together at Prinkipo to resolve their differences. This failure and the chaos and war in Russia prevented any success.[6] The Russian civil war, prolonged and aggravated by foreign intervention and economic blockade, pushed the country further toward disaster. The Bolshevik government, in its desperation to survive, enacted extreme measures to find supplies to support its fledgling Red Army and a rapidly dwindling urban population fleeing to the countryside. A distinguishing feature of the resulting war Communism was food brigades, authorized armed contingents, scavenging the countryside to extract by force enough food to sustain the government and its military forces. Decrees allowed peasants to keep only what they needed for their own basic needs, while the remainder

---

3. Hugh Gibson diary, 2 August 1918, box 2, Gibson Papers, HHPL.

4. To Hapgood, 29 June 1918, f. House, box 9, Hapgood-Reynolds Papers, MD, LC.

5. Gibson diary, 8 November 1918, box 2, Gibson Papers, HHPL.

6. Harold Fisher memorandum, "Relief for Russia: Unsuccessful Attempts to Negotiate a Relief Agreement with Soviet Russia," January 1922, f. 11 (personnel), box 336, ARA, RU, HIA.

(and often more) was confiscated without payment. The villagers responded by sowing and producing smaller quantities of grain. Agricultural production thus declined precipitously in 1919 and 1920, producing famine conditions throughout most of the territory of the former Russian empire. In the meantime, the civil war and the Soviet-Polish War of 1920 were fought over prime agricultural regions in Ukraine, the Volga region, and much of inhabited Siberia with destructive consequences.[7] All of this was then compounded by one of the worst droughts in Russian history in 1921. Through vast areas of the former empire virtually nothing was produced in 1921. With reserves nonexistent, the future was bleak.

Soviet leaders certainly knew about American-sponsored relief efforts during the war and in postwar Eastern Europe, but they were still reluctant to appeal for aid and admit their own economic failures, trusting idealistically on help from the world proletariat. Even if willing and sympathetic, the latter was not in a position to provide much assistance during a postwar depression. Unfortunately, this misplaced idealism delayed more direct appeals until July 1921 when Patriarch Tikhon of the Orthodox Church addressed the world of religion, and Maxim Gorky, an internationally known author, rang the bell, one that was heard loud and clear, for saving Russian people, society, and culture. The latter proclaimed simply that "gloomy days have come to the country of Tolstoy, Dostoevsky, Mendeleev, Pavlov, Mussorgsky, Glinka, etc. . . . I ask all honest European and American people for prompt aid to the Russian people. Give bread and medicine."[8] Nothing could be more direct.

Still, any aid programs for Russia had to overcome serious obstacles. The Red Scare in America in 1919–1920 with the resultant flagrant deportations of many suspect citizens of perceived Russian origin left a dismal legacy of intolerance and bitterness. The expulsion especially of Soviet representative Ludwig Martens left the Soviets hostile toward the United States, as an early business adventurer into the country attested.[9] The advent of a new Republican administration in 1921 under Warren Harding, who was largely ignorant of foreign lands, and with Charles Hughes as secretary of state, did not bode well for relief. But the need was

---

7. The wartime imperial government had already damaged the productive capacity of major agricultural regions by its discriminatory policies against non-Russian populations and confiscations of the lands of its best farmers. See Eric Lohr, *Nationalizing the Russian Empire: The Campaign against Enemy Aliens during World War I* (Cambridge, Mass.: Harvard University Press, 2003), and James W. Long, *From Privileged to Dispossessed: The Volga Germans, 1860–1917* (Lincoln: University of Nebraska Press, 1988).

8. As quoted in Patenaude, *Big Show in Bololand*, 27.

9. Charles Albrecht (Tallinn) to State, 8 July 1921, reporting an interview with Ernest Jennings, vol. 14, DPR Tallinn, RG 84, NA.

obvious, and even the ignorant and conservative can be humane, especially in response to the eloquent appeal of the head of the Orthodox Church in America:

> Unless help comes from outside many millions will die from starvation in a few months. This tremendous disaster makes me forget that my country is under the rule of Bolshevist and that this disaster will probably bring their downfall. At any price the Russian people must be saved from the dreadful decimation awaiting them in the autumn and winter, and I join my voice to those who apply to the American generosity and noble heart in asking you to give to my famine stricken countrymen your help and save them from starvation and death.[10]

Private appeals also came in from all quarters. Donald Lowrie, with the YMCA in Riga, heard from an old friend in Siberia:

> Now the assistance I would crave of you is simply this: from time to time *send me food*. . . . And now will you allow me to give a brief list of articles most absolutely necessary to support a certain degree of health and strength and ability to go on working. Table butter and lard; sugar lump if possible, not granulated; any canned meats—we have not seen meat in three years. *Condensed milk* (very important). Any canned goods like sweet-corn pork and beans, etc. Cocoa, egg-powder. And for pity's sake sweets—any sweets but most especially candy and chocolate. Candy of course not of the very expensive kind, for just now I confess I care more for quantity than quality. . . . Do not laugh at me, just imagine: three years without sugar or anything sweet. The longing for sweets at times is absolutely morbid. I do not dare to ask for white flour because of its weight, but just a couple of pounds now and then would be a great treat.[11]

The writer also ordered candles, since neither they nor kerosene were available. Lowrie added his own analysis. "We have thought that things in Russia couldn't become any worse, therefore, they would surely soon get better: now with the news of a complete failure of harvest . . . we discover a situation where it seems almost impossible to prevent thirty to forty millions of people from starving to

---

10. Platon to Hoover, 29 July 1921, box 534, Commerce, HHPL.
11. Lowrie, quoting Savinsky, to Mother, 12 June 1921, box 1, f. June–July 1921, University of Illinois Archives (hereafter UIA).

death. The whole Volga valley is burnt brown in a drouth [*sic*] such as it has not experienced in history."[12]

Paxton Hibben, a Princeton graduate (with the reputation of being a playboy but now an overly sincere do-gooder, as well as a quasisocialist), managed a trip through the Volga area in June 1921, reporting his grim findings to the American press while serving as his own publicity agent for Russian relief.[13] By July he claimed that his nascent American Committee for the Relief of Russian Children, with the help of the Russian Red Cross, was already feeding 80,000 in the Volga region.

A Decision for Aid

The United States really had no choice but to offer aid after the Soviet appeal to the West. Obviously, it was the only country that had the resources available for the prompt dispatch of massive food shipments. The American Relief Administration (ARA) already existed with a large number of personnel and quantities of supplies in place in Eastern Europe, where the population needs had been stabilized. An established organization, the ARA had already dispensed more than $50 million in aid to refugees, displaced persons, and local populations in East Central Europe, mainly in Poland. A few detachments, American led and directed by Herschel Walker but composed mostly of Poles and Russians, had followed the Polish army into Bolshevik Russia in the summer of 1920, administering to the population, mainly Belorussian, in the occupation zone in and around Minsk.

A Red Army counteroffensive, however, swept over the area and advanced on Warsaw by late July. During a brief armistice and accompanying peace negotiations, an ARA detachment (with a shortwave radio apparatus that refused to function), under direction of Maurice Pate, a veteran of the wartime Belgian relief, passed through the lines into the now Soviet-occupied territory and found Walker and his ARA units still dispensing aid. Pate arrived in Minsk on 16 August 1920, but, since the peace negotiations soon failed, he was arrested and jailed along with the Polish delegates.[14] Soon released from confinement, Pate and Walker, supported by Minsk Bolshevik leaders who appreciated the ARA assistance, and apparently on their own initiative, proceeded on to Moscow, where they hoped to arrange a joint Red Army-ARA program to continue the

12. Lowrie (Riga) to Folks, 16 July 1921, ibid.
13. Hibben, "Report on the Russian Famine 1922" (New York: American Committee for the Relief of Russian Children, 1922), 6–11.
14. Pate reports, 16 and 22 August 1920, f. Polish relief, box 4, Pate Papers, HHPL.

child-feeding program in the Minsk region and perhaps expand it to other cities. Not surprisingly, they met with confusion and disbelief from Chicherin and even from the relatively sophisticated Lunacharsky and Nuorteva, then in charge of Soviet child-feeding programs. Prodded by Arthur Watts of the British Society of Friends, however, Soviet officials agreed to form a jointly operated Russian-American Children's Relief Committee.[15] Unfortunately, nothing came of this opportunity because ARA authorities were even more surprised and unprepared than their Soviet counterparts.

Relief, in fact, was already arriving in Russia from the West in small amounts, and aid groups were forming spontaneously in the United States.[16] A major obstacle, however, was the lack of official high-level recognition that would stimulate contributions and provide leverage with the suspicious Soviet bureaucracy. Several American agencies, most notably the Society of Friends, were already in the field, describing the desperate conditions and doing what they could with limited resources. By January 1921 a third shipment of Friends' supplies had been delivered.[17] Their activities demonstrated what could be done and at the same time shamed the United States into doing more, especially since they were well publicized by Anna Louise Strong, beginning a long newspaper career in the Soviet Union on behalf of the Hearst syndicate.[18] Thomas Thacher, a New York attorney with a social conscience, campaigned for immediate shipments of grain and flour: "There is no need of relief workers or soup kitchens, or condensed milk. Grain and flour in immense quantities are needed; in order to be effective, help must come before the Volga freezes. . . . Anyone who thinks that the Soviet Govt. will be overthrown by hungry peasants from Ufa and Saratov is a fool and a Knave."[19] He proposed an immediate fund drive. Another catalyst for aid to Russia was Allen Wardwell, who was in regular contact with Wilbur Thomas of the Friends.[20]

A YMCA official, noting that the Bolsheviks had modified their attitude toward the West, warned Hoover of the economic consequences of not providing

15. Pate cable from Reval, 10 September 1920, relayed by Brown to Hoover, same date, ibid.

16. For example, D. S. Harding, secretary, American Central Committee for Russian Relief, Chicago Branch, to Cyrus McCormick, 5 January 1921, 2C, box 118, McCormick Papers, SHSW.

17. Wilbur Thomas to Judah Magnes, 12 January 1921, copy in f. Jan.–March 1921, box 17, Robins Papers, SHSW.

18. Strong to Robins, 10 February 1922, f. 1, box 18, ibid. She complained bitterly about State Department obstructions to her return.

19. Thacher to Robins, 27 July 1921, f. April–July 1921, box 17, ibid. He was wrong about the Volga. The lack of rainfall had dropped the water level so much that few barges could pass and only very slowly.

20. Thomas to Wardwell, 9 November 1920, f. Oct.–Dec. 1920, box 6, Wardwell Papers, BA, CU. Thomas also cultivated the premier American relief worker, Jane Addams. To Wardwell, 7 February 1921, f. Jan.–April 1921, ibid.

aid—that the Germans would be there first and score major commercial gains—philanthropy with a cause.[21] That organization led the way in sounding the alarm and had already established in August a base in Riga to furnish Russian relief.[22] And at least one Jewish organization could not understand the delays that they thought, correctly, were due to conflict within the government, namely, between the State Department and Commerce. "It would seem that there has been some slip-up between your organization and the State Department, seeing that each is anxious to have relief work done in Russia, and that each charges the other with responsibility for the failure to do this work."[23]

In Istanbul, Admiral Mark Bristol, chief allied high commissioner for the former Ottoman Empire, thought it was fortunate that the local American Red Cross unit could feed 20,000 refugees during the summer of 1921, though hampered by continuing civil and national upheavals in the Middle East. By September the American Red Cross had expended more than $1,500,000 of relief in the area, and Bristol appealed for more.[24]

He emphasized that "the latest development in Russia is the horrible famine that appears to be gripping the country." With all the crops in South Russia failing, he predicted "that ten million people will die of starvation and disease if assistance does not come from someplace. . . . It appears as if the Bolsheviks themselves are not able to handle this proposition and it must come from the outside."[25] What relief was available was dispensed through the American embassy. The situation was worse in Siberia, where the Red Cross attempted to serve the needs of 30,000 homeless German and Austrian POWs, remnants of the defeated and stranded White armies, and a variety of refugees from the Russian hinterland, probably totaling more than 100,000.[26]

21. Robert Lewis (Cleveland YMCA) to Hoover, 24 March 1921, box 536, Commerce, HHPL.

22. Donald Lowrie (Riga) to his mother, 21 August 1921, f. Aug.–Sept., box 2, Lowrie Papers, UILA.

23. J. L. Magnus to Hoover, 14 January 1921, copy in box 17, Robins Papers, SHSW. Robins headed a vigorous effort among fellow Republicans for American-sponsored relief.

24. Bristol to Newton McCully, 28 July 1921, f. 19–31 July 1921, box 35, Bristol Papers, LC. Admiral Mark Bristol with much experience on the scene had no sympathy for the "reactionary" Anton Deniken, nor the honest but misguided Wrangel. They were "not equal to the task of either defeating Bolshevism, or setting an example that the adherents of Lenine and Trotsky would desert to them." To Charles Crane, 28 July 1921, reel 2, Crane Papers, BA, CU. Bristol to Emmet White (ARC), 25 September 1921, box 873, ARC Papers, RG 200, NA.

25. Ibid. In September 1921 Bristol reported 50,000 Russian refugees in Istanbul alone requiring support. Bristol cable to American Red Cross, box 873, ARC Papers, RG 200, NA. A major handicap was the closing of the special Red Cross unit assigned to the area on 1 October 1921. Arthur Ringland to Brown, 6 April 1922, f. April 1922, box 37, Bristol Papers, MD, LC.

26. Donald Lively to F. P. Keppel, 9 September and 23 October 1920, and to Livingston Farrand, 6 March 1921, box 607, ARC, RG 200, NA. A much neglected area of study is the refugee situation in the Far East where as many as one million Russians were without basic shelter and with little sustenance in 1920–1922, especially concentrated in Harbin, Manchuria.

Meanwhile, Hoover was besieged by friends and associates—and enemies—from the past about what to do about Russia. Philip Norton, a former Committee on Public Information agent in Siberia, regretted the lack of an American initiative abroad during the change of administrations. On his own, Norton contacted a Soviet agent in Stockholm, Professor Georgy Lomonosov, and after that encounter urged that aid be delivered now and not after a problematic Bolshevik demise.[27] Norton admitted that an economic agenda underlay much of American policy toward Russia.

> I know and realize the folly of the communistic experiment. It was organized by Lenin an idealist and was made a thing of horror by some of the men he was obliged to use. I fought the reds largely because of their propaganda in America. The American business men cannot afford to dabble with Russian politics but never the less I would have been glad to see an evolution take place in Russia instead of a revolution . . . I had hoped American commerce might help in a peaceful transition. . . . I am now convinced that it would be years before a revolution even from the inside could succeed. As the people become poorer their opportunity to successfully rise becomes less.
>
> I still think that American enterprise should go to Russia direct. All through Europe I have heard that America has not sufficient brains to do business in Russia direct.[28]

Hoover knew better. Though a fully confirmed anti-Communist, in 1919 he had opposed military intervention and advocated increased trade with Russia.[29] For him the plea for assistance was an invitation to revive trade relations as well. The whole question of Russian relief was complicated by the large number of other desperate refugees scattered especially around the Balkans and the Middle East—Bulgarian, Romanian, Armenian, Greek, and so forth.[30] To their credit, and comprehending the extent of their homeland disaster from their own sources, the anti-Bolshevik Russian émigré groups of disparate orientation virtually unani-

---

27. Norton to Hoover, 31 May 1921 (Vienna) and 2 August 1921 (Berlin), f. Norton, box 451, Commerce, HHPL.

28. Norton to Hoover, 2 August 1921, ibid.

29. He received support and approval of his views from various quarters. For example, E. F. C. Wise, principal British representative on the Supreme Economic Council, to Hoover, 1 April 1921, box 321, Commerce, HHPL.

30. Historian Frank Golder in a series of letters from the region described the sorry conditions of homeless, starving refugees, some of whom were finding a very small support from League of Nations supplements. Golder to Adams, January–April 1921, f. 1, box 11, Golder Papers, HIA.

mously supported any aid that could be provided.[31] This included the still-recognized pre-Bolshevik ambassador to the United States, Boris Bakhmeteff, and his former secretary, Michael Karpovich. With their support, William Redfield, a member of the Wilson Cabinet, lobbied the Harding administration for Russian relief.[32] Bakhmeteff wrote the former provisional government's minister of war, Alexander Guchkov, that it would be unwise to oppose a relief effort that had engendered so much public support in America.[33] And another old Wilsonian, Norman Hapgood, from the beginning urged that, "Of course I feel that relief is right and inevitable, but I wish it might be given with the unmixed motives of the Friends."[34]

From another quarter, Ekaterina Breshko-Breskovskaia, the acknowledged "little grandmother of the Russian Revolution," launched her own small-scale relief operation directed toward Russian/Ukrainian orphans' homes just west across the Russian border in the Ruthenian part of Czechoslovakia. She, of course had good access to information in Russia and relayed it to her American contacts. On 21 July 1921, she appealed to Lyman Brown, head of the ARA in Central Europe, "to extract at any price the consent of the Bolsheviks to the admission of transports with food, medical equipment, and stores of clothing."[35] Samuel Bertron, who had represented New York business circles on the Root Commission in 1917, as chair of the board of the American-Russian Chamber of Commerce, volunteered its services. "Can this organization be helpful, or can I?"[36]

Hoover's personal secretary, Christian Herter, anxious to escape the August Washington heat, wrote his friend Hugh Gibson in Poland,

> This Russian business is making our daily existence just a bit more hectic than it was before, but the Chief [Hoover] is still sailing along most serenely with but very few ruffles on his brow. Just where we are going to get off with the sixty-five ring circus we are now trying to run I don't know, but at least

---

31. See, for example, Philip Carroll (Hamburg) to Walter Lyman Brown, 29 July 1921, reporting on an interview with Alexander Kerensky, box 534, Hoover Papers, Commerce, HHPL. To the question about whether relief might help keep bolshevism alive, Kerensky responded that nothing could, that it was bound to fail. "The Russian mind has a distinct democratic tendency," he said, a point left to be debated. But this belief would have important propaganda value against that regime. Ibid.

32. Redfield to Hughes, 25 July 1921, reporting on communications with Alexander Sack and Karpovich, box 30, ibid.

33. Bakhmeteff to Guchkov, 14 December 1921, box 3, Bakhmeteff Papers, BA, CU.

34. Hapgood to Hoover, 7 August 1921, f. Hapgood, box 252, Commerce, Hoover Papers, HHPL.

35. Breshko-Breskovskaia to Brown, 21 July 1921, box 1, Egbert Papers, HIA. Edward Egbert was her private secretary and main liaison with Americans.

36. Bertron to Hoover, 25 July 1921, f. Bertron, box 50, Commerce, HHPL.

it is somewhat of a satisfaction to feel that every constructive measure so far taken by the Administration has either been initiated by the Chief or in some way shaped by the Chief.[37]

And on 12 August, the Chief himself addressed a concern of Nelson Fell, who had spent many years in prewar Russia as a mining engineer, that relief would only strengthen Bolshevik control, while revealing his policy.

> If, in view of the appalling need which appears to be really genuine, the Allies should all hold back, the Soviet authorities would then be able to raise the cry that Russia is again being blockaded and that the Allies have no sympathy for the Russian people, whether Bolshevik or un-Bolsheviki. Our present evidence of good faith toward the Russian people cannot be construed in any way as a strengthening of the hands of the present authorities inasmuch as all operations that we may conduct will be carried out under our own direction entirely. This will allow of an entering wedge in Russia and will certainly give the whole world an opportunity to point out to the Russian people themselves that their present economic system is hopeless. Of course, charitable aid will only be a drop in the bucket and we will be unable to do anything in the way of permanent economic reconstruction. That, however, must follow in time and be directed from the outside.[38]

So there was an ulterior motive in relief—and a conservative Congress would buy it.

As might be expected, opposition to relief came from a few quarters in the émigré and the politically conservative communities. Foremost among them was Julia Cantacuzene, perhaps because of anticipated competition with her own modest relief effort on behalf of refugees from the revolution and civil war. Raymond Robins complained about this "little American lady [who] was plain Julia Grant before she became a noble lady by marriage . . . protesting relief for starving Russia. Some nobility this!"[39] Actually, she ably defended her concentration on the Russian refugees. "We are giving up trying to do any relief work in Russia proper, as the Bolsheviki are largely occupying that area—but we are helping the destitute refugees who are coming out all along the frontiers by the thousands."[40]

37. Herter to Gibson, 12 August 1921, f. Herter, box 261, ibid.

38. Hoover to Fell, copy, 12 August 1921, ibid.

39. Robins to Gumberg, 29 October 1921, f. New York, Gumberg Papers, SHSW.

40. Cantacuzene to Cyrus McCormick, 1 April 1920, f. American Central Committee for Russian Relief, box 117, McCormick 2C, SHSW.

The Riga Agreement

On 14 July 1921 Fridtjof Nansen responded to Gorky's plea that only the United States could provide the quantity of aid required. Hoover followed with a formal cable to Gorky on 23 July, stressing that the ARA was a private organization prepared to offer assistance to one million people but that a prerequisite of any American famine relief was the release of all American prisoners held in Russia. He stressed its considerable experience of relief in twenty-one countries. A direct request must also be made to the American Relief Administration.[41] Gorky responded on 31 July with an acceptance of the offer by Lev Kamenev on behalf of the Soviet relief committee (Pomgol) and proposed that an ARA representative be sent to Moscow, Riga, or Tallinn. Hoover chose Riga and sent Walter Lyman Brown, chief of ARA operations in Europe, from his headquarters in London for the negotiations. He was joined by Cyril Quinn, in charge of the work in Poland, and by Phillip Carroll of the Baltic region. The head of the Soviet delegation was Maxim Litvinov, deputy commissar of the Peoples Commissariat of Foreign Relations.[42] With Litvinov as chief Soviet negotiator and Secretary of Commerce Hoover leading the American side by proxy, it would be difficult to avoid the conclusion that this was an official Soviet-American agreement that constituted formal diplomatic relations. The Soviet government would pursue this interpretation for the next ten years, while the ARA insisted on its private and unofficial provenance.

Meanwhile, Hoover cabled an international conference on relief that was convening in Geneva of his decision, as well as anticipating the need to rehabilitate transportation, agriculture, and industry in Russia—a tall order. He also dispatched Gardner Richardson from London to Geneva to ensure that the conference participants were well aware of who was in charge.[43] The meeting acknowledged this by simply redrafting Hoover's cable in the form of a resolution.[44] Regardless, the negotiations in Riga began on 10 August, coincident with the release of the American prisoners from their Moscow jails.[45] Unfortunately, more

41. Hoover to Gorky, 23 July 1921, ARA Documents, Pre-Commerce, vol. 1, HHPL.

42. Chicherin to Kamenev, 3 August 1921, in *Rossiia i SShA: torgovo-ekonomicheskie otnosheniia, 1900–1930: sbornik dokumentov* (Moscow: Nauka, 1996), 212–13; copy of Kamenev and Chicherin to Litvinov, conferring his authority to negotiate with ARA, 11 August 1921, vol. 1: 44, Pre-commerce, HHPL.

43. Hoover cables to Brown, to Geneva and to Richardson, 9 August 1921, vol. 1: 44, Pre-commerce, HHPL.

44. Richardson (Geneva) to Hoover, 16 August 1921, ibid.

45. Albrecht (Tallinn) to Evan Young (Riga), 10 August 1921, reporting arrival of the released American prisoners, including Kalamatiano, vol. 14, DPR Tallinn, RG 84, NA. The meeting happened to correspond with a lead article, sympathetic to the Soviet government and supporting famine relief, by Lewis Gannett, "Is Russia Abandoning Communism?" in *The Nation* 113 (10 August 1921): 141–44.

delays resulted as each side consulted at every step with its Moscow and Washington bases. The main issues remaining were the ARA's insistence on freedom to choose its personnel and having complete control over distribution operations in Russia. Litvinov insisted on a veto right over personnel, which Brown firmly rejected. His demand that assistance be restricted to the Volga region was also opposed. To Brown's assurance that the Americans would act in a strictly nonpartisan position, Litvinov responded in what was reported to be a Cockney accent that "Food iz a veppon," which, of course, was true, from both Soviet and American perspectives. Lenin agreed with the need to compromise but still envisioned a Trojan horse coming into his disappointingly limited socialist world.[46]

In spite of this, a stalemate ensued in Riga with the negotiators quibbling over minor details. Hoover's promise that the ARA would not have a political agenda seemed to break the impasse. The size of rations and exactly who would receive them provoked additional debate, necessitating direct communications with an ailing Lenin, who was far from being helpful, as if he were being dragged in reluctantly to deal with his own disaster. Of more importance was Chicherin's not inaccurate charge that Hoover was establishing American sovereignty over a vast portion of Soviet territory. With time of the essence, both parties retreated to vague compromises but acknowledged American control over distribution of supplies, diplomatic immunity status for personnel, along with the right of unimpeded initial surveys of the famine areas. All expenses of operations within Russia were to be borne by the Soviet government, but any suspect hostile individuals, especially subjects of the former Russian empire, were to be excluded from ARA service.

Brown and Litvinov finally agreed to a hurried, wordy, vague, and cumbersome document, and their Riga agreement was duly signed at a public ceremony on 20 August 1921. A great many Soviet subjects (largely not Russian but Tatar, Bashkir, Kazakh, Ukrainian, and Volga German) had perished from starvation and disease in the meantime—but a lot more would be saved as a result of this far-reaching accord. Of the thirty articles, most important were the right of the ARA to bring in "such personnel as it thinks necessary for the efficient administration of relief and that it be assured of full liberty and protection in Russia" (article one), the ARA will have complete freedom in selection of local personnel (article three), and "the personnel in Russia will confine itself strictly to the administration of relief and will engage in no political or commercial activities whatever" (article twenty-six).[47] A subsequent letter clarified some points: that

---

46. Patenaude, *Big Show in Bololand*, 41–44.

47. A copy of the seven-page "agreement" signed by Brown and Litvinov is in vol. 1, ARA, Pre-Commerce, Hoover Papers, HHPL. For a more informal record emphasizing American rights in Russia, f. 1 (rough notes), Carroll Papers, HIA.

only about 100 American personnel would be needed, that all travel within Russia would be cleared in advance, and that any Soviet relief programs in place would continue.[48] Some Americans attending were annoyed at Litvinov's dominant, supercilious, and arrogant behavior at the negotiations, perhaps an understandable facade considering the extent of the concessions.

A YMCA secretary observing from the sidelines in Riga thought that "all the rest of the world is trying to attach itself to the A.R.A. wagon, or to get some part of America's wealth attached to their wagon, to go into Russia to relieve the starving—and incidentally work all sorts of political and economic wires in their own interests. You cannot blame the Russians very much for the suspicions with which they greeted the American delegation here." He added that if the United States were in Europe, the relief agreement would have been impossible. But he was also convinced that the ARA had no political agenda and was "one hundred percent philanthropic, with no other axe to grind."[49]

A bone of contention in the relief agenda was the fact that the Society of Friends was already there dispensing relief and believed that they should take precedence. ARA officials met with representatives of the Friends in August. "They want to continue their work in Russia and they do not want to antagonize or conflict with the ARA." Rickard added, "It must be noted that the Quakers in their operations in Russia have submitted largely to the Soviet regulations. The 150 or more Russian workers who assist them in Moscow were chosen by the Soviet authorities."[50]

At a meeting in Washington of the European Relief Council on 24 August, Hoover easily gained the ascendancy and control over other relief endeavors with some autonomy granted only to the Society of Friends. The session included delegates from the Friends, headed by Wilbur Thomas, the American Red Cross, ARA (Hoover, Haskell, Barnes, and Rickard), Federal Council of Churches, Jewish Joint Distribution Committee, Knights of Columbus, National Catholic Welfare Council, YMCA, and YWCA.[51] Informed of this in Riga, Walter Lyman Brown was awed: "It is going to be by far the biggest and most difficult job we have yet tackled and the potentialities of it are enormous, but I think we can pull

48. Brown to Litvinov, 20 August 1921, ibid.

49. Lowrie (Riga) to mother, 21 August 1921, f. Aug.–Sept. 1921, box 2, Lowrie Papers, UILA.

50. Rickard Memorandum, 17 August 1921, f. 1921–1922, Rickard Files, HIA.

51. Minutes of Washington conference, 24 August 1921, f. Russia 1921, box 534, ARA, RU, HIA.

The YMCA had been working for several months to gain access to Russia. This included a plan drawn up by Brackett Lewis of conditions of accepting an invitation with only very basic guarantees of freedom of action, "tho some additional grant—such as quarters rent-free, priority telegraph rights, priority and free freight transportation—would be very nice." Lewis to Paul Anderson, 22 January 1921, box 6, Anderson Papers, UILA.

it through."[52] Subsequently, in another agreement in New York the American Red Cross agreed to supply $3 million worth of supplies from its stocks in Europe, including an initial requisition of $600,000 from American Red Cross (ARC) sources in Paris.[53] While all these meetings and negotiations were going on, the Society of Friends was busy distributing as much relief as it could with its finger in the dike. Edgar Rickard, the ARA director of relief on the American side, admitted that in August 1921 the Friends Service Committee collected $2,000 a day in small contributions specified for Russia, while the ARA had not yet reached $300. He also noted that Wilbur Thomas had reported that 200,000 garment workers had agreed to donate one-half day's pay to Russian relief.[54] Obviously, the Friends could tap sources beyond the reach of the ARA.

To the Rescue[55]

It did not take long for Hoover's recruit to get into action. The result, in fact, might be compared to the Oklahoma land rush, as the American Relief

52. As quoted in, but not cited, Patenaude, *Big Show in Bololand*, 47.

53. Agreement between ARA and ARC, 2 September 1921, vol. 1, ARA, Pre-Commerce, Hoover Papers, HHPL. J. W. Krueger to John Barton Payne, 11 March 1922, box 869, ARC Papers, RG 200, NA.

54. Rickard memorandum, 17 August 1921, f. 1921–1922, Rickard Papers, HIA. For more details on the "Quaker relief," see David McFadden and Claire Gorfinkel, *Constructive Spirit: Quakers in Revolutionary Russia* (Pasadena, Calif.: Intentional Productions, 2004).

55. Information on the American Relief Administration in Russia is abundant, thanks to Hoover's insistence on thorough and extensive record keeping and reporting and then by providing a home for it at the library he sponsored, the Hoover Institution on War and Peace at Stanford University. More than 700 large boxes of records are filed under the ARA, supplemented by untold numbers of collections of participants, strenuously acquired after the events. In addition, the Commerce files of the Herbert Hoover Presidential Library in Iowa are important, supplemented and largely duplicated in State and Commerce Department files in the National Archives and in the ARA files in Russia. One must conclude from having perused these materials that one of the high priority shipments into Russia during the famine relief, besides food, was paper. Seldom has an operation of this kind been so well documented in all of its ramifications and biases, which, however, poses obvious challenges to the researcher.

Despite the wealth of documentation and the work done on it, the existence of the American Relief Administration and its unique contribution to Soviet-American relations is rarely mentioned— and if then usually erroneously—in basic textbooks on both Russian and American history. Hopefully, Patenaude's *Big Show in Bololand*, and this volume, will correct that injustice. Earlier publications are still useful: Frank Alfred Golder and Lincoln Hutchinson, *On the Trail of the Russian Famine* (Palo Alto, Calif.: Stanford University Press, 1927), Harold H. Fisher, *The Famine in Soviet Russia, 1919–1923: The Operations of the American Relief Administration* (New York: Macmillan, 1927), and Benjamin Weissman, *Herbert Hoover and Famine Relief to Soviet Russia, 1921–1923* (Palo Alto, Calif.: Hoover Institution Press, 1974).

Administration entered Russia in full force, a few hundred within weeks, conquering peacefully a large area of the new Communist world without casualties, what several White armies and divisions of Allied armies had failed to do more than two years earlier with considerable losses. In fact, preparations were well under way at least two weeks earlier, mobilizing the diplomatic and relief organizations in Poland for Russia.[56] The New York office of the ARA at 42 Broadway was besieged with applications for the Russian work weeks before, leading one official to observe to George Barr Baker, a leading Hoover assistant, "All of your friends, my friends, the office boy's friends and everybody's friends want to get a job in Russia." One veteran of relief thought this was "the romantic goal of all the old timers, . . . the ultimate show."[57] That the whole show was portrayed publicly as a "save the children" campaign certainly helped gain supporters. But two unwritten rules applied in regard to acceptance: no women, no Jews. However, there were exceptions, for example, in regard to the former, for those already working for the Society of Friends or who came in under the cloak of the YMCA. Hoover, personally, recruited Colonel William N. Haskell of the U.S. Army to direct the operation in the field because of his military rank and previous experience as ARA director in Romania and Armenia.[58]

Fearing Soviet objections to an army man heading the operation, as well as the other war veterans he brought along, Hoover stressed to Litvinov their valuable experience. No complaints came from that quarter, but many regular ARA men would be persistently resentful of an outsider, his entourage, and his military command demeanor. To his credit, Haskell took his job seriously and listened to and read reports, quickly agreeing that the relief must be extended to adults, after the immediate "save the children" campaign was launched, in order to sustain the next generation.[59] Adults, however, were expected to work in recompense, assisting with relief work or improving sanitation. In Simbirsk on the Volga, for example, many of the adult recipients of aid were assigned to clean the streets, which included removing the bodies of famine victims.[60]

56. Hugh Gibson diary (letters to his mother), 6 and 7 August 1921, f. May 1921–Nov. 1921, box 3, Gibson Papers, HHPL. Quinn of the Child Fund in Poland had already left for Riga to organize the relief on 5 August.

57. Quoted in Patenaude, *Big Show in Bololand*, 49.

58. Hoover to Brown, 19 August 1921, asking him to send Haskell over for "his background as a highly successful organizer used to cooperation with local institutions." Copy in Rickard Papers, f. 1921–1922, HIA. Haskell accepted on condition that at least $50 million be provided. Untitled manuscript, box 1, Haskell Papers, HIA.

59. Haskell to Hoover, 5 November 1921 (cable), f. Russia General, box 534, Commerce, Hoover Papers, HHPL.

60. Circular letter, no. 60, 20 March 1922, ARA, Russian Division, vol. 2, HHPL.

Having secured control of shipments and port facilities, Hoover saw the advantage of a military chain of command to accomplish the immense coordination task ahead, but, to accommodate the goals and wishes of other charitable organizations, a remittance program of food parcels was implemented, whereby the ARA acted as a delivery service in the larger cities, such as Petrograd and Moscow, and among Jewish populations in Ukraine and elsewhere. Anyone could pay the ARA New York office for food to be delivered to relatives, friends, or associates in Russia. He also recruited Russian expertise: Archibald Coolidge from Harvard, Frank Golder from Stanford, Lincoln Hutchinson, an economist from the University of California at Berkeley, and Vernon Kellogg from the University of Kansas. A split among the initial ARA contingent in Russia was soon apparent—between the Russian experts and humanist relievers on one side and the military and technical personnel on the other. Golder, representing one of the former, noted at the beginning, "It was a mistake to put Col. Haskell and his military crowd in command here. The old ARA men chafe under it, and resent it, and as a result the morale is not what it should be. I am very much afraid of the reputation of the ARA. Here is hoping, for Hoover's sake, and for the sake of the United States, that it will work out better than I think it will."[61] In fact, it did, as Haskell took his assignment seriously and related reasonably well to both the academics and relief workers.

An advance guard of ARA men, led by Golder, one of the few Americans immediately on hand who was fluent in Russian, rolled across the frontier on 30 August, arriving in Moscow on 1 September, to establish a headquarters. After some expected initial confusion, one member acknowledged, "Things go better here than we had anticipated. We have an excellent house for our purposes, and the Government is trying to be helpful. There is a mountain of dirt to be removed though, and all of the plumbing and light fixtures have of course long since gone West."[62] As if to impress the Soviet authorities with American efficiency and seriousness, the SS *Phoenix* with the first cargo of 700 tons of ARA supplies docked in Petrograd, also on 1 September, greeted by local astonishment and disorder. Donald Lowrie, on loan from YMCA but fortunately with much Russian experience, managed to save the situation and get the ship unloaded with a minimum of loss by pilfering.[63] Regardless of circumstances, ARA officials felt considerable pressure to measure up to the task. As Cyril Quinn expressed it, "The Russian job

---

61. Golder to Ephraim Adams (Stanford), 3 October 1921, box 11, Golder Papers, HIA. Golder added a few weeks later: "Col. Haskell is not too fond of men who are not strictly under his military orders, and so we tolerate each other." To Adams, 16 November 1921, ibid.

62. Van Arsdale Turner to Albrecht, 5 September 1921, vol. 16, DPR Tallinn, RG 84, NA.

63. Patenaude, *Big Show in Bololand*, 614–15.

will be so much more in the limelight that any failure on our part will have an exaggerated and a disastrous effect. I suppose it is one of the penalties of having done one job well that the people of America will look to us to achieve the same success in Russia, little realizing the great difference between that work and our previous operations and the immense difficulties involved."[64] A second, much larger detachment of personnel, including many journalists, passed through on 14 September with fourteen cars of food, enough to feed 30,000 children for a month—a drop in the bucket.[65] This was part of the first shipload of food, designated for Russia, that had arrived at Riga on 28 August, the first of just under 300,000 tons shipped to Baltic ports for Russian relief in September.[66]

The first task on arrival in "Bololand" was not feeding starving Russians but finding living space from which to operate. In Petrograd this was relatively easy because of massive depopulation, but that city was far from the main famine areas. In Moscow, the main strategic center, the priority requirements of the new government's bureaucracy left an acute scarcity of room. The second priority was to send exploring parties into the famine areas, temporarily relieving the problems of the first, and again led by Golder. Their initial reports quickly removed any doubt that a very serious situation existed and that ARA assistance was needed with all of its possible capability and as soon as possible. As Golder wrote Ephraim Adams,

> The famine is bad beyond all imagination. It is the most heartbreaking situation that I have ever seen. Millions of people are doomed to die, and they are looking death calmly in the face. Next year millions more will die, for little planting is done, the live stock is killed off, and the population is growing weaker. To see Russia makes one wish that he were dead. One asks in vain where are the healthy men, the beautiful women, the cultural life. It is all gone, and in place of it, we have starving, ragged, undersized men and women who are thinking of only one thing, where the next piece of bread is coming from. This is literally true.[67]

64. Quinn (Warsaw) to Brown (Riga), 29 August 1921, vol. 1, ARA, Pre-Commerce, Hoover Papers, HHPL.

65. J. Rives Childs, "Red Days in Russia," 21–23, manuscript in Childs Papers, HIA. Childs was in charge of organizing the train, which included, besides the food cars, three flatcars for trucks and cars and two "saloon" cars for ARA personnel and newspaper correspondents: B. C. Conger (*Philadelphia Ledger*), Walter Duranty (*New York Times*), Ralph Pulitzer (*New York World*), Floyd Gibbons (*Chicago Tribune*), Isaac Don Levine (*Chicago Daily News*), and Bessie Beatty (Inter News Service).

66. ARA: Russian Operations, vol. 5: 99, HHPL. The quick response was facilitated by ample supplies in ARA warehouses in Hamburg and Danzig—and the fact that the major relief in Eastern Europe was completed.

67. Golder to Adams, 3 October 1921, f. 1, box 11, Golder Papers, HIA.

Starving Russian children, 1921. (Prints and Photographs, Library of Congress)

The detailed reports—with pictures—are not suitable bedtime reading, or very pleasant any other time.[68] Stations along the routes were crowded with destitute, hungry people, while men, women, and children were seen falling along the tracks, as the railroads had become magnets for any possible relief or escape. The land was barren and scarcely a horse or cow, or dog or cat—or rat—could be found. One could not walk a block from any hotel in the main famine areas without encountering decaying bodies along the way. Burials were difficult because of the lack of able-bodied men to dig graves. Thousands of homeless and abandoned children wandered in a daze around towns and in the deserted villages or were confined to abominable orphanages with about as many bodies hauled out each day as entered, as their parents had died or given up any possibility of caring for them. A common scene everywhere was women weeping over their lost or abandoned children. Hospitals and clinics, virtually without equipment or medicine, were overwhelmed and virtually helpless to combat the dysentery, cholera, typhus, and more ordinary ailments that accompanied "the great

68. Patenaude has plenty, and the ARA files are full of them, every agent seeming to have a camera.

hunger."[69] Thievery, lawlessness, suicides, and, of course, cannibalism, were rife. The shock—not unexpected but coming so soon and so absolute—to the American inspectors was terrific, and many never recovered from it. None, certainly, would ever forget it.

After more careful examination, Golder found "that the famine is quite local, in spots, and that on the whole it is not as bad as described. It is quite true that thousands will die of hunger this winter, yet it is equally true that right along side of them, at their very door, there is an abundance of things to eat. It is not lack of food, but lack of money and poor distribution." He emphasized that Soviet seizures of grain and the long summer drought were the key factors. Citing Hutchinson's calculations, he thought $15 million would be more than sufficient. "Why all of this hue and cry, why all the political capital made out of it? Perhaps you can answer it. May I repeat again that without foreign aid, thousands more would die than will be the case because the present government cannot, or at least is not, taking care of the situations, though it is doing a good bit. It has been an interesting experience, and I have learned something."[70] Certainly some areas were devastated—and more. A medical report found a village that formerly owned 1,500 cattle and 1,500 horses but now had only 200 cattle and 400 horses. "Bread is made of a seed resembling poppy which has a cathartic action and induces dysentery."[71]

The famine coincided and overlapped with a virtual economic collapse that followed the civil war and involved transportation, distribution, and a disintegrating health service. A big challenge for the ARA was to reestablish a basic infrastructure to facilitate distribution of the needed aid. Donald Lowrie, a veteran of YMCA duty in revolutionary Russia, with the first contingent did not have far to go to find work. "Even three days in this city has been enough to show us that conditions in Petrograd are worse than any American could possibly imagine." He described a great city essentially demolished: ruined buildings, garbage piled high, "pitiful little ghosts of children" in the orphanages they visited.[72] This small contingent stayed in a resurrected hotel until they found an abandoned palace with twenty-three rooms, fully furnished with working fireplaces. Within a month, by the end of September, food kitchens were feeding 15,000 children with more than 40,000 authorized with meal cards waiting in line.[73]

69. The Russian term *the great hunger* rings more true than the innocuous-sounding Western word *famine*.

70. Golder to Adams, 7 November 1921, f. 1, box 11, Golder Papers, HIA.

71. Report of Medical Director, ARA, October 1921, f. ARA report, box 186, ARA, HIA.

72. Lowrie to Mother, 3 September 1921, f. Aug.–Sept. 1921, box 2, Lowrie Papers, UIA.

73. Lowrie to Mother, 29 September 1921, ibid.

While relief poured into Russia, deaths continued to accelerate. Golder reported from the field, "The country is in ruins, and I wish I could see sunshine ahead. So much talking, so much arresting, so much demoralization one finds nowhere else, and while Rome burns the leaders fiddle."[74] A crucial element of the success of the ARA was the ability of Hoover and his chief assistants to recruit talented, experienced people, many of them war or relief veterans ready for another campaign. An excellent example is Dr. Henry Beeuwkes, who would head the medical division of the ARA in Russia with great distinction. Donald Lowrie, who joined the ARA from the YMCA, found Petrograd reeling from lack of almost everything. Meat was simply nonexistent, and the only fish—herring—was rotten.[75] He supervised the examination of 130,000 children in the city, selecting only one-third for the ARA feeding program while noting that at least two-thirds showed signs of "hunger stomach."[76] Many of the American relief workers were clearly not prepared for the scope of the disaster and the shock of seeing it up close. Also exasperating was getting the operation in order, dealing with the Bolshevik authorities at both the top and the bottom, who were certainly even less prepared for the situation. Golder, again, found the best words, "I am thoroughly discouraged with them. It is just talk and talk and more talk. It is not we who are fiddling but they."[77]

Following on the heels of the ARA were many American adventurers and critics. One of the most reputable was Jerome Davis, another old Russia hand, who was convinced by the desperate need: "As far as I could see the famine is real. All the men opposed to the Bolsheviks as well as those favorable admitted that. . . . My general impression was that the Hoover relief work was on the square. I know that he is picking out a good many who are opposed to the Bolsheviks but that was to be expected."[78] Indeed, one of the most important contributions of the ARA, and of considerable consternation to the Bolsheviks, was the employment of about 6,000 Russian subjects as auxiliaries, mostly drawn from the unemployed and destitute ranks of the old Russian intelligentsia—teachers, professors, doctors, lawyers, and so forth—justifiably for their ability to communicate in a non-Russian language. By the Riga agreement they were to be paid by the Soviet government but, most important, their pay was to be augmented by access to ARA food, medicine, and other perks, such as transportation. The motive was clearly written figuratively on the walls of the many soup kitchens—we will save the old Russian culture while saving the children.

74. To Lutz, 15 December 1921, f. ARA report, box 186, ARA, HIA.
75. Lowrie to mother, 4 October 1921, f. Oct.–Nov. 1921, box 2, Lowrie Papers, UILA.
76. October 1921, ibid.
77. To "Miss Eliot," 2 December 1921, f. Eliot, box 12, Golder Papers, HIA.
78. Davis to Robins, 13 September 1921, box 12, Robins Papers, SHSW.

To accomplish the task of saving so many lives, organization was crucial. In Moscow, with Soviet assistance, the ARA found suitable headquarters for central communications and housing in the historic Arbat section of the city. The main building, dubbed the pink house, in the Old Arbat section of Moscow had belonged to a merchant whose current descendants retreated to a back room. The inherited gatekeeper/doorman quickly earned the nickname "Pozhaysta" (a corruption of "please") for his many unfailing, obsequious greetings in and out of the door, while signifying a certain constant in the Russian social order. Everyone saw that there was much work ahead for the ARA, whether in town or country. "Moscow is comparatively well off for food just now, but the reports from the Volga were not at all exaggerated, and it's evident we will have our work cut out for us. In fact we are already in it up to our eyes, hence the brevity of this note."[79]

The situation had not changed much by the time Helen Ogden Lowrie arrived with a contingent of YMCA volunteers that included two women. They were able to find the ARA offices only through the help of Chicherin and obtained quarters at the well-known Savoy with the assistance of American correspondents Walter Duranty and Bessie Beatty. "It used to be a hotel in the old days but it is almost hard to rehabilitate it even in imagination. . . . Poor battered Moscow!!! The streets are so forlorn, even though many of the shops are open and some of the windows quite gay. Others are battered with broken glass and smoky doorways."[80] Also with the YMCA, Jessica Smith, working in the Bashkir region, described a depressing scene: "It looks like the battle of the Marne."[81]

Another finding of the initial surveys was that the hunger extended into Ukraine, the large, vital bread belt of the former Russian Empire, which was not included in the Riga agreement. So, another parallel and somewhat fictitious treaty was negotiated with the "independent" Ukrainian Soviet Republic in Kharkov, after its duly acknowledged appeal for aid and signed on 31 December 1921 with the chair of the Ukrainian Council of Peoples' Commissars, Khristian Rakovsky, adding another $7 million in gold for expanding the ARA responsibility to the region.[82] This stretched ARA capabilities even further and caused more reliance on other agencies, such as Jewish and Catholic, for administration of relief. In the meantime, food and medicine were pouring in, and much of it was quickly dispatched to the worst areas, in the central and middle Volga provinces, where kitchens, supervised by Americans but manned by local inhabitants, pro-

79. Van Arsdale Turner to Albrecht, 5 September 1921, ibid.
80. Ogden to Family, 8 December 1921, f. Ogden, Oct.–Dec. 1921, box 4, Lowrie Papers, UILA. She had served with the YWCA in Moscow in 1917–1918, where she met her husband, Donald Lowrie.
81. Smith folder, 1923, HIA.
82. Original copy in f. 11, box 122, ARA, HIA.

vided a steady ration, emphasizing the children, though many had difficulty finding their way to those dispensing points for lack of shoes and clothing. Hoover, perhaps the first real organization man, applied his well-proven formula for carrying out relief programs in an immediate and efficient manner. Several divisions were headquartered in Moscow to supervise food supplies, medical needs, transportation, and so forth. A historical division ensured that all operations were well recorded and safeguarded for transport to Stanford. It also had the separate mission of gathering all the materials it could on Soviet government and society, past and present.[83] In other words, it was in some ways an unofficial internal intelligence operation with diplomatic and dispatch privileges.

The country was divided into districts, some corresponding to old imperial, and now Soviet, provinces or to newly designated republics such as those of the hard-hit Volga Germans, Tatars, and Bashkirs in the Volga region. The new Soviet administrative units actually helped the ARA to concentrate distribution in the worst areas. The busiest centers quickly became Saratov, Kazan, Simbirsk, and Ufa, the latter serving not only its Bashkir region but also a large part of the Urals, the ARA thus confining its scope to European Russia. At each center a cadre of ARA men supervised the recruiting of local workers for the operation of storage facilities, delivery of daily rations, and kitchens to feed children. Motives for this were mixed; these were the best educated and most sensitive to local conditions, possessed knowledge of both foreign (English, German, and French) and sometimes local (Bashkir, Tatar) languages. They also served a long-range mission of sustaining vital elements of the old Russian culture—and potential resistance to bolshevism. Though paid nominal wages by the Soviet government, according to the Riga agreement, these were supplemented by food and other supplies in kind.

Once in place, this complement of Russian assistants proved their worth, especially since they quickly gained the trust and respect of the local population and knew effective shortcuts in distribution. For example, if children were the target, why not provide meals in their schools, where many of the adult adjunct ARA employees worked? This would motivate the children to attend school and serve as a central distribution point for them as well as their parents. The ARA quickly adapted to this strategy with the blessings of the Soviet leadership and applied it as well to major urban areas such as Petrograd and Moscow, where distribution was much easier, thus supporting education and family integrity with food.[84]

83. This included the purchase from ARA funds of a substantial number of books for the Hoover Collection at the library in Stanford. Golder to Ralph Adams, 8 December 1921, f. 1, box 11, Golder Papers, HIA.

84. Cyril Quinn to Eiduk, 9 March 1922, and Haskell to Eiduk, 18 March 1922, in *RS: 1900–1930*, 232–34.

The Goodrich Missions

With an organization in Russia established and major aid on the way, Hoover wanted an independent survey of the situation and asked an old Republican friend and supporter of Harding, James P. Goodrich, a wealthy small-town banker (Winchester) and former governor of Indiana, to go to Russia and report back in detail. One purpose for Hoover, obviously, was to impress Soviet officials with a demonstration of American political power while avoiding an appearance in Russia himself. Another was to obtain insight on the situation outside the organization. Goodrich was summoned while on vacation at Saratoga Springs on 24 August, immediately after the Riga agreement, and he met with Hoover and Haskell the next day in New York City.[85] After further conferences and a trip back to Indiana on business, Goodrich left for Russia in mid-September. During the crossing he developed a friendship with George Repp, who was investigating the plight of the Volga Germans on behalf of their kin in the United States, and traveled with him into Russia in early October.[86] Near Riga they encountered several carloads of refugee Volga Germans fleeing Russia and gained information about the conditions that lay ahead.

Enduring a cold, miserable journey, they reached Moscow on 5 October. After rest and relaxation (with a guided tour and ballet performance), Goodrich recruited Frank Golder for his experience and Russian language skills, and the three Americans set off for Samara and Saratov, provincial capitals of the lower Volga region, coming face to face with famine along the route and encountering Haskell and Hutchinson in Samara. Delayed by transportation problems and early winter weather, they then continued by boat up the Volga to the major city of the German colony established in the eighteenth century as Ekaterinenstadt (in honor of Catherine the Great) but now renamed Marxstadt after the revolution. Along with Haskell, Merle "Farmer" Murphy remembered Samara as a synonym for filth: "dirty people, dirty streets, mud, slime, refuse."[87] What impressed him most was the clear evidence of deliberately abandoned children.

Goodrich recounted that the German colony, after suffering considerably from Russian discrimination during the world war, had gone from relative prosperity with record crops in 1919 and 1920 to destitution because of government seizure of grain (war Communism) and the worst drought in the history of the region during the summer of 1921. One commune Goodrich visited had lost 20

85. Benjamin D. Rhodes, *James P. Goodrich, Indiana's "Governor Strangelove": A Republican's Infatuation with Soviet Russia* (Selinsgrove, Penn.: Susquehanna University Press, 1996), 48–49.

86. Ibid., 50–51; Goodrich to Hoover, 30 September 1921, box 339, ARA, Russian Unit, HIA.

87. Farmer, "Record of a Russian Year: Daily Life in Soviet Russia," 12 October 1921, p. 9.

percent of its population (1,000 out of 5,000) in just a few months to starvation, cholera, and typhus. This seemed to be the average for the colony, though this would include some who were on the run for the sake of survival. He recorded the disappearance of livestock as an obvious sign of the desperate conditions, as well as the absence of dogs and cats. "No dogs in village—they say they have butchered and eaten all of them."[88] The industrial town of Balzer (tanning, dyeing, and weaving) was left without work and its population of 12,000 down to 8,000.[89] Throughout his diary and letters, however, Goodrich praised government efforts and the socialization process, turning over property of factory owners and landlords to communes. The disaster, he thought, was entirely due to natural consequences—and the civil war.[90]

After needed recuperation in Moscow, Goodrich made a quick trip to Kazan to find more of the same conditions prevailing. Back in Moscow at the end of October, the United States' unofficial ambassador to Soviet Russia wrote a series of letters to Hoover, Secretary of State Hughes, and his wife to be carried in the ARA's diplomatic pouch. He tried to convince Hughes, whom Goodrich considered a doctrinaire anti-Red, of Soviet moderation and progress. To Hoover he was more matter of fact, describing finding a dead peasant with a live child in his arms and "poor hungry looking frightfully emaciated half naked waifs, shivering in the cold raw wind. . . . I could tell you these things until you would be sick at heart as I have been as I saw them, but that would not help the situation, nor aid in the solution of the problem."[91] Goodrich was obviously taken with Russia, not really with Communism, which he thought had failed, but with the people—and they needed a much enlarged relief program. In the meantime, he thought the United States should cooperate with and assist whatever government authority existed.

Within two months of his return, Goodrich was on his way back to Moscow, this time to investigate rumors of infractions, mainly drunkenness, by ARA personnel. A purge resulted, with high-level ARA personnel—Lonergan and Carroll—its chief victims, the latter especially for his well-known imports of large quantities of liquor.[92] Goodrich had also become a convert to closer

88. Goodrich diary, handwritten, 19–21 October 1921, f. diary 1921, box 17, Goodrich Papers, HHPL. Governor Goodrich kept a detailed diary with the idea of writing a book about Russia. He left an incomplete and unpublished manuscript in his papers. Goodrich, "Manuscript on Various Trips to Russia," box 16, ibid.

89. Goodrich (Moscow) to Hughes, 2 November 1921, box 24, ibid.

90. Goodrich diary, 22 October 1921, f. diary 1921, box 17, ibid.

91. As quoted in Rhodes, *James P. Goodrich, Indiana's "Governor Strangelove,* 75.

92. Goodrich (Moscow) to Brown, 10 March 1922, f. Russia ARA, Brown, 1921–1922, box 16, Goodrich Papers, HHPL; Goodrich to Hoover, 6 and 13 March 1922, f. 1 (Goodrich), box 339, ARA RU, HIA.

James P. Goodrich, 1929. (Prints and Photographs,
Library of Congress)

Soviet-American relations, recommending a conference of Hoover, Hughes, and Harding to determine a new, more open policy toward Russia.[93] This trip was apparently less satisfactory in some respects—resentment by ARA officials for being inspected once more, snubbing by Soviet leaders, and greater suffering through bad weather, though Goodrich was impressed with the positive changes since his first visit.[94]

While discussing how to make a higher-level contact with Kamenev, Golder and Goodrich were surprised to receive an invitation at noon on 8 June to a meeting with Radek that evening. After enduring a lecture from their host on American hostility toward Soviet Russia, a longer, more restrained discussion on

93. Goodrich to Hoover, 18 February 1922, ibid.
94. Goodrich to Morton Longnecker, 14 March 1922, f. reports 1922, box 24, Goodrich Papers, HHPL.

general European politics ensued involving Radek, his wife, Goodrich, Golder, and Eiduk, and this seemed to open doors for further frank discourse. Indeed, Goodrich met with Kamenev, Krasin, Litvinov, and others on 19 June in Kamenev's office. Warming to his subject, Goodrich laid out an agenda of redress involving treatment of ARA personnel and Soviet policy. During a heated exchange with Kamenev on the Russian debt obligations, it was clear that the Soviet leaders had little understanding of the issues.[95] Alex Gumberg, who met Goodrich on his return to the United States, regretted that he had not been with him to facilitate connections and because he thought Goodrich meant well and had the ear of Hoover.[96]

Funding

The initial American entry into interior Russian relief cost relatively little, since it was simply an extension of the Central European operation, where ample supplies and personnel were available and, in fact, in surplus. But, as the scale of the problem became known, resupply and financing became political issues. With the backing of Goodrich's public reports and his congressional testimony, and much other publicity about the famine, Hoover appealed to Congress for funds, using an honest, but politically cognizant, campaign "to save the children" as leverage. Surprisingly, the Republican-dominated House of Representatives, generally opposed at this time to any American involvement abroad, not only approved the initial request for $10 million but agreed by a large majority to double that amount. In Moscow, Haskell's assistant Tom Lonergan relayed the news to Eiduk, who immediately informed the highest Soviet authorities.[97]

Although some Congressmen may have thought they were buying out the Bolsheviks with food, most more practically viewed this as a subsidy for the depressed American postwar agricultural sector. Official approval naturally not only gave Hoover leverage to pressure the Soviet government for more support and the prompt delivery of their agreed upon $10 million in gold,[98] but also enhanced

95. Golder memorandum, 9 June 1922, f. 2, box 24, Golder Papers, HIA; memorandum of conference, 19 June 1922, f. 4, ibid.

96. Gumberg to Robins, 21 April 1922, f. 7, box 1, Gumberg Papers, SHSW.

97. Lonergan to Eiduk, 29 December 1921, d. 9, op. 1, f. 1058, GA RF; Eiduk to Lenin, Kamenev, Molotov, Chicherin, Tsiurupa, Lobachev, Dzerzhinskii, Lezhava, Menzxhinskii, Kalinin, and Rakovskii, 29 December 1921, in *RS: 1900–1930*, 225–26.

98. "It cannot be expected that American people will give charity in this volume while Soviet does not strain every resource." Hoover telegram to Brown, 16 December 1921, f. 7, box 324, ARA Papers, HIA. The Soviet gold was transferred through the London branch of Guaranty Trust in three monthly installments to the ARA New York account. See also "Russia Relief, Hearings before the Committee on Foreign Affairs, 13–14 December 1921," Washington, D.C.: GPO, 1921.

his appeal to local organizations in the United States to provide their proper shares. Thanks to Hoover's shrewd manipulation, many ordinary Americans enthusiastically joined the Russian relief effort, quite a turnaround from the Red Scare of only two years before. Adding weight to the cause, the Federal Council of Churches voiced full support of its charities to Russian relief. On behalf of the YMCA, C. V. Hibbard wrote Hoover,

> I feel very strongly that the American Relief Administration is the only group sufficiently comprehensive and representative to have the confidence of the public. In default of their leadership some other group will attempt to rally the national forces and will be I fear only partially successful. Whether it be the newly organized Famine Relief, the Friends or some organization still to be formed I doubt if within the time at our disposal any leadership can be developed which would compare with that of the American Relief Administration.[99]

Not without difficulty, Hoover had already established the principle that all American aid to Russia would be under control of the ARA, to prioritize it and coordinate the purchase and shipping of supplies to Russia. This approach is in sharp contrast with the organization of the American relief program for Russia in 1892–1893, when the operation was largely decentralized and run by volunteers through state committees. Several other important relief organizations, mostly religious charities, were thus subordinated to the ARA headquarters in New York. These included the Society of Friends, centered in Philadelphia; the Catholic charities; the Jewish Joint Distribution Committee (JJDC); the YMCA; the Volga German Relief Society; and the Mennonite Central Relief Fund, each of which contributed well over $1 million through the ARA from their own relief operations.[100] In return, the ARA allowed personnel of these groups a distribution role on the ground in Russia. Other nonreligious donations were, of course, welcomed. At least one vocal anti-Bolshevik, Ralph Easley, protested, seeing "the proposition nothing more nor less than a shrewd scheme to have the eastern tax payers buy $20,000,000 worth of western grain. Of course, it happens that the famine in Russia was a good peg to hang it on. . . . They would just as soon have sent it to Iceland or Terra del Fuego!"[101] So much for altruism in one quarter.

99. Hibbard to Hoover, 21 October 1921, f. 14, box 324, ARA, Russia, HIA.
100. The one million figure for each of these organizations is probably well below the value of their contributions, since much of it came from collections of clothing, blankets, toys, and other items.
101. To Allen Wardwell, 23 January 1922, f. Jan. 1922, Wardwell Papers, BA, CU.

To accommodate a variety of interests, curb opposition to its monopoly, and collect more income, the ARA established a food package service, similar to the later Cooperative for American Relief Everywhere (CARE) enterprise, that allowed any American individual or organization to pay for and have supplies delivered through the ARA to designated individuals and parties in Russia. The JJDC was quick to take advantage of this loophole to send aid to the many destitute Jewish communities in Russia. Already by July 1922, 400,000 food packages had been sold at $100 each, another $4 million to the ARA credit.[102] Congressional appropriation and the package program made possible the quiet extension of the aid to the adult population. By the end of ARA relief in the summer of 1923, more than $65 million had been committed to its work in Russia.[103] That was a lot of money in those times.

Relations with the Soviet Government

One of the most interesting but confusing chapters of the American relief effort to Soviet Russia was the obligatory cooperation with the existing authorities in Russia, no matter how distasteful that might be in the American political scene—or among Soviet authorities. A central problem was determining who they were. For obvious reasons the ARA was initially greeted with suspicion and even hostility by the Bolshevik authorities: American ideological anticommunism, a heritage of armed intervention and support for the anti-Bolshevik causes, the suppression and large-scale deportations of suspected revolutionaries from the United States, and the fear of ARA ulterior motives (the wolf in sheepskin). This suspicion was exacerbated by a perceived weakness and vulnerability by a regime engaged in a transitional policy (the NEP) to no one knew what, though the official view, often repeated, was that this was only a temporary retreat toward the inevitable Communist society. The government/party was divided by left, right, and central positions and essentially left partially leaderless by Lenin's deteriorating health in 1921–1922 but sustained by his vague pronouncements and the halo of genuine idolatry that surrounded him. Commissar for Foreign Relations Chicherin was certainly no dupe and warned Lenin that Hoover was using the publicity about the huge ARA operation in Russia to advance his claim

---

102. *ARA Bulletin*, September 1922.
103. The "Chief" kept his chief informed, claiming that $52,899,000 had already been committed by early February 1922. Hoover to Harding, 9 February 1922, vol. 1: 218, ARA Operations, Pre-Commerce, Hoover Papers, HHPL.

to the Republican nomination for president in 1924, more reason for Russia to go along with the tide.[104]

For reasons unknown, the Soviet authorities delegated inexperienced and politically inept personnel as ARA liaisons. The initial Soviet contact with the ARA, Johann Palmer, was a total failure. A young Latvian who had a reputation as a Cheka executioner, Aleksandr Eiduk, soon replaced him. Energetic but high strung, from the beginning Eiduk understood his role as being commandant of the whole operation and relished the perks—lavish accommodations and a limousine furnished by the ARA. Haskell and company simply appealed to his humanitarian side (which seemed to be nonexistent), ignored him when that failed, and went over his head when necessary.[105] To give Eiduk the benefit of the doubt, he was simply unable to rise to the challenge, but he still signed off on many questionable shipments of aid to nonfamine areas, probably to keep the good things rolling his way. This included $2,000 worth of packages to the Central Physical Observatory in Petrograd.[106] He did, however, rule against the ARA providing relief to remaining Hungarian prisoners of war in Russia and resisted the allocation of $7,500 of supplies to the Jewish community in Minsk, "because famine conditions do not exist there."[107] Surprisingly, he quickly approved many other ethnic shipments—to Volga Germans, including those specifically directed to parish priests, and to Mennonites—and thirty-two parcels for Patriarch Tikhon in Moscow, as well as special consignments to the faculty of the University of Moscow and the cast of the Moscow Art Theater.[108] Nor would he stand in the way of special deliveries of food parcels to American-connected enterprises, such as those from Chicago to the International Harvester factory near Moscow and to the Kyshtim mines in the Urals, where Hoover had investments before the war.[109] No

104. Chicherin to Lenin, 22 November 1922, in *Sovetsko-amerikanskie otnosheniia; gody nepriznaniia, 1918–1926: dokumenty*, edited by G. N. Sevastianov et al. (Moscow: Mezh. fond "demokratiia," 2002 (hereafter SAOGN), 241–42.

105. Patenaude, *Big Show in Bololand*, 108–11. "I think you will agree with Colonel Haskell and myself that our work has just commenced and that we must start strenuously and sincerely to carry out this new program in order to mitigate the suffering of the famine stricken population of the Volga." Lonergan to Eiduk, 29 December 1921, d. 9, op. 1, f. 1058, GARF; Archibald Coolidge, "Liaison Work with the American Relief Administration in Russia, September 1921–February 1922," f. 1 Liaison Div., box 52, ARA, RU, HIA.

106. Haskell to Eiduk, 31 December 1921, and Lonergan to Eiduk, 19 January 1922, d. 103, op. 1, f. 1058, GARF.

107. Elmer Burland to Eiduk, 30 December 1921, and Eiduk to Burland, 6 January 1922, ibid.

108. Haskell to Eiduk, 31 December 1921, and Eiduk to Burland, 14 March 1922, ibid.

109. Hoover admitted "that he had charge of its entire development from the start. The properties that it holds are of enormous value, but the title that it holds is not worth a red cent—unless there is a full and complete abandonment of socialism in Russia." Hoover to John Foster Dulles, 30 January 1922, f. Russia General, box 534, Commerce, HHPL.

wonder Eiduk was overwhelmed and exasperated with ARA tactics; they were simply beyond his control.

The Soviet liaison tried to deal with the enormous transportation problems in coordinating the delivery of large numbers of scarce railcars to ports in both the north and south, long distances from the famine areas. After an urgent appeal on 31 December at a meeting with Haskell, Lonergan, and Coolidge about the shortage of boxcars, Eiduk scheduled a conference with Litvinov on 21 January 1922 on the problem of getting cars across the border into Estonia and Latvia (and getting them back), hoping to increase the number from 250 to 350 a day.[110] But with ARA shipments reaching their height by the end of March and log-jams bringing things to a virtual standstill, Eiduk seemed not able to deal with the situation. An appeal directly to Kamenev brought him on a run to ARA headquarters to listen to complaints. A subsequent conference of Haskell with Kamenev, Dzerzhinsky, and Eiduk on 12 April produced only more Soviet assurances of cooperation in delivering boxcars and facilitating traffic. At this session, Kamenev acknowledged the justice of the complaints and advised Haskell in the future to deal directly with Dzerzhinsky on transportation, while allowing Eiduk little opportunity to speak.[111]

Still, the number of complaints about Eiduk's demeanor, and consequent Soviet recognition of his limited ability to cope with the situation, resulted in his removal in June 1922 and the appointment of a more amenable and sophisticated Latvian, Karl Lander, as the regular go-between. Though also tainted with a recent Cheka background, Lander was an intellectual, a former professor of folklore at the University of Riga, and was much respected in Soviet circles.[112] He began cooperatively responding to special requests, such as one of Dr. Beeuwkes, for the exportation of several Central Asian rugs to the Surgeon General's office in Washington, but also worried Haskell with a long memorandum that transferred more authority to Soviet officials in the districts.[113]

On the other hand, Lander enforced the right to inspect courier runs and found in November and December 1922 several violations, much to the embarrassment of the ARA. Those caught with the most valuable Russian items as personal property were James Rives Childs, one of the most respected ARA men; Earl Dodge, one of Haskell's valued assistants; Van Arsdale Turner in Kazan; and

110. Eiduk to Haskell, 2 February 1922, d. 103, op. 1, f. 1058, GARF.

111. Minutes of conference, 12 April 1922, and Merle Farmer Murphy to Baker, 16 April 1922, f. 1 Baker, box 336, ARA, RU, HIA.

112. Patenaude, *Big Show in Bololand*, 181.

113. Beeuwkes to Lander, 1 November 1922, d. 154 (1), op. 1, f. 1058, GA RF; Haskell to Lyman Brown, 4 October 1922, f. 1 Government relations, box 20, ARA, RU, HIA; and Lander to Haskell, 19 and 24 October 1922, f. 1 Government relations, box 20, ARA, RU, HIA.

Ivar Wahren, also from the Kazan district.[114] All were quickly withdrawn. These violations, though understandably muted in the American records, apparently created a wave of despondency among personnel in Moscow. The four ARA men were probably only token sacrifices to widespread but relatively innocent efforts to gain something tangible out of the Russian experience.[115] These irregularities must be balanced by the genuine sacrifices made by ARA men. In Ufa, Harold Blandy died of typhus and Philip Shield disappeared completely, an apparent victim of highway robbery, perhaps in retaliation to his attempts to curb pilfering.[116] The Shield case, first suspected of being suicide from an involvement with a Russian woman, received much publicity thanks to Walter Duranty's on-the-spot sensationalist coverage.[117] The finger was also pointed at local Soviet authorities who resented his interference in local privilege. Blandy and Shield represented a tip of an iceberg of disease, depression, and unnatural behavior that marred the ARA experience in Russia.

Certainly much of the success of the ARA in Russia should be credited to Lev Kamenev, one of the leading Bolsheviks and member of the Politburo, the inner sanctum of the party, and his wife, Olga (who was also Trotsky's sister), who was in charge of POMGOL, the Soviet relief organization and consequently sympathetic to the efforts of ARA.[118] During Lenin's absence for health reasons in 1922, Kamenev was acting chair of the Council of People's Commissars, the equivalent of Cabinet and National Security Council. Felix Dzerzhinsky, best known for his heading of the infamous Cheka, in another role as commissar of transportation mobilized rail equipment in return for American assistance in the revitalization of that badly damaged and deteriorated system for the common good. Haskell commented, "Djerjinski is all right in this country—he gets things done."[119]

Adding to these assorted personalities involved with Soviet cooperation with the American relief effort was Karl Radek, a colorful Austrian Jew—a hothead of the revolution and a secretary of the Comintern—who mellowed considerably as a visitor-companion of Americans, whom he sought out and whose company

114. Quinn to ARA New York office, 14 December 1921, f. 1, box 20, ARA, RU, HIA. Childs was especially vulnerable since he had been quite outspoken about Soviet obstruction, had married a Russian, and had demonstratively attended religious services. Patenaude, *Big Show in Bololand*, 309–11, 674–81. Golder noted in defending Childs, "Our men are not speculators. Some of us have bought odds and ends, not because they were cheap but because they were Russian." Golder to Herter, 20 December 1921, f. Golder, box 323, ARA, Russia, HIA.

115. Fisher to Herter, citing a letter from Ellingston, 18 January 1923, f. 16, box 324, ARA, RU, HIA.

116. Haskell manuscript, 149, HIA; Patenaude, *Big Show in Bololand*, 313–17.

117. *NYT*, 30 June 1922.

118. A search of the party archive, RGASPI, revealed only one small, inconsequential folder on the Kamenevs, leading Bolsheviks for more than fifteen years.

119. As quoted in Patenaude, *Big Show in Bololand*, 698.

he enjoyed. A maverick, he did not seem to be a planted informer, but he was often found in ARA society. Radek confided to the Americans on one occasion that such conferences as at Genoa (to which he was a delegate) were all talk and a waste of time. He stated that "the Soviet is interested in deeds, not words" and advised the ARA to go directly to Kamenev and Chicherin with any problems.[120] Reporting on another meeting with him, Golder noted, "Radek and I have become quite chummy and he was over for dinner at the Pink House tonight and talked most interestingly to the boys. He is exceedingly intelligent. Lately I have visited him at his home and we have had some interesting conversations."[121] Radek claimed that the Comintern had ordered the American Communist Party "to cease all propaganda in America."[122] He also endeared himself to Golder with his requests for books on American history and politics. On 14 March 1923 they discussed the illness of Lenin. "He is of the opinion that should Lenin die Stalin would become the leader of the Party. He has a very high opinion of the Georgian. . . . In some circles there is complaint against Trotsky that his is not a mind that balances all the pros and cons."[123]

Before the end of the first year of relief, the question of continuation came up. As spokesman for the Communist Party, as well as the Soviet government, Kamenev strongly urged extension through another year.[124] Trouble soon developed about published reports of a very good harvest in 1922 and of Soviet plans to export grain from the 1922 harvest in the midst of a continuing famine, at least in some areas. Kamenev claimed that such reports were exaggerated in a meeting with Quinn on 8 July, but Haskell pressed for further explanation. After conferring with Kamenev and others, Lander came to Haskell with apologies and with another belated appeal for continuation.[125] Kamenev later admitted that, while the ARA continued its relief, exports of $10–15 million worth of agricultural products were planned but solely for the purpose of purchasing implements, replacement livestock, additional foodstuffs, and so forth.[126] Quinn warned Lander that ARA agents would be watching this situation carefully.[127]

120. Golder to Herter, 22 November 1922, f. 2 (Herter), box 24, Golder Papers, HIA.

121. Golder to Fisher, 4 December 1922, f. 8 (Golder), box 323, ARA, Russia, HIA. Radek would become a principal target—and victim—of the Stalin purge trials in the 1930s.

122. Golder to Herter, 2 December 1922, ibid.

123. Golder to Herter, 15 March 1923, f. 10, ibid.

124. Kamenev to Haskell, 23 May 1922, vol. 1: 322, Pre-Commerce, HHPL.

125. Cyril Quinn to Haskell, 9 July 1922; Haskell to Walter Lyman Brown, 4 October 1922; Haskell to Kamenev, 9 October 1922, and Kamenev to Haskell, 13 October 1922; f. 1 Government Relations, box 20, ARA, RU, HIA.

126. Kamenev to Haskell, 6 November 1922, and interview with Kamenev, 8 November 1922, vol. 1, 420–22, ibid.

127. Quinn to Lander, 1 December 1922, f. 3 (grain export), box 21, ARA, RU, HIA.

In January 1923, Hoover denied requests that the ARA expand the campaign of feeding adults by citing documented Soviet exports of grain and questions about the accuracy of crop reports, despite the continuation of famine conditions, and especially the cost and possible negative reaction of a new fund drive. He believed that ongoing relief was capable of dealing with the situation and that a public campaign would only provoke divisive debate.[128] A meeting at his house in Washington that included Wardwell, Baker, Herter, and representatives of the Rockefeller Foundation dealt with the problem of continuation and a major campaign for funding. After Hoover's explanation of Soviet grain exports and his negative opinion on a campaign for funds, the Rockefeller agents promised "not a cent," and the meeting broke up with no conclusion or resolution.[129]

Operations

The flow of supplies through Russian ports, a central organization in Moscow with relatively good cooperation from Soviet authorities, and well-organized district distribution points ensured a basic level of relief through the winter. Anticipated problems were apparent. Payoffs in and around warehouses and on the rails were common to get things moved, as well as losses to common pilfering everywhere, probably to the tune of at least 10 percent of total relief, rationalized as doing a better job in a less official way. Conditions were harsh, and the dangers of disease and lawless abandon were everywhere. Yet, most of the Americans serving with the ARA had an unusual spirit of philanthropy, already well established with a historical record harkening back to the relief program of 1892–1893. They had moments of relief; Golder described their first Thanksgiving Day in Russia:

> Our ARA army officer crowd decided to give a Thanksgiving party, and we have a lot of ballet dancers and other females of that kind, and all the men and women are more than half full of booze, and we are having a happy time. I hear music going now, and I wish I were quietly asleep. The prize guest is Isadora Duncan, and the woman is either drunk or crazy, perhaps both. She is half dressed, and calls to the boys to pull down her chimies. . . . The poor ballet dancers have eaten and drunk everything in sight, and they are still hungry. We are a happy crowd, particularly Professor Hutchinson and Coolidge and I. . . . What may happen before morning I do not know. The

128. Hoover to Allen Burns (National Information Bureau), 29 January 1923 (c), f. 505, box 30, Commerce, HHPL.
129. Memorandum of meeting at Hoover residence, 23 January 1923, ibid.

pitiful part of it all is that we are housed in a museum where there are many rare and beautiful things, finest furniture, and the pigs are crawling all over it, throwing cigarettes around and more like that.[130]

There was obviously some joy in Bololand, and Edwin Hullinger remembered, "In the space of a year, the fox-trot became the big feature of the slowly reviving pleasure life in Moscow. Today, for the first time since the Revolution, Moscow is beginning once in a while to think about happiness."[131]

Much more than food was involved. By December 1922 the Medical Division alone dispensed 450,000 blankets, 700,000 sheets, 600,000 towels, 800,000 pajamas and gowns, 100,000 pairs of hospital slippers, all initially free of vermin and mostly from Red Cross stocks.[132] As ARA men scattered through the countryside to their assigned districts, more details of the situation emerged. Henry Wolfe remembered seeing fifteen bodies in the street during a short walk in Samara and spending a night on the road at the home of a schoolteacher with a cow in his room, because the cow would quickly be dispatched if left out.[133] Hullinger interviewed an intellectual in Simbirsk who said, "I have no force left for writing, my mind is completely exhausted by the physical struggle for existence."[134] Haskell accounted for 300 ARA men in the field with 120,000 Russian assistants, which was probably exaggerated and included many temporary handlers of distribution.[135]

A persisting and one of the most exasperating problems was transportation, not only for the food shipments but simply for personnel to get to and from major cities and from town to country. But all day-to-day work presented obstacles. Golder, in one of his more exasperated moments, complained, "Little by little, they are taking us into camp and running our show. In a thousand and one ways they worry us, they arrest the Russians who work for us, they block us here and side track us there. I dare say that nowhere in Europe have our people suffered so many humiliations and have been appreciated so little as here."[136] Ivar Wahren in Kazan demanded seventy-seven carloads a day to meet the needs, but the next problem was the scarcity of horses to move the supplies into the country. For this, 38,000 were required. In addition was the problem of obtaining and coor-

130. Golder to Lutz, Thanksgiving morning 1921, f. 1, box 11, Golder Papers, HHPL.
131. Hullinger, *The Reforging of Russia* (New York: E. P. Dutton, 1925), 323.
132. ARA report, December 1922, box 869, Red Cross Papers, RG 200, NA.
133. Wolfe, "The Year We Saved the Russians," *This Week Magazine*, 15 February 1959: 9, in box 1, Wolfe Papers, HIA.
134. Hullinger, *Reforging of Russia*, 292.
135. Haskell to Hoover, 27 August 1923, f. 4, box 21, ARA, RU, HIA.
136. To Adams, 30 December 1921, f. 1, box 11, Golder Papers, HIA.

dinating barges on the Volga.[137] Transportation was the linchpin of ARA relief, and the unsung heroes of the whole operation were the traffic managers, Russian and American. Still, famine persisted into 1923. Jessica Smith, working for the Friends, described the dire conditions in the Bashkir region around Ufa: many orphans in awful conditions, villages destitute from government taxes; "a black ominous pall hangs over the valley."[138]

Another dimension of the scope of the ARA in Russia was repatriation of Americans or those who could claim a connection that included numerous relatives of American immigrants. Veteran Russian-American businessman John Lehrs was recruited to oversee this complex program, made more difficult by more stringent American immigration rules. Zenaida Ragozin remained confined to her apartment but, as feisty as usual, thankful for aid food parcels brought to her by ARA Petrograd agent William Harrow. At the end of 1922 she wrote, "To wish anybody a 'Merry Xmas' here under present conditions *here* would be a mochery [sic]; but there is nothing to preclude the very best wishes for the coming New Year."[139] Among the approximately ninety such special cases, mostly Jewish, none denied by Soviet authorities, were Fred Keyes and Samuel and William Caton, trainers who had remained with their horses, and dentist J. Will Lambie, who had fixed the teeth of grand dukes for more than thirty-five years.[140]

At the beginning, some of those on the academic side of the ARA expressed a political agenda critical of the ARA, which was seen as having a motive of overthrowing the Bolshevik regime. Lincoln Hutchinson was representative:

> Looking at it thus, from the inside, it appears to me that in nearly all the official dealings with the problem there has been a fatal failure to recognize some of the essential elements. The governing factor in our attempts at a solution seems to have been a desire to punish and humiliate the gang of ruffians who hold power in Russia today, instead of a clear-cut, single-minded purpose to do everything possible—even to the making of sacrifices—to get Russia started on the road to economic recovery; or, to put it in another way, the tendency has been to identify the two things and to talk and act as though the recovery could begin only after the downfall of the present regime.[141]

137. Wahren (Kazan) to Haskell (Moscow), 26 January 1922, f. 4 Kazan, box 157, ARA, Moscow, HIA.

138. Jessica Smith folder, 18 February 1923, HIA.

139. To ?, nd., f. 1 (Petrograd), box 54, ARA, RU, HIA.

140. Memorandum on Lehrs, ARA 4: 155, HHPL.

141. Hutchinson to Hoover, 3 August 1922, f. Hutchinson, box 24, Goodrich Papers, HHPL.

He added, "The present government of Russia is a melange of visionaries, cut-throats, assassins, thieves and riff-raff so unspeakably rotten that any decent man shrinks from the thought of having any dealings with them." But the population supports it, given the lack of a better alternative.[142] Others would disagree. A cleavage thus resulted in leading ARA personnel between those who praised Soviet cooperation and those who complained about it. These views extended into divergent perspectives on what the Soviet authorities were trying to accomplish in the country.

Within a few months of arrival, a mood of depression descended over many of the ARA personnel closer to the other, more desperate scene in the Russian countryside, no doubt colored by the bitter cold and darkness of winter and the many persisting obstacles. William Kelley on an inspection tour in Ufa reported that one should never touch any children for fear of infection, that they received only bread and rice, or bread and grits, and that in the feeding stations, there was no sound, no talk, no smiles. Ufa should be getting 350 tons a day for six months but that, he realized, was impossible.[143] The winter of 1921–1922 was certainly one of the worst in world history. Easter 1922, however, seemed to be the turning point, more significant to the Russians certainly than to the Americans. But pessimism still prevailed. James Somerville in Simbirsk noted confidentially, "For the idealist, the man who loves to believe the best about human nature, I am sure Russia would prove to be one of the most discouraging countries in the world today. No one trusts anyone else."[144] The Ufa district quickly became known as the shining example of the ARA at its best, credited especially to the district supervisor William Bell, who managed a diverse, multiethnic area with perhaps the worst of the famine results with efficiency and aplomb, winning hearts and souls—and local officials. Above all, he and his inspired staff saved thousands, perhaps millions, of lives.

This depression may have contributed to some of the notoriety that, unfortunately, engulfed the good cause. Alcoholism among some of the leading echelon was prevalent, and several were dismissed from service for repeated flagrant violations both in Moscow and the provinces. Alexis Babin, a former librarian at Cornell University and at the Library of Congress, who had returned to Russia to care for his ailing parents during the war, signed on as a translator in Saratov and was critical of ARA operations, especially of district chief David Kinne, one of Haskell's men, for being frequently drunk, especially during the 1921 Christmas season, which was prolonged to accommodate the Orthodox

---

142. Ibid.
143. Extracts from Kelley letters, 2 and 7 January 1922, f. 5, box 23, Golder Papers, HIA.
144. Somerville to Paul Anderson, 26 June 1922, f. ARA 1921–1923, box 12, Anderson Papers, UILA.

celebration.[145] "The relief work suffers badly."[146] Other cases involved Thomas Lornegan and Philip Carroll, both in the leading echelon of the ARA.[147]

Reassigned to Moscow, Babin was amazed by what he found there—taken by Cadillac to the palazzo Pink House where he found most of the personnel dirty and drunk. In conversation with a local prostitute, "She wondered if all Americans were like those who came with the ARA to Moscow. 'Our Russian young men are not much on morals—I mean about women—but they are angels in comparison with you Americans.'"[148] Though the ARA records clearly support much dereliction of duty unbecoming Americans on a relief expedition, much of the more tawdry activity was swept under the rug. But several violations of the privileges for the diplomatic pouch, involving personal shipments of antiques and other valuable Russian items, resulted in the prompt dismissal of high-level personnel.[149]

Despite personnel problems, less-than-optimal relations with Soviet authorities, and the novelty of the situation, the ARA accomplished extraordinary successes. At the height of its operations in the summer of 1922, it was providing at least one meal a day of American food to at least 10,500,000, including 4,175,000 children. The decent harvest of 1922 allowed the ARA to shift focus to improving medical facilities and to providing for upward of 2,500,000 orphan children, "except in bad crop areas where open kitchens are being continued."[150] On the other side of the ocean the ARA received due credit.[151] The improvement was most visible in urban centers where conditions were described as "unbelievably better."[152] But another report dramatized the general improvement everywhere— no more dead bodies in the street or stations crowded with desperate refugees, and stores open with food available.[153]

Other Relief Operations

Though careful to maintain overall control of the shipping of aid and its distribution in Russia, Hoover allowed independent organizations to work for the

---

145. Babin diary, 29 December 1921 and 6 January 1922, box 1, Babine Papers, MD, LC.
146. Babin diary, 29 December 1921, ibid. Babin recorded some of the worst aspects of the famine: people begging for corpses for food and children eating horse dung. Babin diary, 20 February 1922, ibid.
147. Goodrich to Hoover, 6 March 1922, f. 1922, box 24, Goodrich Papers, HHPL; Patenaude, *Big Show in Bololand*, 130–32.
148. Babin diary, 20 June 1922, Babine Papers, MD, LC.
149. Quinn to ARA New York, 14 December 1922 (confidential), f. 1, box 20, ARA, RU, HIA.
150. George Barr Baker to Herter, 30 January 1923, f. 1 Baker, box 336, ibid.
151. *NYT*, 1 January 1923, 17:8.
152. Fisher to Herter, 18 January 1923, f. 16, box 324, ARA, RU, HIA.
153. William Garner (chief of communications) to Hoover, 24 May 1923, f. Garner, ibid.

same general cause, especially when they had prominent visibility and were co-operative, or in no way conflicted, with the ARA. The largest of these was the Society of Friends, which was given jurisdiction over much of the relief in the Bashkir region. Much resentment remained about ARA assuming overall direction. Anna Haines was especially bitter about Hoover having "told the Friends Service Committee of your intention to bottle up all harbors and railroads to the famine area so that only the American Relief Administrations's supplies would be able to get into Russia." She continued with a blistering attack on ARA policies that elicited a three-page response from Hoover that emphasized the overall need for concerted organization to accomplish their common goals.[154] The Russian Famine Fund, its chief fund-raising arm, based in New York and directed by Allen Wardwell, in a six-month period ending 31 March 1922 collected close to $250,000—no small achievement.[155] Having a long list of prominent people attached to their appeal that included Charles Crane, David Francis, Charles Dana Gibson, Samuel Gompers, Norman Hapgood, Cyrus McCormick, Judah Magnus, Raymond Robins, Thomas Thacher, Norman Thomas, and Charles Tiffany, certainly helped. The Jewish Joint Distribution Committee, happily for Hoover, channeled its resources to the purchase of packages from the ARA that were distributed as designated by the ARA. The location of the administration of all these organizations in New York City facilitated cooperation, despite the obvious handicap of not actually being ARA. Charges that the ARA was arrogant, unappreciative of other efforts, and in general uncooperative were probably justified, but the overall relief effort benefited from centralized direction.

Other relief efforts were led by Julia Grant Cantacuzene, Thomas Whittemore, Admiral Mark and Helen Bristol, and Catherine Breshko-Breskovskaia. These, and especially the YMCA, concentrated on assisting the large number of Russian refugees in Europe and the United States with a special target being to save intellectual bastions of the old Russian culture (YMCA, Cantacuzene, and Bristol) and orphaned children (Breshko-Breskovskaia). The ARA representative in Constantinople emphasized the difference between this operation and that in Russia—no agreement with an established government.[156] Much to her credit, Breshko-Breshkovskaya devoted the waning years of her long life to boarding schools for Russian and Ukrainian refugees in the Ruthenian part of Czechoslovakia, a modest but noble effort. She received modest support from old friends in

154. Haines to Hoover, 19 January 1922, and Hoover to Haines, 23 January 1922, f. Haines, box 324, ibid.

155. Harry Story to Wardwell, 24 April 1922, Wardwell Papers, BA, CU.

156. Arthur Ringland memorandum, 31 August 1922, f. Aug.–Sept. 1922, box 37, Bristol Papers, MD, LC.

the United States, an effort headed by Alice Stone Blackwell. The collections were usually about $100 each, not insignificant, from various Eastern Establishment women.[157]

The American Committee for Relief of Russian Children earned Hoover's special displeasure because of its supervision by Bolshevik-sympathizing Americans, such as Walter Liggett, Paxton Hibben, and Allen Wardwell, and its affiliation with D. H. Dubrowsky, who had replaced the deported Ludwig Martens temporarily as unofficial Soviet representative in the United States. It funneled its relatively modest monetary collections through the Russian Red Cross, which Hoover claimed was entirely controlled by the Soviet government. Nonetheless, this organization continued to provide relief for Russia well into 1923.[158] Hoover also opposed the collecting in the United States for British relief efforts: "So much am I convinced of this that I have strongly criticized any committee here that attempted to collect money for Russian relief or distribution through an English committee, and I believe this is the attitude of the American people."[159]

An old adversary, Paxton Hibben, bluntly denied this with his own documentation from Baker that part of Hoover's opposition to independent relief organizations was his belief that they would be more costly; he boasted directly to "the chief" that his overhead took less than 10 percent of the few thousand dollars that he raised. Hibben was equally annoyed that Hoover attacked him personally rather than in a public forum, such as the United States Senate.[160] Hoover's reputation would indeed be tarnished though only slightly by this effrontery. American Jewish leader Judah Magnus joined Hibben in his resentment of the Hoover monopoly: "I have not been able calmly to accept the mere statement that no more food can be brought in except as Mr. Hoover's organization finds the facilities to bring it in."[161] Hoover responded to Hibben more cordially, emphasizing the need to coordinate shipments of relief but admitted that he was bothered by criticism that he was "not doing it their way. . . . So it goes—but it's no encouragement to interest ones self [sic] in Russia when there are other burdens equally

157. For details see, Blackwell Papers, reel 11, MD, LC. Perhaps the highest amount was $2,500 left in a will to her cause. Blackwell to Breshko-Breskovskaia, 17 December 1929, reel 11 (box 12), ibid.

158. Hibben to Wardwell, 30 January 1923, f. correspondence, Russia, Wardwell Papers, BA, CU.

159. Hoover to Liggett, 23 January 1922, Liggett to Hoover, 26 January 1922, Hoover to Liggett, 27 January 1922, box 185, Thomas J. Walsh/Ericson Papers, MD, LC. Liggett acted as secretary of Walsh and actual director of the American Committee for Russian Famine Relief, but Walsh sided with Hoover, Walsh to Liggett, 23 February 1922, ibid.

160. Patenaude, Big Show in Bololand, 138–39; Hibben to Hoover, f. 15, box 324, ARA, RU, HIA.

161. Magnus to Wardwell, 29 March 1922 (c), f. 2, box 18, Robins Papers, SHSW.

important."[162] Also to his credit, Hoover simply ignored the fringe element, led by Ralph Easley and his National Civic Federation, that opposed any relief whatsoever for Soviet Russia.[163]

More sensitive, but with little publicity, were the efforts of the Jewish Joint Distribution Committee to provide aid to the large and destitute Jewish population in Russia, mostly concentrated in the less afflicted western provinces. Suspicious of an American capitalist or ethnic agenda, the Soviet government, as Haskell noted, "has no use whatsoever for the Joint Distribution Committee. Their past experience with this organization has made them suspicious of it and they are quite opposed to them having the least authority in Russia. They are not prejudiced so much against the Jews as they are against this particular organization."[164] Nevertheless, the loophole of the package distribution system allowed the JJDC to channel considerable relief into Jewish communities in Russia through the ARA, over muted Soviet objections.

Coping with some success with these competing relief problems at home, Hoover tolerated and even cooperated with international charities, especially the Nansen organization, the British Society of Friends, and the Vatican relief effort. Golder and other ARA men objected to Soviet praise of Nansen and his taking the credit for much the ARA accomplished.[165] The British were already operating in the hard-hit Busuluk district of Samara province, while the Vatican grudgingly restricted its relief to the area of Crimea. Though few European resources could be spared for these endeavors, they were nonetheless of great value, lending the Russian relief effort an international character. The British Quakers, led by Arthur Watts, were among the first on the scene and the most successful in rendering aid—without the pomp and circumstance of the ARA.[166]

The financing of Vatican relief came mostly from the United States with its operations on the ground directed by an American Jesuit, Edmund Walsh, delegated to the Vatican. The relief agreement was formally signed on 12 March 1922 in Rome by V. Vorovsky on behalf of the Soviet republic and Pierre Cardinal Gasparri.[167] Directing the Papal relief mission of eleven members in the field, Walsh arrived in Moscow through Berlin in late July to find conditions even

---

162. Hoover to Hibben, 3 February 1922 (c), Ac. 68, 568/1, HHPL.
163. Easley to Hoover, 9 February 1922 (c), f. Easley, box 18, Goodrich Papers, HHPL.
164. Haskell memorandum for Goodrich, 30 March 1922, f. ARA correspondence, box 16, ibid.
165. For example, Golder to Adams, 29 December 1921, f. 1, box 11, Golder Papers, HIA.
166. Michael Asquith, *Famine: Quaker Work in Russia, 1921–1923* (Oxford: Oxford University Press, 1943); "Report on the work of foreign organizations in Samara province," c. 15 June 1922, *RS: 1900–1930*, 234–43; Magnus exaggerated the sum as 5 million pounds. To Wardwell, 29 March 1922 (c), f. 2, box 18, Robins Papers, SHSW.
167. A copy of the agreement is in f. 380, box 6, Walsh Papers, GUA.

worse than expected; he quickly established close ties with ARA personnel.[168] Although somewhat late on the scene, Vatican relief was opportune, focusing on Crimea where relief was most needed in September 1922. Walsh graphically described the arrival of shipments and the suspicion as to motives that accompanied them.[169] In a report to the Vatican in November 1922, he revealed the current statistics of the feeding programs: ARA—4,169,339 children, 6,257,634 adults; British aid—257,727 children, 64,723 adults; Vatican (less precise) 35,000 children, 16,000 adults; the Nansen organization—40,690 children, 35,000 adults; Society of Friends—112,000 children, 180,000 adults.[170] This may reflect an approximate distribution for European Russia, overwhelmingly ARA.

Most of the Vatican food shipments, however, came from purchases in Romania that were shipped directly to Crimea. Unhappy about Vatican relief being restricted at first to Crimea, where local officials were less than cooperative, Walsh was able to provide some aid packages for homeless children in Moscow and then to expand the southern aid to Rostov and Ekaterinoslav.[171] The Vatican was from the beginning interested in using relief as leverage to gain religious concessions, and in that regard it would be disappointed. Walsh continually complained to Soviet authorities that promises, such as reopening Catholic churches in Petrograd and Ukraine, were ignored.[172]

The American Mennonite famine relief came to Russia with less fanfare but with considerable effect. Similar to the Society of Friends and the Vatican efforts in amount and personnel, it was initiated by a separate agreement with Soviet authorities and worked closely with the ARA. Mennonites had a personal connection since many of them had emigrated from Russia and still had relatives in colonies that had been devastated by the civil war in Ukraine, as well as in the famine that followed. As for the Friends and the ARA, they had the advantage of relief experience, local contacts, and sympathetic and supportive organizations in the United States. In the wake of the ARA, the Mennonite Central Committee signed a relief agreement with Lev Kamenev personally on 1 October 1921 and was quickly at work in the field, primarily in southern Ukraine, where the Mennonite colonies were concentrated, but their relief was not confined to them, extending through the Volga region and well into Siberia. Though the committee had reservations about being under the supervision of the ARA, serving the

168. Walsh to Gasparri, 1 August 1922, f. 381, ibid.

169. Walsh to Gasparri, 22 August 1922, ibid.

170. Walsh to Gasparri, 10 November 1922, ibid. The Vatican program soon expanded to 70,000 children. To Gasparri, 11 December 1922, ibid.

171. Walsh to Gasparri, 25 September 1922, ibid.

172. For example, Walsh to Lander, 27 December 1922, f. 383, ibid.

Anna Louise Strong, 1937. (Prints and Photographs, Library of Congress).

clear need for relief took precedence.[173] Supported by a vast array of localized efforts, including the Canadian Mennonite Central Committee, the total North American Mennonite relief amounted to more than two and a half million dollars, plus a huge amount of undervalued contributions in kind of clothing, knitted apparel, blankets, quilts, and so forth from churches all across North America and the unpaid missionary services of Mennonites in Russia.[174] All involved from Hoover and Kamenev on down had great respect for their sincere and nonpolitical dedication to the cause.

A variety of independent American assistance programs overlapped with communal economic assistance and were of considerable variety and range. As one

173. Peter C. Hiebert and Orie O. Miller, *Feeding the Hungry: Russia Famine, 1919–1925* (Scottsdale, Penn.: Mennonite Central Committee, 1929), 59–67.
174. Ibid., 290–330.

example, Anna Louise Strong, who earned a doctorate from the University of Washington, but convinced by the dream of the Bolshevik Revolution, came to Russia to offer her services for relief and building a new society. She moved on to direct the John Reed Children's Colony, which started with ten orphan boys but quickly expanded to fifty-seven.[175]

Most of the authors of these well-conceived or badly conceived minor relief efforts resented the dominance of, and publicity given to, the ARA. This resentment came to a head at a grand dinner staged by the National Information Bureau in New York on 9 February 1923. A number of anti-ARA leaders, such Allen Wardwell and Paxton Hibben, spoke out, but ARA representative Frank Page did not respond to the challenge, to the dismay of other ARA leaders in attendance. According to Harold Fisher, many speakers got carried away into obvious errors and lack of judgment, displaying their general ignorance and prejudices. The main issue was rumors of Soviet plans of exporting grain while relief continued to pour in.[176] Important backing for this rebellion against the ARA came from established religious organizations, and thus the ARA response was understandably muted.[177]

Red Cross and YMCA

Often left out of the picture of direct relief to Russia are the important roles played by the American Red Cross and the YMCA. Both had much experience in Russia, an international focus and organization, and considerable fund-raising clout.[178] Personnel from both organizations entered service with the ARA, and the Red Cross in particular benefited from sales of surplus medicines and other supplies to the ARA. Their main roles, however, were in relief to Russians outside the European Russia districts run by the ARA. On a comparative shoestring, the YMCA in Western Europe directed centers in Berlin, Prague, and Paris that focused on education matters—technical and night schools, correspondence courses, and other cultural activities. A considerable amount of initial ARA aid

175. Anna Louise Strong, *Children of Revolution: Story of the John Reed Children's Colony on the Volga* (Seattle, Wash.: Pigott, 1926), 6–14.

176. Fisher to Herter, 10 February 1923, f. 1, box 337, and Frank Page to Herter, 5 February, f. 13, National Information Bureau, box 332, ARA, RU, HIA; "Reports 8,000,000 Starving in Russia," *NYT*, 10 February 1923: 8, and editorial, "Russian Relief": 12.

177. Ethan Colton to Harper, 10 March 1923, f. 17, box 10, Harper Papers, UC R.

178. As the ARA, the YMCA kept thorough records of its activities; the largest collection (more than 350 boxes) is, not surprisingly, in the Hoover Institution Archives. Most of it, however, pertains to the pre-1921 era.

to Russia came from Red Cross stocks in Europe, mostly medical and hospital supplies, valued at $3,600,000.[179]

American Red Cross assistance to Russian prisoners of war from World War I yet to be repatriated and to the abandoned veterans of the Yudenich offensive in the civil war continued in the Baltic and West Russia, though on a smaller scale under the direction of Riley Allen and Edward Ryan, both veterans of the organization's mission in Siberia during the civil war.[180] The decrease was less true in the former Ottoman Empire where refugees from Armenia and the Greece-Turkey War complicated matters. More than 150,000 refugees had fled Russia across the Black Sea in November 1920, many to be resettled under League of Nations auspices in Slavic countries, mainly Yugoslavia, Czechoslovakia, and Bulgaria (which alone accepted 40,000 for the League's remuneration of five British pounds a head—a substantial reward for a defeated enemy). By March 1921, they were dispersed as follows: Gallipoli 20,000, Lemnos 17,000, Serbia 10,000, Bulgaria 3,000, but 15,000 remained on the Prinkipo Islands in the Sea of Marmora as well as 50,000 on ships in and around Constantinople, all under the general supervision of the American Red Cross with Admiral Mark Bristol in charge.[181] The local chapter of the ARC reported that the number of refugees requiring care decreased from 45,000 on 15 March 1922 to 30,000 on 1 June 1922.[182] A proposal to transfer 40,000 to the United States met with immediate immigration restrictions.[183] Nevertheless, this was a major, if neglected, aspect of American relief that totaled several million dollars, independent of the ARA.

In addition, more than 2,500 of the 30,000 remnants of Wrangel's army, still encamped at Gallipoli under horrible conditions during the winter of 1921–1922, depended on the Constantinople chapter of ARC and Whittemore's Committee for the Education of Russian Children for survival. The USS *Utah*, stationed in the harbor, also made generous gifts.[184] Ernest Bicknell, general director of

179. Frank Page to Bruce Bliven (*New York Globe*), 16 January 1922, box 188, ARC Papers, RG 200, NA.

180. An undated report indicates that the ARC provided more than $8 million in aid to Allied, mainly Russian, prisoners of war during 1919–1921. Box 871, ARA Papers, RG 200, NA.

181. ARC report, 1 March 1921, box 872, ibid.; Bicknell (Paris) to Hill (Washington), 14 October 1921, box 873, ARC, RG 200, NA. Bristol, commander of the American Eastern Mediterranean squadron during the war and then designated by the peace conference as high commissioner for the Ottoman Empire, had earlier assumed an additional role as chair of the local Red Cross chapter; he thus enters into several quadrants of the Middle Eastern equation.

182. ARC Constantinople chapter report, 19 March 1923, box 874, ibid.

183. J. Clafflin Davis (Constantinople) to Emerson, 11 December 1920, ibid.

184. Davis to Bicknell, 31 December 1921, ibid. The full story of this relief effort and the role of the U.S. Navy and especially that of Admiral Bristol and Whittemore in it is yet to be told. Whittemore, a noted American Byzantinist, dedicated much of his time to relief efforts in the Near East during and after World War I.

the ARC in Europe, provided what funds he could and appealed for more from Washington with the response, "Nothing can be done by further references of such appeals to the American Red Cross since we have already spent millions on these refugees and are still spending on them every dollar we can afford for that purpose."[185] Appeals to the ARA at that time were to no avail with jurisdictional excuses. Perhaps there is some irony in the ARA pouring money into Communist Russia while at the same time abandoning those who had fought against it. Unfortunately, funds were running out for both the Red Cross and the navy, perhaps usurped, indirectly, by the ARA campaign in Russia, though a variety of European agencies ultimately contributed to the cause as well as the ARA.[186] Of the ARA operational expenses ($78,000) in this Turkish region from June to December 1923, $35,000 came from the ARA and $15,000 from the League of Nations but only to liquidate operations.[187] A local American Red Cross secretary observed that "these foreign institutions carry politics with their relief work. . . . I am reminded of a cartoon we obtained in Novorossisk just after the ARA decided to go into Russia. It was a caricature of a French waiter bearing an immense platter on the uplifted palm of his hand with a small morsel of bread in the center of the platter entering Russia, and the ghosts of a battalion of soldiers following in the wake."[188]

Admiral Bristol, and especially his wife, Helen, remain unsung heroes of American assistance to Russia. They supervised Red Cross activities and improvised others around Constantinople and the Black Sea, including more or less forced contributions from personnel of the navy under his command for the benefit of destitute Russians in the region.[189] Besides coordination of the ARC and small relief groups for Russian refugees, he advised the ARA on shipping and ports in the Black Sea, wisely choosing Novorossisk, and provided destroyer escorts for ARA supply ships. Bristol realized he was probably exceeding his authority: "A great deal is left to my discretion, and I will use that discretion to the best of my ability to help along in the good work. . . . It is usually my principle not to ask instructions, but to act when I think a thing should be done."[190]

Siberia also remained an especially active provenance for both the YMCA and Red Cross, with unfortunately tragic results, because neither organization had the resources or political clout to deal with the situation, in contrast to that of

185. Hill to Bicknell, 5 December 1921, box 873, ibid.

186. Bristol to Bicknell, 2 June 1922, box 874, ibid.

187. Bicknell to Haskell, 6 April 1923, ibid.

188. Anonymous Secretary to Clara Noyes, 15 June 1923, box 912, ibid.

189. "Sketch of Mrs. Bristol's Relief Work in Constantinople," November 1920–August 1923, f. Aug. 1923, box 40, Bristol Papers, MD, LC.

190. Bristol to Walter Lyman Brown, 21 September 1921, f. Sept. 1921, box 35, ibid.

the ARA in European Russia. A YMCA report described the situation of some remnants of anti-Bolshevik units: "They [the Czechs] did not want to leave them behind and so packed them into boxcars and sent them East under guard, to be handled by the Siberian Government authorities. These are what have been known as 'Trains of Death' among the Red Cross Workers in Siberia. No provision was made for feeding them, for clothing them, or for the necessary sanitary functions, and they had no definite destination."[191] Refugees continued to pour into the remnant of non-Bolshevik Russia, the hapless Far Eastern Republic and—if lucky—on across the border into Manchuria, left much to their own devices with what assistance the Red Cross could manage. Its reports reveal the tragic extent of the problem across the area.[192]

Finis

In early 1923 ARA relations with Soviet authorities grew tense over a refusal to allow ARA official John Lehrs back into the country from Riga, a new round of courier delays, interference with communications, Soviet arrears for their part of the local financing, and other grievances. At a conference on 27 February Kamenev tried to smooth things over with little success, since this event coincided with reports of Soviet grain exports.[193] From published reports of this meeting, Samuel Harper interpreted that the ARA wanted to get out of Russia.[194] Haskell, however, was convinced of the sincerity of the Soviet authorities, especially after his three-hour meeting with Mikhail Kalinin, the Soviet president, and Olga Kameneva, and he noted that Dzerzhinsky had personally interceded to authorize the return of Lehrs to his Moscow post. Kalinin still claimed that more than 8 million were in need of assistance until the next harvest, while admitting that few were in danger of dying of starvation.[195] By the end of April 1923 a consensus of reports from the field indicated that the famine was over, that the situation was much better than anyone had anticipated. "This means then, that the need for

191. R. C. Ostergren, "A Piece of Y Service to Siberian Prisoners of War," f. Russian Work, box 5, Anderson Papers, UILA.

192. For example, Forster to Bicknell, 25 April 1923, enumerating the numbers of refugees in various Manchurian and Chinese provinces, box 874, ARC Papers, RG 200, NA.

193. Quinn to Kamenev, 26 January 1923, and memorandum of 27 February, f. 1, box, 20, ARA, RU, HIA.

194. Harper to Kleifoth, 8 March 1923, f. 17, box 10, Harper Papers, UC-R.

195. Haskell (Moscow) to Hoover (confidential), 6 March 1923, f. 1, box 20 ARA, RU, HIA. Ellingston thought this shed new light on government attitudes: "As I understand it, those relations, which we have believed to be relations of frank ill will, are rather the result of Government preoccupation with other things than famine relief." To Quinn, 2 March 1923, f. 3, ibid.

famine relief—which means the need for the ARA—is much less extensive than we had supposed it would be even at present."[196]

The end of the ARA operation in Soviet Russia was bittersweet. Frank Holden summed up his feelings shortly before departing as a courier with seventy-five large cases of records, "There are a lot of fine people who have been working faithfully and well with us, and I hate to think that this chapter of their life has come to a close. They are good people, and like the French, the women who are given to idealism and clean living far out number the men with the same point of view."[197] Cyril Quinn, while noting the unusual Soviet cooperation at the end, noted, "Life is a mad house, with the show being pulled to pieces about our ears. I shall be supremely grateful when it is all over and I am on my way out of Russia. It has been a memorable experience—but one which I do not care to repeat—at least for a while."[198]

There were other regrets. Summarizing reports from the field, Harold Fisher thought the relief should have been tapered off rather than cut off in the semblance of a hasty military evacuation that Haskell ordered.

> The ARA has been one of the great stabilizing influences in Russia. It has encouraged the non-Communist elements to return to some activity and it has given them hope as they have regarded it as a kind of protector. Its withdrawal will leave these people in the position they were two years ago— hopeless and helpless.
>
> The ARA has succeeded in putting a great number of hospitals and other institutions on their feet and has developed a greater degree of efficiency and service than they have ever known. With our withdrawal all this work will be undone and these institutions will fall back in their former useless state.[199]

Plagued by various political agendas from inside and outside Russia, the ARA gallantly weathered the storms, especially the charge that, while relief flowed in from the United States, Soviet authorities were exporting grain to the world market. In an interview with Haskell in November 1922, Kamenev admitted that around $15 million worth of grain was being exported with the justification, sustained by the ARA, of restoring livestock, horses, and equipment with foreign imports. The ARA supported this explanation, because supplying these items was beyond its authorization. Hoover, nevertheless, protested directly to

196. Ellingston to Hoover, 30 April 1923, ARA, RU, 1: 566, HHPL.
197. Holden (Moscow) to Folks, 7 July 1923, Holden folder, HIA.
198. Quinn to Herter, 4 July 1923, f. 2, box 341, ARA, RU, HIA.
199. Fisher to Herter, 23 May 1923, f. 1 (Fisher), 1923, box 337, ibid.

Lander.[200] Meanwhile, Goodrich, keeping a hand in things to the end, thought Hoover should use the ARA presence to obtain a favorable trade agreement to provide such needs. "I am sure that out of trade relations will come not only a better understanding between the nationals of the two countries and the development of substantial trade between them, . . . I can't talk to Hughes about it. He takes the view of a technical lawyer."[201]

Herbert Hoover was always sensitive to criticism, and the ARA brought quite a bit upon itself and him, and sometimes he lost his perspective. "I have seen the Wardwell Report. It is so involved, the inuendo [sic] is so carefully disguised and it is so painful an effort to prove that everyone helped relieve the Russian famine except the A.R.A., without plainly saying so, that I am convinced nobody will ever understand it." He added, "I understand, however, that various pink groups are trying to get various newspapers to make an assault on the A.R.A. and I have had to intervene with managing editors and show them the inside position on two or three occasions lately."[202] His borderline paranoia rose also to defend his personnel against malfeasance, such as payoffs to American grain corporations: "I, of course, am nauseated by statements of this sort. They can be accredited only to a disturbed mind. If any doubt rests with you I should like to have you examine every document in the Relief Administration, for I know that you will not want to be associated with anything that is not clear as a bell."[203]

Aware of the muffled but still negative publicity involving ARA misuse of diplomatic pouch privileges in December 1922, Hoover quickly approved a plan and specified the overall design for recording on film the ARA in the field in Russia, while its work was still ongoing. Floyd Traynham and his motion picture camera crew were dispatched in January 1923 and had already reached Ufa in mid-February to record for posterity the ARA work in one of the worst areas.[204] Hoover also sent, with little notice, his personal secretary, Christian Herter, for a quick inspection in January. In the meantime, Edgar Rickard of the New York office developed a program to ensure that returning ARA men are "steered in the right direction" in statements regarding ARA policy, that is, managing the news. He directed that a list of possible questions they might face be made—with their correct answers.[205]

200. Haskell to Hoover, citing interview with Kamenev, 8 November 1922, and Hoover to Lander, 18 November 1922, ARA, Russian Division, vol. 1, Pre-Commerce, HHPL.

201. Goodrich to Hoover, 30 January 1923, f. Goodrich, box 240, Commerce, HHPL.

202. Hoover to Goodrich, 7 February 1923., ibid.

203. Hoover to Goodrich, 20 July 1922, ibid.

204. Rickard memorandum (Motion Pictures) to Baker, 3 January 1923, Rickard Papers, HIA; Patenaude, *Big Show in Bololand*, 528–29.

205. Rickard to Baker, 5 July 1923, ibid.

As the program wound down, the Soviet government and the Russian people mellowed toward the United States. Many sensed a Soviet goal of recognition. A naval intelligence report from the Black Sea described a "feeling of friendliness, respect and gratitude which exists towards America as a nation. This feeling though somewhat proverbial even in the days before the Revolution, has certainly been augmented by the aid which America has given to Russia during these, her lean years."[206] On this note, Hoover addressed the International Chamber of Commerce in Washington on 14 May:

> While Russia slowly swings toward the standards that we believe are vital to her recovery and to the point where it is possible to undertake her rebuilding, America has done more than her share. Before the next harvest the American Relief Administration under my directions, will have expended more than fifty million dollars in American charity on the saving of Russian people from starvation and in providing seed for the next harvest. This operation will perhaps do more than save ten millions of humanity from death. It will through this act of charity have saved the soul of the Russian people from an abyss of despair, too terrible for human expression.[207]

The last sentence may be the clue as to what was really on Hoover's mind.

Golder, however, left Russia through Odessa in the south in a pessimistic mood, noting that the Arbat business district, home to the ARA headquarters, had visibly declined in recent months. He observed a corresponding lowering of morale and general physical condition. "The health of the Russian population is not so good as it was because their vitality is greatly diminished." He predicted a serious problem with disease and Soviet ability to deal with it, in the absence of the ARA.[208]

On 16 June Haskell hosted a gala dinner for Chicherin, Radek, Litvinov, Kamenev, Dzerzhinsky, and Lander at the Pink House, which, according to Phil Matthews was a "love feast." "I am sure that the Government considers the occasion as an omen of good luck insofar as recognition is concerned."[209] Rickard and others were appalled by Haskell's praise of Soviet cooperation and positive policies in general but felt that it was awkward to respond for fear of being accused of

---

206. Lt. C. B. Gary (USS *Scorpion*) to Office of Naval Intelligence, 9 April 1923, f. 7, box 713, RG 45, NA.

207. Hoover, "American Relations to Russia," f. Russia 1922, box 535, Commerce, HHPL.

208. Golder (Athens) to Herter, 8 May 1923, f. 10 Golder, box 323, ARA, RU, HIA.

209. Matthews to Golder, 28 June 1923, f. ARA, box 22, Golder Papers, HIA.

bad faith.[210] On 10 July Kamenev issued a formal note of appreciation on behalf of the Soviet government.[211]

Haskell signed off from his tour of unusual duty in Russia with an eloquent tribute to the cause.

To the mind of the Russian common people the American Relief Administration was a miracle of God which came to them in their darkest hour under the stars and stripes. It turned the corner for civilization in Russia. It lifted the Russian peoples from despair to hope. Our medical supplies encouraged the medical profession. Our distribution of literature gave life to the scientists. Our free food packages revived hope in the intelligencia. We purified water systems, disinfected millions of people, opened public baths, repaired roads, required improvement in schools, but above all we demonstrated that at least one organization could exist and succeed in Russia without submission to dictation.[212]

One final duty of the ARA that interfered with an organized departure was to escort visiting politicians who saw the opportunity to benefit from the good graces of both the ARA and the Soviet government in the summer of 1923. Foremost among these was Iowa senator Smith Brookhart, who went to Russia in June on a personal mission totally unprepared for the occasion. Ellingston lamented, "Who is that man Brookhart and why was I picked on to wet-nurse him around Russia? . . . The other members of the American congress who have been turned loose on poor Russia are certainly in need of wet-nurse attendance."[213] After the senator's arrival, he amended his impression and found the senator genuinely interested in Russian conditions, not a Communist sympathizer, but probably to return an advocate of recognition. A tour through Ukraine with the senator

210. Rickard to Page, 20 July 1923, Rickard files, HIA.

211. Kamenev to Hoover, 10 July 1923, f. Russia General, box 535, Commerce, Hoover, HHPL. On the whole the Soviet press also gave credit to the importance of the American relief at the time—with a few exceptions. Aleksandr Zuev in *Pravda*, for example, described the "Arovsty," as ARA administrators were labeled, negatively. One of them referred to as "John" was depicted as fat, dressed entirely in yellow leather, and sticking to rules that denied hungry women of food. Naturally, well-fed and affluent Americans in the midst of Russian poverty and famine inspired resentment and jealousy, especially with suspicious and frustrated government and party officials. Jeffrey Brooks, "The Press and Its Message: Images of America in the 1920s and 1930s," in *Russia in the Era of NEP: Exploration in Soviet Society and Culture*, edited by Sheila Fitzpatrick, Alexander Rabinowitch, and Richard Stites (Bloomington: Indiana University Press, 1984), 145.

212. Haskell to Hoover, f. 4 Haskell, box 21, ARA, RU, HIA.

213. Ellingston to Fisher, 10 June 1923, f. 11, box 30, Commerce, HHPL.

gave Ellingston the opportunity to report on substantially improved agricultural production.[214]

The ARA and other relief to Russia during the two year span from 1921–1923 was remarkable in its philanthropy, scope, ingenuity, and, above all, in its saving of millions of lives while overcoming many obstacles, both Russian and American. Though it did not produce the diplomatic recognition that Soviet officials and American liberals had expected, it warmed many hearts on both sides. Doors were opened for business, cultural exchanges, and journalists—a heritage that would continue through the interwar years and provide a base for the grand alliance that followed.

What did it all mean? Hugh Gibson from Poland expressed one point of view,

> There is much discussion and very real interest in the effect of the American relief work in Russia. The most prominently accepted idea is that the tremendous scale of the American relief, which today is feeding ten million people and is expected shortly to feed eleven million, means nothing other than that America has in large part saved the Bolsheviks from the most terrible of the economic consequences of their program.[215]

He also noted the French concern that the relief allowed the Soviet government to put more resources into the military. "I must admit there is an enormous volume of opinion that supports these points of view, for these supplies release other supplies which the Soviets can then make use of, and to that extent I think our famine relief is useful to the Red authorities."[216] Gibson voiced the opinion, however, that the reverse position of denying aid and expecting the Bolshevik regime to collapse was hopeless.

Many of the ARA workers, especially those occupied primarily with relief and not on the army side, became more benevolent toward the Soviet regime by 1923. They saw the government/party learning from errors, developing a more compassionate view, veering to the right and away from strident revolutionary radicalism. Two of the most visible of the ARA operation in Russia were William Haskell and James Goodrich. Both would become, despite their unceasing belief in the "chief," strong advocates of recognition. Private reports provide ample evidence of this shift also for other personnel of the ARA.[217] Soviet diplomacy

214. Ellingston to Fisher, 29 June 1923, ibid.
215. Gibson to Castle, 23 June 1922, f. 89, box 11, Castle Papers, HHPL.
216. Ibid.
217. See, for example, Harold Fisher to Herter, 1 May 1923, in Ellingston Papers, HIA.

won limited Western support (for example, the Rapallo agreement with Germany in 1922), and launched a publicity campaign to court American business and trade.

Did American aid help save the Communist regime in Russia so that it could perpetrate the many horrors to come? Perhaps, but all historical consequences are relative, and no one in 1922 or 1923 could foresee what was to come. In the short term, humanitarian concerns outweighed the ideological currents to the benefit of millions of the population. To their credit, most Russian émigré factions supported the ARA relief, including Alexander Kerensky. Catherine Breshko-Breshkovskaia was first among them in extending her prayers "to give you long, long years more for the benefit of the Humanity, among which are desolate Russian people."[218]

The Russian Diaspora

The relief problem in Russia was eased to some degree by the exodus of well over a million former inhabitants of the Russian Empire, thus relieving the Bolshevik regime of feeding them. Many fled because of affiliation with, and support for, the losing side in the Civil War. Others, especially from the many non-Russian peoples of the former empire, took advantage of the lack of any central authority over the borderlands to simply flee from the desperate conditions there. Some of both of these constituencies were members of the displaced upper class who were able to leave by their own means, and a smaller group, though quite important culturally and politically, were politicians, academicians, artists, musicians, and so forth, who could not, or would not, accept the conditions and the radical new programs of the Soviet authorities. Few came from the acute famine areas, simply because the people there lacked the means and the physical ability to leave.

Confusion and suffering, nevertheless, accompanied this mass movement, made psychologically worse by the loss of homes, divided families, and forced adaptation to strange new regions and cultures. They ranged from ordinary rank-and-file soldiers of the defeated White armies to the highest of the Russian nobility and were from many widely different ethnic groups. They thus lacked cohesion, set adrift on vast areas of Europe, Asia, and the United States, much of which, after World War I and following economic depression was ill prepared to receive them. Many, naturally, hoped to return to an old—or more acceptable new—

218. Breshkovskaia to Mrs. Herbert Hoover, 15 March 1923, f. Breshkovskaia, box 59, Commerce, HHPL.

Russian officers in Paris learning auto mechanics to become chauffeurs, c. 1928. (W. Chapin Huntington, Homesick Millions*)*

Russia, thus retarding their acceptance of a new future as part of "Russia Abroad."[219]

The numbers and the locations of this exodus are not easy to identify. A partial and approximate accounting for Europe as of early 1922 is as follows: Germany, 250,000; Poland, 200,000; France, 75,000; Romania, 35,000; Bulgaria, 30,000; Yugoslavia, 33,000; Turkey, 30,000; Finland, 20,000; Latvia, 17,000; Estonia, 15,000; Italy, 10,000; Great Britain, 10,000; Czechoslovakia, 5,000. Every country received some, for example, Switzerland 2,500.[220] Relief and assistance came from a variety of sources, with the American Red Cross and YMCA being especially relied upon in Western Europe, but a large number of other international and local agencies were involved. Though the total relief expenditure is difficult to determine, a conservative estimate is that it reached around $10 million. Subsidies of five pounds per head from the League of Nations helped in the resettlement in the Balkans, and the ARA in Eastern Europe helped to prime the pump and set precedents for other relief efforts.

219. For an academic assessment see Marc Raeff, *Russia Abroad: A Cultural History of the Russian Emigration, 1919–1939* (Oxford: Oxford University Press, 1990).
220. Ibid., 202–3.

The numbers would quickly shift through subsequent migrations. By 1930 Germany hosted less than 100,000, while Poland fell to around 80,000 and France rose to close to 200,000. The Balkan states remained the refuge of many of the poorer displaced by the revolution. The European totals dropped in the 1930s owing to the ability of North America—Canada and the United States—to absorb more (around 75,000), many escaping from the anti-Semitic policies of Nazi Germany. But in the Far East, the number resettling in China (including Manchuria) in the 1920s had risen to more than 100,000, assisted by a variety of their own and external relief agencies. The history of assistance to the Russian diaspora caused by the revolution is yet to be fully examined. Exact numbers are again elusive because a number of Russians were already resident in those areas and many were from areas no longer under Bolshevik/Soviet control, for example, the Baltic States, eastern Poland, and western Ukraine.

The Russian diaspora was at that time the largest involuntary resettlement program in modern history, comparable in some respects to the unforced movement of eastern, southern, and midwestern Native Americans to the Great Plains. Assimilation of them into their new environments was, of course, difficult. Through all the mishaps, disorganization, and confusion of the various relief operations on all fronts, the American relief to Russians (including the many ethnic minorities) was a remarkable accomplishment, setting a precedent for more to follow as a result of another war.

Considering the well-recorded contributions of the ARA; the independent efforts of Mennonites, Catholics, Society of Friends, the Red Cross, and the YMCA in the Far East; and additional ARA and other assistance to refugees in Eastern Europe, the total American outlay for Russian assistance, at home and abroad, probably reached more than $100 million,[221] by far the largest national relief program at that time. Many lives were saved, and, perhaps more important, they were given new hope and were able to contribute considerably to a number of countries, especially the Soviet Union, or wherever they would reside. Though this remarkable American effort was intentionally ignored in subsequent Soviet literature—and even in American history—it remained very much a part of millions of beneficiaries.

221. This includes a calculation of around $14 million of Soviet support to the American relief effort, the largest item being just under $8 million for the costs of rail and water transportation from ports to districts. F. 522 (Russian contribution of services), box 31, Commerce, HHPL.

3

Concessions

American views on doing business with Soviet Russia in the early 1920s varied from total opposition to eager anticipation, with a solid middle preferring to wait and see. Some opposed totally for political and ethical reasons, while others believed such concerns were alien to business pursuits. The larger, more multinational companies—such as International Harvester, General Electric, and Ford Motor Company—tended toward a more open stance, carefully studying the situation, gathering information, maintaining connections, considering options, but moving with caution. The near total exclusion of foreign enterprise through the process of Soviet nationalization of industry in 1918 removed most of the big capitalists from the scene, cleared the playing field, and attracted a host of newcomers who saw genuine opportunities. Socialist revolution, ironically, befriended venture capitalism, resulting in the successful careers of unlikely business promoters such as Armand Hammer. Though Americans were more prone than many others to label this new Russia an ideological and moral threat, they also believed more than others in free private enterprise, laissez-faire, "anything goes," in keeping with the American spirit of the 1920s. There was also in the early twentieth century a sense of optimism, of the United States triumphant and a spirit of adventure, of gambling with the odds on winning. Go to Las Vegas, or to Moscow, it was much the same, but Americans, more than any others, were ready to accept the risks.

As before the revolution, American companies were attracted to Russia because of the large potential market, the considerable natural resources, and the willingness of officials to grant special privileges to Americans. They were also experienced in dealing with the problems of space and distance, as well as the recruitment, training, and assimilating of large numbers of rural, semiliterate workers. Soviet experts, such as Ludwig Martens and Leonid Krasin, were certainly aware of the Soviet challenge to transform a largely rural economy to an industrial one. A considerable obstacle certainly remained, since the companies often had little choice and the worker contingents, provided largely by force, were not as conducive to instruction for a new life, especially considering the primitive conditions of most of the new productive centers. How *amerikanizm* could meld with the Russian peasantry remained a central question throughout the 1920s and 1930s.

The new manufacturing centers of Detroit, Cleveland, and Gary, Indiana, and their subsidiary feeders, such as Kokomo, New Castle, and Fort Wayne in Indiana, required the importation of many unskilled laborers from the south and mid-south.[1] The ability to transform rural populations into skilled factory workers was indeed an achievement that impressed leaders throughout the world, but none more so than the Soviets. Though labeled Fordism or Taylorism, the practical accomplishment in the production of large quantities of inexpensive, high-quality vehicles, foods, and other items was genuinely impressive and contributed to the American industrial renaissance.

Though some Bolshevik leaders had seen potential in applying the new American technical achievements to Russia, the main guiding light for an American path for the industrial advancement of Russia came from Lenin himself, who strongly advocated copying the American method and training as most appropriate for the transition of rural peasants into skilled factory workers.[2] The American connection was reinforced by distrust of the former prerevolutionary dependency on Germany, now discredited by military defeat and the emergence of the United States as a global power and by a distrust of their own engineering experts, who were mostly of bourgeois background, who claimed that they could do the job just as well.[3] The vivid impressions of Russian workers in the American industrial heartland added to the stampede to American methods, but they also added a critical tone—and created the myth that with socialist emphasis on equality and absence of class and race discrimination, "we can do it better."[4] Nonrecognition by the American government naturally created an obstacle to the technical transfer promoted by Soviet leaders, but the 1920s nonetheless witnessed a decided shift of Russian economic orientation from Germany and Western Europe to the United States.

Following Martens' embarrassing expulsion in early 1921, a group of businessmen, headed by Emil Jennings of Lehigh Machine Company of Pennsylvania,

---

1. As an undergraduate at Indiana University in the 1950s, one could detect the New Castle accent in the descendants of those recruited in Kentucky and Tennessee for the Chrysler plant in the 1930s.

2. Kendall E. Bailes, "The American Connection: Ideology and the Transfer of American Technology to the Soviet Union, 1917–1941," *Comparative Studies in Society and History* 23, no. 2 (April 1981), 426–27, 434–39.

3. Ibid., 441.

4. Ibid., 438–41.

formed the American Commercial Association to Promote Trade with Russia. The immediate objective was to protect from cancellation agreements already made with Martens. Harold Kellock, the group's executive secretary, explained to a friend that some members had even done business with the Kolchak government but that "if we trade with Russia we must trade with the Russia that is."[5] Jennings' own company had contracted with Martens to supply printing presses worth $4,500,000, but Jennings himself later claimed he had been hoodwinked and condemned Martens as "contemptible and corrupt." He still, however, saw great opportunities in trade with Soviet Russia.[6] Not wanting to lose the initiatives established by Martens and Jennings, Leonid Krasin, as special Soviet trade emissary to the West, called for a meeting with Western businessmen in Copenhagen at the end of May 1920 and emphasized through an associate his hopes that Americans would be represented.[7]

Washington B. Vanderlip of Los Angeles claimed the first chair at the Moscow poker table in late 1920 with a billion-dollar investment in Siberia and the Russian Far East, then still technically outside Soviet control. That fact—and that Vanderlip, an early gold prospector in Kamchatka, with presumed American backing might be able to dislodge Japanese authority in the Far Eastern Republic—caught the interest of Lenin, who gave his initial blessing to what might have been an American corporate takeover of a huge Russian territory. The Soviet leader was apparently misled—by Louise Bryant, among others—into believing that he was dealing with the prominent New York banker Frank Vanderlip, who had also voiced interest in business with Russia, rather than an adventurer with a timely idea but with only modest financial resources.[8] Much publicity about Vanderlip's scheme that involved control of fishing, coal, oil, and other resources for a sixty-year period and a celebrated meeting with Lenin shook up both the diplomatic and business worlds. The American trade commissioner in Warsaw reported much discussion there of Vanderlip's deal and stated that peace with the Bolsheviks meant an inevitable opening of trade.[9]

5. Kellock to Allen Wardwell, 3 May 1920, f. May 1920, box 6, Wardwell Papers, BA, CU.

6. "Martens Predicts Full Recognition," *NYT*, 31 January 1920: 3; and "Jennings Now Says Martens Fooled Him," *NYT*, 6 September 1921: 2.

7. I. G. Osol to Wardwell, 6 May 1920, f. May 1920, box 6 Wardwell Papers, BA, CU.

8. Saul, *War and Revolution: The United States and Russia, 1914–1921* (Lawrence: University Press of Kansas, 2001), 422; Antony C. Sutton, *Western Technology and Soviet Economic Development, 1917–1930* (Palo Alto, Calif.: Stanford University Press, 1968), 296–97. The two Vanderlips were distant cousins, Washington boasting of being a graduate of the "University of Adversity." "Jugglers of World Grants New Race of Business Kings," *NYT*, 1 July 1923: 3.

9. Louis E. Van Norman to R. S. MacElwee (Bureau of Foreign and Domestic Commerce), 7 January 1921, f. Washington Vanderlip, box 1990, RG 151, NA. For the Soviet reaction, see the correspondence published in *Sovetsko-Amerikanskie otnosheniia: gody nepriznaniia, 1918–1926*, edited by G. Sevost'ianov (Moscow: Mezhdunarodnyi fond "Demokratiia," 2002), 144–47.

The Vanderlip concession was reported to involve the lease of 400,000 square miles, most of Kamchatka, for a sixty-year period. This he intended to offer to the United States government, which would have entailed American acquisition of a sizable Asian foothold.[10] Two obstacles remained: one, that the area's strategic ports were then under Japanese occupation, and, second, that the arrangement could become effective only upon recognition of the Soviet government by the United States—an apparent Soviet bribe for recognition. More realistically, the Soviet intention was simply to encourage an already anti-Japanese orientation in Washington in regard to the region. The Soviets sweetened the arrangement by offering to buy $3 billion dollars worth of American goods through Vanderlip to be paid in gold, platinum, furs, and so forth. The *New York Times* was naturally skeptical: "Go to it, you big, glorious son of the Golden West. . . . It is only a Pacific Coast real estate transaction garnished with the flowery phrases that bloom in Los Angeles."[11] The deal remained on paper only, but the ambitious scheme still created a wave of publicity and, despite the discrediting of Vanderlip's financial ability, still attracted the interest of Standard Oil of California in an attempt to revive it in 1922.[12]

Understandably and officially, the State Department, in the face of such ventures, resorted to a conservative position, leaving the door open to business opportunities in Russia—at your own risk—while closing it to diplomatic relations, which many thought would impede commercial arrangements. In response to a query from Secretary of Commerce Herbert Hoover, Hughes stated simply but clearly,

> I do not think it advisable to put any obstacle in the way of any American concern that desires to do business with Russia, or to endeavor to resume management of its property in Russia, always with the understanding that it is acting at its own risk. . . . My judgment is that when business men inquire they should be informed of the conditions in Russia, should be advised that in the present circumstances they must act at their own risk, but that we have no desire to raise any difficulties. In other words, the difficulties that

10. "Billions in It," *NYT*, 19 November 1920: 11; Simon Liberman, *Building Lenin's Russia* (Chicago: University of Chicago Press, 1945), 150–51. A Washington acquaintance sized Vanderlip down. "He is simply a globe trotting mining engineer, making a bare living. He probably represents only a few thousand dollars capital, and would come close to swinging a concession of four square miles than one of 400,000 square miles." R. S. Conrad to State Department, 17 November 1920, roll 136 (861.63/70), M316, RG 59, NA.

11. "Vanderlip's Empire," *NYT*, 1 December 1920: 14.

12. "Standard Oil Joins Vanderlip Project," 11 January 1922: 1. Another dreamer of a Siberian Klondike was Charles Haddon Smith, a veteran of earlier adventures there, who returned in 1922 to investigate and to seek support to oust the Japanese from the State Department. "Siberian Question," *NYT*, 30 April 1922: 36.

exist inhere in the situation, and are not created by us. I do not think this policy will prejudice us in the future.[13]

As for informing of conditions in Russia, Hughes made certain that only the most pessimistic State Department accounts reached the eyes of the president.[14]

The United States' businessman in Washington residence as secretary of commerce, however, would appear to have vested interests in the issue from his prior experience and profits from copper mining in the Urals. As Hoover confessed to John Foster Dulles, then a Wall Street attorney, "I was at one time the engineer for this corporation, and in fact had charge of its entire development from the start. The properties that it holds are of enormous value, but the title that it holds is not worth a red cent—unless there is a full and complete abandonment of socialism in Russia."[15] This could be interpreted as a clearly biased opposition to business with that country, but Hoover remained enigmatic on Russia. He inspired the organization of an East European Division in the Commerce Department that was much more open and objective on Russian issues than its counterpart in the State Department. As busy as he was with the ARA and other matters, he spent much time conferring and corresponding with businessmen about Russia, and on a surprisingly conciliatory, open basis.

To an inquiry from an old, respected friend from Kansas about his assessment of the international situation in the waning days of 1923, Hoover responded, atypically, with a long thoughtful letter, noting, without citing any specific countries, that he saw "an epidemic of dictatorships."

> That is the disease. As a result the people in one country after another in exasperation have welcomed some form of dictatorship. This does not necessarily indicate a failure of sentiment for the principles of liberalism. It is a failure in making practical governmental machinery for their application. . . . Whether the disturbed countries in Europe can recover from their paralysis and return to liberal democracies by better party organization can only be determined by time, and depends upon many factors. One factor is the penetration into the individual mind of the necessity for advance by compromise which successful democracy implies.[16]

13. Hughes to Hoover, 22 March 1922, f. Russian Trade 1922, Box 536, Commerce, HHPL.

14. For example, Hughes to Harding, 26 January 1923, f. 2, Aug. 1922–Dec. 1924, box 6, OEEA, RG 59, NA.

15. Hoover to Dulles, 30 January 1922, f. Russia General 1922, box 534, Commerce, HHPL.

16. Hoover to William Allen White, 28 December 1923, f. Hoover, box 75, C, White Papers, MD, LC.

Perhaps he had Russia especially in mind—and pessimistically—but he knew, as well as anyone, that international business must—and would—go on.

The Commerce Department's Bureau of Foreign and Domestic Commerce, instructed to keep a special eye on Russian activity, sent Laughton Rogers as a special agent to Warsaw and Berlin, where he filed reports on the Russian scene.[17] The result of these and other reports was consternation in Commerce, with Hoover himself doubting the accuracy of statistics for 1922.[18] To add to this confusion, the State Department also reluctantly considered a special fact-finding mission to Russia. As a trial balloon, it sent Meyer Bloomfield, a professor of economics and law at Harvard, to Russia on two trips in 1922, as a personal observer for President Harding. Soviet officials believed he also had a vested interest in Harry Sinclair's early bid for oil-drilling contracts as well as carrying on a fishing expedition for a platinum concession.[19] On 19 February 1923 Bloomfield reported to Harding, Hughes, and Hoover all in one day, apparently pleading the case for American business in Russia. He asked Raymond Robins, through Alexander Gumberg, "to advise Mr. Litvinoff that the only thing to do is to treat the American businessmen, who are trying to do business in Russia, RIGHT."[20]

With the Allied blockade quickly evaporating, a high-level Soviet trade delegation arrived in Copenhagen in early 1920, headed by Assistant Commissar for Foreign Affairs Maxim Litvinov and by Leonid Krasin, who would soon become Soviet Russia's business spearhead into the West. Dapper, suave, and well dressed, Krasin did not fit the Western image of a Bolshevik and set out to take the West by storm, waving gold bars as lightning rods.[21] The going was slow because of

17. Rogers to Hoover, 25 March and 10 September 1922, f. Russia 1922–1923, Box 1987, RG 151 (Records of the Bureau of Foreign and Domestic Commerce), NA.

18. Christian Herter to Durand, 28 April 1923, f. 1923–1927, Foreign and Domestic Commerce, East European Division, box 136, Commerce, HHPL.

19. Litvinov to P. A. Bogdanov and G. M. Krzhizhanovskii, 26 October 1922, in *Sovetsko-Ameri-kanskie otnosheniia, gody nepriznaniia, 1918–1926*, 241.

Sinclair, with eyes wide open to any new business venture and oblivious to its political implications, had supported Martens's early efforts to attract American business, establishing an office in 1918 at 120 Broadway in New York, where Martens gathered his most sympathetic clients. Sutton, *Wall Street and the Bolshevik Revolution* (New Rochelle, N.Y.: Arlington House, 1971), 137, 172.

20. Gumberg to Robins (c), 19 February 1923, f. 9 Jan.–31 March 1923, box. 1, Gumberg Papers, SHSW. Gumberg's impression, based partly on Goodrich's opinion, was that Bloomfield had his own axes to grind rather than devoting time and energy for the president. Gumberg to Goodrich, 24 November 1922, and Goodrich to Gumberg, 27 November 1922, f. Aug.–Dec. 1922, ibid. Goodrich advised, "Bloomfield is on his own, trying to make money."

21. Christine A. White, *British and American Commercial Relations with Soviet Russia, 1918–1924* (Chapel Hill: University of North Carolina Press, 1992), 120–21.

Krasin, an engineer by training and in his fifties in the 1920s, had assisted in negotiating peace with Germany in 1918, with Estonia in 1919, with Britain in 1920–1921, and was a leading delegate to the Genoa and Hague conferences. His premature death in 1926 was a blow to Soviet-Western relations.

British opposition, but the persistent Krasin almost single-handedly opened up the Soviet state to Western commerce with the successful negotiation of a trade treaty with Britain in March 1921. He also managed to antagonize several Bolshevik leaders, among them Litvinov and Kamenev—and even Lenin who had long supported him.[22] At the same time, the inauguration of the New Economic Policy was accompanied by a wave of conciliatory propaganda—and realpolitik—although there would be a later reaction from revolutionary diehards.[23]

The British opening to Soviet Russia registered in Washington with the Commerce Department. Its press release in June 1922 emphasized increased opportunities for American business and an actual expansion in direct trade. "The trade of Russia to-day consists of importing goods and paying out gold from the old Imperial reserve," but minimized the potential results as far below prewar trade. "There is little prospect that Russia will have any more to export in 1922 than she had in 1921. Meantime, the gold reserve is approaching exhaustion and with it is disappearing what might have furnished a start toward reestablishing a workable currency."[24] This was either deliberate disinformation or based on biased and poor research by the department, more typical of the State Department, as Russia continued to export substantial quantities of gold to pay for imports. The report boasted, however, that American trade attained a respectable portion of the Soviet total despite the absence of a trade agreement.[25] When a Soviet textile representative went on a buying spree in late 1923, he gained the impression that the Commerce Department was quite supportive but that the State Department opposed it.[26]

In the meantime, a delegation arrived for the Washington Conference of 1922 representing the technically independent Far Eastern Republic that was sanctioned and approved by the Soviet government. Head of the delegation, the vice minister of foreign affairs and leading Communist in the government, Boris Skvirsky, stayed behind in Washington after absorption of the republic into Soviet Russia to establish a Russian Information Bureau, essentially becoming Martens's temporary replacement as an officially unrecognized Soviet representative.[27] One

22. For the full story, see Timothy Edward O'Connor, *The Engineer of Revolution: L. B. Krasin and the Bolsheviks, 1870–1926* (Boulder, Colo.: Westview Press, 1992).

23. For example, Jonas Lied, *Sidelights on the Economic Situation in Russia* (Moscow: Kushnarev, 1922).

24. "Press release, Trade with Russia," 12 June 1922, f. Russian Trade 1922, box 536, Commerce, HHPL.

25. Ibid.

26. Nogin report, enclosed in Gosplan to Litvinov, 20 February 1924, *Sovetsko-Amerikanskie otnosheniia: gody neprizhaniia, 1918–1926,* 375.

27. Canfield F. Smith, *Vladivostok under Red and White Rule: Revolution and Counterrevolution in the Russian Far East, 1920–1922* (Seattle: University of Washington Press, 1975), 198n17, 218n108.

of his first cases involved the claims of Olaf Swenson & Company of Seattle, which had been trading in Siberian ports, regardless of political authorities during 1920–1922 and then faced fines and exclusion for this from the Far Eastern Republic.[28] He and some others were charged with trading liquor for fur skins in violation of Soviet law. Swenson explained to Senator William Borah, "Under the circumstances we naturally took the only attitude which appeared to be fair to us, that is, we did business at all ports, regardless of political situations at such places."[29] Nevertheless, upon withdrawal of the Hudson's Bay Company's presence, Swenson was considered to be the logical partner for a concession arrangement.[30] In fact, he apparently did have a contract with the Far Eastern Republic to supply the Kommandorski Islands in return for sealskins.[31] Swenson, however, persevered and in 1924 was reported to be near obtaining a concession, a joint Soviet-American venture to replace permanently the presence of the Hudson's Bay Company.

Perhaps advised by sympathizers or on his own initiative because of the prospect of increased business, Skvirsky hired as his secretary and guide-interpreter Alexander Gumberg, who was fluent in both Russian and English and possessed considerable business experience. The Soviet agent also had won the support of influential Washington proponents of recognition of the Soviet government, such as Senator Borah. Skvirsky thus quickly became *the* Soviet diplomat in residence in Washington, providing information on the Soviet republic through his Russian Information Bureau and its organ, *The Russian Review*, and serving as interim economic agent, facilitating the obtaining of visas for Americans, and persistently and cautiously promoting his primary mission: gaining American recognition, a position he would hold until the mission was accomplished in 1933.

Railroads

One of the highest priorities for the Soviet government in reviving the economy after years of war was the railroad transportation system, which even before 1917

28. Swenson to Senator Borah (original), 13 July 1923, f. 1 (July–Sept. 1923), box 2, Gumberg Papers, SHSW. Swenson, an experienced whaler, was a minor hero in the United States for his gallant but futile efforts to rescue Wihjahmar Stefansson's Arctic exploration crew during the summers of 1914 and 1915. "Stefansson Search in Arctic Continues," *NYT*, 9 August 1915: 7.

29. Swenson to Borah, 13 July 1923, box 2, Gumberg Papers, SHSW; "Ships Soviets Seized Had Liquor Cargoes," *NYT*, 21 June 1923: 30.

30. "Plan to Exploit Siberia," *NYT*, 7 May 1924: 33.

31. C. J. Mayer to Bureau of Foreign and Domestic Commerce, 26 June 1922, box 1990, RG 151, NA.

was in a terrible state. The number of serviceable locomotives had declined by more than half despite—and because of—increased demands on the system. That situation was, in fact, a cause of both revolutions that year as the major contributor to food and fuel shortages and consequent runaway inflation. Naturally, Soviet authorities looked to the United States for relief, following the precedents of both the tsarist and provisional governments. The American railroad commission, headed by John F. Stevens, made a survey in May 1917 with the promise of aid. The Russian Railway Service Corps was duly sent into Manchuria and Siberia in early 1918, where its activities, owing to the emerging civil war and Allied intervention, were limited to assisting transport and communication with Kolchak's Omsk government and the Czechoslovak Legion, and continuing its operations into 1922.[32]

The provisional government had dispatched a former imperial railroad official and professor of engineering, Iuri (George) Lomonosov, to the United States to supervise the purchase of locomotives through new American loans extended to Russia in 1917. He then joined the Bakhmeteff delegation in 1917 as its expert on railroad matters. Although delays ensued in filling orders because of the differences in the gauge of tracks and American transportation priorities, several American locomotives were shipped across the Pacific in late 1917 for assembly in Vladivostok and employment on the Trans-Siberian Railroad. In the turmoil that followed, Lomonosov attended a meeting at Madison Square Garden protesting Allied intervention in Russia in June 1918 and was forthwith dismissed by Bakhmeteff.[33] He then cast his lot with the new Bolshevik government in the same capacity and joined Ludwig Martens's staff with his special target being a substantial number of surplus army locomotives that were available for purchase at the end of the war. The result might be made into a comic opera. The full-bearded, rotund professor contrasted sharply, physically and mentally, with Ludwig Martens, who then headed the special Soviet mission to the United States that had set up headquarters in New York, and with Leonid Krasin, briefly commissar of transportation in 1919, before his assignment to head the Soviet Trade Mission in London.[34]

Lenin took a special interest in the Lomonosov mission, since he firmly believed in Soviet reliance on Western economic assistance, on transportation being the highest priority, and on developing close relations with the United States

32. Saul, *War and Revolution*, 142–46, 397–405.

33. "Bolshevist Envoy Acquires a Staff," *NYT*, 1 April 1919: 9. Though Lomonosov may not have been at that time a member of the Russian Social Democratic Party, he had supported it in 1905.

34. The details are expertly presented by Anthony Heywood, *Modernizing Lenin's Russia: Economic Reconstruction, Foreign Trade and the Railways* (Cambridge: Cambridge University Press, 1999).

in particular, and initiated a direct correspondence.[35] He trusted Lomonosov's academic expertise, but he also valued the contributions of Martens and Krasin. Lomonosov also had strong support from Lev Kamenev for reasons not clear, perhaps to curtail and contain Krasin's dominant position in economic relations with the West. Lenin's plans, as well as those of his foreign agents, were undermined, however, by his close associate Grigori Zinoviev, the head of the Comintern, founded in 1919 with world revolution as its ultimate—and even immediate—goal. Zinoviev's prime objective was the support and encouragement of Communist organizations throughout the world, a policy especially resented in the United States, where a volatile and ambitious Communist Party had emerged out of disillusion with the results of the Great War and inspired by utopian views of the Bolshevik Revolution. This duality of Soviet international policy would, of course, be a major obstacle in securing the cooperation of Western governments.

In the meantime, Lomonosov believed he had full authority in the transportation area but, to their dismay, failed to keep either Martens or Krasin informed in regard to his activities.[36] The War Department, pressed by the Russian Division of the State Department, refused to sell the locomotives to the Soviet agent. Lomonosov persisted and developed a scheme to obtain them through the Revalis company in Estonia, but it was Krasin who closed a preliminary deal worth $6 million in gold in April 1920; that, too, eventually failed and the surplus locomotives were ultimately deployed to a limited degree on American rails.[37] Other efforts to purchase locomotives directly from Baldwin, though unopposed by the State Department in regard for the company's depressed economic condition, also fell through. Though Lomonosov and other Soviet engineers clearly preferred the larger and more powerful American engines to European models, they had to settle for improved and larger versions of the latter, which incorporated Baldwin engineering and parts. These units were purchased for substantial amounts of gold from Swedish middlemen, who in turn imported American parts that were shipped to Petrograd and assembled at the large Putilov works there, thus producing Swedish-Russian locomotives of an American style.[38] Lomonosov, falling

35. See for example, Lenin to Lomonosov, 27 January 1922, in *Polnoe sobranie sochinenii V. I. Lenin*, 5th ed., vol. 54 (Moscow: Izpolit, 1965), 144–45. For another list of the correspondence with Lenin, see *Catalogue of the Lomonosoff Collections*, compiled by Hugh A. Aplin (Leeds, UK: Leeds University Press, 1988), 4–5.

36. Martens (New York) to Krasin (London), 6 and 11 August 1920, in *Sovetsko-amerikanskie otnosheniia: gody neprizhaniia, 1918–1926*, 139–44.

37. Heywood, *Modernizing Lenin's Russia*, 90–91.

38. Throughout his brief but tumultuous career as a Soviet economic agent, Lomonosov was aided by his wife, Raisa, who was fluent in English and served as his personal secretary, as described by Raisa Lomonosova to Margaret Robins, 12 October 1922, f. Oct.–Nov. 1922, box 18, Robins Papers, SHSW, and Heywood, *Modernizing Lenin's Russia*, 155.

under a Soviet cloud and left unsupported owing to Lenin's illness, remained abroad, temporarily employed by Krasin to supervise the purchase of German and Swedish locomotives.[39] Since he had essentially failed in his American mission, the Council of People's Commissars formally liquidated the Lomonosov mission on 29 March 1923 and required that it provide a full accounting of all funds and documents by 15 May.[40] Thus one more expert on the United States was lost to the Bolsheviks.

Another early Soviet objective was obtaining cotton, its usual Central Asian source being in a state of disarray. Viktor Nogin, a representative of the All-Russian Textile Syndicate (VTS) arrived in New York in late 1923 to establish an office, its sole purpose being to buy and ship cotton. With the encouragement in Washington of Goodrich, Robins, and Borah, 150,000 bales were purchased in New Orleans and Galveston and shipped indirectly through Bremen to Russia by February 1924, and a branch operation was opened in New Orleans. It is no surprise that this commerce initiated a congressional inquiry.[41] Alexander Gumberg helped arrange the shipments in February and March of well over $4 million in cotton to Russia, but the actual amount, including additional orders, shipping, insurance, and so forth, may have been $40 million.[42]

International Harvester

A few American companies with considerable name recognition were exempted from the wholesale nationalization of foreign and domestic production facilities by the Soviet government in 1919. Chief among them was International Har-

---

39. Walter Duranty, "Public Reprimand for Soviet Official," *NYT*, 27 December 1922: 8. Aplin, intro., *Catalogue of the Lomonosoff Collections*, xvi–xvii.

40. Protocol of Sovnarkom session, 29 March 1923, f. 130, op. 7, d. 1a, GARF. Seeing little future in Soviet administration, Lomonosov and his wife remained abroad in Germany, Italy, and finally Great Britain. They remained sympathetic to the Soviet cause until 1938, when the arrest of so many of their former friends caused them to apply for British citizenship. After spending the war years in London, they sought employment in the United States. He died in Montreal, where a son was living, in 1954. Raisa returned to Britain, eking out an existence in translations until her death in the 1970s. Aplin, *Catalogue of the Lomonosoff Collections*, xvii–xxvi.

41. Letter of Gosplan to Litvinov, 20 February 1924, enclosing report of Nogin from New York, *Sovetsko-amerikanskie otnosheniia: gody neprizhaniia, 1918–1926*, 374–77; "Soviets Buy Gulf Cotton," *NYT*, 12 January 1924: 20. Nogin, the son of a factory clerk, was a respected Soviet economist who supported closer relations with the United States. Unfortunately, he died soon after his return and was buried along the Kremlin wall behind Lenin's tomb, a definite indication of Soviet respect with added condolences from Raymond Robins and Senator William Borah. "Victor Pavlovich Nogin," and "Nogin Buried in Moscow," *NYT*, 23 and 26 May 1924.

42. Gumberg to Goodrich, 20 February 1924, f. Jan.–April 1924, box 2, Gumberg Papers, SHSW; "Textile Industry in Russia Gaining," *NYT*, 4 October 1924: 23.

vester, which had operated a substantial implement factory and assembly plant at Lubertsy in the vicinity of Moscow for about twenty years. After the hiatus of revolution and civil war, in 1920 the company reestablished connections with the management of the plant, which had continued operations through that period, though at a much reduced pace. A special mission to Europe, headed by company president Alexander Legge, Paul Cravath, and Harold McCormick in July 1920, had Russia especially in mind, as Cyrus McCormick Jr.'s secretary revealed. "The first and perhaps the most important subject they have to consider is the Russian question."[43] The Harvester Company also would have sent a representative along with a private mission to Russia organized by Allen Wardwell and supported by Westinghouse, but nothing came of this idea.[44] Similarly, an agent of a rival American implement company, John Deere, considered it important to keep a close watch on the Russian situation, "There is no question in my mind but that the other European Governments are doing everything they can to prepare themselves to get the Russian business both as buyer and seller."[45] It was common knowledge from past experience that Russia was a potentially large market for agricultural machinery.

Though outside the main famine areas, the workers at Lubertsy were not immune from the desperate conditions of the Soviet economy in 1921, especially because of the devastation of agriculture and the consequent decline in demand for equipment. With the beginning of the ARA relief in the late summer of 1921, manager Kruming (of German origin) was able to guarantee deliveries of food by relief packages sent to Lubertsy to maintain operations.[46] The Soviet government was naturally interested in bolstering the agricultural sector[47] and facilitating and encouraging these company initiatives, especially the infusion of capital investment. Another consideration was the fact that the plant had previously imported from the United States vital components, but this stock was exhausted. An interim contract of 1 December 1921 provided that the Soviet government would pay the American company the cost of production of machines plus 10 percent. Obviously, this left the question open of how costs were determined as well as the prompt delivery of essential materials.

The State Department worried about the American company being granted an exclusive concession for manufacturing agricultural implements in Russia,

43. Alice Hoyt to Wardwell, f. June–Sept. 1920, box 6, Wardwell Papers, BA, CU.

44. Legge to Harold McCormick (company president), 20 April 1920, f. 1368, box 8, M90-048 (BA101), IHP, SHSW.

45. William Butterworth to Wardwell, 2 September 1920, Wardwell Papers, BA, CU.

46. Sutton, *Western Technology*, 135–36.

47. Sandomirsky to Peter Bogdanov, Chair, Supreme Council of National Economy, "Regarding the Lubertsy Factory," 9 January 1923, f. 1384, box 8, IHP (M90.048), SHSW.

noting that the offer was verbal but amounted to turning over all agricultural machinery production in Russia to International Harvester. If not accepted, Soviet negotiators threatened, the same arrangement would be offered to a British company.[48] The company and Herbert Hoover, who was kept informed of all negotiations, were also concerned that a subsequent offer would be made to a German enterprise such as Krupp; Poole advised that the German government should be warned that any such connection would be unacceptable.[49] The State Department was clearly perplexed about how to preserve a policy of militant nonrecognition and avoid the loss of considerable American business. Business would come first—Commerce and Hoover over State and Hughes.

Harvester president Legge maintained a neutral position on the Russian plant, trying to keep the factory productive on a cost basis, while searching for a more permanent and secure arrangement with the Soviet agencies, chiefly Selmash (Agricultural Machine Agency). This approach involved shipping in quantities of parts, as well as spares for equipment in the field, as had been normal before the war. Legge continued to keep the secretary of commerce informed. "We have declined since the war to put any real money into Russia, and on the other hand we have not tried to take any out, simply insisting on any new business from the outside being done on a cash basis, of which there has been a little"[50] and enclosed a report of the Lubertsy director, George Sandomirsky, showing that by April 1922 the plant had received less than one quarter (47 billion of 232 billion inflated rubles) of the cost of production. "The situation could be called 'bankruptcy' and the government owes us."[51] Harvester officials concluded, correctly, that the Soviet government was trying to force the company into a major infusion of capital. Hoover's correspondence with Legge was forwarded to Secretary of State Hughes, who asked if he could keep it for future reference.[52] Harvester officials were also discouraged by reports of seizure of their offices and warehouses in Odessa, a major center of their business, despite efforts of local agents to cooperate.[53] In other words, confusion reigned on the Soviet agricultural front.

48. Legge to Hoover, 21 December 1921, f. Russia trade 1921, box 536, Commerce, HHPL; Poole to Hughes, 10 January 1922, f. 1, box 6, OEEA, RG 59, NA.

49. Poole to Hughes, 10 January 1922, f. 1, box 6, DEEA, RG 59, NA.

50. Legge to Hoover, 17 July 1922, f. International Harvester, 1921–1924, box 296, Commerce, HHPL. Legge, a tall and impressively handsome man, had just become president of International Harvester in 1922 and was well known by Hoover for having served on the War Industries Board during World War I. He was generally opposed to doing business with Russia. *Harvester World* 25, nos. 1–2 (January–February 1934): 3–14, a commemorative article after his death in December 1933.

51. Copy, Sandomirsky to T. H. Anderson (Stockholm), 10 May 1922, enclosed in above.

52. Hoover to Hughes, 21 July 1922, and Hughes to Hoover, 28 July 1922, ibid.

53. Legge to Hoover (personal), 30 September 1922, enclosing report from Odessa dated, 22 July, f. Legge, box 367, Commerce, HHPL.

Additional surveys of the situation, including a personal visit by S. G. McAllister, director of Harvester's European business, preceded an important conference in Moscow on 14 December 1922 to consider resuming active direction of Lubertsy between company officials led by George Sandomirsky and Hans Emsch and several Soviet representatives. Davidov, the chair of Selmash and Gurevich of Tsentrosoiuz, noted that prewar production of 35–40,000 machines annually had fallen to below 15 percent and that 1,100,000 gold rubles would be required to increase output to the previous level. Davidov threatened the Harvester representatives that refusal to invest would lead to a recommendation for nationalization. Though initially planning to be passive and only listen to Soviet offers and conditions, the Americans responded that investment of capital was not the only problem but that rejuvenating a marketing division was critical, emphasizing that most of the previous year's production remained in the warehouse unused and unsold. They denied the need for new capital at this time and claimed that Lubertsy continued to operate at a loss because of government delays in paying for deliveries. The conference concluded with no agreement; from a separate source, however, the company learned that the Soviet agencies had in mind a joint venture operation with capital investment divided fifty-fifty.[54] International Harvester was simply reluctant to conclude a concession agreement in the current famine-depressed agricultural climate.

Legge's main concern was with payment for the parts and crucial supporting materials, such as twine for binders, that had been exported to maintain production and repair functions. This was considered a loss in the company's international commerce, despite a contract with Tsentrosoiuz providing for half payment down and the remainder over a three- to twelve-month period.[55] With the major American implement company in trouble with its Russian business, its competitors, foreign and domestic, naturally entered the scene, circling like vultures. Oliver Chill Plow Company of South Bend, Indiana, was among the first, scouting out former Governor Goodrich and sending agents to Russia in early 1922.[56] Several European companies, led by German ones, subsequently entered the competition for Soviet agricultural business, but Tsentrosoiuz preferred International Harvester as a business partner, since it was the world leader in the field—and American. Its representatives went all the way to Chicago in 1923 to

54. "Memorandum of Conference in Company Office, Moscow," 14 December 1922, ibid.

55. Legge to McAllister, 8 September 1923, f. 1370, box 3, IHP, SHSW. Tsentrosoiuz had just placed an order for $457,000 for 1923–1924. "Sales to Centrosojus," Executive Council Report, 11 September 1923, ibid.

56. Goodrich to Hoover, 18 February 1922, f. Goodrich 1922, box 339, RU, ARA, HIA.

negotiate directly with Legge on a contract for $1 million worth of implements for 1924 at cost plus 10 percent profit.[57]

Partly for that reason, International Harvester executives devoted much time and energy to the Russian situation, conferring with Samuel Harper for an hour and half on 12 January 1924.[58] Subsequent negotiations failed to achieve results because of outstanding debts of Tsentrosoiuz for equipment purchased through Harvester's London office, confusion among Soviet agencies, and extraneous charges such as that Sandomirsky, the chief Harvester negotiator, was actually a Soviet citizen, since years ago he had become a Russian subject, a common practice among Western businessmen at the time. The American company refused a Soviet offer to continue operations on the existing contract of cost plus 10 percent because this was only a temporary convenience, never formally agreed upon. The root of the matter was that the company was making no money on its Russian operations. But as McAllister explained to the Chicago office, "I have been quite clear in the matter of not mixing the Harvester Company's claims against the Russian Government with the matter of negotiations to start the operation of the Lubertzy [sic] Works."[59] And later, on the eve of Soviet seizure of the plant, he advised Legge, "We will most certainly use the argument you outline that the stockholders have received nothing for several years out of the Russian activities and if any benefit has been derived it has been by the Russian people and the Russian government and not the International Harvester Company."[60] The Lubertsy plant was formally transferred to Soviet operation on 1 October 1924.[61]

Still, in December, Krasin, a leading Soviet advocate of American business connections and chief manager of business with the West, in his new capacity as Soviet ambassador to Britain, sought out International Harvester president Legge during his visit to London to try to repair the damage inflicted by the negotiation breakdown. He expressed regrets about the failure of negotiations in Moscow while disclaiming any knowledge of details. He was optimistic about the future of Soviet economic development, however, and saw no reason why at least some business could not continue with International Harvester, "making a strong appeal for our carrying on consignment some goods, particularly repair stock, at a convenient point or points, where they could draw on it."[62] Sandomirsky

57. Legge to McAllister, 7 August 1923, f. 1370, box 3, IHP, SHSW.

58. Harper to Kleiforth, 12 January 1924, f. 6, box 11, Harper Papers, UC-Regenstein.

59. McAllister to Perkins, 20 May 1924, f. 1243, box 40, IHP, SHSW.

60. McAllister (Brussels) to Legge, 20 August 1923, box 3, f. 1370, f. Legge, box 367, Commerce, HHPL.

61. J. C. White (Riga) to Hughes, 29 November 1924, vol. 24, DPR Latvia, RG 84, NA.

62. Legge to George Ranney (vice president and treasurer), 15 December 1924, f. 1382, box 8, M90-048 (BA101), IHP, SHSW.

reported personally to Cyrus McCormick Jr. at his Lake Forest home in December 1924 with Harper present, but after a whole day's discussion, the future of the company in Russia was still unsettled.[63]

Legge concluded that his company had simply been caught in a split within Soviet officialdom, that Krasin was being recalled from abroad because of his ties with Trotsky.[64] The final denouement of Harvester direction of a factory in Soviet Russia thus dragged out through 1924. Taking inventories was complicated by trying to determine what belonged to International Harvester and what had been brought in by Soviet agencies in recent years, as well as taking into account the private property left behind by previous company managers. The company still pursued direct sale possibilities, though noting the increased competition from German and Czech concerns, because they offered more favorable credit terms. He urged consideration of a more generous offer—25 percent cash and the balance to be paid over a three- to eighteen-month period, anticipating a gain up to $5 million in sales in 1926.[65]

The question of the company renewing a connection with the Lubertsy plant remained a possibility well after the 1924 Soviet takeover. The Chicago headquarters was impressed by information from a representative of Massey Harris Company that the factory's 1927 program called for the production of 20,000 mowers, 50,000 rakes, 10,000 reapers, and 1,000 binders.[66] Later that year it considered, but rejected, an offer by Bernard Baruch to act for them in resuming a direct connection.[67] With the advent of the First Five Year Plan, however, International Harvester would again play a major role in the advancement of agricultural mechanical progress, signing a contract in 1929 to supply 5,900 tractors.[68] That same year the American company continued to press claims against the Soviet government for its Lubertsy losses, offering to settle for more than 60 million rubles; this offer might have been accepted if Harvester would consider this amount in the greatly inflated rubles of 1917![69]

Fellow partners in old Russian businesses were not as interested in renewing connections. Singer Sewing Machine Company, probably the most visible of foreign concerns in prerevolutionary Russia, because of its household signature machines (*Zinger* in Russian), a dominant architectural legacy of the "dom" on

63. Harper to Rogers, 7 December 1923, f. 1, box 11, Harper Papers, UCR.

64. Legge to Perkins, 24 December 1924, f. 1382, box 8, M90-048 (BA101) IHP, SHSW.

65. "Business in Russia," Sandomirsky memorandum from Brussels to E. A. Brittenham, 3 December 1925, ibid.

66. Executive Council Report no. 27-1, 4 January 1927, box 1, IHP (M90-048, BA 1-01), SHSW.

67. Legge to Baruch, 17 June 1927, ibid.

68. Sutton, *Western Technology, 1917–1930,* 136.

69. Brent Allinson to William Elliott, 8 May 1929, f. 1243, box 40, IHP, SHSW.

Nevsky Prospect in Petrograd, and its multitude of neighborhood shops throughout the country, had little interest in regaining its market, primarily because it
had taken such a financial beating at the beginning and during World War I,
because of erroneous attribution to German—or Jewish—origins. Its main factory at Podolsk, also near Moscow and in operation since 1902, and smaller ones
in Petrograd and Vladivostok continued to produce sewing machines.[70] Because
heavy-duty machines were needed for making military uniforms during the civil
war, the company received payments from the Soviet government, deposited in
company accounts. A bookkeeper described the misery of crowded living quarters, lack of food, disease, and so forth in 1919–1920. The factory provided free
coffins from its carpentry shop.[71]

Unlike International Harvester, Singer had essentially withdrawn from its operations in Russia. For example, chief manager Otto (Otar) Myslik took refuge
abroad while maintaining sporadic contact with a few Singer officials in Russia,
while the American directors pursued claims of more than $100 million against
the Soviet government. Aleksei Miliukov, a brother of Paul Miliukov, tried to
keep the factory in existence until he fled in late 1920.[72] Another officer, Emil
Friedlander, reported that the company had essentially lost control of operations
by November 1919. He stayed on in hopes of a White victory and then was able
to leave by a Soviet exchange with Latvia, his original residence.[73] Singer debt to
its American parent rose precipitously, especially because of its inability to collect
payments for machines sold on credit before the war. As in the case of Harvester,
Singer was not formally nationalized until 1924, but, faced with inability to resume regular operations with complex machinery and to defuse property claims,
the Soviet government returned the main plant to Singer in 1926. Production
quickly rose to 200,000 units in 1927 and to 500,000 by 1929.[74] Singer would
continue sporadically, at least until 1960, to press claims for its losses against the
Soviet government.

Similarly, Westinghouse, which had made air brakes for Russia's expanding
railways since the 1890s, found Russian business unattractive, although its factory, moved from the Petrograd area to Yaroslavl during the war, survived the
revolution and civil war in relatively good condition, verified by Charles Crane's

70. For the background to both International Harvester and Singer operations in Russia, see Fred
V. Carstensen, *American Enterprise in Foreign Markets: Singer and International Harvester in Imperial
Russia* (Chapel Hill: University of North Carolina Press, 1984).

71. Klara Nylander statement, 16 August 1921, f. 1, box 155, Singer Papers, SHSW.

72. Miliukov reports, 30 April 1920, f. 5, box 157, ibid.; Saul, *War and Revolution*, 338–39, 405–6.

73. Friedlander reports to Singer Company, 30 October 1920, f. 5, box 157, and 16 August 1921,
f. 2, box 155, Singer Papers, SHSW.

74. Sutton, *Western Technology, 1917–1930*, 181–82.

personal inspection in 1921.[75] The manager claimed to have good relations with Soviet authorities through 1922, but its efforts to supply workers with food and other necessities instigated charges that they were bribing workers into hostility toward the government. As in the case of the other major American companies, it remained in operation under increasingly tighter Soviet controls and restrictions through 1924.[76]

Electricity

Westinghouse, as well as its main rival, General Electric, also had prerevolutionary interests in serving the Russian demand for electric power that continued and increased in the 1920s, inspired in part by Lenin's trumpeting the importance of electrical advances: "Soviet power equals the electrification of the whole country." Unfortunately for him, that portion of the Russian economy had suffered severely during the revolution and civil war. A high-priority program was pushed forward rather rashly, obscuring the results. American involvement was initially pursued through European affiliates: by Metropolitan-Vickers in the case of Westinghouse and by Swedish and German affiliates of General Electric. In fact, the multinational aspects of these companies may have been especially attractive in Bolshevik circles. Nevertheless, the large number of electric motors, produced mainly at Kharkov, employed American General Electric technology.[77]

Both the inventive genius of General Electric, Charles Steinmetz, and the company president, Maurice Oudin, actively sought out Soviet venture opportunities. In March 1922, the latter informed the State Department that he felt that now was the time to do business with Russia.[78] A new company formed with that in mind, International General Electric, landed several concessions to revamp the Russian production facilities of electrical equipment, such as bulbs, batteries, generators, and motors. Most of these involved revival of existing plants. Before long, however, General Electric and other American companies would be involved in massive expansion of electricity that equated with the Tennessee Valley Authority and rural electrification in the United States. Soviet economists

75. John O. Crane diary, 24–25 July 1921, in David Hapgood, *Charles R. Crane: The Man Who Bet on People* (New York: Institute of Current World Affairs, 2000), 135–39. Crane was the initial manager of what was originally a partnership between Westinghouse and Crane Plumbing of Chicago and Bridgeport, Connecticut.

76. Sutton, *Western Technology, 1917–1930*, 167–68.

77. Ibid., 188–92.

78. Ibid., 185–87.

and planners were not ignorant of these American developments. In more ways than one, they dreamed of electrifying the world!

Arm and Hammer

One of the most controversial persons involved in early and later Soviet-American business was Armand Hammer. An objective account of his role is obscured by his own rather exaggerated and contradictory claims and by attacks of opponents.[79] His name, well known by now in American business history, did not derive from a baking soda company but from the emblem of the American Socialist Party, of which his father Julius, a physician, was a prominent member. As a seemingly meek and docile Columbia University medical school graduate, Armand Hammer emerged in Russia on the caboose of the ARA invasion in September 1921 as a representative of a medical supply company he had organized in New Jersey, Allied Drug and Chemical Company, and as an energetic promoter of whatever might come to the fore. At least he had connections. Ludwig Martens, familiar with Julius Hammer's radical activities, provided assistance, and Boris Reinstein, an old family friend then working in the Commissariat of Foreign Affairs as its American expert, provided introductions to Comintern and other well-connected officials. He was also fortunate to find Boris Mishell to serve as a longterm guide-interpreter. After reaching Moscow by hook and by crook, he immediately seized an opportunity to act as a facilitator for trading Russian commodities for much-needed food from the United States.[80] Exactly why Soviet authorities agreed to this proposal at the very time that shiploads of ARA relief were arriving, or how Hammer could bypass the ARA monopoly on shipping, remains unclear.

Meanwhile, Martens invited Hammer to go along on an investigative expedition into the Urals and personally escorted him for an inspection of an inactive asbestos mine at Alapaevsk, about 200 miles north of Ekaterinburg. Upon Martens's urging, Hammer agreed to rehabilitate it as a concession arrangement. Learning of this and his offer to deliver grain from Martens, Lenin saw a pos-

79. Hammer's own story has been repeated several times in different versions, first in *The Quest of the Romanoff Treasure* (New York: Paisley Press, 1932), and later in his memoir, *Hammer*, as told to Neil Lyndon (New York: G. P. Putnam's Sons, 1987). The chief critical accounts are by Steve Weinberg, *Armand Hammer: The Untold Story, an Unauthorized Biography* (Boston: Little, Brown, 1989), and Edward Jay Epstein, *Dossier: The Secret History of Armand Hammer* (New York: Random House, 1996).

80. Hammer, *The Quest,* passim.

sible breakthrough to American business connections and wanted to meet him. Thus, upon his return to Moscow, Hammer was summoned to the Kremlin on 22 October 1921 for a historic meeting (according to Hammer) with the Soviet leader—an hour-long conversation in English. Lenin, noting Hammer's initial interest in medical relief, observed that what Russia needed was not doctors but business expertise.[81] One direct benefit of this meeting was Hammer's transfer from rather atrocious lodging at the Savoy Hotel to special accommodations at the Government Guest House, a former sugar king's palace. The asbestos concession was duly signed on 28 October, Hammer claiming that it was the first real Soviet-American business contract, a breakthrough on the way to many more concessions.[82]

So, was Armand Hammer on his way to fame and fortune—and notoriety? Not quite. The asbestos venture turned out to be a losing proposition, because of his own inexperience, the remoteness of the resource in the Urals, labor problems, and considerable international competition. He was also having something of a nervous breakdown. The Hammer enterprises were soon on the verge of bankruptcy. Armand's father had been arrested on a medical malpractice suit, perhaps supplemented by his radical activities, and sentenced to Sing Sing. Released early, Julius Hammer soon joined his son in Moscow and played a crucial role, as a proactive American Communist, in rejuvenating the Hammers' Soviet business and was probably, at least for a time, the real brains behind the Hammer business endeavors.[83] Armand Hammer's previous association with Trotsky and Reinstein certainly helped. Taking possession of a vacated ARA building, the Hammers soon held forth in Moscow with lavish dinners and receptions at the Brown Palace, another confiscated property of the former Russian bourgeoisie, displaced by the new international social-capitalists. It became a major social center for Soviet-American contacts and residence of journalists such as Eugene Lyons, and the Mishell family.[84]

81. The meeting is described in some detail in ibid., 57–68, and recounted in other sources. One must wonder how much Hammer absorbed in what was probably a much briefer meeting than he indicated, since a few months later he addressed the Soviet leader as "Nikolai Lenin," an earlier pen name, perhaps failing to note an inscription of "Vladimir Ulianov" on a souvenir photograph presented to him on 10 November. Hammer to Nikolai [sic] Lenin, 11 May 1922, f. 2 (Lenin Papers), op. 1, d. 24795, RGASPI; Lenin photograph in Hammer, *Hammer*, first photograph section, unnumbered page.

82. Bessie Beatty (Moscow) to Gumberg, 2 January 1922, f. Jan.–July 1922, box 1, Gumberg Papers, SHSW.

83. Epstein, *Dossier*, 95–96.

84. Lyons, *Assignment in Utopia* (New York: Harcourt, Brace, 1937) 250, 296, 417. Among the guests were e. e. cummings and the Gene Tunneys.

*Armand Hammer, 1933. (Prints and Photographs,
Library of Congress)*

After organizing a shipment from Riga of Russian goods—mainly furs and almost a ton of caviar—in exchange for the food shipment, Hammer returned to
the United States to reorganize his company for the new business. Out of a complicated transition emerged the Allied American Corporation (Alamerico) as a
major Soviet import-export business and probably, as Epstein claims, a conduit
for transfers of money from the Comintern to the American Workers' [Commu-
nist] Party, charging handsome fees off the top for the service.[85] An agreement
with the Commissariat of Foreign Trade netted a concession for full rights of
trade commerce of $2,400,000 a year with 50 percent of profits remitted to the
Soviet government.[86]

With visions of an open, expanding market, Hammer journeyed to Detroit to
meet with Henry Ford, following up a visit by his father. Despite the automotive

85. Epstein, *Dossier*, 96–103. Unfortunately, Epstein cites only "Russian archives" for his evidence.
86. Walter Duranty, "Soviet Concession to American Firm," *NYT*, 9 July 1923: 3.

entrepreneur's personal and well-known dislike of both Jews and Communists, business opportunities always came first. He contracted Hammer to be the exclusive agent for Ford machines in Russia, with Fordson tractors taking highest priority. Ford definitely saw a future there, and to Hammer's remark that there are virtually no roads in the countryside, he responded in words to the effect, "Bring in the cars and the roads will follow." This had happened in the United States, he observed, but Russia, some would argue, proved to be an exception. For the time being, agriculture was more remunerative. In 1923 more than 600 Fordson tractors were sold to the Soviet Union through Hammer, mostly by transfers of furs to New York.[87] More were to follow in this unusual but profitable Hammer-Ford partnership.

All of these various Hammer ventures yielded little in profits and, in fact, piled up considerable debts, especially when Alamerico was replaced by a wholly Soviet agency, Amtorg (American Trade Corporation) in New York in May 1924, incorporating Arcos-America. An effort to channel Soviet earnings through an Estonian bank also failed. Perhaps feeling that they owed something to the Hammers for their cooperation in transferring money for the Comintern, the Concessions Committee offered them a pencil manufacturing concession. Somewhat by accident Armand Hammer discovered in the summer of 1925 that pencils in Soviet stores sold for an exorbitant amount in comparison to other countries. He went to the concessions committee with a solution—to take over a defunct German pencil factory in Moscow and enlarge it. Knowing nothing about the pencil business, Hammer wisely hired German experts in the field and included housing and other facilities to entice foreign workers to his expansion investment. This concession obviously required considerable capital outlay, and the income would be mainly from the Russian market in rubles. But the government itself was the market for large quantities of Hammer pencils, and, thanks to the hard work and massaging of Armand's brother Victor, Soviet authorities protected the enterprise against any competition to ensure its continued success. Meanwhile, the asbestos venture gained momentum under Julius Hammer's direction with a factory established in Moscow to produce roofing shingles.

Pencils and related office equipment met Soviet needs and paved one path to financial success, and by 1928 quantities of these items were available for export. But another breakthrough came in a Hammer initiative on how to deal with a large quantity of depreciated rubles—unload them on cheap, surplus Russian art that could be sold for good prices in New York. The Hammer Gallery, operated mainly by brothers Victor and Harry in New York, ascended from modest quarters in the Village to the ground floor of the Waldorf Astoria with regular publicity-

87. Epstein, *Dossier*, 95; Hammer, *Quest*, 109–20.

making exhibitions at Lord & Taylor and at a branch gallery in West Palm Beach, Florida.[88] This private venture quickly expanded, as Anastas Mikoyan, whom Armand had met in Rostov in 1923, pushed forward a scheme to dispose of a substantial quantity of Western art, accumulated in museums such as the Hermitage and from noble estates, to support industrialization needs—with the Hammers serving as commission agents.[89] From asbestos to pencils to art, the Hammers had finally found a very profitable niche in the Soviet business world.

The Harriman Concession

Another well-publicized American concession was granted to a much more established and respected businessman, W. Averell Harriman, heir to a railroad empire that had become a multifaceted corporation. His venture into the Soviet wonderland involved the rehabilitation of manganese mines at Chiaturi in northern Georgia on the south slopes of the Caucasus Mountains. Krasin strongly recommended pursuing initial negotiations with Harriman in late 1924, enumerating the advantages but advocating a careful approach. An agreement concluded on 12 July 1925 between Harriman and Leon Trotsky, who had been relegated—briefly—to the supervision of concessions, required a $4 million investment in modernizing the mines, adding a washer plant, a rail system, and an aerial tramway. This all involved another complicated multinational operation with several subcontracts with German companies.[90]

An economic depression in minerals, especially the opening of manganese sources in South America, problems with local Georgian authorities, and poor management in general resulted in losses for the operation. Crucial to the Harriman concession was the failure to obtain sales to U.S. Steel, which opted for cheaper Brazilian and West African manganese. The new head of Amtorg, Saul Bron, attempted to sweeten the pot by purchasing much-needed metals such as copper, lead, and zinc from abroad through Harriman, citing business arrangements with Guggenheim Brothers, American Smelting, and Consolidated Mines as precedents.[91] The Harriman manganese concession was formally liquidated in September 1928 on the eve of the First Five Year Plan. In acknowledgment of a failed concession with an important American business concern, the Soviet agency granted Harriman a $1 million credit for sales of Soviet products abroad.

88. Epstein, *Dossier*, 75–83; Robert C. Williams, *Russian Art and American Money, 1900–1940* (Cambridge, Mass.: Harvard University Press, 1983), 210–18.

89. Epstein, *Dossier*, 127.

90. Sutton, *Western Technology*, 87–90.

91. Bron to Harriman, 20 July 1927, box 14, Harriman Papers, MD, LC.

Ford

By far the best-known American business name in the Soviet Russia of the 1920s was Ford. Bolshevik leaders and their economic advisers, especially Krasin, were mesmerized by the Ford American miracle (*Fordismus*) and its assembly-line production of large numbers of cheap cars for the masses. The first Soviet representative in the United States, Ludwig Martens, in 1919 had Ford on the top of his list. He went to Detroit to meet with Ford executive Charles Sorenson to negotiate on the purchase of about 10,000 Ford tractors at $750 each; they were deemed especially suitable for Soviet farms, either collective or village. He planned to continue the discussion in New York two weeks later—and perhaps to see Henry Ford himself.[92] Nothing, however, came of this, because of the sudden cloak that fell over Martens in regard to the "Red Scare." Nonetheless, a few Ford vehicles—model T's and tractors—made their way into Russia by various routes in the early 1920s.

The first Ford contract directly with the Soviet government came in early 1924, through a Danish subsidiary, to supply 18,000 cars and trucks during that year.[93] With this headstart, the American company would quickly dominate the Soviet market for automobiles, trucks, and tractors, even though it made little effort to promote sales to that country. In late 1925, by another contract with Ford, Amtorg purchased 10,000 Fordson tractors on arrangements demanded by Ford—75 percent down with the remainder due within ten months. The concession provided for setting up a Leningrad factory with Ford equipment for the first local production of tractors.[94] Indeed, agricultural purchases amounted to more than half of all purchases in 1925 and again in 1930. Other years they were around 25 percent of the total.[95]

With business with Soviet Russia taking off, a Ford delegation arrived in Moscow in 1926 to investigate more fully the situation and, to its surprise, found Fords everywhere, sold to Russia mainly by middlemen such as Armand Hammer. As Antony Sutton concluded, "By 1927, more than 85 percent of all trucks and tractors used in the U.S.S.R. were Ford-built from Detroit." In Ukraine, out of 5,700 tractors the government owned, 5,520 were Fordsons. With the negotiation of an additional purchase of $4,500,000 in tractors, plows, and other equipment from

92. Martens to Chicherin, 13 August 1919, *Sovetsko-Amerikanskie otosheniia: gody nepriznaniia, 1918–1926*, 112–13.

93. "Ford Gets Contract with Soviets for Cars," *NYT*, 29 January 1924: 3.

94. "10,000 Ford Tractors to Be Sent to Russia," *NYT*, 15 December 1925: 34, and "Russian Politics and Credits," *NYT*, 28 January 1926: 22.

95. Dana G. Dalrymple, "American Technology and Soviet Agricultural Development, 1924–1933," *Agricultural History* 40, no. 3 (July 1966): 190.

Ford and International Harvester, the number of tractors in service rose to 30,000 in 1926 from 1,250 three years earlier, 98 percent made in the United States.[96] As the delegation quickly discovered, the main drawback of not having a more direct business arrangement was the near absence of servicing, especially since breakdowns under Russian or Ukrainian operation were quite frequent.

The Ford involvement in the Soviet effort to build its own tractors at the Krasnyi Putilovets works in Leningrad was less successful, since the concession involved only technical assistance and a modest number of machines, and it basically failed. In the mid-1920s the Soviet Union still lacked the capital required for a major production facility. Finally, during the First Five Year Plan the Leningrad plant would be completely reequipped with new Ford machinery.[97] For the 1920s, Ford concentrated on developing its American business but with an eye on future international possibilities. The Russians would be first in line, looking to Ford for guidance in its leap into the automobile age with a major automobile and truck assembly plant at Nizhny Novgorod in the 1930s.

Oil

American companies were also major participants in one of the largest and most lucrative of Russian resources, the oil pumped from wells along the west side of the Caspian Sea and from those inland as far as Grozny in the Caucasus region. But after performing major roles in drilling and pipeline construction, the American position in the industry by World War I was overshadowed the Swedish-Russian Nobel Company and a host of smaller Russian companies. Nobel controlled about one-third of the total, especially in refining and shipping. With the collapse of Russian authority in the region during the civil war, the resource seemed to be open for plunder by outside powers with Britain emerging in the forefront; many believed that oil was a chief factor in its involvement in military intervention in Russia. Its chief rival, the French Rothschild empire, had sold its petroleum stake in Russia to Royal Dutch Shell in 1912. Soviet nationalization of the industry forced the withdrawal of Nobel and drew their permanent hostility. With the growing demand in the Asian market for kerosene in view, in 1919 Standard Oil (New Jersey) dipped its toes into the Caspian through a contract with the independent and temporary Azerbaijan republic and, in addition, negotiated a partnership with the Nobels, who had fled to Paris. Standard gambled on

96. "Russia Buys Machines," *NYT*, 22 June 1927: 22.
97. Dalrymple, "American Technology," 140–41.

a Bolshevik defeat with a $14 million purchase of 50 percent of what Nobel had once controlled.[98] Both would turn out to be bad bets.

Turmoil in the Caspian region naturally resulted in a drastic decline in petroleum production with at least half of the wells idle by 1922.[99] After the Red Army extended Soviet control over the region, a Soviet agency, Azneft, was formed with overall jurisdiction of the oil fields and production facilities, and, with the advent of NEP, concessions were soon available. Major world oil companies quickly entered the fray to obtain concessions. The future of the Russian oil fields thus became a major topic at the Genoa economic conference in April 1922 and was considered by Russia, as well as others, to be a chief reason for its failure.[100] Britain (British Petroleum and Royal Dutch Shell) still seemed to hold the upper hand because of the proximity of its interests, equipment, and shipping bases in the Persian Gulf. France, Belgium, and the United States led the opposition with Standard Oil forming a partnership that refused to do business with Soviet Russia unless it recognized its claims. In the meantime, Barnsdall Corporation, employing mainly American workers and equipment, obtained a concession for rejuvenation and new drilling on a large tract in the Baku area through a series of contracts beginning in October 1921. Barnsdall officials in Moscow promised to provide new pumps and deeper rotary drilling to get Russian oil flowing again. Henry Mason Day, the handsome, young, and athletic president of the newly formed International Barnsdall, specifically with Russian business in mind, visited Russia again with seven engineers in July 1922 to sign a final agreement. This involved a considerable investment, valued at a billion dollars by the American company, but it would appear to pay off with a generous percentage of the Soviet oil exports that resulted.[101]

A Department of Commerce internal report of 20 June 1922 concluded that the Soviet oil industry was likely to be divided among two or three foreign concessions but advised that American interests would be best served by the Soviet government having the upper hand, which, in fact, is what happened.[102] Through a series of short-term contracts with several companies, many of them American,

98. White, *British and American Commercial Relations with Soviet Russia*, 103; Jennifer I. Considine and William A. Kerr, *The Russian Oil Economy* (Cheltenham, UK: Edward Elgar, 2002), 19–20.

99. Sutton, *Western Technology*, 17.

100. *Izvestia*, 20 May 1922.

101. While Sutton, *Western Technology*, 20–23, claims Barnsdall lost considerably, the more recent study of Considine and Kerr, *Russian Oil Economy* (p. 25) records a success. "American Obtains Concession," *NYT*, 11 July 1922: 5. The term *international* seemed to have appeal in Soviet quarters—or did Americans simply believe it might—witness International Harvester, International General Electric, International Barnsdall.

102. "Soviet Attitude toward Oil Concessions," memorandum of E. D. Durand, Chief of the East European Division, to Hoover, 20 June 1922, f. Russian Trade 1922, box 536, Commerce, HHPL.

Soviet directors managed to electrify pumps, drill deeper, and expand marketing opportunities. In a joint contract with Azneft, for example, Standard Oil built a new kerosene refinery in Grozny in 1927.[103] One of the major economic successes for the Soviet regime in the 1920s was its ability to retain control of an important resource, to revitalize and expand the industry, and to realize considerable income from the world surge in demand for petroleum products. That same year Amtorg's director urged Vacuum Oil to bid on a contract of $11 million for the construction of a new pipeline through the Caucasus, which also involved Averell Harriman.[104] This led to a strange conflict among the Standard Oil consortium with its leading New Jersey company refusing to buy Soviet oil until that government recognized private property rights, while Standard of New York and Vacuum Oil welcomed Soviet business. The Rockefeller family proclaimed its neutrality, whatever that meant.[105]

The American interest in Soviet oil was not confined to the well-known Caucasus (Baku) field. A relatively new oil company was founded in 1919 by Harry Ford Sinclair, born in West Virginia and raised in Kansas, where he graduated from the University of Kansas in pharmacy. After filling prescriptions and jerking sodas in Independence, he diverted his interests in 1901 to the lucrative Kansas-Oklahoma oil-drilling boom. Well poised in an exploding industry, he had a worldwide vision of petroleum resources in Central America and Africa—and Russia. With oil coursing in his veins, and believing in an even broader worldwide empire, he applied in 1923 for a concession for exploration and development of oil fields on the northern, Soviet half of Sakhalin Island. This was especially attractive to the Soviet agency on concessions and higher authorities, since the project would develop a new resource in the Far East, help consolidate Soviet control of the area, and, above all, exclude the Japanese from this strategically vulnerable area.[106] Political and economic motives were clearly intertwined on the Soviet side. The agreement was at first technically negotiated with the Far Eastern Republic, but with the approval of the Soviet Council of Peoples' Com-

103. Sutton, *Western Technology*, 37.

104. Saul Bron to G. P. Whaley, 2 August 1927, and Harriman to Bron, 10 August 1927, f. Amtorg, box 14, Harriman Papers, MD, LC.

105. "Ivy Lee again Fails to Aid Soviet Cause," *NYT*, 26 July 1927: 3.

106. "Notes from Protocol no. 3 of the Session of Chief Concession Committee," 13 January 1923, and Litvinov to G. L. Piatiakov, vice chair of Gosplan, 26 January 1923, *Sovetsko-amerikanskie otnosheniia: gody neprizhaniia, 1918–1926*, 245–46, 249. Sinclair's Sakhalin project was confined to the northern half, since the southern half belonged to Japan by virtue of the 1905 Treaty of Portsmouth, still in force and recognized. This was also related to the earlier abortive negotiation with Vanderlip in 1920 for a concession in Kamchatka and Northern Sakhalin to counter the Japanese interests. See Chicherin to Lenin, 17 September 1920, in ibid., 152–53.

missars. The republic had become a haven for all sorts of adventurers, mainly Americans seeking Siberian riches.

Oil in the Soviet Far East—then as more recently—could provide Russia with considerable economic and political leverage for markets in China, Korea, and even Japan. The Sinclair contract, signed 25 January 1923, required considerable capital investment, which would not be forthcoming owing to a very competitive oil market and Sinclair's involvement in other risky enterprises, such as Teapot Dome in Wyoming, which propelled him into one of the country's major political scandals. Both Sinclair and Soviet authorities were serious about the Sakhalin prospects, as revealed by considerable documentation about the arrangement in Russian archives and Sinclair's planned excursion to the Baku area with Senator Albert Fall and Mason Day during the summer of 1923.[107] One of the handicaps for any oil company in the 1920s, however, was a world surplus of oil products with many other colonial areas emerging as sources, especially the Persian Gulf. But the rapidly reviving Soviet production could also be blamed. Meanwhile, yet another Sinclair business venture that involved the transport of oil from a proposed concession in Northern Persia through Soviet pipelines to the Black Sea resulted in even more futile negotiations.[108] That too resulted in nothing, exasperating Soviet officials even more with American business. Despite so little result, Harry Sinclair's selling of "medicine oil from Kansas" persona persisted. The Soviet petrol managers still looked to him to bail out various oil production schemes with major loans, while keeping a watchful eye on Standard Oil's manipulations in the international market.[109]

Russia's considerable reserves of other precious metals naturally attracted American attention. Gold-mining concessions led the list, since the Soviet officials were quite anxious to revive and maximize production as a medium to buy goods in the West. Americans who were already experienced about the Siberian potential, such as Charles H. Smith, were first in line, following earlier ventures that resembled the gold rushes of California and Alaska. Most of these speculative American ventures into Siberian goldfields, as earlier, were simply that—forays

---

107. For example, see Sinclair to Piatikov, 18 and 22 July 1923, in *Sovetsko-amerikanskie otnosheniia: gody neprizhaniia, 1918–1926*, 312–23. Alex Gumberg romanticized, "Harry Sinclair and Ex-Secretary Fall will probably have a very nice time doing the races in Moscow. Also they may enjoy the scenery in the Caucasus." Gumberg to Thacher, 5 July 1923, f. 1, box 2, Gumberg Papers, SHSW. See also, "Jugglers of World Grants New Race of Business Kings," *NYT*, 1 July 1923: xx3. The full-page article included pictures of Vanderlip, Sinclair, and Henry Mason Day.

108. A. E. Minkin to Chicherin, 22 December 1923, *Sovetsko-amerikanskie otnosheniia: gody neprizhaniia, 1918–1926*, 353.

109. Litvinov to Ian Berzin, 7 October 1924, ibid., 404–5; Minkin to Piatakov, 14 February 1925, ibid., 420; and Notes from Arens's diary, 2 March 1926, ibid., 483–84. In this expertly edited collection of documents, Sinclair figures prominently.

into the wilderness with little capital backing and even less Soviet cooperation. For example, in January 1924 Joseph Vint secured rights to the Mamyn River area near Chita. This arrangement stemmed from an earlier agreement of Vint and Edmund Parker with the Far Eastern Republic in December 1921. They agreed to furnish dredging equipment and pay one gold ruble per *desiatin* (2.75 acres) of lease and a 5 percent royalty on any gold produced that was to be purchased by the state at the London price minus shipping costs.[110]

Walter L. Brown, a former ARA worker, obtained an even more ambitious concession in the Lena goldfields, taking over a prerevolutionary British enterprise. The negotiations, which lasted more than two years, involved 100,000 acres and resulted in a concession on similar terms as Vint signed on 14 November 1924 by Dzerzhinsky and Litvinov.[111] Another American venturer into this Soviet domain negotiated for the purchase of platinum on behalf of the Wilson Company.[112] He proposed to buy 3,000 ounces of platinum a month for an indefinite period.[113] Nothing of importance seems to have come from these projects. The Soviet government wisely preferred to keep the extraction of any precious minerals under its direct control.

In another traditional energy resource area, American companies were involved on a more modest basis in the rehabilitation of coalmines in the Donetsk Basin in Ukraine, which also had been badly damaged by civil war and the loss of foreign management. Most of these were short term and relatively small auxiliary operations. The major companies involved in Soviet coal were French, British, and German.[114] The Donbas industrial complement, the Kuznetsk Basin in southwestern Siberia, would have a much larger American presence.

Kuzbas

One of the best known and earliest of the projects of production assistance was that of resurrecting coal mines at Kemerovo in southwest Siberia, not far from

110. Secret report of "Concession Committee," 10 February 1924, ibid., 369. G. C. Hansen (Harbin) to State, 17 December 1925, roll 136 (816.63/70), M316, RG59, NA, including copy of agreement of 16 January 1924. Vint spent nine years hoping to strike it rich in Siberia and offered his notes of the experience to President Hoover in 1930. Vint to C. Naramore, 29 October 1930, and Naramore to Hoover, 29 November 1930, box 993, Presidential Papers, HHPL.

111. Coleman (Riga) to State, 12 May 1925, roll 136 (816.63/70), M316, RG59, NA.

112. His name appears as S. Grosbard in Soviet records, Minkin to Chicherin, 12 February 1924, *Sovetsko-amerikanskie otnosheniia: gody neprizhaniia, 1918–1926*, 370–71.

113. Report of the Commissariat of Finance, 21 February 1924, *Sovetsko-amerikanskie otnosheniia: gody neprizhaniia, 1928–1926*, 377–78.

114. Sutton, *Western Technology*, 46–48.

Novosibirsk. The idea was launched by the exiled American radical socialist Bill Haywood in 1921, but its main leadership came from Sebald Rutgers of Rotterdam. Herbert Calvert of Vincennes, Indiana, was the chief American organizer, representing the Society for Technical Aid to Soviet Russia, which quickly grew to more than thirty branches in the United States and would decline just as fast. After submitting a written proposal, these three met directly with Lenin on 19 September 1921 to negotiate a concession.[115] They would take over management of 32,000 acres that included several enterprises in the Kuznetsk Basin and at Nadezhdinsk in the Urals, supplying up to 6,000 young, mostly male American workers. This hodge-podge concession included additional factories in Tomsk and other miscellaneous concerns. Lenin was especially attracted to this offer because of its international socialist character but was skeptical about the requirement of $300,000 in Soviet gold to buy machinery, and because he considered Haywood something of an anarchist. He wisely advised that one of their Soviet attorneys carefully review the proposal.[116] An official contract was, nevertheless, concluded in early 1922 that called for the provision of experienced American workers: 2,800 for Kemerovo and 3,000 for Nadezhdinsk. Though only about 400 Americans actually participated, their management skills are credited with a considerable increase in production at several of the facilities.[117]

Calvert and another convert to the cause, William Barker, hoped to gain the support of the IWW in the United States to provide labor. That organization, then in a state of postwar disorder, also had reservations and only a few backed the endeavor, but enough to form an associated American Agricultural Relief Unit to provide food for the miners. Floyd Ramp, a socialist adventurer from Rosebury, Oregon, joined it. According to his diary, he enjoyed the challenge and was impressed by seeing twenty tractors pulling gang plows across the virgin lands of the steppe.[118] He enthusiastically described riding on a wagon of grain six hours to Kemerovo in cold weather but was not impressed by the confusion he found there. He noted that disc harrows were badly needed.[119] An affiliated American Agricultural Relief Unit, sponsored by Friends of Soviet Russia, contributed $750,000 to this effort in less than a year, Ramp claimed.[120]

115. J. P. Morray, *Project Kuzbas: American Workers in Siberia (1921–1926)* (New York: International Publishers, 1983), 19–34.

116. Ibid., citing Lenin's letters to Valerian Kiubyshev of 19 and 22 September 1921, 60–61.

117. Sutton, *Western Technology*, 48–50. The Riga post reported around fifty American workers passing through to Kuzbas in October 1924. Coleman to State, 7 October 1924, roll 128 (861.55), M316, RG 59, NA.

118. Ramp diary, 28 June 1922, Ramp Papers, Special Collections, University of Oregon Library.

119. May and 9 November 1922, ibid.

120. June 1922, ibid.

The Society of Technical Aid organized five other agricultural communes, mainly in Ukraine, with American volunteers, Communists and sympathizers, who brought in more than $100,000 in equipment. Most of these were short lived as the American pioneers encountered bureaucratic obstacles, ruined estates, and their own lack of experience in agriculture, either Soviet or American style.[121] The first, a group of fifty-one from New York, came in mid-1922 to Tambov province with $36,000 worth of machinery, seeds, and clothing.[122] The California Commune was created in January 1923 in the Donetsk area by workers from the West Coast. Though granted 2,800 acres of rich land and required to remit only 5 percent of production to the state, the American commune was soon bankrupt and dissolved, mainly because of the loss of equipment and supplies on the railroad.[123] An avowed purpose of these American experiments in farm socialism—and the reason Soviet officials welcomed them—was to provide an example not only of progressive socialism but of modern practices to the Russian and Ukrainian villages. Their inhabitants, however, preferred traditional practices, which were restored to a considerable extent during the New Economic Policy. The NEP traditional revival thus confronted and resented the modernist and reformist methods of American idealists.

One of the more interesting projects was inspired not only by modern changes but also by ethnic solidarity. Finnish immigrants in the United States included many socialists who were attracted to the postrevolutionary Russia and its espoused ideals. One group established a farm commune near Petrograd that succumbed to the thievery of local peasants. A more successful one, promoted by Finns from the Seattle region and located north of Petrograd in Karelia, was inhabited by a kindred people to the Finns. The Finnish-American Seattle Commune was thus perhaps the most successful of such experiments, surviving into the collectivization campaign of the 1930s.[124] Despite the infusion of donated American implements and the enthusiasm of their promoters, most of the American agricultural communes were miserable failures. They simply could not transplant American agriculture to the Soviet Russia of the 1920s. Their participants viewed Russia as predominately agrarian but had little knowledge of its social and political background, let alone the more specific elements of soil and climate. Moreover, they had little experience with American agriculture in the first place, resulting in a bad mismatch.

121. Sutton, *Western Technology*, 126–27, 131.

122. "Industrial Emigration from America to Russia," translation from *Ekonomicheskaia Zhizn*, 17 September 1922, J. C. White to State, 19 September 1924, roll 128 (861.55), M136, RG 59, NA.

123. Ibid., 127–28; for official approval of grant, Sovnarkom protocol, 3 April 1923, f. 130, op. 7, d. 1a, GARF.

124. Sutton, *Western Technology*, 128.

An exception to the misplaced idealism of these American Communists was Harold Ware, a graduate of Pennsylvania State University, who had several years of experience in developing industrial farming techniques in Delaware, Pennsylvania, Illinois, and North Dakota. Impressed by the need to reform Russian agriculture to stave off future famines, Ware obtained $75,000 from the American Federated Russian Famine Relief Committee, recruited farm boys from North Dakota, and set off in May 1922 with twenty-two tractors and an assortment of other equipment for a concession near Perm. Five North Dakota boys trained forty Russians in the use of tractors, and they successfully planted 4,000 acres in winter wheat that fall. Their success was promoted by bringing a substantial quantity of American food to feed Russian workers.[125] Ware's Russian reconstruction farms received considerable publicity in both Russia and the United States. He was certainly persistent, launching a campaign in 1925 for contributions of $1,000 for each worker. Even Alex Wiren of the Russian Student Fund considered this opportunity to send a Russian student back to Russia on a constructive mission.[126]

On the basis of this achievement, Ware won another, much larger concession of 23,000 acres in the rich Kuban region. He brought twenty-five American specialists, several tractors, and perhaps the first combined reaper-threshers in Russia with the goal of teaching Russian peasants American methods of mechanical cultivation. Ware informed Theodore Dreiser in 1927 that the venture had been quite successful as part of the drive for the industrialization of agriculture. A larger American contingent included two physicians, two nurses, and a social worker. This still had its limitations: he told Dreiser of a peasant coming in from a neighboring village with a broken scythe, which was mended in their welding shop. Soon others arrived from all over the region to have hand tools fixed. Americans learned to win peasant support by maintaining and encouraging the old ways.[127]

Though Ware, the Kemerovo/Kuzbas project, and a variety of other agricultural communes are perhaps the best known among the socialist-oriented American endeavors with a vaguely romantic and idealistic aura, more immediately practical and successful concerns involved the manufacture of clothing. The Third International Clothing Works was established by radical, mainly Jewish deportees

125. Evans Clark, "American to Modernize Russia's Farming System," *NYT*, 4 January 1925: XX7. This source reported that Lenin took a personal interest in the Perm operation and wrote Ware his congratulations.

126. Wiren to Norman Davis, 24 June 1925, f. Russian Student Fund, 1925–1926, box 48, Davis Papers, MD, LC.

127. "Dakota Farmers Teach Russians New Methods," *NYT*, 5 July 1926: 15; Theodore Dreiser, *Dreiser Looks at Russia* (New York: Horace Liveright, 1928), 139–41. Ware would emerge again in 1929 in charge of one of the largest new collective farms, 120,000 acres. "To Teach Mujiks to Farm," *NYT*, 27 April 1929: 27.

in the early 1920s, with, as the name implies, the goal of serving world revolution. This arrangement was followed by a more substantial concession arranged through the Russian-American Industrial Corporation in Moscow. The corporation was founded by a mainly Jewish socialist labor union, headed by Sidney Hillman, in New York.[128] The New York union financed initial investments from its own treasury, assessed special dues on members, and sold stock in the Russian enterprise. By the end of 1923 the Russian-American Industrial Corporation was operating twenty-five clothing plants in Moscow with 15,000 workers. This business expanded to the establishment of two banks that are credited with transferring more than $20 million by 1927 to support clothing production.[129] These American contributions were more visible than those in the remote agricultural colonies and attracted more attention because of their location in Moscow and immediate results in consumer items.

Because of the diversity of Soviet agencies and the somewhat clandestine operations of individual American enterprises, it is not easy to recapitulate their activities. One American freelance entrepreneur, William Gibson, reported that by negotiating directly with Grigori Zinoviev and his assistant Artzibashev in Petrograd in 1922, he sold 4 million pairs of boots at $6.17 each, 50 percent gold on contract in advance, 43 percent on credit, and 7 percent on delivery. Realizing a handsome profit, he had as many as four shiploads at a time in the harbor.[130] Among other freelance traveling salesmen was Alexander Pincus, who returned to the scene of previous operations in late 1922, tagging along with an international delegation but equipped with a large quantity of samples of goods for sale. During his four-month stay he was granted a concession for a Russian Commercial Trading Company, 25 percent of the stock held by the Soviet government.[131] The company had a Chicago address, but, as with many such fly-by-night operations, nothing seems to have come of it.

American-Russian Chamber of Commerce

Founded in 1916 and composed of representatives of many American companies, the chamber survived through the upheavals of war and revolution to continue

128. Durand to Herter, 13 October 1922, f. Russian trade 1922, box 536, Commerce, HHPL; Sutton, *Western Technology 1917–1930*, 227–29.

129. Sutton, *Western Technology 1917–1930*, 229.

130. William J. Gibson, *Wild Career: My Crowded Years of Adventure in Russia and the Near East* (London: George G. Harrap, 1935), 233–34.

131. "Report on a Visit to Russia," in Pincus to John R. Evans and Company, 1 February 1923, box 1990, Records of the Bureau of Foreign and Domestic Commerce, RG 151, NA.

its advocacy of Russian-American trade and business. During the early Soviet period, however, it was still under control of anti-Bolshevik interests. In reaction a few other short-lived organizations leaned in the other direction, for example, the American Commercial Association to Promote Trade with Russia, directed by Harold Kellock.[132] Its president, Emil Jennings, spent six months in Russia from December 1920 to June 1921 promoting this cause. He found that Russia wanted help but had done much to discourage it by seizing properties.[133]

In the summer of 1926 the American Russian Chamber of Commerce was reorganized to respond to perceived Soviet opportunities and regained its dominant position on the American side of Soviet-American trade by veering to the left to assist and direct American enterprises into Russian business. The new president, Reeve Schley, a vice president of Chase National Bank, provided prestige. Early the following year, it established an office in Moscow under the direction of a general secretary, Charles Haddell Smith, who had long been involved in various Russian-American business ventures and with the management of the Chinese Eastern Railway. He was a committed advocate of Soviet-American business and of diplomatic recognition and conferred about these goals with Aleksei Rykov, Lenin's successor as chair of the Council of Peoples' Commissars in January 1927.[134] Fluent in Russian, Smith knew his way around Moscow and most of the rest of the country. He reported back to the chamber the following year that the Soviet government and economy were stable and that the Moscow office was flourishing and entering the tourist business.[135] Even the Commerce Department as early as 1924 acknowledged the success of American business in penetrating the Soviet market, reaching an annual level of $10 million in exports.[136] There were still limits, however. In 1927 the State Department, responding to a request of J. Edgar Hoover of the Department of Justice, vetoed the sale to a Soviet agency of 200 Liberty aircraft with additional engines.[137] Still, the tide of expansion of Soviet-American trade and business connections was clearly in the direction of expansion.

Another promoter of Russian-American business connections, sometimes operating through the chamber, but more often on his own, was Alex Gumberg,

132. Kellock to Wardwell, 3 May 1920, f. May 1920, box 6, Wardwell Papers, BA, CU.

133. Jennings report, 31 August 1921, vol. 15, DPR, Tallinn, RG 84, NA.

134. "Confer at Moscow on Our Recognition," *NYT*, 11 January 1927: 10.

135. Sutton, *Western Technology*, 284–85; "Soviet Bank Head Tells of Progress," *NYT*, 18 February 1928: 24.

136. L. J. Lewery to Hoover, 19 April 1924, f. Russian trade, 1923–1925, box 536, Commerce, HHPL.

137. J. E. Hoover to MID, 11 August 1927, and Kelley to Secretary of War, 13 September 1927, reel 164, M 316, RG 59, NA.

interpreter-guide for several Americans, starting with Raymond Robins in the revolutionary years 1917–1918, then Goodrich and Senator Joseph France in 1921, and various American businessmen.[138] He was adept at looking for opportunities but not in his dealings with American government officials, who resented his high-handedness—and success—and suspected his motives as the facilitator-in-chief for American business in Russia. Skvirsky was skeptical about all these dealings, reporting that "his government was very tired of adventurers looking for concessions as they have found them to be without substance."[139]

Amtorg

The Soviet pursuit of American business suffered a considerable initial setback with Martens's expulsion. The Lomonosov mission to purchase locomotives also met with little success, and the cotton syndicate promoted by Nogin was something of a breakthrough. The establishment of Arcos in London by Krasin in 1920 to coordinate all business dealings with Britain, however, introduced a new chapter in Soviet economic relations with the West. This awkwardly titled All-Russian Cooperative Trading Society was a novel jump into Western business. At first the United States also fell under its jurisdiction, with Isaac Sherman its first representative in the United States.[140] Soviet leaders quickly judged that this subordination would not work. In late 1922 the Peoples' Commissariat of Foreign Trade dispatched Isai Khurgin (Hoorgin) on a special mission to the United States to sound out commercial contacts—starting simply with caviar for the New York market—and the possibility of a more permanent economic mission.[141] The United States obviously deserved more—and separate—attention; so, to regularize and increase direct Russian-American commerce and maximize American business connections, the Soviet government established a separate trade mission in the United States in November 1924 as Amtorg—the American Trading Corporation—with Khurgin, already on the scene, as its first director. And the casual pedestrian passing by its office on Broadway would never sus-

---

138. Both the Robins and Gumberg papers are in the State Historical Society of Wisconsin in Madison, no doubt due to Professor William Appleman Williams, a long-time professor of history at the University of Wisconsin.

139. Quoted by Charles Marshall to Wardwell, 29 September 1923, box 7, Wardwell Papers, BA, CU.

140. Gumberg to Goodrich, 1 December 1922, f. 8, box 1, Gumberg Papers, SHSW.

141. Protocol no. 36, Session of Main Concession Committee, 30 August 1923, *Sovetsko-Ameri-kanskie otnosheniia: gody neprizhaniia, 1918–1926*, 330–31. Khurgin graduated in mathematics from the University of Kiev, joined the Jewish radical Bund, and became a Bolshevik in 1920.

pect its origin; it would maintain a poorly disguised fiction as an independent company, when it was actually a direct extension of the Soviet Commissariat of Foreign Trade in the United States.

Following the precedent of the Arkos mission in Britain and essentially a successor to Ludwig Martens's efforts of 1918–1920, and then by temporary agencies, Amtorg's mission was to seek out prospective American business opportunities and facilitate negotiation with the appropriate Soviet agencies. From only three initial contacts during its first year, 1925, owing in part to Khurgin's accidental death in August, Amtorg's business contacts rose to around one hundred in 1926 and to considerably more in 1927 under his successor, A. V. Prigarin. The list included major American companies, such as Westinghouse, General Electric, International Harvester, Ford, and Guarantee Trust, as well as many minor ones.[142] Though established somewhat too late for any impact on the era of concessions, Amtorg would become a crucial and adept facilitator of the American contribution to the vast ambitions of the First Five Year Plan and lead the way from the concession process, which was basically designed to revive the economy, to the large construction contracts that would guide the Soviet economy into the modern industrial age. Despite some setbacks to Soviet-American business, Amtorg agents gained experience and remained optimistic about the future.[143]

Assisting the whole process of reestablishing a permanent Soviet presence in the United States was prominent New York attorney Charles Recht, whose assistance to Martens in 1920–1921 without charge, had been much appreciated. By 1925 Amtorg was paying him $500 a month, or $6,000 a year, to steer it clear of legal difficulties in its rapidly expanding business dealings.[144] Unlike Martens's quixotic enterprise, the new Soviet organization was not dependent on American businessmen for advances but had a credit line of $18 million in Gosbank, the Soviet State Bank. Obtaining American private loans on favorable terms, of course, remained a major objective. This helps explain Amtorg's cultivation of friends such as attorney Allen Wardwell, former Republican Congressman Morris Thacher, and bankers Clarence Dillon, Reeve Schley, and James Farrell.[145] Though Washington government circles, especially in the State Department,

---

142. A. V. Prigarin to Commissar of Commerce Lev Kamenev, 29 April 1926, ibid., 510–11; "List of Americans Who Visited USSR and Were Assisted by Amtorg," f. 503, reel 86, M 316, RG 59, NA.

143. Prigarin to Kamenev, 5 March 1926, *Sovetsko-Amerikanskie otnosheniia: gody neprizhaniia, 1918–1926*, 485–89.

144. Litvinov to Krasin, 7 March 1923, ibid., 265; and Skvirskii to Litvinov, 18 February 1926, ibid., 480–81.

145. Prigarin to Kamenev, 5 March and 29 April 1926, ibid., 486, 510–13.

were suspicious from the beginning about its propaganda pursuits and possible links to the American Communist Party, they were reluctant to take on high-ranking Wall Street interests. The Department of Commerce, though continuing its policy of mild discouragement, did not actively oppose the new Soviet business presence. Although few capitalists in the United States found Soviet loans attractive, especially in view of so many other venture opportunities in the 1920s, direct business, paid up front, was another matter. During the 1925 fiscal year, American businesses sold goods worth $68 million to the Russians, more than any other country. In a report of 24 August 1925, Khurgin reported that concentrating on basic trade arrangements had yielded amazing results.[146]

The highest level of Soviet leadership woke up to the reality of the possibilities of an American economic partnership in mid-1926, when the Politburo of the Central Committee of the party devoted most of its session to that issue in a discussion of a report by Commissar of Foreign Affairs Chicherin. A detailed program, approved by this authority, called for a press campaign to highlight its importance, emphasizing especially the growth of American trade vis-à-vis that with Great Britain. Acknowledging the competition in the world grain market, the Politburo saw industrial assistance from the United States as of overriding importance. The propaganda focus would be shifted away from criticism of the United States and directed to cultivating the support of American journalists in Russia. A new direction in foreign policy would be to cooperate as much as possible in China, where both internal and external forces constantly threatened the Soviet influence. A point was made that the favorable views of Senator William Borah toward the Soviet Union should be cultivated and used to advantage.[147]

This new, practical approach also included a reassessment of concessions, and the record was correctly found to be quite mixed, especially the lack of control that existed. Most concessions were completed or canceled.in 1927 and 1928 in preference for Soviet control and monopoly. The leader of this initiative was Anastas Mikoyan, and his new agent as head of Amtorg was Saul Bron, who was especially effective in management and new directions. By this time, Amtorg had more than a hundred full-time employees, many of them Jewish immigrants who knew Russian, supervising and assisting that many more delegates on special missions.

American assistance to the revival of the Soviet economy in the 1920s was indeed considerable. What it involved was mostly the repair and improvement

<hr>

146. Joan Hoff Wilson, *Ideology and Economics: U.S. Relations with the Soviet Union, 1918–1933* (Columbia: University of Missouri Press, 1974), 80–84; Valerii Shishkin, *Stanovlenie vneshnei politiki poslerevoliutsionnoi Rossii (1917–1930 gody) i kapitalisticheskii mir* (St. Petersburg: Bulanin, 2002), 312.

147. Protocol no. 72, 23 July 1926, d. 512, op. 163, f. 17, RGASPI.

of existing infrastructure in mining, oil production, and manufacturing. It added considerably to the success of the New Economic Policy in the 1920s. Concessions, complex in negotiation and operation, proved to have definite limitations. Few on either side were happy with the results, since many were largely the result of previous American economic relations with Russia. But they, along with Soviet infatuation with the United States—especially Lenin's—and with the mirage of American business capabilities, laid the foundation for much of the reliance of the Soviet Union on American expertise during the First Five Year Plan. This is abundantly clear from the large amount of documentation in Russian archives on American business connections, but these records also reveal a considerable naïveté and misplaced faith in an American rescue for the Russian economy.

The concession era reflected the laissez-faire environment of the New Economic Policy. Its distinguishing features were the lack of Soviet development resources and an American search for economic opportunities. Above all, it constituted a feeling out of a Western capitalist presence in an unpredictable socialist world. The success was that workable arrangements between the two were possible. Boris Skvirsky summed it up in a letter to Senator Borah: "Several years ago the government of the U.S.S.R. was encouraging large scale concessions to citizens of foreign states who were financially responsible. The results however were not sufficiently important to warrant a continuation of such a policy."[148]

148. Skvirsky to Borah, 18 March 1932, box 349, Borah Papers, MD, LC.

4

Culture

As in the case of early Soviet-American business relations, a firm foundation already existed in mutual cultural appreciation and contacts, including an American infatuation with the literature and messages, however misinterpreted, of Leo Tolstoy, Fedor Dostoevsky, Ivan Turgenev, Anton Chekhov, and many others. Russians reciprocated in their fascination with American writers such as James Fenimore Cooper, Edgar Allan Poe, Mark Twain, and Jack London, but, most of all, it was a matter of style and an emphasis on the contemporary scene. Russians tired of French dominance of Western culture could look to the United States, where New World cultural centers were emerging in New York, Chicago, San Francisco, and New Orleans. The immediate prerevolutionary Russian period was fertile ground for an American-Russian symbiosis. Americans, finding their way toward a cultural identity, saw Russia, more than any other country with the possible exception of Britain, as possessing the guiding lights: Tchaikovsky, Rimskii-Korsakov, Chaliapin, Chekhov, Gorky, Stanislavsky, Pavlova, all of whom would dominate the pages of the American cultural media and most whom would visit the United States. But what was especially important, the United States—a cultural desert to so many Europeans—contributed as well. The Russian silver age and the American ragtime age melded. Both Russia and the United States were seeking new directions in the cultural sphere—and finding them together.

Despite the official American policy of nonrecognition and a pronounced degree of mutual hostility stemming from the civil war and intervention years, cultural relations between the two countries were surprisingly active and fruitful during the 1920s and 1930s. Americans saw an opportunity for experiment and openness, a vindication of their superior business acumen, while Russians were embarking on a new terrain of revolutionary social progress, casting the old bourgeois culture aside. The vibrancy of both Soviet and American culture in the 1920s meshed to a surprising degree and brought the interchange of individuals and their creativity to a new and unprecedented level. This interaction enhanced and encouraged each country's contribution to the Jazz Age. The old claim that Russia and the United States were the new, progressive, and revolutionary stars shining over the old Europe proved itself in this period.

Moreover, the war and revolution stimulated much discussion of what really had happened in Russia, of where Russia was going, repondering Gogol's immortal question of the mid-nineteenth century, "Whither Russia?" On a late November day of 1921 in Washington, William Boyce Thompson, who led the American Red Cross mission to Russia in 1917, recounted having lunch with Norman Hapgood, a Wilsonian internationalist who had supported an understanding with the Bolsheviks in 1918, and with British writer H. G. Wells. Afterward, he recorded that they walked almost the length of Rock Creek Park, "talking a lot about Russia."[1] Russia would be on many minds in the 1920s—and later—along Rock Creek and elsewhere.

ISADORA!

One American woman would literally take center stage as a symbol of a new direction in experimental art, of a meeting of mind and body, specifically in modern dance, and in Soviet-American cultural exchange. Russia was especially receptive to her free-form dancing, since the country had long excelled in the ballet form, but some in the silver age were seeking to liberate it from its staid classicism. Isadora Duncan had taken Russia by storm as early as 1904, providing some relief from Russia's depressing and losing war in the Far East and giving Russian ballet "a shock from which it could never recover," in the words of Sergei Diaghilev, the most gifted of the Russian radical ballet masters.[2] Her dancing made an even greater impression on the new creative genius of Russian ballet, Mikhail Fokin (Michel Fokine), and the current prima ballerina, Matilda Kshesinskaya, a favorite of Tsar Nicholas II. Though representing the new and modern in dance, along with Ruth St. Denis, she reinterpreted the classical in music, especially that of Tchaikovsky. For the American ragtime and jazz she had nothing but contempt, but combining some of the new and the old endeared her to Russians.

Her first St. Petersburg performance took place, ironically, in the Hall of Nobles, across the street from the elegant Hotel Europe, and was attended by many distinguished royalty and elite, as well as leading lights of Russia's silver age of culture: Diaghilev and Fokin, of course, but also Alexandre Benois, Leon Bakst, and Andrei Bely. Reactions were naturally mixed, ranging from astonishment

1. Thompson to Raymond Robins, 1 December 1921, Additional MS, Robins Papers, SHSW.
2. As quoted in Peter Kurth, *Isadora: A Sensational Life* (Boston: Little, Brown, 2001), 147.

Isadora Duncan and Sergei Esenin, 1922. (Prints and Photographs, Library of Congress)

to outrage. Several critics noted, however, that her reputation for lewdness was misplaced, that her bare legs were merely ordinary.[3] Her second performance was a benefit for the Society for the Prevention of Cruelty to Children, which won accolades from liberal quarters.[4]

Duncan returned to Russia for an even more successful and longer tour in 1908, this time especially impressing the renowned theater director Konstantin Stanislavsky, among others.[5] She was equally mesmerized by performances at his Moscow Art Theater, inspiring rumors of a backstage romance. Popular now in Russia, she returned for another exhausting two-month tour the same year. Her reputation in Russia may also have been enhanced by her liaison and then brief,

3. Ibid., 152–53.

4. Duncan, *My Life* (New York: Boni and Liveright, 1927), 331. Duncan's autobiography is not reliable in regard to dates, as she claimed this event coincided with the beginning of the 1905 revolution.

5. See Stanislavsky's tribute to Duncan and Gordon Craig in his *My Life in Art*, translated by Elizabeth Reynolds Hapgood (New York: Theater Arts Books, 1924), 505–21.

unhappy marriage in 1909 to Paris Singer, a son of the founder of Singer Sewing Machine Company, a name well known in that country. Confined to the United States during the war years, she had become committed to revolutionary change in Russia and, on learning of the abdication of Nicholas II in March 1917, gave an especially inspired performance in New York: "On the night of the Russian Revolution I danced with a terrible fierce joy."[6] Though joining the American patriotic cause in 1917 to the dismay of her leftist friends, she veered further to the left in supporting the Bolshevik victory in November.

With her reputation in innovative dance still undiminished but annoyed by a lack of appreciation for it in the postwar United States, Duncan escaped to Europe, her dancers giving a gala "farewell performance" at Carnegie Hall in June 1919.[7] She opened a school for young dancers in Paris but was not really happy there either. Like some other artists, she was increasingly enamored of the Bolshevik experiment, remembering such good receptions in Russia earlier. Leonid Krasin, one of the most cultured of Bolsheviks, saw her perform in London in April 1921 and in a light conversation afterward suggested that she come to Russia. Apparently upon his advice, she wrote to Anatoly Lunacharsky, the new commissar for education and culture,[8] explaining that she wanted to open a simple dance school for the people:

> I am sick of the bourgeois, commercial art . . . I am sick of the modern the-
> atre, which resembles a house of prostitution more than a temple of art,
> where artists who should occupy the place of high priests are reduced to
> the maneuvers of shop-keepers selling their tears and their very souls for so
> much a night. I want to dance for the masses, for the working people who
> need my art and have never had the money to come and see me.[9]

Lunacharsky promptly cabled a formal invitation to come to Moscow, promising "a school and a thousand children," perhaps seeing an opportunity to unload a few of the many homeless orphans of the civil war, but also in scoring a propaganda victory for the fledgling Soviet state.[10]

After many touching farewells, including a memorable one with the famous London actress Ellen Terry, Duncan embarked for the "promised land" in July. British-born Ivy Litvinov, wife of the assistant commissar of foreign affairs, met

6. Duncan, My Life, 334.

7. "Duncan Dancers Appear," NYT, 11 June 1919: 12.

8. Sheila Fitzpatrick, the leading American authority on Lunacharsky during this period, translated his title as "Commissar of Enlightenment," which more correctly denotes his mission.

9. As quoted in Kurth, Isadora, 405.

10. Ibid., 402–5; "Isadora Duncan to Take Offer from Soviets," NYT, 29 May 1921: 15.

her ship in Tallinn and assisted her across the border. Her destination this time was not the sophisticated St. Petersburg of old, which was now only a ghost of a city, but Moscow, still adjusting to its role as the capital of a rather novel new empire that aspired to transform the world but was still occupied in gathering the remnants of Russia. Arriving in advance of the ARA invasion, she found Soviet Russia disappointing, especially when renewing contact with a tired and dejected Stanislavsky, who was—with difficulty—bridging the transition from the old to the new Russia by staging Tchaikovsky's *Eugene Onegin*, which Duncan considered a waste of his considerable talent. She was also annoyed by a special reception for her held in an ornate palace with guests in formal attire, but she did not object to being provided with an opulent house, built for the Smirnov vodka family at fashionable Prechistenka, no. 20, because of its two large ballrooms. Fittingly, Leonid Krasin was the special guest at her first dinner/entertainment.[11]

Duncan's crusade for the art of revolution first had to contend with famine, the simple fact that few suitable children could be found who had the energy to walk, let alone dance. The arrival of the ARA helped solve that problem, but the numbers were still small. After receiving permission in September to advertise for recruits, ages four to ten, hundreds showed up at her door to audition. She finally resumed performing to gain support and retain her reputation but found herself under attack from different directions. Vsevelod Meyerhold, a former associate of Stanislavsky, declared her "absolutely out-of-date and totally obsolete."[12] To others in the vanguard of socialist culture, her work was mystical and impractical. It did not help matters that with aging and weight gain and performing in a diaphanous gown, critics had a field day with her massive legs and wobbling breasts. Even some of the most accepting found her appearance distasteful. Once the school was established with resident children, she was more at home, especially encouraged by a successful premier from her pupils on Christmas Day 1921, arranged by Ivy Litvinov.

Duncan's Soviet times were highlighted by a developing romance that fall with Sergei Esenin, an imaginist poet of peasant background (which he always stressed), blond and handsome, fifteen years younger than Duncan, and who had two children by an early marriage. A brilliant but tragic figure born of the revolution, Esenin was already well on his way to a premature death—epileptic, alcoholic, dissolute, and disenchanted by the revolution. But, perhaps because of this, Esenin and Duncan found a surprising degree of compatibility (refugees from mutual disappointments)—for about a year. Despite Duncan's vow never to

11. Kurth, *Isadora*, 416–23.
12. Ibid., 423–26.

marry again (after Singer), the couple had a Soviet civil ceremony in April 1922 that legalized their relationship, at least in Russia. Their affair also had the effect of blowing out of proportion the image of Isadora's eccentricity in the West, while in Russia she was blamed, especially by Esenin's imaginist associates and followers, for destroying a popular young poet's career. The United States would soon witness the whole debacle firsthand.[13]

Running out of money, Duncan accepted an offer in May 1922 from budding impresario Sol Hurok for a series of return performances in the United States later that year.[14] Her tour began with a rough flight to Berlin, followed by incongruous receptions, she speaking only English, Esenin only Russian, and featuring a public display of mutual physical and mental abuse.[15] Finally arriving in New York in early October with her Russian poet-husband in tow, she was refused entry, since Washington authorities ruled that she had lost her American citizenship by marrying a Soviet citizen. Their real fear, of course, was that the couple would spread Bolshevik propaganda. Rather than be detained at Ellis Island, she and Esenin stayed on ship entertaining representatives of the press in their stateroom, he with powdered hair and in her embrace.[16] Hurok and her New York fans managed to get them released but only after an embarrassing interrogation at Ellis Island.[17]

Her American tour began with a capacity crowd at Carnegie Hall, and, despite the oppressive heat, she was called back for several encores, climaxing with the first of several political speeches, "Why will America not reach out a hand to Russia as I have given my hand?"[18] The remainder of her American tour was less auspicious, owing in part to her dancing in a salaciously brief red dress that some saw as having either sexual or political connotations—or both. She was banned in Boston by its Irish Catholic mayor, chased out of Chicago, and she stalked off the stage in Brooklyn.[19] Though old fans cheered, critics were not kind.

Out of the limelight but hounded by reporters and bootleggers, Esenin, by all accounts was quite disgraceful. He, nevertheless, recorded his colorful and penetrating impressions that emphasized the wonderment of an electrified Broadway

---

13. Some of this is effectively captured in the American film, *The Loves of Isadora.*

14. *NYT*, 8 May 1922: 22.

15. For the scandalous details, see Kurth, *Isadora*, 444–50.

16. "Isadora Duncan and Husband Detained on Liner," *NYT*, 2 October 1922: 1.

17. This is according to Esenin's foggy reminiscences, published in *Izvestiia* the following summer as "Iron Mirgorod," a New York seen through the prism of Gogol's description of a Russian village. For a translation, see Olga Peters Hasty and Susanne Fusso, *America through Russian Eyes, 1874–1926* (New Haven, Conn.: Yale University Press, 1988), 148–55.

18. "Miss Duncan Dances; 3,000 Cheer Speech," *NYT*, 8 October 1922: 25.

19. "Duncan Dance Ends in a Disappearance," *NYT*, 26 December 1922: 1.

("Not one city in the world has anything like this"), a "Brooklyn Bridge hanging between two cities," and the great contrast between city and country. He noted the African-American influence on popular culture and the music hall world: "The American fox-trot is nothing but a diluted version of a Negro national dance. In other respects the Negroes are a rather primitive people, with very unrestrained manners. The Americans themselves are also a very primitive people when it comes to their own inner culture."[20] More than most Russian observers, he saw the real America in the heartland: "He who knows America by New York and Chicago knows only the holiday America, or exhibition America, so to speak."[21] After Duncan's last performances in New York, she announced she was going back to the land of vodka and black bread and would never return to the United States.[22] And she fulfilled both vows.

But the west-east transit was not easy, with Duncan still short of funds and with Esenin, in modern parlance, "a basket case." On the way back, in fact, they were thrown out of the Hotel Crillon in Paris because of his destruction of furniture.[23] Back in Russia in April 1923, Duncan found less welcome than before and Esenin in even more difficulty, arrested for anti-Semitic slurs. Many of Esenin's followers blamed Duncan for his physical and pathological derangement by American bootleg whiskey and for his precipitous decline into perpetual drunkenness.[24] Duncan tried to divorce him, but it remained debatable whether he complied by Soviet law on his part. In any event they were separated and he remarried. After a serious auto accident near Leningrad in May 1924, she left Russia to save her remaining property in France and find additional resources from friends. Both Esenin and Duncan would die tragically and prematurely, Esenin by his own hand, slashing his wrists, writing his last note with his own blood, and hanging himself in December 1925, while Duncan was thrown from a car by an errant scarf wrapped around a wheel in Nice in September 1927.[25] Their story was a strange, poignant, but fitting preface to the unusual but intriguing Soviet-American cultural relations of the 1920s and 1930s.

20. Esenin, "Iron Mirgorod," in Hasty and Fusso, *America through Russian Eyes*, 153.

21. Ibid.

22. "Isadora Duncan Off, Will Never Return," *NYT*, 4 February 1923: 15. According to the article, a reporter asked with a Gilbert and Sullivan retort: "What Never?" to which she quickly responded, "No, Never."

23. "Isadora's Poet Stirs Riot in Paris Hotel," *NYT*, 16 February 1923: 2.

24. "Essenin again in Jail, This Time in Moscow," *NYT*, 23 November 1923: 3. Ilya Ehrenburg, however, credited Duncan with trying "in vain" to restrain Esenin's excesses. Ehrenburg, *Memoirs: 1921–1941* (Cleveland, Ohio: World, 1964), 24.

25. Esenin had recently remarried to a granddaughter of Leo Tolstoy, but Duncan claimed that they were not formally divorced and that she had left Russia only to earn money and planned to return and work with her real love, Esenin. "Denies Divorcing Yessinin," *NYT*, 2 January 1926: 4.

Balieff and Stanislavsky!

Perhaps as well known as Isadora Duncan in Russia was Konstantin Stanislavsky in the United States. His Moscow Art Theater, formed in 1898, was among the premier repertory companies in the world, thanks to the fame of its director; some would argue it was virtually unchallenged in its mastery of dramatic performance. Unfortunately, and not surprisingly, the theater came under attack in the Soviet Union as bourgeois and retrograde. As early as 1908 inquiries had been made about the possibility of a visit by Stanislavsky and his company to the United States, and in 1914 Norman Hapgood initiated a plan to bring them to New York, but that was precluded by the war.[26] Stanislavsky was also naturally hesitant about performing in Russian abroad, as were potential sponsors. Finally, in 1921, desperate for resources to survive, the theater ventured out of Russia on a tour of Scandinavia, encouraged especially by Alexandra Kollontai, then the Soviet representative in Norway. This trip was a success, but the company remained in dire need of funds, and it was uncertain how the more sophisticated audiences of Paris, London, and New York would take to dramatic productions entirely in Russian.

In the fall of 1921 Morris Gest swept a Russian group onto the New York stage but not yet Stanislavsky. As a longtime representative in Europe of the Hammerstein Brothers, and having his own agency—Comstock and Gest—he "discovered" in Paris a resurrection of a popular Moscow cabaret company in the fall of 1921. Nikita Balieff, described as a tall, rotund, moon-faced, nimble-footed Armenian, had somewhat accidentally found an audience with the after-theater crowd in Moscow, especially the casts, beginning in 1908. Located in a cellar near the Moscow Art Theater[27] at the cabaret Bat and performing Russian-style vaudeville acts, parodying and satirizing the world scene in seemingly improvised acts through the wee hours of the morning, Balieff's troupe attracted enough attention to be invited for a special performance before the high nobility of St. Petersburg.[28]

26. Jean Benedotti, *Stanislavsky: A Biography* (London: Routledge, 1988), 217.

27. The Russian origins may date to the Moscow Art Theater's *kapustniki* (cabbage parties) that ended each winter season beginning in 1902, when the theater was cleared of seats and dinner tables set up. Balieff began his theatrical career as a minor actor in Stanislavsky's cast. Harold B. Segal, *Turn-of-the-Century Cabaret: Paris, Barcelona, Berlin, Munich, Vienna, Cracow, Moscow, St. Petersburg, Zurich* (New York: Columbia University Press, 1987), 256–58.

28. Balieff was not his given name, nor was "Bat" (Letuchaia Mysh) original; one of the best-known cabarets in Europe at the time was the Kabaret Fledermaus in Vienna. For more on the history of cabaret in Russia, see the chapter, "Cabaret in Moscow," in ibid., 255–30. The "bat" name derived from the cellar atmosphere, the "small-great art" claims, and the fact that among the early cabarets in Paris, animal names prevailed, for example, the famous *Chat Noir* (Black Cat). Ibid., 35 et passim.

For a contemporary and colorful description of Moscow's Letuchaia Mysh, see the special commemorative volume, with many illustrations: Nikolai Efros, *Teatr "Letuchaia Mysh" N. F. Balieva: Obzor desiatiletnei khudozhestvennoi raboty pervago russkago teatra-kabare* (Petrograd: "Solntse Rossii," 1918).

Finding his comedy too much for Bolshevik tastes, Balieff left Russia in 1920 at the end of the civil war with a few members of his cast and reassembled his company as *Chauve-Souris*, maintaining the bat name, in Paris in 1921 to great acclaim. After revolution and civil war, perhaps everyone was looking for a good dose of Russian arch comedy and buffoonery—or, as Alexander Woollcott put it, "a bit of Russian larking."[29]

Gest thought their performances in Paris, mostly in Russian but with lively musical accompaniment and a little French thrown in, were the best thing that he had seen in Europe, and he hired Balieff and his company on the spot for a New York engagement.[30] Opening at the new 49th Street Theater in January 1922, the Russian troupe quickly took the city by storm. Will Rogers, among the first to see a performance, credited the Russians with reinvigorating American vaudeville, noting that vaudeville had never before been able to charge more than $1.50 for a seat but that the Russians had filled the orchestra at $5.00 a ticket and were forced to limit advance purchasers to no more than four each because of the great demand.[31] All over New York that season people were talking about the "Great Nikita." On stage, Balieff himself provided whimsical introductions and scampered around in the background delivering inappropriately scornful commentary on the acts and all and sundry—in fractured English.[32] Staging more than 400 performances throughout spring and fall of 1922, the Russians may have set a New York record at the time for successive capacity houses. Besides being wined and dined in society, Balieff also won New York hearts by staging a special benefit for Russian famine relief on 9 April 1922.[33] Clearly, *Chauve-Souris* and

29. Alexander Woollcott, "Say It with Moujik," *NYT*, 6 February 1922: 15. Woollcott described Balieff as a Russian "Humpty-Dumpty," "who had the most disarming smile in all the world." See sketch attached to "Second Thoughts on First Nights," by Woollcott, *NYT*, 12 February 1922: 68. He was especially impressed by the nonchalant "drop-in-for-a-moment atmosphere" of a little restaurant in Moscow, transplanted to New York. Gest and Balieff presented special Tuesday afternoon matinees for the New York theater world, for example, bringing Al Jolson on stage to perform a Russian dance and teasing Doris Keane to make up as Catherine the Great.

30. Woollcott guessed that Gest really wanted to see it another fifty times. Ibid. Gest's judgment was confirmed by Brock Pemberton in "A Tale of Two Cities," *NYT*, 17 July 1921: 8; and by William B. Chase, "The Last Laugh Out of Russia," *NYT*, 15 January 1922: 43.

31. Will Rogers, "Slipping the Lariat Over," *NYT*, 25 February 1923: XX2.

32. Typical introductory remarks included: "To make it more incomprehensible, I will explain," and "I have provided some cool gardens to walk in at intermission. It is called Central Park." "Gay 'Chauve-Souris' Welcomed Back," *NYT*, 4 September 1923: 13. Balieff, the only Russian entertainer to grace the cover of *Time* magazine (10, 2, 17 October 1927) is credited with influencing a whole generation of American comedians that included Bert Lahr, Joe E. Brown, Milton Berle, and George Burns.

33. "500 Russian Artists Write of Gratitude," *NYT*, 28 March 1922: 14. The benefit on 9 April included Al Jolson as ticket taker and Lillian and Dorothy Gish as "program girls." Irving Berlin provided the introductory music on piano.

Nikita Balieff, from Nikolai Efros, Teatr "letuchaia mysh" N. F. Balieva.

the nightclub adaptations that followed it in the 1930s were a dominant feature of New York nightlife—and transcontinental tours—never failing to garner rave reviews and standing-room-only audiences.[34] Balieff would certainly rank high, if not at the top, of the greatest entertainers of the Eastern and Western worlds of that era.

At least part of Balieff's success was the recruitment of other talented Rus-

Balieff and Chauve-Souris would have a long tenure with annual seasons in New York and on world tours in the 1920s and 1930s that always included Paris, and in 1933 Britain and South Africa, until his sudden death in his New York apartment in 1936. His funeral was attended by at least a thousand. "Nikita Balieff, 59, Stage Figure, Dies," *NYT*, 4 September 1936: 19; and "1,000 Attend Service for Nikita Balieff," *NYT*, 8 September 1936: 27.

34. In one of his first theater reviews for the *New York Times*, Brooks Atkinson compared unfavorably another Russian imitator, "Yascha Yushny," with "the early Balieff circuses:" "But leave it to these expatriated Russians to make merry out of trifles. . . . Nothing is jollier than Russian costuming and make-up. . . . It is slight entertainment, a compound of simples." Relish that thought. Atkinson, "The Play," *NYT*, 22 April 1932: 23.

sians, such as the artist Sergei Sudeikin as poster and program creator, Nikolai Remisov as set designer, and Andrei Salama as musical director. Sudeikin would become better known for his illustrated covers for the *New Yorker*. Remisov was the set designer for many Broadway productions and more than thirty Hollywood films during the period of 1939–1965 and created covers for *Vogue*, *Vanity Fair*, and other periodicals. He broke with Balieff in 1924 and established a Russian-themed nightclub, Club Petrushka, painting murals on several floors and directing the gypsy music. After the club was destroyed by fire, he moved on to Chicago, where he spent the next ten years completing works for the Chicago Club, the Casino Club, the Graceland Cemetery Chapel, and the Lake Forest Public Library.[35] Salama composed unique scores for Russian folk songs and made other musical contributions. To foster the creative spirit of the Russian émigré community in the United States, Salama bought a hunting camp near Columbia, New Jersey, in the 1920s and turned it into a Russian summer resort and artist colony, Salamovka, which the family maintained for many years and is now under the direction of the National Park Service.[36]

Chauve-Souris proved that New York audiences would sit through—again and again—performances in Russian. Virtually its only competition was the Ziegfield Follies, also premiering that year, both becoming long-term Broadway productions. Balieff, naturally, was an old friend and admirer of Konstantin Stanislavsky, so Gest thought, why not kick it up a notch? Nikolai Rumiantsev, business manager of the Moscow Art Theater, came to New York by invitation in June 1922 to discuss arrangements with Gest.[37] The American visit would be an extension of a European tour to begin in mid-September 1922. It would be confined to New York and open 8 January 1923 for eight weeks, later to be considerably extended. The company received permission to leave Soviet Russia on the condition that all members return for the fall celebration of its twenty-fifth anniversary in Moscow. Advance publicity carefully noted that this event came on the wake of the Balieff success.[38] An illustrious group of New York socialites subscribed in support of the Moscow theater's appearance, and Richard Crane, American minister to Czechoslovakia, attested to their superb performances in Prague.[39]

Stanislavsky and his company of more than fifty members—preceded by many large crates of stage scenery—arrived on schedule in New York on the steamer *Majestic*, unfortunately docking late on 5 January 1923 to a subdued bread and

35. "Nikolai Remisoff," http:www.usc.edu/isd/archives/arc/finding aids/remisoff/bio.html.
36. Sandy VanDoren, "Register of the Papers of Andrew Salama," Balch Institute for Ethnic Studies of the Historical Society of Pennsylvania, balchinstitute.org/manuscript_guide/html/Salama.
37. "Nikolai Rumiansteff Here," *NYT*, 22 June 1922: 23.
38. Walter Duranty, "Russian Players Coming to America," *NYT*, 28 August 1922: 8.
39. "On the Musovians," *NYT*, 31 December 1922: 73.

Stanislavsky and friends, from left to right: Ivan Moskvin (actor), Stanislavsky, Chaliapin (reclining), Vasily Kachalov (actor), and Sorin (actor), Arnold Genthe photographer, New York, March 1923. (Prints and Photographs, Library of Congress)

salt welcome that included Gest, renowned pianist and composer Sergei Rachmaninoff, Leon Bakst, Balieff and his cast, artist Nicholas Roerich, and Boris Anisfeld, who was then director of stage scenery for the Metropolitan Opera—but many others had given up waiting. The company included a few original members who had left Russia after the revolution but returned to Moscow specifically to participate in the tour. The Jolson Theater on 59th Street seated 2,000 but was sadly deficient in wings and deep stage for the elaborate scenery that the company depended on, and a motley backstage crew had to be assembled, which caused Stanislavsky considerable consternation.[40] Highlighted, and drawing almost as much attention as Stanislavsky, was an original and venerable cast member, Olga Knipper-Chekhova, the widow of the famous playwright whose works would be featured on the program.[41] Her opening performance on 8 January as Tsarevna Irina in Aleksei Tolstoy's *Czar Fyodor* drew predictably rave reviews. She knew

40. Jean Benedetti, *Stanislavski: A Biography* (London: Routledge, 1988), 270. Patrons listed included Mrs. Marshall Field, Walter Damrosch, Charles Dana Gibson, and Frank Polk. "Moscow Art Theatre to Open Here January 8," *NYT*, 27 October 1922: 23.

41. Henry James Forman, "Actress Wife's Mirror of Anton Tchekhoff," *NYT*, 28 January 1923: SM10.

some English and was interviewed in her dressing room by Henry James Forman for his *New York Times* column.[42] She was also the guest of honor at a dinner of the Chekhov Society at Thiessen's landmark restaurant at 14th Street and 3rd Avenue.[43]

Other repertory performances included a wide range of Russian drama from Gorky's *Lower Depths*, Gogol's *Inspector General*, and, of course, Chekhov's *Cherry Orchard* and *Three Sisters*. There was much congratulatory praise in the press for bringing Stanislavsky and the Moscow Art Theater to the United States. Actress Diana Bourbon scored the superiority of the work by actors who never upstaged each other, absent the rivalries and jealousies that predominate on the American stage.[44] The elite of American theater, such as John Barrymore and Lillian Gish, were often in the audience, and Stanislavsky reciprocated by attending many American productions with his old friends Sergei Rachmaninoff and Fyodor Chaliapin.[45] Will Rogers, performing in the Ziegfeld Follies, after suffering the ordeals of a New York February snowstorm, quipped,

> These Russians are having a wonderful season in New York: even the weather is with them. I doubt if a Russian in Summertime would be as attractive. Nobody in New York knows what they are talking about, so it has developed into a fad or game to make your neighbor, sitting around you, think that you know. Nothing outside of Grand Opera in a foreign tongue, has BORED the rich out of more money than these (so called) simple Russian Peasants. . . . The best acting I saw there was by the Audience. When you take three thousand people that act like they like a thing when they don't know what it's all about, that's real acting.[46]

But most of the New York audiences, including Rogers, recognized the quality of the Moscow Art Theater—and welcomed their rare and unusual New York appearances. A biographer noted, "It is impossible to overestimate the impact of the company on the profession."[47] And they left a legacy in inspiring the foundation of the American Laboratory Theater.

The tour was extended to Chicago, Philadelphia, and Boston, where they met their first really hostile reception and where Stanislavsky also signed a contract with Little Brown for his autobiography, *My Life in Art*, which he began to dictate

42. Ibid.
43. "Russian Players Guests," *NYT*, 12 February 1923: 13.
44. Diana Bourbon, "The Russians and the Actor," *NYT*, 11 February 1923: X2.
45. Benedotti, *Stanislavsky*, 269–72.
46. Will Rogers, "Slipping the Lariat Over," *NYT*, 25 February 1923: XX2.
47. Benedetti, *Stanislavsky*, 271.

in his hotel room. In June, after farewell performances in New York,[48] he and the company returned to Europe, but Stanislavsky stayed with his family at European resorts to complete the book[49] and did not go back to Russia as Soviet officials expected. By September he was planning a second tour of Europe and the United States with an entirely new repertoire, adding Ibsen's *An Enemy of the People* and Dostoevsky's *Brothers Karamazov*. Arriving on 7 November 1923, he followed a grueling schedule in New York, then in Philadelphia, where Rachmaninov took him to hear Leopold Stokowski and the Philadelphia Orchestra. The tour widened to include New Haven, Hartford, and again Boston. Back in New York by January 1924 for performances in Brooklyn and Newark, he was invited to the set of a movie that featured Rudolph Valentino and Bebe Daniels. Misunderstanding a polite question, he responded that he thought the acting was "abominable."[50] He would have had few challengers to that opinion.

The highlight of the second American tour of the Moscow Art Theater was a surprising invitation by President Calvin Coolidge to a reception at the White House on 20 March 1924, especially considering that the company was still Soviet and the United States was following a policy of nonrecognition. More important, Stanislavsky met Elizabeth Reynolds Hapgood, who served as his interpreter with the president. He was clearly infatuated with her presence, beauty, and excellent Russian, and they formed the beginning of a lasting professional relationship that would involve collaboration on his best-known published contributions to the acting profession, such as *An Actor Prepares*. This work, written in rough Russian, translated by Elizabeth Hapgood, and edited by her husband, Norman Hapgood, would define method acting and be a key factor of Stanislavsky's legacy in the West. The Hapgoods would subsequently secure the copyrights to all of his works published outside Russia, thus virtually preventing Western access to true, unedited Russian versions published in the Soviet Union.[51] Most, but not all, of the Moscow Art Theater would return to Moscow, along with its director, but Stanislavsky would spend much of the rest of his life between Russia and Western Europe, collaborating with the Hapgoods.

Russian-American cultural connections were also still personified by the vener-

---

48. Charles Crane saw *Three Sisters* at its final appearance of the tour. Crane to daughter Josephine Bradley, 3 June 1923, Crane Papers, reel 1, BAR, CU.

49. Stanislavsky, *My Life in Art*. The frontispiece reads: "I dedicate this book in gratitude to hospitable America as a token and a remembrance from the Moscow Art Theatre which she took so kindly to her heart."

50. Benedetti, *Stanislavsky*, 277–78.

51. Ibid., 279–80, 315–18, 345. A new translation would require payment of rights to the Hapgood estate.

able Zenaida Ragozin, a remarkable historian, orientalist, musician, linguist,[52] and teacher, who had managed to survive war, revolution, and civil war in Petrograd and was an old friend of the Hapgoods and especially Elizabeth's mother Margaret Reynolds, during her many years of residence in New York (1870–1900). Now in her eighties, she welcomed renewed direct contact during the Hapgoods' visit to Russia in 1923 and recounted in some detail the hardships of those postrevolutionary years. Her closest contact during that period was with Methodist minister George Simons, whom she had known for many years, and who was now based in Riga though still making regular visits to Petrograd. Outspoken as usual, Ragozin characterized him as "very timid, and, like most Americans, too narrow and literal, making no allowances, leaving no margin for exceptional cases. Besides, his strength is so overtaxed with care and overwork that he seemed sort of dazed the last time he was here and a little incoherent in his talk."[53] Immobilized by severe arthritis in her last few years, she died in 1924, proud of having outlived Lenin and leaving a still unappreciated legacy in her extensive correspondence on Russia and the United States.[54]

The Russian (Soviet) Information Bureau

A behind-the-scenes agent in arranging Stanislavsky's Washington appearance at the White House was Boris Skvirsky, the representative of the short-lived Far Eastern Republic to the Washington Naval Conference in 1922 who had remained behind to establish what could best be described as "an office of Soviet facilitation" in the American capital. The Russian Information Bureau thus came into existence somewhat spontaneously as a propaganda instrument to be sure, but also to meet practical needs of both countries. Formed in September 1923, it published a biweekly newsletter, the *Russian Review*, the first issue appearing 15 September 1923. The bureau was belatedly given official Soviet status by a directive from the Commissariat of Foreign Affairs in October 1924, with firm instructions to Skvirsky to live in Washington but to visit New York at least once a month. One of the bureau's first tasks, assisted by Roman Veller, was to inaugurate a book

52. Ragozin had survived in part by translating materials into English for the Comintern, noting, "beggars cannot be choosers." Ragozin (Petrograd) to Margaret Reynolds (New York), 22 February 1922, box 9, Hapgood-Reynolds Papers, MD, LC. Several of her closest relatives had perished during the revolution and civil war.

53. Ragozin to Margaret Reynolds, 13 September 1923, ibid. She deserves her own biography, as it encompasses so much of Russian-American cultural relations.

54. For more details, see Saul, *Concord and Conflict: The United States and Russia, 1867–1914* (Lawrence: University Press of Kansas), 1996.

exchange with the Library of Congress, which placed information about the new Soviet regime on high priority. By the end of January 1925, Skvirsky had arranged from his headquarters at 2819 Connecticut Avenue to send twenty-one boxes of American books to Russia through an arrangement with the Library of Congress.[55] Independent of Skvirsky, and with the visits of Stanislavsky and Maykovsky especially, Soviet-American cultural exchanges had indeed taken off.

Skvirsky's bureau soon had a rival—or complement—in an information section of Amtorg in New York, founded in 1925 by Pavel Ziv, who reported that interest in the Soviet Union was enormous despite nonrecognition and negative press.[56] Both Skvirsky and Ziv opposed an attempt by ROSTA, the Soviet telegraph agency, to enter the scene. Veller headed a special mission to establish coordination between the two organizations under Olga Kameneva's cultural organization but stayed, to Skvirsky's regret, only a few months. He succeeded, however, in negotiating, in addition to another book exchange with the Library of Congress, a photographic exchange with the Wide World News Service, which would pay the bureau $10 for each photograph used.[57] By that time Skvirsky's Washington office was widely recognized as the unofficial Soviet embassy in the United States. If anyone wanted anything done that involved Soviet Russia, Skvirsky was the man, with direct contacts with Moscow officials, especially Maxim Litvinov, assistant commissar for foreign relations.

VOKS

Inspired by Lev Kamenev, Leon Trotsky, Karl Radek, Maxim Litvinov, and other "Westerners" in the Soviet leadership, a new independent agency was formed to spearhead and manage Soviet cultural relations with the outside world, meaning the West. The awkwardly named All-Russian Society for Cultural Relations with Foreign Countries, generally referred to by its Russian initials, VOKS, was headed by the outgoing, erudite Olga Kameneva, who was not only Kamenev's wife but also Trotsky's sister.[58] Adding to the organization's prestige was its headquarters in an art nouveau, turn-of-the-century home of a wealthy merchant,

---

55. Undated twelve-page report and Skvirsky to Olga Kameneva, 24 January 1925, d. 5, op. 3, f. 5283, GARF.

56. Ziv (New York) to Kameneva, 27 January 1925, ibid.

57. Skvirsky to Kameneva, 2 October 1925; and Howard Corbett (*New York Times*) to Veller, 8 January 1925, ibid.

58. Efforts to find personal archives of either Lev or Olga Kameneva in Russian archival collections failed, although Olga Kameneva deserves much more attention. Oddly, neither Trotsky, in *My Life*, nor his biographer, Isaac Deutscher, make any substantive references to Kameneva.

where foreign visitors could be received in style.[59] From the beginning, the focus of its international cultural relations was the United States, because of the particular Soviet interest in America (*amerikanizm*), and the intense official desire to obtain formal diplomatic recognition. In the meantime, it would facilitate all kinds of contacts and promote a favorable image of Soviet life in the United States through a variety of channels that included special exhibitions and the formation of American-Russian institutes in New York, Chicago, San Francisco, and Philadelphia.

As for many other Soviet government agencies, VOKS would have its disappointments. Kameneva's desire to tour the United States personally was denied by American rejection of her visa request. The VOKS *Bulletin* circulated in the United States was often too propagandistic and produced negative reactions. Kameneva, who knew English as well as French and German—ably assisted by general secretary Iosif Korinets—was disappointed herself in its regurgitation of simplistic views of Soviet society.[60] Above all, VOKS relied on overworked Soviet agents in the United States, such as Skvirsky, who had many other duties and who were quite cautious in implementing VOKS's ambitious projects.[61] Many of its communications were awkward and unorganized; Scott Nearing sent Kameneva a hand-written note advising that Socialist Party leader Norman Thomas be put on the mailing list for the *Bulletin*, which she then relayed to Skvirsky in Washington a month later.[62] Considering all the other higher priorities of the Soviet government, VOKS ultimately had limited clout, such as its feeble inability to respond to a request for a loan of the panels of artist Marc Chagall from the Jewish Theater in Moscow for a special Chagall exhibition at the Chicago Art Institute.[63]

VOKS was also pestered by a variety of demands from Americans who learned about it through the *Bulletin* or from other sources. In fact, it was taxed beyond its abilities by requests from universities, societies, and individuals. Among the most prominent were the Library of Congress and the Smithsonian Institution and the Hoover Institution at Stanford; though diplomatic relations between the two countries formally did not exist, cultural contacts certainly did. They also included requests from the Workers' [Communist] Party of America, such as one

59. The building was later granted to Maxim Gorky as a town residence shortly before his death and remains well preserved as the Gorky Museum.

60. Junius Wood to Kameneva, 13 April 1926, d. 22, op. 3, t. 5283, GARF.

61. See, for example, Skvirsky to Kameneva, 3 April 1925, d. 5, op. 3, f. 5283, GARF.

62. Nearing to Kameneva, 24 November 1925, and Kameneva to Skvirsky, 2 December 1925, ibid.

63. Christian Brinton to Lipa Niman (VOKS), 15 September 1925, and Kameneva to Brinton, 26 October 1925, ibid.

from a Kansas City worker for admission of his teenage daughter into a Russian university.[64] VOKS also did double duty by explaining American culture to the Soviet audience, a somewhat dangerous pursuit even in the 1920s. Roman Veller, for example, spent much of his brief sojourn in the United States gathering material for a brochure on American folklore.[65] Other diversions arose. Kameneva was at something of a loss as to how to respond to the request of Ernestine Evans and Jessica Smith to stage an exhibit of "working clothes" in Russia.[66] And about the same time dentist Herman Chaynes, noted for his innovations in bridgework, wanted to visit Soviet dental schools, with resulting confusion on what exactly "bridge construction" meant.[67] Fortunately, the Soviet agency responded to the needs of individual American scholars such as John Hazard, Geroid Robinson, and Jesse Clarkson by providing introductions, access to archives, and assistance in securing decent living quarters.[68]

As the number of Americans interested in visiting the Soviet Union rose substantially in the mid and late 1920s, VOKS was simply stretched beyond its capacity to provide service as an information bureau, a promoter of cultural relations abroad, and a tourist bureau that tended to American needs in Russia. The latter absorbed much of its energy, arranging hotels, meals, transportation, guides, and so forth, for various groups and individuals, until at least partially relieved by the formation of Intourist in 1929. Book exchanges on behalf of universities and individual scholars also tied up much time and effort.[69] Once the word was out that there was a welcome entrée to Soviet institutions, many more requests rolled in from universities, scholars, and government institutions such as the Smithsonian. At least there was some monetary reward for these services. VOKS, it could be argued, opened the door to Russia wider than at any time under the tsarist regime. Edward Newman, for example, was one of several to scope Russia with a motion picture camera, with VOKS intervening in several local arrests. He reported his goal as removing ignorance about Soviet Russia: "I hope to show Americans that they are wrong in many respects, perhaps they will have a kindlier feeling after they see my pictures."[70]

Another venture on the irregular plane of Soviet-American cultural relations

64. J. E. Snyder to VOKS, 9 June 1925, d. 6, op. 3, f. 5283, GARF.

65. Kate Conley (Library of Congress) to Vetter, 19 March 1925, ibid.

66. Kameneva to Evans, 25 November 1925, ibid. Smith was the wife of the organizer of the American farm in the Caucasus.

67. Chaynes to Kameneva, 12 August 1925, ibid.

68. See, for example, Matthew Spinka (Chicago Theological Seminary) to VOKS, 12 November 1926, d. 35, and Robinson to VOKS, 14 February 1927, d. 39, op. 5, f. 5283, GARF.

69. Jesse Clarkson to Veller, 12 December 1925, d. 24, op. 3, f. 5283, GARF.

70. Newman to Trevis, 3 September 1926, d. 42, op. 3, f. 5283, GARF.

was due to the initiative of Sherwood Eddy, a strong supporter of closer relations and a veteran secretary of the Young Men's Christian Association, having since 1895 a long involvement in Russia. With a sizable independent income, he had established a record as a dedicated missionary, mainly to India, and as an excellent speaker on behalf of the organization. In 1926 he launched a study seminar to Russia that recruited several university and college faculty and businessmen to tour the new Russia with the cooperation and support of VOKS and with much advance publicity.[71] Although this first organized American invasion of the new Russia was a clear triumph for mutual understanding, by all accounts it was considered simply of propaganda value by the Soviet hosts and the American government.

Eddy wisely sought a cross section of prominent Americans to join his tour, for example, William Allen White of the *Emporia Gazette*, who demurred because of his wife's health, and Walter Lippmann.[72] Perhaps the most prominent and influential member of the group was William Danforth, a Missouri businessman (Ralston Purina), who became a convert to closer Soviet-American relations. Following up his visit by sending samples of seed corn, Danforth wrote, "I am exceedingly anxious to keep my promise because I very much want to aid Russia as far as I possibly can."[73] On his part, Eddy supported the cause of recognition of the Soviet government when it was not yet respectable to do so and used the tour to recruit others to that cause. Thus, upon return he secured a unanimous vote by members of the seminar for recognition and relayed this publicly to President Coolidge. It only had the effect, however, of reconfirming government policy.[74]

The Eddy tours for several successive years were also a magnet for attacks from anti-Bolshevik circles, which only tended to polarize American opinion on Russia. Eddy's cause was certainly not helped by the Soviet expulsion in 1926 of the last YMCA secretary, H. D. Anderson, from Russia.[75] The favorable re-

71. Eddy even warned Herbert Hoover of his venture. Eddy to Hoover, 10 May 1926, f. Sherwood Eddy, box 188, Commerce, HHPL.

72. Eddy to Lippmann, 12 January 1926, f. Sherwood Eddy, box 7, Lippmann Papers, Yale.

73. Danforth to VOKS, 24 December 1926, d. 39, op. 3, f. 5283, GARF. He repeated this even more strongly in his published letters about the trip. "I believe as a Christian nation, it is our moral duty to recognize Russia. . . . Today Russia is looking to America for ideas and standards." *Russia under the Hammer and Sickle: Impressions Written to the Purina Family* (St. Louis, Mo.: Ralston Purina, 1927), 145.

74. "Favor Recognition of the Soviet by U.S.," *NYT*, 13 September 1926: 31. He reported personally to President Coolidge that the group unanimously supported recognition. "Coolidge Is Firm on Soviet Policy," *NYT*, 27 September 1926: 25. Eddy, however, made the mistake of trying to intrude his views into a labor meeting in Detroit and was roundly denounced. "Labor Chiefs Plan to Unionize Men in Auto Industry," *NYT*, 8 October 1926: 1.

75. Copy of "They're after Eddy Again," in d. 27, op. 3, f. 5283, GARF; "Soviet Expels Last Y.M.C.A. Man from Russia Ending Social Work," *NYT*, 22 October 1926: 8; Anderson report to East

sponse to the Eddy seminar, nevertheless, prompted plans for another in 1927 that met with similar success, especially in contrast with one organized by the Communist Workers' Party. [76] By 1928, the "Open Road" production joined the educational tour circuit, emphasizing the participation of young people, a few of whom reported to army military intelligence on their experiences.[77] Frank Golder also came in 1927 to negotiate book transfers on behalf of the Hoover Institution. Exchanges—of a sort and mainly one way—were off but still slowly running. Of special interest was the formation of a committee, headed by Mark Van Doren of Columbia University, to select American books for translation into Russian.[78]

Though the YMCA was excluded from Russia and the official Orthodox Church was under much pressure and actual oppression, the 1920s was a period of unusual freedom of religion in Russia, especially for sects and denominations previously excluded. One of Eddy's missions on his tours was to engage Soviet authorities and audiences in discussion of religious matters. His success during the first visit in achieving an open forum was a triumph that revealed the degree of apparent freedom on religious issues, encouraged missionaries of various sorts, and seemed to demonstrate the openness of authorities. This certainly helped in the recruitment of prominent clergymen to his subsequent tours.

Torn in different, and perhaps too many, directions, short of funds, and losing a power struggle with Amtorg, the new heavyweight on the Soviet-American block, VOKS, recorded its first clear failure by not participating in the sesquicentennial of the American revolution in Philadelphia, despite belated clearance achieved by Governor James Goodrich; nor did it dare accept Scott Nearing's offer of organizing an American branch of VOKS.[79] Skvirsky strongly opposed Nearing's plan, which would include Workers' Party members but supported a proposal of Stanford professor Frank Golder for a separate organization that

---

European Division, 1926, f. Visitors, box 5, East European Division, RG 59, NA. Anderson escorted his family out of Russia, and then was denied a visa to return, despite appeals to Litvinov and Kameneva. It is, in fact, remarkable that the YMCA mission existed well into 1926.

76. J. Louis Engdahl (editor of *Daily Worker*) to Korinets, 25 July 1927, d. 39, op. 3, f. 5283, GARF.

77. See, for example, report of Henry H. Pierce Jr., 29 October 1928, f. 2070–2272, roll 7 (M 1443), RG 165, NA.

78. Van Doren to Kameneva, 20 April 1927, d. 34, op. 3, f. 5283, GARF.

79. Goodrich to Kameneva, 30 November 1925 and Kameneva to Goodrich, 8 December 1925; Kameneva to Skvirsky, 8 February 1926, and Skvirsky to Kameneva, 13 March 1926, d. 22, op. 3, f. 5283, GARF. Goodrich consulted Robert Kelley in the State Department and Herbert Hoover about the lack of invitation to participate; both agreed that an invitation could be issued to VOKS rather than the Soviet government. Goodrich to Kameneva, 23 November 1925, ibid.

would focus on cultural exchange.[80] The number of demands from various American individuals and organizations was almost beyond its capacity. The open and intellectual leadership passed, beginning in 1929 with the ouster of Kameneva and her replacement by an assortment of serious but guarded officials, from Sergei Trevis (1929), a Kameneva protégé, to Daniel Novomirsky and Ivan Petrov (1930), and then to Amdur and Hyman Rovner (1932), all short-timers of limited influence, leaving the agency in disarray and with little trace of its original creative and positive drive by 1933.[81]

Cultural relations between the two countries suffered considerably as a consequence of the eclipse of VOKS. They gradually became a subsidiary of Amtorg's business agenda—and that of the crassly commercial Intourist—not to be fully revived as more or less independent until the Khrushchev-Eisenhower cultural exchanges of the late 1950s. Skvirsky certainly did yeoman duty as a representative of VOKS in the United States in addition to his other duties, and certainly Olga Kameneva deserves an accolade as one of leading Soviet officials who espoused the best hope of a humanist Leninism by promoting genuine and expanded cultural exchanges between East and West. Because of the extraordinary increase in cultural exchanges, VOKS was overwhelmed and its capacity strained. Left vulnerable, much of its early domination of cultural relations in the 1920s passed to other Soviet agencies, such as Sovfilm, and to the newly created Intourist to handle ordinary tourists, creating considerable initial confusion on both sides.[82]

Still, VOKS in the late 1920s was clearly mustering on, handling mainly academic groups and individual and institutional professional exchanges by the early 1930s, such as an extensive printed material transfer initiated by Frank Golder and completed by Harold Fisher for the Hoover Institution.[83] Relinquishing its

80. Skvirsky to Kameneva, 24 March 1926, Kameneva to Skvirsky, 21 April 1926, and Golder to Kameneva, 14 April 1926, ibid.

81. "Illness" seemed to be contagious in the ranks of VOKS. In quick succession, Novomirsky, who became head of the Anglo-American Section in January 1930, reported Petrov to be ill and then Amdur wrote that Novomirsky had resigned on account of health. Novomirsky to Clark, 30 January 1930, d. 109, ibid; and Novomirsky to Harold Fisher, 6 March 1931, and Amdur to Ralph Reynolds, 30 June 1931, d. 171, ibid.

82. Frank Fay to Kameneva, 16 September 1927, op. 3, d. 42, f. 5283, GARF. My efforts to find personal papers of this unsung Soviet heroine in the party archive netted a slim folder of inconsequential trivia. Kameneva certainly deserves more attention than has been accorded her in both Russian and Western revisionism.

83. Fisher to Skvirsky, 26 June 1931, d. 171, ibid. The last communications of Olga Kameneva on behalf of VOKS seem to have involved this exchange in 1929. "Spravka o russko-amerikanskom institute po izucheniiu russkoi revoliutsii pri stenfordskom universitete," *Sovetsko-amerikanskie otnosheniia, gody nepriznaniia, 1927–1933,* edited by G. N. Sevost'ianov et al. (Moscow: Fond "Demokratiia," 2002), 195–200.

original palatial headquarters to accommodate the glorified return of Maxim Gorky, VOKS still had a more modest presence on Trubnikovskii Pereulok, where Novomirsky and office manager Helen Schossberg valiantly continued its mission by fostering exchanges and maintaining contact with the American institutes.[84] But many prospective exchanges and exhibits were canceled for lack of funds and initiative.[85] In the new Stalin regime, cultural interchange was lower priority.

The American Societies for Cultural Relations with Russia

In the meantime, in New York the American Society for Cultural Relations with Russia was organized by Lucy Branham, Graham Taylor, Jerome Davis, and artist Boardman Robinson (who had accompanied John Reed on his first visit to Russia in 1915); Davis, Leopold Stokowski, and John Dewey served as honorary vice presidents. It was essentially a new cultural arm of the American Russian Chamber of Commerce, with its Moscow agent, Charles H. Smith, serving as initial liaison with VOKS.[86] Elizabeth Hapgood presided over the first meeting, held at the Henry Street Settlement House in April 1927. Stokowski spoke on Russian music, and a broad-based advisory board was created that included Robinson, Jane Addams, William Allen White, and Mrs. J. Borden Harriman.[87] All of its leaders were relatively affluent and generally respected, and represented the liberal social causes of mainstream America. Skvirsky, however, was suspicious of its value: "As you know, liberals here are uneven, cautious, and tempering."[88] In any event, VOKS quickly took advantage of this American opportunity, at first soliciting their assistance in organizing an exhibit of Soviet art and literature.[89] Expanded to include handicrafts, theater, science, and industry, the exhibition was opened at the end of January 1928 by Elizabeth Hapgood. She suffered some embarrassment, however, from the difficulty of interpreting the technical Russian of Leon Theremin, a Russian innovator—and one of the first—in electronic music. The event also featured a reception, with comments by socialist Albert

---

84. Fisher to Schossberg, 19 November 1931, d. 171, ibid. Somewhat ironically, considering its founder and its later conservatism, the Hoover Institution was probably the most active in its correspondence and exchanges through VOKS. Both Golder and Fisher were strong advocates of diplomatic recognition in the late 1920s.

85. Clark to Schossberg, 16 September 1931, d. 180, ibid.

86. Smith to Kameneva, 2 March 1927, and Kameneva to Smith, 14 March 1927, d. 34, ibid.

87. "New Society Formed to Interpret Russia," *NYT*, 24 April 1927: 4; Norman Hapgood to Elizabeth Hapgood, 31 July 1927, f. July–Aug. 1927, box 23, Hapgood-Reynolds Papers, MD, LC.

88. Skvirsky to Kameneva, 11 July 1927, d. 34, op. 3, f. 5238, GARF.

89. Korinets to Branham, 31 July 1927, ibid.

Rhys Williams and by budding historian Geroid Robinson, recently back from research in Russia.[90]

During the summer of 1928 Branham herself led a tour of the Soviet Union for the Society with the full cooperation of VOKS and with much press acclaim.[91] The group, organized by Professor K. E. Richter of City College of New York, included a range of university and college presidents and faculty from CCNY, University of Minnesota, Carleton, Amherst, Columbia University, Vassar, and other schools. Perhaps the most illustrious member of the group was John Dewey, making a return trip to Soviet Russia.[92] VOKS leaders were annoyed, however, about Armand Hammer's intervening to offer quarters for the group at his Moscow palace.[93] Dewey, for one, was quite pleased with what he saw: "Speaking for myself I may say that I regard it as one of the wonders of the world that so much has been done in so short a time and against such obstacles."[94] The tour's success was celebrated, subsequently, by a grand reunion at the Astor Hotel in New York on 10 November with 550 present, according to Skvirsky.[95]

The tour was also significant for the future of American music, because of Dewey's contact with Joseph Schillinger, a Leningrad musician and composer in the vanguard of the Jazz Age, who offered to bring a special collection of new and old Russian music to the United States. The result was the cataloguing of more than 400 manuscripts for a new library of Russian music at the society's New York headquarters on East 55th Street during the winter of 1929 that would have, indirectly, a major impact on the American musical world.[96] Schillinger, then in his early thirties, would remain in the United States to be credited with many contributions, including the first American performance later that year of his electronic "Airphonic Suite," on an instrument created by Radio Corporation of America on the directions of Theremin, another recent immigrant from Russia, and accompanied by the Cleveland Symphony Orchestra.[97] Schillinger would be better known for his close collaboration with George Gershwin on the score

90. Elizabeth Hapgood to Norman Hapgood, 30 January 1928, f. Jan.–May 1928, box 23, Hapgood-Reynolds Papers, MD, LC.

91. Kameneva to Korinets, 29 October 1927, ibid.

92. "Educators to Vote on a Soviet Report," *NYT*, 21 June 1928: 8.

93. Skvirsky to Kameneva, 4 March 1928, and Branham to Kameneva, 16 May 1928, d. 52, op. 3, f. 5283, GARF.

94. Dewey to Lunacharsky, 26 July 1928, ibid.

95. Skvirsky to Kameneva, 20 November 1928, ibid.

96. "City to Get Library of Russian Music," *NYT*, 27 January 1929: E7; "Arranges Russian Music," *NYT*, 2 March 1929: 21. According to the initial report, the library included twenty-eight new symphonies, many folk songs, and "even a lullaby about Lenin." *NYT*, 27 January 1929: E7.

97. *NYT*, 17 November 1929: X11.

for *Porgy and Bess,* and for Glen Miller's "Moonlight Serenade," a variation on a Schillinger composition.[98]

The American-Russian interaction on jazz motifs is an interesting result of cultural exchange, culminating in Russia with the ballet of Dmitri Shostakovich, *Golden Age* (1931), and later the big band era of Alexander Tsfasman and Eddie Rosner, "the Louis Armstrong of Russia."[99] Ironically, Stalin liked jazz, Hitler definitely did not, and Franklin Roosevelt was neutral. Many American visitors were pleasantly surprised by evening entertainments in Soviet land. Negley Farson, generally negative about the Russia of 1930, found the roof garden of the old Europe Hotel in Leningrad an oasis of swing. And at the London Hotel restaurant in Odessa, he was entranced by an excellent Russian rendition of "Yes Sir, That's My Baby."[100]

By the late 1920s, the United States was deluged with actual and proposed exhibitions of Russian culture. One of the most ambitious was that of artistic promoter Christian Brinton, who visited Russia in 1925 and again in 1928, and found it "the most progressive and inspiring country."[101] His plan involved a traveling exhibit of 150 to 200 icons, 100 to 175 contemporary paintings since 1910, and an assortment of decorative arts and crafts.[102] Separately, he accumulated a large personal collection of Russian art on display to many invited guests at his residence in Westchester, New York. The National Gallery of Art in Washington, the Art Institute in Chicago, and icon expert Frank Jewitt Mather of Princeton agreed to sponsor Brinton's special exhibit, but it was apparently beyond the scope or ability of VOKS to mount. Cultural relations had its definite limitations, including its promoters on both sides. Perhaps because of this, Lucy Branham was deemed unequal to the expansion and multidimensional communications and was replaced in 1930 by Elizabeth Clark. Skvirsky thought that the whole American operation, like VOKS, was in disarray, unable to cope with the increased Soviet-American cultural traffic.

98. S. Frederick Starr, *Red and Hot: The Fate of Jazz in the Soviet Union, 1917–1980* (New York: Oxford University Press, 1983): 74–75.

99. Rosner was born in Poland and received his musical education in Berlin in the 1920s and was soon recognized as a leading European jazz musician. Back in Warsaw at the time of the German invasion, he escaped east into Soviet territory and soon found himself as a leader of a big Soviet jazz band, becoming the Glenn Miller of Russia by performing behind the front lines of the war; he was singled out for a command performance for Stalin in 1942. "Jazzman from the Gulag," videotape on Rosner, 2001.

100. Farson, *Black Bread and Red Coffins* (New York: Century, 1930), 50, 111. The elevator boy at the Hotel Europe was from Seattle, but nevertheless "watched the parade of a million bedbugs, lice, and cockroaches" in his room. Ibid., 128. He also noted that "when democracy was introduced into Russia it destroyed all the toilets." Ibid., 204.

101. Brinton to Kameneva, 1 May 1928, d. 52, op. 3, f. 5283, GARF.

102. Brinton to Kameneva, 5 September 1928, d. 50, ibid.

A similar, overlapping group with the Society for Cultural Relations sponsored a Russian Bazaar in 1929 that featured arts and crafts of various regions of the Soviet Union, especially of Ukraine and the Caucasus, at a swank address on West 57th Street. Proceeds supported the Paxton Hibben Memorial Hospital Fund for a Crimean treatment center for children with tuberculosis of the bone; Boardman Robinson served as treasurer.[103] Kameneva informed Skvirsky that VOKS should not be directly affiliated with these American sympathizers for good Russian causes but would welcome this and any new organizations' cooperation. Underneath all of these surfaces was a commitment by a substantial portion of the artistic, intellectual American elite to the Soviet program of achieving American recognition, despite disagreement on direction. Perhaps the most challenging new ventures—and successes—involved student exchanges with universities and various cultural organizations, including the Moscow Art Theater.

The American Russian society also faced new challenges with success and the changing times of depression. Two new branches opened in Chicago and Philadelphia in the spring of 1929 but remained somewhat moribund. Stokowski was chosen president in Philadelphia but had little time to devote to it. Skvirsky, obviously struggling with all of these eccentric American entities, saw the replacement of Branham by Elizabeth Clark in New York as a positive move and advised an increase in circulation of publications and films by VOKS, because "she is a serious person."[104] The Chicago affiliate was headed by Jane Addams, Clarence Darrow, Paul Douglas, and historian Charles Merriam of the University of Chicago, but the real impetus of operations and chief motivator was Agnes Jacques, a former Russian language student of Samuel Harper. According to Clark, in New York the chief difficulty everywhere involved inexperience in fund-raising. She noted that her staff had been reduced from six to two and that Branham had taken a long holiday and is "tired and miserable."[105]

Jacques, however, returned from a tour of Russia somewhat disheartened: "I have come back from Russia, most decidedly 'bourgeois' and a great American patriot. This surprises me more than anyone. The reason, of course, is my ability to speak Russian, which enabled me to go off the beaten Soviet path and conduct little investigations of my own. I don't think I made a good impression on the government."[106] Leaping to that challenge, Clark joined an "Open Road" tour

<hr>

103. "Russian Bazaar to Be Permanent," NYT, 20 January 1930: 24. Robinson was at the height of his artistic success with a large mural placed prominently in the new Radio City Music Hall.

104. By May the Philadelphia membership was up to 106 and the Chicago affiliate was "remarkably active." Skvirsky to Kameneva, 29 April and 18 May 1929, d. 61, op. 3, f. 5283, GARF.

105. Clark to Kameneva, 10 May 1929, ibid.

106. Jacques to Harper, 28 September 1928, f. 31, box 13, Harper Papers, UC-R.

of Russia that summer (1929) that reinvigorated her support of Russia: "I am going back [to the United States] with great admiration and faith in Russia."[107] Following several miscommunications and accusations between VOKS and the American New York society, Clark wrote to Skvirsky to complain about the cost of a large luncheon hosted by the society for cinematographer Sergei Eisenstein during the summer of 1930, admitting, "Of course we have been a feeble reed, and though we shall grow in size and strength, the loads we carry must not increase too fast or we will perish again."[108] The Depression would revive its energies to some extent.

In Chicago, however, the institute seemed to be gaining momentum in 1932, thanks to Jacques's initiative but even more to the Depression and more favorable view of a fully employed Soviet Russia. Jesmer claimed that the society "has done more important work, of greater magnitude, and of greater effect, immediate and potential" than ever before. He also advised that he was shutting down all exhibits "as they are never a source of income."[109] Meanwhile, Skvirsky thought that the Philadelphia branch seemed to be more interested in securing travel expenses from VOKS than in pursuing any kind of Soviet agenda. He saw promise in a current reorganization but felt that the Chicago society "exists but is irregular without a paid secretary," going out of his way to maintain communications and paying regular visits, which he felt were not reciprocated.[110] A notable success in New York was an exhibit of Margaret Bourke-White's photographs, "Eyes on Russia," during the winter of 1930–1931. By all accounts it brought the Five Year Plan's construction theme to New York.[111] At about the same time, a modest exhibit of Russian icons, less ambitious than the initial program of Brinton's, at the Chicago Art Institute attracted much favorable attention.[112]

Though VOKS by 1930 was in decline and disarray and its American extensions were also in difficulty because of the Depression, cultural exchanges still expanded in prestige and presence. One bright spot was the organization of a San Francisco branch that launched a successful icon exhibit at the de Young Museum during the summer and fall of 1931. This San Francisco Bureau for Cultural and Economic Relations between the United States and Russia was fortunately boosted by several respected academics: George Day of Occidental College, Harold Fisher of Stanford, and Alexander Kaun of University of California,

107. Clark (Kiev) to F. N. Petrov, 29 August 1929, ibid.

108. Skvirsky to Petrov, 17 June 1930 and Clark to Skvirsky, 11 June 1930, d. 110, ibid. From the context, she was really vexed that VOKS did not pay her way for a visit to Russia.

109. Jesmer to Skvirsky, 6 October 1932, ibid.

110. Skvirsky to Petrov, 17 June 1930, ibid., and to Minlos, 24 December 1930, d. 173, ibid.

111. Clark to Amder, 10 and 16 December 1931, ibid.

112. Jesmer to Clark, 16 October 1931, ibid.

Berkeley.[113] Dr. Ralph Reynolds of San Francisco was an activist president, but he had a large practice, and, as in other places, the real leader was the executive secretary, Rose Isaak. She was the one who actually launched the organization with a talk by Ella Winter that drew a crowd of more than 175 but admitted that "we are getting a few new members but getting money is difficult."[114] The San Francisco institute definitely had the advantage of proximity to Stanford, the Hoover Institution, and the University of California at Berkeley, the only West Coast centers of Russian studies at the time.

Another, fifth American Russian society was organized in Los Angeles under the leadership of J. E. Snyder in 1932, but it found getting off the ground difficult allegedly because of the more hostile atmosphere in that citadel of the new America. Skvirsky thought, however, that VOKS had made a mistake in approving Snyder as director, and an overly energetic secretary, Mary Coleman, was also deemed inadequate, despite her effort to recruit Upton Sinclair. Because of the emerging importance of Hollywood, Skvirsky planned to devote a month there to getting the organization going.[115] Apparently, one of Snyder's motivations in becoming involved was that his daughter had become an assistant to Anna Louise Strong in editing the *Moscow Daily News*.[116]

In San Francisco Isaak was more successful in receiving regular shipments of literature, such as the published speeches of Stalin and the *Moscow Daily News* from Amdur, who hoped to arrange an exchange of publications, since VOKS could no longer afford to subscribe to leading American newspapers.[117] She also staged a highly successful dinner celebrating the fifteenth anniversary of the Bolsheviks' coming to power, claiming 347 in attendance and many turned away. "The audience was most sympathetic in its response to all that was said." VOKS was obviously pleased, judging by Hyman Rovner's request for more in-

113. Reynolds to Skvirsky, 27 April 1931, and Skvirsky to Daniel Novomirsky, 5 May 1931, d. 180, ibid. Dr. Reynolds demonstrated his expertise on health care in the Soviet Union with articles in *Atlantic Monthly*, *Nation*, *Reader's Digest*, and the *American Journal of Public Health*.

114. Isaak to Skvirsky, 13 October 1932, d. 382, ibid. Isaak's appreciation of two postal money orders from Skvirsky is at least one clear piece of evidence of direct Soviet monetary support for these sympathetic cultural societies. "That permits us a clean slate and I'm glad to start that way." Isaak to Skvirsky, 13 September 1932, d. 389, ibid. Winter was a maverick member of the British Labor Party who had been to Russia in 1930.

115. Skvirsky to Petrov, 2 September 1932, d. 385, ibid.

116. Snyder to Skvirsky, 29 November 1930, d. 173, ibid. He claimed also to be developing contacts in Carmel, Santa Cruz, and Palo Alto, nice places to visit. To Novomirsky, ibid.,

117. Isaak to Amdur, 20 February 1933, and Amdur to Isaak, 16 April 1933, d. 382, op. 3, f. 5283, GARF.

formation on the speeches that were delivered on the occasion.[118] The New York American-Russian society discussed having a similar celebration, but one of its old stalwarts, Graham Taylor, advised against it as being too political, especially in the week of a major national election.[119] The New York society rode the wave toward recognition in 1933, reaching a record of more than a thousand members and sponsoring talks by Anna Louise Strong, Maurice Hindus, and Julian Bryan, a well-known veteran producer of travelogues.[120]

On the other hand, one clear sign of the decline of VOKS was its failure to secure a tour by the Philadelphia Orchestra of Russia, in spite of Stokowski's visit to Moscow in late 1931 and his proposal to bring it with the support of American cultural branches and Skvirsky's offer to pay travel expenses. Clark stressed that this would only be an extension of a European tour: "The publicity given to it [in the United States] would be enormous,"[121] but to no avail; VOKS was now without Kameneva and on a very limited budget, and the orchestra, like others, was suffering financial woes from the Depression.[122]

One matter that had been raised frequently in correspondence between VOKS and the American societies and with Skvirsky was a system of student exchanges. Many American students had voiced interest in the prospect, and a few had managed to attend Soviet universities on their own. Even with relations much improved and seemingly headed toward recognition in early 1933, VOKS regretfully declined to participate, clearly on instructions from above. "With regards to the question of American students receiving a course of instruction in our higher educational institutions, it has been thought best, for the time being, not to carry this project through, owing to the lack of accommodations and other reasons.

118. Isaak to Skvirsky, 15 November 1932, and Rovner to Isaak, 29 December 1932, ibid. Notes on the meeting, apparently those requested by Rovner, showed that the main speakers included president Dr. Reynolds, Albert Rhys Williams, Robert Kerner (UC-Berkeley), Harold Fisher (Stanford,) and William Thornton Brown. Notes on 15th Anniversary Dinner, 7 November 1932, d. 389, ibid.

119. Taylor to Skvirsky, 3 November 1932, d. 387, ibid.

120. Beatrice Heiman (Skvirsky's secretary) to E. O. Lerner (Moscow), 29 December 1933, d. 385, ibid. Heiman relieved Skvirsky of much of the correspondence dealing with cultural organizations during the 1931–1933 period leading up to recognition. She would then be the primary secretary for the Soviet ambassador and a woman to be reckoned with.

121. Clark to Bogdanov (Amtorg), 24 March 1931, and Skvirsky to Novomirsky (VOKS), 6 April 1931, d. 180, ibid. Stokowski came to the United States well before the Russian Revolution and became director of the Philadelphia Orchestra in 1913. He, however, constantly emphasized Russian music. An April 1930 concert in New York was all Russian: Glinka, Rimsky-Korsakov, Mussorgsky, Prokofiev, and even Krehn's "Ode to Lenin." "Gives New Russian Music," *NYT*, 5 April 1930: 24.

122. Stokowski to Skvirsky, 18 February 1933, d. 380 (Stokowski), op. 3, f. 5283, GARF. Stokowski had visited Russia in 1931 and, based on conversations, VOKS expected the Philadelphia Orchestra to come, which would have been quite a coup. Bogomazov to Skvirsky, 2 June 1931, d. 170, ibid.

However, we shall raise the matter again with the pertinent organizations at the first opportunity."[123] That opportunity would finally come twenty-five years later with the Eisenhower-Khrushchev agreements of the 1950s.

VOKS clearly faced multiple challenges in hosting a growing number of American delegations to the Soviet Union, the cultivation of American journalists in Moscow, beginning with a positive response to the approach of Junius Wood of the *Chicago Tribune*, who was sympathetic to the cultural exchange programs, despite his newspaper's general anti-Soviet stance.[124] Several special correspondents, such as Jessica Lloyd of the *New York Times*, H. V. Kaltenborn of the *Brooklyn Eagle*, who toured Russia in August 1926 and again in 1929, and Helen Bennett of *McCall's Magazine* in 1930 were grateful for VOKS's guidance.[125] Kameneva, the guiding light of VOKS, however, left the scene in 1929, a victim of the ascendancy of Stalin and her close connections with his chief rivals, Trotsky and Kamenev. Her brief replacement, Petrov, assured Skvirsky of his plans for expansion, providing more assistance to American groups, and to be more systematic and orderly (that is, Stalinist).[126] Several hurried arrangements for Russians to scramble on board the Soviet-American cultural express resulted, especially one involving Sergei Radomsky, which led to embarrassing losses of money.[127] VOKS never recovered from Kameneva's departure, going through a series of mediocre directors and shortages of funds, and in 1931 many contacts with the United States were shifted to a subsidiary, the Anglo-American Center.[128]

Mayakovsky!

Fortunately for the reputation of Soviet arts and letters, Sergei Esenin was not the only representative of the new literary age of the Russian revolution to come to the United States. Besides Stanislavsky and the Moscow Art Theater, a few other Soviet writers, poets, and performing artists visited the United States, though it is true that many were in limbo, not knowing whether to stay in Russia or go abroad—some simply seeking livelihood, while others had a political agenda—seeking support for an alternative to bolshevism. One exception was a dedicated Communist and futurist poet with his own agenda, preceded by advance billing, not by VOKS, but by the Comintern through its newspapers sponsored in the United States.

123. Rovner to Heiman, 23 February 1933, d. 385, ibid.
124. Wood to Kameneva, 19 April 1926, d. 27, op. 3, f. 5283, GARF.
125. Bennett to VOKS, 10 November 1930, d. 109, ibid.
126. Petrov to Skvirsky, 1 October 1929, d. 61, ibid.
127. Skvirsky to S. M. Bogomazov, 29 October 1930, d. 107, ibid.
128. Amdur to Clark, 9 October 1931, d. 180, ibid.

Vladimir Mayakovsky, the poet laureate of the Bolshevik Revolution, first thought of visiting the United States at the end of 1922, when he was then in Paris. He was attracted not by a desire to see the leaders of American politics and culture but rather to observe the leading manifestations of industrialization. The next year, Mayakovsky planned an around-the-world tour but had trouble obtaining a visa for the United States.[129] He came to the United States, mostly on his own initiative, having a substantial bank account of his own—but with VOKS paving the way with advance publicity.[130] He traveled to New York the hard way, sailing from France after a tour of Southern Europe by way of Havana and Mexico City, where he attained a visa (at an exorbitant price), then crossing the border at Laredo and traveling by train straight through St. Louis and Chicago to New York.[131] He was amazed by the speed of transit along the Hudson, the shift to electric power for the entry into New York City, and his arrival at a bustling Grand Central Station, on the evening of 30 July.[132] He went directly to 3 Fifth Avenue where he lodged with Isai Khurgin, director of Amtorg.

Like many other visitors, Mayakovsky was especially impressed by the height of buildings (the Woolworth Tower being the tallest), elevated railways, automats, double-decker buses, "two-pound" Sunday papers, Coney Island, and, above all, "the great white way," the bright lights of Broadway at night. Throughout most of the sightseeing, which he delighted in, he was escorted by a friend, writer, and admirer, David Burliuk, who was familiar with the city.[133] As expected, he saw New York through Bolshevik lenses: the wide gulf between rich and poor, crass materialism, unemployment, racial and immigrant discrimination. Though impressed and supportive of "the industrialization of art," he was not pleased with the result of a homogenized, low-quality, superficial art for the masses. Rather than uplifting, it was downcasting.[134]

At his first performance at the Central Opera House on 14 August, he was typically impressive, living up to his reputation—in size, dress, and demeanor—in delivering an emphatic, stylized Russian monologue before an audience of 2,000. Besides reciting his own poetry, Mayakovsky presented a report on art, theater,

129. Semen Nemrad, *Maiakovskii v Amerike: stranitsy biografii* (Moscow: Sovetskii pisatel', 1970), 17–21.

130. Kameneva to Skvirsky, 31 October 1925, d. 8, op. 3, f. 5283, GARF.

131. Mayakovsky described his impressions of the United States in various articles for Russian newspapers and magazines, assembled later as "My Discovery of America." For an excellent translation, see Hasty and Fusso, *America through Russian Eyes*, 161–209.

132. *Russkii Golos*, 31 July 1925.

133. Hasty and Fusso, *America through Russian Eyes*, 170–75.

134. Nemrad, *Maiakovskii*, 106–10.

and poetry in the USSR.[135] He was then feted by a dinner in his honor by the staff of *New Masses* in Greenwich Village. He found in New York, however, too many middlemen gouging the public and too little courtesy toward women.[136] He remained, however, perplexed and amazed at American progress and ingenuity, as recorded earlier in his "150,000,000." His New York stay was interrupted by the accidental drowning of his host, Khurgin, on 27 August, and he, consequently, felt an obligation to preside at the funeral of his recent acquaintance.[137]

By popular demand, Mayakovsky presented a second lecture and recital of his poetry at the Central Opera House on 10 September to the expected rave reviews from the local Russian press.[138] A few days later he was called on to recite a poem at a grand concert on Coney Island. After a month in New York, Mayakovsky set off on an American four-city tour, performing in each: Cleveland, 29 September; Detroit, 30 September (to do "his honors to Ford"); Chicago, 2 October. His appearance at Temple Hall in Chicago before an overflowing crowd of more than 3,000 was boisterous and full of applause as befitting an audience mainly of American proletariat assembled by the *Daily Worker*. In the meantime, New York was inspiring some of his most memorable verses. *Novyi Mir* sponsored another recital in New York on Sunday afternoon, 4 October, at the Yorkville Casino (East 86th Street). This featured "150,000,000," impressions of the United States written four years earlier, and poetry recently composed in New York: "All Right" and "Brooklyn Bridge."[139] As in the case of the previous performances, this one was ignored by the major New York dailies.

After his Yorkville appearance, Mayakovsky again set off on a whirlwind tour—back by popular demand—that included Pittsburgh, 17 October; Detroit, 18 October; Chicago, 20 October; and Philadelphia, 23 October, before returning once more to New York for another popular, farewell performance at the Yorkville Casino on 25 October, again on a Sunday afternoon, before embarking for France on 28 October. Few Russian visitors could claim to have seen more of the United States in three months—from Rockaway Beach to Lake Michigan to Chesapeake Bay, from the Mexican border to New York's Long Island.[140]

Back in Russia, he publicly complained about the lack of appreciation of the

135. The audience was no doubt mostly Russian speaking, since the event was advertised mainly in the Russian press, especially by *Novyi Mir*. Ibid., 127–30.

136. Ibid., 122; "Fiery Russian Poet Scolds New York," by Louis Rich, *NYT*, 11 October 1925: SM12. Contrary to some accounts, Mayakovsky did not meet leading American writers such as Theodore Dreiser, who was not in New York, or Upton Sinclair, who was in California, during his American tour. He did meet Dreiser in Russia in 1927.

137. Nemrad, *Maiakovskii*, 149–50.

138. Ibid., 150–52; B. Sel'stov, "Maiakovskii o sovetskoi poezii," *Novyi mir*, 14 September 1925.

139. Nemrad, *Maiakovskii*, 175–77.

140. Ibid., 235–40.

arts in the United States and of its materialism, dirt, and waste, echoing a common negative refrain in the Soviet press. Motion pictures, he admitted, were an exception to the otherwise bleak American cultural scene.[141] Though publicly acknowledging the debt of Soviet Russia to the ARA relief program, Mayakovsky was especially impressed with the American "gigantomania" that he had never envisioned as part of Wilsonian America, and portrayed this in his "150,000,000," which glorified the industrialization of the world.[142] Nothing could illustrate this more than his vivid description of Fifth Avenue at rush hour.

Russian Culture Transplanted

Straddling the fence were several highly visible artists of old Russia, most notably Fyodor Chaliapin (Shaliapin), one of the greatest operatic bassos of all time, performing regularly after 1918 for Western audiences but almost always in Russian operas and still claimed by his home crowd in Soviet Russia, headed by Stanislavsky. For eight seasons in the 1920s he was a star performer for the Metropolitan Opera, after special intervention by the State Department to grant him an unlimited visa through Riga.[143] He would eventually return to the Soviet Union in the 1930s and find his final resting place in 1938 in the artist and writers' section of the Novodeviechy Monastery cemetery.

Sergei Rachmaninoff, composer and pianist, was another displaced person of the period, leaving Russia in 1918 at age thirty-five and settling in the United States permanently the following year. Though now devoted mainly to performing, he attracted audiences all across the country to the rich heritage of prerevolutionary Russian music and his own compositions. Among others representing the best traditions of old Russian culture were dowager premier ballerina Anna Pavlova, Rimsky-Korsakov's students Igor Stravinsky and Sergei Prokofiev, and Sergei Diaghilev and his pupil George Balanchine. All would contribute immensely to the revitalization of Russian music and performance in the West, contributing to a legacy of Russian culture that survived revolution and civil war.

Something of a surprise and source of pride to American and other Western sympathizers with the new Soviet experimental culture was that the Gorkys, Mayakovskys, Prokofievs, Chaliapins, and Stanislavskys, though seriously flirting with Western opportunities, would ultimately commit themselves to their Rus-

141. "Red Poet Pictures Us as Dollar Mad," *NYT*, 21 December 1925: 1.
142. Nemrad, *Maiakovskii*, 93.
143. D. C. Poole to Norman Hapgood, 17 September 1921, f. 1921–1927, box 11, Hapgood-Reynolds Papers, MD, LC.

sian homeland or the Soviet revolutionary experiments through the 1930s. They clearly had other alternatives and seriously considered them. Many Americans also appreciated the great contributions of Russians to the American cultural scene. Samuel Harper, despite considering Chaliapin a "despicable person," had to admit that he was simply great, after seeing his performance as Boris Godunov at the Met.[144]

Many of the most illustrious expatriate Russian scholars, musicians, and artists would settle in what they considered more compatible environments in Europe; they included historians Sergei Platonov, Ivan Il'in, Aleksander Presniakov, and Paul Miliukov, artists Chagall and Kandinsky, and composer Igor Stravinsky. The United States could claim its quota, however, especially in the historical field and scattered across the country. The eccentric artist Nicholas Roerich would add color and mystery to the Russian émigré scene on the upper West Side of New York, when he was not at his Tibet retreat.

Jazz!

One major cultural medium of the period went both ways. Though originating in African-American folk culture in the South and lower Midwest at the turn of the century, the new popular music defined an age in both the land of its origin and also in Russia after the 1917 revolution. Both societies were especially free and open to the innovation and development of the new arts. In the United States and to a considerable extent in Europe, the atmosphere of disillusionment that followed World War I promoted a spirit of art for art's sake in the new ghettos of free cultural expression, much of which had prewar antecedents, in the case of music in ragtime. Somewhat surprising is the Russian contribution to the new jazz music of the 1920s, which might be considered a melding of African-American and East European Jewish traditions: Irving Berlin ("Alexander's Ragtime Band") was born in the Russian empire, and the parents of George Gershwin were from St. Petersburg. The melding of African-American folk motifs with Jewish-Russian immigrant talent and motifs was no less than a miracle in the formation of the Jazz Age and its lasting effect on world culture. The new ghettos of Bohemian life and culture—Greenwich Village, SoHo, Monmartre in Paris—had their mirror but less focused images in Russia.

Russia had already been exposed to ragtime and its variations in the early twentieth century through traveling minstrel and individual performers from the United States in areas of popular entertainment such as nightclubs like the

144. Harper to Bakhmeteff, 21 February 1923, f. Harper, box 3, Bakhmeteff Papers, BAR, CU.

Aquarium in Moscow, the circus, and other arenas. Several longtime American residents, such as Frederick Corse, possessed and shared his extensive record collection. The New Economic Policy in 1921 ushered in an era of freedom for the arts, superintended by Lunacharsky, the commissar of enlightenment; many musicians, grounded on a great national cultural tradition that had reached into and developed Slavic folk songs and reverberated in the work of modern innovators such as Rimsky-Korsakov and his pupils Stravinsky and Prokofiev. Revolutionary changes were definitely on the keyboards.

As Soviet Russia opened to the outside with the ARA presence and to travelers in general, news, ideas, and art resumed their normal interaction but were now infected by a new vitality. Among those leading the way was Valentin Parnakh, who was caught up in the frenzy by hearing Louis Mitchell's Jazz Kings in Paris in 1921 and wrote articles in Russian journals praising their innovations. These new sounds found a ready urban audience ready to relax and enjoy dance and modern music in the aftermath of war, revolution, and civil war. Parnakh soon formed a rudimentary band of his own that presented its first performance on 1 October 1922.[145] Russia had modestly entered the Jazz Age. Others would follow, but many contemporaries in the arts—such as Lunacharsky, Stanislavsky, Isadora Duncan, Mayakovsky, and especially Gorky—were still dubious and critical, especially with the sexuality of the dances that accompanied the music. Jazz was boosted, however, by the support of Stanislavsky's rival drama director, Vsevolod Meyerhold, and his Theater of the Revolution and by the continuing influx of new European artists, for example, Kurt Weill, Stefan Weintraub (whose renowned "Syncopators" finally toured Russia in 1935), and other German musicians, who created the world-famous Berlin of the cabaret. Jazz was considered, by some Soviet interpreters at least, ideologically correct, as derived from a protest of African-American oppression in the United States. It symbolized the imperial-colonial conflict laid out in Marxism-Leninism and promoted by Soviet emphasis on colonial oppression.

Russia's "roaring twenties" were really ushered in by the arrival in Moscow in 1925 and 1926 of African-American jazz groups from the United States. First was the Leland and Drayton Revue, which spent six months touring the Soviet Union, leaving bedazzled Soviet audiences in its wake.[146] In February 1926 came Sam Wooding and the Chocolate Kiddies, invited, surprisingly, by the Russian Philharmonic Society. Wooding's jazz band had joined the Chocolate Kiddies, an African-American dance troupe, for a highly successful European tour in

145. Starr, *Red and Hot*, 44–47.

146. Allison Blakely, *Russia and the Negro: Blacks in Russian History and Thought* (Washington, D.C.: Howard University Press, 1986), 156–59.

1925 with a total of more than thirty African-American performers. Arriving from Berlin, the enthusiastic musicians and dancers literally took Communist Russia by storm. Though at first somewhat reluctant to accept the invitation to Russia (the star drummer dropped out) as spouses were left behind, their reception turned out to be the highlight of their European tour. Wooding himself on piano favored the symphonic approach to jazz pioneered by Paul Whiteman and featured in his recordings like "Alabammy Bound." Russian audiences were impressed not only by the novelty of African-Americans demonstrating artistic talent, but also by the acute musicality, sexuality, and natural flamboyance of the group that meshed with the freewheeling cultural atmosphere of the New Economic Policy.[147] Wooding's three-month tour of Soviet Russia (six weeks in Moscow and six weeks in Leningrad) reportedly packed houses, usually hours before the performances.

A budding Russian jazz musician, Arkady Kotliarsky, recalled, however, that Wooding's first and little advertised performance in Leningrad occurred in the half-empty circus building with many spectators dubious after witnessing an orchestra of only ten musicians gradually and lackadaisically assembling on the front of a bare stage. From the first notes, however, the audience was both enraptured and confused, especially when the curtain opened to the jubilant dancing of African-American women. For Kotliarsky it was a revelation; he claims that Sam Wooding's troupe had a tremendous impact on the emergence of Soviet jazz and his own long career as a jazz tenor saxophonist.[148]

American jazz, represented by Wooding in a derivation of its original African-American form, was reinforced by the arrival of Benny Peyton's Jazz Kings, who overlapped with Wooding on the Russian scene in 1926. Peyton's more intimate, improvised performances were a prototype of the Preservation Hall style of New Orleans. His seven-piece band wowed audiences with its renditions of "real" jazz in Moscow, Odessa, Kharkov, and Kiev during the summer of 1926.[149] Russian audiences marveled at the contrast between the comparatively relaxed, more staged, and orchestrated concerts of Wooding and the more exciting and un-

---

147. Ibid., 54–57. Wooding's subsequent career was only modestly successful, considered imitative, into the 1930s, when he dropped out to earn a Master's degree in music at the University of Pennsylvania, reviving his band sporadically. After the death of Duke Ellington, however, he wanted to keep the big band jazz sound alive and reconstituted a thirty-eight-piece ensemble for a sensational reprise of the "Kiddies" in 1975, when he was 79. "Sam Wooding, 79, Brings Back Old Time Sound with '75 Kiddies," NYT, 15 June 1975: 49.

148. Kotliarsky, Spasibo dzhazu: vospominaniia starogo utesovtsa (Leningrad: Khudozhestvennaia literatura, 1990), 5–6. Kotliarsky, a renowned saxophonist with the Leonid Utesov orchestra, begins his memoir with a section entitled "shokoladnye rebiata" (chocolate kiddies).

149. Starr, Red and Hot, 62–66.

Sam Wooding (seated in white) and his orchestra, and the "Chocolate Kiddies," 1926. (Jazz photo gallery, rainerjazz.com)

predictable performances of Peyton. As a result, the artistic, culturally sensitive, and sophisticated worlds of major Russian cities had been thoroughly suffused with American jazz, to reach a crescendo during World War II. The jazz infection would not go into remission until the beginning of the cold war, to reemerge partially in the 1950s and in full force by the 1970s.

American jazz came to Russia directly in the 1920s and in various ways, reaching the largest audiences through silent films. This may seem strange, but many of the most popular silent films shown in Russia were American (Charlie Chaplin and others), and all required musical accompaniment; it seemed natural to provide, usually with piano, current American musical motifs, that is, ragtime and jazz. Exactly how pianists knew what to play is unclear, but sheet music from Tin Pan Alley was sold worldwide. A case in point is Dmitri Shostakovich, who began his musical career playing the piano for silent films in the mid twenties, and most of what he played was in the current popular fashion. Though clearly preferring the classical in his training, he needed financial support. So at "Pi-kadili" and other major cinemas he played far into the night, jazzing up the Leningrad scene.[150] And because he was much more than the pedestrian performer, Shostakovich was soon improvising on jazz motifs, which led to his early and very popular "Tahiti Trot" (Tea for Two) composition (opus 16, 1928), a more classical "Jazz Suite," and the jazz orchestrated *Golden Age* ballet that included another version of "Tahiti Trot"; Shostakovich later repudiated his jazz origins (for political expediency, perhaps), but he really might have been the Russian George Gershwin.

Providing more influx of the American genre were several individual African-Americans who lent their talents and authenticity to Soviet jazz bands. Norval Harrison Allen was one of several. Born and raised in Kentucky, he migrated north to Chicago where he became a barbershop attendant, a butcher, and a steel mill worker. Becoming active in the Chicago branch of the National Association for the Advancement of Colored People (NAACP), he went as a delegate to the International AACP in London in 1925. Returning briefly to Chicago, he had become fascinated by reading about Soviet Russia and, using his own savings, left for Russia in December 1927. Soon running out of money, he signed on with a jazz troupe in Crimea and then Moscow, demonstrating the "Charleston" and buck and wing steps. Then he filled engagements in Leningrad, Minsk, and in the Caucasus. Returning to Moscow in December 1929, he devoted his savings to studying Russia and Russian society, though he was denied entrance to the university. He reported having little contact with other African-Americans, except

---

150. Sofia Moshevich, *Dmitri Shostakovich, Pianist* (Montreal and Kingston: McGill-Queen's University Press, 2004), 37–38.

for Olive Tetts, another performer, but saw them on the streets. After more than a year performing in Russia, he was able to convert his remaining ruble earnings to dollars and pay his own way home.[151]

The African-American cultural impact on Soviet Russia is probably best represented by two women who were longtime residents. Emma Harris toured Russia as a concert singer before World War I and married her manager. She remained a fixture in Moscow after the revolution but abandoned her singing career while maintaining contact with compatriots. More important in terms of jazz was Coretta Alfred, who came to Russia to study at the St. Petersburg Conservatory during World War I. Like Harris, she was a classical opera singer and starred in the title role of Verdi's *Aida* at the Moscow Conservatory in 1921 to much acclaim. She married her pianist, Boris Tietz, and under the name of Coretty Arle-Tietz performed widely around the Soviet Union, especially with Soviet jazz bands in the 1920s and 1930s. She is best remembered for her renditions of spirituals, recording "Sometimes I Feel Like a Motherless Child" and "Roll Jordan Roll" in Kiev in 1933. She was especially known for her concerts of spirituals and jazz for Soviet troops during World War II.[152]

Not surprisingly, there was soon a lively contingent of Russian jazz musicians who established their own "native" expressions, mainly centered in Leningrad, inspired by American performances but also by adherents to new musical motifs, such as the innovative theater director Vsevolod Meyerhold, the young composer Dmitri Shostakovich (already noted), and Valentin Parnakh. Most important, Commissar of Enlightenment Lunacharsky signed on by sponsoring the visit of Leopold Teplitsky to the United States in late 1926, mainly to Philadelphia, Wooding's hometown, where he studied with Paul Whiteman. He returned to form a band that became the nucleus of other many similar ventures that sparked the "Red" Jazz Age through the 1930s.[153] The result was a remarkable Russian contribution to American jazz, especially with Joseph Schillinger coming to the United States in 1929. Though expecting to return, he spent the rest of his life there, adding to the quality and innovation of the American jazz scene through

151. Interview by member of Latvian legation, early 1930, vol. 108, Latvia (1930), RG 84, NA. Maude White was another young African American who won a scholarship from the Negro Research Society of Washington. She first went to Berlin but was denied entry to the university, so she went on to Moscow and spent two years on independent research and study, while also reporting for the *Chicago Defender*.

152 Rainer E. Lotz, *Black People: Entertainers of African Descent in Europe and Germany* (Berlin: Birgit Lotz Verlag, 1997), 196–97. This book includes a CD of early African-American music recordings in Europe; many Russians would have heard them.

153. Starr, *Red and Hot*, 67–73.

his influence on, and contributions to, the work of George Gershwin, Benny Goodman, Glen Miller, and many others.[154]

American Radicals and Soviet Russia

Jazz musicians were, of course, not the only Americans to visit or live in Russia in the 1920s. Most of the others, including several African-Americans, were radical refugees from American society or seekers of their dreams of a new society free of class and race prejudice and discrimination. Quite a few were there because of the 1919–1920 deportations or had fled nearly certain arrest and incarceration. The best-known American resident in that category was "Big Bill" (William D.) Haywood, a former leader of the IWW and a founding member of the American Communist Party from afar in 1921. Jumping bail and emigrating to Russia, he married a Russian, but his activities were limited by severe diabetes; his Moscow apartment was, nevertheless, always open to kinsmen, to whom he was a genuine hero of the American labor movement. Blind in one eye from a childhood accident and wearing a patch, he always commanded attention, despite his illness and alcoholism that led to his premature death at age forty-five in 1927.

The Bolshevik Revolution and the somewhat miraculous survival of the Soviet regime won the admiration and enthusiasm of many other Americans, who were already on the left fringe of American politics. The creation of the Comintern or Third International in 1919 established a Soviet direction, organization, and control of the worldwide Communist movement, to which the American Workers' Party belonged.[155] The result was a succession of American Communists to attend annual Comintern congresses in Moscow and other affiliated meetings, such as Profintern (Trade Union International), constituting a new Soviet Russian intrusion into American political life. An initial division in the party resulted from a challenge to the leadership of Charles Ruthenberg, the son of German immigrants, by a Hungarian émigré and instigator of the abortive 1919 revolution there, Joseph Pogany, who took the name of John Pepper in America. Leading party officials, such as Jay Lovestone (born in Russian Lithuania), Earl Browder, and William Z. Foster, were among those making the obligatory trek to Moscow and were subject to the constant factional strife that prevailed in the American party.[156]

154. Schillinger is acknowledged as a major contributor to (and perhaps the real musicologist of) *Porgy and Bess*.

155. The American Communist Party was forced underground in 1921 to emerge formally as the Workers' Party. They were essentially the same thing.

156. For details, see Theodore Draper, *American Communism and Soviet Russia: The Formative Period* (New York: Viking, 1960).

After benefiting from an initial boost from the revolution and the postwar depression, the American Communists slumped, suffering no doubt from the widespread publicity about Soviet and Comintern funding of their efforts. Running for president, Foster won 33,000 votes in 1924 (to Coolidge's 15,720,000), hardly a threat to the established political parties. Membership in the Workers' Party declined from a high of 13,000 in 1924 to 7,500 in 1926. The party suffered from shifts of direction from bolshevization to Americanization after the 4 July 1926 one hundred and fiftieth anniversary of the Declaration of Independence, and from the divisions and factionalism in the Russian party (Trotsky versus Kamenev versus Bukharin versus Stalin) and within its own ranks.[157] Though Zinoviev, with his imperious demeanor and high falsetto voice, was hard for Americans to accept as the leader of international Communism, his removal by Stalin in 1926 left Soviet direction in disarray. Though receiving modest Comintern subsidies for publications, the American press organs, especially *The Daily Worker*, were in serious financial difficulties through the 1920s.

One success that had both negative and positive aspects for the American party was the recruitment of many African-Americans into the ranks of radical Communism. This resulted mainly from Lenin's emphasis on the colonial areas of Africa and Asia at the Baku Congress of Peoples of the East in 1920 and the subsequent establishment of a Far Eastern Technical University (officially by the mid 1920s the University of Toilers of the East named after Stalin) in Moscow for educating young colonial people of various races in technical skills and in Marxism-Leninism. African-Americans, as an oppressed race, were considered eligible for admission. The Comintern also specified that American Communist delegations to its meetings include black representatives. An assortment of African-Americans thus graced the streets of Moscow in the 1920s as students (an average of about eight per year) or delegates to various meetings, all subsidized by the Comintern. Many of them, however, were not native Americans but were transplanted to the United States from Africa, South America, or the West Indies.[158]

Many of these new adherents were already educated at Tuskegee Institute and other colleges and had also witnessed, through such employment as waiters on dining cars, the racial prejudice in the United States that was especially pronounced in the Ku Klux Klan era of the 1920s and found the relative lack of discrimination in Russia attractive. One of the first and most influential was Claude McKay, a Jamaican who had studied at Tuskegee and Kansas State Agricultural College and was influenced by W. E. B. DuBois. Not a party member, McKay raised money for the trip to Russia from selling his poetry and from friends in the

157. Ibid., 119, 188, 237.
158. See the chapter, "The Black 'Pilgrims,'" in Blakely, *Russia and the Negro*, 81–104.

NAACP, from the Harlem elite, and from Crystal (Mrs. Max) Eastman—along with a modest reporter's retainer from *The Liberator*. Traveling by freighter, he arrived in Petrograd in 1922. Though not an invited delegate, he managed to attend the Fourth Congress of the Comintern in Moscow with the help of Sen Katayama, the leading Japanese delegate to the organization. Dividing his year in Russia between Petrograd and Moscow, McKay cut quite a swath; Zinoviev even asked him to speak at the Congress and then was embarrassed to discover that McKay was not a Communist.[159]

Another African-American who left a detailed record of more than four years in Sovietdom was Harry Haywood [Hall], who grew up in Omaha, Nebraska, relocated with his family to South Chicago, and, after a stint as a railroad diner waiter, was offered a scholarship at the University of Toilers of the East in Moscow, where he studied for a year with his brother, Otto Hall, before being accepted into the more prestigious Lenin University. Although American blacks naturally attracted attention everywhere in Russia and were sometimes mistaken for Uzbeks, they seldom witnessed any signs of racial prejudice. Some, such as Bankole, an Ashanti from Ghana, educated at Pittsburgh's Carnegie Institute, magnified attention to himself by dressing as a British aristocrat, complete with cane and monocle. While Otto Huisman from Dutch Guiana amazed everyone with his fluency in Dutch and English, as well as Russian, Lovett Fort-Whiteman, head of the American party's black section, insisted on mystifying the Chicago southside upon his return from Russia by wearing a Russian peasant belted blouse and speaking a crude Russian to passers by with a Mississippi accent. Walking together down Tverskaya in Moscow, some of these earned an epithet from Russian youth, "jass band," assuming any small group of African-Americans was a musical combo—not a bad guess.[160]

Probably the most prominent African-American Communist and most respected by Soviet recruiters was George Padmore (born Malcolm Ivan Meredith Nurse), originally from Trinidad, but he had studied at Columbia University and Fisk University in Nashville before entering law school at Howard University, where he much impressed one of his professors, Ralph Bunche. He became active in the American Communist Party and was sent to the Soviet Union in 1930 as a delegate to the Fifth Congress of the Red International of Labor Unions, one of seven black members of the thirty American delegates.[161] He was sub-

---

159. Claude McKay, *A Long Way from Home* (New York: Lee Furman, 1937), 153–90.

160. Harry Haywood, *Black Bolshevik: Autobiography of an Afro-American Communist* (Chicago: Liberator Press, 1978), 148–75 et passim; for information on other African-Americans in Russia, such as Leonard Patterson, Jane and John Golden, and George Padmore, see Blakely, *Russia and the Negro*, 85–94.

161. Haywood, *Black Bolshevik*, 328–30. Padmore was overshadowed at the congress by Helen McClain, an attractive, vivacious black needle worker from Philadelphia.

sequently appointed secretary of the International Trade Union Committee of Negro Workers. As a valued member of the Comintern, he was assigned to duties in Europe, was jailed briefly in Germany in 1933, and then deported to Britain. He then came under a cloud for stressing race rather than class in his work and was expelled from the American party.[162]

When feeling homesick, the African-Americans in Moscow could drop in on Bill Haywood, who was always sympathetic, or hunt down Emma Harris, who, stranded in Moscow before the revolution, had presided over an upper-class brothel before being turned into a textile worker after the revolution. Harris, originally from Kentucky, was renowned for her ability to convert local Moscow ingredients into genuine Southern "soul food." She stayed on and endured Soviet life through World War II. Back in the United States, however, the black Bolsheviks confronted racial prejudice as much as class oppression, even from the patronizing attitude of their white Communist brethren, causing another division in the ranks of the American Communist Party. Blacks were prone toward the more pronounced racial concerns of the American Negro Labor Congress organization. This was especially felt by those who had obtained higher education, in the United States, Russia, or both during the Depression.

Russians in the United States

The Russian communities in the United States in the 1920s represented an astonishing assortment of ethnic and political divisions. To some extent they were preformed by earlier immigration and exodus from the Russian empire. Mayakovsky, in 1924, counted 300,000 Russians in New York City, not including the more obvious Jews, Poles, and other ethnic groups originating from the Russian empire; this was probably an exaggeration.[163] Nonetheless, a genuine Russian cultural presence was evident from the more recent addition of refugees from bolshevism, though most of the Russian anti-Bolshevik opposition remained in Europe, concentrated in Paris, Berlin, and Prague, with hopes of an easy and quick return upon the failure of the Communist regime. In the United States, Boris Bakhmeteff, under both public and private pressures, formally resigned his position as ambassador of pre-Bolshevik Russia in 1922, and moved out of the formidable embassy on 16th Street in Washington, taking up residence in New York to pursue, briefly, an unsuccessful career of freelance lecturing and consulting on

162. Blakely, *Russia and the Negro*, 92–94; Haywood, *Black Bolshevik*, 328–30.

163. For an excellent analysis of Russian émigrés, see Mark Raeff's *Russia Abroad: A Cultural History of the Russian Emigration, 1919–1939* (New York: Oxford University Press, 1990).

Russian trade, before being rescued by Columbia University to resume his career as a professor of civil engineering. His financial attaché, Sergei Ughet, however, would continue to conduct the dwindling business of the old provisional government in the United States, drawing for support on the old American loan of 1917, retained in escrow by the Treasury Department; this included the upkeep of the embassy building on 16th Street, which would eventually be transferred to the Soviet government in 1933 in remarkably good condition.

Bakhmeteff's former secretary, Michael Karpovich, made a similar move but had an even more successful transition into American academic life as a professor of Russian history at Harvard University. During his long tenure, he nurtured two generations of advanced students of Russian history. He was joined a few years later by George Vernadsky at Yale and Michael Florinsky at Columbia; they formed a professional triangular nucleus that would make a major contribution to American understanding of the Russian past and the Soviet present. Florinsky was drawn first to London as a research assistant to Bernadotte Schmidt for his work on the Treaty of Brest-Litovsk, then to the United States in 1926 by James T. Shotwell for a volume on the Carnegie Institute's World War I Russia series. He had already begun a regular correspondence with Karpovich, who no doubt played a role in his entry into the United States.[164] Vernadsky was boosted by an already established reputation of scholarship in early Russian history. Perhaps of even greater value was Bakhmeteff's own efforts to preserve the many records of revolution and emigration in a major and still growing manuscript collection in his name at Columbia University.[165] Although Vernadsky would devote most of his career to producing distinguished volumes on early Russian history, while complaining about the lack of interest in Russian history and language by Yale students, Florinsky would concentrate on scholarly works on early twentieth-century Russia and produce one of the finest general histories of Russia through the revolution.

Russians, as other would-be immigrants, would encounter serious obstacles due to American immigration restrictions in the 1920s. An American crusade to preserve the old Russian culture, led by Charles Crane, Mark and Helen Bristol, Julia Cantacuzene-Speransky, Jerome Landfield, and others, forced the lowering of barriers, at least for the professional elites, such as Florinsky and Vernadsky, and

---

164. Florinsky letters to Karpovich, beginning 1924, box 1, and Florinsky to Sergei Sazonov (former foreign minister of Imperial Russia), 19 February 1927, box 4, Florinsky Papers, BA, CU.

165. The archive for many years (1950s through 1970s) was superintended somewhat privately by Lev Magerovsky, who devoted his life to it, but in more recent years it has become part of the rare book and manuscript collection of the university and is under the expert supervision of curator Tanya Cheborateva.

quite a few more who were able to pass through.[166] Crane's long interest in Russia began on a business venture in the 1890s and continued until his death in 1938. Though strongly anti-Bolshevik, he visited the country regularly; in 1930, for example, he managed to purchase the bells from the derelict Danilevsky monastery and donate them to Harvard's Lowell Hall, then under construction.

The Bristols became committed to Russian relief causes, during his stint as commander of the American naval squadron in the Mediterranean, based in Constantinople, during World War I and the Russian civil war, most notably in a truly stupendous effort in dealing with a massive outpouring of refugees at the end of the conflict in 1920. They continued to support private relief efforts during the 1920s concentrated on the intellectual elite.

Another prime example of the survival of Russian tradition and heritage in the United States is Dmitri Fedotoff White, who came to the United States around 1923 as an agent of the Cunard line in Philadelphia.[167] As a veteran of the imperial, provisional government, and Bolshevik navies, he possessed a wealth of experience of those times of turmoil and would apply this knowledge and talent to publications that included one of the best memoirs of the Russian revolution, *Survival through War and Revolution*, and to a wide range of military and naval works.[168] Anatol Mazour would also make a significant contribution to American knowledge of Russian history with books on the Decembrist Revolt and Russian historiography. Arriving with practically no knowledge of English, he was advised to go to the Midwest, to the University of Nebraska, where there would be no temptation to be enveloped by a Russian émigré community, as was the case in New York. He would go on eventually to a professorship at Stanford but left his papers at his alma mater.[169]

The American-Russian exile community, many of them refugees from bolshevism and centered in New York City, would never be cohesive or united due to varied social backgrounds and divided political views. They ranged from World War I and White Civil War veterans, who relished their imperial memories, to a wide variety of former political activists and cultural, ethnic, and religious dissidents. This diaspora featured many of the distinguished losers in the revolution:

---

166. The Russian exile cause was severely weakened by such things as opposition to the American Relief Administration's work to save large numbers of the lower population of the old Russia from starvation.

167. Reginald Hall (Cunard) to White, 5 February 1923, f. Hall, box 1, White Papers, BA, CU.

168. White, *Survival through War and Revolution* (Philadelphia: University of Pennsylvania Press, 1939); his collection in the Bakhmeteff Archive is a valuable émigré record, including White to Bakhmeteff, 17 March 1931, about forming a Russian Luncheon Club, f. Bakhmeteff, box 1, White Papers, BA, CU.

169. Mazour Papers, University of Nebraska Archives.

the old nobility, Constitutional Democrats, Socialist Revolutionaries, Menshe-viks, monarchists, and so forth. In contrast to many earlier immigrants from the Russian empire, their arrival was involuntary. Many initially considered their American residence in the 1920s temporary while expecting a return to the ear-lier and rather forlorn pursuit of Russian grandeur or lost revolutionary causes. They would also be hampered by being a relatively insignificant extension of the similarly divided main centers of "Russia Abroad" in Berlin, Paris, and Prague—and wherever they could find accommodation and a job.[170]

The growing New York Russian community on the upper West Side, already in existence but now bolstered—almost overwhelmed—by the Russian exodus, gravitated toward the St. Nicholas Cathedral on East 92nd Street. A new restau-rant, the Sadko, opened on West 57th Street by Ladyzhinsky, later to be known as the Russian Tea Room, supplemented by a series of cafes on 37th Street and a Russian supper club on 14th Street. The Roerich Museum Apartments at 310 Riverside Drive was another Russian oasis, supported by the generosity of the art-ist.[171] A genuine American effort to absorb a sizable number of misplaced Russian persons was a bright light in an otherwise depressing scene of shock and search for adjustment and acceptance. Though hampered by economic conditions in the 1920s and worsening with the Depression, a surprising number of Russians gained status and made major contributions to American life. Almost all of the prominent Russians in the United States had close relatives remaining in the So-viet Union, some in high places. Michael Florinsky's brother Dmitri, for example, was an official in the Soviet Commissariat of Foreign Relations, until his arrest and exile in the mid 1930s.[172] Michael Rostovstev, a renowned scholar of classical antiquity who had emigrated to the United States before the revolution, had a brother James, also a respected scholar, left behind. Divided families of so many of the displaced, émigré Russians would be one of the most tragic consequences of the Russian Revolution.

The growing number of Russian scholars in the United States, many of whom had participated in the revolution, stimulated a lively discussion of the Russian

170. For the full story of the large Russian exile communities in Europe, see Raeff, *Russia Abroad.*
171. See Alexander Kaun to Harper, 18 December 1928, f. 33, box 13, Harper Papers, UC-R.
172. Florinsky's elder brother was known for his assistance to Americans over many years, having served previously in the Russian consulate in New York. Marguerite Harrison provides an eloquent description: "While spiritually converted to Communism, so he averred, [Dmitri] Florinsky was in ap-pearance a typical boulevardier. He was always dressed in the pink of perfection, with matching ties, handkerchiefs and socks; . . . He was very fond of a hand of bridge or a good game of poker, and he never got up until eleven or twelve in the morning." Harrison, *Marooned in Moscow: The Story of an American Woman Imprisoned in Russia* (New York: Doran, 1921), 112.

scene past and present, often disagreeing but providing an invaluable exchange on what happened and why. Michael Florinsky, for example, took issue with Vasily Golovnin's view of the breakdown of the military forces of the old regime. "He wants to prove that the Russian army was quite sound until the revolution and that the revolution was the real cause of its breakdown. In my opinion the reverse was true; the army was rapidly going to pieces, together with the rest of the political institutions and the social framework of the country, and thus contributed to the revolution which was, indeed, inevitable."[173] Such debates would fuel the fire of discussion on the causes and results of the "revolution of the century" for their American students for many decades and into the next century. In general, the emigration of Russian historians would preserve a truer, more objective history than would emerge under Communist dictate.

The Russian Student Fund

An important stimulus for sustaining Russian culture in the United States and providing cultural continuity for the next generation was the Russian Student Fund, the brainchild of Aleksei Viren (Alexis Wiren), the son of a Russo-Finnish naval commander and sad victim of the February Revolution of 1917 at Kronstadt. The idea was to provide scholarships and leverage for admission of young Russian immigrants without resources to study at American universities and thus qualify for professional careers. He received crucial initial backing from several sources, including Allen Wardwell and former Assistant Secretary of State Frank Polk.[174] The project was given a real boost by a grant of $50,000 from the Laura Spelman Rockefeller Foundation in September 1923.[175] To Samuel Harper, Viren explained, "One of the primary objects of the Russian Student Fund is to establish a group of young Russians who will become a connecting link between Russia and America. . . . Only in such a way will they be able to be true interpreters of American people, ideals and culture; only in this manner when they return to their own country will there be Americans who will keep in touch with them."[176] He was proud to report that ten students had already joined fraternities.[177]

173. Florinsky to Shotwell, 16 July 1930, f. Shotwell, box 4, Florinsky Papers, BA, CU.
174. Viren to Wardwell, 7 May 1923, f. May June, box 7, Wardwell Papers, BA, CU.
175. Small contributions also came from the old Russian embassy—out of the "caretaker" funds of the U.S. Treasury. Ughet to Davis, 7 August 1925, f. Russian Student Fund, 1923–1925, box 48, Davis Papers, MD, LC.
176. Viren to Harper, 16 July 1924, f. 11, box 11, Harper Papers, UC.
177. Ibid.

Viren is owed much credit for devoting most of his life to a deserving cause with only modest resources, expending, for example, only about $25,000 in 1929.[178] However, this spending primed the pump for more support from the institutions themselves. With well-paying jobs and return of funding in mind, the emphasis from the beginning was on the study of engineering and science; the program continued into the 1950s with considerable cumulative impact for Russian youth in the United States. Most important, he had assembled an impressive board of directors that included Norman Davis as chair and Frank Polk (of the Wilson State Department) as vice chair. During the first semester of 1923–1924 ninety Russian students were enrolled in American universities under this program. Columbia University received the most (twelve), while seven each enrolled at Colorado School of Mines and the Massachusetts Institute of Technology. Naturally, technical subjects dominated the fields of study, with seventeen majoring in electrical engineering, ten in mining engineering, and nine in mechanical engineering, but nine were studying agriculture and others were scattered through subjects ranging from education to medicine. Viren had also arranged for General Electric to pay the tuition for future students at Union College in Schenectady.[179]

Viren responded defensively to a skeptical concern of Alex Legge of International Harvester that they should work their own way through college like so many Americans:

> The students are only being given such assistance as they actually require. A lot of them are asking for partial assistance, because through their own means, or through their own work, they are providing for some of their requirements. For instance, in one case, a student only asks for $100 to help him through the year, and some of those who graduated last year have already repaid a portion of the assistance which they received. We certainly shall try to avoid pauperizing any of these fellows, or furnish any of them with automobiles.[180]

He certainly did make rather small contributions go a long way.

Russia Abroad

The great majority of Russians displaced by revolution and civil war remained in Europe, many by choice, expecting to return to Russia upon the collapse of

178. Viren to H. F. Armstrong, 4 November 1929, f. Soviet Union, box 53, Mudd-Princeton.

179. Viren to Davis, 16 November 1923, with attachment, f. Russian Student Fund, box 48, Davis Papers, MD, LC.

180. Viren to Legge, 17 April 1923, ibid.

bolshevism or because they were simply more comfortable in Europe. They were more likely to be familiar with the French or German languages and perhaps to have visited, or at least known more about, European countries than about the United States. Many of the liberal or radical losers of the political upheaval had spent time in exile in Europe before the revolution. It was natural, therefore, for Berlin, Paris, and also Prague, because of its Slavic milieu, to become centers for the Russian refugees. Quite a number of the influx found compatible new homes in the Slavic countries of Bulgaria and Yugoslavia, but economic conditions in the Balkans did not contribute much to their economic welfare.

Because of subsequent European turmoil, some would later emigrate to the United States, including Alexander Kerensky, the head of the last non-Bolshevik Russian government. More notably, this wave of a second generation emigrants included scholars such as David and Alexander Dallin, Richard Pipes, Marc Raeff, Sergei Zenkovsky, and Nicholas Riasanovsky. Several other émigré Russians would have preferred to come to the United States, where opportunities were considered better, but were faced with the considerable obstacle of restricted immigration quotas that had been enacted in the 1920s.[181] A few others, like Emma Goldman, were considered persona non grata, formally forbidden from reentering the United States. She would be forced to spend the rest of her life in France and Canada, though she was buried in Chicago. H. Willoughby Smith, a second-generation Russian-American who had served as American consul in the Caucasus region for several years, was left destitute by the revolution and perhaps best summed up the turmoil of war and revolution: "One of the most deplorable effects of the great war still felt, is that it has broken to atoms so much of our past that we comparatively old men, are left rudderless, sailless, and many backless."[182]

A similar situation existed in Asia, where another flow of refugees from Siberia would result in enlarged Russian concentrations in Harbin and Shanghai. These would become lively communities, incorporating both Red and White perspectives as well as traditional and modern cultures (jazz). As in Europe, turmoil that preceded the war would create a second emigration to North America, mainly to the West Coast. One problem was that the only easy way out was through Japan, which required money and which the Japanese restricted because of resentment of the favored Soviet treatment of Americans and a hostility that dated back to

181. Exceptions were sometimes made for "professionals" and those supported by influential people. A sore point for some was that Russian-Jews were quicker in claiming place in the quotas or finding a way around the restrictions.

182. Smith (Tallinn) to Secretary of State, 27 June 1923, vol. 36, DPR Tallinn, RG 84, NA. He especially lamented his inability to get his Russian wife out of Russia.

the Russo-Japanese War of 1904–1905.[183] A steady trickle of Russians came to the United States during the 1920s and 1930s, settling mainly in the San Francisco and Seattle areas.[184]

The YMCA in Europe

The story of the considerable number of Russians who remained in Europe has already been ably recorded and, in any event, is outside the scope of this study.[185] An exception involves the work of the American YMCA in a continuation of its cultural programs in Russia. At first concentrated in Berlin, it would gradually transfer its operations to Paris. With the benefit of his Russian experience in 1917–1918 and several equally dedicated assistants, Paul Anderson established a Russian Correspondence School in Berlin in 1921 to offer professional courses to young Russian refugees, while at the same time employing several senior Russian émigré scholars. An initial enrollment of 240 quickly expanded to more than a thousand in 1923. Ironically, both the school and its affiliated YMCA summer camps used former prisoner-of-war camps near Berlin that had contained Russians during the war.[186]

Anderson and his cohorts immediately encountered a problem: the Russians were sharply divided between those with strong religious (Orthodox) beliefs and those with none—or who were newly converted to evangelical churches. For the former, a Russian Religious Philosophical Academy was inaugurated with Ivan Il'in and Nicholas Berdiaev as its leaders.[187] The funding came from annual YMCA allocations, leftover World War I contingency funds, some local government sources, special refugee solicitations, and by sales of more than 200 Russian textbooks, mainly on technical and scientific subjects, in the Soviet market.[188]

183. William Turner (U.S. consul, Yokohama) to State, 1 December 1927, 861.111, reel 86, M 316, NA. One who made it that year through Japan was a noted violinist, Efrem Zimbalist.

184. For an excellent description of Russian émigré life in Harbin and Shanghai and emigration to the United States, see Helen Yakobson, *Crossing Borders*.

185. See Raeff, *Russia Abroad*.

186. Pictures and details in f. Russian Correspondence School, 1922–1924, box 6, Anderson Papers, UIA. YMCA leaders John Mott and Ethan Colton had kept close tabs on the Russian refugee situation as it emerged in 1920. See Mott to Friends, 16 June 1920, f. YMCA Newark Conference, February 1920, ibid.

187. Program, 15 January 1924, f. YMCA Hq. Corresp., box 7, ibid.

188. These publications, with author and press undisclosed, were an important source of revenue for the fledgling YMCA Russian press in Berlin and later Paris. It may seem ironic that Soviet funds thus supported Russian émigré scholars and their publications, but such was the order of the day. The income helped finance textbooks in various languages for children of the Russian émigrés.

Serving the large Russian émigré population presented considerable problems for the American YMCA, especially in regard to financial arrangements, which the association was ill-equipped to handle. Nevertheless, its central office as well as those in the field managed to shuffle funds back and forth in somewhat un-orthodox methods to make its resources go further. For example, $50,000 was transferred from the press (textbooks) to support the publication of Russian literature. Ethan Colton in New York regularly scolded Anderson about economy in expenditures.[189]

Thanks to Anderson, Donald Lowrie, and others, the American YMCA was probably more cognizant of the problems of Russian refugees in Europe than any other organization or country. Surveying the Paris region on a trip in December 1923, Anderson estimated that 63,000 Russians were living in and around Berlin and that many young males had just lost their initial jobs in local factories. Veterans of the White armies were having increasing difficulty finding employment, and student stipends were being cut back. "It is almost an epidemic."[190] In his 1925 annual report, Anderson noted that at least 800,000 Russian refugees or immigrants were living in Europe (including Eastern Europe), and many of them were destitute.[191] Another more inclusive survey placed the figure at one million.[192]

Partly for that reason and the concentration of rank-and-file Russian refugees in Paris, the YMCA moved most of its operations to that city in 1924.[193] But the organization was running short of funds, as American philanthropy increasingly withdrew from foreign commitments. The YMCA Press, which had started in Prague in 1922, publishing mainly works in Russian by Russian professional experts, was running into difficulty. The press achieved modest success in printing textbooks for local needs and the Soviet market, or, in other words, no questions asked on either side as the Soviet agencies were desperately short of high-quality textbooks and the YMCA and their authors needed the income.[194] But by the end of 1925 even this operation was running dry of funds. Desperation even forced them to consider selling their franchises to a Soviet agency through Anna Louise Strong and Albert Rhys Williams.[195] Fortunately, that did not happen, and "imca press," under the direction of Edgar MacNaugten, would remain a legitimate and

189. Colton to Anderson, 2, 12, and 19 December 1924, f. 3 YMCA Geneva and Paris 1924, box 8, Anderson Papers, UIA.

190. Anderson, "Report on Trip to Paris, Dec. 16–24, 1923," f. YMCA Press, box 3, ibid.

191. Anderson annual report for 1925, f. Russian work, 1918–1925, box 5, ibid.

192. W. Chapin Huntington, *The Homesick Million: Russia-out-of-Russia* (Boston: Stratford, 1933).

193. f. YMCA, Geneva and Paris, box 8, Anderson Papers, UIA.

194. f. YMCA Press, box 3, ibid.

195. Ibid.

respected voice of Russia abroad through most of the century. The press and its affiliated Russian Literature Service were clearly instrumental in keeping émigré scholarship alive—on a shoestring. Paul Anderson and Donald Lowrie, among other YMCA veterans of Russian service, can certainly lay claim to being the unsung heroes of the Russian refugee emigration.[196]

American Slavic Studies

The elder statesman of Russian studies in the United States in the early twentieth-century was George Kennan, the same name as another recognized scholar at the beginning of the twenty-first century. The first George Kennan, who happened to have the same birthday as the second, 16 February (hence the similarity of names), was now enjoying a modest retirement from a long journalistic career and fame from his exposure of the prison abuses in the Russian empire in the 1880s (*Siberia and the Exile System*). Something of an eccentric (always pencils, never pens), hating cities and loving the country, especially his Baddeck, Nova Scotia, summer retreat,[197] he penned a joint, modest obituary for a friend, Poultney Bigelow, "We both have wandered far and had enjoyable experiences (as well as hard ones); we both have had fair success in literature."[198] Kennan had never enjoyed, however, an academic position or the scholarly prestige attained by his later namesake. As one Kennan passed from the scene in 1924, another, a first cousin twice removed, was just beginning to chart his own long path toward a more sophisticated understanding of Russian-American relations through a diplomatic career.

The widely recognized dean of Russian history in the United States in the 1920s, however, was Archibald Cary Coolidge. He had taught the first course in Russian history at an American university, Harvard, and was active in the initial stages of organizing the American Historical Association and planning sessions on Russia at its annual meetings. The considerable prestige of his university naturally added to his reputation. His contribution to Russian history was largely symbolic and organizational, since his own scholarship was quite modest. The Coolidge legacy came mainly with the inauguration in September 1922 of a new journal, *Foreign Affairs Quarterly*, with the help of Hamilton Fish Armstrong,

196. Lincoln Hutchinson, an ARA veteran, visiting Paris, praised Anderson's accomplishments to Samuel Harper, 29 October 1929, f. 25, box 14, Harper Papers, UC-R.

197. It is now operated as the Broadwater Inn bed and breakfast in Baddeck, in its original form with a wonderful curving staircase.

198. Kennan to Bigelow, box 9, Kennan Papers, MD, LC.

that would focus on the new international consequences of the Soviet presence in the world.[199] It quickly become the most authoritative voice for the American role (some might say imperialism) in the interwar world, sustained especially by the simultaneous formation of the Council on Foreign Relations that sponsored roundtables and lecture series, as well as the journal.

Though the council and its journal contributed considerably to the discussion of Russian issues, it was tainted, according to some accounts, by the inclusion of Ambassador Boris Bakhmeteff and representatives of the State Department, especially Robert Kelley, in its programs, while excluding the most vocal pro-recognitionists.[200] Though Coolidge's scholarly production was relatively modest, he was the elder statesman of the field, open to various points of view and widely respected by the academic community. His sudden death in early 1928 was a definite loss to Russian studies.

Charles Crane remained one of the staunchest friends of Russian refuges and a powerful advocate for the preservation of the best of Russian culture. He continued to fund the faculty position of Samuel Harper at the University of Chicago, reserving an endowment of $250,000 in his fund for that purpose. Other support was scattered and less tangible, doled out in small amounts but with the prospect of more, which kept many waiting on his doorstep—or more likely bombarding his secretary. One interesting legacy inspired by his early infatuation with the Orthodox church and especially its music was the acquisition of the bells from the closed Danilevsky Monastery in Moscow, which were then installed in Lowell Hall at Harvard. When he first heard his transplanted bells in July 1931, Crane was quite pleased with the sound but felt that Americans still had to learn to appreciate them.[201] To promote an understanding of world affairs drastically altered by the emergence of a viable and economically advancing Soviet Union, Crane founded in 1927 the Institute of Current World Affairs, directed by his son-in-law, Walter Rodgers.[202]

199. Coolidge contributed anonymously the first article on Russia in the first issue: "K" [Coolidge], "Russia after Genoa and The Hague," *Foreign Affairs* 1, no. 1 (September 1922), 133–55.

200. See, for example, Coolidge to Kelley, 24 June 1924, and Kelley to Coolidge, 1 July 1924, and subsequent series of letters, f. 5, box 2, Kelley Papers, GU.

201. Crane to JOC [John Crane], 17 April 1930 and 20 July 1931, and to Trustees of Friendship Fund, 25 August 1930, reel 1, Crane Papers, BAR, CU. Harper remained ignorant of the security of his position and the $250,000 endowment that guaranteed it; he was always worried about the annual renewal of the Crane funding of his appointment. Harper Papers, passim, MD, R-UC.

The bells produced controversy in the early twenty-first century, as the restored Danilevsky Monastery, see of the patriarch, wanted them back. Dislodging them from Lowell Hall and transporting them back to Moscow would entail considerable expense, an unresolved legacy of those times.

202. Though he visited Russia several times in the 1920s and 1930s, Charles Crane was increasingly more interested in Far Eastern and Middle Eastern cultures and frequently traveled there, being

A young Harvard scholar, Bruce Hopper, was designated as the institute's Russian resident agent from early 1927 until May 1929 to report to the institute and to Crane personally.[203] He soon found himself in the midst of a new world and reduced to visiting the Hammer pencil factory. He was assisted by Junius Wood but clearly remained in a haze about the passing Soviet scene.[204] Skvirsky remarked to VOKS on the contrast between the liberal orientation of the institute and the conservatism of its patron.[205] Little did he know that Hopper was also serving as an intelligence agent for the State Department. Nevertheless, Hopper delivered eight lectures at the Lowell Institute in 1931, later published, in which he defined recognition as a technical issue: "how and when are we going to become aware of Soviet Russia as a tremendous fact in America's future?" He advised against "allowing those who lost by the Russian Revolution, or those who gained by the Russian Revolution, to interfere too much with our American vision."[206]

A surprisingly large number of Americans in the 1920s had vested interests in Russia because of past experiences, political commitments, and scholarly and artistic professions. Among them were three hundred veteran ARA workers, plus another two hundred connected with the American Red Cross, the Vatican or Mennonite relief program, and the Society of Friends. The ARA had a veterans' organization, as did the Red Cross, that maintained communications and sponsored programs. Herbert Hoover himself was a promoter of their interests, even though the great majority supported recognition and closer relations with the Soviet Union. In answer to a query about granting an honorary degree to ARA

---

kidnapped in Iraq on one occasion. He also contended with family problems: his favorite daughter, Josephine, was deaf; son Richard did not succeed as a diplomat (minister to Czechoslovakia) and retired to a farm in Virginia; his wife went through a difficult conversion to Roman Catholicism and had mental problems; and another daughter, Frances, was separated and then divorced from Jan Masaryk in 1931. Crane still maintained contacts within the American political elite, sending much-welcomed crates of dates to FDR from his Palm Springs, California, estate, where he died in 1938. The Institute on Current World Affairs still functions, and grandson Thomas Crane maintains the Woods Hole family home. Crane Papers, new accessions, BA, CU, and interview with Thomas Crane, October 2002.

203. Hopper to Frank Kellogg, 1930 CV, reel 39, Kellogg Papers, MD, LC.

204. Wood to Harper, 23 February 1927, f. 20, box 11, Harper Papers, UC-R. Wood commented, somewhat facetiously, "He is absorbing atmosphere rapidly. Albert Williams, author, has suggested that they live at Doc. Hammer's pension, the kosher food palace run by that wealthy concessionaire who fled the United States on account of his liberal opinions, according to his chums, and on account of too liberal use of the scalpel, according to NY court records as others say." Ibid. Wood seems to have confused Armand Hammer and his father's records.

205. Hopper to Kameneva, 6 January 1927, and Skvirsky to Korinets, 28 February 1928, d. 43, op. 3, f. 5283, GARF.

206. Hopper, *Pan-Sovietism: The Issue before America* (Boston: Houghton Mifflin, 1931), 1. Hopper was also angling for a position in the State Department. Hopper to Kellogg, 1930 (?), reel 39, Kellogg Papers, MD, LC.

director Edgar Rickard, Hoover responded with his support and added, "If what they want is a character whose name is always in the newspaper headlines they should search elsewhere."[207]

Academic studies of Russia naturally expanded because of the increased attention to the novelty of a Bolshevik Russia that seemed to survive, despite dire predictions, and move in unexpected directions. Samuel Harper at Chicago was a rock of education, both university and the public sector, thanks to his connections with the State Department and the largesse of Crane. Independently, the New York Public Library, already a major resource for Russian studies thanks to its response to serving the concentration of Russian and Jewish emigrant populations in the city, led the way in terms of book acquisitions and exchanges. Inspired by Avrahm Yarmolinsky, the new director of the Slavic Division, Harry Lydenberg, chief reference librarian, set off in September 1923 to acquire books and other materials for the library. This trip perhaps set a new record for territory covered and acquisitions: 12 countries and 26 cities in 155 days. He spent three months in Soviet Russia. The only Soviet official contacted was, appropriately, Lunacharsky, but Lydenberg had free reign with old and new heads of the Academy of Sciences, Sergei Oldenburg and Aleksei Karpinsky, as well as the venerable Zenaida Ragozin. He lectured in October at the Rumiantsev Library in Moscow, soon to be the Lenin Library, and managed to acquire more than 9,000 items for the New York Public Library, considerably enlarging its already impressive collection on Russia.[208]

The 1924 meeting of the American Historical Association in Richmond, Virginia, marked a new beginning for historical scholarship on Russia. The session on Russia featured R. W. Seton Watson of the University of London, Frank Golder of Stanford, Samuel Harper of Chicago, and Robert Kerner of the University of California. Richard Crane hosted the Russian specialists at his nearby farm. Another broader and more political forum, the summer programs at Williamstown, Massachusetts, involved the participation of Bakhmeteff, Harper, Tasker Bliss, and many others, beginning in August 1923. Encouraged by Pares, Seton Watson went on a speaking tour to Chicago, Cleveland, and Boston.[209]

207. Hoover to H. Alexander Smith, 15 February 1927, f. Rickard 1927, box 525, Hoover Papers, Commerce, HHPL.

208. Robert A. Karlowich, "Stranger in a Far Land: Report of a Bookbuying Trip by Harry Miller Lydenberg in Eastern Europe and Russia in 1923–1924," *Bulletin of Research in the Humanities* 87, no. 1 (1986–1987), 182–224; Yarmolinsky to Wardwell, 31 August 1923, f. Aug. 1923–May 1924, box 7, Wardwell Papers, BA, CU.

209. Samuel Harper was annoyed that he got only three days, while Harvard received six. Harper to Kerner, 7 January 1924, f. 9, box 11, Harper Papers, UC-R.

In the meantime, *Foreign Affairs Quarterly* filled the American gap on the new political reality that resulted from the Bolshevik Revolution. The first issue included articles by Elihu Root, Charles Eliot, André Tardieu, Eduard Benes, Victor Chernov, Archibald Coolidge, and Allen Dulles. And Bakhmeteff, Karl Radek, and Paul Miliukov were lined up for the future. Editor Hamilton Fish Armstrong aimed high, hoping to secure articles from Secretary of State Hughes, Edward House, and former president Wilson, as well as Trotsky and Stalin—and had remarkable success. He was disappointed that Thomas Masaryk declined to participate and that, although significant, Charles Crane contributed only $5,000 to the cause.[210] Crane was still a major factor because of his contacts with Wilson, but an article failed to materialize because of the illness and death of the former president. Nevertheless, the council became well established as a promoter of sane and reasoned, though cautious, dialogue on the issues of the times, Soviet Russia certainly being among the chief subjects. Its early emphasis on Russian questions, however, was eclipsed even before the death of Coolidge in 1928.[211] *Foreign Affairs* concentrated on current events—the Soviet and American present situations and recent past.

The historical journal at this time was the *Russian Review* (before its transformation into the *Slavonic and East European Review*), founded and edited by Pares. Almost all American scholars, such as Coolidge, Golder, Harper, and Kerner, had high respect for Pares as the founder of Slavonic studies in the West, assisted by the equally respected R. W. Seton Watson, first in Liverpool, then at the University of London, where they founded the venerable School of Slavonic and East European Studies. All of these Americans, however, somewhat resented Pares' imperial demeanor and wished to be more independent of it. They had the numbers but not the will for many years. In the meantime, they catered to Pares and his somewhat clumsy efforts to support the journal and himself financially. They all anticipated his approach to their university campuses reluctantly—with precious funds scavenged for an honorarium—not only because of having to endure his pomposity but also because he was a notoriously poor speaker.[212] As editor of *the* journal he wielded clout and reputation based more on circumstance (World War I and the revolution) and less on scholarly accomplishment.

210. Coolidge to Armstrong, 2 August and 10 October 1922, box 17, and Armstrong to Coolidge, 27 June 1923, box 18, and House to Armstrong, 16 June 1923, box 35, Armstrong Papers, Mudd. Regarding Crane funding, Coolidge noted, "My relations with the Crane family have several sides to them and require delicate handling." To Armstrong, 9 August 1923, box 18, ibid.

With Crane's sponsorship, Miliukov delivered a series of lectures on Russia in 1928. Miliukov to Harper, 9 May 1928, f. 26, box 13, Harper Papers, UC-R.

211. Coolidge-Armstrong correspondence, 1924–1926, box 19, Armstrong Papers, Mudd-P.

212. Many examples can be found in correspondence, for example, Pares to Harper, 24 January 1923, f. 13, box 10, Harper Papers, UC-R.

Samuel Harper, perhaps Pares' earliest American associate, was especially hard pressed to endure the British scholar's forays into Chicago, where he expected to be hosted by Harper—and his constant pleading for money from American scholars. Harper complained in April 1929, fearing that Pares would tap into Crane's support of Russian studies, "Pares proved more impossible than ever, I do not think he is going to get much support from the Rockefeller Foundation. I do hope you will not let Mr. Crane contribute to any of his plans."[213] Harper complained to Kerner, "Pares has the same old technique of refusing to take in what you are saying, sticking to his ideas, and then when you are discouraged with his treatment of your arguments, calmly assume that you have agreed with him. This is his idea of cooperation."[214] Pares also attempted to woo Florinsky back to England in 1931, as the literature expert on the *Review* and replacement for Dmitri Mirsky, who had defected to the Soviet Union. Florinsky demurred, however, anticipating greater opportunities for Russian expertise in the United States.[215]

A problem on the American side was simply that so many of the Slavic scholars were overworked, fully committed to their research and to extra professional duties, writing for journals, presenting lectures, and going on extended trips to Russia (which was always mentally and physically taxing), not to mention the time-consuming involvements with Russian émigré scholars. Kerner at University of California, Berkeley, was swamped with students, Vernadsky deeply involved in research, Karpovich reviving his scholarship—with difficulty—while Harper maintained a central communications center at his mother's home on Woodlawn Avenue, near the University of Chicago, as well as coping with a mentally unbalanced brother, the illness and death of a sister, and a financially failing farm at Kansasville, Wisconsin. The deaths of two of the founders of American Slavic studies—Coolidge and, soon afterward, Frank Golder—was especially disheartening but also a challenge to those remaining: Harper, Kerner, Robinson, Samuel Cross at Harvard, and others.

Without as many excuses as Harper of extra duties, Geroid Robinson at Columbia complained, "I am disgusted with myself for having got so far down under a mass of work, that only an occasional bubble comes to the surface."[216] Many of his colleagues were exasperated with Robinson's failure to respond to appeals for reviews, conference papers, and articles. "Robinson does not seem to have

213. To Brodie, 10 April 1929, f. 11, box 13, ibid. Harper added that Pares at least seemed to appreciate American "cooperation" but does not understand the word.

214. To Kerner, 31 January 1929, f. 2, ibid.

215. Pares to Florinsky, 16 December 1931, and Florinsky to Pares, 31 December 1931, f. Bernard Pares, box 3, Florinsky Papers, BA, CU.

216. Robinson to Harper, 21 December 1927, f. 12, box 13, Harper Papers, UC-R. Many of his successors in the field can relate to that.

any sense of time or timeliness."[217] But he still produced what was arguably the best book of any of them: *Rural Russia under the Old Regime*. Robinson could also surprise colleagues with a witty remark. "Have you heard this one: [Soviet] agriculture is being very rapidly mechanized. They will soon have a machine gun in every village."[218] More seriously, he noted that the Soviet agricultural experiment (collectivization) has the potential to create mass opposition, a repeat of 1921.[219] Unfortunately, Robinson could never get along with his Columbia colleague Michael Florinsky: "Florinsky just happens to get on my nerves, so the less I say on that subject the better."[220] Nevertheless, the extraordinary American involvement and interest—and émigré input—in things Soviet had laid the foundation for major scholarly advances in Russian history and Slavic studies in general.

The Soviet Open Door

In many ways 1926 was a breakthrough year in Russian-American cultural relations. Mayakovsky had come and gone without a major problem, erasing to some extent the Duncan-Esenin disaster. While Sam Wooding and his Chocolate Kiddies wowed Moscow and Leningrad, VOKS became more or less stabilized with the addition of Ivan Korinets as deputy director.[221] A working modus vivendi had been arranged with Amtorg; Scott Nearing's more radical initiatives had been rebuffed. Above all, the economic and political scene was relatively calm, both domestically and internationally. For example, a program to translate American literature by the society's book committee, both fiction and nonfiction, into Russian was coordinated quietly and without fanfare by Mark Van Doren and Floyd Dell.[222] On another measure of the growing maturity of VOKS, Skvirsky subscribed to the *New York Times*, *New York Herald*, *Chicago Tribune*, and *Book Review Digest* for Kameneva, who was clearly taking seriously her international cultural mission.[223] An example was an arrangement made through Elizabeth Hapgood for the review of Russian books on drama in *Theatre Arts Magazine*.

The first organized American student excursion to the Soviet region was in-

217. Harper to MacMurray, 4 September 1931, f. 20, box 15, ibid.
218. Robinson to Harper, 14 March 1933, f. 3, box 16, ibid.
219. To Harper, 21 December 1929, f. 30, box 14, ibid.
220. Ibid.
221. His official title was "responsible secretary."
222. Korinets to Kameneva, 22 April 1926, d. 22, op. 3, f. 5283, GARF. Noted historian Carl Becker, though agreeing to participate, acknowledged, "I ought to say that I don't read many books on 'History' in the professional sense of that much abused word: and may not be much alive to works supposed to be in my 'field.'" Becker to Dell, 27 April 1926, ibid.
223. Skvirsky to Kameneva, 20 November 1925, ibid.

spired by Nearing, organized by Stephen Duggan of the Institute of International Education, and managed by Elizabeth Van Alstyne, a Barnard College student who initiated the planning in March 1926.[224] VOKS was quick to respond, arranging the requested work in factories during the summer with inexpensive lodging for about twenty students, who set off for their Soviet proletarian adventure at the end of June. The party included three women representing Barnard (Van Alstyne), Michigan, Radcliffe, Columbia, Indiana University, the New York School of Social Work, Northwestern, and Ohio Wesleyan.[225] The group also included at least one African-American, Thomas Dabney, from the Brookwood Labor College.

That same summer a business group went to Russia, organized by Jerome Davis and featuring, among others, William Danforth of Ralston Purina Cereals of St. Louis, but also nonbusiness people such as Kirby Page, Janet Speakman (Society of Friends), Matthew Spinka (Chicago Theological Seminary), and Samuel Cahan, a prominent New York rabbi. In 1927, with exchanges expanding, sympathetic representatives on both sides supported a tour of the United States by Kameneva. Unfortunately but predictably, the State Department responded with its old anti-Bolshevik credo of denial of visa, as it did for many other applicants.[226] But supervision and restriction were also increasing on the Soviet side with the commissariat of foreign affairs raising questions about the proposed visits of historian Jesse Clarkson and several others in April 1927.[227]

"A Russian Tragedy"

Probably the best-known American writer of the 1920s, with competition from Sinclair Lewis and Upton Sinclair left in the dust, was Theodore Dreiser, an abrasive country novelist like many of his Russian predecessors and contemporaries. Rising from the Wabash River valley of Indiana (Terre Haute), Dreiser's depictions of the loss of direction, immorality, and sordidness of middle-class America appealed to the new Soviet Russia, more than perhaps any foreign writer. He represented an American challenge to Chekhov (upper class) and Gorky (lower

---

224. Van Alstyne to Kameneva, 8 March 1926, d. 27, op. 3, f. 5283, GARF.
225. Kameneva to Van Alstyne, 10 May 1926, and Van Alstyne to Litvinov, 11 May 1926, ibid.
226. Skvirsky to Korinets, 28 October 1927, d. 34, op. 3, f. 5238, GARF. The United States had already refused visas to a host of Soviet leaders, such as Sokolnikov, Peatakov, Kollontai, and others.
227. Kagan to Korinets, 3 May 1927, d. 39, ibid. Clarkson did visit Russia and received assistance from VOKS. Trevis to Branham, 22 July 1927, d. 42, ibid.

class) averaged out and rolled into one. By 1927 his works had been translated and published in several Soviet editions and languages.

That year Olga Kameneva singled Dreiser out for an invitation to the grand tenth anniversary celebration of the Russian Revolution, not only to have a distinguished literary presence on hand but also to demonstrate international obligations to conform to copyright formalities and the payment of royalties, the latter an enticement to the former. He departed New York on 19 October for the Soviet world by way of Berlin. He would endure nearly three months of cold weather, poor accommodations, and primitive travel conditions.[228] To Dreiser's credit, few Americans would have ventured into a regimen of sightseeing in Russia in late fall and early winter at any time in its history. Dreiser was not the only major American writer to be invited to the Soviet grand show. Sinclair Lewis and Dorothy Thompson (his wife) came for shorter stays. All of them assembled in the offices of Junius Wood of the *Chicago Daily News* at the Grand Hotel to watch a virtually endless parade. That evening the group celebrated at the spacious apartment of the recognized dean of foreign journalists, Walter Duranty. Wood, Louis Fischer, and Eugene Lyons came to exchange observations and brief the guests on the Soviet world.[229]

Dreiser's meeting with Kameneva resulted in the first of many angry demonstrations, as he had been promised a private guide and free range in seeing the Soviet Union. Kameneva quickly agreed and appointed her assistant, Trevis, in charge of overall arrangements and, fortunately for Dreiser, designated an able and compatible American as personal guide; Ruth Kennell had several years' experience in "Bololand" and knew the language. She not only ushered him through the complications of Soviet bureaucracy in all kinds of weather, but also edited Dreiser's published account of his trip and later provided her own account.[230] She evidently kept the notes of the tour for the writer as well as for herself, lugging along a typewriter. Before departure, Dreiser got off to a good start by signing a contract for the publication of his works in Russian for substantial royalties.

Dreiser was obviously quite impressed by the exotic, primitive, yet grand aspects of the Soviet capital:

228. "Dreiser Sails Tonight for Red Celebration," *NYT*, 19 October 1927: 3; Dreiser, *Dreiser Looks at Russia* (New York: Liveright, 1928), 9–17. That year, Ivy Lee was impressed with the Grand Hotel and especially its eight-piece jazz orchestra. Lee, *Present-Day Russia* (New York: Macmillan, 1928), 15. He also noted that the Commissariat of Foreign Affairs was located in a dilapidated building on a side street.

229. Ruth Epperson Kennell, *Theodore Dreiser and the Soviet Union, 1927–1945: A First-Hand Chronicle* (New York: International Publishers, 1969), 24–28.

230. Ibid.

Rambling, disjointed streets and squares! Numerous and agreeable surprises in the way of open spaces, trees, monuments, vistas. Drab, moth-eaten and yet colorful palaces and once grand private homes, obviously the former residences of capitalists, traders, social parasites, social blood-suckers! Oh, and the churches! 384! Count 'em! With lovely green or gold or brown or red or white or purple pineapply domes. And bell towers packed with a most amazing variety of bells—bells that emit such a clatter of sweet, tinny, somber, even ominous, sounds as never anywhere else issued out of any belfry, I am sure. And cobblestones and general untidiness and casualness.[231]

No doubt Dreiser's views were colored by preconceptions and bias, by Kennell's sympathies, and by Soviet attention to his needs, but American readers might be surprised to find that so many church bells were still ringing in the center of the Comintern capital. And he did report things with some objectivity: "There are beggars in the streets now as there were before the proletariat took charge. Plenty of them! But Lord, how picturesque! The multi-colored and voluminous rags of them! I certainly have seen Joseph's coat of many colors, only in these instances so threadbare and dirty."[232] Poverty viewed through the prism of Soviet colors. But he also frankly found Moscow to be "the dullest city in the world, not even excluding Kansas City."[233]

Dreiser certainly kept busy—or was kept busy by his Soviet hosts. He was not impressed by a modern production of Gogol's *Inspector General* staged by Meyerhold, perhaps because of a cramped theater, and thought that Stanislavsky's presentations were stilted and unfortunately restricted to Soviet works. He found that contemporary American authors, such as Zane Grey, James Curwood, Rex Beach, Jack London, Fanny Hurst, and Edna Ferber, enjoyed considerable popularity and were preferred over Russian classical writers.[234] During a tour of the Kremlin, Dreiser saw Lenin's apartment, interviewed Bukharin, and later visited the primitive, simple apartments of Mayakovsky and Meyerhold. Life in Soviet Russia, he discovered, was fraught with many dangers from medical deficiencies and extreme cold to frequent road accidents: "And wrecks, wrecks, wrecks! I saw six on one trip south to Baku and Batoum—wrecks which implied carelessness and little else."[235] Everywhere, workers were slow and inefficient; he considered

231. Dreiser, *Dreiser Looks at Russia*, 22–23.
232. Ibid., 26.
233. Ibid., 34.
234. Ibid., 35, 67.
235. Ibid., 57.

that "too much was being done for labor and too little for the brains necessary to direct it; that labor was being given an undue share of the fruits of the land."[236] Though known for defending the downtrodden against the power of wealth, Dreiser thought that Soviet socialism had gone too far. All in all, he saw the new Russia for what it was, with "the inescapable atmosphere of espionage and mental as well as social regulation which now pervades every part of that great land."[237] One chapter, in fact, was devoted to the tyranny of Communism, and he found himself defending the capitalists in the United States whom he had often vilified. But Dreiser found much to admire in the aspirations and goals of the regime and in the fortitude—and color—of the Russian people.

Dreiser found travel in the country barely manageable, in fact, unmanageable, and, by both his and Kennell's accounts, he truly did suffer physically and mentally. It was not only the vermin-ridden conditions and lack of heat on trains but the threat of being beaten and robbed; and there was always the constant bickering with officials over permissions. All of this occurred despite Soviet cultural authorities taking special precautions. Some of the problems were due to confusion and transition in VOKS and the inadequacies of its delegated agent, Trevis, who escorted him and Kennell to Leningrad. He was, however, still much impressed by the city of Peter the Great, despite a constant cold fog over the city. Forays into the countryside to the Black Sea and into the Caucasus were frustrating and tiring at that time of year. The difficulties and conditions encountered prompted the writer to dictate to Kennell a steamy letter to VOKS in complaint.[238]

The highlights of Dreiser's visit were naturally meetings with the Russian intellectual elite. Visiting Stanislavsky at his theater, he found the great director dispirited and depressed by being forced—already before socialist realism—into the Soviet mold. No longer could he produce and act in the great classics, and Soviet writers had as yet produced nothing of note, though he still evinced hopes for the future.[239] His interview with Eisenstein was one of the most productive, involving a spirited discussion of films, there and abroad, and the Soviet cinematographer arranged for a special showing of his award-winning *October*. The director commented in regard to controls over his art, "There is strict control as in your country, only here it is political, whereas in the United States it is moral."[240] The meeting with Mayakovsky in his apartment was more elaborate, involving a dinner with a full range of zakuski, vodka and wines, and for the main courses:

236. Ibid., 75.
237. Ibid., 115.
238. Kennell, *Theodore Dreiser and the Soviet Union*, 198–99.
239. Ibid., 197–98.
240. As quoted in ibid., 51.

oxtail soup with piroshki and goose with apples. The climax came with the host pouring a glass of vodka over whipped cream and prune preserves and declaring it *Krem Drayzera*.[241] Not surprisingly the evening turned into a contest of telling ribald jokes, many probably lost in translation.

Back in the United States by the end of January 1928, Dreiser had endured seventy-seven days of the Soviet scene. Although his criticism of Soviet life, accompanied by his gallant defense of the United States in Russia, had perturbed Soviet officials, he now defended the Soviet system against a barrage of complaints from American opponents.[242] He wrote a series of articles for the North American News Agency syndicate, essentially pieces of the book that would be published later that year, which gave a more balanced account. Predictably, letters to the editor attacked the supposed naïveté of his views, claiming he had been virtually brainwashed—far from the case. Nevertheless, Dreiser had opened the Soviet door even more to Americans. In 1931 7,000 tourists would visit the USSR, three quarters of them American.[243]

Film

Lenin placed special emphasis on motion pictures as a means to educate the populace, which still contained many who were illiterate. Along with posters and art, film, cinemas, and projection equipment would receive special state emphasis. The development and availability of the material necessities of showing films coincided with the relaxed era of the New Economic Policy, when people were looking for entertainment as much as for education, and also with the explosive growth of the American cinema industry. It should be no surprise, therefore, that American films dominated the Soviet market, as they did elsewhere in Europe. Though Soviet film directors such as Sergei Eisenstein and Aleksandr Pudovkin were producing higher-quality, innovative films, the American models caught the imagination of a Soviet public looking for escape and entertainment. Exact figures are unavailable, but American films probably captured at least 60 to 65 percent of the Soviet audiences in the 1920s, about the same as for France and Germany.[244]

241. Ibid., 63. According to Kennell, another American guest was astonished by a large bowl of caviar and exclaimed, "Good Lord, that would cost at least 25 dollars in New York." Ibid.,

242. Kennell, *Theodore Dreiser and the Soviet Union*, 214–17.

243. Schlossberg diary, January 1932, d. 372, op. 3, f. 5283, GARF.

244. Denise J. Youngblood, *Soviet Cinema in the Silent Era, 1918–1935* (Ann Arbor, Mich.: UMI Research Press, 1985), 56–58.

Especially popular in Russia were the swashbuckling dramas of Douglas Fairbanks, such as *Thief of Baghdad* and *Mark of Zorro*, and the comedies of Charlie Chaplin, Buster Keaton, and Harold Lloyd. The American success in this market was due to handsome, likable heroes and the product—simply designed and directed films for a mass market—and to a well-developed distribution and advertising system. While the Soviet industry was handicapped in the mass production of film copies, the United States flooded the country with quantities of reels and accompanying poster advertising.[245] The fact that these films were largely silent facilitated audience acceptance. It was fairly simple to substitute Russian captions. The exposure to the United States through film also spurred the invasion of the Jazz Age, as the Soviet people saw the dancing and heard the music.

Some Americans certainly admired the innovative film productions of Sergei Eisenstein, despite their obvious propaganda content. Eisenstein, an engineer by training, quickly rose to the challenge with a series of memorable films, such as *Mother*, *Battleship Potemkin*, and *October*, all of which received favorable reviews in the West. His *Potemkin* had an impact comparable to Balieff and Stanislavsky on the New York scene. A private screening arranged by Amtorg at Wurlitzer Hall on West 42nd Street was a great success. The main problem, in contrast to American films in Russia, was that for some time only one copy of the film existed in the United States, and it was constantly in use.[246] It should come as no surprise, then, that Eisenstein, as well as Mayakovsky and Stanislavsky, would be invited to the United States, arriving to considerable acclaim during the fall of 1930.[247] After the usual wining and dining in New York amid special showings of his films, he was drawn to Hollywood by Paramount to film Dreiser's *American Tragedy*. Matters did not go well between him and the Hollywood moguls, and Eisenstein soon fled to Mexico to produce a film on the Mexican Revolution and its developing society.

Upton Sinclair, who had planned to visit Russia that year, was an initial sponsor and fund-raiser, successfully winning the crucial support of Charles Crane's eldest daughter, Kate Crane-Gartz. He managed to raise $50,000 for the Eisenstein Mexican project but needed more, and so requested a payment of royalties on his books from the Soviet publisher, Gosizdat of $25,000.[248] Eisenstein's delay-

245. Ibid.

246. Gumberg to Clinton Gilbert (*New York Evening Post*), 4 November 1926, f. Oct.–Nov. 1926, box 2, Gumberg Papers, SHSW.

247. "Russia to See Film Play," *NYT*, 3 November 1930: 19.

248. Upton Sinclair, *The Autobiography of Upton Sinclair* (New York: Harcourt, Brace, 1962), 215, 262; Sinclair to Gumberg, 19 June 1931, f. 6, box 5, Gumberg Papers, SHSW. Sinclair had to cancel a planned trip to Russia because of his involvement in the Eisenstein affairs.

ing (perhaps because he did not want to return to Russia[249]) and obstinacy ultimately produced a rift, forcing Sinclair to have him recalled to Russia.[250] He shot
an amazing amount of film documenting Mexican society—mainly peasants and
brightly dressed young women—and its revolutionary past, appearing eventually
as *Thunder over Mexico*, essentially a confusing travelogue that finally opened
in New York to poor reviews, mainly because Eisenstein had little hand in the
final editing.[251] Disenchanted by his American experiences, Eisenstein returned
to Russia, where he was virtually ostracized until handed a contract for a saga of
Alexander Nevsky's successful resistance of a German invasion in the thirteenth
century. This and his final controversial work on a three-part interpretation of
Ivan the Terrible only indirectly related to Soviet-American relations, but they
certainly kept his reputation alive abroad.

In the meantime, with the emergence of a state-controlled socialist realism—
harnessing culture to the political and economic aims of the regime, Soviet film
was becoming even more tainted by propaganda. A case in point was *Today*, a
film released in 1931 that claimed to compare and contrast American and Soviet
life. The American shots were made by a New York Communist showing scenes
of the worst of life in the United States, fairly easy to find in the early Depression.[252] Another example was a Ukrainian silent film, *Jimmie Higgins*, based on
a story by Upton Sinclair, that caused a stir when it was shown in New York in
1933.[253] The famous Nikita Balieff, the best-known Russian actor in the United
States, had little success in filmmaking with a role in an abortive film in New
York and a foray or two into Hollywood that seemed to net only some nice photographs with Charlie Chaplin.[254]

The African-American Invasion of Russia

Another misguided effort at a propaganda film involved a depiction of the "real"
sordid, oppressed life of African-Americans. For this purpose several African-

---

249. Sinclair, *Autobiography*, 262–65.
250. "This matter [the Eisenstein film] dragged out so much longer than we expected, and involved
so many cares, we have had to stay here." Sinclair to Amdur, 19 December 1932, d. 373, op. 3, f.
5283, GARF.
251. "Thunder Over Mexico," *NYT*, 25 September 1933: 18.
252. "Russia and Talkies," *NYT*, 8 March 1931: 112.
253. "A Russian 'Jimmie Higgins,'" *NYT*, 22 February 1933: 25.
254. For the photographs, see Harold B. Segal, *Turn-of-the-Century Cabaret: Paris, Barcelona, Berlin, Munich, Vienna, Cracow, Moscow, St. Petersburg, Zurich* (New York: Columbia University Press,
1987) 273–74, one of Chaplin with Balieff alone, one with the cast of Chauvre-Souris, both of which
are attributed to a "private collection."

Americans were recruited in 1932 to come to Moscow as actors for a film already titled *Black and White*.[255] Among the twenty who sailed on 14 June, however, few could be considered downtrodden or oppressed: four actors, four social workers, four college students, three newspapermen, a farmer, a paperhanger, a singer, a salesman, and an insurance clerk. Best known of the group were poet and novelist Langston Hughes and Henry Lee Moon, editor of the *Amsterdam News*, a Communist-leaning newspaper in Harlem. The official American sponsors, who helped with travel expenses, were prominent Soviet sympathizers: Columbia Teachers' College professor George Counts, Malcolm Cowley, Floyd Dell, and Waldo Frank.[256] Nothing would come of this venture except the exposure of several prominent, idealistic African-Americans to Soviet reality.[257]

Hughes was attracted by the promise of an opportunity to write for film. He was also visiting an old Soviet sympathizer, Lincoln Steffens, in Carmel, California, at the time, who encouraged him to go but warned him about unexpected conditions: "Be sure to take soap and toilet paper for yourself—don't part with it!—and lipsticks and silk stockings to give the girls."[258] He drove coast to coast in record time to make the ship, taking along a typewriter, a Victrola, and a large box of Louis Armstrong, Bessie Smith, Duke Ellington, and Ethel Waters records. The last person up the gangplank, Hughes was surprised to find that most of the contingent were naive, youthful intellectuals, including several attractive young women, many of whom seemed simply along for the adventure. Quartered at the Grand Hotel near the Kremlin, they found plenty to eat but not much variety. The group preferred to gather at the Metropole in the evening where there was a jazz band and "bar-stool girls about."[259] Some of them thought they were all spies, probably the case. Hughes himself wondered about the girls, who did not seem to be prostitutes.

As far as the film project was concerned, Hughes was amazed at the naïveté on both sides and that there was little or no apparent planning, contracts, nor any design. The thousand-page script in Russian was a bafflement. It took three weeks for it to be translated, and in the meantime the troupe enjoyed the sights: theater, opera, and the Park of Culture on the Moscow River with its nude bath-

255. Schlossberg diary for 26 to 31 August 1932, d. 372, op. 3, f. 5238, GARF.

256. "To Aid Soviet Film," *NYT*, 14 June 1932: 26.

257. There were apparently rumors to the effect that American companies, individual engineers, or both, put pressure on the Soviet government to cancel the project. Robert Robinson, with Jonathan Slevin, *Black on Red: My 44 Years Inside the Soviet Union* (Washington, D.C.: Acropolis Books, 1988), 320.

258. Langston Hughes, *I Wonder as I Wander: An Autobiographical Journey* (New York: Thunder's Mouth Press, 1986), 65–66.

259. Ibid., 73.

Langston Hughes, c. 1932. (Prints and Photographs, Library of Congress)

ing beaches.[260] When finally presented with an English translation, Hughes could only laugh at the obvious errors and ignorance about American life. He went over the whole script with a red pencil, and then asked "What is left from which to make a picture?"[261] The film was to be set in Birmingham, Alabama, with working-class black heroes and white bosses as villains. The climax was a scene of a strike by blacks, who radio for aid to Northern allies, who come in the form of white workers from Detroit. As Hughes noted, "These pages of the scenario presented a kind of trade-union version of the Civil War all over again, intended as a great sweeping panorama of contemporary labor battles in

260. Hughes, however, found the tours tedious and managed to escape, at least for a couple of days, to visit with an African-American Soviet worker from Detroit. Robinson, *Black on Red*, 320–21.
261. Hughes, *I Wonder as I Wander*, 77.

America."[262] To top things off, the proposed director of the film was a German who knew little Russian or English and had never seen an African-American before.

Continued protests by the Americans resulted in Hughes being asked to re-write the script. He demurred, saying he had never lived in the South and knew nothing about industry in Birmingham. Another problem was that the cast was expected to sing, but "only a few of us had ever heard a spiritual outside a concert hall, or a work song other than 'Water Boy' in a night club."[263] They, neverthe-less, tried to render a decent version of "Nobody Knows de Trouble I've Seen," "Swing Low, Sweet Chariot," and "All God's Chillun Got Shoes," with accom-panying Russian translation, whatever that could be. The irony of the whole affair was dramatized by one of the group, Silvia, the only real singer, performing spirituals on an antireligious radio station.

One highlight of this new African-American presence in Soviet Russia was meeting those of their race already there, foremost being Emma Harris, named "the mammy of Moscow" by Hughes.[264] She was from Kentucky by way of Brook-lyn and had already been in Moscow for forty years. The whole group knew about her, and, when they got off the train, they automatically shouted, "Let's go see Emma." And, indeed they did, with her welcome, "Bless God! Lord! I'm sure glad to see some Negroes!"[265] She was quite critical of the Stalin regime but still would appear at political rallies—and be cheered—as the token black. Hughes and the others were impressed by her knowledge of the Moscow scene and uncanny abil-ity to fetch the best caviar as well as large amounts of Kentucky bourbon for any occasion. They could not but note the Soviet favoritism toward anything black. Although treated royally and finally developing a good relationship with the German director, Karl Youghams, the Harlem elite were not impressed by the

---

262. Ibid., 79. In the meantime the Soviet film project was quietly dropped. Hugh Cooper, a prominent American engineer who was assisting the electrification of the country, had returned to Russia on the same ship as the American black delegation and learned of their mission. Upon arrival in Moscow, he demanded an interview with the Politburo and harangued several members, includ-ing Molotov and Kaganovich, that any film project that might be construed as anti-American would damage the cause of recognition, especially since it was scheduled for release in 1933. Kaganovich wrote Stalin, "I think we can do without this film." A Politburo decision on 22 August advised that "a complete cancellation of the production of the film 'Black and White' is not to be announced," but relegated it to extensive bureaucratic review, or, in other words, oblivion. Actually the "actors" eventually learned from a small newspaper item of its cancellation but were never told why. *The Sta-lin-Kaganovich Correspondence, 1931–1936*, compiled and edited by R. W. Davies, Oleg V. Khlevniuk, E. A. Rees, Liudmila P. Kosheleva, and Larisa A. Rogovaya (New Haven, Conn.: Yale University Press, 2003), 113–14.

263. Ibid., 80.

264. Blakely, *Russia and the Negro*, 95

265. Hughes, *I Wonder as I Wander*, 83.

Soviet effort to impress, especially after a near riot that occurred on their appearance on an Odessa beach.[266]

Returning to Moscow at the height of the tourist season, the American film ensemble was housed at a small hotel near St. Basil's Cathedral without private baths or dining facilities. Some claimed that Raymond Robins had urged them to withdraw at the very beginning, and most now agreed that he was right. Though Hughes seemed to enjoy the uniqueness of the Russian locale—and being treated as an American novelty—the *New York Herald Tribune* headlined, "Negroes Adrift in 'Uncle Tom's' Russian Cabin."[267] Perhaps because of a far from optimum Moscow exposure, the African-American contingent was given a tour of the Russian great plains of Central Asia, through the Kazakhstan desert to the oases of Samarkand, Tashkent, and Bukhara, encountering another African-American in residence, Bernard Powers, a recent graduate of Howard University in Washington.[268] They were then somewhat taken aback by the Soviet determination to show them their "cotton fields down south," which most of them had never seen before in the United States.

Hughes managed to go off on his own to Ashkabad, which became the highlight of his Russian tour. Here he met German journalist Arthur Koestler and established a compatibility and mutual relationship that gave the region even more exposure through their publications.[269] They continued to travel together through Central Asia, Hughes increasingly miserable because of the wind, dust, and cold in October and November. Lodged in a hotel in Merv, he quoted Koestler, "This filthy hole! It will take more than a revolution to clean up this dive. I can't wash in this stinking water." He compared Koestler's restlessness and curiosity with other writers he had known, such as Richard Wright and Harlan Ellison.[270]

266. Ibid., 95.

267. Ibid., 96.

268. Ibid., 104–5.

269. Ibid, 114–17. As Hughes tells the story, in the hotel in Askhabad he was playing on his portable phonograph one of the many jazz recordings he carried with him to listen to while typing up some notes, when he heard a knock on the door, and, expecting a friend, yelled, "Come on in." Koestler, also a fan of jazz, entered and introduced himself. They spent the evening together listening to records and sharing camel sausage. Hughes described his attendance with Koestler of a trial of Turkmen "saboteurs" the next day; he entitled that section of his memoir, adroitly, "Darkness Before Noon," after Koestler's famous exposé of the later Soviet purge trials.

270. Ibid., 119–20. Hughes wrote a number of short, descriptive articles and longer works for both Soviet and American publications, for example: "Moscow and Me: A Noted American Writer Relates his Experiences," *International Literature* 4 (September 1933), 60–66; "Going South in Russia," *The Crisis* 41 (June 1934), 162–63; *A Negro Looks at Central Asia* (Moscow and Leningrad: Cooperative Publishing Society of Foreign Workers in the U.S.S.R., 1934). These were essentially summarized in *I Wonder as I Wander*. Besides Hughes's memoirs, this account is based on an excellent survey by David Chioni Moore, "Colored Dispatches from the Uzbek Border: Langston Hughes' Relevance, 1933–2002," in *Callaloo: A Journal of African Diaspora Arts and Letters* 25, No. 4 (Fall 2002), 1115–35, which

On the other extreme of the moving picture industry was Cecil B. DeMille and his extravaganza approach to filmmaking. Stalinist cinema directors were intrigued by his grand scale use of propaganda and by the possibility of capturing the idea of grandeur sweep for their own purposes. The result was another American foray into the Soviet world that was, of course, more than welcoming to the premier Hollywood director. His 1931 and 1932 visits paved the way, however, for the reception of many American films into Soviet *kinos*, which in turn would influence Soviet cinematography, not perhaps in the right direction.[271] One thing that Soviet and American culture had in common was the infatuation with doing things on a grand scale and with the creation of exaggerated, idealized images of life, socialist realism American style, anything to help people forget for a while the drudgery and hardships of their life.

Without question DeMille carried clout and dollars, but the best-known Hollywood visitor to Russia in those years, a motion picture in himself, was Harpo Marx, the silent member of the Marx Brothers. Arriving in Moscow in November 1933, he was well aware that he was not the only Marx familiar to Soviet authorities—and made the most of it. The nature of his acting was at first misunderstood, and he had to endure a tryout at the Moscow Art Theater until it was made clear that his act involved comedy pantomime, vaudeville style.[272] He then had a successful tour playing to packed houses in Moscow, Leningrad, and places in between and beyond.

Another popular film medium was documentaries, and Soviet Russia was a popular subject. E. M. Newman, who had pioneered with motion pictures in Russia as early as 1911, led the way during the summer of 1927, traveling widely though about half of his film was shot in Leningrad and vicinity. Threatened with arrest several times in remote areas, Newman managed to talk his way out and bring most of his footage home to provide a unique picture of Russia, warts and all, at the end of the NEP.[273] Julien Bryan made Russia his subject in more

---

includes a marvelous picture of Hughes and Koestler (in suit and tie) picking cotton in Uzbekistan. Additional material is available in the Langston Hughes Papers, in the Yale Collection of American Literature, Beinecke Rare Book and Manuscript Library at Yale University, which were not consulted.

271. De Mille to Petrov, 12 December 1931, d. 420, op. 3, f. 5283, GARF. In this letter, De Mille thanked VOKS for its support, adding, "I shall hope to repay that country by bringing to my countrymen a knowledge of the work you are so splendidly doing."

272. Harpo Marx, with Rowland Barber, *Harpo Speaks!* (New York: Limelight Editions, 2000), 309–11. He delighted in relating that he was sitting in a Moscow hotel room having tea when his visit became official, that is, when the recognition agreement was signed.

273. Newman to Trevis, 3 September 1927, d. 42, ibid. Unfortunately, most of this is preserved only in over 300 still pictures in the account of his Soviet adventure. Newman, *Seeing Russia* (New York: Funk & Wagnalls, 1928).

than one travelogue. His films, especially *Russia as It Is* (1933), were more formal and official, more patronizing, positive, and sympathetic but nevertheless remain valuable documents of a Russia in transition during the First Five Year Plan. Perhaps the most memorable photographer of Soviet Russia in transition, however, was Margaret Bourke-White, who captured the transition of an overwhelmingly agricultural country into an industrial age, with dramatic pictures of dams, factories, people—of Russia on the move.[274]

Journalists

Before the revolution, the American press was represented only by itinerant correspondents, few spending more than a few weeks in the country. That would change after 1920. The American resident reporters of the Soviet scene were a mixed lot, but whatever their deficiencies, they gave Americans the most accurate news possible from the Russia of the 1920s and 1930s. The chief anchor, to the grief of some at the time and more later, was British-born Walter Duranty. He held that position because of the clout of his employer, the *New York Times*, and because of his longevity in the Soviet reporting jungle. Beginning in 1921, he operated from a large, if not lavish, apartment and information center that looked both ways. He courted Soviet authorities and befriended numerous American visitors with his hospitality, won favors from most of both, and collected any bits of information they may have been able to provide. More important, by cultivating Soviet authorities and portraying the country's life in a generally favorable way, he gained special access to government and party counsels. His overlordship of American reportage was clearly too much for some competitors to take, one commenting that he was lucky to have escaped from "Duranty's Inferno." Without question, Duranty took advantage of his position and connections while sending a fascinating quantity of information about the Soviet Union, always having an open line to his paper in New York and its editors' respect for his reports.[275] While other reporters could often not find print space for their observations, Duranty was always there, prominently placed in the *New York Times*.

As some other journalists, Duranty would sometimes rush his cables to New York without fully checking the facts. Alex Gumberg once took him to task

274. See Margaret Bourke-White, *Eyes on Russia* (New York: Simon and Schuster, 1931).

275. Acknowledging his deficiencies in regard to neglecting, or intentionally missing, aspects of the Soviet scene, such as the wholesale murder of masses of peasants during collectivization, he provided the American public and many others privately with information that they might not have had about the Soviet Union. William Allen White, for example, credited him as the key inside source on his own fairly accurate account of the famine losses.

for inaccuracies in an article on the Ford contract for the car factory at Nizhny Novgorod, but also acknowledged, "In my opinion, you have given us the best interpretation of Russia's progress, difficulties and problems that we have yet had from anyone."[276] Another journalist who dipped in and out of Russia and was the subject of scorn from the "experts" was Fred Knickerbocker, who wrote a critical series on Russia for the *New York Evening Post* in late 1930. He claimed to know it all after a relatively brief tour.

Second in line to Duranty in rank and in column inches was probably Eugene Lyons, who was more sophisticated and intellectual in his reporting from Russia and traveled much throughout the country. He was also sympathetic to the Soviet Union as a veteran editor of the Soviet press agency, TASS, in the United States. He was recruited by the United Press in 1928 to establish a Moscow bureau because of his contacts and closeness to Soviet officials, though he soon became disillusioned by what he saw in Russia.[277] Like Duranty, he established an imposing command post—in the Armand Hammer mansion.[278] Considered by many to have the most objective views on Russia, Lyons still came to the conclusion, after an hour's interview with Stalin in 1930, that "I like that man."[279] Close behind him in the scale of reporting on Russia were certainly William Henry Chamberlin of the *Christian Science Monitor*, freelance journalist Maurice Hindus, William Stoneman of the *Chicago Daily News*, and Louis Fischer of the *New Republic*. In terms of scholarship and lasting contributions, the works of Fischer and Hindus stand out. While Fischer produced a memorable biography of Lenin, Hindus recorded sympathetically the turmoil of the First Five Year Plan in the countryside in *Red Bread* and *Humanity Uprooted*.

276. Gumberg to Duranty, 20 January 1930, f. 3, box 4, Gumberg Papers, SHSW.

277. Barbara S. Mahoney, *Dispatches and Dictators: Ralph Barnes for the Herald Tribune* (Corvallis: Oregon State University Press, 2002), 56–60; Whitman Bassow, *The Moscow Correspondents: Reporting on Russia from the Revolution to Glasnost* (New York: Paragon House, 1989), 65–69.

278. See Lyons, *Assignment in Utopia* (New York: Harcourt, Brace, 1937), 285–331. American and other Western correspondents in Russia maintained a cosmopolitan, generally quite active social life with frequent, lavish parties sustained by an ability to exchange money on the black market and buy all kinds of goods at a special store for foreigners. Soviet authorities catered to their whims with these advantages in addition to lavish accommodations, at least until 1933. But life in Moscow for the large number of American reporters had its ups and downs. James Abbe, a short-term correspondent-photographer of the scene, described how Gene Lyons was forced to give up much of his large space, on Hammer's orders, to *Moscow News* and its staff of forty, who cooked their meals on his stove. Still, an un-Soviet bourgeois lifestyle prevailed in the colony with rounds of entertainments in their spacious rooms or at the Metropole Hotel bar featuring gypsy orchestras, Soviet ballerinas, and a typical 1920s cabaret atmosphere. For more descriptions of this high life of jazz age Moscow, see Abbe, *I Photograph Russia* (London: George G. Harrap, 1935), 179–88.

279. Lyons, *Assignment in Utopia*, 389.

In 1931, with more Americans coming to Russia out of curiosity or on business, the *New York Herald Tribune* established an office in Moscow to compete with the *Times*, headed by Ralph Barnes. The big news item was the collectivization campaign and the devastating famine resulting from that and a severe drought. Though aware of the immense loss of life, Duranty downplayed its importance, most likely in the interests of maintaining his contacts in the Soviet government. Stoneman and Barnes traveled through the south of Russia, guided by Hindus, to report on the scope of the famine and sent their reports through visiting German businessmen. They were soon summoned for a warning and dressing down by the chief Soviet Press official, Konstantin Umansky, later ambassador to the United States.[280]

Duranty, Lyons, Hindus, Fischer, and Chamberlin all wrote books as well as regular columns that developed their reputations, as well as earning them more royalties. Hindus clearly scored best on that front, both in royalties as well as reviews.[281] Probably the best regarded by American visitors, if they could find him in his room in the Grand Hotel, was Junius Wood of the *Chicago Tribune*, who was always willing to share his electric hot plate.[282] Unlike the other long-term journalists, however, Wood never learned Russian. Other transient journalists were usually lodged in the Lux Hotel, which Lyons termed "an overcrowded tenement."[283] One notable characteristic was the tendency to help each other out, providing leads, such as Hindus providing essential leads in 1931 to Barnes for an exclusive interview with Stalin's wife, Nadia Alliluleva.[284] Clearly, Americans who read the major newspapers and journals should have been well informed, if not always with the greatest accuracy, of progress in the Soviet Union. No other foreign correspondents, not even Malcolm Muggeridge of the *Manchester Guardian*, could do any better.

By this time the "Great Offensive," as Hindus termed it, was already launched and had become the focus of news reports. Vladimir Mayakovsky, during his visit to the United States in 1925, recorded in advance the spirit of this new age of materialism that, he thought, both the United States and Soviet Russia were pioneering, symbolized by the Brooklyn Bridge.

---

280. Bassow, *The Moscow Correspondents*, 67–69. Umansky would later be the Soviet ambassador to the United States in 1939.

281. Bernard Pares observed, in reference to *Mother Russia*: "The difference between him [Hindus] and Chamberlin is that he has grit and Chamberlin has not, so that, whereas Hindus' hesitations to judge are informing, the other man's seem to me only compromises." To Harper, 14 November 1929, f. 27, box 14, Harper Papers, UC-R.

282. Ray Long, *An Editor Looks at Russia: One Unprejudiced View of the Land of the Soviets* (New York: Ray Long and Richard Smith, 1931), 17.

283. Lyons, *Assignment in Utopia*, 70.

284. Mahoney, *Dispatches and Dictators*, 66–67.

Give, Coolidge,
a shout of joy!
I too will spare no words
about good things.
Blush
at my praise,
go red as our flag,
however
united-states-
of-
america you may be
As a crazed believer
enters
a church,
retreats
into a monastery cell,
austere and plain;
so I,
in graying evening
haze,
humbly set foot
on Brooklyn Bridge.
. . . .
I am proud
of just this
mile of steel;
upon it,
my visions come to life, erect—
here's a fight
for construction
instead of style,
an austere disposition
of bolts
and steel.[285]

285. Mayakovsky, *The Bedbug and Selected Poetry*, translated by George Reavey (Bloomington: Indiana University Press, 1975), 173–77.

5

Construction

The 1920s represented an experiment in a mixed capitalist/socialist system, a relaxation from the stress of war Communism and the civil war for Soviet Russia. Much of the ordinary, day-to-day economy was returned to private individuals and companies, with the "commanding heights," the very large industries, retained under state control and operation. The result was a remarkable recovery of the economic life of the country from the depths of a virtually complete collapse by 1921 and from the effects of the catastrophic famine. But Russia was still and increasingly behind the rest of the world, especially the United States, in industrial growth and basic living standards. The Communist promise of a utopia had proved quite ephemeral. Its success in some areas, however, offered some promise. The question again was the eternal Russian question, "What is to be done?" or better, "What is to be done now?"

The great industrialization debate was the result. Many leading Bolsheviks, led by Trotsky, believed the socialist agenda, which they had acquired but retreated from in the NEP, demanded a new revolution of economic construction. Lenin in 1917, in *The Threatening Catastrophe and How to Fight It*, acknowledged that special pressures existed for Russia to repair economic damage and build a new economic structure, because of the effects of the war in setting back the economy and because of its expected postrevolutionary leadership of the world to be the guiding light for making socialism work. When and how remained the questions, and there were sharp divisions. The American model of rapid industrialization was often cited and gradually won out, thanks to Lenin, Krzhizhanovsky, Krasin, Lomonosov, and others. The history of looking to an American model went back to Sergei Witte, Petr Stolypin, and their many supporters.

A major architect of the American emphasis in the First Five Year Plan was Nikolai Ossinsky, also known as Valerian Obolenskii-Osinskii, a descendant of the old nobility who lent his expertise to Bolshevik economic planning as early as 1917.[1] A respected economist and member of the Academy of Sciences, Ossinsky served as the first chair of the Supreme Council of the National Economy of the Russian Soviet Federated Socialist Republic (RSFSR) in 1917–1918 and subsequently as commissar of agriculture of the USSR in the mid-1920s, as well as the first Soviet ambassador to Sweden for two years. Fluent in English, he had long admired American progress in both agriculture and industry and observed the country firsthand for six months in 1925.[2] He served as chair of the Central Statistical Bureau and as an ally of Valerian Kuibyshev, a rising Stalin protégé. In 1927 he launched a major campaign for the "automobilization" of the USSR, but he was denied a visa to enter the United States to examine automobile construction in 1928, because he had attended a Comintern congress as an economic expert, despite efforts made on his behalf by former governor of Indiana James Goodrich.[3]

Ossinsky emerged in the middle of the First Five Year Plan as the chair of the All-Union Automobile and Tractor Industries Corporation in charge of overall planning for new projects at Nizhny Novgorod and Chelyabinsk, mainly because of his investigative tour of the United States in 1927. By his own account, "he started an extensive and energetic campaign for the motorization of Russian transport and agriculture. I am known in my country as the outstanding advocate of American gasoline, automobiles and tractors and of American methods of manufacture thereof."[4]

An essential component of the great transformation was collectivization of agriculture, certainly a major diversion from the American model, though one might reflect that a considerable reduction of the number of "peasant" sharecroppers was one consequence of American industrialization. On paper Soviet collectivization appeared to be a simple transition from the Russian communal village to a socialized form. The idea was to reconstitute the traditional village land tillage into a more centrally managed farm with large fields that could accommodate

1. On his own letterhead, he listed his name in Russian as V. V. Obolenskii-Osinskii and in French as V. Obolensky-Ossinsky. In Soviet documents the name is "Ossinskii." For simplicity, "Ossinsky," which he used in signing correspondence, is used in the text.

2. Goodrich to Alexander Gumberg, with letter of introduction, 10 August 1925, f. 7, box 2, Gumberg Papers, SHSW; *Sovetsko-Amerikanskie otnosheniia, gody nepriznaniia, 1918–1926: dokumenty*, edited by G. N. Sevost'ianov et al. (Moscow: Mezhdunarodnyi Fond 'Demokratiia,' 2002), 543, n.1. Ossinsky offered to return to the United States in January 1928, but the offer was vetoed by the Politburo. Politburo protocol, 30 November 1927, f. 17, op. 163, d. 662, RGASPI.

3. Rhodes, *James P. Goodrich, Indiana's "Governor Strangelove": A Republican's Infatuation with Soviet Russia* (Selinsgrove, Penn.: Susquehanna University Press, 1996), 156. Ossinsky to Goodrich, 16 November 1927, f. Russia Ossinsky, box 20 Goodrich Papers, HHPL. As many others associated with economic planning, Ossinsky would be arrested and executed in 1938.

4. Ossinsky to Borah, 7 March 1930, f. Osinskii, box 20, Borah Papers, MD, LC.

the new machinery that industrialization—and American technology—would provide. Labor saved from mechanized agriculture would be absorbed into the new industrial workforce. The plan called for a 20 percent conversion rate from the old village to the new farms within five years, predicated on the expectation that modern equipment could be supplied in that quantity. The result would actually be more like 60 percent collectivization, with the needed equipment provided for less than 5 percent of the total. The real problem was local opposition to the principle of socializing the property of the peasants, especially from the kulaks or the wealthiest element. The reaction to local opposition was the use of force by organizers sent to the countryside, with especially destructive results. Rather than give up their farm animals and poultry for the collective farm, peasants slaughtered them; rather than sow large fields for the collective, little sowing was done.[5]

Some Americans saw imminent disaster ahead in the new agricultural program. Among the first was one of the few American experts on Russian land use, Professor Geroid T. Robinson of Columbia University, who predicted that the new agricultural experiment had the potential for creating mass opposition and that the crisis situation of 1921 in the wake of war Communism had reappeared in greater force in 1928.[6] He would continue to warn of the consequences of all-out collectivization, but he was still only a young student of the Russian scene. Another voice of apprehension represented a deep knowledge of peasant society; Maurice Hindus, a prolific author on the Soviet transformation, witnessed the large-scale opposition to collectivization. He wrote privately to Harper,

> I do know that its failure would plunge Russia into a holocaust. Certainly there are features in the practical control of the movement that fill one again and again with discouragement. But that too is nothing new in Russia. After all they are trafersing [sic] an uncharted sea of social reorganization and blunders are inevitable. It is only a question of the capacity of the Russian leaders to learn from these blunders and also of their ability to finance the vast projects involved.[7]

Nor was he alone in predicting dire consequences from the new Soviet agricultural policy of the First Five Year Plan. Spending some time in Berlin on his way

---

5. For a detailed analysis, see R. W. Davies, *The Socialist Offensive: The Collectivization of Soviet Agriculture, 1929–1930* (Cambridge, Mass.: Harvard University Press, 1980).

6. Robinson to Samuel Harper, 21 December 1929, f. 30, box 14, Harper Papers, UC-Regenstein.

7. To Harper, 3 February 1930, f. 36, ibid. Hindus had just published two major books on the subject: *Broken Earth* and *Humanity Uprooted*.

into Russia in April 1930, Harper found everyone in deep depression, expecting a serious upheaval in Russia but realizing that an extension of the NEP would not work. Little spring planting was expected in Russia that year and production shortfalls all but certain.[8] His correspondence reflected a deep pessimism regarding the Soviet forced economic program. Moscow correspondent Eugene Lyons also saw 1928 and the launching of the First Five Year Plan as the critical year in Stalin's consolidation of power. "The Russia which it created in the next few years was as different from the one bequeathed by Lenin as it was from tsarist Russia."[9]

For Americans on the scene, an overlap clearly existed between the era of concession arrangements of the New Economic Policy and that of construction contracts of the Five Year Plan. By 1930 Averell Harriman had managed to bail out of the unprofitable manganese concession, but the negotiated agreement with Soviet officials resulted in Harriman holding bonds worth $3,450,000 on the mining equipment that he had introduced to be paid off on schedule fifteen years later. The arrangement also involved a Harriman loan of a million dollars to support the continued operation of the Caucasian mines. Harriman's conclusion that those doing business with Russia were subject to "the grandest aggregation of corruption, incompetence, and utter brutality that the world has seen for centuries" did not deter others or even him from considering other ventures.[10] Harriman was still worried about payments coming in on schedule in 1930 but would not discuss the matter openly.[11] However, he would be the first to admit that the new Soviet program raised real possibilities for American business.

Dneprostroi

The challenge of harnessing the long stretch of shallow rapids on the Dnepr River below Kiev extends back many years in Russian history. The wide rapids (*zaporozhe*) dotted with hundreds of islands were unnavigable and nearly impos-

---

8. Harper (Berlin) to Walter Lichtenstein (Chicago National Bank), 17 April 1930, f. 1, box 15, ibid.

9. Eugene Lyons, *Assignment in Utopia* (New York: Harcourt, Brace, 1937), 152. There is, of course, some hindsight in this judgment.

10. Rudy Abramson, *Spanning the Century: The Life of W. Averell Harriman, 1891–1986* (New York: Morrow, 1992), 163.

11. Harriman to Ivy Lee, 18 June 1930, f. Ivy Lee, box 71, Harriman Papers, MD, LC. He was apparently disgusted enough with his Russian experience to resign from membership in the American-Russian Chamber of Commerce, much to the regret of its president, Hugh Cooper. Cooper to Harriman, 21 June 1921, f. Am.-Russ. Chamber of Commerce, box 14, Harriman Papers, MD, LC.

sible to bridge because of spring floods. The wild area became the base of the Za-
porozhian (or Ukrainian) Cossacks in the sixteenth and seventeenth centuries.
Able to manipulate the rapids on horseback and finding natural refuges on the
islands, they presented a formidable opposition to the seventeenth-century Russian conquest of Ukraine. Once that was accomplished, somewhat by treachery,
Russian rulers faced another challenge: how to make the Dnepr navigable up to
Kiev from the Black Sea, which under Catherine the Great virtually became a
Russian lake. Nothing could really be done at the time owing to cost and lack of
technical ability. Catherine allegedly visited the area on her famous trip to the
Black Sea and pointed out where and what should be done.[12] It was better, her
predecessor Peter the Great had thought, to concentrate on building a canal to
connect the Volga and the Don Rivers to reach the Black Sea from interior Russia. Though a start was made with Western help, both the Volga-Don and Dnepr
projects would await their fulfillment in Stalin's Five Year Plans.[13]

In the late nineteenth century a new agenda was ushered in for both Russia
and Ukraine. The industrialization of Russia, promoted especially by the program
of Minister of Finance Sergei Witte, led to the development of the Donets Basin (Donbas) in East Ukraine with its rich coalfields, about one hundred miles
east of the Dnepr, as a major steel-producing region. Simultaneously, advances in
hydroelectric engineering inspired a new desire to harness the Dnepr to supply
electricity to the Donbas. Preliminary plans in the early twentieth century were
suspended by war and revolution. The ultimate victor of that tumultuous period
was Vladimir Lenin, who had a vision regarding the importance of electricity
and coined the phrase: "Communism is Soviet Power and the electrification of
the whole Country." The Dnepr River rapids loomed large as a target, but little
could be done in the relatively unplanned, free, and capital-short New Economic
Policy. For Leon Trotsky, a strong proponent of planned and controlled economic
planning with specific goals, the Dnepr project represented the best possible fulfillment of Lenin's credo, and he pushed as long as he could for a grand electrification for the Soviet Union.[14]

In 1926, Russian engineering professor Ivan Aleksandrov came to the United
States to study various hydroelectric projects completed and under way. Colonel
Hugh Cooper had supervised major dam projects at Niagara Falls on the Cana-

---

12. Hugh Cooper, "Russia," an address to the Society of American Military Engineers at the Engineers Club of Philadelphia, 25 February 1931, *Engineers and Engineering* 48, no. 4 (April 1931), 78.

13. For details on the considerable progress that Russia had already made toward electrification,
see Jonathan Coopersmith, *The Electrification of Russia, 1880–1926* (Ithaca, N.Y.: Cornell University
Press, 1992).

14. For the ideological background and Trotsky's role, see Ann D. Rassweiler, *The Generation of
Power: The History of Dnepostroi* (New York: Oxford University Press, 1988), 20–49.

dian side, on the Mississippi at Keokuk, Iowa, and finally at his biggest project in the United States, the Muscle Shoals dam on the Tennessee River in northern Alabama. He naturally attracted the Russian envoy's attention, and Cooper agreed to provide an on-site assessment of a Dnepr dam project.[15] He and his team of engineers inspected the Dnepr site and delivered a positive report in August 1926, but government and party leaders were aghast at the estimated cost.

The death of Felix Dzerzhinsky in 1926 and his replacement within the meager pool of economic expertise in the bureaucracy by Valerian Kuibyshev may have been decisive, since Kuibyshev was enthralled by Cooper's report, both for the Dnepr project and for the approaching Stalin crash industrialization program.[16] In fact, the daunting task of constructing the largest dam yet conceived with the required mass assembly workers may have appealed to Stalin's particular fantasy and actually helped to precipitate the Five Year Plan with all its manifestations of collectivization, famine, and regimentation of Soviet life. The project also obviously would transform a large area of central Ukraine, mobilize thousands of workers, and create a large infrastructure of industrialization. Foreign expertise could not be provided under a concession agreement, since the electricity produced could not be sold abroad. It would have to be done by a consulting contract with hard cash up front, paid for by increased Soviet exports.

Cooper's enthusiasm and optimism about the project in personal interviews with Stalin won him the contract as supervising engineer in early 1928 just as the Five Year Plan was being launched. Dneprostroi, in fact, was a central pilot project of the plan. With the aid of Soviet engineers and his own New York staff, Cooper drew up the plans for construction to be accomplished by a vast array of mobilized labor, many drafted from nearby or displaced Ukrainian peasants who opposed collectivization, and from young people, including enthusiastic Communists from Kiev and other cities. Even Cooper was daunted by the scope of the endeavor. It took the combined capacities of Siemens Engineering of Germany and International General Electric to provide the several sets of 77,500 kWh turbines.[17] The dam itself would be 200 feet high and nearly a mile long. By far the

15. The "colonel" title comes legitimately from his command of an engineering corps project of building port facilities at Bordeaux in France for unloading American men and supplies in 1917–1918.

16. Rassweiler, *Generation of Power*, 50–55; "Colonel H. L. Cooper Hopeful of Russia," *NYT*, 2 October 1926: 1, and James C. Young, "Soviet Power Project Rivals Muscle Shoals," *NYT*, 17 October 1926: 8.

17. Sutton, *Western Technology and Soviet Economic Development, 1917–1930* (Palo Alto, Calif.: Stanford University Press, 1968), 203–4. Veteran journalist H. V. Kaltenborn, after an extensive tour of the new industrial regions, quoted Cooper, "The men governing this country aren't normal. There is scarcely a man in the government who hasn't spent years of his life in jail. . . . I feel we should give these people a chance to try out their theories. You cannot make them change. Any changes that come in Russia will have to come from within." Kaltenborn, *Fifty Fabulous Years, 1900–1950: A Personal Review* (New York: G. P. Putnam's Sons, 1950), 150–51.

largest hydroelectric project in the world at the time, it exceeded Muscle Shoals on the Tennessee River by 35 percent. The $100 million project would produce electricity for industry in the Donbas but would also provide an important strategic crossing of the river over the dam, especially considering the large lake that was formed and could not be bridged. It also fulfilled the dream of Catherine the Great of making the Dnepr navigable up to Kiev by means of locks that lifted vessels 140 feet, while also meeting some irrigation needs for Ukrainian agriculture.[18] Above all, it would be a cardinal accomplishment for the Stalin revolution upon its completion in 1932.

More than any project, Dneprostroi nailed down the inauguration of Stalin's ideas for a planned economy, thanks to the American engineering capability that left its initials in Soviet concrete. A representative of the Donets Basin Coal Corporation came from the United States in 1927 to examine the mines and to promote new ones. He was much impressed by the best of the lot, the Amerikanska mine.[19] Renowned photographer Margaret Bourke-White visited the dam site in 1931 to record much evidence of the American presence, including Cooper himself, several of the American contingent's Chevrolets, and Cooper's imports of chocolates, shoes, socks, and Victrola records to provide an air of American popular culture for the construction community.[20] She probably did not miss the presence of the large amount of heavy American equipment: steam shovels, pneumatic drills, and 48 forty-ton locomotive cranes brought in from the United States, which Cooper admitted spent much of the first year fishing each other out of the ditch. One pleasant surprise was the high quality of Ukrainian cement, though the sand for it had to be brought 200 miles from the shores of the Black Sea.[21] Cooper himself made at least six trips of an average of two months each during the first five years of the project. The "Cooper Dam" was elaborately dedicated as "Stalin Dam"—with Cooper present—on 10 October 1932, as a dramatic marking of the conclusion of the First Five Year Plan, which in many other ways was a major economic disaster. The dam symbolized the triumph of engineering, the rise of Stalinism, and, ironically, the passing into retirement of an engineer president in the United States. Now simply Dneprostroi, it is still the largest producer of electricity in Ukraine.

18. Cooper, "Russia," 78–79; Albert Creighton to Robert Kelley, 29 July 1931, box 5, Office of East European Affairs (hereafter OEEA), USSR, RG 59, NA. Creighton visited the site and interviewed the resident Cooper engineer Thompson. Another Cooper engineer, William Emegass, dissented, claiming that Cooper was showered with favors, flattered by Soviet officials, and was allowed to see only the best; in short, he was treated like royalty. Louis Susseldorff to State Department, 10 January 1929, case file 861,50, reel 139, M 316, NA.

19. Adolf Carl Noe, *Golden Days of Soviet Russia* (Chicago: Thomas S. Rockwell, 1931), 23.

20. Bourke-White, *Eyes on Russia* (New York: Simon and Schuster, 1931), 73–87.

21. Cooper, "Russia," 78–79.

The dam had its critics at the time and later, deservedly. The facility was publicized as having a power output of 756,000 kW when completed, but not all of the turbines could work throughout the year because of seasonal low water. All ten of them could operate for only three months and only two year around. The *New York Times* reported that constant supply of only 180,000 kW could be maintained on a regular basis and that this would need to be supplemented by steam-powered turbines.[22] Though an impressive structure to all who saw it, one must question whether it was worth the cost. But as with the other gigantomania projects of the First Five Year Plan, the propaganda value was immense, especially when it seemed to sanctify both American engineering and Soviet long-range planning, a big step forward in the Hoover "damnization" of the world.

Another result of Cooper's Russian experience was his ardent support of diplomatic recognition of the Soviet Union by the United States, as early as 1928.[23] His fame—or notoriety—meant that he could not easily be ignored, and he received responses to his appeals on this subject from presidents and secretaries of state. Former Secretary of State Frank Kellogg in 1932 confided to Cooper that he now was much closer to his views. "You of course understand that I always thought that you knew more about Russia than any other American."[24] Fittingly, Cooper would act as master of ceremonies at the grand banquet in New York in November 1933 for Maxim Litvinov in celebration of the conclusion of the agreement for diplomatic recognition.

Shakhtostroi (Mine Construction)

A necessary accompaniment to the big Dnepr River dam project was the rehabilitation of the Donets Basin coal mines, the foundation of the industrial region. All were in bad condition and had been poorly and cheaply constructed in the first place. The initial debate concerned whether to concentrate on rehabilitating and modernizing existing mines or to start from scratch with new ones. Essentially both would be done, but again the Soviets called upon American expertise, beginning with the inspection visits of George E. Stuart of Stuart, James,

22. "Soviet Giant," *NYT*, 3 May 1932: 20.

23. "Col. Cooper Urges Soviet Recognition," *NYT*, 16 May 1928: 41.

24. Kellogg to Cooper, 29 November 1932, reel 47, Kellogg Papers, MD, LC (originals in Minnesota Historical Society, St. Paul). Cooper also had an entrée into the Franklin Roosevelt family through his brother Dexter, also a hydroelectric engineer, who had a summer house across the road from the Roosevelts on Campobello Island, and would claim some fame in his own right for a pioneering project to harness the tides of the Bay of Fundy to produce electricity and received WPA funds for it in the 1930s.

Hugh Cooper at Dneprostroi, 1932. (Prints and Photographs, Library of Congress)

and Cooke, Engineers, of 17 Battery Place in New York, in late 1926 and early 1927. The initial survey and proposal resulted in a series of technical assistance contracts, the first with Donugol (Don coal) signed in June 1927. It was reported to be worth more than $15 million.[25]

The Stuart company sent twelve engineers to establish a base in Kharkov to carry out a major program of advice on mine reconstruction in 1927. They began with a critique of the various antiquated equipment and practices, such as varied gauges of rails and coal cars used at the mines and urged standardization. The opposition of local Russian engineers to change was also highlighted in their reports and may have influenced the arrest of more than fifty Russian mining engineers in the following year and the subsequent *shakhty* trials, presaging the purge trials ten years later and condemning many innocent Russians to death or oblivion in prison. Stuart, James, and Cooke would obtain at least one substantial contract for a new mining shaft, but many of the foreign contracts would go to German or British companies. Two other American companies, however, would obtain

25. Picture of signing in *Coal Age News*, 7 July 1927, in Stuart Papers, f. 28, box 3, HIA; *New York Evening Post*, 14 July 1927, ibid. By October Stuart had returned from his third trip to Soviet Russia. Stuart to Harper, 22 October 1927, f. 7, box 13, Harper Papers, UC-R.

major coal-mine contracts in the Donets area: Roberts and Shaefer and Allen and Garcia both based in Chicago.[26]

Stuart concluded his Russian engagement with an agreement with Shakh-tostroi for a 10,000-mile inspection tour of mines in 1931. That tour resulted in a lengthy critical report that was translated into Russian and 10,000 copies circulated, creating something of a sensation.[27] More important, Stuart became an active promoter of business with Russia and of recognition, emphasizing, "If imitation be the sincerest flattery, then the Russian nation has paid the United States its highest compliment in that it has patterned its industrial development almost exclusively upon our methods."[28] He also drew an interesting interconnection between American engineering, the First Five Year Plan, and the New Deal. In an address on the importance of central planning to the Engineers Club of Philadelphia in 1933, he stressed, "Central Planning is essentially American in its origin, and Russia borrowed it from us as she did many of the elements of her Five Year Plan." He then added, in reference to the American Depression and the Roosevelt administration, "We are now passing out of <u>drifting</u> into an era of <u>planning</u>," citing Russia as the best example to follow: "She owes to it her existence as a nation today."[29] He would later remind anyone who wanted to hear about his success as an entrepreneur in Stalin's Russia. In actuality, the Soviet plan involved the forced mobilization of large numbers of workers and an often irrational kind of economic planning that bore little resemblance to American agricultural and industrial developments.

Tracktorstroi

As electricity rang bells within Soviet leadership, agricultural modernization was another major goal but was more likely to invoke moans rather than joy. The history of such modernization extends well back into the nineteenth century, when Russia faced considerable competition from the United States in grain sales abroad and the backwardness of methods and equipment placed their economic

26. Sutton, *Western Technology 1917–1930*, 53–54. They maintained around fifty mining engineers in Russia over a five-year period.

27. Stuart, "Industry in Russia and the United States," presented to the Thursday Club in New York, 26 January 1933, f. 14, box 2, Stuart Papers, HIA.

28. Stuart, "Industrial Condition in Russia," nd, f. 12, ibid. Stuart also took many motion pictures of the Russian scene and showed them to various audiences, for example, at the American Museum of Natural History and at the Teachers Club in New York, Stuart to Gumberg, 23 October 1929, f. 1, box 4, Gumberg Papers, SHSW.

29. Stuart, "National, Industrial, and Managed," 28 March 1933, f. 11, box 1, Stuart Papers, HIA. Underlining in original.

balance of trade at a clear disadvantage. In the past various delegations abroad and their reports on what should be done came to little because of the entrenched peasant socioeconomic tradition as well as other state priorities.[30] This would essentially remain the case under Soviet rule. But an effort would be made in the First Five Year Plan by collectivization of agriculture—with disastrous human consequences—to create the needed labor, while also providing grain exports to pay for the vast construction projects. To borrow from Lenin's electricity formula, Soviet power plus American agricultural mechanization equaled collectivization of the whole country. Peasant resistance and communal village land policy played a role; they stood in the way of "tractorization" as an important subcategory of *Amerikanizm*, so it was believed. As with the Dnepr dam project, discussion on agricultural modernization began at least as early as 1926. The Dnepr rapids and the Ukrainian peasantry had to be conquered.

Seeking the best models to transform the economic life of the country, Soviet authorities looked mainly to the United States. In 1928 two separate Soviet delegations came to the United States, with tractors and a plant near Stalingrad already in the planning stages as goals. The second came fortified with money, $17,500,000, to buy machines for the new plant.[31] After collectivization was launched that fall, however, plans expanded from a plant with a capacity of only 10,000 tractors a year to 20,000 tractors annually and finally to double even that and hired the Detroit construction company of Albert Kahn to build the factory. Actually, several other companies would be involved, with McClintock and Marshall supplying materials and John Calder, who had built the Ford Dearborn complex and was more recently overseeing the erection of the Hudson department store in Detroit, supervising construction.[32] Calder reported that "we have put up steel faster than I have known in America" and predicted that the plant would be completed well ahead of schedule.[33] This was indeed the case, with an opening ceremony on 18 June 1930, though the first International Harvester model Farmall had already rolled off the line on 1 May. Receiving congratulations personally from Stalin, Calder moved on to Chelyabinsk, while several other American engineers remained to supervise the Stalingrad plant.[34]

---

30. An example is that the need for grain storage facilities at central terminals and at ports was perceived as early as the 1880s and repeated a number of times, but development never materialized, not even in the Soviet planning era.

31. "Soviet Engineers Here," *NYT*, 16 July 1928: 19, and same title, 5 November 1928: 39.

32. "Soviet Plans Factory to Build Tractors," *NYT*, 5 May 1929: 24; Sutton, *Western Technology 1917–1930*, 186–87.

33. Duranty, "Big Farm Outlay Planned by Soviets," *NYT*, 13 December 1929: 11.

34. Duranty, "Soviet Celebrates New Tractor Plant," *NYT*, 19 June 1930: 7.

Production did not go well at Stalingrad, probably because, in the rush to completion, management neglected the training of personnel to run the assembly operations, and other construction projects were taking priority. American engineer John Becker was quite critical of the operation of the plant in an article published in a leading Russian economic journal, *Za Industrializatii*, which exposed gross mismanagement and cost overruns.[35] Andrew Smith, visiting the plant as a member of a foreign Communist delegation in 1933, found production at 400 tractors a day, but the plant filled with dirt and disorder, virtually no safety standards, and many of the tractors rusting in a field. For the low quality, the director frankly blamed Moscow and the stress on quantity production targets.[36] The Soviet planners had also counted on the expertise of a variety of individual contractors and skilled technicians, but faced instead a large turnover and an unstable labor supply. More than three hundred Americans initially served as examples to guide and train Soviet workers. At the height of construction about 450 Americans, including wives and children, lived near the factory on the outskirts of the city; 325 were employed directly by Amtorg, but another 40–50 were sent by American companies to fulfill contracts.[37]

Two other, similar large tractor factories were designed by Americans in Kharkov in Ukraine and at Chelyabinsk in the Urals. International Harvester (model Farmall 15/30) furnished the assembly equipment at Stalingrad and Kharkov. The tracked Caterpillar was the model for the heavier tractors to be built at Chelyabinsk, an early example of Soviet planners copying an American model, coining anew the term *copycat*.[38] Amtorg purchased 1,300 sixty-horsepower Caterpillar tractors and arranged for exchanges of technicians and engineers. Caterpillar opened an office in Moscow to coordinate and deal with problems of employment and repair of their tractors. The extent of the Peoria, Illinois, company's involvement with the Chelyabinsk plant remains unclear. Soviet engineers apparently were going it alone for the most part, with the assistance of some individually contracted Caterpillar technicians—with disastrous results—until John Calder came to the rescue. Chelyabinsk, nevertheless, was the sole producer of Caterpillar-type tractors (Stalinets S-60) in the Soviet Union through the 1930s.[39] It

35. Duranty commented that if this had been written by a Russian, he would have been shot. "Finds Soviet Plant Badly Managed," *NYT*, 9 October 1930: 5.

36. Andrew Smith, *I Was a Soviet Worker* (London: Robert Hale, 1937), 173–74.

37. John Wiley to Robert Kelley, 7 November 1930, f. Reports of visitors to Russia, box 5, OEEA, RG 59, NA.

38. One report credits a Soviet engineer in Detroit acquiring a Caterpillar, taking it apart, and designing a production plant on the basis of this. Sutton, *Western Technology 1917–1930*, 190.

39. Ibid. Eugene Lyons described Calder: "as honest a man as ever drew a Soviet payroll." *Assignment in Utopia*, 574.

made some sense to build a heavy tractor plant in Chelyabinsk to use the production of steel at Magnitogorsk, not far away, although the only rail connection with Magnitogorsk was a very rough line. Moreover, the plant was designed for conversion to military tank production, well in the rear of any hostile attack.

As in the case of Ford and other major contractors, the arrangements for the tractor plants specified the training of Soviet workers at their American facilities. In June 1930, of 575 Soviet technicians in the United States, about 150, or 15 percent, were in agricultural industries, the largest contingent of 33 representing the Chelyabinsk plant in Peoria, Illinois. The Stalingrad factory sent 16 and Kharkov 12 of these experts.[40] While providing this training assistance and superintending the construction of factories, the American companies reaped the benefits of substantial sales of agricultural equipment, rising gradually from the major start in 1925 of over $7 million to the Five Year Plan purchases of 1929, 1930, and 1931. In the peak year of 1930 the Soviet Union expended more than $42 million for agricultural machinery, almost $36 million of it for tractors, in the United States, certainly of major importance, if not survival, for those companies during the Depression. Almost 95 percent of the total imports of tractors and parts in these years came from the United States.[41] Terms were also favorable with initial sales in the mid-1920s on the basis of 75 percent cash up front. By 1930 the normal terms were 25 percent down and the remainder in equal installments over the following three years.[42] Though Ford, International Harvester, and Caterpillar were dominant, more than 175 American companies were involved, including several other sites such as the Selmashstroi enterprise at Rostov.

Meanwhile, Ford took on the difficult task of remodeling the Krasnaia Putilovits plant (former Putilov factory) in Leningrad with Americans in supervisory roles. The Fordson tractor that was produced there, however, was considered quite inferior to the Stalingrad Farmall, which would be the principal Soviet collective farm tractor through the 1940s.[43] The Leningrad failure was due more to the antiquated and poorly adapted facility, as Charles Sorensen had pointed out, and an inadequate labor force, than to any inherent problem with Fordson.[44] Similarly, Farmall engines would predominate in new assembly plants in Rostov on Don and in Novosibirsk for the production of Holt combine harvesters, both plants supervised mainly by American technical experts. All these factories, ex-

40. Dana Dalrymple, "American Technology and Soviet Agricultural Development, 1924–1933," *Agricultural History* 40, no. 3 (July 1966), 191.

41. Ibid., 192–93.

42. Ibid., 202.

43. Ibid., 189–91.

44. Duranty, "Soviet Plans Lag on Three 'Fronts,'" *NYT*, 4 January 1930: 5.

cepting Kharkov (which was quickly overrun), were shifted to military production during World War II to considerable Soviet benefit.

The Kharkov plant, under the direction of American engineer Leon Swa-
jian, who had supervised the construction of the Ford River Rouge plant, fared
somewhat better than the others, thanks largely to learning from experience.[45]
Construction there was still slowed by the famine disaster afflicting Ukraine in
1931–1933, which affected labor supply. An American adviser, one of around a
hundred, at Kharkov observed the new restrictions imposed on travel and the
walls and gates that were erected in an attempt to prevent workers from seeing
the horrific results of collectivization in the nearby countryside. When he complained about these conditions that were still being reported from the Ukrainian
countryside, he was told, "That is unfortunate, but the glorious future of the Soviet Union will justify that," and, subsequently, he was simply told to mind his
own business.[46] Visiting the site in 1934, Louis Fischer found production up to
145 tractors a day—not impressive by American standards. He was impressed
enough by the evidence of the new constructive command economy to comment, "I never saw Russia when it was Czarist, but I saw Czarist Russia when it
was Soviet."[47] To cover the interim and guarantee quality, the Soviet Union had
purchased more than 20,000 American tractors in 1929 alone.[48]

The construction of the Stalingrad tractor plant involved more Americans—
and more complaints—than any other single project. John Becker complained
that 50 percent were "toughs," 25 percent "thugs." His conclusion was that "it
was all 'Topsey-turvey.'"[49] Another report indicated continuous problems, such as
a strike by American workers for cigarettes.[50] Other American implement companies, such as Oliver and Deere, achieved more modest success in sales to the

45. Dalrymple, "American Technology," 190–93.
46. Fred E. Beal, *Proletarian Journey: New England, Gastonia, Moscow* (New York: Hillman-Curl,
1937), 308, 331.
47. Fischer, *Soviet Journey* (New York: Harrison Smith and Robert Haas, 1935), 166. This supported his prediction two years earlier that by 1933 the Kharkov plant would be producing 50,000
tractors a year. He added that Stalingrad would be turning out another 50,000, Leningrad 30,000,
and Chelyabinsk 60,000. The Soviet Union would thus be the number one manufacturer of tractors
in the world annually at close to 200,000 and imports from the United States would be reduced to
zero, though the plants would still rely for a few more years on the purchase of American machinery
and raw materials. Of course, the Depression had reduced American production of tractors. Fischer,
Machines and Men in Russia (New York: Harrison Smith, 1932), 39.
48. Gumberg to Joseph Cotton (State Department), 10 December 1929, f. 1, box 4, Gumberg
Papers, SHSW.
49. John Wiley (Warsaw) to Kelley, 7 November 1930, box 5, OEEA, RG 59, NA. Wiley was
reporting on a conversation with a tool designer named John Becker who had completed only six
months of a year contract at Stalingrad.
50. Letter of Ed Addleton, 8 August 1930, ibid.

Soviet Union, which still certainly helped them stave off the worst effects of the Depression. And the J. I. Case Company took on a major role in the production of Soviet Holt combine harvesters, supplied with engines from the Hercules Company at a plant in Rostov on Don.[51]

Although problems would continue to plague Soviet tractor production, the American analysts in Riga recorded major gains in assembled tractors: 1927, 1,275; 1929, 9,000; 1931, 38,000; 1932, 50,000; 1934, 95,000. The emphasis was increasingly on the larger tractors, with Caterpillar type rising from 500 in 1932 to 34,000 in 1936. Of 210,000 tractors employed in Soviet agriculture in 1936, the breakdown is as follows: STZ (Stalingrad) IH 15/30 119,000; IH 10/20 16,000; Fordson (Leningrad) 38,000; IH 22/36 8,200; John Deere 7,250; Case 4,700; Oliver 2,000. Obviously, American tractors dominated the field in sales and production.[52]

Tractors and plants for their construction were the major American contributions to the Soviet Five Year Plan in size and volume, but Americans could be found on the new collective farms and in allied industries: fertilizer plants (DuPont and Nitrogen Engineering Corporation); irrigation projects centered near Tashkent (Arthur Power Davis, Lyman Bishop, and W. L. Gorton); cotton (J. A. Bremer and C. B. Olberg); meatpacking (Armour and Edward Innes and James Barr); hogs (Raymond Douglas). Many other Americans advised and were employed in the food-processing industries.[53]

Magnitostroi

Steel was obviously a key to any new drive for heavy industrialization, but as in the case of dams, the Soviet government had little technical capability to draw on. The Dnepr dam electric project was linked to the Donbas industrial region, which was already well established during the 1890s on the basis of its rich coal deposits and the Krivoi Rog iron ore not far away. But much remained to be done in terms of reviving and modernizing the plants and improving the railroads. Naturally, Western technology was needed. Freyn Engineering of Chicago was hired as initial consultants, but the first contract went to a Hammer-type entrepreneur, Percival Farquhar, a financier who knew little about engineering but saw a promising linkage of resources with electrical power and won a contract

---

51. Sutton, *Western Technology 1917–1930*, 191–93.

52. Soviet tractor production statistics, 1937, 866.12-R, box 5, RFSP, Riga 1936–1937 (Russia Series), RG 84, NA.

53. Dalrymple, "American Technology," 197–203.

for modernization in October 1927, about the same time that Freyn engineers, independently, had established a base in Leningrad.[54] They called the Farquhar project into question and ultimately replaced it with a technology transfer agreement in October 1928 at the beginning of the Five Year Plan. The updating and modernizing of plants and railroads in the Donbas ultimately involved many American, German, and other companies.[55]

In another location farther away in Southwestern Siberia, another "Donbas" was developing, again with a natural correlation of coal and iron ore. The local supply of coal was the catalyst, augmented by new finds in Central Asia (Karaganda), and with iron ore from the Urals. Freyn Engineering was again called on to supervise the expansion of production facilities that had already attracted American utopian ventures in the 1920s. The new region, known as the Kuznetsk Basin (Kuzbas), had the advantage of starting more or less from scratch, with the latest technology and safely remote from any military invasion from east or west. Freyn contracted to build a big iron production facility with a capacity of one million tons a year, a $40 million project.[56] With E. P. Everhard, assisted by more than seventy Freyn engineers, and employing the American Martin system of blast furnaces, the Kuznetsk (renamed Stalinsk upon completion) steel complex achieved a production of 450,000 tons annually. It was by most accounts one of the most successful Soviet-American joint ventures during the First Five Year Plan.[57] A second section of Kuznetsk was soon launched but this time under Soviet direction with less success. It included a significant amount of foreign equipment with Western technical assistance and Soviet duplication of Freyn designs.

Probably the best known of the Five Year Plan's gigantic industrial endeavors, however, was the building of a new steel complex in the southern Urals where literally nothing existed except a large quantity of iron ore and a few Bashkir and Kirghiz villages.[58] As in the case of Dneprostroi, preliminary plans were initiated in 1926 with test drilling to survey the extent of the ore resources. The project would require the mobilization and transport of many workers as virtually forced labor, which would have been impossible during NEP. Once the new direction

54. Henry J. Freyn first visited Sovietdom in February with company engineers Roger Foote and Waldemar Stark. Freyn to Harper, 1 February 1927, f. 30 box 12, Harper Papers, UC-R.

55. Sutton, *Western Technology 1917–1930*, 72–75; Farquhar Papers, HIA.

56. Sutton, *Western Technology 1917–1930*, 62–65, 74. Several German companies were also involved.

57. Ibid., 77–79.

58. The project is best known by the recounting of personal experiences at the site by John Scott in *Behind the Urals: An American Worker in Russia's City of Steel* (Bloomington: Indiana University Press, 1989).

Soviet workers, pulling logs up the mountainside at Magnitogorsk, seen in the background, 1930. (Louis Fischer, Men and Machines, *photo by Marguerite Bourke-White)*

to a planned economy was launched, American expertise was again sought. On the recommendation of Amtorg, Arthur McKee and Company of Cleveland sent experts, headed by Max MacMurray, to inspect the site during the spring of 1930. They agreed to design and supervise the construction of a series of plants and a mile-long dam across the Ural River that would provide electrical power on a $2,500,000 contract, just for the designs.[59] The company cleared one large floor in a building on Euclid Avenue in Cleveland for drawing up the plans, and a large staff worked furiously through April, May, and June 1930 to keep on schedule with a commission of Soviet engineers, headed by V. Smolianinov, the first director of Magnitogorsk.[60]

Overall direction at Magnitogorsk was under R. W. Stuck of McKee, but one of the best descriptions of the operation is by William Haven, who, accompanied by his wife, arrived on site along with ten other McKee engineers on 1 June 1930 as vice president for operations. They lived in comparative comfort (butter,

59. William A. Haven, "The Russian Contract," typescript, 1964, Western Reserve Historical Society (hereafter WRHS), Cleveland.
60. Haven, "Magnitogorsk: Some Comments on the Design and Construction of a Mining and Metallurgical Plant for the USSR," f. 2, box 5, Haven Papers, WRHS.

eggs, and milk plentiful) while directing a crew of about twenty-five American engineers.[61] He still complained of the accommodations: flies, lack of refrigeration, and the general confusion, while advising others on what to bring: baseballs and gloves, tennis rackets, and footballs or soccer balls. The McKee group was initially lodged in the log houses of displaced peasants in the original villages, and then in hastily constructed stucco bungalows for special guests.[62] In contrast to Cooper's experience at Dneprostroi, Haven encountered confusion, disorder, poor cement, and a host of other problems—one bungle after another. Worst was the severe weather, not only the cold winters but also the heat of summer and heavy rains in the fall. More than 60,000 inexperienced and reluctant workers who descended on the scene added to the strain.[63]

Returning the following year, Haven traveled from Moscow to Sverdlovsk with his wife on a ten-passenger airplane with Wright engines and Soviet body, then by train to Magnitogorsk. This time they had relatively commodious quarters: a five-room apartment with a water heater in the bathroom! They dined in a common *stolovaya* (dining hall) with McKee engineers. He was impressed with the progress and captured much of it on film.[64] Construction fell behind schedule, however, because of mismanagement by Soviet administrators. John Calder was dispatched by Stalmost to correct the situation, but he too ran into opposition. "The whole job is at sixes and sevens, and everything is in a muddle."[65] Loud complaints from him and Haven reached the Soviet and American press and resulted in one more American site inspector, Hugh Cooper, who sided with the other Americans, and reputedly achieved a turnover in Soviet managers. Calder then supervised an unusual construction of a blast furnace on a horizontal level— rather than building from the ground up—followed by its hazardous raising into place by cranes that were mired in thick mud.[66]

Haven stayed until the first blast furnace began operation in March 1932 and

61. Haven to Sherry and Company, 4 June 1931, and to Hayes, 11 May 1932, f. 1 (business correspondence), box 1, Haven Papers, WRHS.

62. "Magnitogorsk: Some Comments on the Design and Construction of a Mining and Metallurgical Plant for the USSR," box 5, ibid.

63. Haven noted that the population grew while he was there from 5,000 to 150,000 in two years. Ibid.

64. Haven to Sherry and Company, 4 June 1931, f. 1, business correspondence, box 1, ibid. Among other McKee engineers on site were Fred Hays, Charlie Springer, Andy Crump, Alex Graybaugh, George Dewey, Jack Middleton, Jack Harris, Warren Smith, Sam Morton, Walter Ellis, and B. M. McKechnie. Hays to Haven, 6 May 1932, ibid.

65. As quoted by Duranty, "Big Soviet Project Found Mismanaged," *NYT*, 18 August 1931: 9.

66. Duranty, "American Experts Win Soviet Victory," *NYT*, 26 August 1931: 10; Duranty, "Soviet Steel Plant Called Labor Epic," *NYT*, 18 October 1931: 56.

reported that it worked fine, that it was the best furnace feed he had ever seen, and that "the blowing in" had been celebrated all over Russia; no wonder, considering the enormous publicity given to the First Five Year Plan's "battle for ferrous metallurgy." After his departure, a friend complained about the slow work, rain every day, and the constant bridge games among the Americans. They were now "obliged to follow a conservative policy in regard to foreign expenditures."[67] Back home Haven sympathized with many of the McKee-Magnitogorsk engineers who were now out of work. The Soviet project had at least delayed the impact of the Depression on them by a couple of years.

John Scott's account of an American "behind the Urals" at Magnitogorsk lent special notoriety to the project from the perspective of an ordinary worker, though it was not published until 1942. A graduate of the University of Wisconsin and refugee from the Depression, Scott was intrigued by the Soviet plan for industrialization and enthusiastically joined the effort, first as a welder, and then as a director of a section of the plant. Fortunately, he brought much American clothing with him, including long underwear, but gave most of it away. "I worked in Magnitogorsk with the common soldiers, the steel workers, the simple folk who sweated and shed tears and blood."[68] Many problems involving various foreign involvement and disagreements between McKee and Soviet authorities caused major time extensions, so that the plants were not fully operational until 1934. Though plant construction had moved ahead, the city—accommodations for workers—was still practically nonexistent at the end of 1931. A constant shortage of skilled labor was the result. The expansion of managerial personnel, "office rats," and a shortage of basic supplies because of dependency on the one-track railroad from Chelyabinsk were persistent problems throughout the history of building Magnitogorsk.

Many other Americans were working through the difficult circumstances at Magnitogorsk, as skilled workers like Scott or as engineers, especially in supervising the coke-making facilities. At the latter Philip Getter of Pittsburgh reported that there were seventy American engineers at the steel plant and sixteen at the coke works in 1931. He complained of the delays and inability to import food that had been promised.[69] Another American at the coke plant reported that there was no heat in his building, that the only meat available was horse or

67. Bendt family to Haven, 21 July 1932, Haven to G. L. Pringle, 28 August 1932, f. 1, box 1, Haven Papers, WRHS.

68. John Scott, *Behind the Urals*, 6.

69. George Messersmith (Berlin, consul general) to State, 30 November 1932, reporting on a conversation with Getter on 25 November, reel 67, T 1249, RG 59.

goat, and that the only labor consisted of 40,000 convicts.[70] Several agreed that progress was hampered by a conservative policy—because of cost overruns.[71] The problems were immense in regard to supply of both labor, mostly involuntary, and material. McKee withstood some of the blame from Soviet authorities, who claimed that they had been able to come up with designs much quicker, failing to note that they were simply copying those of Freyn Engineering for Kuznetsk that did not fit the operation at Magnitogorsk.[72]

Anna Louise Strong wrote in *Moscow News* that Soviet engineers had been able to take advantage of the McKee contributions to the building of Magnitogorsk by copying all the plans. Robert Baker responded to the claim,

> I think it is probably true that the Russians may have copied more drawings in three months than we made in an entire year, but from the reports which we are receiving they lost a great deal of their labor, and had the drawings been followed as prepared by them they would have lost many rubles.
>
> I suppose that any one doing business over there is quite likely to require defense from time to time. We are not very much concerned about such statements for the reason that some of the higher officials, particularly Meshlauk [*sic*], Chairman of the Supreme Economic Council, has advised me not to lay too much stress on articles of the sort.[73]

With much celebration, however, the blast furnaces at Magnitogorsk commenced operations in April 1932, though with many mishaps; an initial discharge of molten iron, for example, was dumped prematurely onto a railroad track, blocking all entrance to the plant for several days.[74] A follow-up report noted, "very poor organization. . . . It is just about as erratic and jumpy as a worn out model T."[75] A major problem was that Soviet political economists and authorities kept changing the target figures and making alterations in the grand concepts despite the existence of previous detailed plans.

The Magnitogorsk enterprise, steel complex and new city, was one of the most complex, difficult, and costly of all the gigantomania efforts of the First Five Year Plan. It was quite different from the projects in Kharkov, Stalingrad, Leningrad, Nizhny Novgorod, even Chelyabinsk, which could draw on a substantial urban

70. Ibid., interview with Vally Stadelman on 28 November 1932.

71. Haven to G. L. Pringle, 28 August 1932, f. 1, box 1, Haven Papers, WRHS.

72. "American to Advise Soviet on Building," *NYT*, 27 May 1931: 8.

73. Robert Baker, secretary and treasurer of McKee & Co., to John Carmody, 31 July 1931, box 39, Carmody Papers, FRPL.

74. Ibid.

75. S. Morton to Haven, 15 November 1932, ibid.

population as well as a populated countryside. The steel complex rose in rough terrain, where there were few settlers, poor transportation, and a legendary Siberian climate. Because of these obstacles, and the conceived grand proportion of the enterprise, Magnitogorsk received more publicity in the Soviet press as well as abroad than any other project. Much of the heralded Five Year Plan was clearly at stake in terms of proving the efficacy of a planned industrial economy. The project required a vast mobilization of labor, most of which was untrained and resistant to the conditions that prevailed. The pressure to win the "battle for ferrous metallurgy" cost hundreds of lives, while creating vast confusion on site, resulting in hastily and poorly constructed key features such as blast furnaces that had to be repeatedly rebuilt. The mix of displaced kulaks and other victims of collectivization, recently demobilized soldiers, inexperienced graduates of technical schools, non-Russian ethnic recruits, and foreign workers, along with short-term American engineers as supervisors, provided an unsteady, unreliable, and fluctuating labor force. It was more than McKee Engineering and even the American miracle constructor John Calder could cope with. Behind schedule, and with frequently changing directors, who were confronted with orders to speed up and make deadlines, it is a wonder that pig iron, steel, and rolled steel were eventually produced in substantial quantities by 1934.[76]

Autostroi

Less known but more interesting in many ways was the construction of the largest automobile plant in the world at the time near the village of Monastyrka, thirteen miles north of Nizhny Novgorod on the Oka River.[77] Soviet officials, beginning with Lenin, had long been infatuated with Henry Ford and his assembly-line technique of construction that produced basic, inexpensive, and durable vehicles, namely, the Model T. Ford, reciprocated with a vision of a grand Eurasian market. A truck model of the Model T had already been produced for the Red Army on a limited basis from parts at a Petrograd factory during the civil war. Many more cars and trucks were purchased directly from Ford in the 1920s. Championing the cause was Nikolai Ossinsky, who pushed hard to include an

76. For a full examination, complete with many pictures, see Stephen Kotkin, *Magnetic Mountain: Stalinism as a Civilization* (Berkeley: University of California Press, 1995).

77. Nizhny Novgorod was the third-largest city in Soviet Russia, centrally located with a port on the Volga River with good rail connections, and had experience with American engineering through a locomotive plant initiated by Baldwin at Sormovo at the end of the nineteenth century. Saul, *Concord and Conflict: The United States and Russia, 1867–1914* (Lawrence: University Press of Kansas, 1996), 409.

emphasis on automobile and truck production in the new industrialization effort. To really enter the automobile age, a natural goal of the Five Year Plan was thus to have a large mass production factory of their own.

A small Soviet commission visited the Ford plant at Dearborn in early 1928 but seemed to have little idea about how to begin negotiations, especially since none of the six members knew English. As a Ford official recounted, "I might just as well have been talking to a delegation from Mars."[78] Soon, however, a more expert group arrived, headed by the vice chair of the Supreme Council of National Economy, Valery Mezhlauk, along with the head of Amtorg, Saul Bron, to begin serious discussions. They obviously had authority for a major commitment. Mezhlauk, about forty and fluent in English, gave an impressive performance about the Five Year Plan, stressing American opportunities in a talk arranged by Freyn at the City Club in Chicago.[79] Following up, Charles Sorensen, the Ford executive in charge of production, visited Russia during a European tour in the summer of 1929 for a series of Kremlin meetings with Anastas Mikoyan, Mezhlauk, and others, interrupted by a visit to Nizhny Novgorod.[80] The chief Ford concern was the supply of materials to the site, one Soviet officials evaded by conducting them on an inspection trip to Leningrad. When asked about what could be done to improve production at the Putilovets factory there, Sorensen responded that they should bring in a keg of dynamite and clear it out.[81]

In the meantime, a debate ensued in Moscow among party and economic authorities over whether the Ford model was the one to choose, where to build the plant, and how much to commit to the project. The big planners, Kuibyshev and Ossinsky, won out and favored Ford because of its simpler design and Ford's apparent support of the Soviet idea of industrialization, and also the site of Nizhny Novgorod because of the region's large agricultural population, much of which would be released by collectivization for industrial labor. By mid-1929, Kuibyshev and other allies of Stalin were in ascendancy over moderates such as Bukharin.[82] The conclusion was to build the largest automobile factory in the world, with

---

78. Charles E. Sorensen, with Samuel T. Williamson, *My Forty Years with Ford* (New York: Norton, 1956), 194.

79. Memorandum of Walter Lichtenstein, nd, f. 8, box 13, Harper Papers, UC-R.

80. Ibid., 199. The State Department kept close surveillance on all of this American business activity. Coleman (Riga) to State Department, 25 June 1929, reel 164, M 316, NA. And, of course, it was especially watching Austin, McKee, and all other major and minor American involvements with the Soviet Union. For the full story of Ford in Russia, see Kurt S. Schultz, "Building the 'Soviet Detroit': The Construction of the Nizhnii-Novgorod Automobile Factory, 1927–1932," *Slavic Review* 49, no. 2 (summer 1990), 200–12.

81. Sorensen, *My Forty Years with Ford*, 202.

82. Schultz, "Building the 'Soviet Detroit,'" 203. Ossinsky argued in a series of articles for crash industrialization and emphasized use of the American model.

American engineering. The Supreme Economic Council approved Ossinsky's proposal to increase the planned output of Model A cars and Model AA trucks to 130,000 annually, the bulk of them to be trucks.[83] To supervise the arrangements, Ossinsky applied for an American visa in Riga but was denied, despite the fact that it had been approved in 1926 and he was offering several hundred million dollars in contracts.

He was forced to come to Canada instead and established an office in Windsor, Ontario, across the river from Detroit, to negotiate with American car, truck, and tractor manufacturers there. Naturally, he was not happy, having been already wined and dined by German and British businessmen at their factories. "Presidents of American corporations have to come to me, automobiles must be shipped temporarily to Windsor for my inspection and the Ford Canadian plant is a substitute of the River Rouge factory for my study purposes. It is a funny situation, but I do not know whether I am the comical person in this play staged by overzealous officials, or somebody else."[84] To Senator Borah, he complained, "Although I am an advocate of modern American technique, it is only natural, after my experience here, that I should look with more sympathy to cooperation with European producers than with American manufacturers whom I practically cannot reach or become acquainted with. Would this be in the interests, from a business point of view, I ask you, of either my country of yours?"[85]

Also in Moscow, the Soviet engineers rejected Sorensen's offer to build in Russia the new V-8 model Ford then on the drawing boards for being too complicated. A contract was then signed for Ford to deliver $30 million in Model A cars to Russia, 74,000 units in components over a four-year period, and to provide machinery and instruction on how to use the equipment that would be furnished for assembling the Model A at the new Nizhny Novgorod plant.[86] As if to ward off criticism about undermining American auto exports by helping the Soviet Union build their own, Henry Ford commented typically, "No matter where industry prospers, whether in India or China, or Russia, all the world is bound to catch some good from it."[87] He probably also had in mind that the Soviet vehicles would be behind the times, already practically a relic of the automobile age, and would never be able to compete with Ford in sales abroad.

There was still a problem. The Ford Company manufactured cars but did not

83. Schultz, "Building the 'Soviet Detroit,'" 204–5.

84. Ossinsky to Goodrich, 3 March 1930, f. Russia Ossinsky, box 20, Goodrich Papers, HHPL. He invited Goodrich to visit him in Windsor. Ossinsky also complained to Borah about how ridiculous his situation was.

85. Ossinsky (Windsor, Canada) to Goodrich, 7 March 1930, ibid.

86. "Ford Sells $30,000,000 in Cars to Russia and Agrees to Help Soviet Build Factory," *NYT*, 1 June 1929: 1.

87. As quoted in ibid.

build factories. The natural solution was to refer the Russians to Albert and Moritz Kahn, architects of Detroit, who had designed several Ford, Packard, and Hudson plants. Amtorg was also aware of another possibility: the Austin Company of Cleveland that had just completed a large, thirty-five acre factory for General Motors' Pontiac Six. Perhaps because negotiations were already under way with Kahn to build another factory (the Stalingrad tractor plant), Austin had an advantage. Coincidentally, the vice president of the Austin Company, George A. Bryant Jr., had already scheduled a visit to the Soviet Union on an Amtorg-sponsored tour for American businessmen and became impressed by the opportunities.[88] He and Fred Coleman, another Austin engineer, detached themselves from the tour to negotiate with Soviet authorities. They found that everything going through an interpreter "tries patience sorely."[89] The resulting contract, signed 23 August, called for construction to begin in April 1930, specified that the Soviets would provide the site, the workers, and the materials, while Austin would engineer and supervise the whole project from beginning to end for $40 million, paid in monthly installments.[90] Subsequent additions to the contract raised the production goal to 120,000 vehicles (cars and trucks) a year.

What may have especially intrigued the Soviet negotiators was the Austin plan—or rather, method—of designing the whole project, down to the last nut and bolt, on the drawing boards before any construction began, a process initiated by founder Samuel Austin and refined by current president Wilfred Austin. This was *plan*, American style, that fit well with the Soviet obsession with the same general idea of economic planning.[91] Another factor was the Austin emphasis on trust, that all depended on a working relationship in which both sides of the agreement would understand that cooperation was essential for mutual gain.[92] The first several months of the contract were devoted entirely to about 120 engineers and drafters working around the clock on one large floor of a rented building in Cleveland, much like what McKee did for Magnitogorsk.[93] And in fulfillment of a clause in the contract, a delegation of Soviet engineers

88. Bryant to his wife, 16 July and 11 August 1929, f. Bryant letters, box 1, Austin Company Archives (hereafter ACA), Cleveland.

89. Bryant to his wife, 16 August 1929, ibid.

90. "Austin Will Build Russia a Detroit," *Cleveland Plain Dealer*, 5 September 1929, f. GAZ project, box 1, ACA.

91. The Austin Company is still in operation in Cleveland, designing airports, factories, office complexes, and so forth. The logo is an A over M—Austin Method—credited to founder Samuel Austin. Fortunately, it preserved many of the records and engineering plans of the Soviet period, though it is no longer under Austin family direction and are now in the Western Reserve Historical Society.

92. Richard Cartwright Austin, *Building Utopia: Erecting Russia's First Modern City, 1930* (Kent, Ohio: Kent State University Press, 2004), 10–15.

93. Photograph in Austin Papers.

Austin engineers on site, 1931. Allan Austin is third from left. (ACR, courtesy Western Reserve Historical Society)

came to Cleveland to see how it was done. All of this was accompanied by angry exchanges of letters on the nature and scope of authority on the project, a major problem being that Austin had to deal with two competing Soviet agencies, *met-alstroi*, in charge of construction, and *autostroi*, which had overall responsibility for the resultant production.

The first Austin contingent to arrive on the Nizhny Novgorod scene was headed by Bryant and included Allan Austin, son of the company president and recent Yale graduate with his new bride Margretta, David Kempfer, Harry Miter, and several other Austin men and women. After a few days in Moscow and a slow trip to Nizhny, they journeyed out to the site and found only a wide, flat field in the middle of nowhere. They lodged in a hotel in town while several buildings, dubbed Austingrad, were erected adjacent to the factory site.[94] These consisted of stuccoed duplexes with nearby laundry, bakery, and a clubhouse, where the Austinites met frequently for teas, card games, films, and so forth, during construction. The women eventually added the refinements of a wood-floor tennis court and a miniature golf course for outdoor entertainment and exercise.

Work on the factory commenced on 2 May 1930 with much fanfare, 5,000 attending the elaborate May Day ceremony, which involved twenty-five renditions of the "Internationale." In addition to Communist officials from Moscow and the surrounding country, Allan Austin reported, "There were old, solid-looking aproned stone-masons there who looked as tho they might have worked on the

94. Transcript of interview by Martin Greif of David Kempfer, 8 November 1976, f. GAZ project, box 1, ACA.

Austin Company wives playing tennis, 1931. (ACR, courtesy Western Reserve Historical Society, Cleveland, Ohio)

Parthenon."[95] He described the scene during the summer in considerable detail, especially the regular and always challenging shopping with his wife in the local markets. But they could not find many things that they needed, so he sent a list of items to his parents to bring with them on a planned visit later in the summer; it was headed by "mosquito bite dope," flashlight batteries, an electric hotplate, toilet paper (many rolls), toothbrushes, thumb tacks, ungentine, dental floss (25 yards), and ant powder, several boxes. His wife added baking powder, Crisco, vinegar, spices, Certo, any kind of canned goods, and several clothing items—wool socks, heavy underwear, pajamas, stockings, and, especially, a garter belt, size 16.[96] American social life was clearly maintained with certain accommodation to the Russian scene. To celebrate the first month of work on the "city," thirty-eight Americans and the leading Russians were entertained at the clubhouse in grand fashion.[97] Allan Austin reported that his wife found life better than she expected; and they all enjoyed a "jolly, big Thanksgiving dinner."[98]

Starting in 1930 with 16,000 workers living in makeshift tenements and rising

95. Allan Austin to Wilfred Austin, 2 May 1930, f. 1930, ibid.

96. Attachments to A. Austin to W. Austin, 15 May 1930, ibid. He added, "Generally speaking, trunks are a nuisance in travelling, especially in France, and Russia, where they do not seem to be set up to handle them properly. Hand baggage, even of large size, is prefferable [sic], and you always know you have it."

97. A. Austin to W. Austin, 31 May 1930, ibid.

98. A. Austin to W. Austin, 24 November 1920, ibid.

to 40,000 in 1931, what would soon become known as GAZ (State Automobile Factory), the largest automotive plant in the world at the time, finally began to take off. One of the stellar accomplishments on the Soviet road to the automobile age was the building of a concrete highway, the first in Russia, from the plant site to the housing area and to the Oka River—also to serve as a trial road for the Soviet Model A's. The plant itself would encompass six football fields, the largest of its kind, challenged in size only by the tractor plant being erected at the same time in Chelyabinsk. William Haskell, who visited the construction site, noted serious problems with labor and supplies. Labor was inefficient owing to being new and young. Railroads were severely taxed to bring in supplies.[99]

The most novel part of the whole project, however, was the building of a model socialist city according to a design that won first place in an All-Union Soviet competition. The young Allan Austin, son of the company president, was in charge of the construction of this model city that would house 50,000 workers for the factory. Each unit consisted of eight four-story apartment buildings, the fourth floor devoted to dormitories for young, single workers. The roofs were railed and "designed for sunbathing, enthusiastically practiced here." The facility was complete with a large central kitchen factory, nurseries, schools, adult reading rooms for night classes, and with 70 percent of the ground area reserved for parks and athletic fields.[100] Austin wrote his father, "We have an ambitious construction schedule ahead of us, and it will keep the Russkies sweating to keep up to it, and us sweating to keep after them to maintain it."[101] Despite a slow start, by September eleven apartment buildings had been erected.[102] In contrast with Magnitogorsk the housing project was keeping pace with factory construction.

The model city still exists in somewhat dilapidated state, though its more luxurious appendages were never finished.[103] Apartments for worker families consisted of the bare necessities with virtually no kitchen facilities (only for tea), since all were expected to eat in communal dining halls in each building, supplied from a central food factory. Schools, parks, and daycare centers were amply provided, at least on paper.[104] While all of this was going on in the Russian boondocks, Ford engineers were at work in downtown Nizhny setting up a prototype assembly line

99. Memoirs, vol. 3, Haskell Papers, HIA.

100. Allan Austin, "Socialism's Model City," f. Russian Project, ibid. Several pictures of the "city" from Richard Austin's visit of 1999 are in *Building Utopia*.

101. Allan Austin to Wilfred Austin, 19 May 1930, f. 1930, box 1, ACA. Allan noted that this letter was going back with one of the Austin engineers and would not be censored. Among the workforce assigned to the project, Austin found a group of Finns from Jersey City.

102. A. Austin to W. Austin, 26 September 1930, ibid.

103. Allen's son Richard visited the site in 2001. Austin videotape, ibid.

104. Ibid. For full details of the construction of the model city, see Austin, *Building Utopia*, 47–58.

to train Russian workers, with tools, fixtures, and so forth, sent from Michigan. Someone noted that this equipment was basically surplus, since Ford was revamping its American plants for new V-8 models. The Nizhny Ford crew managed to assemble more than a thousand Fords from components shipped to the site. A teacher from the Soviet Society for the Ford Engineers found food and clothes scarce but theater and social life vibrant.[105] The Austinites were impressed with a Nizhny production of *Rose Marie*, set in Canada, even though they had to spend the night in their cars, since the pontoon bridge across the Oka had been opened for night river traffic by the time they reached it.[106]

The Americans encountered a new challenge in the large number of women laborers, about 25 percent of the total, but Bryant was impressed by the Soviet effort and determination. "Here in the Soviet is being tried out the greatest industrial and humanitarian romance in the world. It has all passed beyond the experimental stage, but the accomplishment will take time." If they reach even 50 percent of their goal, "it will be the greatest industrial feat ever accomplished in the world." Bryant admitted that the whole Nizhny project could be done for half the cost in the United States.[107] Revisiting the site in 1931, he was amazed at the progress and the general state of the Austinites in residence: "Most keep themselves happy, a few keep themselves and everybody else miserable; just selfish that's all."[108] Despite many problems and disputes with Soviet authorities, the plant was completed on schedule in early 1932 with its Ford assembly machinery installed, rolling off the first Soviet Model A's, the "GAZ 1," in February.[109] The Austin company was paid regularly and on time, through Chase Bank in New York. The project received much publicity in the United States, especially in the syndicated articles of Milly Bennett.[110]

The training of many Soviet engineers and technicians at the Ford River Rouge

105. Margaret Wettlin, *Fifty Russian Winters: An American Woman's Life in the Soviet Union* (New York: Pharos Books, 1992), 8–10.

106. A. Austin to W. Austin, 17 June 1930, f. 1930, box 1, ACA; "Building Autostroi," videotape of Austin films of construction, box 2, ACA.

107. As quoted in Albert Creighton to Robert Kelley, 19 July 1931, box 5, OEEA, USSR, RG 59, NA. The Austin Company, headed by Bryant and Allan Austin, was active in promoting American business in Russia by favorable articles and editorials in various newspapers.

108. Bryant to Edith Bryant, 30 April 1931, f. Bryant, box 1, ACA.

109. The GAZ factory is still the largest producer of automobiles in Russia today, best known for its basic "family car," the Volga, which is also the main taxicab of Russia. The Austin plant structure was largely destroyed by German air raids in 1941, but the equipment remained mostly intact and was used to assemble the Studebaker trucks shipped to the Soviet Union under the lend-lease agreement. The plant was rebuilt after the war essentially on the same plan. GAZ Museum Archives videotape, box 2, ACA, which shows the German bombing.

110. For example, her "U.S. Engineers at Nizhny Novgorod," Long Beach, Calif., *Press Telegram*, 23 August 1931, f. newspaper clippings, box 1, ACA. Allan Austin was also proud of receiving $100

The Austin Company Club House, 1931. (ACR, courtesy Western Reserve Historical Society, Cleveland, Ohio)

plant also proved essential to Soviet car production.[111] One annoyance was that the chief Soviet engineer at the Nizhny plant, Stepan Dybets, who had already spent six months in Detroit, was denied a subsequent visa to return because he had admitted being a party member.[112] Despite this and the completion of the plant on schedule, Soviet automotive assembly endured a series of difficulties because of oversight and supply problems. Instead of the 120,000 units expected annually, *autostroi* turned out around 30,000 cars and trucks in the last year of the First Five Year Plan.[113] The infrastructure, however, was in place, though it would take several years of worker training and administrative experience to obtain at least half of the original target. The big planners had, nevertheless, achieved more than what their small planners had envisaged.[114]

Production reports of 1936 document the change. In 1932 only 32 passenger

for two articles he wrote for the *New York Times* magazine section. Transcript of Allan Austin interview by Martin Greif, 4 August 1976, box 1, ACA.

111. One of them was Alexander Kamenev, the son of Lev Kamenev and Olga Kameneva. A. Kamenev to his wife on Ford stationery, 31 January 1931, d. 178 (Kamenev family correspondence), op. 2, f. 323, RGASPI.

112. Stuart scrapbook, box 3, Stuart Papers, HIA. Actually the real reason was probably that Dybets was an IWW agitator in the United States who had been arrested and deported to Russia in 1919. He, as many others blamed for shortcomings in the industrialization drive, would face a much grimmer fate in 1937. Harold Denny, "More Executions Hinted in Moscow," *NYT*, 19 June 1937: 6.

113. Bryant was quick to claim that the problems in no way diminished Austin's accomplishment. To Arthur Engle, 12 April 1932, f. GAZ, box 1, ACA.

114. Schultz, "Building the 'Soviet Detroit,'" 211–12; GAZ video, ACA. See also, Richard Austin, son of Allan Austin, *Building Utopia*.

cars were produced in the Soviet Union, while 3,170, mainly Fords, were assembled from foreign (American) parts; by 1934 domestic production was more
than 17,000. The change was more dramatic in truck production, which was
emphasized at the Nizhny Novgorod GAZ plant: one-and-a-half-ton Ford AA:
1931, 1,268; 1932, 7,500; 1933, 16,500; 1934, 32,200. For the larger two-and-a-
half-ton trucks: 1931, 1,600; 1932, 15,150; 1933, 20,000.[115] These figures show
that Soviet Russia was clearly ushered (rushed) into the automotive age, with an
emphasis on trucks to serve industry and a possible military role. To top it off,
Maurice Pate, veteran of an early 1920 venture, arrived in 1932 to investigate
possible sales of asphalt-laying machinery.[116]

Other Americans in Comrade Stalin's New Russia

Besides the major American companies such as Freyn, Stuart, McKee, Austin,
Ford, International Harvester, Cooper Engineering, and General Electric, many
others were contracted for smaller projects, and many individual Americans by
their own will or through Amtorg's persuasion joined the Soviet construction
mania. The estimates of numbers range from at least 1,000 to more than 6,000
depending on classification and period, probably the former for those present at
one time, the latter for the total of the period of the First Five Year Plan, 1928–
1932, most of them contracted by Amtorg for their specific expertise or those
who were simply seeking challenging employment during the Depression. A figure of 3,000 for 1930 is probably reliable. Their experiences varied considerably,
often depending on where they were assigned. Fortunately, many left a record of
their experiences. Nearly all were newcomers to the Soviet and Russian world.

For example, Bill Shatoff, expatriate American, had been committed to the
Soviet construction cause since 1917. He had left Russia in 1907 and made a
name for himself as an IWW agitator across the United States. He was placed
in charge of railroads in the Petrograd area in 1918 and helped Trotsky stem
the advance on Petrograd of a White army. He then went east to serve the Far
Eastern Republic as minister of transportation. After several other ventures, such
as being director of state banks in the Rostov region, he was placed in charge of
another of the giant projects of the First Five Year Plan, the Turk-Sib Railroad, a
930-mile line to connect the existing railroad from the west at Tashkent through
Alma-Ata in Kazakhstan to connect with the Trans-Siberian at Novosibirsk,

115. Soviet car and truck production, 1936, 866.14-R, box 5 (vol. 324), RFSP, Riga 1936–1938
(Russia Series), RG 84.
116. Pate, f. Russian trip observations, 1932, box 6, Pate Papers, HHPL.

which opened ahead of schedule on 1 May 1930. Heavy-set, charismatic, and somewhat elusive, Shatoff combined a genuine expertise in railroad engineering with American determination and drive, while retaining fond memories of things American, especially open fireplaces.[117] Having been entrusted with, and accomplishing, one of the largest and most difficult projects of the First Five Year Plan, he would disappear during the purges in 1937.[118]

George Burrell, a petroleum engineer, was assigned to the oil production and refinery center of Grozny in the Caucasus, a city established as a Russian industrial and administrative center in an area where the native population, Chechens, was traditionally hostile to Russians and Russianization and its successor, Sovietization. About a dozen American engineers lived with wives in a new and fairly comfortable apartment complex. According to Burrell, they worked well together in general and with the Russian oil experts on the scene in expanding Russian oil production and exports, which were vital in paying for all the imported construction.[119] He admitted that a few malcontents caused problems for Russian authorities, but their wives kept the community together and formed an American clubhouse in one of the buildings. Even a golfcourse was laid out for the foreign contingent, rarely to be used because of work and weather. Burrell's account of his eighteen-month tour included a description of the destruction of the Cathedral of Christ the Savior in Moscow, rebuilt in recent years; the migration of many Chechens into what had been a mainly Russian city; the arrest of many other Chechens for their opposition to collectivization; his favorable impression of the building of new hospitals and clinics and camps for orphans; and the arrest and shooting of several local Soviet engineers.[120] Above all he was impressed by the large Soviet military presence in Grozny and the drafting (forcing) of Chechen women to dig the ditches for oil pipelines.[121]

By contrast, Fred Beal, a New England mill worker with a history of labor organization there and in the South (the Gastonia, South Carolina, strike), related his experiences of being swallowed up by the Five Year Plan. Sponsored by the American Workers' Party, Beal arrived in Leningrad in July 1930, observing that

117. Anna Louise Strong, "The Anarchist Who Builds an Empire," *NYT*, 9 March 1930: 84. He told Strong that if he ever had a "bourgeois" visiting card it would read, "Bill Shatoff, Social Engineering, graduate, U.S.A., the greatest industrial college in the world, specializing, temporarily, in Soviet Russia."

118. Anna Louise Strong, *The Soviets Conquer Wheat: The Drama of Collective Farming* (New York: Henry Holt, 1931), 171. Walter Duranty, hearing a rumor that Shatoff had been arrested, was told in response to an enquiry that the "a" in Shatoff had been changed to an "o". "Moscow Is Filled with Spying Tales," *NYT*, 19 September 1937: 66.

119. George A. Burrell, *An American Engineer Looks at Russia* (Boston: Stratford, 1932), 84–92.

120. Ibid., 119–207.

121. Ibid., 175, 188.

he found more exploiters there than workers. He was immediately upset by the Comintern confusion and indecision about his assignment.[122] First he attended a Red International Labor meeting in Moscow, dismayed that the American party had been instructed to have one-third of the delegation black.[123] Beal then left for Tashkent to build a cotton gin, where he was appalled by the use of child labor in the textile mills.[124] Returning the following year, he wound up in Kharkov at the tractor plant, editing a newspaper, *Tempo*, for the foreign community and becoming thoroughly disenchanted with Soviet industrial bungling and inhumanity. He managed to make his escape through Odessa and back home in October 1933.[125]

Another American adventurer, Zara Witkin, an experienced engineer from Oakland, California, was initially sympathetic to the Russian Revolution. But his real motive for going to the Soviet Union under the auspices of Amtorg was to track down Emma Tsesarskaya, a Soviet movie star with whom he had become obsessed after seeing her in a film, *Her Way*. With the help of journalist Eugene Lyons in Moscow, he was able to meet her and actually have a brief relationship.[126] Romantic encounters by Americans in Stalin's Russia included those of Margaret Wettlin of Newark, New Jersey, who went to Russia in the summer of 1932 to find a job as a teacher in a school at Nizhny Novgorod for Ford engineers. She met and married Andrei Efremov in Moscow and stayed on for several years as a guide and assistant for American engineers.[127] She was only one of many American women to wander into Russia in the 1930s with idealistic if not romantic pursuits in mind.

Another venturer into the quagmire of Russian industrialization was John Pelikan, representing the Union Switch and Signal Company of Swissvale,

122. Beal, *Proletarian Journey*, 130–58.

123. Beal, *Proletarian Journey*, 245–47. He was impressed especially by a beautiful "Jenny" from Philadelphia, who wore silk dresses and good shoes, hardly what the Soviet authorities expected from the downtrodden, exploited ethnic minority in the United States.

124. Ibid., 250–54.

125. Ibid., 319–40. Beal's account is suspect because of his sharp shift against communism. According to Myra Page, who was on the return ship with him in 1931 and knew him in Russia, he already had a bad reputation in American communist circles. In Russia he expected to find everything perfect. "He wanted to live off the system and have everyone look up to him and give big parties for him. When he didn't get the adulation he thought he deserved, he turned away from the Party and said, 'This whole thing's a fake.'" Christina Looper Baker, *In a Generous Spirit: A First-Person Biography of Myra Page* (Urbana: University of Illinois Press, 1996), 120. He certainly would not have endeared himself to his former comrades by comments such as, "The American Communist Colony in Moscow was a little Bohemia worshiping vodka and Stalin. . . . I found it a round of drinking bouts done by cliques." Beal, *Proletarian Journey*, 258.

126. Zara Witkin, *An American Engineer in Stalin's Russia: The Memoirs of Zara Witkin, 1932–1934*, edited by Michael Gelb (Berkeley: University of California Press, 1991), 3–7.

127. Wettlin, *Fifty Russian Winters*, 16–26.

Pennsylvania. He was assigned to supervise the installation of modern signaling equipment on the Moscow-Volokolamsk railroad by a contract signed in January 1930, after many delays, owing to Soviet bureaucratic inefficiency, poor wiring, and the timing. The work had to be subsequently postponed until after the spring thaw.[128] For this comparatively modest project, Pelikan would supervise the work alone, receiving a salary of $600 a month (above his usual $275), remitted from Amtorg and deposited in his local bank account, as well as expenses provided in Moscow, the total not to exceed $1,000 a month. Only 25 Russian engineers and 250 workers were involved on the project. Pelikan valiantly struggled with the assignment in miserable conditions through 1931, while adding complications by marrying a Russian. Ensuing efforts to gain a visa for her to leave Russia and enter the United States disclosed a passport violation in that he had innocently claimed birth in Chicago while he had actually been born in the Czech area of the Hapsburg Empire and brought with his family as an infant and had never completed naturalization papers. His wife was eventually allowed to leave Russia and, after some deliberation and challenges, the American immigration officials simply dropped their case.[129]

Myra Page (pen name of Dorothy Gary), a young idealist and Communist, depicted her adventures in an autobiographical novel.[130] She and her husband (John Markey) met as sociology graduate students at the University of Minnesota and would become caught up in social causes of the Depression era and joined the Workers' Party. She researched the Gastonia, North Carolina, textile strike, resulting in a novel set in the South, *Gathering Storm*, published by International Publishers in Moscow, that was quite successful.[131] They visited the Soviet Union first in 1928, and joined the study group that included John Dewey, for whom they had great admiration, but it provoked several encounters with him on views of the country they were seeing.[132] The Markeys returned to Moscow in September 1931 for a two-year stay. While he became an adviser to collective farms, working with Harold Ware, she was a contract reporter for left-wing periodicals in the United States, such as *Working Women*, and for *Moscow News*. His illness

128. F. 1930, Pelikan Papers (one box), HIA.

129. F. 1931 and f. 1932, ibid.

130. Page, *Moscow Yankee*, reprint edition (Urbana: University of Illinois Press, 1995).

131. See Dorothy Myra Page, *Gathering Storm* (Moscow: International Publishers, 1932). The book was actually published by Russian-American Communist Alexander Trachtenberg of New York, but he used facilities open to him in Moscow to avoid tax and other problems. Myra Gary, her real family name, was searching for a pen name and chose Dorothy Page initially. Baker, *In a Generous Spirit*, 110–15.

132. Baker, *In a Generous Spirit*, 95–96.

and months of recuperation on the Black Sea gave her the opportunity to write two books in 1932 promoting a positive view of the First Five Year Plan.[133]

The number of American companies involved in the Soviet Five Year Plans constituted virtually a who's who of American business. DuPont built a nitric acid plant, and the Hercules Powder Company contributed to the construction of a nitrocellulose plant, both of which had military implications. General Electric, behind the scenes, was a major contributor to the Five Year Plan, not only in providing turbines for Dneprostroi but also, on Cooper's recommendation, establishing American electrical standards in Russia. He regarded Cooper "as good an American as I know."[134] General Electric also furnished diesel electric locomotives for the new Tashkent railroad. The State Department played a minor role in monitoring American exports, opposing the sale of Wright airplane engines but approving the sale of thirty cargo vessels to Soviet Russia by the Shipping Board.[135] Black & Decker sent a specialist to instruct Russians on the use of electric drills and grinders.[136]

The best-known American engineer in Russia, apart from Cooper, was John Calder, who supervised the construction of the Stalingrad tractor plant and impressed Soviet authorities with his ability to complete the task ahead of schedule. He came to Russia with experience in building automobile factories for Ford and Packard and quickly won the praise of fellow engineers and Soviet officials, including Stalin.[137] After Stalingrad, he supervised the completion of the heavy tractor plant at Chelyabinsk and then became the chief consultant to the Soviet head of construction, Soiuzstroi, and finally chief consultant in 1931 to the Soviet steel trust, Stalmost, with a chief supervisory role over the troubled Magnitogorsk project.[138]

Margaret Bourke-White interviewed Calder in early 1932 and reported that part of his success was due to his ample use of swearing at employees, which was magnified by a woman interpreter into Russian. She described him as "lean bodied, 52, with a restless energy that flows out inexhaustedly [sic]," and as saying, "In

133. Baker, *In a Generous Spirit*, 119–39; Page, *Soviet Main Street* (Moscow: Cooperative Publishing Society, 1933). The Markeys left the party but remained social activists until their passing in the 1990s when they were in their nineties. For pictures and additional family history, see Baker, *In a Generous Spirit*.

134. Owen Young to William R. Castle (State Department), 7 August 1930, f. policy book, box 7, OEEA, RG 59, NA.

135. Robert Kelley memorandum, 13 November 1929, ibid.

136. John Abbink to Carmody, 1 April 1931, f. Russian trip, box 39, John M. Carmody Papers, FRPL.

137. Duranty, "Soviet Celebrates New Tractor Plant," *NYT*, 19 June 1930: 7; Walter Rukeyser, *Working for the Soviets: An American Engineer in Russia* (New York: Covici-friede, 1932), 219.

138. "American to Advise Soviet on Building," *NYT*, 27 May 1931: 8; and "American to Build 90 Soviet Steel Plants," *NYT*, 2 June 1931: 1.

spite of the conferences, meetings, the talk, Stalingrad must be built."[139] Unlike Cooper, Calder stayed on the job at the construction sites with only two assistants, James McElroy from Detroit, a graduate of Michigan State, and "Spencer." John Carmody recalled that Mezhlauk considered Calder "the best American engineer who had come to Russia."[140] Carmody, however, found Calder in Chelyabinsk depressed and worried about the failure of steel shipments to arrive. He was on his way to see Mezhlauk in Moscow to complain. McElroy, in conversation with Carmody in Moscow, suspected that Calder was either an American spy or a Soviet agent or both.[141] Carmody reflected,

> We found ourselves in complete agreement on one point: Jack [Calder] was a consummate liar, an accomplished one. He was not a professional engineer; he was a competent rough and trouble construction "boss". He was precisely what the Russians needed when he was there; their engineers were too theoretical then and too timid, Jack was mater-of fact, brusque, and without fear. The Russians understood him and he understood them and Walter Duranty and Knickerbocker. He served Russia well.[142]

Calder left Russia in April 1933, planning to return the following fall but apparently did not. He had sacrificed much of his productive life to the fulfillment of Stalin's Five Year Plan, just what the Soviet managers wanted.

John Littlepage also left a substantial mark on the First Five Year Plan. An expert on gold mining, which was a crucial industry in providing export support for the import of technology, he was appointed to a supervisory position in Moscow to coordinate the working of the many gold mines in Siberia and the Far East.[143] As assistant territorial commissioner in Alaska with special expertise in mining, Littlepage was approached by Amtorg in the autumn of 1927 as a consultant for gold mining in Siberia. This was a high-priority item in the plan because of its importance in paying for costly imports. Though apparently a quiet, unassuming

139. Bourke-White, "Where the Worker Can Drop the Boss," *NYT*, 27 March 1932: SM 8–10.

140. Carmody, "Russian Trip 1931—Experiences with John K. Calder," 6 June 1958, Carmody Papers, FRPL.

141. Ibid. No subsequent evidence for this allegation can be found.

142. Ibid.

143. His story is told in Littlepage, with Demaree Bess, *In Search of Soviet Gold* (New York: Harcourt, Brace, 1938). Bess, who actually wrote the book, admitted to Samuel Harper that he endured many difficulties, because Littlepage, soon after his return to the United States, simply disappeared. "I talked to him at great length on all sorts of subjects to get his point of view and his ideas. But he didn't give me enough actual material in the three weeks I had with him to make a whole book; and I had to include some of my own fitted to his mental pictures." Bess to Harper, 18 April 1938, f. 18, box 20, Harper Papers, UC-R.

man, he got things done and was given credit by Stalin with the rare order of Red Banner of Labor in 1935, near the end of his seven years serving the Soviet state. He had to be pressed to write about his experiences, which turned out to be an excellent survey of the pros and cons of Soviet economic management.[144]

Among the many other American experts contributing to the fulfillment of the First Five Year Plan was Walter Rukeyser, who was assigned to Azbest, the former, short-lived Armand Hammer asbestos concession in the Urals, located about thirty-five miles east of Sverdlovsk (Ekaterinburg), but he and his wife were delayed for weeks in Moscow. He quickly realized that the GPU was the best-organized operation in the country and appreciated their assistance when called upon.[145] He found in 1930 the whole country swarming with foreigners, hotels crowded, the streets full of Fords. A Russian he met in a dining car advised him, "To Americanize Russia—that seems to be the objective—therefore tell the people how far ahead technically America still is."[146] Though the new mill at Azbest was German—from Krupp—Rukeyser pioneered the American style of extraction of ore by steam shovels with locomotive rail relays to the plant. The chief handicap was ill-suited equipment and poor management of labor, but he was impressed with the new apartments for 40,000 workers.[147] Rukeyser at least took advantage of the opportunity to see quite a bit of the Soviet Union.

Along with Rukeyser's, many other accounts were published on American experiences in Russia during the First Five Year Plan. Another of interest is that by Eve Grady, the wife of an engineer who was assigned to the tractor plant in Kharkov but had ample opportunity to examine the Soviet scene. Though the book is dedicated, perhaps somewhat ironically, to "Joseph Stalin who made this book possible," the reflections are a mélange of positive and negative. She noted the many kulaks and other peasants "being killed off," rotting potatoes on poorly managed collective farms, the Russian engineers who were simply disappearing in the GPU "rounding up of 'plotters,'" catching "13,530 sparrows," and the many American engineers who were chafing under senseless restrictions and the ubiquitous bootlegging of food in order to survive.[148] Kharkov, perhaps more than other provincial Soviet cities, lacked many American necessities, such as coffee, soap, paper, and ink.[149]

144. Michael Florinsky, "Nine Years in Russia," review of above *In Search of Gold*, *NYT*, 23 August 1938: 104.

145. Rukeyser, *Working for the Soviets*, 26–29. Unlike most Americans working for the Soviets, Rukeyser had an Ivy League education: Princeton, 1916; Columbia, 1918.

146. Ibid., 96.

147. Ibid., 259–61.

148. Eve Garrette, *Seeing Red* (New York: Brewer, Warren, 1931).

149. Adolf Carl Noe, *Golden Days of Soviet Russia* (Chicago: Thomas S. Rockwell, 1931), 63–67.

Many American workers were in Russia not because of Amtorg's recruitment devices, nor for the love of socialist construction, but simply to find jobs in the Depression years. Octave Imer, working in Donbas, felt his situation was typical, "given prospects for employment in the United States." He advised that no one should sign up for more than one year because of conditions that went from bad to worse and that services provided should be specified in advance: light, heat, water, and individual stoves in accommodations. One should demand, he cautioned, first-class travel all the way to the workplace, paid in advance.[150] Jane Seymour, a Canadian who went in 1931 with her husband who was working for an American company, however, noted, "No sensible person went to Moscow expecting the comforts and conveniences we had been accustomed to at home. . . . There was no valid reason why any set of men should have."[151] Many were initially sponsored by the American Communist Party but became desperate once their initial stipends were exhausted and while the Soviet bureaucracy deliberated on what to do with them. Most had no alternative but to stay and endure their fate, taking solace in acquiring Soviet wives. They would be a major headache for the American embassy after 1933, when they tried to return home, especially since many had taken Soviet citizenship.[152]

Other Americans, as in the past, were intrigued by the challenges of Siberia, similar to those of the American West, but even larger and more daunting, especially after the economic sweeping of previous development by the revolution. Hugo Huppert saw Novosibirsk firsthand in 1931 as "the world's youngest big city."[153] He witnessed the Five Year Plan's drive to produce quantities of the Holt model harvesting combine there. The Kuznetsk combine drive was intended to furnish equipment for the cultivation of new lands in Central Asia, successful to a limited degree, but which would finally come to fruition in the Virgin Lands campaign launched by Nikita Khrushchev in the 1950s.

Myra Page perhaps best portrayed the perspective of American women in a little-disguised autobiographical novel, *Moscow Yankee*. Most of the American female contingent were along for the ride, accompanying husband-engineers, but, as Page, were sometimes caught up in the socialist construction and its goals. Though few, if any, ever worked in a Soviet factory, they empathized with and admired the many Russian women who did. For Page, Anna Louise Strong, and others, this new echelon of trained workers represented the true heroes of the

---

150. Imer to John Mulvaney, 11 September 1930, box 5, OEEA, RG 59, NA.

151. Seymour, *In the Moscow Manner* (London: Denis Archer, 1935), 188.

152. Lyons, *Assignment in Utopia*, 521–53.

153. Hugo Huppert, *Men of Siberia: Sketchbook from the Kuzbas* (New York: International Publishers, 1934), 47.

Stalin revolution, demonstrating the genuine workplace contributions of women. In Russia, women were finally realizing their potential and achieving an equality still remote in the Western world. The irony in *Moscow Yankee* is that the American wives enjoyed a special status as socialite companions to male engineers while praising the hard life and drudgery of the Soviet women. Page, with all her sympathy for socialist construction, duly noted that women, in addition to full-time factory work, were expected to maintain the household as before.[154]

Some American engineers (it is difficult to know how many) felt they had been misled by Amtorg and cheated by the terms of their contract being in rubles or simply by their negligence and naïveté. An example is G. L. Nicholson of St. Louis who, with his family, spent a miserable two years (by his account) working in Russia and became a strong advocate of nonrecognition in 1933, too late to make a difference.[155] Many American workers stayed on, however, to make the best of it, for example, John Scott at Magnitogorsk, Fred Moe at Chelyabinsk, and Baldwin at Kharkov. The American reaction to the Five Year Plan experience was obviously varied: convinced Communists became conservative oppositionists; unknowing opportunists found the light of positive construction and a fully employed society; businesses took what they could get and were thankful for it. One can agree at least partly with Beal's comment, "All kinds of driftwood from the United States floated into the Soviet Union."[156]

To many bewildered Americans contracted by Amtorg and sailing off into the Soviet sunrise, Charles H. Smith, an old Siberia gold-mining speculator and a representative of the American Russian Chamber of Commerce, was a lifesaver in terms of providing advice and orientation. "He was most surprisingly outspoken on Russian matters and we gathered that he has considerable power in Russia due to the fact that he is the nearest thing to direct contact between American business and the Russian Government."[157] Knowing Russia—and the language—from long experience, he was a clear asset to many bewildered Americans in Stalin's Russia. But he could also be tiring and was showing his age, Alex Gumberg noting, "We hope to have a live wire in Smith's place soon."[158] He was dismissed from his post late in 1930: "I am rather amused by the old man's stupidity—I mean our friend, Smith. I have looked after the old man for a number of years and helped him get jobs."[159]

154. Page, *Moscow Yankee.*
155. Nicholson to Senator Bennet Clark of Missouri, 8 July 1933, copy in box 22, OEEA, RG 59, NA.
156. Beal, *Proletarian Journey*, 276–77.
157. Report of R. B. Hosken, 15 October 1928, ibid.
158. Gumberg to Duranty, 20 January 1920, f. 3, box 4, Gumberg Papers, SHSW.
159. Gumberg to Fischer, 9 April 1930, f. 6, ibid.

John Carmody, the editor of *Factory and Industrial Management*, embarked for Russia to check on the American engineering pursuits in April 1931, armed with letters of introduction from Bogdanov of Amtorg, Mezhlauk, Walter Rukeyser, and others and with the assistance of Samuel Harper. He set his own itinerary, traveling more than 10,000 miles around the country.[160] Accompanied by Junius Wood, he toured the Nizhny Novgorod plant site, Stalingrad, Chelyabinsk, where he met John Calder, and Magnitorgorsk and wrote a series of articles on his trip that were somewhat critical of the Soviet management of the operations but was praised by veteran engineer Hugh Cooper: "You have handled your subject with great fairness and intelligence, and I hope the Russian engineers will read what you have said with profit to themselves and to their country, and that American engineers contemplating a visit to Russia will read over very carefully what you have presented before they make any contracts for service of any kind with this great opportunity."[161] A criticism of an article by Anna Louise Strong in *Moscow News* also won him credits in the Soviet-American business community.

Of course, American engineers and companies were not the only foreign contributors to the Soviet Five Year Plan. The other major presences were British and German. The former were especially involved in electrical powerplants and aircraft engineering, especially by Arcos contracts with the Metropolitan-Vickers Company for installation of electrical equipment and lines in major cities. In contrast to the relatively clean record of the Americans, at least officially, the British engineers encountered Soviet oppression firsthand in a round of arrests in early 1933. They appeared to be scapegoats for some of the failures of performance goals at the end of the First Five Year Plan but were forced into the ignominy of primitive incarceration and public show trials.[162] Their only crime was in trying to protect Soviet engineer colleagues. They were finally simply deported. All in all, within the foreign involvement in Soviet Russia, Americans represented well over 50 percent of the personnel and contract contributions to the First Five Year Plan, a total probably in excess of one billion dollars in business. British experts were also found in the oil industry in the Caspian Sea area, while

160. Carmody to John Snure, 1 April 1931, f. Russian trip, and letters of introduction, f. Letters, and Carmody to S. S. Shipman (Amtorg), 29 March 1931, and to Harper, 27 July 1931, box 39, Carmody Papers, FRPL. In the letter to Shipman, Carmody viewed Russian workers as "more awkward and less efficient" than he had expected.

161. Cooper to Carmody, 17 September 1931, f. Russia, ibid.

162. For a stirring firsthand account of one of those British engineers arrested and tried, see Allan Monkhouse, *Moscow, 1911–1933, Being the Memoirs of Allan Monkhouse* (London: Victor Gollancz, 1933). Monkhouse was arrested on 11 March 1933 at 9:15 PM as he was finishing his dinner and taken directly to the OGPU Lubianka prison. Ibid., 288–301. After trial, forced confession, and so forth, he was simply deported, and Vickers continued to do business with the USSR. See also, Sutton, *Western Technology 1917–1930*, 170–71.

Germans predominated in other electrical operations, especially at the Electric Works in Moscow.[163]

Amtorg

The American Trading Corporation in New York was hard pressed to keep up with the demands from Moscow for American engineering and skilled worker talent and to keep track of purchases and contracts. From expenditures in 1925–1926 of just over $13 million dollars, by 1929 the amount had grown to almost $50 million. It did not initiate, was not warned, and was clearly unprepared for the huge Soviet commitment to American engineering. Not surprisingly, it had to improvise, expanding to meet the demands, which later brought upon it critical scrutiny. A Communist Party inspection in early 1929 found that of 338 full-time employees in the New York office, 274 or 81 percent were Jewish, only 42 (13 percent) were Russian, 12 American, and scattered others, including four Irish. The report was critical of its operation, especially of its high composition of Jews, and that there was no practice of self-criticism, no party work, no wall newspapers, a normal way of disseminating information. It also thought salaries were too high and the staff poorly trained and lacking in technical expertise. Of 24 who were designated as engineers, 8 were deemed unqualified.[164] Another inspection in 1930 set a clear goal that staff include more young Soviet specialists, with at least 60 percent being members of the party, but recognized the difficulty of finding qualified people with knowledge of English who could be spared for assignment in the United States.[165]

Peter Bogdanov, who replaced Bron as head of Amtorg in late 1929, regularly complained about the lack of expertise of personnel sent from Moscow.[166] The head of the chemical section, he noted, was sixty-three, knew some English, but did not seem to have any chemical background.[167] Bogdanov appealed directly to Molotov and Kaganovich in regard to sending expert economists with full authority to make business arrangements with American companies. He complained that some real experts assigned to New York never showed up or were

163. See Sergei Zhuravlev, *"Malen'kie liudi' i "Bol'shaia istoriia"*: *Isnostrantsy moskovskogo Elektroza-voda v sovetskom obshchestve 1920-kh-1930-kh gg.* (Moscow: Rosspen, 2000).

164. Report on Amtorg, dated 1 February 1929, d. 47, op. 74, f. 17, RGASPI.

165. Report on Amtorg, dated 28 September 1930, ibid.

166. Bron was reassigned to be the head of Arcos in London.

167. Bogdanov to Moskvin and Moroz, 5 November 1929, ibid. Bron was transferred to London to direct Arcos, which had clearly become a second fiddle to Amtorg.

quickly withdrawn.[168] Another report by A. Vasilev complained about the deluge of commissions and delegations coming to New York, for which Amtorg had to provide costly housing and transportation but that they had little expertise and only interfered with assistance to genuine delegates such as Mezhlauk.[169] His appeals apparently fell on deaf ears or were simply lost somewhere in the Soviet bureaucratic machinery. Bogdanov also suffered from the fact that, according to several sources, 10 percent of his personnel were OGPU (or police) agents.[170]

To make matters more difficult, the Comintern was independently seeking volunteers from the American Workers' Party, most of whom were ideologically deficient as well as technically ignorant. Amtorg was, of course, expected to provide guidance and assistance for this naive contingent. Ivan Poliakov, the Moscow Gosplan supervisor of Amtorg operations, was especially vehement about the failure of the American agency to respond to criticism and direction. He especially noted that workers were sent to the United States without knowing the language, then were scattered around a large city, not meeting among themselves, not knowing the economic and political conditions of the country, and quickly adopting a "capitalist form of work."[171] He compared these workers with soldiers at the front lines, noting that the best we have are left to drift around in a capitalist world. No wonder there was a high turnover of personnel in New York.

Poliakov was especially critical of the acquisition of model designs from Caterpillar for the plant in Chelyabinsk without details, that the American company was paid for just a model. "They think they have done their job and can blame Amtorg for not providing answers." He concluded, "It is simply not in condition to cope with such enormous tasks."[172] His final blast was that Amtorg had not been provided with a single qualified engineer: "We do not need general workers, good party people, service personnel but fully qualified engineers. . . . In the course of the last several months, I have done everything possible to bring attention to all instances on the situation of people in Amtorg, but so far without result."[173]

The year 1931 was the high point of Amtorg's activity. Alex Gumberg kept a chronicle of orders placed that year in the United States, and it was clearly im-

---

168. Bogdanov to Molotov, et al., 18 November 1929, ibid.

169. Vasilev report, 1 February 1929, ibid.

170. Bogdanov's brother, Alexander, was in charge of the Seattle office of Amtorg. He had come to New York to purchase equipment for a Kamchatka enterprise in 1928 and remained behind. Harold Fisher memorandum, 8 August 1930, box 19, Fisher Papers, HIA.

171. Poliakov to Central Committee, CPSU, 28 June 1929, and to Mikoyan, 22 August 1929, ibid.

172. Poliakov to M. G. Gurevich (VSNKh), 20 September 1929, ibid.

173. Ibid.

pressive. The report extending from the beginning of the year was fifty-five pages long with about twenty-five orders listed on each page, ranging from $150,000 to just over $1,000,000 and not including any of the large, long-term contracts. Calculating an average of $250,000 for each, the total would come close to half a billion dollars. The list missed few companies that were on the New York Stock exchange and included Bucyrus Erie Company of Milwaukee, Hercules Motors, Caterpillar Tractor, Marion Steam Shovel, Cincinnati Grinders, Baldwin Locomotive, Sperry Gyroscope, Timken Axel Company, and many others, as well as General Motors, General Electric, and Ford.[174] Not all orders would be filled. Still, the total was huge and came at an especially important time for the financial survival of the American companies.

The Consolidated Machine Tool Corporation of America in Rochester, New York, was especially appreciative of Soviet orders through Amtorg, noting that many of its workers had been suffering because of the Depression.

> Conditions would have been worse still had it not been for a number of orders received from Amtorg Trading Corporation for machinery for Russia. This business was taken on the basis of extended credit—final payments being made nine months from date of shipment. Every payment and obligation has been promptly met and our business relations have been satisfactory in every way, in fact we wish all of our customers would be as satisfactory to do business with.[175]

But by 1932, Amtorg was demanding better terms. "At the present time Amtorg Trading Corporation have several hundred thousand dollars of additional business to place with us, but are unable to do this without much longer credits than previously—credits nearer to the length of time to what are offered by European manufacturers. We are not financially in a position to do this, and cannot get banks here to consider in view of existing conditions."[176] The American economic boom engendered by Soviet construction was drawing to an end.

The natural question arising from this orgy of Soviet purchasing abroad is how did they pay for it? The answer is in the export of two major items much in demand—gold and oil. Both had played a role in the payment of Russian industrialization before World War I, so it was natural for Soviet economists to target these for revival and rehabilitation after the devastating effects of the war and civil war.

174. "Russian Orders Placed with American Firms," f. 3, 1931, box 5, Gumberg Papers, SHSW.

175. Consolidated Machine Tool to Borah, 7 January 1932, f. Russia Dec. 1931–Feb. 1932, box 349, Borah Papers, MD, LC.

176. Ibid.

The value of Russian gold production in 1913 was around $55 million but had plummeted to only $2,500,000 in 1921. By 1934 it had reached $135 million on an annual basis, well above the prewar figures.[177] The USSR was now second only to South Africa in gold production, having surpassed American and Canadian levels. Also important were shipments of timber and wood products, manganese, platinum, grain, and art (through the Hammer galleries).

The Five Year Plan in Crisis

Perhaps the grandiose goals of the First Five Year Plan could never have been accomplished without American engineering and skilled labor. The cost, however, was tremendous and caused complaints and reconsiderations among both Soviet officials and American advisers. From the relatively safe laboratories of Ivan Pavlov, famous physiologist, W. Horsley Gantt reported "dissatisfaction with Stalin and his policy in general and that it was growing rapidly. . . . Everybody has become hopeless and tired of suffering. But [there is] no sign of aggressive spirit."[178]

The great explosion of American presence in Russia in 1928–1932 was of considerable benefit to both countries at the time, but the exhaustion of Soviet financial ability and dissatisfaction of many Americans with the conditions there signaled the end of the road. The Soviet grand vision and design caught the fancy of many Americans, individually and as enterprises. Some were genuinely devoted to the cause of construction, while many others were simply in it to make a buck. Both countries backed off at about the same time. The Soviet leaders felt that they had paid too much in direct contracts and terms of financing. Henry D. Baker, in a letter to the *New York Times*, astutely noted the Soviet demand for better terms, such as credit on purchases for three to five years, in contrast to full or 75 percent cash. Another point was that Soviet demand for American products such as cotton had drastically declined owing to problems in the neglected textile industry.[179] Most American companies and individuals met the considerable challenges with success but were reluctant to continue. The First Five Year Plan offered a unique opportunity for Soviet-American cooperation on a grand scale. Both rose to the occasion but were exhausted by it. Nevertheless, the ex-

177. Soviet gold production report, 1936, 863.4, box 5, RFSP, Riga 1936–1938 (Russia Series), RG 84, NA.

178. Coleman (Riga) to State Department, 4 June 1929, quoting Gantt, box 24, OEEA, RG 59, NA.

179. Henry D. Baker, Letters to the Editor, "Our Loss of Russian Business Not Viewed as a Calamity," *NYT*, 20 July 1930: E2.

perience provided a new and more extensive involvement of the two countries, greater than ever before in their histories.

The American Press

The whole "great leap forward" by the Soviet Union in the First Five Year Plan attracted a historic record of coverage of Russia in the American press. The great construction projects, the involvement of many American companies and individuals in them, contrasted with the United States, which was suffering decline in the economy and massive unemployment. Newspapers profited from a barrage of articles on the successful Soviet experiment. Heading the list with almost daily accounts of Soviet achievements was Walter Duranty of the *New York Times*, but most other regular correspondents followed suit, taking advantage of the many opportunities to visit construction sites and report in detail on American engineers in action. Most, of course, were reporting from Russia under observation and were sensitive to maintaining their jobs. In later years, some, especially Duranty, would be accused of tailoring their columns to please Soviet authorities.

Louis Fischer and Maurice Hindus were probably most successful in straddling the fence in noting both the positive accounts of Soviet accomplishments as well as their human costs. Both were also adept at quickly adapting their observations into books that were even more effective in portraying a massive economic transformation, but their overall views were generally positive. William Chamberlin, reporting for the *Christian Science Monitor*, published perhaps the most perceptive series on the Soviet transformation, but with the safety of having left the country with no plans to return. The most critical series, by Knickerbocker, for the *New York Evening Post*, was also written after an extensive tour of the country. All American reporters had unusually free access to information because of Soviet proclivity to things American. There were obviously important exceptions and Soviet authorities had certainly learned the art of manipulating the news. The American newspaper readers—and there were many—could count on almost daily news on events in Russia, reported by telegraph the day after. They could not help but be impressed by reading descriptions of the huge crowds celebrating the launching of various construction projects, while many of their own kind were standing in soup lines or burning worthless stocks and bonds.

Louis Kon, reporting to a Canadian Pacific official, coined a positive epitaph to the Stalin economic revolution: "The present regime in the Soviet Union is as strong as reinforced concrete." Nothing could or should stand in its way, but he should have quickly added, "with cracks." Louis Fischer, in comparing his 1932 tour of Russia with one in 1934, saw improvement and more stability, but he also described a pattern that had sunk in and would plague socialist construction—lackadaisical or nonexistent production at the beginning of the month and then a fourth week of storming to meet the goal.[180] The big problems of the Five Year Plan were, first, factories can be built, grand projects designed, mines developed, but it is another thing to get them to work; second, the purchase of much-needed expertise, design, and equipment was based on an ability to pay for it through the export of raw materials on a depressed market, resources rapidly diminishing; third, the assumption that an enthusiastic labor force released from peasant villages would respond to the challenges of a new adventure. These expectations were dashed by an inexperienced, overconfident, and forceful administration that alienated workers, made many mistakes, and had little interest in correcting them. The new technocrats lacked technical knowledge. They appreciated the value of American business, engineering talent, and managerial ability but could not duplicate the educational structure and basic ingenuity behind it.

180. Fischer, *Soviet Journey*, 25.

6

Recognition

By 1930 the arguments against recognition of the Soviet Union by the United States were definitely weakening. The early widespread belief that the Bolshevik regime was transitory and soon to fail and fall had disappeared into Trotsky's "dustbin of history," into which he himself, a leading advocate of world revolution, had also sunk. The radical proponents on the Soviet side—Trotsky and Zinoviev, especially—were thus cast away of any illusion of power. The Comintern, formerly a loose cannon on the world scene, or so perceived by many Americans, especially by those Americans in government offices, had been restrained and tamed into supporting the goals and interests of the Soviet state, which were fairly traditional realpolitik. Where now was the internal threat to the American system or society? Some still thought it existed and saw an increased danger in the viability and rise of the Soviet Union as an economic and military power. The old ideological advocacy of world revolution was now backed by traditional political strength. But there was also the argument that a new power, especially flexing economic muscle, required a diplomatic presence.

After conducting several tours of Russia in the 1920s, Sherwood Eddy was even more devoted to the cause of recognition.

> At the close of our trip three years ago when we took a vote of our party after going over all the evidence, they were unanimous for recognition on the basis of the Coolidge proposal. Our present party would be equally unanimous but they would go far beyond the Coolidge proposals and not include the irrelevant question of propaganda as a condition. If I was hundred per cent for recognition three years ago, I am two hundred per cent for it now, but for different reasons.[1]

---

1. Eddy to Robins (strictly private), 17 August 1929, f. 31, box 2, Eddy Papers, YDSA.

He saw financial isolation, a fear psychosis, defensive militarism, and the alleged Red Terror as the main problems. He admitted that the legacy of the great famine of 1920–1922 was still much in evidence but claimed there were also many new signs of hope and progress. Eddy clearly was in the forefront of advocating recognition with a genuine cloak of respectability and increased opportunities for travel to Russia.

On another front, American businesses and individuals had benefited from the Soviet great leap forward, with generally good results for both sides. Many would come back from their Five Year Plan adventures with cash in hand and as strong advocates of recognition. "We can do good business with them," was the refrain. They considered nonrecognition simply out of date and misguided, an unwarranted policy. Cultural relations also attained a very high level with much mutual benefit and little indication of any possible nefarious infiltration of Communism into American culture. In fact, the evidence pointed the other way; *amerikanizm* and all it represented was gaining rapid headway in that "wicked" Communist world. Much of this was simply credited to the engineering of the world with the stress on gigantomania in dams, factories, buildings, and society. In Hegelian terms, achieving the goal of an ideal Communist society brought antitheses along with the consequences, as Aldous Huxley emphasized in *Brave New World* (1932), on the eve of American recognition of the Soviet Union.

More concretely, openings in the impasse in official relations had already appeared during the Hoover administration. First was the Kellogg-Briand Pact, which proposed to gather guarantees against the conduct of war without using all possible avenues of avoiding it. Though it was based on a Franco-American "Western" initiative, Secretary of State Frank Kellogg insisted that all nations be invited to become signatories, and the Soviet Union, to some embarrassment, was the first to join. This, unfortunately, was Kellogg's swan song as secretary of state.[2] His successor, Henry Stimson, hinted at a reconciliation with Russia in 1929, based on commercial possibilities, but that was all. Cloaked in careful rhetoric, it was ignored by the Soviets to the regret of some American advocates of recognition.[3] Upon rumor of a special mission of businessmen being sent to Russia in April 1929, Kelley assured Harper that the State Department had no knowledge of this: "The Secretary stated at the same time that no change was

2. In an exchange of letters with Castle in 1933, Kellogg claimed the initiative in making the pact universal and indicated that he had mellowed considerably toward the Soviet Union. Kellogg to Castle, 12 May and 5 June 1933, and Castle to Kellogg, 1, 8, and 18 May 1933, reel 47, Kellogg Papers, MD, LC. Kellogg also wrote that he was planning his memoirs "to set the record straight," but, unfortunately, he never did.

3. Gumberg to Reeve Schley, 17 December 1929, f. 1, box 4, Gumberg Papers, SHSW.

contemplated in our policy with regard to the recognition of the Soviet Government."[4]

The American side subsequently was resigned to the fact that recognition
would not be considered while Hoover was president. Alex Gumberg reported,
"It is rumored in Washington that the President is alleged to have said that no
one will dare mention recognition in this Administration."[5] He thought that
Kellogg was otherwise disposed but handcuffed by an already determined presidential policy. Kellogg's assistant, William Castle, was more forthcoming, "I do
not believe that recognition of the Soviet government or the stationing of a
representative of this Government in Moscow . . . would make it possible for the
Soviet authorities appreciably to increase their purchases in the United States."[6]
Stanley Washburn, a voice from the World War I scene in Russia, sent President Hoover a copy of a 1920 letter to Harding that warned about the threat to
American democratic principles: "Russia happens to be the local habitat where
this Pandora's box of evils was opened, but its field of activity is not confined to
Russia but is aimed, as they themselves assert, at the entire world."[7]

Gumberg thought that Stimson was headed in the right direction and amenable to recognition. He interpreted one Stimson study in 1931 as a slap in the
face to Robert Kelley, the conservative head of the East European Division of the
State Department.

> He was [and still is], for almost ten years, the expert of the Department
> on Russia. He boasts of his knowledge of the language and familiarity with
> all developments there. It would seem that, under such able supervision,
> they would have all the facts. Of course, Kelley, who is intelligent but very
> prejudiced, could not year after year talk about the 'fall' of the Soviet gov-
> ernment. He had to change his line occasionally, I suppose, but I imagine
> that whatever his line was, it was always against the restoration of relation
> between the two countries. If the Department really makes an effort to study
> the problem, Kelley will be an obstacle to the last ditch, or perhaps he will
> become chagrined and quit.[8]

4. Kelley to Harper, 19 April 1929, f. 11, box 14, Harper Papers, UC-R.
5. Ibid.
6. Castle to Doan, 11 November 1932, f. Correspondence relations with Russia, box 22, FG 59.
7. Memorandum to Harding, 20 June 1920, enclosed in Washburn to Hoover, 10 October 1930, f.
Corres, Russia, box 993, Hoover, Presidential, HHPL.
8. Gumberg to Robins, 13 March 1931, f. 5 box 5, Gumberg Papers, SHSW. It is truly unfortunate
that Kelley, America's main State Department expert on Russia and a genuinely erudite scholar, if
there ever was one in the State Department, had such hostile, prejudiced views toward the Soviet
Union.

Kelley was indeed opposed to the "last ditch" to recognition but would yield to accommodation to the extent that he would have to, and, sadly, served to the end as the alter ego of Father Edmund Walsh of Georgetown as the die hard anti-Communist in the State Department. When Admiral Mark Bristol returned from his post as commander of the Pacific fleet by way of Siberia and European Russia in 1930, the State Department, upon Kelley's recommendation, ruled that such travel by American officers was not to be permitted, a slap in the face to a distinguished naval career.[9] On the other hand, Kelley, still a true professional, supplied information that trade with the Soviet Union had risen in value from $7 million in 1923 to $114 million in 1930 and the number of tourist visitors from the United States was up from around 2,000 in 1929 to 4,500 in 1931, all arguments for recognition.[10]

In the meantime, if one needed a special action, such as getting a relative out of the Soviet Union, William Borah was the man. His senatorial office in Washington virtually constituted a substitute State Department as far as Soviet Russia was concerned, as fellow congressmen from both parties frequently referred constituents to him if it involved a Russian problem. Consequently, he conducted a considerable correspondence directly with Litvinov in Moscow or indirectly through Skvirsky about Americans, or relatives of Americans, stranded in the Soviet Union; and most of them were promptly resolved. Quite clearly, Soviet authorities were anxious to please Borah, and many congressmen knew it.[11] Borah, however, was an adroit and prominent politician with many other matters on his agenda. When questioned by Jerome Davis in March 1929 about launching a campaign for recognition, Borah replied, "I have a feeling it is a little early yet to bring this matter forward. So many other things are pressing."[12]

The Stalin Mystique

The impression conveyed by those involved in the massive construction efforts, as well as those influenced by the positive depictions of Walter Duranty and

A few years later, Henry Stimson, who had supported nonrecognition in the Hoover administration as secretary of state, revealed over lunch with President Roosevelt that he welcomed his recognition of the Soviet Union, that it was "wise and good." Stimson diary, 17 May 1934, xxvii: 32, reel 5, Stimson Papers, MD, LC.

9. Wilbur Carr to Kelley, 28 June 1930, box 22, DEEA, RG 59, NA.

10. Kelley to Carr, 9 February 1933, f. 5, box 3, Kelley Papers, GUA.

11. For examples of this direct correspondence with the Soviet Commissariat of Foreign Affairs, see f. Russia, 1930–1931 (several folders), box 325 and 326, and f. Russia, March–May 1932, box 349, Borah Papers, MD, LC. As a rough tally, around 100 separate cases were involved.

12. Borah to Davis, 20 March 1929, f. Russia 1928–1929, box 284, ibid.

other journalists, was admiration for a leader moving a country ahead in the right way, that is, in what was viewed as an American direction: giant enterprises, full employment, and major advances in technical skills and social welfare—housing, free medical care, and educational opportunities. To many Americans and Europeans in the early 1930s, who were dismayed by the food lines in their streets, the Soviet economic miracle looked good in comparison, if not the ultimate solution. Some had questions about this being the accomplishment of a nondemocratic, dictatorial regime, but it was one that simply did not seem to pose any direct threat to the American political course, which, it could be claimed, was also turning toward a managed system. Part of this was certainly an admiration for an increasingly mechanistic society of efficiency and order, whether achieved by Mussolini in Italy or Stalin in Russia. Hitler, autobahns, and gas chambers, purges and labor camps, were around the corner. The 1930s were perhaps the decisive, formative years of the twentieth century—and beyond.

Americans certainly had mixed feelings about the new Soviet leader. Some considered him the best of the worst evils, an improvement on Trotsky, but few knew much about a Bukharin alternative, a more moderate NEP-type progression for Russia.[13] In any event, the die had been cast—Russia was on the road to a Stalin plan of social revolution and economic construction, regardless of costs. Former ambassador Bakhmeteff drew another picture of a man carrying out the logical Leninist direction: "Many people think Stalin is first of all an opportunist and that he will do the same in the present instance as he did with Trotsky. Kill the 'right' opposition [Bukharin] and then carry their policy." But he disagreed: "Stalin appears to me to be a straight revolutionary Bolshevist by tradition and upbringing. The difference between him and Rykoff and others lies exactly in the fact that he is hard boiled while they are not."[14] The Stalin regime, he might have added, possessed at least the semblance of stability, especially in world affairs, with a Western-leaning Litvinov as commissar of foreign affairs beginning officially in 1930.

Even before the Republican defeat in the 1932 election, signs and rumors appeared that recognition was not far off. Phillip Simms of the *New York World Telegram* headlined, "U.S. Held Ready to Send Commission to Study Soviet." He noted four reasons for the current consideration of recognition: (1) aggression in

13. Nikolai Bukharin was an old Bolshevik who had been left of Lenin in the early years of the Bolshevik regime but had become the strongest advocate of Lenin's New Economic Policy of mixed socialism-capitalism in the 1920s. He believed that Trotsky's planned economy with collectivization and an emphasis on industrialization that Stalin would adopt (after Trotsky was out of the picture by deportation). For more on Bukharin's program of avoiding the human costs of the Stalinist regime, see Stephen F. Cohen, *Bukharin and the Bolshevik Revolution, 1888–1938* (New York: Norton, 1973).

14. Bakhmeteff to Harper, 15 April 1929, f. 11, box 13, Harper Papers, UC-R.

the Far East; (2) business prospects; (3) the rise of Jeffersonian principles; and (4) the fact that Russia was ready to negotiate.[15] There was no shortage of prominent Americans ready to clamber on board an American Soviet express.

The State Department

From Secretary of State Frank Kellogg on down, the American "ministry of foreign affairs" remained adamantly opposed to recognition, led by Robert Kelley of the Division of East European Affairs and backed by Father Edmund Walsh of Georgetown's School of Foreign Policy. This position, however, had entered a softer stage, with little public pronouncement and a sense of inevitability. The new man in the small department block devoted to Russian affairs was Alfred Kumler, a sophisticated and able lawyer from Evanston, Indiana, who was much more open to discussion and options than the Poole-Landfield-Hughes regime of the early 1920s and who worked full time on Russia but was still committed to nonrecognition. He was fond of extended strolls through Rock Creek Park with Sam Harper and many others, with Russia on their minds.[16] Unfortunately, while crossing a bridge over the park on one of his many walks in 1928, he was struck and killed by an automobile, thus depriving the country of one of its most promising leading lights on foreign affairs.[17] An even greater loss was the sudden death of Robert E. Olds, a veteran of Hoover's American Relief Administration in Russia, who served as undersecretary of state in 1927–1928; proponents of recognition had found him especially receptive.[18]

During the 1932 election campaign, Hoover asked Assistant Secretary of State William R. Castle Jr. to draw up a statement on recognition, in case Roosevelt made an issue of it. Castle, who had been in the department since 1919, mainly concerned with Western European affairs, advised the president not to make Comintern propaganda an issue, "since that is discounted by a large number of the intelligent people of this country." Also, he felt it wise to ignore the debts owed the United States by Russia, "since those debts have been pretty well wiped off the books." In the brief statement prepared for possible campaign use, nonrecog-

15. *New York World Telegram*, 19 August 1932, clipping in f. Russia June–Nov. 1932, box 350, Borah Papers, MD, LC.

16. Kumler to Harper, 9 and 21 January 1928, f. 14, box 13, ibid. This walk was six miles. Kumler was one of those relaxed, convivial individuals rare in the State Department. In the spring of 1927, he invited Harper for a visit: "The cherry blossoms are out and there is a bottle on the shelf. But you know what happens to cherry blossoms and bottles. So don't put off your visit." To Harper, 27 April, 1927, f. 11, box 13, ibid.

17. Jane Bassett to Harper, 26 November 1928, f. 37, ibid.

18. Gumberg to Schley, 20 July 1927, f. 2, box 3, Gumberg Papers, SHSW.

nition was boiled down to "A vast majority of the American people oppose recognition of any government which, failing to respect the institutions and the form of government of its neighbors interferes with their internal affairs."[19] Fortunately perhaps for Hoover, Roosevelt did not bring up the subject in 1932. Later, in early 1933 when the director of the department's Far Eastern Division suggested that recognition might be in order in regard to Japanese aggression, Castle responded that there were many other arguments against recognition.

> It is quite obvious, furthermore, that it would be entirely improper for the President, at the very end of his term in office, to take action in a matter as important as this which would definitely bind the next Administration and might be very distasteful to that Administration. It is obvious, therefore, that the question of Russian recognition will have to remain in abeyance until after the 4th of March.[20]

With the advent of the Roosevelt administration, the department shifted—but not very much. Cordell Hull, the new secretary of state, was socially progressive but administratively conservative; his credo would be: "don't rock the boat," keep foreign affairs in tranquility while major domestic reforms were in progress. The foreign priority would be his particular interest in Latin/South America. Kelley remained posted on the solid rock of American expertise on Russia and also of nonrecognition—very resistant to being moved. He and his office spent much time organizing the arguments against recognition.[21] That policy was still strongly entrenched. A friend of the president, after attending a postelection celebration in December 1932, wrote, "It seems to be generally understood that you are committed to the recognition of Russia. I hope this is not so, or that if you do do it, you will take your time. The Bolshevist Government may be very plausible and innocent but, up to date, the Third International is really the power behind the throne."[22] Old nonrecognitionists would not simply fade away.

The current was thus clear to all; recognition was on the agenda, and the appointment of William Phillips, a veteran of the Woodrow Wilson administration, as the new undersecretary of state brought in a strong supporter of recognition for the president. Walter Lippmann saw it coming: "The recognition of a country is not a moral act but an act of realism. The question of the advantages to Ameri-

19. Castle to Hoover, 17 August 1932, f. 192 Hoover, 1931–1932, box 24, Castle Papers, HHPL.

20. Castle to Morris Lazaron, 3 February 1933, f. 95 Russia, 1931–1933, box 12, ibid.

21. See the large file, "Correspondence Relating to Russia, 1920–1933," box 25, OEEA, RG 59, NA.

22. Samuel Lloyd to "Frank," 17 December 1932, f. Russia 1933, box 1, POF 220, RFPL.

can trade that might flow from recognizing Soviet Russia is an open one. The subject might be left for the next administration to deal with as seems expedient at the time."[23] Also, historian William Dodd of the University of Chicago, ambassador-designate to the important post in Germany, supported recognition and discussed it with secretary-designate Hull on 1 March. He learned at that time that William Bullitt was already being considered as the future ambassador to the Soviet Union.[24] What was left was to get the country in gear to accept an inevitable development and gain as many concessions as possible.

Setbacks

The Soviet cause for recognition did not fare well either in the public arena. It seemed that the initial and rather reasoned debate over recognition had deteriorated into a war of words and vicious exchanges. The Soviet Union was behaving with more confidence, to the annoyance of many Americans. There was a sense that the lines were being drawn in the sand, the pistols ready. Proponents of recognition had been frustrated by the Hoover administration's deaf ears, rarely receiving responses, such as to a quite sophisticated proposal for a bipartisan commission to Russia by Samuel Reading Bertron, a New York banker who had served as an economic member of the Root mission to Russia in 1917.[25] Still committed to Wilsonian internationalism and active in the American-Russian Chamber of Commerce, he remained a consistent and respected advocate of recognition.

Any move—or drift—toward recognition obviously had to contend with an initial uphill fight. First of all, the opposition to recognition became more militant and actually gained strength with a religious and defensive political reaction. Another influential voice that the president was forced to acknowledge was that of Charles Crane, a major supporter of the last Democratic president (Wilson), a founding member of the Root mission, and a strong opponent of recognition. He had a longtime interest in the Orthodox Church in all its aspects and much resented the Bolshevik restrictions on its activities. In a letter to the editor of

23. "Memorandum of talk at lunch with WL," 28 October 1932, f. Lippmann, box 41, H. F. Armstrong Papers, Mudd-P. The Lippmanns and the Armstrongs were close friends; Lippmann later married Armstrong's widow.

Though supporting a change in administration, Lippmann backed Newton Baker for the Democratic nomination and was annoyed that he was ignored after the election of Roosevelt. Lippmann to Baker, 11 January 1933, f. 1933 Lippmann, box 149, Baker Papers, MD, LC. Lippmann had served as an assistant to Baker in the War Department during World War I.

24. Dodd to Harper, 11 August 1933, recounting his meeting, f. 11, box 15, ibid.

25. Bertron to Hoover (personal), 5 November 1930, presidential personal file, f. Bertron, box 6, HHPL.

Commonweal in May 1933, he asserted that an important but less recognized part of the Five Year Plan was its attack on religion.

> They started in their Five Year Plan of destroying all the churches in Russia. They don't boast very much of this part of their plan, but it is an integral part of it. This year especially is given over to destroying all religious literature. . . . They have kept an entirely air-tight wall around all of the pure Russian people so that no voice of suffering could reach the outside world and the people inside the wall could reach the outside world and the people inside the wall know nothing of what is going on in the outside world.[26]

His influence in Washington was limited in 1933, however, by his misplaced praise of the new German leader, Adolf Hitler, whom Roosevelt despised.[27]

Alex Gumberg, while claiming that an anti-Soviet campaign did not exist, admitted that "Hamilton Fish, who has political ambitions, has tried to capitalize the Russian problem as a means for keeping himself before the public. Fish, in fact, was a new and effective obstacle to recognition with much support from New England. The so-called unemployed riots, which occurred early in March [1930], and then the May Day demonstrations each year gave him an excellent opportunity to start a big noise about 'Communism' and 'revolutionary activities.'"[28] Increasingly, American politicians and conservative causes were seizing on any possibilities—such as blaming Communism and Soviet policies for American problems—and there were many of them during the Depression. Gumberg's friend Robins disagreed, seeing "a concerted drive here and abroad against the Soviet State."[29] To complicate matters, *Pravda* delivered a direct attack on Gumberg in early February, which Gumberg and Fischer blamed on Charles H. Smith and Eugene Lyons in Moscow.[30]

The largest of these was the issue of the Soviet dumping of products such as wood pulp and manganese on the American market, which opponents claimed—with some justification—had been produced by convict labor. The main culprit was perceived to be the export of forest products, chiefly wood pulp, at low prices to the United States. This rather minor issue in terms of dollars, became a major focus of congressional investigation by the Fish Committee in 1930, resulting

26. Crane to Editor, *Commonweal*, 2 May 1933, reel 1, Crane Papers, BA, CU.
27. Crane to FDR, 18 May and 11 July 1933, f. Charles Crane, PPF 462, FRPL. In the latter Crane wrote how pleased he was "at the wonderful way you are managing our relations with Germany."
28. Gumberg to Fischer, 20 August 1930, f. 9, box 4, Gumberg Papers, SHSW.
29. Robins to Gumberg, 2 March 1930, f. 5, ibid.
30. Fischer to Gumberg, 15 April 1930, and Gumberg to Yazikov, 9 April 1930, f. 6, ibid.

in much extremely negative publicity. The resulting legislation forbidding the importation of any products produced by convict labor was clearly aimed only at the Soviet Union. That year's tour of Russia sponsored by the American-Russian Chamber of Commerce had to be canceled because so many businessmen dropped out, fearing government reprisals.[31] The result of this anti-Soviet pressure was that the Treasury Department issued a new order in November 1930 that importers of Russian pulpwood would have to prove that it was not produced by convict or forced labor, a near impossibility. As Theodore Wallen noted in the *New York Herald Tribune*, "The new regulation puts the shoe on the other foot: it puts the burden of proof on the importer and hence, . . . on Soviet Russia."[32]

Hugh Cooper, the former engineer-in-Russian-residence, acting on behalf of the American-Russian Chamber of Commerce, organized a conference to refute the new government regulations and plead the case of the advantages of Soviet-American trade on the whole. A resolution was passed that began as follows:

WHEREAS the Regulations promulgated by the Treasury Department on November 24th, 1930, in respect to convict made goods, already have caused a substantial disruption of American-Russian trade by creating uncertainties which have not only prevented the consummation of important contracts but constitute a particularly serious obstacle to the continuance of this trade because of the possibility of summary embargo apparently permitted by the Regulations and the lack of any specific interpretation of the formalities and credentials required of the American importers engaged in Russian Trade.[33]

This resolution was followed by a visit of representatives of the American-Russian Chamber of Commerce, headed by Cooper and Allan Wardwell on 23 January 1931, to the Treasury Department about the new regulations. They were met by William Castle, assistant secretary of state, Robert Kelley, and by a Mr. Mills, undersecretary of the treasury, who seemed to know little about the issues at hand. Though nothing came of the meeting, Mills indicated a willingness to receive concrete suggestions from the Chamber.[34]

Another powerful and vocal opponent of recognition right up to the last minute was Edmund Walsh, a veteran of the Vatican relief program in the early 1920s and who now directed the School of Foreign Affairs at Georgetown, a primary

31. Gumberg to Fischer, 20 August 1930, f. 9, ibid.
32. Wallen, "U.S. Fortifies Barriers on Convict Goods," *New York Herald Tribune*, clipping in f. 1, box 5, ibid.
33. "Minutes of Conference in Consideration of American Russian Trade Held in the City of New York," 18 December 1930, f. 2, box 5, Gumberg Papers, SHSW.
34. Memorandum of conference, 23 January 1931, OEEA, box 23, RG 59.

producer of foreign service personnel for the State Department and a regular lecturer at the Army War College.[35] Entrenched in Washington and influential, especially and ironically, in the largely Protestant-oriented Republican administrations, he was an eloquent and willing speaker on that cause, even if often betraying his ignorance of the situation. Crane, for one, was much impressed with him, as Harper related, "Mr. C. dropped in last evening and we had a pleasant hour. I did one tactless thing. He had seen Walsh in Washington and was most enthusiastic 'about this man who knows more about Russia than anyone else in the country.' I told him I had found Walsh very unreliable and unscholarly, and had been obliged to come out in sharp criticism of his writings. This seemed to hurt Mr. C's feelings a bit. Perhaps I should have kept still."[36]

The argument that the great expansion in trade and business connections in the early years of the First Five Year Plan should have diplomatic recognition to facilitate further expansion was dampened by a decrease in trade in 1931, mainly due to expected production from new factories that would replace imports, especially of agricultural implements. At least, this was the analysis that Gumberg relayed to Borah.[37] The other factor, however, was that European countries were taking advantage of the situation of American nonrecognition to offer better credit terms to the Soviet Union. Borah chose to take the long-term approach, noting that American exports to Russia had exceeded imports by five times during the 1923–1930 period—and were growing.[38] More persuasive was the view, expressed by many in the business community, that "the Soviet Government is firmly in power for years to come."[39]

One of the greatest setbacks to recognition was the continuing reports and direct evidence of discrimination and oppression of minority peoples. Most of the information was contained by Soviet restriction on emigration, but in late 1929 an exodus of more than 5,000 Volga Germans caused something of a sensation, especially since they passed through Latvia and were interrogated by the members of the American listening post. "No event connected with Soviet Russia has made such a profound impression upon the people in this part of Europe as the passage through their midst of thousands of so-called German colonists, on their

35. Some had doubts about this close association. See, for example, Tasker Bliss to Hamilton Fish Armstrong, 26 January 1927, f. Tasker Bliss, box 8, Armstrong Papers, Mudd-P.

36. To Brodie, 22 October 1931, f. 27, box 16, Harper Papers, UC-R. Crane periodically visited Chicago and would stop over with Harper and his mother, going to and from seeing his daughter and family in Madison, Wisconsin.

37. To Borah, 13 August 1931, f. Russia 1931, box 326, Borah Papers, MD, LC.

38. To Ogden Mills (Secretary of the Treasury), 26 March 1932, f. Russia 1932, box 349, ibid.

39. Arthur Coyle (United States Lines) to Borah, 19 December 1928, f. Russia 1928–1929, box 284, ibid.

way from their former houses in Russia to an undetermined location."[40] Reflecting this division, John Van Antwerp MacMurray, director of the Walter Hines Page School of International Relations at Johns Hopkins, returned from a trip to Russia in the fall of 1932 somewhat bewildered:

> It was a fascinating experience, but as exhausting as being in the cheering section at a big football game for a fortnight on end, merely to be in Russia and to try to understand something of the temper of the people. And having been deafened by loud speakers, and dazzled by the red banners, I confess that I am more uncertain than ever what the great experiment is really all about, and whether or not it is really progressing.[41]

CPUSA

One of the most ubiquitous charges against recognition was that the Comintern, claimed to be a Soviet government agency, financed the activities of the Communist Party of the United States of America (CPUSA). Subsequent investigations have proved some truth to this charge. Most of the funding went to the subvention of publications, such as the works of Lenin, and providing basic expenses of leaders' attendance at Comintern congresses and tours of the great Soviet achievements, trips that often produced negative impressions. For anyone who has scanned at least a portion of the vast, disorganized, and repetitive party records, this was essentially money down the drain.[42] They prove at least that the American Communist Party was an ineffective, much divided and divisive organization that had practically no impact on American social, political, or economic life.[43] At most, the CPUSA performed as a cover for some clumsy intelligence gathering but was seldom trusted by Soviet authorities even for that.

If the Comintern was disenchanted and distrustful of the American party, the Americans were equally disdainful of the operations of the supposedly in-

---

40. Coleman (Riga) to Secretary of State, 19 December 1929, f. 861.56/86, roll 128, M316, RG 59, NA.

41. MacMurray to Harper, 28 October 1932, f. 26, box 17, Harper Papers, UC-R.

42. The records of the CPUSA were regularly sent to the Comintern headquarters in Moscow, where they were seldom read, and simply filed—and misfiled—away. Not long ago they were microfilmed from the party archive (RGASPI) by a Hoover Institution-Library of Congress project, and later placed online, largely a waste of time and money.

43. See, for example, "On factionalism in the US party," 28 February 1927, d. 998, op. 1, f. 515, reel 74, CPUSA Papers, MD, LC. Americans were forced to listen to such lectures as one by Bukharin who stressed, "There is very little Marxism in the American Party." Ibid. There was probably general agreement on that point.

ternational directorate. A report of an anonymous "Zigzag," apparently Bertram Wolfe, who attended a Comintern meeting, claimed that "not the slightest effort was made to clarify political issues." Jay Lovestone wrote, sarcastically, after a visit to Moscow, "We had to do a little writing in Moscow. Everybody against factionalization, for collective actions."[44] The party naturally gained membership but little else with the advent of the Depression. A party directive awkwardly acknowledged, "Speaking generally there is abstract sympathy for our movement more than any other time, [but] we have no sufficient forces to utilize this sympathy."[45] Many prominent American Communists, such as Wolfe and Lovestone, soon became defectors or dissidents, leaving the party with the inept and pedestrian leadership of Earl Browder and William Foster.

Much was still made by opponents of recognition that the Comintern was financing the political goal of the CPUSA, which was to capture political power, the same as other parties. Some transfers of funds have been documented, but they were rather insignificant amounts and mainly designated for the publications of the works of Lenin and other more contemporary literature, which hardly anybody read.[46] Comintern's investments in the world revolution were definitely reigned in, while the American party constantly complained of shortages of funds. Whatever funds can be accounted for were a drop in the bucket compared with what Amtorg was investing in contracts with American capitalists.

Another bone of contention fostered by the Comintern concerned activism among the American blacks. The leadership of the CPUSA, dominated by mostly old and some new white socialists in the North, was quite unenthusiastic about meeting the challenge of recruiting among either Northern or Southern African-Americans. They resented Comintern directives to include a quota of blacks in the American delegations to various Soviet- and Comintern-sponsored tours. The real problem in finding support for Communism among African-Americans is that few were convinced that this road would really lead to immediate progress in civil rights, while the NAACP had essentially captured the main ground, abhorred Communism—or direction from outside—and chose to work within the American political infrastructure, in which there were many white sympathizers. African-American activists tended to be pro-Soviet in response to propaganda about equal rights under socialism but basically neutral in terms of governmental recognition of the Soviet Union.

---

44. Ibid.

45. Language department memo, February 1931, d. 2337, reel 178, ibid.

46. Harvey Klehr, John Earl Haynes, and Fridrickh Igorevich Firsov, *The Secret World of American Communism* (New Haven, Conn.: Yale University Press, 1995), 29–34. Actually, not much was secret about all of this.

Perhaps the greatest damage to the prospects for recognition, however, was the devastation in the countryside caused by collectivization that in combination with a severe drought created a massive loss of life, which the Soviet regime could not deal with—or consciously avoided. Bill Stoneman of the *Chicago Daily News* estimated the loss of life at 30 percent in Ukraine, North Caucasus, and some other parts of the country. "It must have been a ghastly spring in the villages," he noted.[47] And, surely, it was. Why should the United States recognize an obviously failing system?

The Far East

Russia became a major disrupting factor in East Asia in the last decade of the nineteenth century, when the Trans-Siberian Railroad was launched and finally completed after 1905. Already a naval fleet existed in the area, based at Vladivostok. The Russian position was strengthened by the acquisition of a lease on Port Arthur and a portion of the Liatung Peninsula, strategically located in the Yellow Sea and a guardian of Southern Manchuria. Japan was also developing economic and military power, and viewed the increased Russian presence as a direct challenge, especially with the building of the Trans-Siberian shortcut, the Chinese Eastern Railway (CER), from Chita to Vladivostok through the middle of Manchuria. As an imperialistic stroke into China it was similar to the American Panama Canal, but it had even greater implications as a Russian dominance in Northern China. Harbin, as the central administrative center of the Chinese Eastern and also of the Russo-Asiatic Bank, quickly became the principal Russian stronghold in Manchuria and North China. The failure of Russia to take Japanese objections seriously led to the Russo-Japanese War (1904–1905), resulting in a considerable Russian military and political setback in the region.[48]

Though severe, this setback, and the consequent loss of Port Arthur to Japan, was temporary. The Chinese Revolution of 1911 and growing instability on the Asian mainland in general invited a series of Great Power interventions. Because it was integral to the Trans-Siberian—as an avenue into Russia, as well as a Russian penetration into China—the Chinese Eastern Railway remained under Russian administration and grew in prominence and profitability with the

47. To Harper, 12 October 1933, f. 13, box 16, Harper Papers, UC-R.
48. The following is based on several sources but especially: George Alexander Lensen, *The Damned Inheritance: The Soviet Union and the Manchurian Crises, 1924–1935* (Tallahassee, Fla.: Diplomatic Press, 1974); and Peter S. H. Tang, *Russian and Soviet Policy in Manchuria and Outer Mongolia, 1911–1931* (Durham, N.C.: Duke University Press, 1959).

completion of the Trans-Siberian and the growing market potential in the area. It became a vital and secure link for supplies and communications through Russia during World War I. Repercussions from the Russian Revolution in 1917 resulted in the breakdown of central authority in Siberia and the Russian Far East, including Manchuria. The Russian Civil War produced several contending governments: Kolchak in central Siberia in Omsk; a renegade White Cossack general, Semenov, at Chita; a motley conglomeration of Western forces centered around Vladivostok; and a substantial Japanese army of around 75,000 in Manchuria and Siberia. With troops situated at strategic points along the Trans-Siberian and the Chinese Eastern, Japan played various sides against each other in an attempt to secure a mainland empire. As the civil war wound down, the White armies collapsed, and American and other Western contingents withdrew, leaving the Japanese holding much of the territory under arbitrary authority. A joint Allied—but mainly American—special railway corps was present until 1921, maintaining a precarious technical control over the CER in Manchuria. Western pressure combined with the creation of a temporary but comparatively stable Far Eastern Republic that included much of Eastern Siberia forced the withdrawal of the Japanese forces by 1922, leaving a vacuum of power that both China and Soviet Russia attempted to fill, the latter gaining control of the CER.

A new complication for both the Soviet Union and China was the large number of refugees, mostly remnants of anti-Bolshevik forces, that descended on Harbin in Manchuria and Shanghai in China. In Harbin, for example, there were essentially three cities: White Russian, Red Russian, and Chinese—and a surprising degree of harmony, at least in social and cultural life. The main factor that allowed a major resurgence of Soviet presence, however, was an alliance with Chiang Kai-shek's Kuomintang in the 1920s. Both strove to regain position and strength with China obtaining Soviet military aid and advice, and the Soviet Union hoping to take advantage of the major growth in the Chinese Communist Party, which was part of the Kuomintang political alliance. Chiang's sudden and surprising attack and repression of the Communists in 1927 naturally caused a crisis in the relations and a breaking off of the close relations with Soviet Russia.

With its strong position in China suddenly virtually destroyed, the Soviet Union attempted to shore up its strength in the borderlands, especially in Mongolia, where a strong Chinese resettlement campaign was under way and the Manchu and other contenders for power in dissolution. After a series of confrontations with local authorities, the Russians gained the upper hand and by 1930 had essentially installed a Soviet government in Mongolia. In the meantime, however, the Chinese had taken the offensive in Manchuria, promoting a regional government in Mukden and virtually seizing the Chinese Eastern Railway.

The Chinese, however, understood that the viability of the railroad depended on Russian traffic and sought a compromise that preserved at least a temporary nominal Soviet authority. The situation was ripe for Japanese intervention.

In September 1931, a Japanese army officer from Dairen (Port Arthur) was killed while leading a foray into Manchuria by a Chinese detachment; this provided the excuse for a major Japanese invasion and occupation of Manchuria, which neither Soviet nor Chinese forces were prepared to confront. The sudden, if not unexpected, Japanese seizure of a large tract of the Asian mainland bordering on the Soviet Union naturally struck sensitive nerves in Moscow. The United States, of course, was concerned about the emergence of an expansive Japanese Asian empire on its Pacific horizon. The illusion of controlling or restricting this new presence in Asia was only that, another dilemma for both American and Soviet foreign policy—how to deal with a successful penetration of Asia by Japan. All of this came at a crucial time during the winter of 1931–1932 with the Soviet Union mired in a faltering First Five Year Plan and the United States in the midst of the worst stage of the Great Depression and also engrossed in an exceptionally consequential election campaign.

If the view of the eastern sunrise from Moscow did not bode well, the western sunset was perhaps even more clouded. The rise of the National Socialist Party in Germany by election victory and the ascendancy of its rabidly aggressive leader, Adolf Hitler, were of obvious concern to the Soviet leadership in early 1933, since much of his party's political propaganda had been directed against Communists of all kinds and with the goal of acquiring Russian territory. Fortunately, the Soviet Union now had a foreign minister, Maxim Litvinov, with an agenda, ideological and political, for curbing fascism with Western alliances, termed *collective security*. Precedents for a Franco-Russian alliance were well rooted in history, and most recently in the background of World War I, but this was not so easy to accomplish in the early 1930s, considering the reluctance of major Western countries such as France, Britain, and the United States to side with a Communist power and its alleged and at least partially proved history of supporting revolution in their countries.

France, of course, was quite concerned about the German national resurgence and designs of at least altering, if not nullifying, the Versailles arrangement, such as revoking the demilitarized zone along the Rhine. Soviet Russia, by invitation, became a defender of the Paris peace, though it had not participated in it, at the Geneva meeting on disarmament in 1932 and in direct negotiations with France. The Soviet Union was suddenly threatened on two sides. Karl Radek, the Western-oriented radical maverick in the Soviet camp, in private conversation with Norman Davis in Geneva pressed the point of the importance of U.S. recognition to get Japan to back off. Radek believed that "Japan was determined to attack Russia." He asked Davis to ask Stimson to meet with Litvinov informally about this. On the golf course the next day, Stimson agreed but only if the meeting was natural or accidental.[49] Apparently it did not happen.

These discussions became especially intense in mid-1933 after the Hitler ascendancy in Germany. When Germany withdrew from the League of Nations that summer, France asked Soviet Russia to join—which it did. Thus the preparations for a Franco-Soviet alliance were contemporary to the negotiations for recognition with the United States. Litvinov's visits to Paris for serious discussions on the "German problem," in February, July, and again in October on his way to the United States, revealed one clear weakness: France would do nothing for the Soviet problems in the Far East in dealing with an equally (to Germany) resurgent Japan. Where else could Litvinov go in regard to this problem?

The Roosevelt Election and Recognition

Shortly after Franklin Roosevelt's nomination as the Democratic Party candidate for the presidency, a surprise player entered the recognition game: William C. Bullitt, who had a brief exposure on the Russian-American scene many years earlier, in 1919, when he was sent to confer with Soviet leaders, including Lenin, about arrangements to settle issues relative to the destructive Russian Civil War and the deliberations in Paris. His participation caused something of a minor furor, since it had not been directly sanctioned by President Wilson but was the brainchild of Colonel House and others who thought leaving Russia out of the negotiations in Paris was ludicrous. He had also been accompanied by maverick socialist Lincoln Steffens, which did not help the cause of the delegation in Paris. After this brief but dramatic venture into politics, Bullitt became "a playboy of the Western world," drawing some attention by marrying Louise Bryant, widow of John Reed, but otherwise living in comfortable European exile through the 1920s.

Seeing an opportunity to again be of service, he approached his old patron, Colonel House and secured his support. On his own, Bullitt went on a tour of Europe, familiar ground to him, but this time with political conditions uppermost in mind. He informed Louis Wehle, a Harvard classmate and old friend of Franklin Roosevelt, of his availability, and Wehle offered Bullitt's assistance as a resource on European affairs, which was promptly accepted, in courtly Roosevelt fashion:

49. Stimson diary, 24 April 1932, xxi, 148–49, reel 5, Stimson Papers, MD, LC. Originals at Yale University. Later that year Stimson prepared a strong statement against Japanese aggression in the Far East, which Hoover vetoed, in the midst of the presidential election campaign, because an inclusion of the League of Nations would offend William Randolph Hearst. "If he is going to run his campaign according to what Hearst says, why I must stay out of it." Diary, 27 July 1932, xxiii: 104, ibid.

"I am most anxious to avail myself of your help."[50] On Wehle's suggestion, Bullitt became a roving secret ambassador for the president-elect, making two more trips to Europe, in November 1932 and again in January 1933, sounding out various issues related to debts, recognition of the USSR, and relations with Japan.[51] His mission was leaked to the press, providing Bullitt with not unwanted publicity. Though more pressing business of the new administration eclipsed his activities, Bullitt would soon secure a position in the administration as a special assistant (a title that would avoid the necessity of Senate confirmation) in the State Department, thus strategically placing a knight on the recognition chessboard.[52]

As in previous interwar elections, recognition of the Soviet Union was not a public issue. Behind the scenes there was discussion and expectation that a Roosevelt victory would lead to recognition. Just how many votes that may have brought him cannot be known. Some Republican supporters may have switched sides on the presidential vote, but most would have remained loyal to the chief, despite their disagreement on the matter. On old veteran of Democratic politics, Al Smith, made his position quite clear during the campaign and after the victory: "I believe that we ought to recognize Russia; I do not know any reason for not doing it. . . . I do not believe in being against them just because they have a form of government that we do not like."[53] Bainbridge Colby, another prominent Democrat who laid the foundation for nonrecognition as secretary of state at the end of the Wilson administration, stuck by his original position, claiming that the basis of the policy was not ideological but was because Russia had become "an enemy state" constantly attempting to overthrow the government of the United States.[54] The press continued to be divided, with the *Washington Post* leading support for the cause of past administrations, but the majority of the press seemed to have passed to the side of recognition. The Roosevelt election spurred editorial debate for various recognition efforts, for example, the organization of an Independent Committee for the Recognition of Soviet Russia, composed mostly of academic scholars.[55]

50. FDR to Bullitt, 12 September 1932, f. Bullitt, PPF 1124, FRPL.

51. Edward M. Bennett, *Recognition of Russia: An American Foreign Policy Dilemma* (Walthan, Mass.: Blaisdell, 1970), 105–7.

52. Bullitt to FDR, 10 April 1933, f. 1932–1941, PPF 1124, FRPL. Bullitt was not the only American to scout the Soviet scene with recognition in mind in 1932. William B. Lancaster, a director of National City Bank of New York, arrived in June with the settlement of his bank's considerable debt cancellations in mind. During his stay of six weeks he was given special consideration by the Soviet leaders, as a leading American capitalist, which he was. *The Stalin-Kaganovich Correspondence, 1931–1936*, 129–30.

53. "Al Smith on Russia," *Literary Digest*, 18 March 1933.

54. Ibid.

55. The latter was led by a longtime pro-Soviet professor, Frederick Schuman of the University of Wisconsin. Schuman to Harper, 9 March 1933, f. 2, box 13, Harper Papers, UC-R.

One of the first to press the issue of recognition on the president-elect was S. R. Bertron. On the fifteenth anniversary of the Bolshevik Revolution, he wrote to FDR, "The campaign you conducted has been marvelous. You surely must be a man of iron to have endured it and come through as you have. . . . When you do have leisure, I hope that you will let me discuss the Debt and the Russian problems with you, as being two of the most pressing and important problems of your Administration."[56] Receiving no response, Bertron persisted with a request to introduce him to Hugh Cooper, "today the best posted American on Russian affairs of anyone here and has a very intimate acquaintance with most of the leaders in Russia. He would like immensely to present the picture to you as he sees it for your future consideration, and I am positive your time would not be wasted."[57] Disappointed again—because of FDR's busy schedule and higher priorities—Bertron added in another letter, "Cooper and I merely wanted to present to you a unanimous vote, on the question of Russian recognition, by the members of the American-Russian Chamber of Commerce, comprising about 150 of the leading manufacturers throughout the country, and to answer any questions which you may care to ask regarding Russian affairs."[58]

Sumner Welles, a close confidante of FDR, also pressed the case for recognition in January 1933. He summarized the advantages in being able to gain some of the trade now possessed by Britain and Germany and as leverage in "adjusting the Manchurian problem" with Japan and reported on an extended conversation with Skvirsky. "What you may deem worthy of your consideration, however, is the fact that I gained the very definite impression from my conversation with Mr. Skvirsky that the Soviet Government is desperately anxious to obtain recognition by the United States at the earliest possible date."[59] Welles added his opinion that this desire was at least in part due to the fact that the "domestic situation in Russia at the present time is more precarious than it has been in many years," in combination with the increased tension with Japan.[60] Some cautioned against recognition on the same grounds, that it would antagonize that power. John O'Laughlin reported, after a conversation with Matsuoka, "Japan will resent

56. Bertron to FDR, 7 November 1932, f. 1931–1933, PPF 907, FRPL.

57. To FDR, 10 January 1933, ibid.

58. To FDR, 16 January 1933, ibid. Samuel Harper, who met Cooper at his dam in 1932, was cautious. "He is new at the game he is now playing—high international politics, the intermediary between Stalin and Hoover (& Roosevelt)—and is a bit unprepared and therefore naive in his newly assumed role." Harper to Walter Rogers, 5 November 1932, f. 27, box 17, Harper Papers, UC-R.

59. Welles to Roosevelt, 12 January 1933, f. Roosevelt, box 149, Welles Papers, FRPL Skvirsky stressed the advantages of expanded trade for the United States.

60. Ibid.

American recognition of Moscow . . . [and] will look upon it as a move to curb our natural development."[61]

A surprising new advocate of recognition was DeWitt Clinton Poole, one of the early architects of nonrecognition in the State Department. In a speech to the Foreign Policy Association in Boston on 18 February 1933, "Should the United States Now Recognize Soviet Russia?" he answered with a definite "yes."[62] He saw the world situation as quite changed since the early 1920s, no doubt reflecting his own shift to a prominent academic post at Princeton University. Like the president, he was especially concerned about the German and Japanese authoritarian threats. Though less often articulated, many others felt the same way. In October, upon request of the Associated Press, Poole provided a public statement that began, "President's invitation to Russian Government to enter into discussions with view to finding mutually satisfactory basis for establishment of official relations seems to me timely and wise," and cited his Boston speech.[63] Privately, Poole advised Harper, "It seems to me that Roosevelt has in fact adopted the wise course of negotiating before placing the final seal upon the act of recognition. Recognition will almost certainly follow."[64]

As might be expected, another to knock on the new president's door—actually by a telephone line—on behalf of recognition was Hugh Cooper. With the help of Senator George Norris and Cooper's sister-in-law Gertrude (Mrs. Dexter Cooper), who was an old family friend of the Roosevelts, Cooper conversed with the president on 14 April 1933, discussing the need for recognition but also plugging for his brother's idea for a Bay of Fundy (Campobello Island) tidal power project, which would soon receive funding from the Works Progress Administration.[65] Just what was said in regard to recognition is not known, but at least he probably kept the iron in the fire. Others with different commitments, such as William Haskell, former director of the ARA relief mission, and Professor Jerome Davis of Yale, hoped that recognition would soon follow the inauguration.[66]

One of the first off the block to the Soviet Union was an original proponent of recognition, Raymond Robins, who was naturally enthralled in 1933 by new

61. O'Laughlin to Hoover, f. Hoover, October 1933, box 43, O'Laughlin Papers, HHPL.

62. Text of Poole speech, 18 February 1933, f. 4, box 7, DeWitt Clinton Poole Papers, SHSW.

63. Enclosure in Poole to Harper, 24 October 1933, f. Poole, box 18, Harper Papers, UC-R.

64. Poole to Harper, ibid.

65. Norris to Marvin McIntyre (president's secretary), 31 March 1933; McIntyre to Cooper, 6 April 1933; Cooper to McIntyre, 11 April 1933; Gertrude to Franklin, 13 April 1933; and Cooper to Senator Frederick Hale, 19 April 1933, PPF 1766 (Dexter Cooper), FRPL.

66. Haskell to Louis Howe, 16 March 1933, and Davis to Howe, 15 March 1933, f. Russia, Jan.–Aug. 1933, box 2, POF 220a, FRPL. Louis McHenry Howe, a trusted friend of the president, shared secretarial duties at the White House with Marvin ("Mac") McIntyre.

prospects after his long pursuit of an apparent mirage. Despite health problems, he set off in April to gather more ammunition for recognition. Arriving in Leningrad on the SS *Felix Dzerzhinsky* in time for the May Day celebrations, he waxed beyond eloquent: "The belief in *tomorrow*, in the day of Liberation, in the Good Time coming out of all the struggle and suffering of this present time and dark past, this is the fundamental quality of the Soviet Mind! A vast Hope, however long delayed may be its realization, a Hope in which is the daring and the dreaming of a million years!"[67] He, of course, would lend his somewhat weakened voice (as a maverick Republican) to the cause of recognition, and already in May he backed the "radical" William Bullitt to be the first ambassador. All of these advocates obviously warmed the president toward recognition, a clear sign being his invitation to John Calder, one of the prominent engineers in Russia, for lunch at the White House on 6 June.[68]

In the meantime, proponents of recognition received a boost from a detailed May survey by the American Foundation. From an undefined sampling of 152 businessmen, 78 were recorded in favor of recognition, 56 opposed, and 16 undecided; of 108 newspaper publishers, 65 were in favor, 17 opposed, and 26 undecided; of 28 religious leaders, 20 supported recognition, 6 opposed, and 2 were undecided; finally, of 139 "university men" surveyed, 118 were in favor, only 12 opposed, and 9 were undecided. Of prominent historians, Charles Beard, Bernadotte Schmitt, and Sidney Fay supported recognition, while Michael Rostovtseff opposed.[69]

There was also heartening news on the economic front from Henry Morgenthau. The Reconstruction Finance Corporation announced in June the completion of a sale of 70,000 bales of cotton to a Soviet agency at favorable terms of 30 percent cash and the remainder in one year at 5 percent interest.[70] A few weeks later, the White Motor Company announced the sale of 5,000 heavy trucks to the Soviet Union for around $15 million.[71] Almost everyone thought that recognition would increase the already considerable American business in the USSR.

In July 1933, with nothing definite yet from the administration in regard to recognition, the pressure on the president gained momentum. The United States Board of Trade, an influential middle-of-the-road business organization that must have included quite a few Republicans, took a public stand in favor of recognition: "The menace to our form of government from Soviet Russia seems in-

67. Robins, essay on 1933 trip, f. 1, box 1, Robins Addition, SHSW.

68. William Phillips to FDR, 5 June 1933, briefing him on Calder, f. Russia Jan.–Aug. 1933, box 2, POF 220a, FRPL.

69. F. American Foundation survey, 25 May 1933, box 42, Carmody Papers, FRPL.

70. Jesse Jones, RFC, to FDR, 24 June 1933, f. Jan.–Aug. 1933, box 2, POF 220a, FRPL.

71. Everett Gardner to McIntyre, 6 September 1933, f. Sept.–Oct. 1933, ibid.

significant in contrast with the destructive forces in our midst with which the administration is now so courageously battling. The more we comprehend the motives and practices of the Soviet government and people, the better we shall be equipped to applaud or decry them."[72]

More directly, women's rights advocate Esther Lape approached her old friend Eleanor Roosevelt on the subject of recognition and then requested an interview with the president at Hyde Park by a group representing the Committee on Russian-American Relations of the American Foundation. The membership of the committee constituted a virtual who's who of longtime proponents of recognition, including Hugh Cooper, Allen Wardwell, Haskell, Paul Cravath, Roland Morris (former ambassador to Japan), and Roscoe Pound. Lape wrote, "That your own interest in recognition is, of course, assumed by the group; what they want is not to discuss with you the general question of recognition but to present their views and their information as to general approaches to the present situation, and as to certain immediate practical possibilities which they consider to be of great importance."[73] Roosevelt responded at the end of July by inviting her personally for a chat but demurred about hosting a delegation: "I feel I should not see the group of which you speak. I could have no group come to me at Hyde Park, or anywhere for that matter, really privately. It would be taken as an out and out announcement of recognition."[74] The president was still cautious on the issue.

Although the Catholic Church remained opposed to recognition in general, partly because of the large anti-Bolshevik Polish and Lithuanian constituencies, Protestant denominations, excepting Baptists, were in support. The missionary-minded Mennonite Central Committee in Kansas sent a delegation to Washington to support recognition, their agenda led by the prospect of opening up better communications with brethren and relatives in Soviet Russia and providing relief.[75] Recognition might also open up more possibilities for emigration of Mennonites from Soviet Russia.[76] The American Volga Relief Society in Lincoln, Nebraska, saw similar opportunities, while Jewish groups were divided between the more orthodox in opposition while others for business, relief, and other reasons joined the recognition camp.

72. Clark Hardeman, vice president, to Borah, 8 July 1933, f. Russia, box 371, Borah Papers, MD, LC. Fiorello LaGuardia was another vice president.

73. Lape to Roosevelt (addressed as Franklin), 21 July 1933, box 2, POF 220a, FRPL. Lape had consulted earlier with Samuel Harper about recognition. To Harper, 13 March 1933, f. 3, box 16, Harper Papers, UC-R.

74. Franklin to "Esther," 28 July 1933, box 2, POF 220a, FRPL.

75. P. C. Hiebert to Borah, 7 April 1933, ibid.

76. Levi Mumaw to Adam Wyant, 18 April 1930, f. Russia Dec. 1929–May 1930, box 304, Borah Papers, MD, LC. He noted that 3,800 had recently arrived in Germany but more emigrants were unlikely.

Though officials in the State Department did not look forward to recognition, most accepted the probability and made adjustments. Behind the scenes, one hurdle was cleared—the transfer of all former Russian government property in the United States to the temporary care of the department in August by Sergei Ughet. He also arranged to move out of the old embassy building in Washington more than 500 boxes of records of the World War I Supply Commission and other materials stored in the embassy.[77] Only on the eve of the recognition negotiations did he resign formally—with an old world flourish, "I deem it a paramount duty to express my deep appreciation for the unfailing consideration with which I have been treated at the Department of State."[78] There were, however, still unresolved claims against the previous Russian government that would keep Ughet busy, though he managed to transfer some of them to the new American presence in Moscow, to Bullitt's later chagrin.

The business sector was also somewhat divided on recognition, with considerable negative reaction coming from some individuals who had worked on various construction projects in Soviet Russia, but some of these could be dismissed as self-serving. C. Chamberlain Carter of Lehigh Portland Cement Company, however, offered to provide film footage of twenty-five American engineers in Russia, despite many disappointing experiences, "for I am sure you will gain from these films a much truer picture of the actual situation in Russia than is possible from the many contradictory reports constantly being circulated."[79] In the meantime Julian Bryan returned from another film tour through Russia that was being shown to wide audiences.[80] Another example is Mendel Glickman of Milwaukee, who had supervised more than 300 other Americans at the Stalingrad Tractor factory; he complained to Borah about the miserable conditions there but admitted that he was considering requesting a return of his expenses.[81] He offered his services to help with the problems of additional contract arrangements with Soviet agencies. G. L. Nicholson of St. Louis chimed in with complaints about being hounded by the OGPU (successor of the Cheka and forerunner of the NKVD), cheated out of about a thousand dollars owed him, and for the misery

77. "Ughet Assignment," 25 August 1933, and Ughet to Packer, 25 August 1933, f. Ughet, box 31, DEEA, RG 59, NA. Considering the timing of the Ughet transfer of the embassy building, an August meeting of Hull with FDR at Hyde Park may have signaled a definite commitment to seek recognition. The heat and general recess from Washington at that time, however, delayed implementation.

78. Ughet to Kelley, 21 October 1933, f. Ughet, box 22, ibid.

79. Carter to Howe, 5 July 1933, Russia, January–August 1933, box 2, POF 220a, FRPL.

80. An effort to arrange a special showing for the president in October was unsuccessful. McIntyre to Bryan, 29 October 1933, f. Sept.–Oct. 1933, ibid.

81. Glickman to Borah, 28 October 1931, f. Russia, box 326, Borah Papers, MD, LC.

of life he and his family, including three children, endured. The bottom line was that a condition of recognition should be the payment of money owed him.[82]

Andrew Smith, of Slovak background, who signed on with Amtorg for a job in Novosibirsk in 1933, sharply attacked the primitive conditions, favoritism, and inefficiency he found there and managed to get transferred back to Moscow, where he worked at Elektrozavod (the main city power plant).[83] He traveled around the country to Stalingrad and to Nizhny Novgorod to visit plants and to spend time at resorts on the Black Sea with his ill wife. His was a far from flattering picture of Soviet working conditions in the Second Five Year Plan that began in 1933.[84] Although some American workers were demoralized and antagonistic, the chief engineers, with a few exceptions, were overwhelmingly positive about their experience and made this known.

The appointment of Henry Morgenthau as secretary of the treasury, however, had brought another ally of recognition into the field in promoting trade with Russia—most important, an arrangement with limited credits for the purchase of $75 million of American cotton; this registered in the Depression South. Taking a lesson from Herbert Hoover's bypassing of the State Department in the 1920s, Roosevelt used Morgenthau as a wedge. The secretary met frequently with Bullitt in September and October, with Skvirsky sometimes included, specifically on preparing for recognition. The back door to the State Department had been breeched.

Most of the Russian émigré community in the United States naturally remained opposed to recognition and had become even more vocal; they now had gained position and confidence from long-term settlement adjustment and were better organized than previously, mainly in the United Russian National Organization in America, which included affiliates such as the Russian Womens' League of Republican Party, chaired by Xenia Bickoff. Boris Brasol, one of the original strong opponents of recognition in the United States, was a leading member of the organization.[85] Such conservative representatives of the old Russian regime still carried weight and had consoled themselves in the face of Bolshevik survival and growing strength with the existence of American nonrecognition. But they were now preparing for a strategic retreat, capable of only last gasp measures that fell on deaf ears in the American public and in the Roosevelt administration.

As reports of recognition discussions spread, opponents such as the American Legion, the National Civic Federation (Ralph Easley), the Washington Society

82. Nicholson to Senator Bennett Clark, 8 July 1933, box 22, OEEA, RG 59, NA.
83. Andrew Smith, I Was a Soviet Worker (London: Robert Hale, 1937), 23, 80–86.
84. Ibid., 173–201.
85. F. 1933, box 2, Brasol Papers, MD, LC.

of Sons of the American Revolution, the Catholic Church, and the American Federation of Labor redoubled their efforts and were uniting. They were hampered to some extent by being associated with the still powerful Ku Klux Klan in this endeavor. At the national convention of the Legion in Washington on 18 April 1933, Walsh, Fish, and William Green (American Federation of Labor) spoke strongly against recognition—and this was relayed to the president by the National Commander in due course.[86] Walter Steele, editor of the conservative Washington-based *National Republic*, emphasized the coming Communist onslaught on the United States with recognition opening the door.[87] John Spargo, probably the most inveterate anti-Bolshevik, warned "that the Power we are about to recognize officially is not the Government of Russia. It is not the Government of any particular and defined sovereignty. It is not a question of recognizing the Government of Russia, but of recognizing a power which has no fixed and defined sovereignty at all. There is absolutely no basis in international law, nor any shadow of precedent in our history, for the recognition of such a Power."[88] And in the State Department, the specter of Cuban unrest incited by Communists was raised as a delaying tactic, so at least Henry Morgenthau believed.[89]

Sam Harper, after a foray into a very confused Washington, was also alarmed about this late counteroffensive against recognition. He wrote his former colleague and ambassador, William Dodd:

> My guesses were right. First, the question of recognition was much to the fore, and I made the round of the old and new authorities, receiving very cordial welcomes from all, especially from Mr. Hull. Had the big chief been in town I believe the Secretary would have put me through to him. And what is going to happen respecting recognition? I will admit, I do not know, for just as the plan of procedure seemed to have been reached, the Cuban situation comes into the picture, the delay has given the antis a chance to get busy—Catholics, American Legion and so forth.[90]

Impatient with the State Department's foot dragging, and after consulting with Skvirsky through Morgenthau and Bullitt to ensure that an overture would be

86. Louis Johnson (Legión) to FDR, 17 June 1933, enclosed in Phillips to Howe, 7 July 1933, box 2, POF 220a, FRPL.

87. To Moore, f. Russia 1933, box 18, Moore Papers, FRPL. The *National Republic*, published in Washington, would also be a persistent opponent of recognition up to the end. See William Huie, "Why Recognize the Soviets?" *National Republic* 21 (September 1933), 12.

88. Spargo to FDR, 5 July 1933, box 2, POF, 220a, FRPL.

89. Robert E. Bowers, "Hull, Russian Subversion in Cuba, and Recognition of the USSR," *Journal of American History* 53, no. 3 (December 1966), 542–50.

90. Harper to Dodd, 7 October 1933, f. 13, box 18, Harper Papers, UC-R.

welcome, on 3 October 1933 Roosevelt took the bull by the horns and drafted a note to "President" Mikhail Kalinin[91] in Moscow that he would welcome receiving a representative of the Soviet Union in regard to talks toward recognition, but, as an afterthought, he asked Hull to review it.[92] In final form the message read, "Since the beginning of my Administration, I have contemplated the desirability of an effort to end the present abnormal relations between the hundred and twenty-five million people of the United States and the hundred and sixty million people of Russia." The response was prompt and direct, indicating that the Soviet chief of foreign affairs, Maxim Litvinov, would soon be on his way. "There is no doubt that difficulties, present or arising, between our two countries can be solved only when direct relations exist between them; and that, on the other hand, they have no chance for solution in the absence of such relations."[93] Upon this acceptance, a public announcement was issued on 20 October. Skvirsky must have danced all night, but he gave major credit to Senator Borah:

> When President Roosevelt made his announcement yesterday, it occurred to me that you more than any other American would appreciate the full significance of his happy overture. I felt that you would agree with me that the cause of peace was well served in this move. . . .
>
> You have been the pioneer in Washington in the matter of Soviet relations and I feel that this development owes more to your persistent spade work than to any other factor. Your open door and your sympathetic understanding have been most heartening to me during the long period of waiting, and I want now to express my deep gratitude for your consistent kindness.[94]

Also indicative of the move toward recognition was the appointment of John Van Antwerp MacMurray as minister to Latvia in October 1933. He was acknowledged to be a leading American expert on foreign affairs as director of the Walter Hines Page School of International Relations at Johns Hopkins University. In a personal letter to an old Russia hand, J. Butler Wright, now assigned

91. Kalinin was chair of the USSR Supreme Soviet (the nominal state legislature), making him technically "head of state." He was essentially a figurehead with virtually no direct authority on any matter of importance. From peasant background, he had successfully adapted to the sophisticated social graces required by the job and kept clear of political squabbles, which probably accounts for his surviving in the position until his natural death in 1946.

92. "Here is my effort at a suggested letter to Kalinin to be submitted in draft form to see what kind of reply he would make if we sent it—what to you think? No hurry. Monday will do." FDR to Hull, nd [in sequence of 3 October], reel 10, correspondence, Hull Papers, MD, LC.

93. Bennett, *Recognition*, 112–13.

94. To Borah, 21 October 1933, f. Russia (Aug.–Nov. 1933), box 371, Borah Papers, MD, LC.

to head the legation in Montevideo, he noted that William Phillips told him that this was the best that he could expect. He feared that Riga would not be a good springboard. To Samuel Harper, he noted, "Riga is the world's worst agglomeration of spies and Black Hundreds, and that its exclusive industry is the fabrication of mare's nests."[95] "But Riga it is"—the main current observation post for Russia—and he noted rumors that this was preliminary to his being named ambassador to Russia. "Needless to say, I shall consider such an appointment the most interesting and responsible one in our Service, and should be overjoyed if it worked out."[96] Unfortunately, he would not be chosen, though he would have been a much better choice than the one who was.

MacMurray knew, however, "that our first ambassador will be some prominent liberal or parlor Bolshevik whose sympathy with the Soviets can be capitalized for political purposes."[97] He left New York—with his 1929 Packard on board—for Riga on 8 November 1933, not waiting for the outcome of the recognition negotiations that were just beginning.[98] Either MacMurray or Wright would have been more professional choices for a Moscow mission. In the interim the stalwart Felix Cole in Riga was still manning the last bastion of American intelligence on the Soviet Union: "Despite any further instruction on which may come along later I am for the time being carrying on with the usual process of reporting on Russian matters."[99] And he would continue to do so for several years.

The Role of Newspaper Editors: William Allen White and Henry Justin Allen

In the meantime, the press climbed on board the bandwagon, led by two Kansas newspaper men. One of William Allen White's best-known books, *The Martial Adventures of Henry and Me*, published in 1918, recorded his fictionalized experiences with those of fellow Kansas newspaper publisher Henry Justin Allen as Red Cross representatives behind the lines in 1917 France. They were among the first on hand to welcome contingents of American troops to the Great War. White captured the tenor of the times, the pathos and horror of the war with feeling, objectivity, and humor. He described the sound and shock of an oncom-

95. To Harper, 6 September 1933, f. 12, box 18, Harper Papers, UC-R.

96. MacMurray to Wright, 11 October 1933, f. 10–23 Oct. 1933, box 51, MacMurray Papers, Mudd-P.

97. Ibid. The former American consul in Vladivostok, John Caldwell, heard the rumor of MacMurray's appointment to Russia in faraway Sydney, Australia. Caldwell to MacMurray, 26 October 1933, box 51, ibid.

98. Shipping paper, ibid.

99. Cole to MacMurray, 20 November 1933, f. 1–20 Nov. 1933, ibid.

ing shell on the front as like picking up the Haynes' hardware store down the street in Emporia, shaking it up, and dropping it back down. This book certified White's reputation as a preeminent journalist and master of the American experience who bravely reached out into the international sphere. His longtime friend and political alter ego, Henry Allen, seemed to be along for the ride, but he stayed on in Europe through 1918 and rode the publicity of the book into victory in the Kansas gubernatorial election in 1918, thanks also to White's skillful campaign management.

White, somewhat by coincidence, developed a serious interest in Russian affairs from conversations with Samuel Harper on their return passage to the United States in 1917. Harper had just left revolutionary Russia, where he had served as a chief adviser to Ambassador David Francis and to the Root mission, which the Wilson administration had sent to welcome a new provisional government that was expected to add credence to an American commitment to the conflict in order to make the world safe for democracy. Always fully committed to the support of public education, White arranged a lecture tour in early 1918 for Harper through the central states, namely, Colorado and Kansas, and his lectures in Colorado Springs, Denver, Boulder, Manhattan, Lawrence, and Emporia met with great success.[100] He retained contacts with Harper and the major and minor figures of American political life in subsequent years. As an observer at the Paris peace conference, he had observed, "Always to the north [hangs] the unsettled black cloud of Russia."[101]

His interest in Russia was reflected in his columns and correspondence through the 1920s, inspired by his close relationship with Herbert Hoover, with maverick Republican Raymond Robins, and with Walter Lippmann, Colonel Edward House, and Charles Crane. In general, White opposed the blockade of Soviet Russia by the Paris powers in 1919, strongly objected to military intervention, and dismissed as ridiculous any serious Communist threat to the United States during the Red Scare, consistently arguing that the best antidote to Communism was American social and economic advancement. He welcomed the substantial aid to Russia provided by Hoover's American Relief Administration. Through channels, he let it be known that he would be at the service of any special government mission to Russia that might be sent to resolve political and economic issues, and he planned a personal visit to that country with Walter Lippmann in 1926 but withdrew owing to his wife's illness.[102]

---

100. White to Harper, 15 February 1918, box 4, Harper Papers, UC-R. Harper's tour was originally to include Nebraska, Oklahoma, and even Texas but was abbreviated for lack of time.

101. "Realists or Idealists," *Emporia Gazette*, 1 February 1919.

102. Lippmann to White, 25 January 1926, and White to Lippmann, 7 June 1926, f. Lippmann, box C107, White Papers, MD, LC.

Many members of the Eastern establishment looked forward to White's semi-annual visits to Washington, Philadelphia, Princeton, and New York. And the ten scheduled Santa Fe Railroad trains a day that stopped in Emporia delivered a who's who of American politics to his front porch. He wrote and received an average of more than twenty letters each a day, as anyone who has ventured into the 700 boxes of the White papers at the Library of Congress can attest, and this does not count the numerous telegrams and White's obsession with the use of local as well as long-distance telephone lines. He lived by the typewriter, the telephone, and, of course, the printing press. Some of William Allen White's dedication to addressing major national issues and his belief in the importance of informing the public on international affairs naturally rubbed off onto Henry Allen, publisher of the *Wichita Beacon* and an associate crusader in striving for an honest and viable progressive Republican Party in Kansas. Allen might have been White, except that White was first, having already won national recognition putting Allen—and another Kansas editor-politician, Arthur Capper—in his shadow. After his two terms as governor, Allen's interest in international issues was apparently reignited while serving as a fill-in senator from Kansas in the early thirties.

White and Allen often took to the road, speaking at all sorts of occasions. Few texts can be found, as both disliked prepared speeches. When Carl Ackerman (another veteran of revolutionary Russia), then editor of the *New York Times*, asked White for a copy of a speech he made in Philadelphia, White responded that he had none. "It was a blithe, gay, irresponsible, impromptu melee in which I left the young people to ask questions and I answered, which is my favorite indoor sport."[103] White also had a taste of real politics, when, in 1924, he ran for governor not really to be in office but to lead a campaign against the Ku Klux Klan, winning yet more credits among the Eastern liberal establishment. When Colonel House questioned him about his political ambitions, White responded, "As you know I never wanted to be Governor. There were moments when I thought it would be a grand thing to be Governor, just for what I could do to help the men and women in the state educational institutions live a free and happy life."[104]

What to do about a Soviet, Communist Russia was an issue for everyone on the national scene after 1917, an issue many tried to ignore. Not White, nor Allen. In his 1924 biography of Woodrow Wilson, White reserved his sharpest criticism for Wilson's handling of the Russian Question. "He could have stopped that *debacle*, but Russia was a friend who questioned his imperious will, and so became an enemy. . . . It was his first major blunder; the first time he let his spirit,

---

103. White to Carl Ackerman, March 14, 1924, f. Ackerman, box C80, White Papers, MD, LC.

104. White to House, 25 November 1924, f. House, box C82, White Papers, MD, LC. White was a long-term member of the Kansas Board of Regents.

his happy Irish spirit, be guided by the dour Scot within him."[105] Allen and White were convinced that the old rationale for nonrecognition was fading and the ascendancy of Franklin Roosevelt to the presidency would bring about a change, so they went to Russia in 1933 to bolster that agenda.

Both were biased. White thought all along that intervention, blockades, nonrecognition, and public ostracism were bad ideas. They made little rational sense. Allen went further in praising the accomplishments of a new, progressive Russia that was digressing from the prerevolutionary one, with impressive constructive advances in the 1930s. White had longtime friends and associates, such as Norman Hapgood, Theodore Dreiser, Raymond Robins, Sinclair Lewis, and Edna Ferber, who had similar views and who had visited Russia and reported favorably on what they saw. Ferber had just returned from Russia as White was preparing to leave and perhaps inspired him to complete the trip. "It is incredible, and the most interesting thing I've seen in my life," she wrote to White.[106] He agreed, after his trip: "We stayed there two weeks—two gorgeous weeks—and saw the world turned upside down."[107]

Going to Russia in 1933 was not such a novel, nor yet an easy adventure. Experienced tour manager Sherwood Eddy promised Allen an opportunity to visit a Russian collective farm and wondered if he could bring along other senators.[108] As if trying to find an American comparison that would attract Allen, he wrote, "It's like visiting a western border mining camp."[109] Eddy's seminar eventually numbered about thirty in 1933, but most joined for only part of the trip and skipped in and out. Allen, in fact, went to Bucharest first to visit friends and then by train into Ukraine and Russia. William Allen White's foray into the Communist world was directly from London by passage on a Soviet ship to Leningrad. Later, he recounted his impressions for readers of the *Gazette*. "The Soviet ship was as Russian as Russia. Our first meal was breakfast." He described an impressive quantity and variety of cold meats and cheeses and copious egg dishes, and, he added, "a quart bowl of caviar. The second or third morning they put on two bowls of caviar, one pink caviar which I mistook for currant jam. . . . All through the meal were two kinds of bread—white bread and Russian black bread, sour, heavy, unpalatable bread that I tried to eat toasted but it almost broke my teeth." The Intourist official who rescued the White party from a hotel impasse in Lenin-

105. White, *Woodrow Wilson: The Man, His Times, His Tasks* (Boston: Houghton Mifflin, 1924), 364.
106. Ferber to White, 7 August 1933, f. Ferber, box C202, White Papers, MD, LC.
107. White to Ferber, 23 October 1933, ibid.
108. Eddy to Allen, 11 May 1933, f. Russia correspondence, box C135, Allen Papers, MD, LC.
109. Allen to White, 18 May 1933, ibid.

grad turned out to be former avid reader of the *Gazette*—in Leavenworth. White was quick to respond, "federal or state [prison]?" "Federal, I was a Wobblie."[110]

White and Allen spent separately two to three weeks in Stalin's Russia in August 1933 with their wives. While Allen, who came overland from Romania, stayed with Eddy's tour group and saw more of the countryside, White spent more of his time dining and talking with resident Moscow correspondents, Walter Duranty, Eugene Lyons, and especially Maurice Hindus, and drew upon their considerable knowledge of the Russian scene. He made good use of his time and connections and skillfully mined his sources. He, as well as Allen, had made arrangements with press syndicates to write columns that would essentially pay their way; neither sent material directly from Russia but waited until after recrossing the border. They thus had an advantage over the resident correspondents by avoiding any Soviet interference, and they had no plans to return in the near future that might be compromised.

White had a large guaranteed audience for his Russian articles with the prominent North American Agency, which included major subscribers, such as the *New York Times* and the *Washington Post*.[111] But Allen lined up the *New York Evening Post*, which had the largest circulation in the country at the time, and the *Detroit Free Press*, whose publisher was an old friend, among others.[112] Grove Patterson, editor of the *Free Press*, who was also along with the group, actively promoted Allen's columns in more than a dozen other newspapers, earning Allen's gratitude.[113] Though many others had visited Russia in the early 1930s and wrote about their experiences, White and Allen probably had the largest readership of any visiting American journalists during that period and at a time when Russia was drawing much attention.

White broke into print first, on 1 October, with a center column on the front page of the *New York Times*, "New Russia Found Much Like the Old." He opened by describing an interview with the editor of *Izvestia* and that person's early revolutionary efforts to obtain funds for underground publications and noted that at the same time Stalin was raising money by robbing banks.[114] White, a keen student of history, cited historical precedents for Americans assisting Russia (such as John Paul Jones in the time of Catherine the Great) and noted that Russians now encountered similar problems as Jones in providing technical assistance. "They

110. "Some Notes on Russia," *Emporia Daily Gazette*, 27 October 1933.

111. White's close association with editor Carl Ackerman of the *New York Times* and dean of the Columbia University School of Journalism no doubt was a factor.

112. Allen to M. A. Raines, 30 October 1933, and Allen to Bengay, 5 May 1933, f. Russia correspondence, box C135, Allen Papers, MD, LC.

113. Patterson to Allen, 19 October 1933, and Allen to Patterson, 3 November 1933, ibid.

114. "New Russia Found Much Like the Old," *New York Times*, 1 October 1933.

are invariably met with secret sabotage, with studied indifference, with intrigue, neglect and an inflexible incompetence which is a heaven-sent gift to the Russians. They have no sense of efficiency as Americans know the word. Unlike the English, the Russians are willing to try anything once and spoil it."[115] But White added,

> The machine moves; Russia goes on. The great industrial enterprises on the rivers and in the mountains and in the new cities that have grown up on the plains are actually functioning. They are turning out finished products, they are transforming wood and stone and steel into houses, iron into trucks, tractors and automobiles, copper into electric cables, and chaos into a civilization. It is not the American kind of civilization which clicks with precision. It jumps and rattles just as Paul Jones found it bumped and rattled in Catherine's day. But it stands up and marches.[116]

White recited a mixed review of admiration for effort and achievement in the industrialization campaign but cautioned about what it would mean in the long run. He was convinced that Russians backed the regime and looked forward to the results of their efforts.

Henry Allen followed White by a day, featured on 2 October, also on the front page, in the *New York Evening Post* with a banner headline, "Senator Allen Looks into the Real Russia." His article eschewed history and claimed to tell it like it was now, admitting that members of the tour group could find evidence to bolster whatever preconceived notions they had. The excellent and free nurseries and kindergartens were especially impressive, he reported. "But a Doubting Thomas could go to Moscow on a rainy night and find at midnight in every one of many districts bedraggled lines of men and women, many with children, waiting until stores opened in the morning so they could get their allotted quantity of bread and coal oil."[117] He was impressed by the number of recent graves in village cemeteries and the pinched faces of peasant children. He promised to tell in future articles of the government's thorough liquidation of kulaks and of any counter-revolutionary activity. But the tone was generally positive: "The ideas that Russia borrows from us as she travels to the right, as well as the notions we may borrow from her as we travel toward the left will be kept in mind during these articles."[118] It was an early version of the convergence theory.

---

115. Ibid.
116. Ibid.
117. *New York Evening Post*, 2 October 1933.
118. Ibid.

In their respective series of articles that followed, White and Allen were clearly not gullible Kansans in the land of Oz. Allen's 6 October article, "Soviet Industrializes as Farmer Pays the Way: 5-Year Plan Still in Dream Stage," emphasized the shortcomings and terrible human costs that Stalin's Russia was enduring.[119] Even more graphically, White enumerated the loss of life due to collectivization and the accompanying famine. He cited various estimates, siding with Duranty's figure of 5 million during the two preceding years, higher than most Western press reports at the time.[120] Foreign trade adviser to the Department of Agriculture Smith Brookhart thought this was an exaggeration,[121] but White verified that number with Duranty after he returned to the United States in November. Allen, meanwhile, headlined, "4,000,000 Kulaks Wiped out in Russia."[122] The famine, both agreed, was a terrible thing, partly balanced by the great opportunities for employment in industry that contrasted sharply with the situation in the United States in 1933. White concluded,

> Probably, when history is written on the year 1933, the historian, if he gives any attention to the 15 years between 1918 and 1933, will write 'in these years, for the first time on earth, a civilization developed without the aid of capitalists. It began to work.' Then, to be fair, history will bite her pencil and finally add these qualifying words: 'After a fashion.'[123]

These sympathetic, perhaps pro-Soviet articles did not pass without criticism. Several letters to the editors took issue with comments such as White referring to Stalin as a "benevolent dictator."[124] But the authors had already acknowledged many faults of the system. Another writer thought Allen greatly exaggerated the commercial benefits of recognition, emphasizing that Americans could have this without recognition, if they wanted and could pay for it. Both White and Allen were emphatic in supporting official recognition, thus lending powerful middle-American Republican voices to Roosevelt's initiative. On 21 October the *Washington Post* headlined, "Soviet Accepts U.S. Invitation to Hold Recognition Parley; Moscow Hails Roosevelt Step." This was a fitting welcome home for the Kansans, who stepped off the *Vulcania* in New York that very day.[125]

119. *New York Evening Post*, 6 October 1933 (five columns on p. 12).
120. "A Man-Made Famine," *Emporia Daily Gazette*, 7 October 1933.
121. Brookhart to White, 4 November 1933, box C206, White Papers, MD, LC.
122. *New York Evening Post*, 13 October 1933: 30.
123. *Emporia Daily Gazette*, 7 October 1933.
124. "Life Among the Tyrants," *Emporia Daily Gazette*, 25 October 1933.
125. *New York Herald Tribune*, 20 October 1933.

In several ways, Allen's reporting was more resourceful, informative, opinionated, and focused on portraying an up and coming Russia that the United States could and should do business with. It was also more extensive with separate detailed articles on Russian food supply, religious affairs, labor, agriculture, and finance.[126] Even conservative columnist Drew Pearson commended Allen for his direct approach: "Just a line to tell you how much I have enjoyed reading your swell stories on Russia. They certainly have been timely and have shown to some of us upstarts that we shall have to advance a lot further before we can equal some of the old time bears like you."[127]

Allen and White returned to print after their return to Kansas, Allen for a national audience with a full page article in the Sunday *New York Times*, 5 November 1933, "The Meaning of Recognition for Russia and for the U.S." In this he listed his reasons for supporting the Roosevelt initiative: Russia's move to the right, withdrawing from pushing world revolution; a major increase in Russian-American commerce with Russia providing the United States with raw materials and importing manufactured goods, thus countering opposition from labor unions; excellent business with Russia already helping American companies, citing especially General Electric; the fact that France, the only major democracy left in continental Europe, was establishing closer relations, and finally—and most important—to facilitate joint action to counter Japanese aggression in Asia. The latter was also a primary motive of Soviet interest in a closer relationship with the United States, and it was no accident that the soon-to-be-named first Soviet ambassador, Alexander Troyanovsky, had served five years as Soviet envoy to Japan but was currently working in the commissariat in Moscow and available for reassignment.

White again beat Allen to the punch, but only for readers of the *Emporia Gazette*, which, of course, included more than a hometown audience. In an editorial apparently dispatched by telegraph upon landing in New York, White fully supported recognition:

> There is no reason why Russia should not be recognized at this time by the United States. . . . No other party in any other European country has been in charge of government so long. There is no danger of a spread of communist propaganda in America. The communists are too busy with their own

126. *New York Evening Post*, 5, 7, 12, 13, and 14 October 1933.

127. Pearson to Allen, 18 November 1933, f. 1933, box C37, Allen Papers, MD, LC. Pearson was from Kansas and his mother and father had attended Baker University with Allen. Pearson to White, 1 April 1933, f. Drew Pearson, Box C204, White Papers, MD, LC.

problems to have much time or money to waste trying to organize a communist revolution in the United States.

He followed with a list of "It may be said" that included: "It may be said that the communists do not recognize the Christian God. Neither do the Turks nor the Japanese nor the Egyptians whom we recognize." This was a refrain in both Allen and White's arguments for recognition, as well as:

Russia needs moral support in her contest with Japan. American recognition will give Russia that moral support before the world. Russia needs to buy American heavy machinery. She wants particularly American Goods. . . . From every standpoint the recognition of Russia is common sense. It would have been common sense in Harding's day. It would have been wise if Coolidge or Hoover had recognized Russia. It is not only wise but it is highly necessary that the American senate shall back up the obvious intention of President Roosevelt to recognize the Soviets.[128]

They also repeatedly pointed out that fascism was just as cruel, hostile to American ideals, and undemocratic as Communism, yet the United States recognized fascist Italy and Germany.

On a practical level, White and Allen argued that recognition, accompanied with substantial credits, would reduce Russia's need to export grain to pay for industrialization, thus not only allowing Russia to feed its people better but raise the demand for American wheat and profits for the Kansas farmer, an argument that became widespread throughout the Central Plains. The Kansas duo naturally responded to invitations to speak on these issues, at which Allen especially excelled. One of his first appearances, within a week of his arrival in New York, was at a special convocation at the University of Kansas in Lawrence on 26 October, on the topic, "Russia as I Saw It." The *University Daily Kansan* advised in advance that "no student can afford to miss hearing him,"[129] and apparently few did, as Chancellor Lindley reported to White, "We had Henry Allen for convocation recently, and he made, as always, a great speech. Twenty-five hundred students were there."[130] The *Kansan* headlined a full column on 27 October with "Henry Allen Says Soviet Recognition Essential to U.S."[131] He spoke in Topeka,

128. "Russian Recognition," *Emporia Daily Gazette*, 21 October 1933.

129. *University Daily Kansan*, 26 October 1933.

130. Lindley to White, 7 November 1933, f. Lindley, box C204, White Papers, MD, LC.

131. See "For Recognition: Henry J. Allen Returned from Russia," *Lawrence Daily Journal*, 27 October 1933.

Ottawa, and, of course, in his hometown at the University of Wichita, where he made a dramatic impression, according to the dean of education.[132]

Significantly, White and Allen came from solidly Republican middle America. They emphasized economic and diplomatic gains to be won and acknowledged the injustices of the past. Their writings and public engagements were vital in shaping an American acceptance of normal relations with a Communist regime. Other reporters adding their voices to the chorus based on recent visits to Russia were Bill Stoneman of the *Chicago Daily News*, Bob Davis of the *New York Sun*, and Whiting Williams of the *Saturday Evening Post*. Though not syndicated, they captured audiences in two of the most important urban centers and a popular national readership. Both Stoneman and Davis echoed White and Allen in support for recognition.[133] All of these special correspondents were perhaps more trusted by readers than Duranty, Lyons, and other resident reporters, since their columns were written after they had left the country. In several other major newspapers of this period little opposition to recognition could be found.

Joining the press assault on nonrecognition was Sherwood Eddy, who had just completed his tenth trip to Soviet Russia. Recounting the 1933 tour to friends, he emphasized how open and cooperative Soviet officials had become, beginning with Radek and Mezhlauk. He acknowledged the restrictions on freedom and hardships of daily life but claimed that great progress had been made. "In spite of the evils of the system which we all recognize and deplore I believe that recognition would make for the recovery of trade, prosperity and peace, especially in the Far East. I do not believe that, according to the traditional practice of our government, recognition implies approval of policy but the establishment of normal economic and political relations."[134]

Always mindful of the press, Roosevelt asked William Phillips in September to conduct a survey on the matter of recognition. Phillips reported back that the Division of Current Information in the State Department conducted a survey of 300 newspapers over a thirty-day period in September and October and found surprisingly little editorial discussion of the matter. "However, as far as it goes, the memorandum seems to indicate that the New England and North Atlantic States

---

132. "It was enlightening as well as entertaining." Leslie Sipple, Dean College of Education, 1 November 1933, f. Russia, box C135, Allen Papers, MD, LC.

133. Stoneman (Helsingfors) to Harper, 12 October 1933, f. 13, box 16, Harper Papers, UC-R. Davis' reports may have been especially bolstering to the president, since he forwarded those published and advance copies of the twelve columns that appeared beginning with 24 October. They were especially positive about progress in the USSR. Davis to FDR, 27 October 1933, box 2, POF 220a, FRPL.

134. To friends, 20 September 1933, f. 79, box 4, Eddy Papers, YDS. Eddy regularly reported on his guided tours to friends. See, for example, one for 1929, f. 75, box 3, ibid.

do not appear to be enthusiastically in favor of recognition; that the majority of the Southern and Mid-Western States are in favor of recognition and that the Pacific Coast States are somewhat indifferent."[135]

Preparing for Recognition

Serious preparations for negotiating diplomatic recognition had to wait until the end of summer, when it was comfortable to return to aired-out offices in Washington. Secretary of State Cordell Hull was expecting this task and not particularly looking forward to it. On precisely the last day of summer, he warned the president of the complications ahead. "There are a whole series of questions arising out of differences between the economic and social structure of the United States and Russia, especially the existence of a State monopoly of foreign trade in Russia, which require settlement by agreement." He observed that the Soviet government wanted mainly two things: credits or loans and diplomatic recognition, which was desired as a "factor in preventing a Japanese attack on the Maritime Provinces." Hull strongly advised the president to use these Soviet goals as leverage to gain agreement on other issues.[136]

Hull delegated most of the detailed study to his assistant secretary, Judge R. Walton Moore, since he was soon to depart on a tour of South America, and to Roosevelt's personal assistant in the department, William Bullitt. A first draft of Moore's observations was passed to Hull on 4 October 1933. The first paragraph noted, "It seems clear that there should and must be recognition eventually, provided there is assurance that the Russian Government will not directly or indirectly make any effort to affect the political institutions or integrity of the United States." A second paragraph emphasized that the British experience demonstrated that it was much easier to achieve conditions before recognition than afterward. In another section of the three-page document, a list of items to be discussed included "the alleged desire of Russia to Undermine our System of government" and "the personal property rights of our nationals in Russia." The latter was corrected to add the words "and religious" after "personal."[137]

135. Phillips to FDR, 19 October 1933, f. Russia 1933, box 1, POF 220, Russia, FRPL.

136. Hull to FDR, 21 September 1933, f. Russia Sept.–Oct. 1933, 220a, POF, FRPL.

137. Moore draft for the secretary, 4 October 1933, f. Russia, April–Oct. 1933, box 18, Moore Papers, FRPL. A few days before, Joseph Conry, who had spent several years in Russia on economic matters, wrote Louis Howe, the president's secretary, that he had just talked with Bullitt in the department, concluding, "As you know, the President is approaching final determination on the matter of recognition of Russia" and saw the appointment of Morgenthau as additional proof. To Howe, f. Russia Sept.–Oct., box 2, POF 220a, FRPL. Moore, a former long-term congressman from Virginia, had only joined the State Department in September.

Proponents of recognition kept the fire burning. Raymond Robins, responding to a telephone call from Hull that the president sought his advice, encamped at the Lafayette Hotel by 13 October. After conferring with Hull, he sent word that he was waiting to see the president and "to give him what information he has on Russian situation."[138] Despite the crush of new business, the president opened his door to Robins that very day, thanked him for his information, and hoped to see him again soon.[139] According to Robins the interview lasted forty-five minutes, unusually long for FDR: "Friendly and co-operative I found his mind, and toward me personally cordial and apparently confidential, with a trusting attitude. . . . The end of the interview with the President spelled VICTORY for the fifteen years struggle on the Russian question."[140] Robins immediately went to New York to confer with Gumberg and Bogdanov of Amtorg to send a direct cable to Stalin that signaled that the lantern was lit.[141] Indeed, the Robins interview must have strengthened the president's resolve to issue the invitation a few days later. On 2 November, Robins followed up by sending FDR a copy of Hindus's *Great Offensive*. Another veteran Republican, Meyer Bloomfield, surfaced to recall to the president that he had resided in the same house as Litvinov ten years earlier, when he had been sent to Russia by President Harding.[142]

Several hurdles still lay in the path of recognition on both sides. In Washington, Father Edmund Walsh, like Kelley, was a powerful voice of Roman Catholicism and, more important, exercised clout in foreign affairs education as director of the School of Foreign Affairs at Georgetown. In July before an American Legion convention and as late as mid-September in a radio address, Walsh spoke strongly against recognition, accusing the Soviets of "making fallacious [claims] . . . to get a fat slice of our National Recovery funds for the purposes of world revolution" and of buying American cotton in order to dump it at "cut-throat prices to enter into ruinous competition with American cotton in the market of the world."[143] That latter charge did not make much economic sense, and wheels were clearly spinning in October in regard to Walsh and other religious opponents of recognition. Walsh saw the handwriting on the wall and planned to make the most of the situation through Walter Hooke, who wrote to McIntyre,

138. Memorandum to FDR, 13 October 1933, f. Russia 1933, box 1, POF 220, Russia, FRPL.

139. Robins to FDR, 14 October 1933, and FDR to Robins, 17 October 1933, ibid. For additional description of these meetings, see Salzman, *Reform and Revolution: The Life and Times of Raymond Robins* (Kent, Ohio: Kent State University Press, 1991), 359–61.

140. Robins to his wife, 16 October 1933, as quoted in Salzman, *Reform and Revolution*, 360.

141. Salzman, *Reform and Revolution*, 360.

142. Bloomfield to FDR, 21 October 1933, f. Sept.–Oct. 1933, POF 220a, FRPL.

143. Walsh radio address, "Soviet Russia and American Trade," National Grange Home Program, 16 September 1933, f. 341, box 5, Walsh Papers, GUA.

Father Walsh authorizes me to say that he was prepared to place the A. F. of Labor, the American Legion, the Bishop [James] Freeman Committee and the Catholics squarely behind the Administration's program for Russia, solely on economic grounds, and with reasonable protection of our own interests. . . . Father Walsh can and is anxious to furnish certain information so I hope in your own way you will arrange a conference directly with the President.[144]

Adroit politician that he was, through McIntyre Roosevelt invited Walsh to a conference at the White House on Friday afternoon, 18 October. Though, as usual, no record of the conversation was made, a deal was obviously struck. Roosevelt would put religious matters in the forefront of the negotiations; Walsh would back off from opposition to recognition, submit a memorandum to the president on the religious issues, and cancel several scheduled lectures on the topic.[145] Both gained by the compromise, and muting Walsh's opposition to recognition was indeed a truly presidential accomplishment. As Edward Bennett shrewdly observed, "Father Walsh's cooperation on the matter emerged as one of the major coups of the President in preparing public opinion for recognition and in insuring minimal opposition from the important pressure groups."[146]

Besieged by inquiries on the subject, Walsh issued a press release on 21 October, which concluded, "President Roosevelt has simply called for a conference to discuss the grave difficulties existing between two sovereign states. These obstacles, in his own language, are 'serious but not insoluble'. Should they be solved, I would be the first to support renewed diplomatic relations."[147] The Roosevelt-Walsh bargain was not a prerequisite to recognition, but it certainly eased the way and diminished possible political reactions, even from Robert Kelley and others in the State Department. With an arch opponent on board, other oaks standing in the road gave way. Such a U-turn by Walsh could not occur without complications, and Walsh asked for an emergency meeting with the president on 30 October, trusting they could be straightened out.[148]

With Litvinov literally on the horizon, Hull assured the president on 27 October, "I have really given a great deal of attention to our problems with Russia,

144. Hooke to McIntyre, 15 October 1933, f. Sept.–Oct. 1933, box 2, POF 220a, FRPL. Bishop Freeman was the leading Presbyterian clergyman in Washington.

145. Walsh to McIntyre, 21 October 1933, ibid.

146. Bennett, *Recognition of Russia*, 94.

147. Enclosure in Walsh to McIntyre, 21 October 1933, box 2, POF 220a, FRPL; copy in f. 414, box 6, Walsh Papers, GUA.

148. McIntyre confidential memo for the president, 30 October 1933, f. Russia 1933, box 1, POF 220, FRPL.

dating back from your inauguration, and I am undertaking for another week or ten days to give every attention to the important necessity of carefully developing every technical and other phase of all the preliminary subjects and questions of which you should be fully in possession for purposes of preliminary conversations with the Russian representative."[149] The State Department was hopping. On 30 October a thirty-one-page memorandum on the retroactive legal effects of recognition prepared by Green Hackworth, legal counsel of the department, appeared on Moore's desk.[150] The department seemed to be at something of a loss in terms of preparing for the Soviet agenda, except that settlement of religious, debt, and credit issues should come first.

In the meantime, Smith Brookhart, a former senator from Iowa and a longtime advocate of recognition, held several preliminary conferences with Walsh, centering on the matter of clergy being held in Soviet prisons. The response from Moscow was cooperative: "Let Walsh specify who is in prison on account of religion and where. We will consider his proposition." With the assistance of Skvirsky, lists were drawn up and rechecked. Walsh wrote the president, "This answer from Moscow is valuable as indicating at least a tendency on the part of the Soviets to listen to the recommendations outlined in the Memorandum, and which we all devoutly hope you can persuade Mr. Litvinov to accept."[151]

Though negotiators deliberately avoided the issue of Japanese aggression in the Far East (Manchuria), everyone on-site had it in mind—definitely a dark shadow hanging over both Washington and Moscow. A colonel of Headquarters Third Corps, U.S. Army (Baltimore) perhaps expressed it best: "If our relations in the Pacific are ever broken, Russia benevolently neutral would be much more preferable to Russia malevolently neutral" and "while we have nothing in common with their principles of government, we can say the same of Turkey, meaning thereby that there are other ends to be achieved."[152] More astute observers would place the threat of a new aggressive Germany at the top of the list of the reasons to recognize Russia. In any event, realpolitik was ascending.

In addition to Hugh Cooper, several other prominent Americans involved in the era of construction in Russia added their support for recognition in direct communications to the president. They included Charles Stuart, John Calder, Alexander McKee, and Thomas Campbell. All offered their assistance, the latter, a big Montana farmer who had been involved in agricultural consultations in

149. Hull, memorandum for the president, 27 October 1933, f. Department File, State, Hull, box 73, PSF, FRPL.

150. F. Russia, April–October 1933, box 18, Moore Papers, FRPL.

151. Walsh to Roosevelt, 7 November 1933, f. 417, box 6, Walsh Papers, GUA.

152. Colonel C. A. Seoane, to Moore, 23 October 1933, f. Russia, 1933, box 18, Moore Papers, FRPL.

Russia, being especially emphatic in praising the president's overture to Kalinin: "This should have been done long ago, and I am sure might have been done had not there been so much objection from our International Bankers and other concentrations of wealth in the hands of a few. I know President and Mrs. Kelenin [sic] very well. Mrs. Campbell and I have been entertained by them in their home several times and they are splendid, lovely people."[153]

Getting down to business in the dreary State Department offices, drawing on the expertise of Kelley and Bullitt and the legal advice of Hackworth, Moore drew up a working memorandum for Hull and the president on 28 October. He understood that a separate agreement would "operate concurrently with recognition and constitute the condition on which recognition is to be granted." This was the basis of an important brainstorming session in his office on Monday morning, 30 October, with Bullitt, Hackworth, and Kelley. Among the points they outlined: relations "shall be subject to the principles and processes of international law"; U.S. citizens will have rights equivalent to those granted to Russians; "the clause against subversive propaganda should be made as definite as possible"; "the religious rights of Americans now or hereafter in Russia, should be protected as strongly as possible"; "debts and private claims must be subject to open discussion and arbitration." This included military damage claims from intervention. Bullitt, Kelley, and Hackworth had a lively exchange on this issue, with Kelley scoring a point: "I feel that if there is any chance of an agreement here, the Russians will be willing to drop them." On another issue, Kelley warned against including anything in the final document involving any promise of credits. Bullitt replied, "No, but I think we ought to have it 'by the ears' to be brought into the discussion." In other words, he expected much to be discussed behind the scenes. They also agreed on a clause forbidding propaganda against each other's governments.[154]

As the negotiation approached, other influential voices were heard. Charles Crane advocated somewhat naively that a prerequisite for recognition be guaranteed religious freedom in all respects. He also advised Colonel House to caution FDR to go slow on recognition.[155] The progressive Secretary of Agriculture Henry Wallace, out of the picture as far as negotiations were concerned, wanted

153. To FDR, f. Russia Sept.–Oct., 26 October 1933, box 2, POF 220a, FRPL. Calder had lunch with the president earlier, on 6 June, the topic of conversation readily predictable. Phillips to FDR, briefing the president, 5 June 1933, f. Russia Jan.–Aug. 1933, ibid.

154. Notes of conference in Moore's office, and Moore to Hull, 30 October 1933, f. Russia, box 18 Moore Papers, FRPL.

155. Crane to FDR, telegram, 6 November 1933, box 2, POF 220a, FRPL; to House, 3 April 1933, reel 1, Crane Papers, BA-CU.

an agreement on a limitation on Russian wheat exports.[156] Both would be ignored as impractical or not germane to the central discussion at hand. S. Reading Bertron, chair of the American-Russian Chamber of Commerce, telegraphed the president:

> Please accept heartiest congratulations recent steps taken resumption diplomatic relations with Russia thus should lead to great economic and political advantages to both countries stop President Wilson said to me when he asked me to serve on Russian diplomatic mission that he believed close friendship between two great diplomatic nations geographically located as Russia and America would one day go far toward controlling destinies of world stop your wise action may well lead to realization of his vision.[157]

The Commissar Arrives

The dean of the American press in Moscow, Walter Duranty, managed (of course) to accompany Litvinov on his voyage across the Atlantic and to arrange a lunch and a news conference aboard ship, at which the Soviet commissar displayed his diplomatic bearing. Asked about Germany and Japan, he answered simply that the Soviet Union opposed all aggression wherever. Questioned about the outcome of his mission, he quickly noted that it would depend on the Americans, that they would learn the result from a joint pronouncement with President Roosevelt. He impressed everyone with his willingness to answer all questions, including personal ones, though evasively.[158]

Litvinov demonstrated his chess skills by outwitting his assistant Ivan Divilkovskii on several occasions, well covered by the American press. The Soviet commissar was coming equipped with a chessboard. He also arrived in a dense fog, climatically and diplomatically. Accompanied by a scrambling assortment of news personnel and conveyed by launch past an invisible Statue of Liberty, the Soviet delegation was met, according to Divilkovskii, by a team of six large secret service agents wearing identical sports jackets and chewing gum.[159] Adroit to the occasion and following the Roosevelt precedent of people to people, upon his inauspicious landing in New York, Litvinov stated to the press,

156. Wallace to FDR, 7 November 1933, box 2, POF 220a, FRPL.
157. Bertron to FDR, 21 October 1933, ibid.
158. Zinovy Sheinis, *Maxim Litvinov*, translated by Vic Schneierson (Moscow: Progress, 1990), 236–38.
159. As cited in ibid., 239.

I am stepping on to the soil of the great American Republic deeply aware of the honor of bringing greetings to the American people from the peoples of the Soviet Union as their official representative. I am conscious of the fact that, in a sense, I am making the first breach in the artificial barrier that had for sixteen years hindered normal intercourse between the peoples of our two countries.[160]

After landing in New York on 7 November 1933, the anniversary of the Bolshevik seizure of power in 1917, the Soviet delegation went immediately to Washington, where it was met the same day at Union Station by Robert Kelley and Jefferson Patterson. Most of them lodged with Boris Skvirsky, who was clearly looking forward to relinquishing his post as unofficial ambassador. On 9 November the Soviet commissar made a formal call on the secretary of state. As a witness described the scene, "The department was all agog this morning over the arrival of Mr. Litvinoff for a conference with the Secretary."[161] Clerks lined the stairways, pushed aside by more plainclothes and police officers than he had ever seen. Within hours, delayed by a previously scheduled tea by Mrs. Roosevelt, Litvinov was walking up the steps of the front portico of the White House and ushered in to meet the president, who was already seated at the dining table. As Roosevelt struggled to rise, Litvinov hurried forward to shake his hand and wish him well. No Russian bear hugs were reported—but cordiality definitely reigned that evening.[162]

After all the hoopla and both long-term and short-term preparations, the actual signing of the recognition agreement should have been only a formality. This was far from the case. Litvinov came equipped for hard bargaining, proposing at the opening of conversations that there be no references to any past claims or issues on either side, along the lines of the Soviet Rapallo treaty with Germany in 1922. Moore and other representatives of the department, fearing the president would give in for the sake of an accomplishment, were aghast, but they were hampered by the president's instructions—that none of this should go to Congress for debate and approval or rejection.

John O'Laughlin, a close friend and adviser to Herbert Hoover, summarized the negotiations succinctly to the former president: "He [Litvinov] will be in-

---

160. Ibid., 238.

161. Jefferson Patterson, *Diplomatic Duty and Diversion* (Cambridge, Mass.: Riverside Press, 1956), 178.

162. Probably on this occasion, prompted by knowledge of the president's stamp collecting hobby, Litvinov presented a handsome album of all Soviet postal stamps issued to that date. The album, as witnessed by the author, is carefully preserved at the Roosevelt Presidential Library in its original state but has never been on display.

Boris Skvirsky greeting Maxim Litvinov, November 1933. (Prints and Photographs, Library of Congress)

terested in securing credits, the Administration in granting them for the benefit of our farm products. The Administration also will require assurances that Red propaganda will not be conducted and will discuss the debts of the Ancien Regime."[163] A few days later, he noted the delay due to Roosevelt's insistence on religious freedom for Americans. "The result is that the negotiations are being drawn out and there is no certainty that recognition will be effected," but he was confident it would finally be achieved because of the Japanese situation: "Japan of course is hostile to recognition and has not failed to communicate her viewpoint to this Government."[164]

163. O'Laughlin to Hoover, 4 November 1933, f. Nov. 1933, box 43, O'Laughlin Papers, MD, LC.
164. O'Laughlin to Hoover, 13 November 1933, ibid.

Litvinov and Roosevelt cartoon, 1933. (Prints and Photographs, Library of Congress)

The first substantive meeting of the American and Soviet delegations occurred on 10 November, beginning with a morning-long discussion of generalities, one of which was equal protection for American citizens under Soviet law. No problem was raised on that score. Though with much more experience than any of his counterparts, Litvinov claimed to be nervous and apprehensive, especially when confronted by a hard-line policy on the debt issue by Bullitt, who asserted that most of the American loans to Russia had been expended to defeat Germany. Litvinov's expected counter was that they were also used to kill other Russians—in the civil war. It had become clear that Litvinov was demanding unconditional recognition without reference to debts due and Russian counterclaims, but this the American side could not agree with.

The matter of the debt came to a head on the morning of 15 November in an intense two-hour discussion between Litvinov and Bullitt, who threatened the Soviet commissar with the "Johnson Bill" then before Congress that would forbid loans to countries in default of indebtedness (it would be passed the following April) and insisted that a low sum such as $50 million could not be accepted. Litvinov asked him what amount would be acceptable, and, anticipating the answer, "You will say $150,000,000." He then hinted at a compromise of $100 million. In his hurried report to FDR, Bullit thought that he had been too gentle with Litvinov and offered to meet with the president to plan the strategy for the crucial session that afternoon at 2 PM.[165] As Moore noted, "He is thus not willing to make any of the agreements which we so carefully prepared during the ten days preceding his arrival and he is anxious to place us in the same position occupied by other nations which accorded recognition and then found that they were unable to reach settlements or to save their nationals from injustice."[166] Essentially, Litvinov had shrewdly nullified the home court advantage and scored points.

On the sensitive topic of religious freedom, Litvinov quickly agreed that Americans would have complete freedom to practice their beliefs in Russia. He professed that this was also the case for Soviet citizens but a matter of domestic concern in which the United States had no right to interfere. The American side could not press the point while promoting its main agenda, the direct interference of Comintern- and Soviet-initiated propaganda into American society, with the response being the usual disclaimer that the Soviet state had nothing to do with this and would not in the future. So much for that record. In the afternoon meeting on 15 November, Litvinov and Roosevelt came to a "gentlemen's agreement" that the specifics of the debt amount (probably $100 million) and a substantial loan with added interest to apply toward satisfying this debt would be worked out in further negotiations. This set the stage for the formal exchange of notes on 16 November that provided the "seal" on recognition.

Without going into the details of tedious negotiations that followed and the time wasted on the American side in preparing an agenda for achieving concessions, Litvinov simply won the chess game, outmaneuvering the overconfident Americans and capturing the opponent's two knights (debt and credits), the

165. Bullitt to FDR, 15 November 1933, *FRUS: Soviet Union, 1933–1939* (Washington, D.C.: GPO, 1952), 25–26; memorandum of FDR to Litvinov, 15 November 1933, ibid., 26–27; Hugh D. Phillips, *Between the Revolution and the West: A Political Biography of Maxim M. Litvinov* (Boulder, Colo.: Westview, 1982), 131–32.

Roosevelt had insisted that no formal recorded minutes of his meetings with Litvinov be kept, to allow for an informal, freewheeling atmosphere. Fortunately, several messages and memoranda provide insights, though they were brief and hastily written. Litvinov apparently followed suit, keeping his negotiations in the dark as far as Moscow was concerned, since there is a gap in the published documents for the crucial period of negotiations, recording only the formal exchanges of notes. See *Sovetsko-Amerikanskie otnosheniia, 1927–1933*, 709–12.

166. Moore memorandum for Hull, 9 November 1933, f. Russia 1933, box 18, Moore Papers, FRPL. Moore added, "Personally I have for some time favored recognition but in my judgment it is unthinkable that there are any advantages that could accrue from it being granted unconditionally which would satisfy the American public or fail to produce a dangerous reaction." Ibid.

American side winning only a "guarantee" or "promise" that the match would be resumed at a later date, that is, the debt issue specifically remained open for further negotiation. The Roosevelt administration simply could not afford to lose the main point, recognition, and the Soviets knew it. Raymond Robins saw the need for compromise: "TIME seems to me of moment in these negotiations. If some matters involve delay they should be referred to a commission AFTER Recognition." He could not avoid expressing his own view, going back many years: "What an hour in the life of this nation and the world!"[167] The ultimate winner, it could be claimed, however, was the United States, which established a permanent and annoying new presence in the heart of the Soviet Union.

Reaction to Recognition

Moore succinctly summarized the results to Hull in South America:

> The recognition of the Soviet Government on terms arranged by the President seems to meet general approval. That the Roman Catholics are not disapproving is evidenced by a statement from Father Walsh, who has heretofore been very hostile toward recognition, but is now commending the President for the terms on which it was created. Representative Fish is about the only one of the old antagonistic group who has expressed severe criticism, and that he bases largely on the possibility that our Government may make loans to the Soviet.[168]

He added that the department was beginning to work on fixing the debt figure at "not in excess" of $150 million and that he fully approved the president's appointment of Bullitt as the first ambassador.

After such a long era of sharply divided opinion on the diplomatic recognition of the government of the Soviet Union, response to the actual event was relatively quiet. Some Republicans who had advocated for it were dismayed and embarrassed by the fact that it was accomplished by a party they had so recently campaigned against. Governor Goodrich wrote the president, "I have delayed writing you relative to the Recognition of Russia. Although I am not of your political faith, as you know, I want to congratulate you upon the invitation extended to Russia to send someone here to discuss the matter."[169] In fact, this ac-

---

167. Robins to Borah, 1 December 1933, f. Robins, box 401, Borah Papers, MD, LC.
168. Moore to Hull, 27 November 1933, reel 10, Hull Papers, MD, LC.
169. Goodrich to Roosevelt, 6 November 1933, f. FDR, box 15, Goodrich Papers, HHPL.

complishment had the effect of reducing criticism from a substantial quarter of that party for other new policies of the Roosevelt administration, thus making it difficult for the Republican Party to unite in opposition to the New Deal and in the next presidential campaign.

A charter member of the American proponents of recognition deserved and received a private meeting on 11 November with Litvinov. Raymond Robins described it as a lifelong fulfillment to his friend Gumberg,

> I saw Litvinov for a little visit at Skvirsky's. He was very cordial. [In?] One or two little matters I may have been some use, otherwise it was just a friendly meeting. He admitted that I was right and he wrong when we last talked together at the Foreign Office in Moscow [in May]. He is very well, finds the matter of "face saving" a bit irksome, but I tried to have him see how wise it was for the situation over here. He has no idea of the opposition that did exist to the Soviet Union in this country. I think this week marks the end of the 16 years battle.[170]

He wrote his wife in similar fashion and again after the formal signing of the agreement on 16 November, "At last, VICTORY!"[171] And after the deal was final and all the papers signed, he wrote Gumberg, "Congratulations old Comrade and dear friend for this culmination of your wise, brave, unfaltering labors for the common good of your homeland and your adopted country."[172] Robins, lifelong Republican, waiting for an opportunity to return to the White House, congratulated the president "for your great move for international peace, economic recovery and control of price levels in the international market by *recognition of the Soviet Union*."[173]

Not surprisingly, the American Communist Party welcomed recognition as a victory of its program, but warned that militancy should be renewed. "Recognition . . . is neither a guarantee of permanent peace or of the permanence of normal relations. On the contrary, the more advantages the Proletarian State gains from the diplomatic and economic relations with the capitalist countries the sooner the capitalist countries will try to attack it. . . . The task of defending the Soviet Union becomes therefore, more important after recognition."[174] While attributing the American decision to a poor economy and hopes for in-

---

170. Robins to Gumberg, 12 November 1933, f. 2, box 7, Gumberg Papers, HHPL.

171. As quoted in Salzman, *Reform and Revolution*, 361.

172. To Gumberg, 18 November 1933, f. 2, box 7, Gumberg Papers, HHPL.

173. Robins to Roosevelt, 29 November 1933, POF220a, box 2, FRPL.

174. "Recognition and the Task of the Communists," 12 December 1933, Central Committee CPUSA, f. 575, op. 1, d. 3123, reel 243, CPUSA Papers, MD, LC.

creased Soviet trade, the party congratulated itself that Litvinov had granted virtually no concessions. The party could also look forward to easier entry and exit from its acknowledged center. The party had just held a plenum meeting of its central committee in New York in mid-October; attention was focused almost entirely on self-criticism. Membership was listed at about 30,000 but only 18,500 were paying dues. *The Daily Worker* remained a major problem with circulation down to under 30,000, a small fraction of that of big city dailies. An effort to raise $40,000 to improve and enlarge the paper had netted only $8,000, and the *Worker* was deeply in debt and in danger of closing. Regarding other matters, the minutes recorded much discussion of the failure to recruit black members with the campaign against the NAACP backfiring; the New York membership was guilty of "extreme sophistication" (too intellectual, perhaps).[175] There was no mention of impending recognition, though a sense of being neglected and sacrificed to Soviet state interests prevailed.

The American Communist Party had taken little advantage of the large-scale unemployment that accompanied the Depression, nor had it capitalized on the awakening of African-Americans and the beginning of the civil rights movement. The death of Charles Ruthenberg in 1927, Foster's heart attack during the 1932 election campaign, and the demise of Lovestone and his faction had left the party virtually leaderless and in disarray. The removal of Zinoviev and then Bukharin from Comintern leadership also damaged the American connection with Moscow, especially since Stalin made clear on several occasions his dislike for his North American affiliate and its factionalism.[176]

Clinton DeWitt Poole, an early supporter of the policy of nonrecognition in the State Department, now directing the School of Public and International Affairs at Princeton University, remained skeptical about the future of Soviet-American relations, especially in regard to the expected granting of credits, but agreed "that it would be a calamity to get L[itvinov] over here and then miscarry."[177] A chorus of others in the Hamilton Fish–oriented press warned of the consequences of recognition in all its conservative religious and political dimensions. They predicted that it would have lasting effects—as indeed it would into the cold war era. On a more reasoned plane, Bainbridge Colby, one of the original architects of nonrecognition, wrote an old supporter of that policy, John Spargo, that Litvinov had claimed that he made no concessions. "I cannot but feel that we have made a botch of it, although I would be very happy if events should

---

175. Minutes of Plenum of Central Committee, 14–15 October 1933, d. 3120, ibid.

176. Draper, *American Communism and Soviet Russia: The Formative Period* (New York: Viking, 1960), 394 et passim.

177. Poole to Harper, 14 November 1933, f. 16, box 18, Harper Papers, UC-R.

prove otherwise. The reversal of a diplomatic policy seems a slight thing compared with the philosophy of repudiation which seems to have taken possession of us."[178] J. F. T. O'Connor, comptroller of the currency, monitored the views of religious groups and informed the president through McIntyre on 13 December that there was a significant shift by both Catholic and Protestant groups. A speaker at one forum declared, "Roosevelt has put God back into Russia." He added, "From other sources I get information that the whole country is gradually approving the President's policy of recognition."[179]

William R. Castle Jr., the last official defender of the policy of nonrecognition, as assistant secretary of state in the Hoover administration, announced that he had no quarrel with the present administration recognizing Soviets, admitting that "it is no longer possible to say that it does not represent the wishes of the people."[180] He defended recognition as the correct policy now, but warned that little would come of it in regard to increased trade or reduction of propaganda. Original reasons that the Soviet government was a tool of Germany (Rapallo) and did not honor its financial obligations, he noted, were no longer valid. Former President Hoover himself refused to condone recognition, responding to inquiries with a gruff rejoinder: "Read the Bill of Rights." To Castle, he was a bit more explicit, "To me the Bill of Rights is the heart of the Constitution."[181]

Percival Baxter, former reform governor of Maine and veteran of four visits to the Soviet union, perhaps had the best and last word on the general situation, recalling the dream of an American path for Russia: "Folks often say to me, 'After all, have not the Russians made progress,' and my reply is that they have after a fashion, but how much farther ahead would they now be had they devoted their energies toward building a state on a sound foundation of representative government and upon sound principles of public economy."[182]

The formality of diplomatic recognition did not solve many problems between the two countries, since they were essentially waved aside for later discussion. The State Department, somewhat reluctantly, took on the challenging issues of debts and credits. Moore advised Phillips to assure the president that the work had

178. Colby to Spargo, 8 December 1933, f. 1933, box 29, Colby Papers, MD, LC.

179. O'Connor to McIntyre, 13 December 1933, f. December 1933, box 2, POF, FRPL.

180. Castle memorandum, undated, f. 303 Soviet Recognition, box 34 (articles and speeches), Castle Papers, HHPL. This may have been the text for an address at Goucher College in Baltimore on 4 November 1933, in which he added, "And if after recognition there should be the urge to extend vast credits the American people should consider whether this use of their money will, or will not, actually work toward a permanent as distinguished from a very temporary improvement in a few industries." Talk at Goucher College, 4 November 1933, f. 247 July–Dec. 1933, box 29 (articles and speeches), ibid.

181. Hoover to Castle, 15 November 1933, f. 194 1933–1937, box 24, ibid.

182. Baxter to Hoover, 21 December 1933, f. Baxter, box 14, Post-Presidential Papers, HHPL.

the daily attention of Kelley, Hackworth, Wiley, and himself, but that this also involved much consultation with the Treasury Department, Franklin Field of the Bank of Manhattan, and John Hancock of Lehman Brothers. A memorandum, drafted on 5 December, suggested some roundabout ways of dealing with payment of American claims, relying especially on intermediate transfers through the re-payment of German credit loans, a rather complicated procedure.[183] In a follow-up note, Moore assured, "The situation is being carefully explored with the hope that a plan can be devised not involving the employment of the funds or credit of our Government or with a minimum resort to that expedient."[184] All of this smacked of expediency and failed to deal with the basic issues.

From Warm Springs, Georgia, with the help of Bullitt, President Roosevelt extended his farewell best wishes to Litvinov.

> It has been a great personal pleasure to me to meet you and I trust that some day I shall again have the pleasure of welcoming you in America. [He would—on 8 December 1941.] On your return to your country I hope that you will convey to President Kalinin my greetings and best wishes.
>
> I am profoundly gratified that our conversations should have resulted in the restoration of normal relations between our peoples and I trust that these relations will grow closer and more intimate with each passing year. The cooperation of our governments in the great work of preserving peace should be the corner stone of an enduring friendship.[185]

Before departing, Litvinov called on Senator Borah, who was in bed with a cold, and at the State Department with William Phillips, Hull having managed to escape from the recognition scene on a mission to South America.[186]

Back in New York the old cohorts for recognition gathered for a grand celebra-tion banquet for Litvinov at the Waldorf Astoria on 24 November. Hugh Cooper served as master of ceremonies, and most of the left fringe of New York society attended. Robins, of course, was there, regretting the absence of Borah, "Never have I felt the absence of any man from a setting as much as your absence from the head of the table last Friday night at the Waldorf-Astoria. It was a tremen-

183. Memorandum of Moore, 5 December 1933, in Phillips to FDR, 6 December 1933, POF220a, FRPL.

184. Moore to Phillips, 7 December 1933, f. Russia, Dec. 1933, box 18, Moore Papers, FRPL.

185. FDR to Litvinov, 23 November 1933, f. Russia, POF220a, FRPL. Bullitt sent the revised draft to FDR for his signature and asked that it be returned to him at the State Department so that he could deliver it personally to Litvinov. Bullitt to FDR, 22 November 1933, ibid. Bullitt began his journey to Moscow soon afterward.

186. "Litvinoff Makes Farewell Calls," *New York Times*, 23 November 1933: 9.

"We did it." Hugh Cooper and Maxim Litvinov,
November 1933. (Prints and Photographs, Library of
Congress)

dous scene and had you been present and spoken—it would have been perfect.
Litvinov did an able job, and so did Colonel Cooper—but your absence was felt
and deplored by all who knew the situation and cared, in that rare gathering."[187]
James Goodrich, also deservedly invited, disagreed, finding Cooper as toastmaster
"ponderous and tedious." Robins, however, was his old self, "all fire and enthusiasm," and Litvinov was temperate and well balanced. He too was doubtful about
solving the debt-credit problem. His final thought was, "Russia & America together can do much for the peace of the world."[188]

187. Robins to Borah, 26 November 1933, f. Robins, box 401, Borah Papers, MD, LC.
188. Goodrich, f. Diaries, 1933, 24 November 1933, box 3, Goodrich Papers, HHPL.

The American Embassy

Speculation on who would occupy the post as the first formal representative of the United States to the Soviet Union hovered in the background of all the negotiations for recognition. Early candidates, Samuel Harper (proposed by several from the academic community) and Jerome Davis of Yale (self-proclaimed), were quickly eliminated. Davis assured Borah that he had always supported the cause of recognition.[189] Earlier, in hopes of consideration for the post, Davis had provided the president with his own rather complicated agenda for the expected negotiation on recognition. He specifically pressed the point, "Stalin and the Soviet Government feel that America should have recognized them long ago. A new administration has the opportunity to win their good-will. The longer we wait the more we lose this potential psychologic advantage, which is distinctly important."[190] Borah supported Robins for ambassador, a quaint idea: "Our friend Jerome Davis is asking the place. If there is positively no chance for you I would be for him. I think although the truth is I will have nothing to say about it, one way or the other."[191] But Davis was a professor of religious studies, a background unlikely to elicit a congenial Soviet reception.

After conferring with Hull about his own appointment to Germany in March, William Dodd, while promoting the cause of his colleague at the University of Chicago, suspected that William Bullitt was already the choice. Several voices were raised in opposition, because of Bullitt's reputation as pro-Soviet, his marriage to Louise Bryant and divorce, and his playboy reputation in European society. Raymond Moley, however, thought that his appointment would reverse an injustice done him in 1919, when he was "cut politically dead by party chieftains."[192] Reintroduced to him by FDR in February 1933, Moley found him "pleasant, keen-minded, idealistic, and widely informed. On the other hand, he had a deep and somewhat disturbing strain in him."[193] The actual announcement of Bullitt had to await the final agreement on recognition. The State Department could take solace in its ability to designate Bullitt's staff.

189. Davis began his campaign to be ambassador before the Roosevelt inauguration. Davis to Borah, 13 and 15 February 1933, f. Russia, box 371, Borah Papers, MD, LC.

190. Davis to Howe, 23 March 1933, with attached memorandum, ibid.

191. Borah to Robins, 8 November 1933, box 371, Borah Papers, MD, LC. Davis had few friends in the academic community. Geroid Robinson quipped, "There is a good deal to be said for getting him out of the country—but why wish him on the Russians?" To Harper, 8 November 1933, f. 15, box 16, Harper Papers, UC-R.

192. Moley, *After Seven Years* (New York: Harper, 1939), 135.

193. Ibid, 136. For more details on the Bullitt appointment, see Michael Cassella-Blackburn, *The Donkey, the Carrot, and the Club: William C. Bullitt and Soviet-American Relations, 1917–1948* (Westport, Conn.: Praeger, 2004), 99–105.

Traveling with Litvinov, Bullitt arrived in Moscow on 11 December 1933 with a few assistants, including the twenty-nine-year-old George F. Kennan, who quickly impressed Soviet officials, as well as Bullitt, with his knowledge of Russian and his calm and deliberate manner.[194] The party was welcomed at the Moscow station by Troyanovsky, Ivan Divilkovskii, and Dmitri Florinskii (brother of the Columbia University historian), all from the Commissariat of Foreign Affairs, and escorted to the venerable National Hotel, where they found the stars and stripes draped over the entrance. Bullitt was lodged in the same suite he had occupied as a tourist in 1914. He formally presented his credentials to Kalinin on 14 December.

We have been received with the greatest kindness and a cordiality which has impressed us all. I presented my letters of credence to Mr. Kalinin this morning and had a thoroughly delightful conversation with him. . . . The Soviet Government is cooperating in every possible way to help us in establishing the embassy as soon as possible, but with the best will in the world I do not see how we can install ourselves here and get to work seriously before the first half of February, and I hope that you will continue the customary Russian reports from the Legation in Riga until we are thoroughly established.[195]

Things seemed to be off to a good start.

Almost immediately, Kennan and Bullitt found a house built by a Moscow merchant in 1914 with large central halls but only five bedrooms. The Commissariat of Foreign Affairs used it to lodge some of its staff, including at various times Chicherin, Litvinov, and Krestinsky. Attracted to the ambience of the large

194. Bullitt wrote to the American minister to Latvia, "I have rarely been so impressed by the ability and character of a man of his age. His Russian seems to be perfect and he should be, unless I am mistaken, the wheel horse of the embassy here. That will mean that I shall have to take him away from you. I apologize, but to my mind he is essential." To John Van Antwerp MacMurray, 14 December 1933, f. Bullitt, box 51, MacMurray Papers, Mudd-P.

More than fifty years later, Kennan recounted strolling on the platform of a station just over the border in Soviet Russia with Litvinov, who seemed unusually solemn. He explained simply that this was his hometown. Kennan's point was that Americans do not normally think of Soviet officials as having hometowns. Author's notes of speech in Kiev at meeting celebrating the fiftieth anniversary of recognition, August 1984.

195. Bullitt to John Van Antwerp MacMurray, 14 December 1933, f. Bullitt, box 51, MacMurray Papers, Mudd-P. MacMurray in Riga agreed, "He [Kennan] is a very able and fine youngster, and it is with many regrets that we see him leave us to take up this opportunity of doing the Russian work for which he has been preparing himself." MacMurray to Bullitt, 2 January 1934, f. 1–15 January 1934, ibid. He added two weeks later, "Kennan is the most valuable asset that we can have in Russia for a good many years to come," but warned that he was of frail health and may not live long. Right on the former, wrong on the latter. MacMurray to Bullitt, f. 16–31 Jan., box 52, ibid.

*"Hats on, off to Russia." William Bullitt and FDR, probably at
Washington's Union Station, 1933. (Prints and Photographs,
Library of Congress)*

reception area and ballrooms were many of the Soviet elite in the 1920s: Lenin, Trotsky, Stalin, Kamenev, and others.[196] The commissariat was probably reluctant to relinquish it to the United States, but sacrifices had to be made. As "Spaso House," it became the first residence of the ambassador and temporary embassy, and is still the domicile of the current American ambassador to the Russian Federation. The embassy building proper, however, proved more difficult and would apparently have to be built from scratch, available not before May. Keith Merrill, another assistant, was in charge of that problem. In quick order, Bullitt endured a regimen of welcoming events: a reception at the Foreign Commissariat, a meeting with "Premier" Molotov (chair of the Council of Commissars), who rarely received ambassadors, and a formal dinner hosted by Litvinov, featuring, as he related to Roosevelt, "many toasts to you and me."[197]

196. Rebecca Matlock, *"Spaso-Khaus" Liudi i vstrechi: zapiski zheny amerikanskogo posla*, translated by T. Kudriavtseva (Moscow: Eksmo: Algoritm, 2004), 64–66.

197. Bullitt to FDR, 1 January 1934, f. Russia 1934, box 49, PSF, FRPL.

George Kennan, c. 1940. (Prints and Photographs, Library of Congress)

Bullitt managed to squeeze in time to lay a wreath at the grave of John Reed below the Kremlin wall, just before the formal dinner on 20 December in the Kremlin, hosted by Commissar of Defense Klimenty Voroshilov, "one of the most charming persons that I have ever met," and who had "an immense sense of humor."[198] Ushered in by Soviet (Cadillac) limousine, the American party was met by a receiving line of Stalin, Kalinin, Molotov, and Litvinov. The latter whispered

198. Ibid. Note the preserving of the fiction of official contacts with government and not party officials. Of course, all Soviet state officials were also high in the party, but Stalin held no state office at this time and until 1941. This dichotomy of party and state naturally caused problems for all diplomatic representatives, who could not officially approach the real person of power directly. British Foreign Secretary Anthony Eden recorded his dilemma in early 1935, after arriving in Moscow on a mission to try to save Collective Security. He finally achieved an unofficial, informal meeting with Stalin in Molotov's apartment in the Kremlin. Eden, as well as the few others privileged to attain this goal, were duly impressed by Stalin's grasp of details, his intelligence, craftiness, and willingness to listen. Anthony Eden, *Facing the Dictators: The Memoirs of Anthony Eden, Earl of Avon* (Boston: Houghton Mifflin, 1962), 170–75.

to Bullitt, "This is the whole 'gang' that really runs things." His first introduction to Stalin was brief and perfunctory, but "I noticed from time to time he looked in my direction out of the corner of his eye, as if he were sizing me up before coming to close quarters." He had somehow expected a big man with a strong voice and was surprised to find a diminutive figure dressed in a plain soldier's uniform, smoking a large pipe, which he held throughout the dinner. Bullitt was impressed with his eyes: "They are small, intensely shrewd and continuously smiling. . . . When he laughs lips curl in a curiously canine manner. . . . With Lenin one felt at once that one was in the presence of a great man; with Stalin I felt I was talking to a wiry Gipsy with roots and emotions beyond my experience."[199]

At the dinner table, Bullitt was placed between Mrs. Voroshilov and Litvinov with Stalin on the other side of the lady and Kalinin directly across from him. With protocol out of the way and everyone understanding who was in charge, Stalin rose first to offer a toast, "To President Roosevelt, who in spite of the mute growls of the Fishes [a jibe at Hamilton Fish] dared to recognize the Soviet Union." Bullitt toasted Kalinin, then Molotov to Bullitt, "The health of one who comes to us as a new Ambassador but an old friend." On his part, Litvinov reminded Bullitt that one must empty the glass each time and observed that after quite a few no one would seem to care that he [Litvinov] was not one of the "gang." Bullitt reported that he still managed a considerable conversation with Stalin across Mrs. Voroshilov, who must have been rather uncomfortable. One of the final toasts was again offered by Stalin—to the health and prosperity of the American army and navy, the president, and the whole United States. Bullitt responded with one to the memory of Lenin and the continued success of the Soviet Union.

With everyone considerably well toasted and mellowed by vodka, the conversation turned rather openly to Soviet concern about Japanese aggression in the Far East, with Stalin rather abruptly, to Bullitt's surprise, emphasizing the importance of arranging an immediate American shipment of 250,000 tons of rails for the double-tracking of the Trans-Siberian Railroad, noting that American rails are much heavier than Russian; they would even be happy to accept used ones. Stalin added, according to Bullitt, "Without those rails we shall beat the Japanese, but if we have the rails it will be easier."[200] He stressed that this should be done as soon as possible through Amtorg. Bullitt was clearly impressed with Stalin's shrewdness, inflexible will, and "the quality of intuition in extraordinary measure. . . . Moreover, like every real statesman I have known, he has the quality of being able to treat the most serious things with a joke and a twinkle in his

199. Matlock, *"Spaso-Khaus,"* 64–66.
200. Ibid.

eye."[201] Stalin escorted Bullitt to the door after the long evening and asked if there was anything he needed. Bullitt brought up the problem of finding an embassy building, and Stalin quickly responded, "You shall have it."[202]

The Soviet Embassy

Getting into position to carry on the normal routine of diplomatic relations was easier for Troyanovsky and his entourage, since the old Russian embassy sat waiting in Washington at 1119 16th Street in remarkably good condition. Built for the Pullman (of railroad fame) family, it was occupied only by John Hays Hammond before sale to the Russian imperial government to house its last ambassador to the United States, George Bakhmetev, and his American wife. It was a stately mansion, the personification of American capitalism, which the Soviet embassy would occupy for many years.

The greeting party for Ambassador Troyanovsky at Union Station on 7 January 1934 again consisted of Kelley and Patterson, the latter describing the new envoy as short, plump, and Asiatic looking.[203] He formally presented his credentials to the president at the White House on the following day, thus completing the last formality of recognition.[204] The ambassador then spent a few weeks getting around the country, for example, addressing the Foreign Policy Association in Cincinnati on 2 April, emphasizing the Soviet quest for peace but adding, "We will not surrender a foot of our land as the price for peace," and stressing the dangerous threats of "nationalisms of every kind—political, economic, spiritual."[205]

After some refurbishing and waiting on new furnishings from Moscow museums, the Troyanovskys moved into the embassy on 6 April, just before hosting a grand reception on 12 April.[206] Despite discussion in some quarters about whether to appear, well over 500 turned up to partake of lavish buffets on three floors—and it was not crowded. Besides cabinet members, such as Hull and Morgenthau, the full diplomatic corps, most of the State Department, and Mrs.

---

201. Ibid.

202. Ibid. The embassy apart from Spaso House would go through a long process, including one plan to model the main building on Monticello and embassy housing on the University of Virginia. Kelley to Charles A. Murphy, 22 May 1934, f. I-F-3, box 25, DEEA, RG 59.

203. Patterson, *Diplomatic Duty and Diversion*, 184.

204. The official copies of the speeches on that occasion are in f. Russia, 1934–1939, box 1, POF 220 Russia, FRPL. Though the recognition agreement was signed in November 1933, the completed accord did not take place until that day in January 1934.

205. "Troyanovsky Sees Grave War Danger," *New York Times*, 3 April 1933: 3.

206. "Embassy Occupied by Troyanovsky," *New York Times*, 7 April 1934: 3.

Woodrow Wilson, there were many predictable out of towners: Bertron, Alex Gumberg, Ivy Lee, and General William Graves, commander of the American Expeditionary Force in Siberia in 1918–1919.[207] All were impressed by a centrally positioned bust of Lenin and a large photograph of Stalin, and the nicely attired Mr. and Mrs. Ambassador at the head of the reception line. Large quantities of champagne, vodka, and caviar were consumed—and as Patterson noted, "with the gilt wood work and brocade curtains, the effect could not be less proletarian. I did not notice that anyone was deterred by a scruple from attending."[208]

The launch of official diplomatic recognition between two great powers that spanned a major ocean and most of two continents was a major event of the twentieth century, setting the stage for a period of accommodation that would eventually, not without difficulty, produce the grand alliance of World War II. With the recognition achievement in mind, William Allen White gave the president credit, "He certainly is strong for 'drammer', combining all the gracious qualities of John Barrymore with the showmanship of Barnum."[209]

The American Moscow Scene

Bullitt, accompanied by his daughter, left New York on 15 February 1934, arriving in early March to establish residence in the Soviet capital at Spaso House, which had to be shared with several other embassy personnel. Resolution on the matters of debts and credits proved to be more difficult than expected, as Litvinov turned allusive and recalcitrant. Secretary of State Hull approved Bullitt's delays in establishing consulates. "Confidentially, you may think it desirable to intimate in your own way to Litvinov that if the understanding had while he was here is to be repudiated it may not be worthwhile to provide any consulates or proceed in certain other respects."[210] They agreed that no negotiations on these matters would be conducted in Washington with Troyanovsky. After the cards were dealt, Bullitt bid one no trump and Litvinov passed. In the meantime one positive note was the establishment of an American consul general's office in Moscow in March 1934.

207. "Soviet Envoy Host at Brilliant Fete," *New York Times*, 11 April 1934: 14. The article included a large portrait of Mrs. Troyanovsky and a picture of the grand salon. Patterson, *Diplomatic Duty and Diversion*, 184, gives the attendance as around 1,000.

208. Patterson, *Diplomatic Duty and Diversion*, 186.

209. White to Julian Street, 21 February 1934, f. 11 White, box 48, Street Papers, Firestone Library, Princeton.

210. Hull to Bullitt, 9 April 1934, f. Russia 1934, box 49, PSF, FRPL.

Felix Cole, director, Riga "Listening Post," 1928. (Prints and Photographs, Library of Congress)

Obviously disappointed that he could not tie up quickly the loose ends of the recognition agreement, Bullitt reported privately to Kelley that the Commissariat of Foreign Affairs "seem inclined to be just as nasty as possible," but that "Brother Stalin" and the Kremlin in general "are extremely friendly."[211] He found Voroshilov (commissar of defense) extremely friendly; he guessed that Litvinov was placing highest priority on achieving a French alliance in 1934 and that the

211. To Kelley, 20 June 1934, f. 8, box 3, Kelley Papers, GUA. Kelley had already warned Mac-Murray that Bullitt would not be able to immediately take over the work of the Latvian legation. Kelley to MacMurray, 14 February 1934, f. Feb. 1934, box 52, MacMurray Papers, MUDD-P.

American issues were displaced in importance for the time being. Bullitt also suspected a Jewish bias: "It would be simple enough to say that the Russians are fond of us whereas the Jews are not, and that the Narkomindel, being composed completely of Hebrews now that Karakhan and Sokolnikov have been thrown out, is just engaged in being itself, but the explanation is too easy and to my mind does not explain anything."[212]

In the meantime, Bullitt struggled with the problem of getting established physically in Moscow. Loy Henderson, one of the original staff, noted that "we are extremely busy at the present time here, endeavoring to set up a machine that will function."[213] By mid-May, Bullitt complained, "not one stick of furniture for my house has yet arrived." He enjoyed Spaso House, nevertheless, and the social life, sharing it with most of the regular personnel. He was sympathetic toward the embassy women, especially the wives of Kennan, Wiley, and Ward, the latter of Russian imperial origin and extremely unhappy in this "foreign" land.[214] Still, the beginnings of an American diplomatic presence in Soviet Russia were not auspicious for anything more than being "distant friends." As a consequence, the Riga listening post remained in operation. Kelley informed MacMurray that "the Riga office is hanging . . . between heaven and earth in consequence of the establishment of the Moscow embassy." He was working hard to continue financing for the personnel there.[215] Cole, advised by Bullitt, was more explicit that, because of administrative problems in Moscow, it would be some time before the Riga work could be transferred, despite MacMurray's desire to reduce it.[216]

One of the unsung heroes of the recognition process was certainly Felix Cole, who, while directing the Riga listening post, prepared much material for the background work in Washington and who was content to stay on to manage the Riga office. Though maintaining a famously disorganized office with papers scattered everywhere, he had a knack of inspiring support and loyalty from his staff

212. Ibid.

213. Henderson to MacMurray, 15 March 1934, f. 1–15 March 1934, ibid. Kennan was more explicit: "You can imagine the confusion that results from dumping a staff of over forty people into a place like Moscow before any apartments, furniture, appropriation or transportation facilities are available for their use." To MacMurray, 15 March 1934, ibid.

214. Bullitt to Moore, 14 May 1934, f. Moore, box 94, PSF, FRPL.

215. Kelley to MacMurray, 2 April 1934, f. April 1934, box 52, MacMurray Papers,

216. MacMurray to Bullitt, 22 March 1934, f. 16–31 March, and Cole to MacMurray, f. April 1934, 14 April, ibid. Later that year nothing had changed. Cole advised MacMurray that Wiley had written "that no action be taken, for the time being, in regard to the transfer of the Russian work to Moscow pending a full discussion of the matter in Washington with Mr. Bullitt." Cole to MacMurray, f. 11–30 November, box 54, ibid. But Cole had already been ordered to Moscow for discussion of the transfer of the Riga operation but "I venture that after this little burst the matter may again go to sleep for sometime." Ibid.

and an insight into what could be done in the way of research on Soviet affairs.[217] On a well-deserved home rest after the arrival of MacMurray, Cole wrote in reference to the assignment of a new assistant, "That is much better than wasting a trained Russian student in the Moscow mad-house."[218] Riga would continue to be the main source of information on the Soviet Union through the 1930s.

217. Interview with George F. Kennan, Princeton, November 2002.
218. Cole (Montclair, New Jersey) to MacMurray, 18 July 1934, f. 12–31 July 1934, box 53, MacMurray Papers, MUDD-P. MacMurray advised the department, confidentially, not to send Cole back to Riga, because of his wife's mental breakdown. To T. M. Wilson, 9 August 1934, f. 1–20 Aug. 1934, ibid.

7

Accommodation

Diplomatic relations had finally been established between two of the major countries of the twentieth century, first with the agreement between President Roosevelt and Commissar of Foreign Affairs Litvinov in November 1933 and then formally with the presentation of credentials by Ambassador Alexander Troyanovsky, the Soviet ambassador designate, in January 1934 in Washington. Thus the latter year is the official date for the resumption of relations. Secretary of State Hull, returned from his trip to Latin America, was pleased with the smoothness of Troyanovsky's formal call at the department on 24 January.[1] A few months were subsequently devoted to "settling in" and renovating the embassy, more for the Americans than for the Soviets because of a lack of an embassy building in Moscow.[2]

After Bullitt's brief, ceremonial trip to Moscow in December, he returned with several staff members in March 1934: John Wiley, second in command as counselor, had been a career diplomat since 1920, with his previous expertise mainly involving Western Europe; Loy Henderson served as first secretary; and as third secretaries were a trio of young but genuine Russian experts with a knowledge of the language—Charles ("Chip") Bohlen, George F. Kennan, and Bertel Kuniholm.[3] Kennan was the most academic, planning a biography of Anton Chekhov (which he never completed). He and Bohlen quickly immersed themselves in the fascinating political and cultural scene. In charge of consular affairs was Elbridge Dubrow, another experienced career officer. Rounding out the main echelon was Charles ("Charlie") Thayer, who had skipped out on an army obligation (as a graduate of West Point) to be a tourist in Russia dedicated to learning about the

1. Hull memorandum of conversation, 24 January 1934, f. Russia, reel 32, Hull Papers, MD, LC.

2. Much of the following is based on the excellent recent works by Grigorii N. Sevost'ianov, *Moskva-Vashington: Diplomaticheskie otnosheniia, 1933–1936* (Moscow: Nauka, 2002), and Michael Cassella-Blackburn, *The Donkey, the Carrot, and the Club: William C. Bullitt and Soviet-American Relations, 1917–1948* (Westport, Conn.: Praeger, 2004).

3. Charles E. Bohlen, *Witness to History, 1929–1969* (New York: Norton, 1973), 16–17.

country and the language. Kennan discovered him at the National Hotel and signed him on as a messenger, who buzzed around Moscow on a battered Harley-Davidson motorcycle.[4] Thayer could be counted on to add humor to the many difficult situations the staff faced.[5] Also of considerable assistance in the settling-in process was George Andreychin, a Bulgarian immigrant to the United States who was expelled as a dangerous "Wobblie" and found himself marooned in Soviet Russia. Now working for Intourist, he became the embassy's troubleshooter with local bureaucrats.[6] Bullitt was fortunate to have found such a capable and varied crew that could establish a respectable, yet colorful diplomatic presence in Moscow in relatively short order. Another source of relief were the American journalists, which included Duranty, Chamberlin, Stoneman, and Barnes. They were quite familiar with the Soviet scene and how to get things done, as well as fond of informal parties that included Russians—and the new diplomatic contingent.[7]

Bohlen, in turn, found Bullitt a congenial person but overly worried about finances.[8] His initial experience was "an experience": "In Moscow . . . my god things here in the embassy are in an awful mess as everything has to be started from scratch."[9] He found himself living with the ambassador and in charge of the house—Spaso House; the shops were better than expected but the transportation was horrible—the streets were torn up due to the building of the new metro. Nevertheless, "I have never had more fun or interest in my life."[10] He was impressed by a dinner Bullitt hosted for Red Army: "No other embassy in Russia has ever been able to get them to come and to have Voroshilov show us how they are making eyes at us," and especially by Marshall Budenny's foot-long mustaches.[11] Bohlen, however, found Bullitt difficult to work with, having little organizational skill, summarizing him as "brilliant but volatile," and "as a result we have had considerable more disorganization than was necessary."[12] Kennan accepted Bullitt as he was, the misplaced playboy of the eastern world.[13]

Bullitt and his staff would be plagued by a host of problems associated with the locale but also with Americans clamoring to get on board a new ship sailing in

4. Kennan, *Memoirs, 1925–1950* (Boston: Little, Brown, 1967), 59.

5. For proof, see his memoir: Charles W. Thayer, *Bears in the Caviar* (Philadelphia, Pa.: Lippincott, 1950).

6. Bohlen, *Witness to History*, 22–23.

7. Kennan, *Memoirs*, 60.

8. Bohlen to his mother, 6 March 1934, f. letters to mother, box 36, Bohlen Papers, MD, LC.

9. March 1934, ibid.

10. April 1934, ibid.

11. Ibid.

12. Ibid.

13. Interview with George F. Kennan, Princeton, November 2000.

old waters. Following a precedent of his predecessor, David Francis, in acquiring a cheap Model T Ford, probably unknowingly, Bullitt ordered a $600 Plymouth for his own use in Moscow.[14] After a few months, Bullitt reported privately, "A good many of the staff had their nerves a bit frayed by the physical difficulties of life here and by the difficulties of dealing with the Russian Government, but the men . . . back from holidays seem to have dropped into their places as if this were an entirely normal post."[15] Bohlen, for example, spent a whole day careening through the muddy streets of Moscow in search of coat hangers for the ambassador.[16]

Apparently reluctant to turn to the business at hand, Bullitt asked Kennan to review the *Daily Worker* for the use of propaganda in violation of the recognition treaty. Obviously miffed by this tedious assignment, Kennan responded,

> The whole thing is absolutely unnecessary. . . . The existence of the headquarters of the III International in Moscow is in itself a flat violation of the pledge. We could have protested the day after recognition, or at any time since, on the basis of material in the files of the Department, and could still protest on this basis without any reference to the *Daily Worker*. . . . The point is not whether we have a right to protest but whether it is expedient to do so.[17]

This would remain a principle of doing business in Moscow for Kennan and others, a case of learning on the job and taking everything in stride. Kennan, nevertheless, developed a profile and analysis of the Soviet Communist Party, earning him a well-deserved commendation.[18] Left unsaid was probably Kennan's thought that this was an assignment for that outfit in Riga.

The Riga Outpost

Regarding that "listening post" under the direction of Felix Cole, adjustments had to be made, since it now was connected to a direct Moscow line. After some con

14. Bullitt to Chrysler, 16 July 1934, f. 879.6, vol. 426, USSR 1934, RG 84, NA. Another source claims that the ambassador's car was a Hudson Terraplane roadster. Wiley to Kelley, 18 May 1934, f. Department of State 1933–1934, box 1, Wiley Papers, FRPL. Considering the dates of the reports, the Plymouth probably replaced the impractical roadster.

15. Bullitt to Kelley, 28 August 1934, f. 8, box 3, Kelley Papers, GUA.

16. Bohlen, *Witness to History*, 19.

17. Kennan to Bullitt (confidential), nd., f. 800.13, vol. 421, ibid.

18. Moore to Henderson, 31 July 1936, f. 800-B, vol. 354, USSR 1936, RG 84, NA.

sideration in 1934 of moving the Riga operations to Moscow, both the Moscow embassy and the Riga legation agreed that this service should continue where it was, if for no other reason than the lack of space in Moscow. Wiley added, "Moreover, I very much question whether it would be advisable to have it here, even if we had adequate accommodations. The research section could not function to best advantage in this atmosphere, one lacking every element of cloistered calm. The work would be subject to constant and distracting interruptions and the more people we have here, the more enslaved we become by the chores and tasks of administration."[19] Kennan, Bohlen, and company, short of staff and contending with all the living problems in Moscow, had plenty to keep them busy without having to do translations and analyses for the State Department, but there were problems in separating the jurisdictions and the duplicate purchases of books and periodicals. Kennan asked Cole to provide him with a card index of the Riga library, but Cole demurred, "since that would involve making up several thousand cards."[20]

John Van Antwerp MacMurray, a former foreign services officer, left his post as director of the Page School for International Relations at Johns Hopkins to accept an appointment as minister to the Baltic States in 1933, not long before the recognition agreement was signed. In many ways his job was even more difficult than Bullitt's. Though the legation was centered in Riga, it was responsible for two other quite different countries besides Latvia—Estonia and Lithuania—that necessitated frequent trips to Tallinn and Kaunas and attendance at state functions in all three countries. He later reflected to Herbert Feis, "These three little nations are very new, very self-conscious, very much inclined to carry a chip on the shoulder, and very jealous as to the degree of deference paid to them. . . . They are at the best, a very difficult people to get on terms with."[21] It did not help that they were all aware that much of the activity of the legation involved intelligence research on the Soviet Union. MacMurray also had to devote much time in 1934 to a previously assigned project study of the wheat export market for the State Department.[22]

MacMurray inherited a well-entrenched "nest of vipers," the Russian Section, on the third floor, superintended by Felix Cole, a forty-seven-year-old graduate of Harvard (1910). All things considered, they worked in relative harmony, though

19. Wiley to Kelley, 6 November 1934, f. Correspondence with East European Division, box 1, Wiley Papers, FRPL.
20. Cole to Kennan, 3 June 1936, f. 020, box 1, Riga 1936, Russia Series, RG 84, NA. Kennan described Cole as an amazingly bright but completely disorganized person, whose office was piled with books and papers in apparent total disarray. Interview with Kennan, November 2000.
21. MacMurray to Feis, 10 January 1936, f. 1–7 Jan., box 57, MacMurray Papers, Mudd-P.
22. Ibid.

most dispatches back to the Kelley "Division" in Washington and communications with Moscow passed across his desk. In some ways he was relieved not to be in a backwater but on the mainstream. He also faced a more than usual thinly manned diplomatic post. When the consul in Kaunas had a mental breakdown (an apparently frequent occurrence on the diplomatic frontiers), he asked Cole, next in rank, to drop everything and take over temporarily.[23] And when MacMurray was absent, Cole was in charge of the legation. Riga was also on one of the main routes into Soviet land, so there was a constant stream of American visitors and assorted agents and adventurers going in and coming out through Latvia.

Perhaps the worst ordeal for MacMurray and other members of the staff, however, was dealing with Donald Day, reporter for the *Chicago Tribune* on Russia, who had chosen to set up headquarters in the comfort of Riga rather than in Moscow. He was a pest in more ways than one, descending on the legation at odd times, sneaking up to the third floor to pry out information, and then being extremely critical of Bullitt, MacMurray, and any other Americans who seemed to cross his path.[24] Day was notorious both in Latvia through a number of years but also in the United States for his grossly inaccurate and critical (and largely made up) commentaries on Soviet affairs. Coleman, MacMurray's precedessor, considered him an "untrustworthy, immoral, and a dishonest reporter."[25] And Kelley recalled how Day had tried to bribe him to get secret material in the early 1920s.[26]

The Russian Section itself consisted of Cole, former Moscow businessman John Lehrs, John Perts, William Gwynn (a veteran ARA man), and Edward Page, each responsible for certain types of activities—a total of fourteen personnel, including eight translators.[27] Kelley threatened a reduction in staff in 1934 to increase budget for the new embassy in Moscow, but that was soon rescinded. The Riga consulate, however, was forced to give up its separate building and move into the legation, thus putting an additional squeeze on available space. This was partly resolved by refinishing the attic and moving part of the Russian Section into it.[28]

23. MacMurray to Cole, 22 January 1935, f. 15–24 Jan., box 54, ibid.

24. See, for example, MacMurray to F. W. B. Coleman (his predecessor), 15 January 1935, ibid.

25. Coleman to MacMurray, 31 January 1935, f. 25 Jan.–5 Feb. 1935, box 55, ibid.

26. Kelley to MacMurray, 4 February 1935, ibid.

27. Section list, f. 8–11 Jan. 1936, box 57, MacMurray Papers, Mudd-P. Perts, a Latvian fluent in Russian and English, complained to MacMurray in 1935 about his salary, which had remained constant at $45 a month for thirteen years. To MacMurray, f. 17–35 May 1935, box 56, ibid.

28. Packer memorandum, 24 January 1937, box 6 (124.2-R), Riga 1937 (Russia Section), RFSP, RG 84, NA.

The Embassy in Moscow

Bullitt, expecting to spend most of his time successfully concluding the unfinished business of the recognition agreement, was apparently surprised to face many mundane issues and overtures, now opened up by formal recognition. Champ Pickens, a well-known jack of all athletic trades, wrote to Bullitt, noting the ambassador's interest in baseball, to offer his services in introducing that sport, as well as track and tennis to Russia.[29] Bullitt responded by putting him off, that it would not be possible this year.[30] Pickens would pursue sports exchanges with Russia well into 1937, offering to bring over an all-star cast of American athletes that would include a soccer team and a female athlete, Helen Stephens, a high-school student from Fulton, Missouri, who had taken the United States by surprise by upsetting the premier American woman athlete at the time in the fifty-yard dash.[31]

Bullitt was also not happy about being dragged into trivial pursuits in arranging five concerts in Leningrad and five in Moscow for the Westminster Choir from Princeton University in the fall of 1934, nor even the proposal to bring in the Yale Glee Club from his own alma mater.[32] Nor was he enthusiastic about dealing with Theodore Dreiser's plea for delinquent royalty payments for his books published in Russian.[33] Another distraction was the affair of the Mangean dance troupe, protesting a contract arranged by Alexander Basy that proved highly unsatisfactory, at least from the point of view of the manager, Hazel Speer.[34] After many hours of negotiation, Loy Henderson finally worked out a compromise in regard to recompense for performances. It seemed that anyone who was anybody now wanted to travel to the Soviet Union. Henderson contended, among others, with Frank Lloyd Wright being held up and thoroughly inspected at the Soviet border, where he had papers seized after attending a conference in Moscow.[35]

29. Pickens to Bullitt, 4 May 1934, vol. 423 (840), DPR USSR, ibid. Bullitt had indeed tried unsuccessfully to introduce baseball to the Soviet Union during the summer of 1934. Bohlen, *Witness to History*, 23.

30. Bullitt to Pickens, 24 May 1934, vol. 423 (840), DPR USSR, RG 84, NA.

31. "Miss Walsh Bows in 50-Meter Dash," *New York Times*, 23 March 1935: 22; Davies to Pickens, 10 March 1937, f. 10–12 March 1937, box 4, Davies Papers, MD, LC.

32. Albert Morsini to Bullitt, 12 June 1934, vol. 423 (840.6), DPR, USSR, RG 84, NA.

33. Dreiser to Bullitt, 27 February 1935, vol. 337 (350), ibid.

34. Speer to Henderson, 26 May 1935; and a fourteen-page description of the situation, Henderson to State, 18 June 1935, vol. 435, ibid. The main problem was a complicated arrangement by Basy with a Soviet agency, GOMEZ, the State Combine for Musical, Vaudeville, and Circus Entertainments. Henderson warned that such entertainment groups should come only after being well informed of contracts and conditions.

35. Henderson to Drexel Biddle, 24 June 1937, vol. 381 (811.1), DPR USSR, RG 84, NA.

The embassy was fortunate to have John Wiley—a highly regarded professional diplomat with several years service in Poland, Germany, and Spain—in charge of affairs through the prolonged absences of Bullitt. He had been promoted for a Moscow position by Walter Duranty just after Roosevelt's election.[36] Arriving soon after Bullitt in March 1934, Wiley became his most reliable and experienced assistant. Wiley quickly adjusted to the scene and was relaying valuable information, for example, regarding the mission of Evgeny Rubinov of the foreign commissariat to the United States, recommending that Kelley see him and introduce him to Phillips and Moore. "He has shown a very cooperative spirit and the smooth running of our business with the Foreign Office will depend to a considerable degree on him."[37]

Wiley was also in charge of daily operations, which were a mounting frustration in the early months of the embassy. Transportation came first, but the embassy's order for the first-class Cadillacs went astray, and the embassy had to depend on high-priced rentals of Lincolns from Intourist and trucks from Torgsin, the department store for foreigners. He finally managed to get two Pontiacs and a Chevrolet truck delivered at the end of April. To Kelley, he complained, "We have got a numerous personnel, and during the initial period of establishing the Embassy, one shipment after another arrives; they have to be cleared, delivered, and unpacked. People are running to and fro all day long. The Spaso House and the Savoy Hotel are widely separated. Official calls are endless and distances vast."[38]

As late as the end of June, Wiley noted that the National Hotel, where several embassy personnel were still lodged, was a "robbers' den." Mokhovaya House, an apartment building hastily completed in 1934, was usurped by the large number of American military personnel who spent most of their time monopolizing vehicles and seeing the sights. Anticipating the need for security in Moscow, a sizable guard contingent had been sent, to Wiley's regret. The marines were, he expected, to uphold the highest traditions of the corps. "As I understand it though, these traditions are to grab for themselves everything that is not securely nailed down and not to do very much for others. Nimmer [the Marine attaché] has been looking after his men with great ability. His men have been looking after him with equally great ability and, as far as the embassy is concerned, they

36. Kelley to Wiley, 30 January 1930, f. Department of State 1933–1934, box 1, Wiley Papers, FRPL.
37. Wiley to Kelley, 3 April 1934, f. Correspondence with Division of East European Affairs, 1934–1936, ibid. Evgeny Rubinin, in the Soviet diplomatic corps since 1920, had special responsibility at this time for Western Europe and the United States. A rare survival of the purges that decimated the commissariat, he died in his late eighties in 1981.
38. Wiley to Kelley, 18 May 1934 (private), ibid.

almost might not be here except for the space they take up and the trouble they cause."[39] Nimmer and the American air corps under Lieutenant Henry White turned sour on Russia rather quickly.[40] Neither the Americans nor Soviets lamented their departure. Wiley did not indicate which was worse, Soviet bureaucracy or the plague of marines, but noted that the latter could be corrected by immediate withdrawal. Adding to the strain was a special air corps demonstration crew, complete with the latest military aircraft, occupying quarters intended for embassy personnel.[41]

Wiley was also concerned about the infringement on the proper activities of the embassy by visiting businessmen, who saw new opportunities in a Soviet Russia provided with diplomatic staff. He recommended to Bullitt a limitation on the embassy's service.

> While Russia presents interest, as a field of endeavor, to the great corporations, it is unfortunately the case that it is equally attractive to the fly-by-night type of American promoter. . . . While I consider it entirely fitting and proper, something to be most encouraged, that the Embassy give all proper aid and information to American business men, I think the business of running after them, giving them advice, making appointments for them, escorting them thereto, or acting as interpreters is most dangerous. We might easily get ourselves into a most equivocal and embarrassing situation; in a position where we might be held responsible, when things go awry, and, perhaps, properly blamed by the American interests and Soviet agencies involved; severally and jointly.[42]

He added that he had excellent relations with the most prominent business people and that Henderson had been of great assistance. "In his methodical way, he has managed to produce factual data which has been much appreciated on several occasions. He has never failed to create a dignified, competent and sincere impression."[43]

But there was also some relief. In July Wiley arranged a polo match that included teams of Red Army Cossacks along with the participation of embassy clown Charlie Thayer, who had played on the army team at West Point, with the ambassador as umpire and attended by Litvinov and Commissar of Defense

39. Wiley to Kelley, 29 June 1934, ibid.
40. Wiley to Bullitt, 1 December 1934, box 2, Wiley Papers, FRPL.
41. Ibid. The new American colony in Moscow was not a happy lot, largely of its own making.
42. Wiley to Bullitt, 1 December 1934, box 2, ibid.
43. Ibid.

Voroshilov. Dinner followed at Spaso House, lasting well into the night, with an excellent floorshow in the ballroom with exotic dancers, ballerinas, and gypsy music.[44] Perhaps Soviet-American relations for the 1930s reached its height—or nadir—that night. Spaso House survived, along with Wiley, who continued to provide droll and insightful comments on the scene. Escaping briefly to Leningrad—"After Moscow, Leningrad looks like civilization"—and reflecting on a roundup of homosexuals in August as Stalin's NEP, "New Erotic Policy."[45]

On the more serious matter of the everlasting debt-credit question, Wiley saw two courses of action: (1) drop the whole thing "like a dull thud", or (2) "revise our position and enter into negotiations on a new and altered basis."[46] He already thought there was little chance that the Soviet Union would accept the strict American terms; Wiley sided with the latter and worked out an interest arrangement on credits that would at least go a ways in paying the debt, while noting that the "Soviet economy is becoming progressively more and more independent of the outside world."[47] More important, Wiley kept the State Department informed of affairs in Moscow through personal, unofficial correspondence (as shown earlier), especially with Robert Kelley, an old friend.

On the cultural front, one of the biggest projects that the embassy supported was a proposal to bring a special All Union Soviet ballet troupe, numbering more than a hundred, for a six-week engagement at the Metropolitan Opera in 1935. The Met offered $12,000 a week and all travel expenses, but the Soviets asked for $30,000, while voicing concern that "the girls would be spoiled while in America and would no longer be satisfied with Soviet living and working conditions."[48] This and other similar cases occupied an inordinate amount of the new American embassy's time in Moscow. Another group of twelve African-American performers, headed by New York teacher Adolph Hodge, created a Soviet sensation and a big American embassy headache.[49]

The establishment of an embassy in Moscow certainly increased and inspired more American forays into the land of the Soviets under the partly mistaken belief that it would be more open than ever before. Veteran documentary producer Julien Bryan was back to shoot more film than ever before—10,000 feet—for his typically titled *Russia as It Is Today*, and noted travel chronicler, Richard Halliburton, dropped into the Moscow scene to produce more hyperbole: "Russia! I've

44. Wiley to Kelley, 27 July 1934, ibid.; Bohlen, *Witness to History*, 23–24.
45. To Kelley, 14 and 21 August, box 2, Wiley Papers, FRPL.
46. Wiley to Kelley, 14 August 1934 (Personal and strictly confidential), f. East European Division, box 1, ibid.
47. Ibid.
48. Henderson to State, 28 May 1935, ibid.
49. Henderson to State, 1 August 1936, vol. 363, ibid.

seen Russia, and now I can believe in miracles, for there is no word to describe the picture of Russia today, other than miraculous"; but he added, "I do not mean that the picture is miraculously beautiful. In many ways it is unbelievably ugly."[50] As before, many Americans would have mixed and confused feelings about what they saw.

Most of these American venturers called on the embassy, perhaps just to touch base, but more often to solicit assistance, which the embassy staff did its best to accommodate. In regard to more serious business, the embassy was somewhat in the dark, with personnel necessarily spending much of their time contending with day-to-day realities, traveling around the country to get a feel for the land, and then taking "needed" rests in the West. For example, in early 1937, George Kennan planned to write a report on Soviet antireligious policy but had to take over the work of a colleague who was on vacation; Henderson asked if Riga could do it, but the staff there was already overloaded.[51] Henderson himself, however, spent more than two years on the job in Moscow before taking a vacation in the West.[52]

As a consequence, the expected transfer of the Riga intelligence listening post to Moscow was delayed and finally cancelled as not realistic; it would be much better for it to remain on "free" soil. Fortunately, the Riga staff was adept and innovative, seeking out various avenues of approach to Soviet sources, now assisted by a resident Moscow contingent with a regular courier service between Moscow and Riga. One example is a report of more than 600 pages on the Seventh Comintern Congress held in late 1935.[53] Some found fault with too much occupation with trivia and information that could be found much earlier in the pages of daily newspapers.

The new Moscow post certainly had some advantages in collecting information for Riga and Washington. A special resource on Soviet internal conditions was Dr. Hans Schiller, the agricultural attaché of the German embassy, who spent much of his time roaming through the Soviet countryside and establishing contacts with descendants of German settlers on the Volga and around the Black Sea. He was quite free and open to share his findings with the American newcomers.[54] He presided over handsome, if not lavish, quarters in Moscow (when

50. Halliburton, "Russia—Yea and Nay," 22 December 1934, box 21, Stine Papers, HHPL; flyer for Bryan film, d. 805, op. 3, f. 5283, GARF.

51. Henderson to Packer, 24 February 1937, box 7 (802), Riga 1937 (Russia Series), RFSP, RG 84, NA.

52. Henderson to Gwynn, 28 February 1936, box 4 (804.44), Riga 1936, ibid.

53. MacMurray to Hull, 10 January 1936, box 3 (800-R), Riga 1936, ibid.

54. Schiller was no stranger to American experts on Russia, since he had published several long articles on collectivization that were translated by the Department of Commerce. Ropes to Harper, 19 May 1933, f. 8, box 18, Harper Papers, UC-R.

he was there).[55] Because of his many contacts and unique expertise on Russia, beginning with the direction of an agricultural colony sponsored by Krupp in the 1920s—and the developing tensions with Berlin—he was expelled by the Soviet government in 1936, because of his intimate knowledge of internal conditions.[56] Another reliable source on Soviet agriculture was Louis G. Michael, who had been studying Russian grain production since 1910 and was now serving as American agricultural attaché in Belgrade with most of Eastern Europe under his jurisdiction.[57] Materials provided by Schiller, Michael, and other sources were included in a detailed Riga report on Soviet wheat exports that showed a high point of sales abroad in 1930 (nearly 700 million metric tons), falling off to around 150 million in 1931, 1932, and 1933 and to only 11 million in 1934, then back up to 125 million tons in 1935.[58] The data prove that grain exports were vital in paying for the import of technology and especially American engineering for Five Year Plan projects and that substantial shipments continued during the height of the famine until 1934, when little more could be found in the countryside.

Credits and Loans

Meanwhile, Bullitt became increasingly exasperated with the failure of Litvinov and other Soviet officials to come through with promises to negotiate realistically on the debt/credit issue. Impatience, in fact, was Bullitt's greatest weakness. This had clearly become the major disappointment in the new relationship. In Moscow, where it was expected that the details would be resolved, Litvinov proved to be recalcitrant, elusive, and busy with other affairs. To Bullitt's chagrin, the negotiations passed to Washington where Troyanovsky seemed initially to be more flexible. In conversation with the ambassador on 26 March 1934, Hull expressed the American disappointment.

55. Henderson to State, 8 October 1935, vol. 436 (848), ibid., and interview with Heinrich Stammler, December 2004, Lawrence, Kansas, who lived in the Schiller house, while serving as a junior attaché in the German embassy in 1934. The National Socialist government program reached out to any Germans outside the Third Reich, especially the Volga Germans in the middle of the Soviet state. A center in Stuttgart maintained contacts and published much information on "brethren" Aryans in the Russian heartland.

56. Henderson to State, 31 December 1936, vol. 352 (310), ibid.

57. Saul, *Concord and Conflict: The United States and Russia, 1867–1914* (Lawrence: University Press of Kansas, 1996), 553.

58. MacMurray to Hull, 8 January 1936, box 5 (861.31-R), Riga 1936–1937, RFSP, RG 84, NA. Figures that included rye, barley, and other grains were just over one billion tons in 1930, just under 500 million in 1931, 240 million in 1932, almost 300 million in 1933, 67 million in 1934, and 263 million in 1935. Ibid.

I stated to the ambassador that I must be entirely frank and say that the President, Mr. Bullitt, Assistant Secretary Moore, and others who participated in the Russian debt conversations with Mr. Litvinoff when he was here during last November, were greatly surprised and keenly disappointed to learn that Mr. Litvinoff offered a contention and a version of the debt understanding, entered into at the time of his visit here, entirely different from anything the American officials thought they were discussing and entirely different from anything they were thinking about.[59]

Three weeks later, after consulting with Moscow, the Soviet ambassador claimed that Litvinov's understanding with the president was that the debt was $75 million, but if that was a problem it could be raised to $150 million.[60] Troyanovsky added that Litvinov was "very much disturbed" about American allegations that he had changed his position. The State Department typically took a hard line, Litvinov and Troyanovsky were at odds, and Bullitt was imprisoned in Moscow's Spaso House, licking his wounds and planning an escape.[61] Although American officials (Department of State) thought Litvinov had reneged on his agreement, the Soviet side was disappointed that the credit possibilities were considerably reduced by the restrictions placed on the Export-Import Bank, which was created to handle the transactions.

The central problem remaining was to agree on a formula concerning the amount of the debt owed, the conditions of the loan, and the interest to be paid. Both sides understood that, to avoid obligations to other claimants on debts, the Soviet Union would obtain long-term loans through a special American government Export-Import Bank with an "added on" interest, which would eventually repay the debt over a period of years. This subterfuge did not sit well with either side, nor especially with Congress, resulting in eventual failure. Another problem was that the "bank," looking for something to do, was trying to supervise, that is, regulate, the operations of Amtorg, a Soviet but technically private business operation. Negotiations on the debt/loan continued through 1934 with various compromises involving the amount of the debt, the percentage of interest, and the issuance of credits, all fluctuating in both Moscow and Washington but to the satisfaction of none.[62] The State Department and Bullitt were at odds, and so

---

59. Hull memorandum of conversation, 26 March 1934, reel 32, Hull Papers, MD, LC.
60. Hull memorandum of conversation, 16 April 1934, ibid.
61. For the full story, see Cassella-Blackburn, *The Donkey, the Carrot, and the Club*, 129–40.
62. For an excellent, detailed analysis of the Export-Import Bank, see Frederick C. Adams, *Economic Diplomacy: The Export-Import Bank and American Foreign Policy, 1934–1939* (Columbia: University of Missouri Press, 1976). The bank did serve a function in development loans to Latin America, Hull's primary concern.

were Litvinov and Troyanovsky, both of whom, along with Bullitt, were hoping to score a victory. If Bullitt and Troyanovsky could have met in mid-Atlantic, would something have been resolved? No chance. Any more moderate Soviet position depended on Litvinov and Stalin, and Litvinov was increasingly occupied with the European political scene. And Stalin obviously had other things on his agenda.

Meanwhile, Bullitt took solace in a long return home in October 1934 on the Trans-Siberian Railroad and across the Pacific.[63] The American State Department, still trying to stem its thoroughly broached dike of nonrecognition, wanted debts paid first and before any credit consideration. There it rested, with the Soviet side becoming less desperate for the credits, while the debt issue waned on the American side. To escape further fruitless negotiations Troyanovsky also took long trips and reported to Hull about his journey through the Far East and the coolness he found in Japan because of his appointment to the United States. The ambassador generally avoided any discussion of the debt issue.[64] Krestinsky, commissar for foreign trade, advised Troyanovsky in July 1935 that he considered the discussion at an impasse.[65] As if he had not already reached that conclusion.

Litvinov, having scored a triumph in Washington, moved on to a bigger, more challenging game, making speeches in the League of Nations, proposing the creation of a special disarmament organization in Geneva, and, above all, pursuing a French alliance, the linchpin of his collective security strategy to rally opposition to the reconstituted German menace under Adolf Hitler's leadership that had already emerged in early 1933. In the meantime, John Wiley, Loy Henderson, and others of the Moscow staff negotiated fruitlessly with Litvinov's subordinates about trade agreements, the unresolved debt problem, which everyone was becoming sick of, and mundane local problems. Meanwhile, Henderson cultivated Ambassador von Schulenberg at the German embassy, considering him the best informed of diplomatic representatives on Russian affairs.[66] By the end of 1936, with the Spanish civil war occupying much Soviet attention, Henderson found Litvinov ill at ease and with a considerable loss of confidence.[67] The purges and public trials were reducing contacts and trust on both sides. In the meantime,

63. George Kennan described Bullitt as "charming, brilliant, well-educated, imaginative, a man of the world capable of holding his own intellectually with anyone, including such great intellects of the Communist movement as Radek and Bukharin, . . . His greatest weakness as a diplomatist (and it was the natural counterpart of his virtues) was impatience." *Memoirs*, 79.

64. Hull Memorandum, 28 January 1935, f. Russia, reel 32, Hull Papers, MD, LC.

65. G. N. Sevostianov, *Moskva-Vashington: Diplomaticheskie otnosheniia* (Moscow: Nauka, 2002), 97. Bullitt to Wiley, 19 October 1934, f. Davies, box 2, Wiley Papers, FRPL.

66. Henderson memo on interview with von Schulenberg, 19 November 1936, f. 310, vol. 352, USSR 1936, RG 84, NA.

67. Henderson memo, 30 December 1936, ibid.

Soviet-American relations shifted to a side track, although the soviet commissar of food, Anastas Mikoyan, after a tour of the states in 1936, announced to Hull that he was pleased with the hospitality, which was "much more agreeable" than in Europe.[68]

Back in Washington

Though it is still not perfectly clear, the Soviet side preferred to negotiate the outstanding differences in Washington and sent a special emissary in April 1934 to clear some of the hurdles. Exactly what Evgeny Rubinin's mission was all about is not clear (at least Hull among others was perplexed); he was duly, though not enthusiastically, received by the State Department as an official guest representing the Soviet government. Kelley remarked, "He struck me as a very intelligent person and appeared to be very sympathetically inclined towards the United States."[69] Rubinin, whom no one in Washington had ever heard of before, was introduced to the officials at the State Department, as well as the president, and his hosts even gave him a special tour of Mount Vernon and Alexandria. Nothing seemed to result, though Bullitt was heartened by a conversation with Rubinin, upon his return to Moscow, and with Krestinsky, the foreign commissariat's expert on trade: "Krestinsky talked more like a human being than either he or Litvinov has up to date."[70]

During Bullitt's absence in 1935, however, Wiley found Rubinin increasingly difficult to deal with on the debt/credit issue.

> The difficulties inherent in conducting affairs with the Narkomindel [commissariat of foreign affairs] are fantastic. For example; every conversation with Rubinin leads to an *impasse*; to a point where one would like to ask whether he is being downright cynical or just plain stupid. He talks to us in the tones of "Dr. Pangloss", the philosopher in "Candide", and there doesn't seem to be anything that one can do about it.[71]

Litvinov was busy pursuing collective security in Europe and apparently delegated the United States to Rubinin.

---

68. Hull memo, 12 October 1936, f. Russia, reel 32, Hull Papers, MD, LC.

69. Kelley to Wiley, 1 May 1934, f. East European Division, box 1, Wiley Papers, FRPL. See also, "Soviet Debt Move Hinted in Capital," *New York Times*, 28 April 1934: 7.

70. Bullitt to Kelley, 28 August 1934, f. 8, box 3, Kelley Papers, GUA.

71. Wiley to Kelley, 16 March 1935, f. Correspondence, box 1, Wiley Papers, FRPL.

Third-party locations seemed to promise more progress than Moscow or Washington. Hugh Wilson, U.S. ambassador to Germany, dined privately with Litvinov, by the latter's invitation, in Geneva on 20 November 1934; Litvinov seemed to have more important things on his mind than matters of debt and credit. He began by emphasizing the continuing threat of Japanese aggression in the east, despite the Soviet sale of the Chinese Eastern Railroad. His foremost objective was obtaining American support for a permanent peace organization, noting the weakness of the Kellogg-Briand Pact and the League of Nations, of which the United States was not a member but clearly conscious of. Above all, he made yet another plea for collective security against Germany. "Throughout the conversation Litvinov displayed the most complete distrust of Germany. To him, so long as there is a Hitler regime, just so long is Germany a mad dog that can't be trusted, with whom no agreements can be made, and whose ambition can only be checked by a ring of determined neighbors."[72]

The issues of debt and credit would not die nor easily fade away. Bullitt was clearly incensed with both Litvinov and Troyanovsky for lack of progress in early 1935, while on leave in Washington. Both Bullitt and Troyanovsky seemed to spend little time at their posts. After extended delays, Troyanovsky returned from Moscow in December 1934 the long way via Japan and Hawaii. Wiley thought that this route was ordered by the Kremlin to check on the state of Soviet-Japanese relations in the wake of the recognition agreement.[73] Bullitt complained, "We are still waiting for Troyanovsky and he is making it more obvious than ever that he is not anxious to come to Washington and fling a flat refusal at the Secretary of State." Suffering from illness and exhaustion, Bullitt was reluctant to return to Russia in 1935. He added, "The good will that has been built up for the Soviets in this country in the past three or four years has been demolished by the failure of trade to materialize and the number of shootings growing out of the Kirov murder."[74]

Indeed, the assassination of Sergei Kirov, generally regarded as number two to Stalin in the Soviet hierarchy, in December 1934, and the executions without formal trial of those accused of being involved had a major effect on Soviet-American relations. Bullitt reported to Wiley in Moscow,

> The executions have produced a really astonishing effect in this country. I have met not one American since I have been here who has a good word

72. Wilson to Norman Davis (head of American delegation to General Disarmament Conference), 21 November 1934, f. Norman Davis, box 1, Wilson Papers, HHPL.

73. Wiley to Bullitt, 26 November 1934, box 2, Wiley Papers, FRPL.

74. Bullitt to Wiley, 21 January 1935, ibid.

for the Soviet Union, even the enthusiasts for recognition to whom I have talked have all come to me wagging their heads and saying that if the question of recognition were to come up now, it unquestionably would be disapproved by the entire nation. The feeling against tyranny and summary executions remains, thank God, very strong in this country. Litvinov probably doesn't know it but a snotty policy towards us now would be resented by this country much more violently than at any time since recognition.[75]

After long delay awaiting the return of the Soviet ambassador, on 31 January 1935, Hull initiated a discussion with Troyanovsky, with Moore, Kelley, and Bullitt attending. The secretary proposed a much reduced debt recognition and payment over a longer period but that any credits extended would be under control of the Export-Import Bank. He was quite disappointed that the Soviet ambassador flatly turned it down. "In view of the present attitude of the Soviet Government, I feel that we cannot encourage the hope that any agreement is now possible. . . . There seems to be scarcely any reason to doubt that the negotiation which seemed so promising at the start must now be regarded as having come to an end."[76] Bullitt had guessed correctly that the conversation would be brief and obstructive.[77] From Moscow, Litvinov quickly responded that the problem was the failure of a "promise" of an unrestricted loan.[78] He was certainly not happy that the United States cancelled plans for opening a consul general office and scaled back considerably the personnel of the embassy to one of the smallest in Europe, over the protests of Bullitt and Wiley.[79]

In the Shadow of the Kremlin

In the Moscow embassy, John Wiley, second in command to Bullitt, whose leave was extended by a streptococcus infection, met with Litvinov on 5 February 1935 and found him calm and without concern over the impasse on the debt issue. The commissar thought it was best to "put it on ice" for awhile and referred, vaguely, to political changes that might affect the situation, referring to his long-sought alliance with France, which he was about to conclude.[80] Wiley reacted quickly with a thoughtful appraisal of the factors obstructing settlement: an Eastern or

---

75. Bullitt to Wiley, 7 January 1935, ibid.
76. Hull press announcement, 31 January 1935, vol. 436 (851), RG 84, NA.
77. Bullitt to Wiley, 21 January 1935, box 2, Wiley Papers, FRPL.
78. Wiley (Moscow) to Hull, 3 February 1935, ibid.
79. Wiley to Kelley, 2 April 1935, f. DEEA, box 1, ibid.
80. Wiley to Hull, 6 February 1935, ibid.

Asiatic mentality in respect to finances; caution in respect to foreign commitments; reluctance to recognize obligations from a previous Russian government; fear of reviving old claims by other governments; and resistance to any country gaining favor by a monopoly privilege. He noted that Litvinov seemed to emphasize the importance of the first and last. Wiley also sensed that the foreign commissar was under fire for having promised too much in Washington.[81]

On the same date, Wiley wrote privately to Bullitt, voicing his opinion that Litvinov's coolness was mostly for show in reaction to the breaking off of negotiations on credit arrangements.

> As for Litvinov's *sang-froid* over our drastic decision, I suppose it is window dressing rather than a manifestation of indifference genuinely felt. Credit terms elsewhere will stiffen; opponents of rapprochement in France will derive encouragement and, last but not least, the voice of conciliation in Japan may become squeaky rather than more persuasive.
>
> Our only hope is either to modify our position, which seems most unlikely and inadvisable, or to dig our toes in and regard developments with philosophical detachment.[82]

He added, "The recent and sudden death of two members of the Politburo, Kirov and Kuibyshev, has undoubtedly altered things considerably." He thought the result was to bring Stalin and Voroshilov closer together.[83]

As if the American embassy did not have enough to contend with on the Moscow scene, Harper appeared in late 1934 and left quite critical of its operation, as Wiley thought, "perhaps having a drop too many." He reported to Kelley, "though he had kind words to say of Loy and me, he damned everybody else individually and collectively. He also took quite a crack at you and thought that you had made a fatal mistake 'in view of the Soviet attitude towards you' in not extending your recent trip as far as Moscow in order to appease matters."[84] Wiley was especially annoyed with Harper, since he had gone out of his way to entertain him, inviting him as a guest with Troyanovsky, and that he had accused embassy personnel of "drinking a great deal." "This is an outstanding example of the pot calling the kettle black. While there is a good deal of drinking in Moscow, the staff on the whole handles itself extremely well."[85]

---

81. Ibid.; Wiley to Bullitt, 31 January 1935, box 2, ibid.
82. Wiley to Bullitt, 6 February 1935, ibid.
83. Ibid.
84. Wiley to Kelley, 19 January 1935, ibid.
85. Ibid.

Bullitt was even more incensed by Samuel Harper's sharp criticism of the American mission in Moscow during his October 1934 visit, which he had deposited at the State Department in early January. Harper claimed that embassy personnel, including Wiley, were alcoholic, carousing at the Metropole Hotel, and "pawing" women. For Bullitt the worst Harper charge was that he had abandoned Ivy Litvinov at dinner in order to turn over his wine cellar to girls from the Bolshoi Ballet. He was puzzled about these charges, until Kelley informed him that Harper had borne a grudge against Bullitt since that venture to Russia in 1919.[86] More likely, it was caused by Harper being passed over for the ambassadorial appointment or for a position as adviser in Moscow similar to the one he had held with Francis in 1917.

Meanwhile, a quite sober Wiley thought that the Russian concern about outside threats was genuine. "As near as I can make out, the fear of foreign attack in the Soviet Union is not simulated but is genuine, I doubt very much whether Soviet anxiety has been chiefly centered in the Far East for the last year or two. The 'bogey man' is Aryan, not Asiatic."[87] He also detected a rift between Litvinov and Troyanovsky: "without doubt, he and Litvinov impacted like stags in rut."[88] This and the fact that the big leaders were all away delayed Troyanovsky's return to Washington. Wiley also thought that those in the Kremlin questioned Litvinov's Western policy as a "reckless burning of all bridges between the Red Army and the Reichswehr and to letting himself be taken bag and baggage into the French camp."[89]

In the interim, social graces were not avoided. Wiley and his wife spent a pleasant weekend cross-country skiing at the Litvinov dacha outside Moscow in February 1935. He felt, however, a strain, that it was a pro forma invitation. Walter Duranty's interview with Litvinov on 16 February 1935 elicited the comment that Bullitt harbored an anti-Russian prejudice from his Polish wife, to which Duranty responded that Litvinov must be biased toward Britain because of his British wife. Litvinov was miffed and expressed anger and disappointment in the American positions on debt and credit, flatly saying that Roosevelt had betrayed

---

86. Bullitt to Wiley, 7 January 1935, box 2, Wiley Papers, FRPL. There was probably some truth to Harper's allegations. Bohlen reported that "there were usually two or three ballerinas running around the Embassy." Bohlen, *Witness to History*, 20.

87. Wiley to Kelley, 18 January 1935, ibid.

88. Wiley to Bullitt, 26 November 1934, ibid. Wiley added, "As to Troyanovsky, I think he is very pleased with himself, patting himself on the back for having been able to extract really important concessions from the American Government. . . . From having observed Troyanovsky at length, I have gained the impression that he is a very independent *Tovarish* who knows his way through the intricacies of the Party hierarchy and is a person with whom one should reckon."

89. Ibid.

him. Duranty requested permission to publish this, which the commissar refused, but he went ahead anyway, and it was passed by the censors.[90]

In the meantime, upon his return to Moscow, Bullitt consoled himself with entertaining the high and low of the Soviet regime, who probably also found solace in Spaso House and its abundant buffets, a Western oasis in the middle of Moscow. Bukharin and Radek were regular visitors to Spaso House in 1935—not wise perhaps for their futures.[91] Among the topics of conversation was fishing, an avid hobby of Robert Kelley, who was planning a trip to Russia "to see for himself." Bullitt reported, "If you are still intent on trout fishing, Bukharin tells me that any season is good in the Caucasus but that the streams are relatively small so that a little casting rod rather than a large one is desirable."[92] One might wish, for the sake of a story, that Stalin had chimed in to recommend a certain stream in Georgia. It is clear, however, that American resident diplomats and visitors fished and hunted regularly in the Soviet hinterland for more than political game, probably with no better success.

Meanwhile, Wiley, perhaps losing his patience, as had Bullitt, reported to the ambassador that the 1935 Comintern Congress in August was "clearly a breach of the pledges given by Litvinov to the President" regarding propaganda activities on behalf of Communist subversion.[93] This evoked a formal protest by Bullitt to an absent Litvinov, which in turn elicited a quick response from Krestinsky that the Comintern was totally independent from the Soviet government. Bullitt was clearly becoming disillusioned with the scene and convinced that the Soviet leaders put world revolution and the advancement of the Comintern crusade in first place, a turnaround from his position in 1933. In contrast, his staff, especially Kennan, Bohlen, and Henderson, leaned toward viewing the foremost Soviet objectives as state security. Faymonville and the new ambassador, Joseph Davies, were even more inclined in this direction.[94] This was not so much a contradiction as an assessment of current priorities in reaction to the aggressive postures of Germany and Japan.

90. Wiley to Bullitt, 21 February 1935, ibid.

91. Bullitt to Armstrong, 27 April 1935, box 13, Armstrong Papers, Mudd-P. One embarrassment was that the embassy's chief manager, Stewart, was caught with 1,262 pairs of stockings and 19 watches to sell on the underground economy. After intervention by Wiley, he was allowed to leave the country, after paying a heavy fine. Wiley to Hull, 16 March 1935, f. 350, vol. 431 (1935), RG 84, NA.

92. Bullitt to Kelley, 8 June 1935, f. 8, box 3, Kelley Papers, GUA.

93. Wiley to Bullitt, 20 August 1935; Bullitt to Litvinov, 25 August 1935; and Krestinsky to Bullitt, 27 August 1935, f. 800, vol. 433 (1935), RG 84, NA. Bullitt had been especially incensed by Earl Browder's fiery speech at the opening of the 1935 Comintern congress. Bullitt to Hull, 29 July 1935, ibid.

94. For an excellent appraisal, see Thomas R. Maddux, *Years of Estrangement: American Relations with the Soviet Union, 1933–1941* (Tallahassee: University Presses of Florida, 1980), 46–51.

One of the most successful of the American contingent in Moscow in terms of engagement with the Soviet world was military attaché Major Phillip Faymonville, who had previous experience in Russia while serving with the American Expeditionary Force in Siberia in 1918–1920 and had visited the country in 1927. Fluent in Russian, he went out of his way to cultivate contacts in the Soviet military and was met with surprising openness and cooperation. Though living with the Kennans and others in the American compound, he established his own agenda and operated very much independent of the embassy, filing many but brief reports to army intelligence in Washington. Faymonville was also frequently called upon by the Soviet authorities to mediate problems with American businessmen.[95] Wiley, among others in the diplomat section, constantly complained about the military personnel. He did not understand "why Faymonville and company ride on the State department running board," while "we see nothing they report."[96]

Another problem was the health of George Kennan, the workhorse of the embassy. Wiley thought he should have a long leave in Washington—but on second thought, considering the expense and his low salary, he should be allowed special leave in Vienna. He feared that Kennan's life would be considerably shortened by the stress and strain that he had to endure in Moscow.[97] The American embassy could not spare many, since it stood at the low end of personnel in Europe: London 108, Paris 90, Warsaw 78, Berlin 70, Moscow 58.[98]

Business as Usual?

With essentially a hiatus existing in 1935 regarding the unfinished important business, the embassy was forced to turn its attention to the routine, in other words, become a normal diplomatic agency in a foreign country, concerned mainly with visitor problems, traveling American entertainments—such as the Mangean troupe—and individuals of all sorts who wandered in or felt stranded in an extremely foreign milieu. Many of these instances were passed down through channels, typically from a family member to a senator to the State Department to the Moscow embassy. There were quite a number of them, owing to the shakeout of émigrés, refugees, escapees, and so forth, that swarmed over Europe, Asia, and the United States from the former Russian empire. The largest number involved

95. Kubliako conversation with Donald Stephens, d. 810, op. 3, f. 5283, GARF.
96. Wiley to Kelley, 27 November 1934, f. Correspondence, box 1, Wiley Papers, FRPL.
97. Wiley to Bullitt, 7 February 1935, box 2, Wiley Papers, FRPL. Kennan would still be quite active and productive seventy years later, outliving everyone associated with the Soviet or American government in the 1930s.
98. Kelley to Carr, 23 February 1937, f. 5, box 3, GU. He was pleading for more appointments to Moscow.

the leftover American workers and engineers on construction projects and other enterprises.

The Hazel Mangean Four, and the Alexander Basy affair connected to it, continued to plague the embassy, thanks to the shaky but persistent direction of Basy, who was simply trying to seize an opportunity to benefit financially from the popularity of American acts in Russia. He was also the agent for the Cleveland Orpheus Choir that performed at the Conservatory Hall in Moscow on 20 September 1935.[99] Basy came over to try to straighten out affairs, pester the embassy about his problems, and create more of them by his ambitious promises to Soviet organizations.[100]

These tensions and obligations were relieved by cultural and social events and, especially, by staff member Charles Thayer, "the clown of the embassy," who provided a hilarious account of his experiences during a visit to the State Horse Farm near Tula, the former estate of Obolensky-Shakhovsky. This was no small enterprise, accommodating more than 650 superior Orlov trotters.[101] Unofficial American contacts with the Soviet Union were unfortunately largely reduced to such matters, though Bullitt, understandably, developed a special interest in supporting a projected visit by the Tuskegee Institute choir, whose purpose was "to interpret to the world the achievements and aspirations of the American Negro and to promote the interests of good-will between the races of mankind."[102]

VOKS continued to superintend these American cultural excursions into Sovietland but no longer occupied front and center. The agency, headed by Olga Kameneva through most of the 1920s, was now directed by Aleksandr Arosov, an experienced diplomat, from 1934 until his arrest in 1938. His assistant, Ilia Amdur, maintained regular contacts with the American Russian institutes in the United States, but they were no longer as active as before recognition. One problem was long delays in getting Soviet publications, with requests four months overdue in 1936.[103] Another consequence was the high number of arrests within this organization in connection with the purges.

Falling by the wayside in the debt negotiations were numerous small claims, which may indeed have contributed to its failure. Veteran State Department official Frank Polk regretted the inability to provide for a variety of genuine small claims for seizures of property: "What I am really concerned about . . . is the posi-

99. Wiley to Hull, 13 April 1935, f. 840.6, vol. 435, RG 84, NA.

100. Ibid.

101. Henderson to Hull, 25 September 1936, f. 861, vol. 368, RG 84, NA.

102. Bullitt to Arosov (VOKS), 12 June 1934, d. 518, op. 3, f. 5283, GARF. Arosov responded by assuring him that he was doing everything possible to prepare for their arrival, 12 June 1934, ibid.

103. Consul General Zhan (John, Ivan, or Jean) Arens (or Ahrens) to Cherniavskii (Arosov's assistant), 21 May 1936, Sovetsko-amerikanskie otnosheniia, 1934–1939 (2003), 448–49.

tion of numerous smaller claimants and the damage done to the sanctity of private property in international law, which it is one of the interests of this country to uphold."[104] Of course, this is exactly what Litvinov did not want to contend with—an endless array of petty claims, many based on dubious past business involvements and upon an opening for recompense with recognition—and Polk must have known that.

Though regular business contacts were much reduced from the period before recognition and on a much lower profile, they were still evident. International Business Machines, for example, was doing quite well with sales in Russia. The longtime consultant for American businesses, Charles H. Smith, was still in action, now finding it easier to negotiate visas, such as one in 1937 for mining engineer Norman Chambers, who was negotiating for the sale of oil-drilling equipment.[105] Similar to Smith was Albert Johnson, who had been involved with the ARA relief in the early 1920s and who also served as an adviser to American companies but was considered a nuisance by the embassy, despite having rendered assistance in getting it established. The Soviet government, as well as the embassy, wanted to be rid of him.[106] Many Americans who had come to Russia in the early 1930s during the Depression and now wanted to go home kept the embassy staff busy.

In February 1937 a detailed report on Americans resident in Russia was filed. It recorded 555 native American citizens and 249 additional naturalized and 48 children. Fifty had Soviet wives, 27 had Soviet husbands, and 26 were African-Americans. Soviet organizations employed 475. Of 872 individuals listed, 92 were students and 34 were teachers. One of the students was John Hazard, future professor of Soviet government at Columbia University, and included were resident journalists, such as Louis Fischer and Harold Denny, and the embassy staff.[107] Obviously, quite a few were missed in the count.

Spies

Intelligence agents, or rather gatherers, were active on both sides. Obviously, with so many Americans in the Soviet Union as workers, engineers, diplomats, and tourists, plenty of opportunities existed for collecting information on the inner workings of the country. Soviet authorities were quite forthcoming with their own data and views, at least until the height of the purges. The problem

104. Polk to FDR, 1 November 1935, POF 220, FRPL.
105. Smith to embassy, 20 May 1937, f. 811.1, vol. 380, USSR 1937, RG 84, NA.
106. Davies to Hull, 15 July 1937, and Elbridge Dubrow memorandum, 15 July 1937, ibid.
107. A. I. Ward to Hull, 11 February 1937, vol. 371, DPR USSR 1937, ibid.

was separating actuality from propaganda. Few of the Americans could be labeled "spies" who were assigned specific targets, perhaps the only exception being the military attachés, such as Faymonville, but that was their recognized job. The result of the openness of the Soviet territory and the curiosity of Americans about that region resulted in a deluge of information and views, quite a bit of it published in article or book form, or left in unsolicited conversations or reports with government officials at various posts abroad or in Washington. The Riga listening post was the more systematic collector of such information through analysis of the Soviet press and debriefing of travelers. It apparently did not "run" agents, at least not on a regular basis, into Russia, simply because it had more than it could digest in over-the-counter materials. The main problem was that Americans and other foreigners could be suspect saboteurs and spies, especially because so many Soviet citizens were also under suspicion by the large network of NKVD agents in the country.

The situation of Soviet agents in the United States was different because of the much greater availability of information unclouded by intentional falsification. The problem, not unlike that of Americans trying to decipher the Soviet reality, was the overwhelming amount of it and the Soviet handicap in seeing the United States through an ideological prism. Clearly, however, the Soviet quest for sensitive information had a distinct advantage in established state agencies of its own or under the oversight of the Comintern: Amtorg, Intourist, the Communist Party of the United States. Quite a number of separate official missions appeared in the United States to gather information about industries, agriculture, and so forth, quite openly and generally with little restriction, to the consternation of a relatively feeble FBI.

Of course, a different and more serious dimension of Soviet intelligence activities in the United States existed, partly because of the latent but still active faith of many Americans in Communist world revolution, with the United States as a prime target, and also because of the presence of many real sympathizers with that cause and the Soviet experiment in general. As we now know, underground intelligence rings focused on gathering and relaying strategic information and infiltrating American government and private organizations with future opportunities in mind. As early as 1927, the FBI had under surveillance the dentist office of Dr. Philip Rosenbliett at 88 West 119th Street in New York, where military agents—Albert Winter, Peter Lawson, and B. N. Volynsky—were collecting information on Liberty aircraft engines, among other things.[108] This ring was ini-

---

108. J. Edgar Hoover to Robert Kelley, DEEA, 19 August 1927, roll 164 (861.796/33), M316, RG 59, NA. Rosenbliett is perhaps best known for recruiting one of the most notorious Soviet agents in the United States, Whittaker Chambers.

tially directed by Felix Wolf (Nikolai Krebs) of Soviet military intelligence under an Amtorg cover.[109] Other active Soviet intelligence centers in the 1930s were directed by Jacob Golos (connected with Intourist), along with his lover Elizabeth Bentley (who later worked in the Pentagon), Gaik Ovakimian (Amtorg), and Harry Gold.[110] The value of information relayed from these sources remains debatable. At least, they managed to frustrate and alarm the FBI and the congressional Dies Committee.

New developments in the early 1930s revived the idea of a Communist menace to many Americans, especially those in that government agency headed by J. Edgar Hoover. First was the disillusionment of many young, educated, and unemployed with the failures of the capitalist system in the Depression era, who saw the Soviet industrial and social progress in reality and as a mirage, as a possible alternative. Second was the accompanying Popular Front policy of the Comintern that turned the Communist Party activities into a milder-seeming socialist program with various quasi-Communist organizations that attracted youth and the disenchanted world-wide. By blurring the perceptions of who was and was not Communist, the Popular Front to some represented a "Trojan Horse," undermining the already economically and politically threatened institutions of the liberal West from the Left and the Right. By 1936 and the failure of the Litvinov program of Collective Security, however, the distinctions were made clearer, at least in political rhetoric as an opposition to totalitarianism, loosely defined. Many of the "fellow travelers" on the socialist path sought another road.

Among the correspondents and diplomats in Moscow, spying and bugging were regular topics of conversation. The American embassy was routinely collecting information on the Soviet scene through various channels, many unofficial, but most rather ordinary. In a conversation on the subject with Albert Rhys Williams in the embassy in 1937, Joseph Barnes of the *Herald Tribune*, to make a point, accused all embassy personnel of spying in the hearing of a nearby clerk, who then replied "that I did not do anything which I could not do just as well in Washington or in Kansas if it were possible to receive the daily Soviet newspapers there."[111] From a cursory review of the immense records of the CPUSA, the only conclusion is that little Soviet money came into the United States on behalf of

109. Raymond W. Leonard, *Secret Soldiers of the Revolution: Soviet Military Intelligence, 1918–1933* (Westport, Conn.: Greenwood Press, 1999), 109.

110. Katherine A. S. Sibley, *Red Spies in America: Stolen Secrets and the Dawn of the Cold War* (Lawrence: University Press of Kansas, 2004), 72–77. Because of the recent and very thorough studies of the subject by Leonard and Sibley, and another in press by Vladimir Pozniakov, this work contains only a brief summary of matters of intelligence.

111. Billings memorandum, 10 December 1937, vol. 384 (820.02), DPR USSR 1937, RG 84, NA.

world revolution. One clear piece of evidence is funds that came through the Hammers and other sympathizers to support publications in the United States, especially International Publishers in New York that began as early as 1920. One of its major publications was the *Collected Works of V. I. Lenin* in English, a massive undertaking with volume 18 on "the imperialist war" appearing only in 1930, edited by Alexander Trachtenberg, a respected New York socialist.

Mission to Moscow

William Bullitt, once a leading catalyst of recognition but now disillusioned and dejected, pulled out of the Moscow scene, resigning in the summer of 1936 to be compensated with a more congenial post as ambassador to France. The Moscow post was then offered to George Messersmith, a career foreign service officer, but he declined. FDR then turned to Joseph Davies, a prominent Wisconsin lawyer married to a wealthy businesswoman and art collector, Marjorie Meriwether Post, who, having inherited the Post cereal fortune, pioneered frozen foods (Birdseye) and amassed a professionally selected and valuable collection of art, emphasizing French and Russian paintings, porcelain, and other objects for her Hillwood estate in Washington specially designed to house her collections for public and private view.[112]

Davies, in contrast to Bullitt, had virtually no prior knowledge of Russia and was quite surprised to receive an invitation to lunch at the White House in August 1936.[113] After even more than the usual preparation delays, Davies was confirmed as the second ambassador to the Soviet Union in November. After a dinner in their honor by Troyanovsky in mid-December and an extensive briefing by Alex Gumberg, they began their slow trip to Moscow through Berlin with his daughter by an earlier marriage and the ubiquitous Walter Duranty sharing ship space.[114] Duranty advised him that Bullitt antagonized Litvinov with his bullheadedness and to drop the debt question as futile, since it was tied to outstanding debts with other countries.[115]

---

112. Jesse H. Stiller, *George S. Messersmith: Diplomat of Democracy* (Chapel Hill: University of North Carolina Press, 1987), 93–94. He feared for his weak stomach and his wife's interest in comfortable surroundings, though if he had been promised a later transfer to Berlin—as Davies was—he might have accepted. Davies corresponded regularly with his two daughters by a previous marriage, the eldest married to Senator Millard Tydings, the youngest a student at Vassar, and with stepdaughter Nadenia Hutton (daughter of E. F. Hutton), who was left in charge of Hillwood.

113. Davies diary, 28 August 1936, box 3, Davies Papers, MD, LC.

114. Ibid., 5 January 1937.

115. Davies to Hull, 19 January 1937, ibid.

Arriving at Spaso House in January 1937, he found it in decrepit condition, much worse for the Bullitt wear, but the city was a surprise, full of activity. George Kennan relates the embassy staff's initial negative impression of Davies:

> Suffice it to say that he drew from the first instant our distrust and dislike, not so much personally . . . but from the standpoint of his fitness of the office and of his motivation in accepting it. We doubted his seriousness. We doubted that he shared our own sense of the importance of the Soviet-American relationship. We saw every evidence that his motives in accepting the post were personal and political and ulterior to any sense of the solemnity of the task itself.[116]

That evening, as Kennan relates, the staff met in Henderson's apartment to consider resigning in a body in protest. He also warned the ambassador "that members of the Soviet Foreign Service are subject to an entirely different set of behavior in Moscow than they are at other posts."

Davies, nonetheless, was promptly and cordially received by Litvinov's assistant, Nikolai Krestinsky, at the foreign commissariat. One of his first exposures to the new political reality of the Stalin era, however, was to attend a great purge trial, the one generally referred to at the time as the "Radek case." Kennan drove him to the scene late in the evening of 24 January and provided the interpretation. He was amazed that Davies believed the prosecutor's case that they were all guilty.[117] But to William Phillips, then ambassador in Rome, Davies wrote that the trial was "shockingly horrible."[118] The new ambassador's meeting with "President" Kalinin to present his credentials at the end of January was brief and perfunctory, but Kalinin went out of his way to emphasize the strength of the country and the success of the new Five Year Plan.[119] To his old friend, Colonel House, Davies admitted that "there are more stores and shops open than I have been led to believe." He and his wife had already begun a campaign to collect art

116. Kennan, *Memoirs*, 82. For a balanced assessment of Davies in Russia, see Elizabeth Kimball MacLean, *Joseph E. Davies: Envoy to the Soviets* (Westport, Conn.: Praeger, 1992).

117. Kennan, *Memoirs*, 83; Davies diary, 24 January 1937, Davies Papers, MD, LC. Kennan's view is contradicted by Davies's contemporary impression: "The treason trial was horrible beyond words because of its terrifying disclosure of what a dictatorship and a police state can do to deprive the individual of not only liberty, but life, and even worse, those intellectual and spiritual freedoms which free people value more than life." To House, 27 January 1937, f. Jan. 1937, box 3, Davies Papers, MD, LC.

118. To Phillips, 12 February 1937, ibid. He was impressed enough by the proceedings to collect a number of volumes of the transcript of the trial in English and send them to the president and others. Davies to James Roosevelt, 19 February 1937, ibid.

119. Davies to FDR, 25 January 1937, and Diary, 25 January 1937, ibid.

of various kinds, she emphasizing eighteenth- and nineteenth-century artifacts, he the contemporary Soviet art, which he donated to his alma mater, the University of Wisconsin.[120] In appraising his staff, the new ambassador reported that "Henderson is a very great comfort. He is highly efficient, has a very capable, broad-minded outlook and his judgement is most sound." His main concern had to do with George Kennan:

> Kennan is of the scholarly type, most capable and thorough, and he has done a perfectly splendid job here, as is quite evident from his work, with which you are familiar. The difficulty lies in the fact that Kennan is not at all strong and well . . . and suffers from duodenal ulcer. . . . He is of a rather high-gear, nervous type, and quite frankly I think that he has been here quite long enough—perhaps too long for his own good. . . . Quite frankly both Henderson and I feel that the loss to us here would be a most serious one and we would be seriously handicapped for a time. [121]

Davies had a pleasant meeting with Litvinov, just back from Geneva, on 4 February and, upon his suggestion, invited Secretary of State Hull to visit Moscow. "During the course of the conversation he said that he failed to understand why England and France were continually making overtures to Hitler. . . . Hitler's policy was still that outlined in his book, 'Mein Kampf,' and he continued to be dominated by a lust for conquest."[122] The new ambassador received the definite impression that Litvinov was quite concerned about France, Britain, and Germany composing their differences.

Davies spent the next afternoon at the dacha of Commissar of Foreign Trade Arkady Rozengolts enjoying a lavish eleven-course lunch. As in the case of Bullitt's dinner at the Voroshilovs' Kremlin apartment soon after his arrival, Davies was surprised at the number of Soviet dignitaries on hand—Voroshilov, Tukhachevsky, Mikoyan, prosecutor Vyshinsky, trial judge Vasily Ulrich, and others—but Stalin was absent.[123] He noted that the conversation was mostly in German, which they all understood. Davies was quite impressed, as Bullitt before him, with Voroshilov. After lunch, Rozengolts turned the conversation to the debt

---

120. To House, 27 January 1937, and Diary, 28 January 1937, ibid. The Joseph Davies art collection of more than a hundred mostly contemporary Soviet paintings is preserved, and partly displayed, at the university's art museum. The Hillwood estate-museum in Washington speaks for his wife's more extensive and discriminate collecting.

121. Davies to Kelly, 10 February 1937, f. Feb., box 3, Davies Papers, MD, LC. Many felt that Kennan would not live long.

122. Davies to Hull (telegram), 5 February, f. Russia 1937, box 22, PSF Confidential, FRPL.

123. Davies diary, 5 February 1937, and memorandum, 6 February, and to Steve Early (president's secretary), 8 February, ibid.

issue, reiterating the Soviet position that there was no moral obligation to pay the "Kerensky debt" and emphasizing that both France and Britain had agreed to leave the debt out of credit discussions. He further insisted that the November 1933 discussion had resulted in a gentleman's agreement guaranteeing a credit arrangement. Davies denied this but hoped the disagreement would not cloud the relationship.[124] Making a formal call on Molotov on 25 February, he was surprised to find Litvinov there and anxious to resume discussion of the debt-credit issue.[125]

In spite of Kennan and Bohlen's dislike for Davies's lack of professionalism and naïveté as a diplomat, Davies learned quickly on the job and saw through the Soviet camouflage of the show trials.

> On the face of things everything is quiet. There is nothing unusual on the streets or among the crowds you see, but there are constant rumors, both unverified and authenticated, of prominent people in all sections of life being in prison or liquidated. They seem intent on making men free here even if they have to put every man in prison to do it. It is an extraordinary combination of the strongest, highest altruistic devotion to a purpose of elevating mankind and the proletariat, and the most ruthless, tyrannical cruelty.[126]

He also took seriously the task of learning about the country, though at least some of the travels were motivated by his and his wife's collecting of art, spending a couple of weeks in Leningrad in late February and early March and then leaving in mid March, not the best time for travel in Russia, for a southern tour with Faymonville and other staff members and several American journalists.[127] He visited the "Cooper Dam" and the American-built tractor factory in Kharkov, and visited five cities, expressing his admiration for Soviet achievements along the way. Back in Moscow, he conferred with Litvinov about exporting paintings and listened to another diatribe against Hitler but the same day had lunch with the German ambassador, Friedrich-Werner von Schulenberg.[128]

Marjorie Post endured a tour of Madam Molotov's perfume factory, while the ambassador was shown a new plan for the rebuilding of Moscow. They were both impressed by the commission shops where much old and new Russian art could be

124. Davies to Hull, 18 February 1937, ibid.

125. Davies to FDR, 25 February 1937, f. 21–28 Feb., ibid.

126. To Sumner Welles, 10 July 1937, f. Davies, box 40, Welles Papers, FRPL.

127. To FDR, 5 March 1937, f. March, box 4, Davies Papers, MD, LC.

128. Diary, 26 March 1937, ibid. At Dnepropetrovsk, Davies acquired an eighteenth-century icon of St. George and the dragon, which he presented to the president as a gift. Davies to FDR, 1 December 1938, PPF, 1381, FRPL, and personal viewing at Roosevelt Museum, Hyde Park.

*Marjorie Meriwether Post Davies, c. 1938. (Prints and
Photographs, Library of Congress)*

purchased.[129] Called home for consultation by Hull, Davies called first on his old
friend Colonel House, whom he found quite feeble, but "his knowledge of Europe
is extraordinary."[130] Davies gained from him and others that there was much un-
ease about the world situation and that history seemed to be at a crossroads.

The Purges

Upon Davies's return to Moscow in April 1937, the purge atmosphere had become
almost overwhelming. To stem reaction, perhaps, Molotov's wife staged a luncheon

129. Davies to Eleanor Roosevelt, 22 March 1937, f. 22 March 1937, box 4, Davies Papers,
MD, LC.
130. Davies diary, 12 April 1937, f. April, ibid.

for Marjorie Davies at the lavish Molotov dacha. She reported that the dacha was really a modern French-style villa. "The service of the food were of the very best and unusual, even for a similar occasion in France, England or the United States."[131] The correspondent for the *Christian Science Monitor*, Demaree Bess, had reported to Henderson how upset he was about the arrest of Lydia Nekrasova in April, shortly after visiting her apartment in Moscow, and he feared it was because he had given her copies of the *Times* and *Monitor* to take to friends.[132] Davies was shocked to learn in London in June of the arrest of Marshall Tukhachevsky on charges of sabotage and spying for Germany and Japan.[133] He correctly guessed that another major purge trial was in the making. He was also not happy to learn upon his return that a listening device had been discovered in Spaso House above his bedroom.[134] He reported confidentially and indirectly to FDR,

> Everything over here is topsy turvy. It is either black or white. One could write a brief on the good things they are doing and trying to do, but a dictatorship and a police state brings far more evil than it attempts to cure. Their professed fine purposes are being besmirched by this horrible blood letting. The idea that is prevalent among diplomats—that this regime is about to fall to pieces—as I see it is wishful thinking. The facts here, in my opinion, do not sustain it.[135]

Caught in the sweep of arrests were a few innocent Americans such as Albert Melville Troyer, an agricultural expert on citrus and graduate of the University of Nebraska, who was seized in his apartment in July 1937. The embassy could do little about it, despite appeals of Nebraska Senator Edward Burke, since Troyer had voluntarily given up his American passport and taken Soviet citizenship shortly before his arrest.[136] Robert Petty, an American petroleum engineer working for Glavneft in Baku, was also refused an exit visa, apparently because he was expected to testify against imprisoned Soviet engineers.[137] Davies commented to his friend "Birney" (Bernard Baruch) that "when they adopt a policy they pursue

131. Diary, 8 April 1937, ibid.
132. Bess to Henderson, 3 May 1937, f. 891, vol. 394, DPR Russia 1937, RG 84, NA.
133. Diary, 13 June 1937, f. June, box 5, Davies Papers, MD, LC.
134. Diary, 28 June 1937, ibid.
135. Davies to Marvin McIntyre (personal and confidential), 6 October 1937, f. October, box 6, ibid. The discovery of the bugging of the house is a hilarious account of the staff, mainly Kennan and Thayer, stretching a silk thread across the attic that set off an alarm in a room below in order to catch one of the Soviet employees in the act. Thayer memos, 28 May, 12 June, and 24 June 1937, f. 820.01, vol. 382, DPR USSR 1937, RG 84, NA.
136. Ward to Burke, 10 September 1937, vol. 399, DPR Russia 1937, RG 84, NA.
137. An embassy official sent to investigate found him drunk in a Moscow hotel, apparently suffering from the strain. Ward to State Department, 3 December 1937, vol. 380 (811.1), ibid.

"*Red Salute*," *R. A. Lewis cartoon.* (Milwaukee Journal, *15 June 1937*)

it intensively and permit nothing to stand in their way."[138] Davies escaped the Moscow hysteria with weekend sailing on the Baltic with journalists and other invited Americans on his wife's yacht, *Sea Cloud*, which he had brought over, its arrival cleared personally by Litvinov. He was also fond of showing the latest Hollywood films to special guests on the yacht and at Spaso House.

Davies still captured the atmosphere of the purges, especially the arrests, quick trial, and executions of several army generals, including Tukhachevsky in July 1937 and the dismissal of Rozengolts as commissar of foreign trade only a few months after he had provided such a friendly atmosphere for discussion. He thought that the charges against the officers were not justified but that Stalin was not blamed by any of the diplomatic corps for them. He traced the purges back to the Kirov assassination, correctly predicted that Bukharin would be next,

138. To Baruch, 10 July 1937, f. July, box 5, Davies Papers, MD, LC.

while considering the Stalin regime stronger than ever.[139] Meanwhile, Litvinov repeated his concerns about the failure of the Western democracies to stand up to Hitler and predicted correctly the demise of Czechoslovakia, not this year but the next.[140] When Davies asked Litvinov about the perceived weakness of the USSR because of the purges, the commissar quickly responded:

> He asserted vigorously that there was no governmental weakness here but actual strength which in his opinion was demonstrated by the fact that probably no other country in the world could have sustained the loss through death and removal of so many heads of military and civil branches of government because of treason and still preserve its stability, direction, and force to the degree where "business went on as usual every day."[141]

Cruising on the Baltic in August and on to France in September to sail on the Mediterranean offered relief from hearing of more arrests and executions in Moscow. Loy Henderson was left to report the depressing details to Washington, acknowledging that there was no way he could compile a complete or accurate list and noting that it included several friends, such as the past and present heads of VOKS. Harold Fisher thought that the arrest and execution of Sergei Trevis was due to his brash and "show off" manner.[142] On other seas, the Soviet authorities in Vladivostok rendered unprecedented hospitality to the visit of an American Pacific squadron, the cruiser *Augusta* and four destroyers at the end of July 1937.[143] The *Augusta* was open for visitors, which elicited favorable comments in both *Pravda* and *Izvestiia* (issues of 30 July).

Davies was finally back in Moscow on 4 October 1937 to summon Duranty, Anna Louise Strong, Joseph Barnes, and a few other journalists to hear more bad news about the purges and the dismal course of the Spanish civil war, in which the Soviet Union was the most active supporter of the antifascist Republican coalition.[144] He found a definitely more repressed atmosphere in Moscow and looked forward to his return to Washington and reporting to the president. "Perhaps you don't believe it, but I never worked harder in my life. But I do know that

139. Davies to Hull, 28 July 1937, ibid.

140. Davies to Hull, 10 July 1937, f. Russia 1937, box 22, PSF Confidential, FRPL.

141. Ibid.

142. Henderson to Hull, 2 October 1937, vol. 373, DPR USSR 1937, RG 84, NA; Fisher Memorandum, "Soviet Was Built on Ruthless Policy," 5 June 1937, f. W. H. Chamberlin, box 3, Harold Fisher Papers, HIA.

143. Admiral H. E. Yarnell to Davies, 30 July 1937, and Faymonville (who was there for the occasion) memo, 17 August 1937, vol. 384 (833), DPR USSR, RG 84, NA. Faymonville found Vladivostok "poor, dirty, and in disrepair."

144. Davies diary, 4 October 1937, f. Oct., box 6, Davies Papers, MD, LC.

I have an extraordinary amount of information first-hand that will be of value to the Boss in his assessment of the situation in Europe."[145]

Litvinov seemed to be unusually attentive to him, hosting a private luncheon for the American ambassador on 30 October, where he relayed more information on his fears of German and Japanese aggression during an extended conversation.[146] He also provided Davies with a ringside seat for the upcoming festivities celebrating the twentieth anniversary of the revolution and hosting a luncheon afterward at his dacha on 9 November, reciprocated by one for Litvinov at Spaso House on 11 November.[147] Davies was impressed by the lovely French-style villa. Litvinov expressed himself quite frankly about Japanese and German aggression and the betrayal of collective security by the British (well before the Munich conference). The result was a consolidation of the Anti-Comintern Pact.[148] When asked about the effect of the large-scale purge of army officers, Litvinov could only respond, "The army is devoted to the Party. Its loyalty is not to the generals, but to the country."[149] What else could he say? The ambassador had taken special note of who was on the Lenin mausoleum: Stalin, Molotov, Kalinin, Dimitrov, Voroshilov, Budenny on 7 November. Gone were many of the familiar Bolshevik figures of the past. A week later another long list of arrests was published that included "anyone who have [sic] doubts about current policy."[150]

Reflecting on the parade itself, Davies was clearly overwhelmed by the show of armed forces descending from three avenues upon Red Square: "What was frighteningly impressive 'from where I sat' was the Secret Police of four or five thousand men as they marched past in company formation. . . . Of course, 'Red' was all over the place and everywhere throughout the milling crowd of thousands were the blue or green-capped Secret Police."[151] This would sound familiar to anyone who saw Leni Riefenstahl's depiction of the Nuremburg National Socialist rally of that same year, *Triumph of the Will*. "Huge battleship tanks dashing across the Square at high speed were the sensation of the day."[152]

145. Davies to McIntyre, 6 October 1937, PPF, FRPL.

146. Davies to his wife, 30 October 1937, ibid. That evening the young people were thrilled by the music of a Rimsky Korsakov opera. Davies had planned to leave again for home in November but stayed longer upon a special request of the president, because his absences had aroused criticism in Washington. Davies to McIntyre (FDR's secretary), 28 August 1937, and McIntyre to Davies, 22 September 1937, f. 1381, PPF, FRPL. The latter communication was no doubt dictated by the president.

147. To Hull, 11 and 15 November 1937, f. Nov., box 6, Davies Papers, MD, LC.

148. Davies diary, 9 November 1937, ibid.

149. Ibid.

150. To Hull, 16 November, ibid.

151. Diary, 10 November, ibid.

152. Ibid.

Even in the absence of his wife, Joseph Davies maintained a lively guest schedule at Spaso House during the winter and was perhaps even more receptive to the
liberal-radical Americans than Bullitt. He was fascinated by the dinner repartee
of veteran American-Soviet supporters Albert Rhys Williams and Anna Louise
Strong in the wake of the November 7 anniversary festivities. He commented
about his impression of Strong, "She is about fifty years of age and looks much
older. She evidently was a beautiful girl, but now her eyes are sad and there are
strong lines in her face. I think the disillusionment she and Williams have experienced has rather hardened them both."[153]

Colonel Faymonville took Davies and his guests to the ballet at the Bolshoi
Theater during the weeklong celebrations: "I do not think any place in the world
could afford anything equal to the ballet we saw last night."[154] It was this incon-
gruity of mass purges and high culture that confused and amazed many Americans
on the scene in 1937 and 1938. Davies was also impressed by a young journalist,
Whittaker, whom he found to be a brilliant conversationalist. "He was full of
information. It was a rich mind and I got a lot out of it. He bats around with the
young people and he and EK [his younger daughter] and the staff discussed the
international situation till all hours of the morning at the Gypsy Night Club."[155]
Do the NKVD files have a recording of this? In any event the American colony in
Moscow celebrated Armistice Day by a tea at Spaso House. But there was clearly
an uneasy sense of the end of tranquility.

While back at home in January 1938, Davies read Litvinov's diatribe in the
press about the weakness of the League of Nations, that it had been transformed
into "a world-wide farcical Spanish Non-Intervention Committee," and noted,
"His extraordinary capacity for phrases struck me again."[156] Meanwhile, Troyanovsky reported back from a long vacation in Russia on 11 December 1937 to
Hull, who questioned him about how and why so many readily confessed during
the purge trials. The Soviet ambassador responded that he had just discussed this
with J. Edgar Hoover, who claimed the same phenomena—mass confessions—
in the United States. Hull disagreed—and complained of customs delays and
searches of embassy personnel in Moscow.[157] When he heard about this American protest, Davies was upset, writing to Hull that these were trivial matters,
most of them already resolved.[158] But he would later revive protests over several

153. To his wife, Marjorie Meriwether Post, 13 November, ibid. Davies noted that Strong (as his
wife) was an Oberlin College graduate and had never given up her American citizenship.
154. Ibid.
155. Ibid.
156. Davies diary, 2 February 1938, f. 1–14 Feb., box 7, Davies Papers, MD, LC.
157. Hull memorandum, 11 December 1937, reel 32, Hull Papers, MD, LC.
158. To Hull, 4 March 1938, f. 1–5 March, box 7, Davies Papers, MD, LC.

incidents late in 1937 and in early 1938. For example, future Columbia University professor John Hazard had notes, pictures, and credentials taken from him at the border in December 1937, and Montfort Melchior's manuscript on Voltaire was seized, also at the border.[159] Several other veterans noted the shift to a more formal relationship in the background of the purges of 1937–1938.

The March 1938 purge of the right wing of the party in the 1920s was especially upsetting to many Americans because it involved more friends and the more ideologically compatible of the old Bolsheviks. Davies observed to his daughter,

> There is a strong presumption that these defendants have been somehow induced to testify in this incredible manner by duress or coercion. However as these proceedings develop, it seems to be a fact that a conspiracy did exist and had been in the making ever since Lenin died due to the struggle for power among his followers. It is a commentary upon the horror of a police state. . . . All through the trial I fairly itched to cross-examine and test the credibility of witnesses and possibly break down their testimony through their own contradictions. Never was I so impressed with the value of the protections of the Bill of Rights and our Constitutional protections for the individual.[160]

Davies may have been unfairly criticized by Kennan and others as too gullible and overly sympathetic, but one thing was clear—life was far from normal in Moscow.

Some of the clumsy Soviet attempts to obtain information—or simply to frustrate resident Americans—contained elements of humor. For example, in June 1937, Charlie Thayer discovered a microphone hidden in the ceiling above the Davies' bedroom at Spaso House and a wire extending to a movie projection room. Kennan, Dubrow, and Thayer then engaged in an elaborate amateur game of "catch the spy" with thin thread stretched across an attic floor that triggered an alarm in the basement. This involved quite a bit of ingenuity and time, with the three spy catchers in turn standing watch at night. At least it gave them something to do to break the tedium. Early in August they caught a doorman, Samuel Lieberman, in the attic. Though almost certainly a Soviet spy but now compromised, he retained his job at the residence.[161] In the meantime, Faymonville, somewhat cut off from his Soviet contacts after the military purge, served

---

159. Memoranda, f. 350, vol. 400, DPR USSR, RG 84, NA.
160. To Bijou, 6 March 1938, f. 6–10 March 1938, box 7, Davies Papers, MD, LC.
161. Thayer memoranda, 28 May, 12 and 24 June, and 17 July 1937, vol. 382 (820.01), ibid. This embassy file report included pictures of the microphone, made in Leningrad.

as a handsome, uniformed escort for the comings and goings of Davies's wife and daughter and perhaps a source of information on that subject to Soviet intelligence for whatever it was worth.

The State Department, Moscow, and Riga

Davies also confronted major changes in personnel and administration in 1937.

Arthur Bliss Lane replaced MacMurray, who had been an astute guide to Bullitt as minister to the Baltic States. He immediately inserted himself as a key adviser on Soviet affairs in the interlude between Bullitt and Davies in Moscow in an effort to reverse the disappointing decline in Soviet-American trade. Lane recommended the revival of the Export-Import Bank by issuing bonds for Russian credits that might be partially covered by Soviet gold, while noting obstacles in the reluctance of Molotov and Rozengolts, commissar for foreign trade, to make commitments and the fact that Amtorg was "over the hill," concentrating mainly on propaganda. He was encouraged by a Riga study that showed that more than 900 American firms received Soviet orders in 1935, 69 exceeding more than $100,000 in value.[162]

Four of the leading American experts on Russian and Soviet affairs—Robert Kelley, George Kennan, Charles Bohlen, and Felix Cole—were removed from their long-term posts as Russian experts and reassigned. Cole in Riga was replaced at the end of 1936 by Earl Packer from the East European Division of the State Department, who proceeded to reorganize and streamline the operations of the Russian Section to the dismay of some of the veteran personnel. Foremost on his agenda was to coordinate more closely with the mission in Moscow, a goal to be commended but not easy to achieve with a new ambassador in residence and other reassignments being effected. Taking over in late 1936, he wisely waited a few months before journeying to Moscow "to work out a concrete scheme of cooperation between the two missions" with Henderson.[163] He also set about changing the subject area responsibilities of the staff to specific delegated reports in an attempt to remove a serious backlog in workload. To his credit he campaigned for additional staff and increases in salary, which were long overdue. He could do nothing, however, about Donald Day's continuing misrepresentation of what was going on in Riga and the Soviet Union generally for the *Chicago Tribune*, a constant frustration for American officials in Riga for more than twenty

---

162. Lane to Hull, 15 July 1936, box 2 (613-R-U.S.), Riga 1936, RFSP, RG 84, NA.
163. Packer memorandum, 24 January 1937, box 6 (124.2-R), Riga 1937 (Russian Section), RFSP, RG 84, NA.

years, despite Packer's long conversation with him in January 1937.[164] Day clearly added to his paper's reputation as one of the most conservative and unreliable newspapers in the United States on international affairs. Unfortunately, it had a wide circulation.

Robert Kelley was dismissed from his position as director of the Division of East European Affairs in July 1937 and relegated to the Turkish embassy, where he languished until 1945, when he transferred to the CIA to reemerge as a cold warrior in the Truman administration. His division was merged with the West European Office, and the extensive library on Russia that Kelley had built up was transferred to the Library of Congress and merged into its general collection. By several accounts, Kelley was the victim of Soviet private manipulations and a new direction in American foreign policy.[165] Most of all, however, it was his long-term opposition to recognition that continued to dominate his attitude toward the Soviet Union.

The president, buoyed by his reelection in 1936, and sensing that Kelley, along with Bullitt, had sabotaged the expected close friendship with the Soviet Union after recognition, had moved to reorganize the State Department's oversight of Soviet policy in 1937 by closing down the Division on East European Affairs with the help of a new trusted adviser, Sumner Welles.[166] Kelley's temporary replacement was Orsen Nielsen, who had little expertise in the area; he immediately informed Earl Packer that many of the Riga reports were "not worth the time and effort" and that there was continuing conflict of interest with the Moscow embassy and recommended a total reorganization.[167] Packer abrasively responded, "I can assure you that the relations between the Embassy and the Legation have never been better; that as far as the Russian Section is concerned, we all feel that it is only an extension of the Moscow embassy."[168] George Kennan, meanwhile, had been recalled to Washington, replaced by Angus Ward, to man the newly created "Russian desk" in the reconstituted European Division, where he was definitely not happy. He shared an office, however, with a congenial old Princeton classmate who was in charge of Polish and Baltic affairs. "We whiled away the official doldrums with the continuation of the philosophic and political discussion we had inaugurated as college sophomores, twelve years earlier."[169] It would seem to many that the whole Soviet Union had descended into official doldrums, at least as far as the State Department was concerned.

164. Packer to Hull, 18 January 1937, ibid.
165. See Bohlen, *Witness to History*, 39–41, and Kennan, *Memoirs*, 83–85, both Kelley protégés.
166. Frederic L. Propas, "Creating a Hard Line toward Russia: The Training of State Department Soviet Experts, 1927–1937," *Diplomatic History* 8, no. 3 (summer 1984), 225–26.
167. Nielsen to Packer, 19 August 1937, box 6, Riga 1937 (Russian Section), RFSP, RG 84, NA.
168. Packer to Nielsen, 1 October 1937, ibid.
169. Kennan, *Memoirs*, 85.

In addition to these official personnel changes, the Moscow press corps also evolved. One of the most respected of the old guard, William Henry Chamberlin, was transferred to Tokyo in 1936, replaced by Demaree Bess for the *Christian Science Monitor*. Anna Louise Strong retired from her founding editorship of the *Moscow Daily News* that year, bitter about her suspicions of being undermined by the embassy.[170] Eugene Lyons, Ralph Barnes, and several other veteran Moscow journalists sought more comfortable surroundings. Even Walter Duranty was given relief by newcomer Harold Denny for the *New York Times*. The United States was left with less experienced journalistic expertise in Russia at a time when it was most needed.

To occupy time and pursue the old agenda, Henderson continued to massage the old debt question in 1937 in lengthy and apparently not very serious discussions in the Foreign Commissariat, bickering about the amount of debt to be paid, the length of term of repayment, the rate of interest to be added, and the amount of credit to be extended and how it would be channeled. He suggested a formula of Soviet payment of $100 million over twenty years at four and a half percent interest, with an added supplement of two and a half to three and a half percent. If agreed to, $200 million in credit would be available.[171] The commissariat simply avoided discussion; the whole matter was off the list.

The Gathering Storm

Davies returned to his Moscow post again at the end of February 1938 to report on continued shortages of food, especially butter and fats, and the emergency military shipments of food and equipment to the Far East. He was not surprised to learn of the arrest and charges of treason against Bukharin, Rykov, Rakovsky, and others of the former right opposition. "Generally speaking, the present regime is regarded here as more firmly entrenched than ever. Press, radio and other propaganda media, army and secret police all are working overtime and toward the same end. Heaven protect freedom and individual under such a condition!"[172] He had lunch with Litvinov at his country dacha on 1 March and was present the following day for the opening of another show trial, saddened to see old friends, Krestinsky and Rozengolts, among the accused and facing certain death. Krestinsky amazed the audience at the first session of the court by loudly recanting his

---

170. Angus Ward memorandum, 21 November 1937, vol. 381 (811.1), DPR Russia, RG 84, NA.

171. Henderson to Davies, 8 March 1937, vol. 386 (851), ibid.

172. Davies to Sumner Welles, 1 March 1938, f. Davies, box 45, Welles Papers, FRPL. Such comments seem to refute the impression by some critics that Davies was a dupe of the Soviets.

signed confession, but the next day he claimed he had been confused and stood by the original confession.[173] One can guess what went on in the interim.

On 4 March Davies invited Litvinov for tea during an intermission in this last major purge trial.

> Alone in the library, I referred to the trial and told him how shocked I had been to see these men whom I personally knew and respected faced with death for treason. His comment was that the government had to protect itself against traitors who, however, misguidedly, were nevertheless conspiring with Germany and Japan. Litvinov said that he had been greatly shocked by the arrest of Krestinsky and some of the others, but he could not understand why any man should confess to treason, a crime which he knew was punishable by death, unless he was in fact guilty. After all, he said, 'a man could die only once.'[174]

Davies continued to attend the trial, finding the experience "interesting intellectually, although emotionally horrifying."[175]

Davies was surprised at the attention he received from Litvinov, having conferences with him on 14 and 23 March, all apparently in anticipation of Davies leaving his post. The commissar and his daughter paid a special call at Spaso House on 26 March. No wonder Davies stressed to Hull his opinion that the American mission was favored over all others.[176] April also brought several changes in staff, with Alexander Kirk designated as first counselor. The Davies family persisted in seeing Moscow sights, before departing on 15 May for Odessa, where the *Sea Cloud*, having been brought in from the Mediterranean, was waiting them for a Black Sea cruise with calls at Batum, Sochi ("the Atlantic City of Russia"), and Yalta.[177]

To Sumner Welles in March, Davies repeated the gist of a conversation with "a high authority in Central Europe": "It was to the effect that there existed a firm understanding between Hitler and Mussolini on a quid pro quo basis; that England would not fight; that neither Mussolini nor Hitler wanted war because of their economic condition, but that both would 'get away' with their aggressive demands in Central Europe and in the Mediterranean, respectively, and that

173. Bohlen, *Witness to History*, 50–51.

174. Diary, 4 March 1938, box 7, ibid. Davies and his wife visited the Litvinov dacha on 2 March: "In talking to me he expressed complete disgust with the weakness of the Western democratic powers in dealing with Japan." 3 March, ibid.

175. Diary, 8 March, ibid.

176. Dairy entries and Davies to Hull, 1 April 1938, f. 1–5 April, ibid.

177. Dairy entries in May, Box 8, ibid.

a fascist peace would be imposed in Europe." He added, "All these predictions seem to be in the process of complete fulfillment."[178] As far as Moscow is concerned, "There is . . . a generally begrudging admission that the Soviet regime is more firmly entrenched than it has been for some time and that Stalin and his group have complete control of the Army, Secret Police, and all forms of propaganda."[179]

Reflecting his several discussions with Litvinov, Davies wrote McIntyre (for the president),

> The fascist powers set out to isolate and quarantine this Government here, raising the bogeyman of communism; the pot calling the kettle black. They have succeeded remarkably well in Europe and in the world and are getting away with it. Of course, that breaks the power of the London-Paris-Moscow axis as a force to impose an equilibrium in Europe. The risk which the European democracies are taking, all dependent upon the success of Chamberlain's plan, is tremendous. Unless Chamberlain is successful, Europe in all probability will be completely fascist with the exception of England and the Soviet Union.[180]

Davies also found Soviet military authorities expecting war with Germany or Japan or both. "It is quite clear that the soviet military leaders are gravely impressed with the seriousness of their situation. While they do not anticipate immediate trouble, they believe it is inevitable and are addressing themselves seriously and insistently to preparations."[181]

In his June 1938 final report he concluded that "Communism holds no serious threat to the United States. Friendly relations in the future may be of great general value." The cult of the personality was clearly in evidence: "The arch protector of the masses, 'Father Stalin,' is being constantly extolled. Communism has been drilled into all from childhood as a religion."[182] He also cited Faymonville's April report that the Soviet military capability had been little affected by the purges and, in general, presented an optimistic report on Soviet conditions. In other respects Davies was obviously ready to abandon the unsteady Soviet ship for what he hoped would be an easier assignment in Belgium.

178. Davies to Welles, 26 March 1938 (personal and confidential), f. 4 Davies, box 45, Welles Papers, FRPL.

179. Ibid.

180. Davies to McIntyre, 4 April 1938, PPF 1381, FRPL.

181. Ibid.

182. Davies, "Final Summary and Report on the Soviet Union Prior to Departure," vol. 401, DPR Russia, RG 84, NA. This sixty-one-page report deserves close examination.

In late spring 1938, Joseph Davies resigned as ambassador, taking his formal farewells in June, relieved to be out of the thick of it and into the more normal routine of American life. His departure was reminiscent of Bullitt's reception in December 1933. Davies went to see Kalinin and Molotov in the Kremlin on 5 June to be surprised by the sudden appearance of Stalin.

> Well, when he came in, of course, I stood up and approached him. He greeted me cordially with a smile and great simplicity, but also with real dignity. He gives the impression of a strong mind which is composed and wise. . . . A child would like to sit on his lap and a dog would sidle up to him. It is difficult to associate his personality and this impression of kindness and gentle simplicity with what has occurred here in connection with the purges and shootings of the Red Army generals and so forth.[183]

They conversed, just the two of them with an interpreter, at a table for more than two hours. Davies was impressed by his relaxed, sly humor. Some of the repartee concerned Mrs. Davies's wealth and what she was doing with it. What was Stalin really trying to convey in his meeting with Davies in the summer of 1938? Most likely, it was another overture to create or solidify an understanding or alliance in opposition to German and Japanese aggression. It is interesting that this came not long before the Munich Conference—and that nothing came of it.

Davies's mission to Russia ended with a formal dinner hosted by the Litvinovs on 7 June and two lengthy discussions with Molotov, no doubt a required followup to the meeting with Stalin, on the eighth and ninth. The old issue of debt and credit also came up again, raised by Molotov, with an offer sanctioned by Stalin that the indebtedness be reduced to $50 million paid in equal installments over twenty years with no interest added, except for a 10 percent assessment on the whole at the beginning. But this all depended on the old demand of a credit from the United States of $200 million for ten years.[184] Clearly, Soviet leaders were anxious to mend fences with the United States during the first half of 1938.

Ambassador Davies retained warm memories and many artistic mementoes of his experiences in Russia and would immortalize them in his memoir, *Mission to Moscow*, later to be performed on stage and in the cinema, romanticizing his Russian experiences through the lens of the approaching World War II alliance and atmosphere of good old Uncle Joe Stalin. To his stepdaughter, he reflected, "The Russian experience is over. It was crowded with action, interest and fascination. It is and was a memorable experience—perhaps in a small way an historical one."[185]

183. To his daughter, 9 June 1938, f. June, box 8, Davies Papers, MD, LC.
184. Molotov to Davies, 9 June 1938, ibid.
185. Davies to Nadenia Hutton (stepdaughter), 10 June 1938, ibid.

8

Alliance

The Soviet Union and the United States were both concerned about the changing political face of Europe and its extensions into the imperial world. This was especially true for the Soviet Union, as it touched more directly on American as well as world interests and security. The Anti-Comintern Pact of 1936 that included the three most aggressive countries—Germany, Italy, and Japan—was obviously aimed against the East Asian power. National Socialist rhetoric, Hitler's own "plan" clearly stated in *Mein Kampf* for acquiring "living space" in the East, and his ruthless suppression of the German Communist Party had thrown the gauntlet in the face of Soviet Russia. The German chancellor, with the help of an expert diplomatic staff, was steadily and successfully undermining the restrictions imposed by the Versailles terms of 1919. The remilitarization of the Rhineland, an *anschluss* (annexation) of Austria into what was proclaimed as the Third Reich, led to pressures on Poland about expanding transit rights through the "corridor" between the main part of Germany and East Prussia that had been carved out at the Paris conference in 1919 to assure Polish access to the sea.

Meanwhile, Litvinov's pursuit of "collective security" to confront this German challenge and produce a defensive military alliance achieved some success with treaties with France and Czechoslovakia. The missing anchor, however, was Great Britain, which chose first to abstain from continental alliances and then to seek an accommodation with Germany. Expanding Litvinov's idea of collective security arrangements to other smaller countries (such as Albania) was considered foolhardy by both France and Britain, leaving them exposed and vulnerable. The first real test of Soviet policy and the Litvinov agenda was in Spain, where a Republican government, suffering under the economic hardships of the Depression, faced a serious challenge from a military and fascist-inspired clique headed by General Francisco Franco. The resultant civil war was a contest between "the democratic countries" and fascist-style authoritarianism. Despite the altruism of many volunteers, who included Ernest Hemingway and George Orwell, and a considerably more realistic injection of Soviet direct military assistance, that cause was lost by the summer of 1938. Germany supported effectively its "right side" while the Soviet Union blundered into a confused situation, combating a strong Trotskyite presence as well as the Franco forces.

The Soviet Union's military capability and Litvinov's stewardship of its foreign policy were especially jeopardized by the Spanish civil war experiences and by the continuation of mixed signals that posed legitimate questions. The Soviet Union's support of the Republican side won some friends in the West but ended in complete failure, partly because of its own blunders. Where really did the Soviet Union stand in relation to international issues? Was the Soviet Union democratic? Little evidence, apart from the much publicized "paper" Stalin constitution of 1936, could be summoned to support it. Was it pursuing the old goal of world revolution? The rhetoric was there, but not the will. Still, Litvinov endeavored to place his country on the "good side" in international relations. On the other hand, the wholesale Soviet purges of 1937–1938 that included so many respected political and cultured people placed his country almost beyond the tolerance of Western moral standards. Whatever the explanation for them—and there are many—the results seriously damaged the goals of Soviet foreign policy, however poorly they were defined, and left the country vulnerable in its isolation to a power with a concrete agenda, that is, Germany. The purge destruction of much of the high command of the Red Army, including the best-known Soviet military leader, Marshall Mikhail Tukhachevsky, could not but severely damage the Soviet Union as a credible military ally. The United States was still on the fringe of all this, but many Americans, in and out of government, were quickly awakening to the dangers inherent in this situation that was leading to the Munich capitulation to Hitler in 1938.

Because of the heightened international crisis after the beginning of the Spanish civil war, Japanese expansion into Manchuria, and the remilitarization of the Rhineland, the Soviet Union was frantically updating its military preparedness. For bolstering its naval presence in the Pacific, it naturally looked to the United States because of its leadership in the field and convenience of delivery. In August 1937 Moscow negotiated for the construction of warships with the Carp Export and Import Corporation, created for the purpose, as the purchasing agents for one or more modern battleships in the United States.[1] The negotiations dragged out for months, involving Soviet changes of specifications and many conversations with officials in the Department of State and the Navy Department. The latter finally indicated that the American government would not oppose the deal, so,

---

1. According to the *New York Times*, Samuel Carp was a brother-in-law of Molotov. Hanson Baldwin, "Russia Now Seeking 3 Battleships Here," *NYT*, 8 August 1937: 1.

finally, William Francis Gibbs, a naval architect, was approached to draw up the plans and Bethlehem Steel to construct the ship. A proviso was that Gibbs's design be transmitted to the Department of State's Office of Arms and Munitions Control and relayed to Navy to ascertain that no military secrets were compromised.

At a cabinet meeting on 29 April 1938, approval was granted for the construction of a Soviet 45,000 ton battleship, equipped with sixteen-inch guns, though the Gibbs design called for a ship of 62,000 tons with eighteen-inch guns. This led to additional delays. On 8 June Hull sought the president's advice on several matters pertaining to the proposed Soviet naval construction. On the question of whether the United States should object to Gibbs's plans for the larger ship being sold to the Soviet government, FDR first wrote "Yes," but then crossed it out and indicated "No." On the matter of allowing the construction of the smaller battleship, the president noted, "Yes." One condition was that the United States could commandeer the vessels in case of emergency. Since the project would involve the Soviet expenditure of more than $200 million, the president indicated that government departments should "give all help" to the project.[2] Despite all the negotiations and the final approval, nothing came of the project. It was superseded by events.

The Munich Conference

In his design of an expanded Aryan empire, Hitler seized upon the existence of a substantial German minority that had been left by the peace of 1919 inside the new state of Czechoslovakia. These "Sudeten" Germans on the western and northern borders were attracted to the idea of a revitalized, nationalistic Germany and agitated for inclusion in it. This was no small matter since they occupied an area of strategic military importance and constituted more than 20 percent of the total population of the country. Pressures grew on both sides during the summer of 1938 to transfer the people and their territory into the Third Reich in a major revision of the peace settlement.[3]

2. FDR hand-written notations on Hull and Charles Edison (acting secretary of navy) to FDR, 8 June 1938, POF 200, FRPL.

3. The Wilsonian principle of national self-determination of peoples, proclaimed at the Paris peace negotiations, had given in to strategic defensive considerations—and general sentiment in favor of Czechs and Slovaks (Thomas Masaryk). After World War II the problem would be solved more drastically by forced removal of the German population from the territory that was restored to Czechoslovakia.

During the summer of 1938 diplomatic encounters between British Prime Minister Neville Chamberlain, Hitler, and French officials led to a meeting in Munich in late October. The result was the appeasement of Germany on the Sudeten question and the sacrifice of Czechoslovakia in the interests, Chamberlain claimed, of preserving peace. Perhaps just as important, the Munich agreement undermined and virtually destroyed the collective security policy of Litvinov. The United States stood by, out of range of the big guns and flimsy pieces of Chamberlain paper that seemed to prevail over Europe. There was not even an American ambassador in Moscow for more than a year that included the Munich deliberations. The reaction was a wakeup call to many in the academic world. Sir Bernard Pares delivered a typical condemnation of the British policy: "Chamberlain is an honest but ignorant man. . . . He is emotional and out for peace on provincial Birmingham lines."[4]

Confusion and missed signals dominated Soviet relations with Washington. In January 1938, Secretary of State Cordell Hull delivered a strong protest against the transparent Soviet activism in support of the American Communist Party, but then immediately and seriously considered a request for Soviet purchase of an American-built battleship.[5] And Hull voiced his regret about the lack of coordination on the part of Britain and France in opposing German aggression.[6] The Munich agreement had left everything up in the air, and Litvinov's policy of collective security was especially left hanging. Davies shrewdly observed on the Munich agreement, "This isolation of Russia is probably more serious to the democracies of Europe than to the Soviet Union. The officials purport to be indifferent to this development, except as they regret it on account of collective security and its effect on world peace."

Nonintervention

The kaleidoscope of European events left many in the United States more than ever convinced of the virtues of isolationism. Another blow to the faltering cause of collective resistance to fascist aggression came in May 1939 with the dismissal of Maxim Litvinov as Soviet commissar of foreign affairs. He had been a real

4. Pares to Harper, 2 December 1938, f. 30, box 20, Harper Papers, UC-R. For an excellent reassessment of Munich that takes into consideration the Soviet perception, see Hugh Ragsdale, *The Soviets, the Munich Crisis, and the Coming of World War II* (Cambridge: Cambridge University Press, 2004).
5. Hull memos of conversations with Troyanovsky, 13 January and 26 March 1938, reel 32, Hull Papers, MD, LC.
6. Hull memo, 2 April 1940, ibid.

survivor in the Stalin regime, valued for his ability to put a good face on Soviet activities abroad. Unfortunately, his courting of a Western alliance system
had been virtually demolished by the Munich betrayal and the defeat in Spain.
His pursuit of informal as well as formal relations did not sit well with his boss,
the chair of the Council of Peoples' Commissars (equivalent to prime minister)
Molotov, whom Stalin depended upon in guiding governmental affairs through
the upheavals of the purges and the Five-Year plans. The Americans opposed
to involvement in Europe or Asia still included an impressive array of political
authorities, led by Herbert Hoover, Senator Borah, and Charles Lindbergh. Another loyal ally of Hoover, former Undersecretary of State (1931–1933) William
R. Castle Jr., even campaigned for appeasement of Japan—to keep Soviet Russia
out of the Pacific—during the 1939–1941 period.[7]

Litvinov's old and trusted friend, Ambassador to Britain Ivan Maisky, had just
returned to Moscow to witness a meeting between Litvinov, Stalin, and Molotov
on 27 April 1939: "It was the first time I saw the relationship between Litvinov,
Stalin, and Molotov. The atmosphere was strained to the extreme. Though Stalin
looked outwardly calm, puffing on his pipe all the time, it was obvious he was annoyed with Litvinov. As for Molotov, he was simply vicious, attacking Litvinov
and accusing him of everything under the sun." In his tirade against his foreign
affairs chief, he centered on a conversation of Maisky with the Finnish foreign
minister on his way back from London, which Stalin noted was clearly unauthorized. Litvinov replied, "Comrade Stalin, it was an ordinary conversation between
two diplomats; he could not avoid it."[8] A few days later the Foreign Commissariat was surrounded by NKVD guards and Litvinov summarily dismissed from
his post (technically forced to resign). His dacha was simultaneously surrounded
and searched. His life was spared simply because his execution would have produced a world outcry.[9] Litvinov clearly could use a rest, considering his "hands
on" conduct of foreign policy, which meant many trips abroad, frequent consultations with his own ambassadors as well as the foreign ones in Moscow, and, when
at home, his presence was required at nearly all weekly meetings of the Politburo.
During his exile from May 1939 until July 1941, when he was recalled to active
service, Litvinov saw few people, was usually attended by a guard, but was able to

7. Davies to MacIntyre, 4 April 1939, f. 1381, PPF, FRPL. Alfred L. Castle, *Diplomatic Realism:
William R. Castle Jr. and American Foreign Policy, 1919–1953* (Honolulu, Hawaii: Samuel N. and Mary
Castle Foundation, 1999), 111–12.

8. As quoted in Zinovy Sheinis, *Maxim Litvinov*, translated by Vic Schneierson (Moscow: Progress,
1990), 294.

9. Litvinov managed to call Lavrenty Beria, Peoples' Commissar of Internal Affairs (NKVD) to
ask about the guards. Beria laughed, "You're valuable, Maxim Maximovich. We must guard you."
Ibid., 295.

*Laurence Steinhardt and family, 1939. (Prints and
Photographs, Library of Congress)*

attend cultural events. On 23 August 1939, at a performance of *Swan Lake* at the
Bolshoi Theater, he was chagrined to see Molotov and German Foreign Minister
Joachim von Ribbentrop together in the state box.[10]

Molotov took over the foreign office and cleaned house of the Litvinov staff,
most of whom did not fare as well as their patron. He had clearly despised Litvinov for many years for his dominance of a foreign policy that charted a Western
democratic path in contrast with his own sympathy for Germany, and he quickly
installed loyal cohorts, few of whom had any experience in foreign affairs, simply
because he could not trust any selections of Litvinov, who had controlled the
selection process for well over ten years. The purges had also taken their toll on
many of the old guard who had foreign experience, such as Boris Skvirsky and
Karl Radek. Molotov brought in Andrei Vyshinsky, better known as the chief

10. Ibid., 297–98.

prosecutor for the purge trials, as his chief lieutenant and effective acting commissar; Semen Losovsky served as an aide as well as a young Andrei Gromyko, who had at least a modest ability in English and handled the "American desk" with practically no prior experience in diplomacy or knowledge of the country involved. Fortunately, Molotov had enough sense to retain the veteran diplomats abroad, such as Maisky and Umansky, though Maisky complained that his personal meetings and attendance at social functions were greatly limited by new rules.[11] He was also too busy with his job as "premier" to spend much time at the commissariat.

In the aftermath of the "cleansing" of the foreign commissariat, a new American ambassador took up residence at Spaso House. Laurence Steinhardt, a prominent New York attorney and friend of FDR with no diplomatic experience, would endure and survive a tumultuous and difficult period in international affairs. Litvinov's former "friends," Britain, France, and the United States, were virtually cut off from the commissariat of foreign affairs. In a rare visit to the commissariat in April 1941, Ambassador Steinhardt complained bitterly to Lozovsky about the lack of communications (regarding three detained American women) and in general a forced isolation, to which the vague response was that he would look into it; at least, he reported on the conversation to Stalin, Molotov, Vyshinsky, and so forth.[12]

American Slavic Studies

During the rapid advance of American scholarship in the 1920s and 1930s, the study of Russian history and culture matured considerably. Some of this certainly can be credited to the influx of Russian émigré scholars such as Michael Florinsky, George Vernadsky, and Michael Karpovich, at Columbia, Yale, and Harvard Universities, respectively. Their accomplishments in terms of research and publication and the training of students were truly impressive. But just as much credit should go to the native, largely self-trained cadre that included Samuel Harper at Chicago, Samuel Cross at Harvard, Geroid Robinson at Columbia, and Robert Kerner at University of California, Berkeley. Younger scholars, benefiting from their leadership and support, were rising: Bruce Hopper at Harvard, John Hazard at the University of Chicago and then Columbia, Bertram Maxwell at Washburn

11. Ivan Maisky, *Memoirs of a Soviet Ambassador: The War 1939–1943*, translated by Andrew Rothstein (London: Hutchinson, 1967), 211.

12. Losovsky report of conversation with Steinhardt to Stalin et al., 15 April 1941, DVP, 23, 1 (2 March–22 June 1941), 573–75. Steinhardt took the occasion to warn about an impending German attack on the Soviet Union, which was duly relayed to Stalin in Losovsky's report.

University in Topeka, and many others. Harper, perhaps because of his seniority or location in the middle of the country, became the nucleus of a Russian academic circle. He had the advantage of independent support (Charles Crane paid his annual salary through the Friendship Fund at the University of Chicago on condition that his teaching be devoted entirely to Russian language and culture) for his position and for travel to Russia—and made the most of it.[13] Crane also supported the legal studies of John Hazard, with degrees from both Harvard and Yale, in Soviet Russia for several years and helped him secure his first teaching assignment in the Law Department at the University of Chicago.

Because of his location in Chicago, Harper acted as a communications center for American Slavic studies and with officials of the State Department such as Kelley and Kennan and various others associated with groups such as the American Russian Institute or the American Russian Chamber of Commerce. Kennan noted in a letter dated 21 October 1937 that he was immersed in the department in Washington, "So I have inherited many of the cares of Bob [Kelley] and Pack [Packer] and former generations," and that he had found a house in Alexandria for himself and his family.[14] Harper's previously strained relations with former mentor Bernard Pares were repaired and more cordial in the late 1930s. Pares confided his impressions of a long-delayed trip to the new Soviet Russia in 1937 with the view "that Stalin is flattening out [the party] into something broader and more natural." He thought the great masses were supporting Stalin and that he "was knocking out the world revolutionary extremists" such as Radek and Zinoviev.[15]

Sir Bernard Pares and Samuel Harper continued to work on establishing special student rates with Intourist with only modest, hard-earned success for reduced accommodation charges—and for only a few. In contrast to the strain in relations between the two scholars in the 1920s, they became quite friendly in the late 1930s. Probably a relief from money worries through comparatively lavish accommodation in the new Senate House of the University of London for the School of Slavonic Studies, funded by the Rockefeller Foundation, mellowed Pares—or perhaps it was his knighthood.[16] Crane was happy about this development: "I am glad of your working with Pares. No one else understands Russia bet-

13. Crane was concerned about the university diverting Harper to other subjects and, therefore, kept his support limited to an annual basis, which, of course, worried Harper about his future.

14. Kennan to Harper, 21 October 1937, f. 8, box 20, Harper Papers, UC-R. Kennan invited him to dinner the day after Thanksgiving: "It happens that I shall be a bachelor for that day, so we will not have to bore Annelise with discussions about Russia." Kennan to Harper, f. 10, ibid.

15. Pares to Harper, 2 November 1937, f. 9, ibid.

16. Harper was certainly impressed—and envious. To his mother, 14 April 1939, f. 8, box 21, ibid.

ter than he and he keeps the main points still in good perspective."[17] Whenever Pares was remiss in communication, which was often, his loyal secretary, Dorothy Galton, filled in, maintaining the trans-Atlantic Slavic link, which was later important for the war effort.

American scholarship on Russia matured considerably in the 1930s, thanks to the input of émigré scholars such as Florinsky and Vernadsky, but also by the high-quality work of Americans dedicated to the cause. Many of their works still stand as classics: Robinson's *Rural Russia under the Old Regime*, Harper's *Civic Training in Russia*, Samuel Cross's works on Pushkin, and many others stand out. It was only natural that these scholars would discuss the idea of a regular journal, but progress was slow, owing to a division on leadership and the election of an editor, especially between Robert Kerner at the University of California and the East Coast elite. Although Kerner felt isolated and neglected in Berkeley, he clearly had the largest enrollments in Russian history in the country. Harper, Cross, and others found him arrogant and authoritarian. The rift delayed the production of a journal. There were other problems. Robinson was always busy, others irascible.[18] Finally, to their surprise, an émigré historian, Dmitri von Mohrenshildt, launched *The Russian Review* in December 1941.

World's Fair

Rebuffed at Munich and seeing that collective security was in shambles, the Soviet Union turned to another opportunity and planned to make a statement at the New York World's Fair of 1939. Designed as a showcase of scientific progress on a broad expanse of Flushing Meadows, it was barely squeezed in before the eruption of war in Europe. Soviet participation was planned well in advance to showcase its industrial and social advancements, reflecting the grandiose designs of the Five Year Plans and of socialist realism. Advance notices boasted that the central pavilion would cover one and two-thirds acres and require 1,200 tons of steel. Already by early December 1938 the Soviet flag had been raised on the steel skeleton.[19]

Although the fair was not scheduled to open until 30 April 1939, Soviet "president" Kalinin sent a special message at the end of January that the fair

17. Crane to Harper, 10 March 1938, f. 17, box 20, ibid.

18. Robinson remarked about one of the newcomers in the field: "Jesse Clarkson is one of the keenest destructive critics that I know—one of the hardest men in the world to meet in an argument. . . . I like him and admire his ability greatly." Robinson to Harper, f. 26, ibid.

19. *NYT*, 23 November and 6 December 1938.

would advance "international collaboration so necessary to safeguard peace" and announced a dedication ceremony for a Soviet heroic statue commemorating industry and labor. The event included 600 Soviet workers engaged on the construction. The Red Army Chorus and the Piatnitsky Peoples' Chorus, accompanied by the Grand Symphony Orchestra, inaugurated the festivities with "The Internationale" and "The Star Spangled Banner."[20] This was clearly the largest congregation ever of Soviet citizens in the United States.

The Soviet pavilion was truly impressive, probably the largest of all contributions from foreign participants. The central feature was a 269-foot pillar of red marble, the same kind as that in Lenin's tomb, topped by a 79-foot steel statue of a worker with one arm extended holding a red star, the tallest edifice at the fair, excepting the famous 700-foot Trylon, the symbol of the fair—along with the perisphere.[21]

One disappointment was that a much-anticipated direct Moscow–New York flight, which was to land in New York on the day of the opening, crash-landed instead on an island off the New Brunswick coast, owing to the freezing up of instruments during the 27,000-foot altitude flight on the Arctic circle route. The two aviators, Brigadier General Vladimir Kokinaki and Major Mikhail Gordienko, though badly shaken, were rescued and duly delivered to the fair on schedule to much fanfare.[22] They gave brief and much applauded speeches on the occasion, as the Lindberghs of Russia.

The Soviet pavilion was formally dedicated on 16 May by Soviet chargé d'affaires Konstantin Umansky. The semicircular structure included nine varieties of marble and enclosed 100,000 square feet of space, the entrance naturally flanked by large relief statues of Lenin and Stalin. The exhibits featured an exact, full-size replica of a Moscow metro station, miniatures of Moscow Art Theater stage productions, numerous vintage Palekh boxes, a collection of Chukchi bone carvings, dioramas of Magnitogorsk and a collective farm, a painting of the Soviet countryside that claimed to be one of the largest single canvasses in the world (53 × 30 feet), and many pictures depicting the revolutionary history of Russia, beginning with a dramatic presentation of the Bloody Sunday tragedy of January 1905.[23] All in all, the Soviet representations at the fair in its own pavilion and in other buildings reflected the broad gigantomania of the Five Year Plans

20. "Soviet Officials to Hail Fair Today," *NYT*, 29 January 1939: 27; and "Soviet Greets U.S. in Salute to the Fair," *NYT*, 30 January 1939: 15.

21. "Nations in Parade," *NYT*, 1 May 1939: 1. The statue was dubbed by fair workers "Big Joe" and "The Bronx Express Strap Hanger."

22. "Russian Aviators Rescued Arrived," *NYT*, 1 May 1939: 1; and "Two Soviet Fliers Deliver Their Country's Greetings," *NYT*, 2 May 1939: 17.

23. "Huge Steel Statue Tops Soviet Center," *NYT*, 17 May 1939: 2.

in scale—and poor taste—but generally fit well with the scope and character of the fair itself.

The Crane Legacy

American interest in Russia and the Soviet Union had been quietly promoted by the philanthropist Charles R. Crane, who made his twenty-third visit, his last, to that country in 1937. From the beginning of the century he had supported the career of Samuel Harper, professor of Russian studies at the University of Chicago, as well as that of other scholars such as Bruce Hopper at Harvard and John Hazard. His endowed Institute of Current World Affairs not only paid Harper's salary at Chicago, but also subsidized his several trips to the Soviet Union. In return Harper filed reports on his observations of his six sojourns to the Soviet Union, the last in the summer of 1939, which were circulated by the institute to a select company of experts, growing to about a hundred, including the leading officials of the Soviet embassy.

Although Harper was generally sympathetic to the Soviet industrial and social progress and a supporter of recognition, Crane remained an old school conservative (though always a Democrat), anti-Bolshevik, and opposed to recognition. He had, as one author noted, "a faith in people" to observe carefully, gather facts, and interpret them, though this certainly had its bias, a clear anti-Semitism. Though Crane preferred personal contacts on the phone or over lunch and in personal conversation, he expressed his beliefs well in a rare written letter to the president on the occasion of his second inauguration.

> The American people have a wonderful faculty for reliable hunches which are much more important than the most brilliant intellectual calculations. They have peeked around the corner to the left and seen only the dramatic part—the tragedies. Now you have led them around the corner and will show them how to manage the tremendous world movement to the Left in real American fashion so that they will face the new adventure calmly, then like it, and finally conquer it, making a better, stronger America. To bring about this new spirit is the work of the next four years and nothing else counts in comparison. The people believe that you have seen a vision and they absolutely trust you.[24]

24. Crane to FDR, 20 January 1937, PPF 462, FRPL.

Charles Crane represented a special, though not rare, perspective: Russia was important, its culture was certainly worth studying, and its political evolution was important for research in depth. Hence, Crane continued his support of Samuel Harper, funding his salary through the Friendship Fund and his trips to Russia in the 1930s, despite Harper's drift toward a pro-Soviet stance. Though this was probably his greatest contribution to Russian studies, in terms of the number of years and total cost, Crane also sponsored many cultural events that featured major Russian performers, both Soviet and émigré.[25] In return for protection against having to teach anything outside Russian studies, Harper felt obliged to deliver lectures, appear at conferences, and host a variety people with Slavic interests who passed through Chicago.

Crane's background and views were certainly not lost on Soviet officials. Umansky was especially attentive to clearing his visa in 1937. He wrote Harper, "Since I want to make his stay in Moscow as pleasant as possible I would ask you very much to give me any pertinent data about him, his past and present activities and especially his sentiments toward and interest in the U.S.S.R., his special interest in research work. . . . I recall that you told me quite a good deal about him but it seems to have slipped my mind."[26]

The American-Russian Institute

Of the several pro-Soviet cultural organizations established in the 1920s affiliated with VOKS (the Soviet agency in charge of cultural relations with the West), only the one in New York continued to be active through the late 1930s. It hosted exhibits, sponsored film series, and wined and dined visiting Soviet citizens of note. Perhaps the most visible exhibit was a traveling collection of 50 oils and 190 other items of contemporary Soviet art that opened at the Pennsylvania Museum in Philadelphia to quite favorable reviews under the joint patronage of ambassadors Troyanovsky and Bullitt. Christian Brinton, a vice chair of the American-Russian Institute, oversaw the operation.[27] After a long tour of the country, including stops in such outposts as Toledo, Kalamazoo, and Denton, Texas, as well as Los Angeles and San Francisco, the exhibit finally concluded

25. A real assessment of the Charles Crane contribution to Russian-American relations in the twentieth century remains to be written. His papers, in segments, have only recently been assimilated in the Bakhmeteff Archive at Columbia University. This task is complicated by the fact that Crane had many other interests, especially in the Far East and Middle East.

26. Umansky to Harper, 14 April 1937, f. 35, box 19, Harper Papers, UC-R.

27. Edward Jewell, "Philadelphia Sees Soviet Art Exhibit" *NYT*, 15 December 1934: 11.

in November 1936 on the thirty-third floor of the Squibbs Building in New York.[28]

In April 1936, the institute hosted a reception for the wife of the Soviet premier, Olga Karpovskaya-Molotova, after her lunch at the White House with Eleanor Roosevelt, and at the conclusion of her two-month tour of the country. In charge of a perfume and cosmetic industry in Russia, Madam Molotov noted at the event, "Russian women like make-up and deluxe toiletries and can afford them. All you have to do is to show them how to use them."[29] The institute could be counted on to relieve the anti-Soviet State Department from such duties as greeting three Soviet aviators who flew in over the Arctic to receive a hero's welcome. After a visit with the president in Washington, they arrived in New York on 30 June 1937 for a grand reception at the Waldorf-Astoria, hosted by the American Russian Institute and the American Geographic Society. Lowell Thomas served as toastmaster for the occasion.[30] At this gathering of more than one thousand, Ambassador Troyanovsky took advantage of the occasion to criticize American policy in regard to the Soviet Union as too critical of its peace objectives.[31]

The American Russian Institute continued to act as a social agent for the improvement of Soviet-American relations, arranging cultural events and exhibitions, usually at the American Museum of Natural History, and hosting political receptions. For example, on 21 June 1939, it hosted a luncheon in honor of both the Steinhardts and Umanskys at the Waldorf Astoria with little press notice.[32] Naturally, it suffered an eclipse during the Baltic and Finnish incursions but recovered in the spotlight after June 1941. Perhaps the highlight of the institute's cultural career was the sponsorship of a benefit concert of Russian music at Carnegie Hall on 30 April 1941 for Soviet military casualties, featuring the premiere of a Shostakovich quintet for piano and strings. The show was stolen, however, by Paul Robeson singing folk songs in Russian and by Benny Goodman on his clarinet joining with the Roth String Quartet on Prokofiev's "Overture on Yiddish Themes" in a jazz rendition. The *New York Times* reporter of the occasion was clearly dazzled.[33]

28. "News of Art," *NYT*, 13 November 1936: 21.

29. "Wife of Molotov Ends American Tour," *NYT*, 2 April 1936: 16.

30. "City Will Welcome Soviet Fliers Today," *NYT*, 30 June 1937: 17.

31. "Envoy Denounces Attacks on Soviet," *NYT*, 1 July 1937: 17.

32. William O. Field (ARI) to Steinhardt, 24 and 31 May 1939, f. D–F, box 27, Steinhardt Papers, MD, LC.

33. Howard Taubman, "Music of Russia Heard in Concert," *NYT*, 30 April 1941: 22.

The Nazi-Soviet Pact

Behind the supposedly surprise arrangement reached by Commissar of Foreign Affairs Vyacheslav Molotov and German Foreign Minister Joachim von Ribbentrop on 22 August 1939 was a curious, yet to be fully explained, American connection. The general perception is that the Munich Agreement led the Soviet Union, seeing France folding into the British orbit, to abandon the apparent lost cause of collective security and seek an arrangement with Germany. The removal of Litvinov as commissar of foreign relations in May 1939, to be replaced by Molotov, who was more than the henchman of Stalin, definitely inclined more toward Germany, going back to the 1920s Rapallo accord. Could American intervention have prevented this pact and all that followed? Possibly. There was at least an attempt: Welles wrote Steinhardt on 4 August, personally and confidentially, that "the President said that if war were now to break out in Europe and in the Far East and were the axis powers to gain a victory, the position of both the United States and the Soviet Union would inevitably and immediately and materially be affected thereby."[34] Welles stressed the importance of this message to be delivered immediately to Molotov. Unfortunately, Steinhardt was still several days away from arriving at his post, and the message was eclipsed by events.

A report by Ambassador Steinhardt, dated just six days before the signing of the pact, provides some indication of the new Soviet direction. He had just presented his credentials to Molotov on 10 August and learned subsequently that Umansky, who had preceded him to Moscow by three weeks, had left the impression with Molotov, from his own conversation with the president, that a new direct communication would come through Steinhardt, who conferred again with Molotov on the afternoon of 16 August.[35] He brought, instead, a message from Welles (not the president) and was assured by the commissar that "the views . . . were of great interest and value to his Government, which considers the situation in Europe at the present time to be most serious."[36] He continued, "The president could not help but feel that if a satisfactory agreement against aggression on the part of other European powers were reached, it would prove to have a decidedly stabilizing effect in the interest of world peace, in the maintenance of which, of course, the United States as well as the Soviet Union had a fundamental interest."[37]

34. Welles to Steinhardt, 4 August 1939 (personal and confidential), f. V–Z, box 27, Steinhardt Papers, MD, LC.

35. Steinhardt to Welles (personal and strictly confidential), 16 August 1939, f. USSR 1938–1940, box 166, Welles Papers, FRPL.

36. Ibid.

37. Welles to Steinhardt, 4 August 1939, f. V–Z, box 27 Steinhardt Papers, MD, LC.

Molotov indicated his disappointment in the negotiations with Britain, according to Steinhardt, who took verbatim notes: "We are not interested in declarations. We are desirous that the present negotiations lead to a determination of action to be taken under specific conditions or circumstances—and that there shall be mutual obligations to counteract an aggression." Molotov added, hinting at a German arrangement, "We would not go into any agreement aiming at an attack on anybody." The commissar expressed his exasperation that the delays in the negotiations with Britain and France were not the fault of the Soviet Union.[38] Steinhardt added his own interpretation of his conversation and in consideration of the atmosphere at the time.

That while the Soviet authorities are genuinely desirous that peace should be preserved, they are particularly anxious to avoid being drawn into any European conflict—at least at the beginning, if for no other reason than because of their internal difficulties and the threat to their political as well as economic program which would result from the outbreak of a general European war at the present time, the guiding principle of their European policy being to assure the non-violation of their frontiers; and they are deliberately carrying on negotiations with the French and British on the one hand and the Germans on the other, in the hope of thereby avoiding the outbreak of war before the beginning of October.[39]

Steinhardt added that he was impressed by various indications of considerable concern about conflict in the Far East.

In the meantime, Hull met with Umansky, who returned to Washington in September, and took the opportunity to stress how damaging the new Soviet relationship with Germany was. "I . . . said that it was a matter of great disappointment that we could not have the cooperation of Russia to a much fuller and broader extent than we have had during the past seven years, especially in view of the far-reaching extent to which we have gone to encourage and induce such broader cooperation for peace and mutual welfare."[40]

38. Ibid.

39. Ibid. The Nazi-Soviet Pact shook the Western democracies, with Stalin and Hitler soon getting equal billing as evil geniuses. It must have been a toss-up for *Time Magazine's* man of the year, but Stalin won the featured place on the cover that included an allusion to Ivan the Terrible. *Time Magazine*, 1 January 1940.

40. Hull memorandum, 12 June 1940, reel 32, Hull Papers, MD, LC.

And the Band Played On

The American and Soviet cultural worlds continued to have much in common, despite the strictures and limitations of socialist realism and the Soviet regimentation of the arts to support constructive endeavors. Some of the interconnection was fostered by the ideals of the socialist dreams that a substantial number of Americans believed were being created by Soviet planning. Soviet progress, however, confronted the reality of economic depression and recession in the arts, though perhaps much distorted by media promotion. Facing the reality of the United States in the 1930s, Soviet achievements could be attractive to young artists—and productive. Pete Seeger recalled in an interview on National Public Radio that the inspiration for one of his classics, "Where Have All the Flowers Gone," came from a line in Mikhail Sholokhov's *And Quiet Flows the Don* that he read in the 1930s, after he had joined the Young Communists.[41]

No better example of the mirror reflections of culture can be found than in popular music. The jazz tradition that spread to Soviet Russia in the 1920s had endured the critical opposition of socialist realism, which focused on the suggestive dances that accompanied many jazz performances. They contributed to a negative influence on youth, who were expected to be model Young Pioneers and Komsomol dedicated to the ideological and construction goals of the party-state. But American-style jazz remained alive and well at the end of the 1930s, thanks to talented musicians such as Alexander Tsfasmann, Leonid Utesev, Iakov Skomorovsky, Leopold Teplitsky, Georgy Landsberg, Genrikh Tepilovsky, and Aleksei Semenov. They directed popular swing bands and jazz combos, such as Semenov's "Original Dixieland Jass Band." They were mainly centered in Leningrad but with several others in Moscow and quite a few in provincial cities such as Odessa, notorious as a beehive of jazz.[42] Despite being labeled as bourgeois or worse, jazz orchestras prevailed, simply because many Communist leaders liked them, including Stalin himself. To prove the point, one of the most popular Soviet jazz bands during the war, in both recordings and performances, was the All-Soviet Red Flag Baltic Fleet Orchestra.

This development, which paralleled the American big band era, was given a decisive boost, surprisingly, by the Nazi-Soviet Pact. In the chaos of a doubly invaded Poland, Eddy (Adolph-Addy) Rosner managed to escape Warsaw and

41. NPR interview, 2 July 2005.
42. For an excellent historical survey of the Leningrad/St. Petersburg jazz scene, see Vladimir Feiertag, *Dzhaz ot Leningrada do Peterburga* (St. Petersburg: Kul'tInformPress, 1999). See also, Richard Stites, "Frontline Entertainment," in *Culture and Entertainment in Wartime Russia*, edited by Richard Stites (Bloomington: Indiana University Press, 1995), 134–35.

get on the Soviet side of the lines. As a Jew and a jazz musician he knew what the alternative would be. Of Polish-Jewish heritage Rosner grew up and received his musical education in Berlin in the 1920s.[43] Though trained in classical violin and piano, he quickly gravitated to jazz and the trumpet (or more precisely, the coronet). Joining the Weintraub Syncopators, the most popular jazz combo of Berlin's cabaret era, he toured the world, including New York, with the band on the German-America Line, meeting the much-admired Louis Armstrong during a tour of Italy. In a subsequent correspondence between the two, Armstrong called him the "white Louis Armstrong," while Armstrong became the "black Eddy Rosner."[44] By the late 1930s he had settled in Warsaw as a popular jazz band conductor, while also touring a diminishingly free Europe. Arriving in Russia across a yet to be defined border in 1939, with his reputation preceding him, Rosner quickly re-formed his orchestra and would play to full houses behind the Soviet lines during the war. Though often compared to Louis Armstrong, he was more like Harry James or Glen Miller and their orchestras in terms of style and improvisations.[45] A highlight of his wartime engagements was a command performance for Joseph Stalin, who proved to be a fan—for a while.

It might be claimed that jazz won the war, since it dominated mass entertainment in all the Allied countries and was the most popular relaxation for military personnel and others, the American Miller and the "Russian" Rosner being the key examples. Anything associated with jazz or swing bands was officially banned in Germany, Japan, and Italy, where patriotic anthems prevailed.

Moscow Time

For those residing at Spaso House and manning the American outpost in Moscow in 1939–1940, the situation was confused, to say the least. Captain Frank

43. His original first name, ironically, was Adolf, shortened to Addy, then Eddy.

44. According to some reports, during the meeting in Italy, Rosner entered a trumpet contest with Armstrong and came in a close second. Though the American influence was clearly dominant in Soviet popular music, some Russian motifs seeped into the American jazz scene. Two of Louis Armstrong's classics were his jazz renditions of "Dark Eyes" (Ochi Chernyi) and "Russian Lullaby," which he first heard as a child from a Russian Jewish family in New Orleans. Small world!

45. See the excellent video documentary, *The Jazzman from the Gulag*, French production in English, 1999. The title derives from the fact that Rosner was arrested and sentenced to the Gulag in 1946 for a foolhardy attempt to return to Germany—and because of the association of jazz with the United States during the height of the cold war. To no one's surprise, he re-formed his band (most members having also been incarcerated) in the Gulag with the encouragement of prison authorities and played the camps. Released in the 1950s, he again became a popular big band conductor (theme song "Caravan"), finally obtaining permission in the mid-1970s to return to Berlin, where he died suddenly two years later.

Hayne, Faymonville's replacement as military attaché, found dealing with the commissariat of defense far from satisfactory in 1939. He regretted his inability to maintain Faymonville's associations with the Soviet military, noting that he had been allowed only one visit to a Soviet military facility, the Frunze Academy, in his sixteen months on assignment. "I am almost certain that he [Faymonville] was the only military attaché here who had such contacts."[46] And no one would repeat his accomplishment.

In the meantime, the president and his closest advisers on foreign relations, Harry Hopkins and Sumner Welles, appeared to distrust the State Department's core of Russian experts as being too rigid and anti-Soviet, shaped in the Kelley mold. They, in turn, would castigate Roosevelt, Hopkins, Davies, and others as naive, inexperienced, and susceptible to Soviet propaganda. One side saw the situation through the perspective of the more immediate reality of world politics, the other at least partly through the prism of the cold war, when they penned their memoirs of the period. For example, "Chip" Bohlen wrote about Joseph Davies: "He never even faintly understood the purges, going far toward accepting the official Soviet version of the existence of a conspiracy against the state. Moreover, he and his wife treated the staff as hired help and rarely listened to its views."[47]

Both opposing positions, exaggerated by personal feelings, were produced largely in retrospect. The State Department professionals were typically conservative in their analyses and tempered by their experiences in Moscow. For example, in early 1939 Henderson wrote Samuel Harper,

> I do not believe that it is necessary for me to go into the reasons for what may be called the present industrial stagnation of the Soviet economy. You are sufficiently acquainted with the inherent defects of the Russian people, the effects of the purge on industry, and the increasing hesitancy of Soviet officials to accept responsibility. . . .
>
> Although I do not believe that conditions are as bad as some of the sensationalists are saying, I do believe that industry is functioning far from satisfactorily and that, if Soviet figures can be believed, it is safe to say that heavy industry is encountering difficulty in maintaining the level obtained in 1936.[48]

He has subsequently been designated, somewhat ironically, as a *Russian* jazz legend: hear a revival of his recordings on a 2004 CD—"Antologiia dzhaza: dzhaz-orkestr Eddi Rosnera," released appropriately in St. Petersburg.

46. Frank Hayne to Col. J. A. Crane, 17 February 1939, f. 2450-D-7, box 1378, MID, RG 165, NA.
47. Bohlen, *Witness to History, 1929–1969* (New York: Norton, 1973), 91.
48. Henderson to Harper, 13 February 1939, f. 10, box 18, Harper Papers, UC-R.

While the department veterans were looking at all the damage done by the purges and forced industrialization, Roosevelt, Hopkins, Davies, and Welles saw a relationship in need of nurturing in the interests of responding to world politics, that is, the Hitler menace.

During the winter of 1939–1940, the State Department, Roosevelt's advisers, and the general public were united in their concern about the Soviet attack on Finland, which had won American allegiance through its payment of war debts and was considered a rare democratic bastion on the Soviet border. Americans almost unanimously cheered the Finns for their resistance—and the Soviet Union suffered a major blow to its prestige that would linger into the lending assistance in 1941. Additional press outcries followed about the Soviet occupation in late 1939 of the Baltic states, which had received special American support but remained hopelessly divided and decidedly pro-German. The Soviet move into Latvia also had the effect of shutting down permanently the long-existing Riga "listening post," which had provided valuable information on the Soviet Union and had never been supplanted by the embassy in Moscow.

As a result especially of the Soviet attack on Finland but with the simultaneous aggressive actions of Germany, Italy, and Japan also in mind, the president declared in late 1939 a "moral embargo" on export of goods from the United States, particularly anything that could be of military use, to the nondemocratic world. American companies were simply asked to reconsider contracts under way or new orders pending. Most of them should not be concerned about loss of business since Britain and France were purchasing such items in large quantities. The Soviet Union was most affected by this measure, or so its agents claimed, because it was belatedly in the midst of a crash rearmament program, and, as in times past, was relying on American imports of supplies and technology. Two examples were the focus of a series of Soviet protests—machine tools and airplane engines. The first involved a large number of orders placed with a variety of manufacturers, while the second centered on the Wright Aeronautical Company of Patterson, New Jersey. The contract dating back to 1937 with Wright involved not only the purchase of engines obviously for military aircraft but also the presence of at least fifteen Soviet technicians as permanent "observers" in the Wright plant. Soviet defense of the right to "do business as usual" and to maintain the contract with Wright would keep Umansky busy in Washington and Steinhardt in Moscow and pain to the State Department.[49]

The attention given to these cases may have obscured other major commercial transactions. Sir Stafford Cripps, arriving as the new British ambassador to

49. See a number of documents in *FRUS: Diplomatic Papers 1940*, vol. 3 (Washington, D.C.: GPO, 1958).

Moscow in early 1940, complained to Steinhardt that more than 100,000 tons of American cotton had been imported by the Soviet Union to be delivered, or to replace Soviet cotton exported, to Germany under the trade terms of the pact. In fact, as in the case of other embargoes, third parties could find ways around restrictions. These sensitive trade issues were accompanied by a variety of petty problems, ranging from Soviet intransigence in granting exit visas to Soviet spouses of Americans and in requiring the embassy to go to the central telegraph office to make any long-distance call. In regard to the latter, FDR commented, "I am wondering whether we might apply the same rule to the Russian Embassy here—or at least tell Oumansky we are thinking of doing it. What is sauce for the goose might well be sauce for him too!"[50]

Ambassador Steinhardt was clearly dismayed to hear that Umansky claimed in Washington after his return that everything was normal in the Soviet capital after the Nazi-Soviet pact was signed. "I may dispose of his remark that 'in Moscow no one would know that there is a war going on anywhere in the world' with the observation that it is possible for internal conditions to be so bad that not even a war can make them any worse." He also disposed of Umansky's assertion that he had close relations with Steinhardt in Moscow by noting that there had been only three brief and inconsequential encounters.[51] Clearly, an element of unreality occupied the world on the eve of the second great war of the twentieth century. George Kennan, on assignment from his post in Berlin to inspect American property (the old embassy building) in Prague, wrote nostalgically of walking "about these venerable, shabby streets" that seemed to survive everything.[52] And much ultimately would.

In the aftermath of the fall of France and the apparently formidable totalitarian advance that included the Nazi-Soviet Pact, FDR, advised by Sumner Welles, sought a mechanism to place the United States in firm opposition to this onslaught, before it was too late. In December 1940 he called (literally, by telephone) upon Republican William Allen White, the "sage of Emporia," Kansas, and longtime conscience of middle America, to head the awkwardly labeled Committee to Defend America by Aiding the Allies (more generally referred to subsequently as the "William Allen White Committee"). With chapters in nearly every state, the "committee" soon became a force in inspiring American attention to a world that seemed to be turning against its long-endowed democratic

50. FDR memorandum for Hull, 10 January 1940, ibid., 245.
51. Steinhardt to Welles, 11 January 1940, f. USSR 1938–1940, box 166, Welles Papers, FRPL. Among other frustrations, Steinhardt complained of the Soviet refusal to allow contact with the crew of the *City of Flint*, detained in a Soviet port.
52. Kennan to Jeanette Hotchkiss, 7 December 1940, f. 1940, box 28, Kennan Papers, Mudd-P.

principles. Many of the initial supporters of the committee, including White, wanted to take an aggressive position in regard to a war that was being won by Germany, not with the idea of direct military involvement, but, on the contrary, to advance American interests and preparedness in regard to any peace settlements; above all, they opposed direct military involvement. As the first six months of 1941 unfolded with aggression clearly unchecked, a split developed in the loose organization of the committee between those continuing to place high priority on avoiding military commitments and those now ready to become more directly engaged. White, unsuccessfully trying to steer a middle course, resigned his leadership post, but he would continue to adhere to its initial ideals and actively support lend-lease in 1941 to the Allies, including Russia, after the German invasion in June.

In the United States, Soviet acts of aggression against its immediate neighbors—part of the bargain with Nazi Germany—naturally were received with much animosity.[53] The new regime in the Molotov commissariat had a minimally objective perspective on foreign affairs, and Umansky, who should have known better, was apparently astonished by the American reaction, especially by obstructions placed in the path of Soviet orders for military supplies in the United States. In a heated discussion with Acting Secretary of State Welles on 27 July 1940, Umansky complained that many items were refused licenses for export to the Soviet Union while the same ones were being quickly authorized for shipment to Britain. Welles responded forcefully that the United States was reluctant "to approve exports of materials which could assist governments indulging in the practice of bombing civilian populations from the air [referring to Finland]."[54]

By this time Ambassador Konstantin Umansky, who replaced Troyanovsky in 1939, had quickly earned the reputation as the most difficult, if not the worst, diplomat in the United States, perhaps the world. His behavior in constantly beleaguering State Department officials—and the president—and in issuing obviously false statements and claims alienated everyone. The Soviet Union could not have been served worse at a crucial time. The wonder is that an alliance in 1941 resulted in spite of him. To give Umansky a little credit, it was a difficult time, well beyond his grasp, and he had little support, Andrei Gromyko being his chief assistant; and he was usually at a loss for words, his English being virtually nonexistent.

53. A Gallup poll at the end of December showed Americans supporting Finland by an overwhelming margin of 88 to 1, while one year previously general sentiment was four to one in favor of the Soviets. "Soviet Drop in Favor in U.S. Found Sharp," *NYT*, 1 January 1940: 14.

54. Welles memorandum of conversation, 27 July 1940, f. USSR 1938–1940, box 166, Welles Papers, FRPL.

Neither Faymonville, who had been in touch with many high-level Soviet officers, nor other contemporary American experts on the Soviet Union foresaw any danger of a Soviet preemptive attack on Germany in 1940 or 1941. Loy Henderson, among the best of the experts, personally doubted the possibility of any immediate conflict at the end of March 1941, certainly not on Soviet initiative. It would be, he advised Steinhardt in Moscow, of Germany's choosing, "not as a result of any desire on the part of the Soviet Union."[55] Though Soviet strategic planning called for a surprise counteroffensive on an initial attack and training stressed the morale advantage of attack, the idea that the Soviet Union would carry out an offensive on its own against Germany was absurd. The Red Army was in no condition to mount an attack, as the results of the German invasion clearly demonstrated. Defeat, which would have been inevitable, would have had much worse consequences than defending against the invasion that actually occurred. Of course, military planners considered mounting a surprise counteroffensive, which appeared on the record as an offensive. And, indeed, Soviet counteroffensives at Smolensk and Moscow in 1941 netted considerable results in terms of a boost to Soviet morale and destruction of part of the best of the German army.

Making the transition from a stance of opposing totalitarian regimes in general was not easy for Americans, though. Fortunately, the Roosevelt administration had not employed a clearly antitotalitarian policy during the 1939–1941 interim. Winston Churchill certainly helped in providing the light in a timely and characteristically rhetorical way, no doubt with an American audience in mind.

> I see Russian soldiers standing on the threshold of their native land guarding the fields which their fathers have tilled from time immemorial. I see them guarding their homes, where mothers and wives pray. Ah yes, for there are times when all pray for the safety of the loved ones, for the return of the bread winner, of the champion, of the protector. I see the 10,000 villages in Russia where the means of existence is wrung so hardly from the soil, but where there are still primordial human joys, where maidens laugh and children play. I see advancing upon all this the invidious onslaught of the Nazi war machine, with its clanging, heal-clicking, dandified Prussian officers, its crafty expert agents, fresh from the cutting and cowing down of a dozen countries.[56]

55. Henderson to Steinhardt, 31 March 1941, box 33, Steinhardt Papers, MD, LC. Benjamin L. Alpers expressed the impact of Barbarossa well: "The Nazi invasion of the Soviet Union remade World War II; it could no longer be a war against totalitarianism." Alpers, *Dictators, Democracy, and American Public Culture: Envisioning the Totalitarian Enemy, 1920s–1950s* (Chapel Hill: University of North Carolina Press, 2003), 156.
56. As quoted in ibid., 253–54.

How could patriotic, romantically inclined Americans resist this? The conservative *New York Post* commented that some might say that we are now allied with communism, but the prime minister has provided the answer.

Barbarossa

Information on the German plans for invasion of Russia came to Moscow from many sources, including Soviet intelligence. Several high-ranking officers, especially from air force general Ivan Proskurov, who served as chief of Soviet military intelligence, warned repeatedly of an approaching invasion. Though proved correct, he would be arrested and shot without trial later in 1941 for his efforts. Earlier in mid-May Sumner Welles, the effective secretary of state for European affairs, summoned Soviet ambassador in Washington Umansky to inform him with emphasis of reliable intelligence from sources in Berlin and from decoded intercepts of German communications of the details of an invasion coming in mid-June. The same information was relayed through Steinhardt in Moscow to Lozovsky in the Foreign Commissariat (Molotov typically being unavailable), who dismissed the news as superficial and discredited. More poured in from other sources, the British being more tentative, but Soviet officials had no real reason to doubt the American communications. Why were so many indications of a coming invasion from reliable American sources apparently ignored? Stalin's suspicion of any foreign reports may have been the key factor, especially since the invasion did not occur as was predicted by many reports in May. Then he also may simply have hoped—knowing his military was unprepared—that it would not occur as late as 15 June, too late, as his intelligence sources indicated, for the Germans to accomplish the objective of taking Moscow that year.[57] Wrong about avoiding an invasion and right as it was too late, as it turned out. But verifiable indications of an imminent attack increased in June, becoming absolutely positive a few days before, yet Stalin apparently ignored them.[58]

The massive German invasion of Russia on 22 June 1941 was, nonetheless, a surprise on many sides; some, though surprisingly few, saw the war as an opportunity to get rid of both Russia and Communism. A more typical American response came from the Committee to Defend America: "The German attack on Russia should finally convince all doubting Americans: first that Hitler is plan-

57. David E. Murphy, *What Stalin Knew: The Enigma of Barbarossa* (New Haven, Conn.: Yale University Press, 2005), 146–47. Interestingly, any mention of these American warnings for this period is strangely absent from the recently published documents from the Soviet foreign affairs archives: *Dokumenty vneshnei politiki, 1940–22 iiunia 1941* (Moscow: Mezhdu-Otnosh., 1998), 681–98.
58. Ibid., 170–72.

ning on world domination and that he will commit any crime to achieve it."[59] But many Americans were confused about allegiances, best expressed by Bullitt, now evacuated from his post as ambassador in Paris. He wrote the president personally, emphasizing his continued animosity toward the Soviet Union:

> The line you took when Germany attacked the Soviet Union—that of giving support to anyone (even a criminal) fighting Hitler—was, of course, sound. But the emotions aroused by the spectacle of Nazis fighting Bolsheviks were so conflicting that most people needed a lot more guidance than they got. Public opinion is now befuddled. The feeling has begun to spread that we no longer need to hurry our war preparations and that the communists have become the friends of democracy.[60]

He went on to stress that Communists in the United States were just as dangerous as ever.

A Gallup poll taken in mid-July 1941 clearly reflected American sentiment: 4 percent supported Germany, 72 percent for Russia, with the rest undecided, an overwhelming American sympathy for the Soviet side. But on the question of which would win, the result was 47 percent Germany, 22 percent Russia, 8 percent a stalemate. Gallup concluded from the comments recorded that "it goes without saying the American sympathy for Russia is not based on any love for communism. . . . Russia is not imperialistic, but Germany is. Russia, even if she won, would not invade the United States, whereas Germany probably would."[61] The poll also showed little difference among classes or religious groups with only a slight leaning of Catholics toward Germany.

Major Ivan Yeaton, the American military attaché in Moscow, was absolutely certain that the Soviet Union would quickly fall to the German invasion and reiterated this conviction through the end of 1941, when he was finally replaced. Though apparently having knowledge of Russian, he rarely used it, seldom contacting Soviet military officials and never reading anything published in Russian because he considered it propaganda. He distrusted others in the embassy and refused to communicate anything confidential to Ambassador Steinhardt.[62] In short, he represented the worst of all possible attachés in Soviet Russia at this time, totally anti-Soviet and never relenting from his prediction of Soviet defeat. Fortunately, his reports were eventually discounted. He was the total opposite

---

59. Press release, 23 June 1941, f. state and local, CDA, box 34, Mudd-P.
60. Bullitt to FDR, 1 July 1941, PPF 1124, FRPL.
61. George Gallup, "Victory for Russia Found in Survey," NYT, 13 July 1941: 2.
62. Yeaton to Sherman Miles, 5 June 1941, f. 2610-D-20, MID, RG 65, NA.

of the pro-Soviet Faymonville and left the Soviet military very confused as to American objectives. He forcefully opposed lend-lease while he was the key military person in Moscow in 1941. To give him a little credit, few others could see through the fog of Soviet propaganda, assess the military reality, and predict the position of the United States during the summer of 1941. But he certainly did major, fortunately not irreparable, damage to the cause of defeating Germany.

In August, with the situation more than critical for Soviet survival, Washington still seemed to be in the dark. Loy Henderson advised Steinhardt that the "military people here [Washington] were convinced that Moscow would fall before the first of August. Now no one seems to know anything about anything." Henderson thought, however, that "Hitler made what may be a fatal mistake in attacking the Soviet Union" and that even if he won, the "cost in men and supplies may almost fatally weaken Germany."[63] A good prediction.

Lend-Lease

The idea of extending a special large military loan to a foreign country emerged in response to the desperate situation of Britain under air attack during the winter and spring of 1939–1940. Britain obviously had critical supply needs to maintain its defense, recover from the damage, and prepare for a possible invasion. Many orders had been filled and shipments made, but Britain had exhausted its means of repayment. In proposing the scheme of lend-lease, President Roosevelt used this analogy: if your neighbor's house was on fire, you would naturally lend him your hose, without guarantee that it would come back. Congress approved a commitment for lend-lease to Britain and Greece, which the president signed on 11 March 1941. The bill was intentionally lacking in specifics that would allow temporary aid to other countries. An additional, more selfish argument was that British and other orders, including Russian, had lifted American industry considerably, boosting economic recovery, which should be maintained for the welfare of the American economy.

It then became only a matter of extension after the German invasion in June to expand lend-lease to the Soviet Union three months later. Fortunately, the immediate German threat to Britain was drastically reduced by that invasion, and some of the aid committed could be reassigned. Conferences on American supplies to Soviet Russia began almost immediately through Molotov's rare direct contact with Steinhardt in Moscow and by a forceful presentation to Sumner Welles from Soviet Ambassador Umansky in Washington on 30 June, who, on

63. Henderson to Steinhardt, 18 August 1941, f. G–I, box 33, Steinhardt Papers, MD, LC.

instructions from Moscow, put warplanes first, since most of the Soviet air force had been destroyed on the ground during the initial attack, and fuel at the top of the list.[64] Harry Hopkins also lent support and went to Moscow in July for a firsthand inspection.

Winston Churchill and his ambassador in Moscow, Sir Stafford Cripps, were essential supporters of the granting of American aid. Roosevelt's loyal assistant, Harry Hopkins, was quickly on his way to Moscow in July to ascertain immediate needs and demonstrate moral support. Upon return he would accompany the president—and represent the Soviet Union in absentia—at the first summit, the meeting of Roosevelt and Churchill at Placentia Bay in August, which produced the Atlantic Charter but also, perhaps more important, confirmed the need for immediate aid to Russia.[65] Harriman, in Moscow, approved by a formal protocol on 1 October 1941 the already ongoing lend-lease to Russia. But the startup of lend-lease was slow and complicated.

American provision of aid in emergency was not a new idea. Large shipments of food were sent to relieve famine in 1893, which few would probably remember. Many more on both sides, however, were well aware of the massive distributions under the American Relief Administration in 1921–1923. This time, though, enemies controlled the most direct routes, through the Baltic or Black Seas. Three alternate paths were quickly inaugurated: the old, established route across the North Atlantic and following the Gulf Stream over Scandinavia to the established ports of Murmansk and Archangel. A second was the long way across the South Atlantic and around Africa to the Persian Gulf, then overland through Iran to the Caspian Sea. A third, used extensively during World War I, was across the North Pacific to Vladivostok. The Persian Gulf access took time to develop in shipping and ports and transit across Iran, and the Pacific route depended on Japan upholding the May 1941 Neutrality Pact with the USSR and the supply of new Liberty ships from the Kaiser shipyards in California and the arrival of Soviet crews to staff them. Initially, the Arctic route was the most important in delivering supplies to the crucial Moscow front and in providing a moral uplift to the Red Army. The main problem was finding the ships, both for cargo and as armed convoy escorts.

One of the little recognized aspects of the 1941 lend-lease effort was setting up production and supply controls in the United States. For example, instructions

64. Umansky to Molotov, 30 June 1941, DVP, 24 (Moscow: Ministry of Foreign Affairs, 2000), 81–83. The hastily assembled list of highest priority included 3,000 single-motor pursuit planes, 3,000 bombers, 20,000 anti-aircraft guns, and, perhaps most important, $30 million worth of machine tools. Umansky to Welles, 30 June 1941, f. 11 (USSR 1941), box 166, Welles Papers, FRPL.

65. For the full story, see Theodore A. Wilson, *The First Summit: Roosevelt and Churchill at Placentia Bay 1941* (Boston: Houghton Mifflin, 1969).

were issued to Detroit to cut automobile production by half to release metal supplies for other needs, for example, tanks. This would be an important preparation
for the war that the United States was soon to fight on a large scale. Still, this
move encountered much local opposition, and the transition to military production was slow. In late July a Soviet military delegation flew from Prestwick,
Scotland, to Montreal, Canada (a seventeen-hour trip), and then to the United
States. Delegation members were clearly confused by American refusal to respond quickly to requests. They dealt primarily with Sumner Welles and Dean
Acheson in the State Department. Only the request for aviation fuel and oil
products—115,000 tons—could be fulfilled at that time. Not even the sympathetic Faymonville could provide much assistance. He told them that production
and political obstacles were slowing the response, the latter involving British
refusal to give up designated military supplies.[66]

General Fedor Golikov recalled with bitterness the difficult circumstances,
stalled or delayed meetings, few and vague commitments, and, according to him,
a definite American reluctance to support the Soviet war effort. The major problem, though he only partly realized it, was that so much had already been committed to Britain.[67] But he was also correct in detecting U.S. reluctance to send
important material "down the drain," expecting a Soviet collapse, predicted by
State Department experts, and a possible repeat of the 1918 situation, when Allied forces were detailed to Russia to prevent valuable supplies in Murmansk,
Archangel, and Vladivostok from falling into German hands. After much pressure, Welles promised the Soviet delegation an unspecified number of Curtiss
P-40 fighters and Lockheed-Hudson bombers. Then came the news that most of
these planes were yet unassembled in Britain and unarmed; the weapons would
be provided by the British, despite Soviet objections.[68] Soviet officials were naturally dismayed by this turn of events.

The Harriman Mission

To consolidate and extend the lend-lease arrangements and clearly demonstrate
American support for the Soviet efforts to resist the German invasion, Roosevelt
asked Averell Harriman, a prominent businessman and Democratic supporter
with some Russian experience, to head a special mission to Moscow at the end

66. F. I. Golikov, On a Military Mission to Great Britain and the United States, translated by Nadezhda
Bureva (Moscow: Progress, 1987), 60–61.
   67. Ibid., 46–55.
   68. Ibid., 61–64.

of August 1941.[69] Backing Harriman as a personal envoy of the president was his personal aide, Edward Page Jr., a veteran of the Riga listening post, accompanied by a special military escort comprising Major General James Burns, Major General George Brett, and Admiral William Standley. Colonel Philip Faymonville, the American officer most experienced with the Soviet scene, headed a larger contingent to coordinate the shipments of military supplies. Several others tagged along, including the veteran pro-Soviet New York attorney Allen Wardwell, representing the American Red Cross, which was involved in the aid programs.[70] Ambassador Steinhardt especially welcomed an old friend, Admiral Standley, not suspecting that Standley would soon replace him as ambassador, and hoped that he and the other leaders of the delegation would stay with him at Spaso House.[71] Left out of this important mission were the State Department's real Russian experts: Kelley was in Ankara, Bohlen in Tokyo, Kennan in Berlin, and Henderson was overworked in the department.

Steinhardt and British ambassador Stafford Cripps made advance arrangements. The former advised Hull that all forty-five members of the mission should bring flashlights and batteries, as well as recent issues of the *New York Times* and weekly magazines.[72] Five leading members of the American delegation would stay at Spaso House while the others would room at the National Hotel. In the meantime, wheels were turning in Washington and London to provide shipments to Russia.[73] Roosevelt's chief assistants in rounding up equipment were Harry Hopkins and Brigadier General Sidney Spaulding. The latter reported that 5,000 tanks could be made available, 1,000 immediately from current army stock, while Hopkins guaranteed the shipment of 10,000 tons of plate armor at the rate of 1,000 tons a month.[74] Hopkins also noted for Harriman's benefit in Moscow that between the end of June and 13 September $20 million in supplies had been shipped to the Soviet Union, chiefly airplane fuel and ammunition.[75]

69. Telegram to Harriman, 29 August 1941, POF 220, FRPL.
70. Harriman to Winant, 2 September 1941, f. Harriman Mission, box 31, OEEA, RG 59, NA.
71. Steinhardt to Standley, 4 September 1941, ibid.
72. Steinhardt to Hull, 7 September 1941, ibid.
73. Hull for President to Harriman, 19 September 1941, ibid.
74. Spaulding to Hull, 20 September 1941, and Hopkins to Harriman, 23 September 1941, ibid.
75. Hopkins to Harriman, 24 September 1941, ibid. The best study of the lend-lease specifically to the Soviet Union is still that of Robert Huhn Jones, *The Roads to Russia: United States Lend-Lease to the Soviet Union* (Norman: University of Oklahoma Press, 1968). For a revisionist account that enlarges considerably the role of lend-lease in the Soviet war effort, see Albert L. Weeks, *Russia's Life-Saver: Lend-Lease Aid to the U.S.S.R. in World War II* (Lanham, Md.: Lexington Books, 2004). This is done mainly by revising downward Soviet production figures. In fact, most trucks and warplanes, major items in the supply effort, were delivered in large components and assembled in the Soviet Union, and thus were counted both as lend-lease and Soviet production.

"Avoiding Eye Contact?" Harriman and Stalin, 1941. (Prints and Photographs, Library of Congress)

The journey was not an easy one for all concerned. Harriman first flew to London, where he met with Churchill and accepted the mission as a joint one with Lord Beaverbrook, minister of supply. A British contingent was also included. Though some of the staff went by B-24 at high altitude over Scandinavia to Moscow, by Beaverbrook's insistence, he and Harriman and others boarded the Cruiser *London* in Scotland for an equally perilous transit through bad weather into the Arctic to Archangel. Page and Faymonville landed in Moscow on 24 September as the advance guard. Symbolic of the cause, several of the promised P-40s released by the British, went on board the cruiser to be reassembled under direction of American experts in Archangel. On 28 September, Harriman and Beaverbrook flew from there on a Russian bomber, which, in spite of a fighter escort, encountered heavy antiaircraft fire in the vicinity of Moscow, apparently the gunners assuming any plane in the sky must be German.[76]

76. Steinhardt to Hull, 28 September 1941, f. 1941, box 31, DEEA, RG 59, NA. When Stalin stressed the need for antiaircraft guns, Harriman responded coolly that Moscow seemed well supplied. Rudy Abramson, *Spanning the Century: The Life of W. Averell Harriman, 1891–1886* (New York: William Morrow), p. 192.

Harriman/Stalin cartoon. (Prints and Photographs, Library of Congress)

The delegation came prepared with a billion dollar list to present to Stalin. What remained was to coordinate the demands with the realities of production and shipping. Harriman, though lacking clear authorization, signed a protocol agreeing to the massive lend-lease shipments on 1 October. Heading the list were trucks, scout cars, 1,800 warplanes, 2,250 tanks, 562,000 miles of telephone wire, and large amounts of explosives. Steinhardt and Cripps escorted Harriman and Beaverbrook to the Kremlin on the evening of 29 September for the meeting with Stalin, who was now acting in an official state role as chair of the Council of Peoples' Commissar (replacing Molotov). They were surprised to find Litvinov acting as interpreter and, more objectionable, the ever-present Umansky.[77] With German guns in the distance, the proceedings went quickly, but ended with a typical Russian/Soviet banquet on 3 October with nearly 100 guests treated to more than thirty toasts. Steinhardt reported that Stalin greeted most of them personally during the event, which lasted until 1:00 AM.[78] Harriman, as instructed,

77. Steinhardt to Hull, 29 September 1941, f. 1941, box 31, DEEA, RG 59, NA.
78. Steinhardt to Hull, 3 October 1941, ibid.

pressed the point of religious freedom to Stalin and in more detail to Molotov, who Steinhardt felt was "paying lip service" while not making any commitment,[79] but was also convinced of the necessity of speeding deliveries, with highest priorities on fighter planes and barbed wire.[80] The Allied delegation, probably suffering from the abundance of toasts, left early the next morning by the same way they had come through even worse weather, arriving back in England, most in ill health—little wonder.[81]

Harriman had left part of his staff back in Moscow with Faymonville in charge of the coordination of lend-lease under Brown's direction. In the meantime, however, Harry Hopkins had maneuvered control of the Soviet part of lend-lease to the army's Division of Defense Aid Reports. The special envoy was annoyed to learn in London that Faymonville was now acting without direct supervision, reporting directly back to Washington. He immediately objected by cable to Hopkins. "I left Burns in Moscow as my assistant with others working under him and planned to work out on my return to Washington detail of the manner in which you wished them to begin. I am convinced that Faymonville is not heavy enough to swing the supply job alone. There must be a man with more balanced experience to whom he would be a competent and useful assistant."[82]

Soon after the departure of the Harriman mission—and with German forces closing in on Moscow—most of the American embassy retreated to Kuibyshev (formerly and currently Samara), the designated alternative capital on the Volga about 400 miles east, in the case of the fall of Moscow. Some Soviet offices, including the commissariat of foreign affairs and other embassies, had already been evacuated to Kuibyshev by October 1941, as the battle of Moscow loomed. From there, Steinhardt departed on a long journey home at the beginning of November by way of Singapore and the Pacific; he had done his duty under difficult circumstances.

One of the Soviet officials who assisted with the Harriman/Beaverbrook meetings on the Soviet side was none other than Maxim Litvinov, who had been called back into service in the commissariat as an adviser on Allied relations after the German invasion, quite a turn of events for the author of collective security,

---

79. Steinhardt to Hull, 4 October 1941, ibid.

80. Harriman to Hopkins, 4 October 1941, ibid.

81. Ibid., 290–94. Harriman was very ill on the voyage.

82. Winant (American ambassador to Britain) to Hull (Harriman for Hopkins), 11 October 1941, f. Harriman Mission, box 31, DEEA, RG 59, NA. One sorry final note to the mission was that a direct message from Roosevelt to Stalin was delayed by bad weather in Canada and then relayed by a low-priority code, apparently intercepted by the Germans, who learned of it before Stalin received it. Harriman was unjustly accused of leaking it through German agents. Drew Pearson and Walter Winchell made the most of this in radio broadcasts, earning Harriman's wrath. Harriman to Stephen Early, 29 October 1941, POF 220, FRPL.

which was now coming into existence in a new form, a military alliance by the necessity of clear aggression. During the conversations, Stalin had complained about Steinhardt, and Harriman responded with criticism of Umansky's conduct in Washington. Perhaps Harriman or someone else in the American contingent suggested that the cause of delivering American supplies to the Soviet Union might be advanced by the presence of a prominent and well-known Soviet political figure personally known to President Roosevelt. Or, perhaps, Stalin himself perceived such an advantage. Nevertheless, late one night in early November, Molotov called the foreign commissariat office in Kuibyshev with instructions to deliver a message to Litvinov that he had been appointed deputy commissar of foreign affairs *and* ambassador to the United States; he was to come to Moscow immediately, a plane standing by.[83]

Litvinov left Kuibyshev on the morning of 9 November 1941 for one more fateful meeting with Stalin in the Kremlin. Upon landing, he was escorted immediately to Stalin's large office, where Molotov sat in the background. This time Stalin did all the talking, recalling their past history together. Stalin expressed his concern that Roosevelt was not that keen on aiding the Soviet Union and that this mission to Washington involved first and foremost the speeding of more war supplies to the Eastern Front. Litvinov clearly agreed to serve his country any way he could, his only hesitation was about Umansky, who would be displaced; he was told not to worry, that the commissariat would find a place for him (he was demoted to Mexico). Litvinov returned to Kuibyshev to prepare quickly for his new assignment.[84]

Following the same route that Steinhardt took a few days earlier, Litvinov and his wife, Ivy, departed on 12 November 1941 for the United States. Their flight was delayed in Tehran, Baghdad, and Cairo, which he blamed on the British, and then passed through Singapore, island hopping across the Pacific to Midway, Guam, and Hawaii, where he toured the military barracks, with somewhat ominous clouds in the sky, at Honolulu on 4 December.[85] The Litvinovs finally arrived in San Francisco on the sixth. They immediately boarded a plane for Washington, arriving on the morning of the seventh of December with much fanfare, including a live radio broadcast interview. Litvinov then went to a luncheon with his old American friend, Joseph Davies, which was interrupted by the news of the Japanese attack on Pearl Harbor. They exchanged impressions of what this meant. Davies recalled, "I asked him how he felt about it. He said that had the United States come into the war earlier it would have undoubtedly

83. Sheinis, *Maxim Litvinov*, 305–8.
84. Ibid., 310–12.
85. Ibid., 312–14; Kirk to Hull, 19 November 1941, box 33, Steinhardt Papers, MD, LC.

thwarted Hitler. He was not so sure that it was advantageous now. I gathered that what was in the back of his mind was that this development would prevent the delivery of vital war materials to Britain and Russia."[86]

Despite an obviously busy schedule at that time for the American commander in chief and the secretary of state, Litvinov presented his credentials the next day to Cordell Hull and called by appointment at the White House on the president, who casually invited him and his wife for bridge that evening.[87] The alliance was sealed by a bid of two hearts over two clubs. Friends for the time being, by necessity.

86. As quoted in William L. Klingaman, *1941: Our Lives in a World on the Edge* (New York: Harper and Row, 1989), 418.

87. Litvinov was well known for his skill at bridge as well as chess.

Bibliography

Manuscript Sources

Augusta, Maine
    Maine State Library
        Percival Baxter Scrapbooks
Cambridge, Massachusetts
    Harvard University, Houghton Library
        Louise Bryant
        Joseph Grew
Champaign-Urbana, Illinois
    University of Illinois Special Collections and Archives (UIA)
        Paul Anderson
        Donald Lowrie
        Russian Student Fund
        YMCA
Chicago, Illinois
    University of Chicago, Regenstein Library, Manuscript Division (UC-R)
        Samuel Harper
Cleveland, Ohio
    Austin Company Archives
        GAZ/Nizhny Novgorod files (transferred May 1905 to WRHS below)
        Austin family
    Western Reserve Historical Society (WRHS)
        Austin Company Archives (transferred from above, 2005)
        William A. Haven (Alexander McKee Co.)
Eugene, Oregon
    University of Oregon Special Collections
        Floyd Ramp
        Anna Louise Strong
Hyde Park, New York
    Franklin Roosevelt Presidential Library [FRPL]
        Adolph Berle
        John Carmody
        R. Walton Moore
        Henry Morgenthau

Personal Secretary's File
President's Official File
President's Personal File
Sumner Welles
John C. Wiley
Madison, Wisconsin
State Historical Society of Wisconsin (SHSW)
Hannah Campbell
Alexander Gumberg
Cyrus McCormick
International Harvester
DeWitt Clinton Poole
Raymond Robins
Edward Ross
Singer Company
Moscow
Arkhiv Vneshnei Politiki Rossiskoi Federatsii (AVPRF)
f. 011, op. 4, p. 24, d. 5; p. 25, d. 17 (Umanskii diary), 1.
f. 0129, op. 2, p. 23, d. 293; op. 17, d. 1, d. 129; op. 18, d. 130a; op. 20, d. 1, 2, 3; op. 21, d. 2, 3; op. 22, d. 136; op. 24, p. 138a, d. 2, 4; op. 25, d. 1; op. 26, d. 11; op. 26a, d. (031)3;
f. 059, 1939, op. 1, p. 296, d. 2048; d. 2049, 2050; p. 297, d. 2050; p. 313, d. 2154; p. 320, d. 2199, 1. 41–58; d. 2200, 1. 19–22; d. 2201, 1. 172–74; 2202, 1. 52 f. 072, op. 17, p. 105, d. 65 (United States in Belgium) op. 14, d. 83
f. 06, op. 1, p. 14, d. 155; d. 15; p. 15, d. 158; 1. 155–73; op. 2, p. 23, d. 293; p. 24, d. 23; op. 3, d. 21; op. 4, d. 22
Gosudarstvennyi Arkhiv Rossiskoi Federatsii (GARF)
f. 130, op. 7a, d. la (American commune)
f. 386, op. 1, d. 1176 (American commune)
f. 583, op. 3, d. 34 (Russian engineers in US)
f. 1058, op. 1, d. 2, d. 52; d. 71; d. 154; d. 162; d. 187; d. 243, d. 803 (ARA) f. 1064, op. 6, d. 26 (ARA)
f. 1065, op. 3, d. 90 (ARA)
f. 5283, op. 3, d. 22, 34, 39–43, 110-16, 120,124, 170–75, 327, 372-496 (VOKS) f. 5446, op. 1, d. 32, 1. 299; d. 43; d. 45 (Hammer concession)
f. 8350, op. 3, d. 83, d. 486 (Hammer concession)
Rossiskii tsentr khranenii i izucheniia dokumentov noveishei istorii (RTsKhIDNI)
Rossiiskii gosudarstvennyi arkhiv sotsial'no-politicheskoi istorii (RGASPI)
f. 2, op. 1, d. 24795 (Hammer concession)
f. 5, op. 1, d. 1176 (concessions) f. 17, op. 74, d. 9, 47
f. 17, op. 162, d. 1–4, 6–9, 11–16
f. 17, op. 163, d. 345, 548–660 (Politburo protocols)
f. 17, op. 120, d. 37, 1. 84
f. 484, op. 7, d. 28
f. 495, op. 18, d. 65–66; op. 73, d. 69; f. 74, d. 465; op. 184, d. 3
f. 534, op. 3, d. 523, 1. 213; op. 4, d. 4; op. 4, d. 393; op. 8, d. 194 (Profintern mission)
Russkoi Gosudarstvennyi Arkhiv Ekonomiki [RGAE]
f. 413, op. 10, d. 359–364
f. 3270, op. 2, d. 25–26 (Arkos)
New Haven, Connecticut
Sterling Library, Special Collections, Yale University
William Bullitt
Edward House

              Robert Lansing
              Walter Lippmann
Yale Divinity School Library, Special Collections
              Sherwood Eddy
              John R. Mott
              Student World Council of Churches
New York
      Columbia University, Manuscripts and Rare Books
              Bakhmeteff Archive
                    Boris Bakhmeteff
                    Ekaterina Breshko-Breshkovskaia
                    Nicolas Murray Butler
                    Jane Perry Clark Carey
                    Charles R. Crane
                    John O. Crane
                    Dmitri Fedotoff-White
                    Michael Florinsky
                    Michael Karpovich
                    Thomas Thacher
                    Evgeny Ughet
                    Allen Wardwell
                    John Wiley
                    Adam Yarmolinsky
              Oral History Project
                    Boris Bakhmeteff
                    Malcolm Davis
                    DeWitt Clinton Poole
                    Stanley Washburn
      New York Public Library, Manuscript Division (NYPL)
              Ekaterina Breshko-Breshkovskaia
              Harold Fleming
              Emma Goldman (microfilm)
              Isabel Hapgood
              George Kennan
              Nikolai Khrabov
              Thomas Thacher
              Lillian Wald
      New York Public Library at Lincoln Center
              Billy Rose Theater Collection
              Elizabeth Hapgood
Newton, Kansas
      Bethel College Mennonite Historical Archive and Library
              Christian Kreibiel Papers
              Mennonite Central Relief Committee
Princeton, New Jersey
      Princeton University
              Seeley-Mudd Library (Mudd-P)
              Hamilton Fish Armstrong
              Arthur Bullard
              Committee to Defend America
              Council on Foreign Relations Allen Dulles
              John Foster Dulles

George F. Kennan
John Van Antwerp McMurray
J. Butler Wright
Firestone Library
Julian Street
Stanford, California
Stanford University
Hoover Institution Archives [HIA]
American Red Cross
American Relief Administration, Russia Unit
Nancy Babb
George Barr Baker
Walter Russell Batzell
Philip M. Carroll
James Rives Childs
Frederick B. Coleman
Ethan Colton
George M. Day
Edward Egbert
Percival Farquahar
Phillip Faymonville
Harold Fisher
Harold Fleming
Frank Golder
William N. Haskell
Lincoln Hutchinson
Merle F. Murphy
John A. Pelikan
Jessica Smith
Charles E. Stuart
Ivan Yeaton
Washington, D.C.
Georgetown University Library (Special Collections)
Richard Crane
Robert F. Kelley
John F. Stevens
Edmund Walsh
Library of Congress, Manuscript Division
Alexis Babine
Newton Baker
Alice Stone Blackwell (microfilm)
Charles Bohlen
William Borah
Basil Brasol
Mark and Helen Bristol
Bainbridge Colby
Communist Party of the United States (microfilm) [CPUSA]
Calvin Coolidge (microfilm)
Joseph Davies
Norman Davis
Herman Hagedorn
W. Averell Harriman

Leland Harrison
Cordell Hull (microfilm)
Frank Kellogg (microfilm)
George Kennan
Robert Lansing
Breckenridge Long
George W. Norris
John C. O'Laughlin
Laurence Steinhardt
Henry Stimson diaries (microfilm)
Thomas J. Walsh
National Archives
RG 59 Department of State
Internal Conditions of Russia and the Soviet Union, 1910–1929 (M316), Political Relations between US and Soviet Union, 1910–1929 (M330), Internal Conditions of USSR, 1930–1939 (T1249)
Office (or Division) of East European Affairs
RG 84 Diplomatic Post Records
Riga, Latvia, legation
Riga, Latvia, consulate, Russian Series
Tallinn consulate
Vyborg consulate
USSR embassy
RG 151 Department of Commerce
RG 165 Office of Military Intelligence (M1194)
Military Intelligence Division (M1443)
RG 166 Foreign Agricultural Services
RG 200 American Red Cross
West Branch, Iowa
Herbert Hoover Presidential Library (HHPL)
American Relief Administration
William R. Castle
Commerce Papers
Hugh Gibson
James P. Goodrich
Postpresidential Papers
Presidential Papers
Westbrook Pegler
Edgar Rickard Diaries
Truman Smith (Katherine Smith Manuscript)

Newspapers and Journals

Atlantic Monthly
Chicago Daily News
Chicago Tribune
Christian Science Monitor
Cleveland Plain Dealer
Current History
Detroit Free Press

Emporia Gazette
Foreign Affairs Quarterly
Kansas City Star
Milwaukee Journal
Moscow News
New Republic
New York Evening Post
New York Herald Tribune
New York Times (NYT)
Pravda
Saturday Evening Post
Time Magazine
The Worker

Documentary Collections and Reference Works

America through Russian Eyes, 1874–1926. Edited and translated by Olga Peters Hasty and Susanne Fusso. New Haven, Conn.: Yale University Press, 1988.
"ARA k nam idet bez zadnikh myslei, no bozni s Nei brudet mnogo: deiatel'nost' Amerikanskoi administratsii pomoshchi v Rossii, 1921–1923," Istoricheskii Arkhiv 1993, no. 6: 76–95.
Catalogue of the Lomonosoff Collections. Compiled by Hugh A. Aplin. Leeds, UK: Leeds University Press, 1988.
Collected Works of V. I. Lenin. 24 vols. New York: International Publishers, 1927–1935.
Documents on Russian-American Relations: Washington to Eisenhower. Edited by Stanley S. Jados. Washington, D.C.: Catholic University of America Press, 1965.
Documents of Soviet-American Relations. 4 vols. Edited by Harold J. Goldberg. Gulf Breeze, Fla.: Academic International Press, 1993–2001.
Dokumenty vneshnei politiki, SSSR [DVP] 1917–1941, vols. 1–24. Moscow: Mezh. Otn., various years.
For the President, Personal and Sacred: Correspondence between Franklin D. Roosevelt and William C. Bullitt. Edited by Orville Bullitt. Boston: Houghton Mifflin, 1972.
Foreign Relations of the United States, Diplomatic Papers: The Soviet Union, 1933–1939. Washington, D.C.: GPO, 1952.
Franklin D. Roosevelt and Foreign Affairs. 17 vols. Edited by Edgar B. Nixon. Cambridge, Mass.: Belknap Press (Harvard), 1969
From the Morgenthau Diaries: Years of Crisis, 1928–1938. Edited by John Morton Blum. Boston, 1959.
Historical Dictionary from the Great War to the Great Depression. By Neil A. Wynn. Lanham, Md.: Scarecrow Press, 2003.
Hugh Gibson, 1883–1954: Extracts from His Letters and Anecdotes from His Friends. Edited by Perrin C. Galpin. New York: Belgian American Educational Foundation, Inc., 1956.
Istoriia otechestva v dokumentakh, 1917–1993 gg. Part 2: 1921–1939. Compiled by Lidiia Larina. Moscow: Ilbi, 1994.
"Iz istorii sovetsko-amerikanskikh kul'turnykh i ekonomicheskikh sviazei (1931–1937 gg.)." Istoricheskii Arkhiv, no. 1, 1961.
"Jazzman from the Gulag," video documentary on Eddie Rosner. Paris, 1999.
Makers of the Russian Revolution: Biographies of Bolshevik Leaders. Edited by Georges Haupt and Jean-Jacques Marie. Ithaca, N.Y.: Cornell University Press, 1969.
Making Things Work; Russian American Economic Relations, 1900–1930. Stanford, Calif.: Hoover Institution Press, 1992.
Opisannanie v vechnost'; velikii russkii istorik M. I. Rostovtsev v SshA.. Edited by G. M. Bongard-Levin. Lewiston, N.Y.: Edward Mellen Press, 1999.

Papers Relating to the Foreign Relations of the United States. Japan: 1931–1941. 2 vols. Washington, D.C.: GPO, 1943.

Polnoe sobranie sochinenii V. I. Lenin. 55 vols. Moscow: Izpolit.

Register of the Department of State, 1922–1941. Washington, D.C.: GPO, 1922–1941.

Rossiia i SShA: torgova ekonomicheskie otnosheniia, 1900–1930. Edited by G. N. Sevost'ianov. Moscow: Nauka, 1996.

Rossiia i SShA: torgova ekonomicheskie otnosheniia, 1934–1941. Edited by G. N. Sevost'ianov. Moscow: Nauka, 2001.

Rossiia i SShA: torgovo-ekonomicheskie otnosheniia, 1900–1930: sbornik dokumentov. Moscow: Nauka, 1996.

Russia Reported by Walter Duranty. Selected and arranged by Gustavus Tuckerman, Jr. London: Victor Gollancz, 1934.

A Russian Civil War Diary: Alexis Babine in Saratov, 1917–1922. Edited by Donald J. Raleigh. Durham, N.C.: Duke University Press, 1988.

Sovetsko-Amerikanskie otnosheniia, gody nepriznaniia, 1918–1926: dokumenty. Edited by G. N. Sevost'ianov et al. Moscow: Mezhdunarodnyi Fond 'Demokratiia,' 2002.

Sovetsko-Amerikanskie otnosheniia, gody nepriznaniia, 1927–1933: dokumenty. Edited by G. N. Sevost'ianov et al. Moscow: Mezhdunarodnyi Fond 'Demokratiia,' 2002.

Sovetsko-Amerikanskie otnosheniia, 1934–1939: dokumenty. Edited by G. N. Sevost'ianov et al. Moscow: Mezhdunarodnyi fond 'demokratiia,' 2003.

Soviet Peace Efforts on the Eve of World War II: Documents and Records. Edited by A. A. Gromyko et al. Moscow: Progress, 1976.

The Stalin-Kaganovich Correspondence, 1931–1936. Compiled and edited by R. W. Davies, Oleg Khlevniuk, E. A. Rees, Liudmilla Kosheleva, and Larisa A. Rogovaya. New Haven, Conn.: Yale University Press, 2003.

Stalin's Letters to Molotov, 1925–1936. Edited by Lars T. Lih, Oleg V. Naumov, and Oleg V. Khlevniuk. New Haven, Conn.: Yale University Press, 1995.

Ten Years in Japan; A Contemporary Record Drawn from the Diaries and Private and Official Papers of Joseph Grew, United States Ambassador to Japan, 1932–1942. New York: Simon and Schuster, 1944.

Vneshniaia volitika SSSR; rechi i zaiavleniia 1927–1935. Edited by Maxim Litvinov. Moscow: Gos-sots-ekon-izdat, 1935.

Who Was Who in America. Vol. 1: *1897–1942;* Vol. 2: *1943–1950.* Chicago: Marquis Company, 1966.

Who Was Who in American Politics. Edited by Dan and Inez Morris. New York: Hawthorne Books, 1974.

Who's Who in Russia Since 1900. Compiled by Martin McCauley. London: Routledge, 1997.

Memoirs and Contemporary Accounts

Abbe, James E. *I Photograph Russia.* London: George G. Harrap, 1935.

Anderson, Paul B. *No East or West.* Paris: YMCA Press, 1985.

Armstrong, Hamilton Fish. *Peace and Counterpeace from Wilson to Hitler: Memoirs of Hamilton Fish Armstrong.* New York: Harper and Row, 1971.

Babine, Alexis. *A Russian Civil War Diary: Alex Babine in Saratov, 1917–1922.* Edited by Donald Raleigh. Durham, N.C.: Duke University Press, 1988.

Baker, Christina Looper. *In a Generous Spirit: A First-Person Biography of Myra Page.* Urbana: University of Illinois Press, 1996.

Beal, Fred E. *Proletarian Journey: New England, Gastonia, Moscow.* New York: Hillman-Curl, 1937.

Bliven, Bruce. *Twentieth Century Unlimited: From the Vantage Point of Fifty Years.* Philadelphia: Lippincott, 1950.

Bohlen, Charles. *Witness to History, 1929–1969.* New York: Norton, 1973.

Bourke-White, Margaret. *Eyes on Russia.* New York: Simon and Schuster, 1931.

———. *Portrait of Myself.* New York: Simon and Schuster, 1963.

Brown, John. *I Saw for Myself.* London: Selwyn and Blount, 1935.

Bryant, Louise. *Mirrors of Moscow.* New York, 1923.

Bullitt, William C. *It's Not Done.* New York, 1926. (Fiction)

Burrell, George A. *An American Engineer Looks at Russia.* Boston: Stratford, 1932.

Cantacuzene. See Kantakuzen.

Chamberlin, William Henry. *Collectivism: A False Utopia.* New York: Macmillan, 1937.

———. *Russia's Iron Age.* Boston: Little, Brown, 1934.

Chesterton, Mrs. Cecil. *My Russian Adventure.* Philadelphia: J. B. Lippincott, 1931.

Colby, Bainbridge. *The Close of Woodrow Wilson's Administration and the Final Years.* New York: Mitchell Kennerley, 1930.

Colton, Ethan T. *Forty Years with Russians.* New York: Association Press, 1940.

Coolidge, Archibald Cary ["K"]. "Russia after Genoa and The Hague." *Foreign Affairs* 1, no. 1 (September 1922), 133–55.

Cooper, Hugh. "Russia." *Engineers and Engineering* 48, no. 4 (April 1931), 76–86.

Counts, George S. *A Ford Crosses Soviet Russia.* Boston: Stratford, 1930.

Danforth, William H. *Russia under the Hammer and Sickle: Impressions Written to the Purina Family.* St. Louis, Mo.: Ralston Purina, 1927.

Davies, Joseph. *Mission to Moscow.* New York: Simon and Schuster, 1941.

Davies, R. W. *The Socialist Offensive: The Collectivisation of Soviet Agriculture, 1929–1930.* Cambridge, Mass.: Harvard University Press, 1980.

Dewey, John. *Impressions of Soviet Russia and the Revolutionary World Mexico-China-Turkey.* New York: New Republic, 1929.

Dexter, Byron. *The Years of Opportunity: The League of Nations, 1920–1926.* New York: Viking, 1967.

Dodd, William E., and Martha Dodd. *Ambassador Dodd's Diary, 1933–1938.* New York: Harcourt Brace, 1941.

Dreiser, Theodore. *Dreiser Looks at Russia.* New York: Liveright, 1928.

Duncan, Isadora. *My Life.* New York: Boni and Liveright, 1927.

Duranty, Walter. *I Write as I Please.* New York: Simon and Schuster, 1935.

Eden, Anthony. *The Memoirs of Anthony Eden, Earl of Avon: Facing the Dictators, 1923–1938.* Boston: Houghton Mifflin, 1962.

Eddy, Sherwood George. *The Challenge of Russia.* New York: Farrar and Rinehart, 1931.

———. *Eighty Adventurous Years: An Autobiography.* New York: Harper and Brothers, 1955.

Efros, Nikolai. *Teatr "Letuchaia Mysh" N. F. Balieva: Obzor desiatiletnei khudozhestvennoi raboty pervago russkago teatra-kabare.* Petrograd: "Solntse Rossii," 1918.

Ehrenburg, Ilya. *Memoirs: 1921–1941.* Translated by Tatania Shebunina. Cleveland, Ohio: World, 1964.

Farson, Negley. *Black Bread and Red Coffins.* New York: Century, 1930.

Fischer, Louis. *Machines and Men in Russia.* New York: Harrison Smith, 1932.

———. *Men and Politics: Europe between the Two World Wars.* New York: Harper Colophon, 1966.

———. *Soviet Journey.* New York: Harrison Smith and Robert Haas, 1935.

Fisher, Harold H. *The Famine in Soviet Russia, 1919–1923: The Operations of the American Relief Administration.* New York: Macmillan, 1927.

Frear, James A. *Forty Years of Progressive Public Service: Reasonably Filled with Thorns and Flowers.* Washington, D.C.: Associated Writers, 1937.

Friedman, Elisha M. *Russia in Transition: A Business Man's Appraisal.* New York: Viking Press, 1932.

Gauvreau, Emile. *What So Proudly We Hailed.* New York: Macaulay, 1935.

Gibson, William J. *Wild Career: My Crowded Years of Adventure in Russia and the Near East.* London: George G. Harrap, 1935.

Golder, Frank Alfred, and Lincoln Hutchinson. *On the Trail of the Russian Famine.* Stanford, Calif.: Stanford University Press, 1927.

Goldman, Emma. *My Disillusionment in Russia*. Intro. by Rebecca West. New York: Thomas Y. Crowell (Apollo), 1950.

Golikov, F. I. *On a Military Mission to Great Britain and the United States*. Translated by Nadezhda Bureva. Moscow: Progress, 1987.

Grady, Eve Garette. *Seeing Red*. New York: Brewer, Warren, 1931.

Grew, Joseph. *Ten Years in Japan: A Contemporary World*. New York: Simon and Schuster, 1944.

———. *Turbulent Years: A Diplomatic Record of Forty Years, 1904–1945*. Two vols. London: Hammond, 1953.

Gromyko, Anatoly. *Pamiatnoe*. Vol. 1. Moscow: Nauka, 1988.

Gruber, Ruth. *I Went to the Soviet Arctic*. Revised edition. New York: Viking Press, 1944.

Halle, Fannina W. *Woman in Soviet Russia*. London: Routledge, 1933.

Hammer, Armand. *The Quest of the Romanoff Treasure*. New York: Paisley Press, 1932.

Hammer, Armand, with Neil Lyndon. *Hammer*. New York: G. P. Putnam's, 1988.

Hammond, John Hays. *The Autobiography of John Hays Hammond*. New York: Farrar and Rinehart, 1935.

Hapgood, Norman. *The Changing Years: Reminiscences of Norman Hapgood*. New York: Farrar and Rinehart, 1933.

Harper, Samuel. *The Russia I Believed In: The Memoirs of Samuel N. Harper, 1902–1941*. Edited by Paul Harper. Chicago: University of Chicago Press, 1945.

Harriman, Mrs. J. Borden. *From Pinafores to Politics*. New York: Henry Holt, 1923.

Harriman, W. Averell. *America and Russia in a Changing World: A Half-Century of Personal Observation*. Garden City, N.Y.: Doubleday and Company, 1971.

Harriman, W. Averell, and Ellie Abel. *Special Envoy to Churchill and Stalin, 1941–1946*. New York: Random House, 1975.

Harrison, Marguerite. *Marooned in Moscow: The Story of an American Woman Imprisoned in Russia*. New York: Doran, 1921.

———. *There's Always Tomorrow: The Story of a Checkered Life*. New York: Farrar and Rinehart, 1935.

Haywood, Harry. *Black Bolshevik: Autobiography of an Afro-American Communist*. Chicago: Liberator Press, 1978.

Henderson, Loy. *A Question of Trust: The Origins of U.S.-Soviet Relations — The Memoirs of Loy W. Henderson*. Edited by George W. Baer. Stanford, Calif.: Hoover Institution Press, 1986.

Herniss, Chris and Cliff. *To the Soviet Union in 1937 and Now*. Moscow: Novosti, 1981.

Hiebert, Peter Cornelius, and Orie O. Miller. *Feeding the Hungry: Russia Famine, 1919–1925*. Scottsdale, Penn.: Mennonite Central Committee, 1929.

Hindus, Maurice. *Red Bread*. New York: Jonathan Cape and Harrison Smith, 1931.

Hoover, Herbert. *The Cabinet and the Presidency, 1920–1933*. Volume 2 of *The Memoirs of Herbert Hoover*. New York: Macmillan, 1952.

Hopper, Bruce. *Pan-Sovietism: The Issue before America*. Boston: Houghton Mifflin, 1931.

Hughes, Langston. *I Wonder as I Wander: An Autobiographical Journey*. New York: Thunder's Mouth Press, 1986.

———. *Moscow and Me: A Noted American Writer Relates His Experiences*. Moscow: International Union of Revolutionary Writers, 1933.

Hull, Cordell. *The Memoirs of Cordell Hull*. 2 vols. New York: Macmillan, 1948.

Hullinger, Edwin Ware. *The Reforging of Russia*. New York: E. P. Dutton, 1925.

Huntington, W. Chapin. *The Homesick Million: Russia-out-of-Russia*. Boston: Stratford, 1933.

Huppert, Hugo. *Men of Siberia: Sketchbook from the Kuzbas*. New York: International Publishers, 1934.

Ickes, Harold L. *The Secret Diary of Harold L. Ickes*. 3 vols. New York: Macmillan, 1948.

Ilf, Ilya, and Eugene Petrov. *Little Golden America: Two Famous Soviet Humourists Survey the United States*. London: George Routledge and Sons, 1946.

Ilyin, Olga. *White Road: A Russian Odyssey, 1919–1923*. New York: Holt, Rinehart, and Winston, 1984.

Johnson, Robert Underwood. *Remembered Yesterdays*. Boston: Little, Brown, 1923.

Kaltenborn, Hubert V. *Fifty Fabulous Years, 1900–1950: A Personal Review*. New York: Putnam's, 1950.

Kantakuzen, Julia Grant. *Revolutionary Days, Including Passages from My Life Here and There, 1876–1917, by Princess Julia Cantacuzene, Countess Speransky, Nee Grant*. Edited by Terence Emmons. Chicago: R. R. Donnelley, 1999.

Kennan, George F. *At a Century's End: Reflections 1982–1995*. New York: W. W. Norton, 1996.

———. *Memoirs, 1925–1950*. Boston: Houghton Mifflin, 1970.

———. *Sketches from a Life*. New York: Pantheon, 1989.

Killen, Linda. *The Russian Bureau: A Case Study in Wilsonian Diplomacy*. Lexington: University Press of Kentucky, 1983.

Knickerbocker, Hubert R. *The Red Trade Menace: Progress of the Soviet Five-Year Plan*. New York: Dodd, Mead, 1931.

Kotliarskii, Arkadii. *Spasibo dzhazu: vospominaniia starogo utesovtsa*. Leningrad: Khudozhestvennaia literatura, 1990.

Krivitsky, Walter G. *In Stalin's Secret Service: An Exposé of Russia's Secret Policies by the Former Chief of the Soviet Intelligence in Western Europe*. New York: Harper and Brothers, 1930.

Leder, Mary M. *My Life in Stalinist Russia: An American Woman Looks Back*. Edited by Laurie Bernstein. Bloomington: Indiana University Press, 2001.

Lee, Ivy. *Present-Day Russia*. New York: Macmillan, 1928.

———. *USSR: A World Enigma*. New York: privately printed, 1927.

Levine, Isaac Don. *Eyewitness to History: Memoirs and Reflections of a Foreign Correspondent for Half a Century*. New York: Hawthorne Books, 1973.

Liberman, Simon. *Building Lenin's Russia*. Chicago: University of Chicago Press, 1945.

Lied, Jonas. *Sidelights on the Economic Situation in Russia*. Moscow: Kushnarev, 1922.

Lindberg, Anne Morrow. *North to the Orient*. New York: Harcourt, Brace, 1935.

Littlepage, John, with Demaree Bess. *In Search of Soviet Gold*. New York: Harcourt Brace, 1938.

Litvinov, Maxim. *Notes for a Journal*. Introduction by E. H. Carr. New York: William Morrow, 1955.

Lohr, Eric. *Nationalizing the Russian Empire: The Campaign Against against Enemy Aliens During during World War I*. Cambridge, Mass.: Harvard University Press, 2003.

Long, James W. *From Privileged to Dispossessed: The Volga Germans, 1860–1917*. Lincoln: University of Nebraska Press, 1988.

Long, Ray. *An Editor Looks at Russia: One Unprejudiced View of the Land of the Soviets*. New York: Ray Long and Richard Smith, 1931.

Lyons, Eugene. *Assignment in Utopia*. New York: Harcourt, Brace, 1937.

Mackenzie, F. A. *Russia before Dawn*. London: T. Fisher Unwin, 1923.

Maisky, Ivan. *Memoirs of a Soviet Ambassador: The War 1939–1943*. Translated by Andrew Rothstein. London: Hutchinson, 1967.

Manning, Ethel. *Forever Wandering*. New York: E. P. Dutton, 1935.

Marshall, Mildred Widmer. *Two Oregon Schoolma'ams, around the World, 1937, Via Trans-Siberian Railroad*. Woodburn, Ore.: Widdy Publishing, 1985.

Marx, Harpo, with Rowland Barber. *Harpo Speaks!* New York: Limelight Editions, 2000.

Mayakovsky, Vladimir. *The Bedbug and Selected Poetry*. Edited by Patricia Blake, and translated by George Reavey. Bloomington: Indiana University Press, 1975.

McCullagh, Francis. *A Prisoner of the Reds: The Story of a British Officer Captured in Siberia*. New York: E. P. Dutton, 1922.

McKay, Claude. *A Long Way from Home*. New York: Lee, Furman, 1937.

Moen, Lars. *Are You Going to Russia?* London: Chapman and Hall, 1934.

Moley, Raymond. *After Seven Years*. New York: Harper, 1939.

Monkhouse, Allan. *Moscow, 1911–1933: Being the Memoirs of Allan Monkhouse*. London: Victor Gollancz, 1933.

Nabokov, Nicolas. *Bagazh: Memoirs of a Russian Cosmopolitan*. New York: Atheneum, 1975.

Newman, Edward Manuel. *Seeing Russia*. New York: Funk & Wagnalls, 1928.

Nicolson, Harold. *Diaries and Letters*. Vols. 1–2. New York: Atheneum, 1967.

Nobile, Umberto. *My Five Years with Soviet Airships*. Akron, Ohio: Lighter-Than-Air Society, 1987.

Noe, Adolf Carl. *Golden Days of Soviet Russia*. Illustrations by Edmund Giesbert. Chicago: Thomas S. Rockwell, 1931.

Page, Kirby. *Kirby Page, Social Evangelist: The Autobiography of a 20th Century Prophet for Peace*. Nyack, N.Y.: Fellowship Press, 1975.

Page, Dorothy Myra. *Gathering Storm*. Moscow: International Publishers, 1932.

———. *Moscow Yankee*. Introduction by Barbara Foley. Urbana: University of Illinois Press, 1995 (autobiographical novel set in 1931–1932).

———. *Soviet Main Street*. Moscow: International Press, 1933.

Patterson, Jefferson. *Diplomatic Duty and Diversion*. Cambridge, Mass.: Riverside Press, 1956.

Phillips, William. *Ventures in Diplomacy*. Portland, Maine: Anthoensen Press, 1952.

Ponafidine, Emma Cochran. *Russia—My Home: An Intimate Record of Personal Experiences before, during, and after the Bolshevist Revolution*. Indianapolis, Ind.: Bobbs-Merrill, 1931.

Remple, Henry D. *From Bolshevik Russia to America: A Mennonite Family Story*. Sioux Falls, S.D.: Pine Hill Press, 2001.

Reuther, Victor G. *The Brothers Reuther and the Story of the UAW: A Memoir*. Boston: Houghton Mifflin, 1976.

Robinson, Robert, with Jonathan Slavin. *Black on Red: My 44 Years Inside the Soviet Union*. Washington, D.C.: Acropolis, 1988.

Rukeyser, Walter Arnold. *Working for the Soviets: An American Engineer in Russia*. New York: Covici-friede, 1932.

Schlesinger, Arthur M., Jr. *A Life in the 20th Century: Innocent Beginnings, 1917–1950*. Boston: Houghton Mifflin, 2000.

Scott, John. *Behind the Urals: An American Worker in Russia's City of Steel*. Bloomington: Indiana University Press, 1989.

Seymour, June. *In the Moscow Manner*. London: Denis Archer, 1935.

Shaliapin, Fedor. *Maska i dusha*. Moscow: Vagrius, 1997.

Shirer, William L. *20th Century Journey: The Nightmare Years, 1930–1940: A Memoir of the Life and Times*. Boston: Little, Brown, 1984.

Sinclair, Upton. *The Autobiography of Upton Sinclair*. New York: Harcourt, Brace, 1962.

———. *World's End*. New York: Literary Guild, 1940 (Fiction with references to Bullitt).

Skariatina, Irma (Mrs. Victor Blakeslee). *First to Go Back: An Aristocrat in Soviet Russia*. Indianapolis: Bobbs-Merrill, 1933.

Smith, Andrew. *I Was a Soviet Worker*. London: Robert Hale, 1937.

Sorensen, Charles E., with Samuel T. Williamson. *My Forty Years with Ford*. New York: Norton, 1956.

Sorokin, Pitirim A. *A Long Journey: The Autobiography of Pitirim Sorokin*. New Haven, Conn.: College and University Press, 1963.

———. *Russia and the United States*. New York: E. P. Dutton, 1944.

Stalin, J. V. *Problems of Leninism*. Peking: Foreign Languages Press, 1976.

Stanislavsky, Constantin. *My Life in Art*. Translated by Elizabeth Reynolds Hapgood. New York: Theater Arts Books, 1924.

Steffens, Lincoln. *The Autobiography of Lincoln Steffens*. New York: Harcourt, Brace, 1931.

Strong, Anna Louise. *Children of Revolution: Story of the John Reed Children's Colony on the Volga*. Seattle, Wash.: Pigott, 1926.

———. *I Change Worlds: The Remaking of an American*. New York: Garden City Publishing Co., 1937.

———. *Remaking an American*. Moscow: Cooperation Publ. Society, 1935. [first edition of above].

———. *The Soviets Conquer Wheat: The Drama of Collective Farming*. New York: Henry Holt, 1931.

Sulzberger, Cyrus L. *A Long Row of Candles: Memoirs and Diaries*. Toronto: Macmillan, 1969.

Thayer, Charles W. *Bears in the Caviar*. Philadelphia, Pa.: Lippincott, 1950.
Troianovskii, O. A. *Cherez gody i rasstoianiia: Istoriia odnoi s"em'i*. Moscow: Vagrius, 1997.
Trotsky, Leon. *My Life*. New York: Grosset and Dunlap, 1960.
Welles, Sumner. *A Time for Decision*. New York: Harper and Brothers, 1944.
Wettlin, Margaret. *Fifty Russian Winters: An American Woman's Life in the Soviet Union*. New York: Pharos, 1992.
White, Dmitri Fedotoff. *Survival through War and Revolution*. Philadelphia: University of Pennsylvania Press, 1939.
White, William Allen. *The Autobiography of William Allen White*. New York: Macmillan, 1946.
———. *Woodrow Wilson: The Man, His Times, His Tasks*. Boston: Houghton Mifflin, 1924.
Williams, Albert Rhys. *The Soviets*. New York: Harcourt Brace, 1937.
Witkin, Zara. *An American Engineer in Stalin's Russia: The Memoirs of Zara Witkin, 1932–1934*. Edited by Michael Gelb. Berkeley: University of California Press, 1991.
Wooding, Samuel. "Eight Years Abroad with a Jazz Band." *The Etude* (April 1939), 233–34, 282.
Yakobson, Helen. *Crossing Borders: From Revolutionary Russia to China to America*. Tenafly, N.J.: Hermitage, 1994.

Scholarly Sources on Soviet-American Relations

Abbott, Lawrence F. *The Story of NYLIC: A History of the Origin and Development of the New York Life Insurance Company from 1845 to 1929*. New York: The Company, 1930.
Abramson, Rudy. *Spanning the Century: The Life of W. Averell Harriman, 1891–1986*. New York: Morrow, 1992.
Adams, Frederick C. *Economic Diplomacy: The Export-Import Bank and American Foreign Policy, 1933–1939*. Columbia: University of Missouri Press, 1976.
Alexander, Robert Jackson. *The Right Opposition: The Lovestoneites and the International Communist Opposition of the 1930s*. Westport, Conn.: Greenwood Press, 1981.
Alpers, Benjamin L. *Dictators, Democracy, and American Public Culture: Envisioning the Totalitarian Enemy, 1920s–1950s*. Chapel Hill: University of North Carolina Press, 2003.
Ashby, LeRoy. *Spearless Leader: Senator Borah and the Progressive Movement in the 1920s*. Urbana: University of Illinois Press, 1972.
Asquith, Michael. *Famine: Quaker Work in Russia, 1921–1923*. Oxford: Oxford University Press, 1943.
Austin, Richard Cartwright. *Building Utopia: Erecting Russia's First Modern City, 1930*. Kent, Ohio: Kent State University Press, 2004.
Bailes, Kendall E. "The American Connection: Ideology and the Transfer of American Technology to the Soviet Union, 1917–1941." *Comparative Studies in Society and History* 23, no. 2 (April 1981), 426–39.
Bailey, Geoffrey. *The Conspirators*. New York: Harper and Brothers, 1960.
Baker, Christina Looper. *In a Generous Spirit: A First-Person Biography of Myra Page*. Urbana: University of Illinois Press, 1996.
Ball, Alan M. *Imagining America: Influence and Images in Twentieth-Century Russia*. Lanham, M.D.: Rowman and Littlefield, 2003.
Barnes, Harper. *Standing on a Volcano: The Life and Times of David Rowland Francis*. St. Louis: Missouri Historical Society, 2001.
Bassow, Whitman. *The Moscow Correspondents: Reporting on Russia from the Revolution to Glasnost*. New York: Paragon House, 1989.
Beitzell, Robert. *The Uneasy Alliance: America, Britain, and Russia, 1941–1943*. New York: Knopf, 1972.
Benedotti, Jean. *Stanislavsky: A Biography*. London: Routledge, 1988.
Bennett, Edward M. *Franklin D. Roosevelt and the Search for Security: American-Soviet Relations, 1933–1939*. Wilmington, Del.: Scholarly Resources, 1985.

———. *Franklin D. Roosevelt and the Search for Victory: American-Soviet Relations, 1939–1945.* Studies in International History. Edited by Warren Kimball. Wilmington, Del.: Scholarly Resources, 1990.

———. *Recognition of Russia: An American Foreign Policy Dilemma.* Waltham, Mass.: Blaisdell, 1970.

Bishop, Donald G. *The Roosevelt-Litvinov Agreements: The American View.* Syracuse, N.Y.: Syracuse University Press, 1965.

Black, Conrad. *Franklin Delano Roosevelt: Champion of Freedom.* New York: Public Affairs, 2003.

Blakely, Allison. *Russia and the Negro: Blacks in Russian History and Thought.* Washington, D.C.: Howard University Press, 1986.

Boe, Jonathan E. *American Business: The Response to the Soviet Union, 1933–1947.* New York: Garland, 1987.

Bogomolov, O. T. *Razvitie ekonomicheskikh sviazei s zarulezhnvmi stranam.* Moscow: Nauk, 1957.

Bolkhovitinov, Nikolai N. "Zhizn' i deiatel'nost' G. V. Vernadskogo (1887–1973) i ego arkhiv." Sapporo, Japan: Slavic Research Center, Hokkaido University, 2002.

Bowers, Robert E. "American Diplomacy, the 1933 Wheat Conference and Recognition of the Soviet Union." *Agricultural History* 40 (January 1966), 39–52.

———. "Hull, Russian Subversion in Cuba, and Recognition of the USSR." *Journal of American History* 52, no. 3 (December 1966), 542–55.

———. "Senator Arthur Robinson of Indiana Vindicated: William Bullitt's Secret Mission to Europe." *Indiana Magazine of History* 41 (September 1965), 189–204.

Boyle, Peter G. *American-Soviet Relations: From the Russian Revolution to the Fall of Communism.* London: Routledge, 1993.

Brands, H. W. *Inside the Cold War: Loy Henderson and the Rise of the American Empire, 1918–1961.* New York: Oxford University Press, 1991.

Braun, Edward. *The Theatre of Meyerhold: Revolution on the Modern Stage.* New York: Drama Book Specialists, 1979.

Brooks, Jeffrey. "The Press and Its Message: Images of America in the 1920s and 1930s." In *Russia in the Era of NEP: Explorations in Soviet Society and Culture.* Bloomington: Indiana University Press, 1991.

Browder, Robert Paul. *The Origins of Soviet-American Diplomacy.* Princeton, N.J.: Princeton University Press, 1953.

Brown, Anthony Cave. *The Last Hero: Wild Bill Donovan.* New York: Times Books, 1982.

Brownell, Will, and Richard Billings. *So Close to Greatness: The First Biography of William C. Bullitt.* New York: Macmillan, 1987.

Buckingham, Peter H. *America Sees Red: Anticommunism in America, 1870s to 1980s: A Review of Issues and References.* Claremont, Calif.: Regina Books, 1988.

Buehler, E. C., B. W. Maxwell, George R. R. Pflaum, comps. *Selected Articles on Recognition of Soviet Russia.* New York: H. W. Wilson Company, 1931.

Bullitt, William C., and Sigmund Freud. *Thomas Woodrow Wilson: A Psychological Study.* Boston: Houghton Mifflin, 1966.

Butler, William E. *The Soviet Union and the Law of the Sea.* Baltimore, Md.: Johns Hopkins Press, 1971.

Byrnes, Robert F. *Awakening American Education to the World: The Role of Archibald Cary Coolidge, 1866–1928.* Notre Dame, Ind.: University of Notre Dame Press, 1982.

Capelotti, P. J. *Our Man in the Crimea: Commander Hugo Koehler and the Russian Civil War.* Columbia: University of South Carolina Press, 1991.

Carley, Michael Jabara. *1939: The Alliance That Never Was and the Coming of World War II.* Chicago: Ivan Dee, 1999.

Carstensen, Fred V. *American Enterprise in Foreign Markets: Singer and International Harvester in Imperial Russia.* Chapel Hill: University of North Carolina Press, 1984.

Cassella-Blackburn, Michael. *The Donkey, the Carrot, and the Club: William C. Bullitt and Soviet-American Relations, 1917–1948.* Westport, Conn.: Praeger, 2004.

Castle, Alfred L. *Diplomatic Realism: William R. Castle, Jr. and American Foreign Policy, 1919–1933.* Honolulu: University of Hawaii Press, 1999.

Carr, E. H. *Twilight of the Comintern, 1930–1934*. New York: Pantheon, 1982.

Carstensen, Fred V. *American Enterprise in Foreign Markets: Singer and International Harvester in Imperial Russia*. Chapel Hill: University of North Carolina Press, 1984.

Caute, David. *The Fellow Travelers: A Postscript to the Enlightenment*. New York: Harper and Row, 1973.

Chubarian, A. O., ed. *Voina i politika, 1939–1941*. Moscow: Nauka, 1999.

Cohen, Stephen F. *Bukharin and the Bolshevik Revolution: A Political Biography, 1888–1938*. New York: Norton, 1973.

Cohen, Warren I. *Empire without Tears: America's Foreign Relations, 1921–1933*. Philadelphia: Temple University Press, 1987.

Cole, William. *Roosevelt and the Isolationists*. Lincoln: University of Nebraska Press, 1983.

Considine, Jennifer I., and William A. Kerr. *The Russian Oil Economy*. Cheltenham, UK: Edward Elgar, 2002.

Coopersmith, Jonathan. *The Electrification of Russia, 1880–1926*. Ithaca, N.Y.: Cornell University Press, 1992.

Craig, Gordon A., and Felix Gilbert, eds. *The Diplomats: 1919–1939*. 2 vols. Princeton, N.J.: Princeton University Press, 1953.

Dallek, Robert. *Franklin D. Roosevelt and American Foreign Policy, 1932–1945*. New York: Knopf, 1979.

Dalrymple, Dana. "American Technology and Soviet Agricultural Development, 1924–1933." *Agricultural History* 40, no. 3 (July 1966), 187–206.

Davies, Jessie. *Isadora Duncan's Russian Husband or Child of the Terrible Years*. Liverpool: Lincoln Davies, 1990.

Davis, Donald E., and Eugene Trani. *The First Cold War: The Legacy of Woodrow Wilson and U.S. Soviet Relations*. Columbia: University of Missouri Press, 2002.

Davis, Kenneth S. *FDR: The New Deal Years, 1933–1937*. New York: Random House, 1986.

Dawson, Raymond H. *The Decision to Aid Russia, 1941*. Chapel Hill: University of North Carolina Press, 1959.

Dearborn, Mary V. *Queen of Bohemia: The Life of Louise Bryant*. Boston: Houghton Mifflin, 1996.

DeSantis, Hugh. *The Diplomacy of Silence: The American Foreign Service, the Soviet Union and the Cold War, 1933–1947*. Chicago: University of Chicago Press, 1980.

Desmond, Robert W. *Crisis and Conflict: World News Reporting between Two Wars, 1920–1940*. Iowa City: University of Iowa Press, 1982.

———. *Tides of War: World News Reporting, 1931–1945*. Iowa City: University of Iowa Press, 1984.

Dexter, Byron. *The Years of Opportunity: The League of Nations, 1920–1926*. New York: Viking, 1967.

Divine, Robert A. *The Illusion of Neutrality*. Chicago: University of Chicago Press, 1962.

Dorn, Harold. "Hugh Lincoln Cooper and the First Detente," *Technology and Culture* 20 (1979), 322–47.

Draper, Theodore. *American Communism and Soviet Russia: The Formative Period*. New York: Viking, 1960.

Dubie, Alain. *Frank A. Golder: An Adventure of a Historian in Quest of Russian History*. Boulder, Colo.: East European Monographs, 1989.

Dukes, Paul. *The USA in the Making of the USSR: The Washington Conference, 1921–1922, and "Uninvited Russia."* London: Routledge/Curzon, 2004.

Dunn, Dennis J. *Caught between Roosevelt and Stalin: America's Ambassadors to Moscow*. Lexington: University Press of Kentucky, 1998.

Eagles, Keith David. *Ambassador Joseph E. Davies and American-Soviet Relations, 1937–1941*. New York: Garland, 1984.

Edwards, Jerome E. *The Foreign Policy of Col. McCormick's Tribune, 1929–1941*. Reno: University of Nevada Press, 1971.

Efros, Nikolai. *Teatr "Letuchaia Mysh" N. F. Balieva: Obzor desiatiletnei khodozhestvennoi raboty pervago russkago teatra-kabare*. Petrograd: Solntse Rossii, 1918.

Egorova, N. I. *Izoliatsionizm i evropeiskaia politika SShA, 1933–1941*. Moscow: Institut vseobshchei istorii, AN, 1995.

Engerman, David Charles. *Modernization from the Other Shore: American Intellectuals and the Romance of Russian Development*. Cambridge, Mass.: Harvard University Press, 2003.

Epstein, Edward Jay. *Dossier: The Secret History of Armand Hammer*. New York: Random House, 1996.

Farnsworth, Beatrice. *William C. Bullitt and the Soviet Union*. Bloomington: Indiana University Press, 1967.

Feiertag, Vladimir. *Dzhaz ot Leningrada do Peterburga*. St. Petersburg: Kul'tInformPress, 1999.

Feis, Herbert. *1933: Characters in Crisis*. Boston: Little, Brown, 1966.

———. *Churchill, Roosevelt, Stalin: The War They Fought and the Peace They Sought*. Princeton, N.J.: Princeton University Press, 1957.

Ferrell, Robert. *American Diplomacy in the Great Depression: Hoover-Stimson Foreign Policy. 1929–1933*. New Haven, Conn.: Yale University Press, 1957.

———. *Peace in Their Time: The Origins of the Kellogg-Briand Pact*. New Haven, Conn.: Yale University Press, 1952.

———. *The Presidency of Calvin Coolidge*. Lawrence: University Press of Kansas, 1998.

Figes, Orlando. *Natasha's Dance: A Cultural History of Russia*. New York: Henry Holt, 2002.

———. *A People's Tragedy: The Russian Revolution, 1891–1924*. New York: Penguin, 1996.

Filene, Peter G. *Americans and the Soviet Experiment, 1917–1933*. Cambridge, Mass.: Harvard University Press, 1967.

Fisher, Charles. *The Columnists*. New York: Howell, Soskin, 1944.

Fisher, Harold H. *The Famine in Soviet Russia, 1919–1923: The Operations of the American Relief Administration*. New York: Macmillan, 1927.

Fitzpatrick, Sheila, Alexander Rabinowitch, and Richard Stites, eds. *Russia in the Era of NEP: Explorations in Soviet Society and Culture*. Bloomington: Indiana University Press, 1991.

Friedheim, Robert F. *The Seattle General Strike*. Seattle: University of Washington Press, 1964.

Foglesong, David. *America's Secret War against Bolshevism: U.S. Intervention in the Russian Civil War, 1917–1920*. Chapel Hill: University of North Carolina Press, 1995.

———. "Xenephon Kalamatiano: An American Spy in Revolutionary Russia?" *Intelligence and National Security* 6, no. 1 (January 1991), 154–95.

Friedheim, Robert F. *The Seattle General Strike*. Seattle: University of Washington Press, 1964.

Furaev, V. K. *Sovetsko-amerikanskie otnosheniia, 1917–1939*. Moscow: Nauka, 1964.

Furniss, Edgar S. "Russia in World Politics." *Current History* 38 (July 1933), 374–77.

Gaddis, John Lewis. *Russia, the Soviet Union, and the United States: An Interpretive History*. Second edition. New York: John Wiley, 1992.

Gaiduk, Ilia V. "Sovremennaia istoricheskaia sovetologiia SShA: Metodologiia i pratiki izucheniia sovetsko-amerikanskikh otnoshenii (1917–1941 gg.)." Dissertation, Moscow University, 1990.

Gardner, Lloyd. *Architects of Illusion: Men and Ideas in American Foreign Policy, 1941–1949*. Chicago: Quadrangle Books, 1970.

———. *Economic Aspects of New Deal Diplomacy*. Madison: University of Wisconsin Press, 1964.

———. *Safe for Democracy: The Anglo-American Response to Revolution, 1913–1923*. New York: Oxford University Press, 1983.

Gardner, Virginia. *"Friend and Lover": The Life of Louise Bryant*. New York: Horizon, 1982.

Garrett, Garet. *Defend America First: The Antiwar Editorials of the Saturday Evening Post, 1939–1942*. Caldwell, Idaho: Caxton Press, 2003.

Gellman, Irwin F. *Secret Affairs: Franklin Roosevelt, Cordell Hull, and Sumner Welles*. Baltimore, Md.: Johns Hopkins University Press, 1995.

Getty, J. Arch, and Oleg V. Naumov. *The Road to Terror: Stalin and the Self-Destruction of the Bolsheviks, 1932–1939*. New Haven, Conn.: Yale University Press, 1999.

Glad, Betty. *Charles Evans Hughes and the Illusions of Innocence: a Study in American Diplomacy*. Urbana: University of Illinois Press, 1966.

Glantz, Mary E. *FDR and the Soviet Union: The President's Battles over Foreign Policy*. Lawrence: University Press of Kansas, 2005.

Glenny, Michael, and Norman Stone, eds. *The Other Russia: The Experience of Exile*. New York: Viking, 1991.

Gorodetsky, Gabriel. *Grand Delusion: Stalin and the German Invasion of Russia*. New Haven: Yale University Press, 1999.

Gorsuch, Anne. *Flappers and Foxtrotters: Soviet Youth in the "Roaring Twenties."* Carl Beck Papers, no. 1102. Pittsburgh, Penn.: University of Pittsburgh Press, 1994.

Grant, Natalie. "The Russian Section: A Window on the Soviet Union." *Diplomatic History* 2, no. 1 (Winter 1978), 107–15.

Haight, John McVickar, Jr. *American Aid to France, 1938–1940*. New York: Atheneum, 1970.

Hanby, Alonzo L. *For the Survival of Democracy: Franklin Roosevelt and the World Crisis of the 1930s*. New York: Free Press, 2004.

Hapgood, David. *Charles R. Crane: The Man Who Bet on People*. New York: Institute of Current World Affairs, 2000.

Harrison, Marguerite. *Marooned in Moscow: The Story of an American Woman Imprisoned in Russia*. New York: George H. Doran, 1921.

Harrington, Daniel F. "Kennan, Bohlen, and the Riga Axioms." *Diplomatic History* 2, no. 4 (fall 1978), 423–37.

Haslam, Jonathan. *Soviet Foreign Policy, 1930–1933: The Impact of the Depression*. New York: St. Martins, 1983.

———. *The Soviet Union and the Struggle for Collective Security in Europe, 1933–1939*. New York: St. Martins, 1984.

———. *The Soviet Union and the Threat from the East, 1933–1941: Moscow, Tokyo, and the Prelude to the Pacific War*. Basingstoke, UK: Macmillan, 1992.

Hatfield, Senator Mark O., comp. *Herbert Hoover Reassessed: Essays Commemorating the Fiftieth Anniversary of the Inauguration of Our Thirty-First President*. Washington: GPO, 1981.

Heale, M. J. *American Anticommunism: Combating the Enemy Within, 1830–1970*. Baltimore: Johns Hopkins University Press, 1990.

Heinrichs, Waldo H., Jr. *American Ambassador: Joseph C. Grew and the Development of the United States Diplomatic Tradition*. Boston: Little, Brown, 1966.

———. *Threshold of War: Franklin D. Roosevelt and American Entry into World War II*. New York: Oxford University Press, 1988.

Herndon, James S., and Joseph O. Baylen. "Col. Philip R. Faymonville and the Red Army, 1934–1943." *Slavic Review* 34, no. 3 (September 1975), 483–505.

Herzstein, Robert E. *Roosevelt and Hitler: Prelude to War*. New York: Paragon House, 1989.

Heywood, Anthony. *Modernizing Lenin's Russia: Economic Reconstruction, Foreign Trade and the Railways*. Cambridge: Cambridge University Press, 1999.

Hindus, Maurice. *Broken Earth*. London: T. J. Unwin, 1926.

———. *Humanity Uprooted*. New York: Cape and H. Smith, 1930.

Hochman, Jonathon. *The Soviet Union and the Failure of the Collective Security, 1933–1938*. Ithaca, N.Y.: Cornell University Press, 1984.

Hogan, Michael J. *The Ambiguous Legacy: U.S. Foreign Relations in the "American Century."* Cambridge, UK: Cambridge University Press, 1999.

Hughes, Thomas P. *American Genesis: A Century of Invention and Technological Enthusiasm, 1870–1970*. New York: Viking, 1989.

Iriye, Akira. *After Imperialism: The Search for a New Order in the Far East, 1921–1931*. Chicago: Imprint Publications, 1990.

Isaacson, Walter, and Evan Thomas. *The Wise Men: Six Friends and the World They Made: Acheson, Bohlen, Harriman, Kennan, Lovett, McCloy*. New York: Simon and Schuster (Touchstone), 1986.

Israelian, V. "Bolshaia troika: SSSR, SshA, Angliia 1941–1942 gody." *Soviet Union/Union Sovietique* 18, 1–3 (1991), 123–37.

Ivanov, Robert. *Stalin i soiuzniki, 1941–1945 gg.* Smolensk: Rusich, 2000.

Jacobson, Jon. *When the Soviet Union Entered World Politics.* Berkeley: University of California Press, 1994.

Jones, Robert Huhn. *The Roads to Russia: United States Lend-Lease to the Soviet Union.* Norman: University of Oklahoma Press, 1969.

Josephson, Matthew. *Sidney Hillman: Statesman of American Labor.* Garden City, N.Y.: Doubleday, 1952.

Kagedan, Allan L. "American Jews and the Soviet Experiment: The Agro-Joint Project, 1924–1937," *Jewish Social Studies* 43, no. 2 (1981), 153–64.

Karlowich, Robert A. "Stranger in a Far Land: Report of a Bookbuying Trip by Harry Miller Lydenberg in Eastern Europe and Russia in 1923–1924." *Bulletin of Research in the Humanities* 87, no. 1 (1986–1987), 182–224.

Kasinec, Edward. "H. B. Khavkina (1871–1949): American Library Ideas in Russia and the Development of Soviet Librarianship." *Libri* 37, no. 1 (1987), 59–71.

Keenan, Claudia J. "The Education of an Intellectual: George S. Counts and Turn-of-the-Century Kansas." *Kansas History* 25, no. 4 (winter 2002–2003), 258–71.

Kennan, George F. *Russia and the West under Lenin and Stalin.* Boston: Little, Brown, 1961.

Kennell, Ruth Epperson. *Theodore Dreiser and the Soviet Union, 1927–1945; A First-Hand Chronicle.* New York: International Publishers, 1969.

Kern, Gary. *Death in Washington: Walter G. Krivitsky and the Stalin Terror.* New York: Enigma Books, 2003.

Ketchum, Richard M. *The Borrowed Years, 1938–1941: America on the Way to War.* New York: Random House, 1989.

Khanga, Yelena, with Susan Jacoby. *Soul to Soul: A Black American Family, 1865–1992.* New York: Norton, 1992.

Killen, Linda. *The Russian Bureau: A Case Study in Wilsonian Diplomacy.* Lexington: University Press of Kentucky, 1983.

Kimball, Warren F. *Forged in War: Roosevelt, Churchill, and the Second World War.* New York: Morrow, 1997.

———. *The Most Unsordid Act: Lend-Lease, 1939–1941.* Baltimore, Md.: Johns Hopkins University Press, 1969.

Klehr, Harvey. *The Heyday of American Communism: The Depression Decade.* New York: Basic Books, 1984.

Klehr, Harvey, John Earl Haynes, and Fridrikh Igorevich Firsov. *The Secret World of American Communism.* Russian documents translated by Timothy D. Sergay. New Haven, Conn.: Yale University Press, 1995.

Klingaman, William K. *1941: Our Lives in a World on the Edge.* New York: Harper and Row, 1989.

Kluger, Richard. *The Life and Death of the New York Herald Tribune.* New York: Knopf, 1986.

Kotkin, Stephen. *Magnetic Mountain: Stalinism as a Civilization.* Berkeley: University of California Press, 1995.

Krzhizhanovsky, Gleb M. *The Basis of the Technological Economic Plan of Reconstruction of the U.S.S.R.* Moscow: Cooperative Publishing Society, 1931.

Kurth, Peter. *Isadora: A Sensational Life.* Boston: Little, Brown, 2001.

Kutulas, Judy. *The Long War: The Intellectual People's Front and Anti-Stalinism, 1930–1940.* Durham: Duke University Press, 1995.

Lacey, Robert. *Ford: The Men and the Machine.* Boston: Little, Brown, 1986.

LaFeber, Walter. *The American Age: United States Foreign Policy at Home and Abroad.* Second edition. New York: W. W. Norton, 1989.

Langer, John Daniel. "The Harriman-Beaverbrook Mission and the Debate over Unconditional Aid for the Soviet Union, 1941." *Journal of Contemporary History* 14, no. 3 (July 1979), 463–82.

———. "The 'Red General': Philip R. Faymonville and the Soviet Union, 1917–1952." *Prologue* 8, no. 4 (winter 1976), 208–21.

Langer, William L., and S. Everett Gleason. *The Undeclared War, 1940–1941: The World Crisis and American Foreign Policy*. Gloucester, Mass.: Peter Smith reprint, 1968.

Lasch, Christopher. *The American Liberals and the Russian Revolution*. New York: Columbia University Press, 1962.

———. *The New Radicalism in America, 1889–1963: The Intellectual as a Social Type*. New York: Knopf, 1965.

Lensen, George Alexander. *The Damned Inheritance: The Soviet Union and the Manchurian Crises, 1924–1935*. Tallahassee, Fla.: Diplomatic Press, 1974.

Leonard, Raymond W. *Secret Soldiers of the Revolution: Soviet Military Intelligence, 1918–1933*. Westport, Conn.: Greenwood Press, 1999.

Leuchtenburg, William E. *Franklin D. Roosevelt and the New Deal, 1932–1940*. New York: Harper and Row, 1963.

Levering, Ralph B. *American Opinion and the Russian Alliance, 1939–1945*. Chapel Hill: University of North Carolina Press, 1976.

Levin, N. Gordon. *Woodrow Wilson and World Politics: America's Response to War and Revolution*. New York: Oxford University Press, 1968.

Libbey, James K. *Alexander Gumberg and Soviet American Relations, 1917–1933*. Lexington: University of Kentucky Press, 1977.

———. *American-Russian Economic Relations: A Survey of Issues and References*. Claremont, Calif.: Regina Books, 1989.

———. *Russian-American Economic Relations, 1763–1999*. Gulf Breeze, Fla.: Academic International Press, 1999.

Lohr, Eric. *Nationalizing the Russian Empire: The Campaign against Enemy Aliens during World War I*. Cambridge, Mass.: Harvard University Press, 2003.

Long, James W. *From Privileged to Dispossessed: The Volga Germans, 1860–1017*. Lincoln: University of Nebraska Press, 1988.

Lotz, Rainer. *Black People: Entertainers of African Descent in Europe and Germany*. Bonn: Birgit Lotz Verlag, 1997.

Luskin, John. *Lippmann, Liberty and the Press*. University: University of Alabama Press, 1972.

Lyons, Eugene. *Herbert Hoover: A Biography*. Garden City, N.Y.: Doubleday, 1964.

MacLean, Elizabeth Kimball. "Joseph E. Davies and Soviet-American Relations, 1941–1943." *Diplomatic History* 4, no. 4 (fall 1980), 73–93.

———. *Joseph E. Davies: Envoy to the Soviets*. Westport, Conn.: Praeger, 1992.

MacMillan, Margaret. *Paris 1919: Six Months That Changed the World*. New York: Random House, 2002.

Maddox, Robert James. *William E. Borah and American Foreign Policy*. Baton Rouge: Louisiana State University Press, 1969.

Maddux, Thomas. "American Diplomats and the Soviet Experiment: The View from the Moscow Embassy, 1934–1939." *South Atlantic Quarterly* 74, no. 4 (autumn 1975), 468–87.

———. "Watching Stalin Maneuver between Hitler and the West: American Diplomats and Soviet Diplomacy, 1934–1939." *Diplomatic History* 1, no. 2 (Spring 1977), 140–54.

———. *Years of Estrangement: American Relations with the Soviet Union, 1933–1941*. Tallahassee: University Presses of Florida, 1980.

Mahoney, Barbara S. *Dispatches and Dictators: Ralph Barnes for the Herald Tribune*. Corvallis: Oregon State University Press, 2002.

Manykin, A. S. *Izoliatsionizm i formirovanie vneshnepoliticheskii kursa SShA (1923–1929)*. Moscow: Izd-vo MGU, 1980.

March, G. Patrick. *Eastern Destiny: Russia in Asia and the North Pacific*. Westport, Conn.: Praeger, 1996.

Margolies, Sylvia R. *The Pilgrimage to Russia: The Soviet Union and the Treatment of Foreigners, 1924–1937*. Madison: University of Wisconsin Press, 1968.

Marks, Steven G. *How Russia Shaped the Modern World: From Art to Anti-Semitism, Ballet to Bolshevism*. Princeton, N.J.: Princeton University Press, 2003.

Marushkin, Boris. *Amerikanskaia politika po otnosheniiu k Sovetskoi Rossii posle Oktabr'skoi revolutsii.* Moscow: Nauk, 1961.

Matlock, Rebecca [Metlok, Rebekka]. *"Spaso-Khaus": Liudi i vstrechi: zapiski zheni amerikanskogo posla.* Translated by T. Kudriavtseva. Moscow: Eksmo: Aloriritm, 2004.

Maxwell, Bertram W. *The Soviet State: A Study of Bolshevik Rule.* Topeka, Kans.: Steves and Wayburn, 1934.

Mayer, Arno. *Politics and Diplomacy of Peacemaking: Containment and Counterrevolution at Versailles.* New York: Knopf, 1967.

Mayers, David. *The Ambassadors and America's Soviet Policy.* New York: Oxford University Press, 1995.

———. *George Kennan and the Dilemmas of US Foreign Policy.* New York: Oxford University Press, 1988.

McCauley, Martin. *Who's Who in Russia Since 1900.* London: Routledge, 1997.

McKenna, Kevin J. *All the Views Fit to Print: Changing Images of the U.S. in Pravda Political Cartoons, 1917–1991.* New York: Peter Lang, 2001.

McDaniel, George William. *Smith Wildman Brookhart: Iowa's Renegade Republican.* Ames: Iowa State University Press, 1995.

McFadden, David W. *Alternative Paths: Soviets and Americans, 1917–1920.* New York: Oxford University Press, 1993.

———, and Claire Gorfinkel. *Constructive Spirit: Quakers in Revolutionary Russia.* Overview by Sergei Nikitin. Pasadena, Calif.: Intentional Productions, 2004.

McKenna, Marian C. *Borah.* Ann Arbor: University of Michigan Press, 1961.

McVay, Gordon. *Esenin: A Life.* New York: Paragon, 1988.

Meiburger, Anne Vincent. *Efforts of Raymond Robins toward Recognition of Soviet Russia and the Outlawry of War, 1917–1933.* Washington, D.C.: Catholic University of America Press, 1958.

Miner, Steven Merritt. *Between Churchill and Stalin: The Soviet Union, Great Britain, and the Origins of the Grand Alliance.* Chapel Hill: University of North Carolina Press, 1988.

Mokhovikova, G. V. *L. V. Genderson i sovetsko-amerikanskie otnosheniia v 30-e god.* Novgorod, 1995.

Montefiore, Simon Sebag. *Stalin: The Court of the Red Tsar.* New York: Knopf, 2004.

Moore, David Chioni. "Colored Dispatches from the Uzbek Border: Langston Hughes' Relevance, 1933–2002." *Callaloo* 25, 4 (Fall 2002), 1115–35.

Morison, Elting E. *Turmoil and Tradition: A Study of the Life and Times of Henry L. Stimson.* Boston: Houghton Mifflin, 1960.

Morray, J. P. *Project Kuzbas: American Workers in Siberia (1921–1926).* New York: International Publishers, 1983.

Moshevich, Sofia. *Dmitri Shostakovich, Pianist.* Montreal and Kingston: McGill-Queen's University Press, 2004.

Mosley, Leonard. *Dulles: A Biography of Eleanor, Allen, and John Foster Dulles and Their Family Network.* New York: Dial Press, 1978.

Mott, Col. T. Bentley. *Myron T. Herrick, Friend of France: An Autobiographical Biography.* Garden City, N.Y.: Doubleday, 1938.

Murphy, David E. *What Stalin Knew: The Enigma of Barbarossa.* New Haven, Conn.: Yale University Press, 2005.

Nadzharov, D. G. *Neitralitet SShA (1935–1941).* Moscow: Nauka, 1990.

Nadzhalov, D. G. "Peripetii Sovetsko-Amerikanskikh otnoshenii, 1933–1939 gg." In *Russkoe otkrytie Ameriki: Sbornik statei posviashchennyi 70-letiiu akademika Nikolaia Nikolaevicha Bolkhovitinova.* Moscow: Rosspen, 2002.

Nemrad, Semen. *Maiakovskii v Amerike: stranitsy biografii.* Moscow: Sovetskii pisatel', 1970.

Nitoburg, E. L. "Sud'by russkikh immigrantov vtoroi volny v Amerike." *Otechestvennye zapiski* 2 (2003), 102–13.

O'Connor, Timothy Edward. *Diplomacy and Revolution: G. V. Chicherin and Soviet Foreign Affairs, 1918–1930.* Ames: Iowa State University Press, 1988.

———. *The Engineer of Revolution: L. B. Krasin and the Bolsheviks, 1870–1926.* Boulder, Colo.: Westview, 1992.

Overy, Richard. *The Dictators: Hitler's Germany, Stalin's Russia.* New York: Norton, 2004.

———. *Russia's War: A History of the Soviet War Effort, 1941–1945.* New York: Penguin, 1997.

Parrott, Bruce. *Politics and Technology in the Soviet Union.* Bloomington: Indiana University Press, 1985.

Patenaude, Bertrand M. *The Big Show in Bololand: The American Relief Expedition to Soviet Russia in the Famine of 1921.* Stanford, Calif.: Stanford University Press, 2002.

Peterson, Dale E. *Up from Bondage: The Literatures of Russian and African American Soul.* Durham, N.C.: Duke University Press, 2000.

Phillips, Hugh D. *Between the Revolution and the West: A Political Biography of Maxim M. Litvinov.* Boulder, Colo.: Westview, 1992.

———. "Rapprochement and Estrangement: The United States in Soviet Foreign Policy in the 1930s." In *Soviet-U.S. Relations, 1933–1942,* 9–17. Moscow: Progress, 1989.

Pleshakov, Constantine. *Stalin's Folly: The Secret History of the German Invasion of Russia, June 1941.* Boston: Houghton Mifflin, 2005.

Pozniakov, Vladimir. "Enemy at the Gates: Soviet Military Intelligence in the Inter-War Period and Its Forecasts of Future War, 1921–1941." In *Annali della Fondazione Giangacomo Feltrinelli: Russia in the Age of Wars, 1914–1941,* 215–33. Milan: Feltrinelli, 2000.

Propas, Frederic L. "Creating a Hard Line toward Russia: The Training of State Department Soviet Experts, 1927–1937." *Diplomatic History* 8, no. 3 (summer 1984), 209–26.

Proskurin, A., comp. *Vozvrashchennye imena.* 2 vols. Moscow: Novosti, 1989.

Raack, R. C. *Stalin's Drive to the West, 1938–1945: The Origins of the Cold War.* Stanford: Stanford University Press, 1995.

Radosh, Ronald. "John Spargo and Wilson's Russian Policy, 1920," *Journal of American History* 52, no. 3 (December 1965), 548–65.

Raeff, Marc. *Russia Abroad: A Cultural History of the Russian Emigration, 1919–1939.* New York: Oxford University Press, 1990.

Ragsdale, Hugh. "Soviet Military Preparations and Policy in the Munich Crisis: New Evidence." *Jahrbucher fur Geschichte Osteuropas* 47, no. 2 (1999), 210–26.

———. *The Soviets, the Munich Crisis, and the Coming of World War II.* Cambridge: Cambridge University Press, 2004.

Raleigh, Donald J. *Experiencing Russia's Civil War: Politics, Society, and Revolutionary Culture in Saratov, 1917–1922.* Princeton, N.J.: Princeton University Press, 2002.

Rassweiler, Anne. *The Generation of Power: The History of Dneprostroi.* New York: Oxford University Press, 1988.

Rhodes, Benjamin D. *James P. Goodrich, Indiana's "Governor Strangelove": A Republican's Infatuation with Soviet Russia.* Selinsgrove, Penn.: Susquehanna University Press, 1996.

———. "The Perils of a Foreign Service Clerk: The Career of Karin Sante Korsstrom," *Prologue: Quarterly of the National Archives* 20, no. 1 (spring 1988), 24–41.

Richman, John. *The United States and the Soviet Union: The Decision to Recognize.* Raleigh: North Carolina State University Press, 1980.

Roberts, Henry L. "Maxim Litvinov." In *The Diplomats, 1919–1939,* edited by Gordon A. Craig and Felix Gilbert: 344–77. Princeton, N.J.: Princeton University Press, 1953.

Robinson, Edgar Eugene, and Vaughn Davis Bornet. *Herbert Hoover: President of the United States.* Stanford: Hoover Institution Press, 1975.

Rogger, Hans. "*Amerikanizm* and the Economic Development of Russia." *Comparative Studies in Society and History* 23, no. 1 (July 1981), 382–420.

Rosenberg, William G., and Lewis H. Siegelbaum, eds. *Social Dimensions of Soviet Industrialization.* Bloomington: Indiana University Press, 1993.

Ruddy, T. Michael. *The Cautious Diplomat: Charles E. Bohlen and the Soviet Union 1929–1969.* Kent, Ohio: Kent State University Press, 1986.

Russell, Francis. *The Shadow of Blooming Grove: Warren G. Harding in His Times.* New York: McGraw-Hill, 1968.

Salzman, Neil V. *Reform and Revolution: The Life and Times of Raymond Robins*. Kent, Ohio: Kent State University Press, 1991.

Sanders, Marion K. *Dorothy Thompson: A Legend in Her Time*. Boston: Houghton Mifflin, 1973.

Saul, Norman E. *Concord and Conflict: The United States and Russia, 1867–1914*. Lawrence: University Press of Kansas, 1996.

———. *Distant Friends: The United States and Russia, 1763–1867*. Lawrence: University Press of Kansas, 1991.

———. *War and Revolution: The United States and Russia, 1914–1921*. Lawrence: University Press of Kansas, 2001.

Schmidt, Regin. *Red Scare: FBI and the Origins of Anticommunism in the United States, 1919–1943*. Copenhagen: Museum Tusculanum Press, University of Copenhagen, 2000.

Schultz, Kurt S. "Building the 'Soviet Detroit': The Construction of the Nizhnii-Novgorod Automobile Factory, 1927–1932." *Slavic Review* 49, no. 2 (summer 1990), 200–12.

Schulzinger, Robert D. *The Making of the Diplomatic Mind: The Training, Outlook, and Style of United States Foreign Service Officers, 1908–1931*. Middletown, Conn.: Wesleyan University Press, 1975.

Segal, Harold B. *Turn-of-the-Century Cabaret: Paris, Barcelona, Berlin, Munich, Vienna, Cracow, Moscow, St. Petersburg, Zurich*. New York: Columbia University Press, 1987.

Sevost'ianov, Grigorii. "Missiia M. M. Litvinova v Vashington v 1933: novye materialy." *Novaia i noveishaia istoriia* 3 (1994), 148–79.

———. *Moskva-Vashington: Diplomaticheskie otnosheniia, 1933–1936*. Moscow: Nauka, 2002.

———. "Sudba soglasheniia Rusvelt-Litvinov o dolgakh i creditakh, 1934–1935 gg.: novii dokumentii." *Novaia i noveishaia istoriia* 2 (1995), 121–22.

Sheinis, Zinovy. *Maxim Litvinov*. Translated by Vic Schneierson. Moscow: Progress, 1990.

Shiro, William L. *The Nightmare Years: 1930–1940*. Vol. 2: *20th Century Journey: A Memoir of a Life and the Times*. Boston: Little, Brown, 1984.

Shishkin, V. A. *Stanovlenie vneshnei politiki poslerevoliutsionnoi Rossii (1917–1930 gody) i kapitalisticheskii mir: ot revoliutsionnogo Azapadnichestva' k Anatsional-bol'shevizmu*. St. Petersburg: Bulanin, 2002.

Shpotov, Boris M. ""Bolezni rosta' ili 'sindrom knopki': kak prizhivalis' SSSR amerikanskie promyshlennye tekhnologii v gody pervoi piatiletki." In *Russkoe otkrytie Ameriki: Sbornik statei posviashchennyi 70-letiiu akadmika Nikolaia Nikolaevicha Bolckhovitinova*. Moscow: Rosspen, 2002. Shvedov, S. "Obraz Genri Forda v sovetskoi publitsistike 1920–1930-kh godov: vospriiate i transformatsiia tsennostei chuzhoi kultury." In *Vzaimodeistvie kul'tur SSSR I SShA xviii-xx vv*. Edited by O. E. Turganova. Moscow: Nauka, 1987.

Sibley, Katherine A. S. *Red Spies in America: Stolen Secrets and the Dawn of the Cold War*. Lawrence: University Press of Kansas, 2004.

Siegel, Katherine A. S. *Loans and Legitimacy: The Evolution of Soviet-American Relations, 1919–1933*. Lexington: University Press of Kentucky, 1996.

Singer, C. Gregg. *The Unholy Alliance*. New Rochelle: Arlington House, 1973.

Smith, Canfield F. *Vladivostok under Red and White Rule: Revolution and Counterrevolution in the Russian Far East, 1920–1922*. Seattle: University of Washington Press, 1974.

Smith, Gene. *When the Cheering Stopped: The Last Years of Woodrow Wilson*. New York: William Morrow, 1964.

Sparks, Nemmy, and Ruth Epperson Kennell. "Americans at Kuzbas, 1922–1924," *New World Review* 39 (fall 1971), 68–98.

Spence, Richard B. "The Tragic Fate of Kalamatiano: America's Man in Moscow." *International Journal of Intelligence and Counterintelligence* 12, no. 3 (fall 1999), 346–74.

Stafford, David. *Roosevelt and Churchill: Men of Secrets*. Woodstock, N.Y.: Overlook Press, 2000.

Starr, S. Frederick. *Red and Hot: The Fate of Jazz in the Soviet Union, 1917–1980*. New York: Oxford University Press, 1983.

Steel, Ronald. *Walter Lippmann and the American Century*. Boston: Little, Brown, 1980.

Stephanson, Anders. *George F. Kennan and the Art of Foreign Policy*. Cambridge, Mass.: Harvard University Press, 1989.

Stiller, Jesse H. *George S. Messersmith: Diplomat of Democracy*. Chapel Hill: University of North Carolina Press, 1987.

Stites, Richard. "Frontline Entertainment." In *Culture and Entertainment in Wartime Russia*. Edited by Richard Stites. Bloomington: Indiana University Press, 1995.

———. *Soviet Popular Culture: Entertainment and Society since 1900*. Cambridge, UK: Cambridge University Press, 1992.

Sutton, Antony. *Wall Street and the Bolshevik Revolution*. New Rochelle, N.Y.: Arlington House, 1971.

———. *Western Technology and Soviet Economic Development, 1917–1930*. Palo Alto, Calif.: Stanford University Press, 1968.

———. *Western Technology and Soviet Economic Development, 1930 to 1945*. Palo Alto, Calif.: Stanford University Press, 1971.

Tang, Peter S. H. *Russian and Soviet Policy in Manchuria and Outer Mongolia, 1911–1931*. Durham, N.C.: Duke University Press, 1959.

Taubman, William. *Stalin's American Policy: From Entente to Detente to Cold War*. New York: W. W. Norton, 1982.

Taylor, Sally J. *Stalin's Apologist. Walter Duranty: The New York Times's Man in Moscow*. New York: Oxford University Press, 1990.

Trani, Eugene P., and David L. Wilson. *The Presidency of Warren G. Harding*. Lawrence: University Press of Kansas, 1977.

Travis, Frederick F. *George Keenan and the American-Russian Relationship, 1865–1924*. Athens: Ohio University Press, 1990.

Tsikhilashvili, Nana. Sh., and David Ch. Engerman, "Amerikanskaia pomoshch' Rossii v 1921–1923 godakh: konflikty i sotrushnechestov." *Amerikanskii Ezhegodnik 1995*, 191–213.

Tsvietkov, Hlib Mykolaiovych. *Shestnadtsat' let nepriznaniia: Politika SshA v otnoshenii Sov. gosudarstva v 1917–1933 gg*. Kiev: Izd-vo Kiev Un-ta, 1971.

Tucker, Robert C. *Stalin in Power: The Revolution from Above, 1928–1941*. New York: Norton, 1990.

Uldricks, Teddy. *Diplomacy and Ideology: The Origins of Soviet Foreign Relations, 1917–1930*. London: Sage, 1979.

Ullman, Richard H. "The Davies Mission and United States-Soviet Relations, 1937–1941." *World Politics 9*, no. 2 (January 1957), 220–39.

Unterberger, Betty Miller. *The United States, Revolutionary Russia, and the Rise of Czechoslovakia*. Chapel Hill: University of North Carolina Press, 1989.

Utkin, A. I. *Diplomatiia Ruzvel'ta*. Sverdlovsk: Izd-vo Uralskogo universiteta, 1990.

———. *Rossiia nad bezdnoi: 1918 g.–dekabr 1941 g*. Smolensk: Rusich, 2000.

Von Laue, Theodore. "Soviet Diplomacy: G. V. Chicherin, Peoples Commissar for Foreign Affairs, 1918–1930," in vol. 1., *The Diplomats, 1919–1939*. Edited by Gordon A. Craig and Felix Gilbert. New York: Atheneum, 1974.

Watt, Donald Cameron. *How War Came: The Immediate Origins of the Second World War, 1938–1939*. New York: Pantheon, 1989.

Weeks, Albert L. *Russia's Life-Saver: Lend-Lease Aid to the U.S.S.R. in World War II*. Lanham, Md.: Lexington Books, 2004.

———. *Stalin's Other War: Soviet Grand Strategy, 1939–1941*. Lanham, Md.: Rowman and Littlefield, 2002.

Weeks, Charles J., Jr. *An American Naval Diplomat in Revolutionary Russia: The Life and Times of Vice Admiral Newton A. McCully*. Annapolis, Md.: Naval Institute Press, 1993.

Wehle, Louis. *Hidden Threads of History: Wilson through Roosevelt*. New York: Macmillan, 1953.

Weil, Martin. *A Pretty Good Club: The Founding Fathers of the U.S. Foreign Service*. New York: W. W. Norton, 1978.

Weinberg, Steve. *Armand Hammer: The Untold Story, an Unauthorized Biography*. Boston: Little, Brown, 1989.

Weinstein, Allen, and Alexander Vassiliev. *The Haunted Wood: Soviet Espionage in America—The Stalin Era*. New York: Random House, 1999.

Weissman, Benjamin B. *Herbert Hoover and Famine Relief to Soviet Russia, 1921–1923*. Palo Alto, Calif.: Hoover Institution Press, 1974.

White, Christine. *British and American Commercial Relations with Soviet Russia, 1918–1924*. Chapel Hill: University of North Carolina Press, 1992.

Williams, Robert C. *Russian Art and American Money, 1900–1940*. Cambridge, Mass.: Harvard University Press, 1983.

Williams, William Appleman. *American-Russian Relations, 1781–1946*. New York: Rinehart, 1952.

———. *The Tragedy of American Diplomacy*. Cleveland, Ohio: World, 1959.

Wilson, Joan Hoff. *American Business and Foreign Policy, 1920–1933*. Lexington: University Press of Kentucky, 1971.

———. *Ideology and Economics: U.S. Relations with the Soviet Union, 1918–1933*. Columbia: University of Missouri Press, 1974.

Wilson, Theodore A. *The First Summit: Roosevelt and Churchill at Placentia Bay 1941*. Boston: Houghton Mifflin, 1969.

———. "In Aid of America's Interests: The Provision of Lend-Lease to the Soviet Union, 1941–1942." In *Soviet-U.S. Relations, 1933–1942*. Moscow: Progress, 1989.

Youngblood, Denise J. *Movies for the Masses: Popular Cinema and Soviet Society in the 1920s*. Cambridge, UK: Cambridge University Press, 1992.

———. *Soviet Cinema in the Silent Era, 1918–1935*. Ann Arbor, Mich.: UMI Research Press, 1985.

Zhuravlev, Sergei. *"Malenk'ie liudi" i "bol'shaia istoriia": Inostrantsy moskovskogo elektrozavoda v sovetskom obshchestve 1920-kh—1930—kh gg*. Moscow: Rosspen, 2000.

Index